Python for Finance

Second Edition

Financial modeling and quantitative analysis explained

Yuxing Yan

BIRMINGHAM - MUMBAI

Python for Finance
Second Edition

First published: April 2014

Second edition: June 2017

Production reference: 1270617

Published by Packt Publishing Ltd.
Livery Place
35 Livery Street
Birmingham B3 2PB, UK.

ISBN 978-1-78712-569-8

www.packtpub.com

Credits

Author
Yuxing Yan

Reviewers
Dr. Param Jeet
Nabih Ibrahim Bawazir, M.Sc.
Joran Beasley

Commissioning Editor
Amey Varangaonkar

Acquisition Editor
Tushar Gupta

Content Development Editor
Amrita Noronha

Technical Editor
Akash Patel

Copy Editor
Safis Editing

Project Coordinator
Shweta H Birwatkar

Proofreader
Safis Editing

Indexer
Mariammal Chettiyar

Graphics
Tania Dutta

Production Coordinator
Nilesh Mohite

Cover Work
Nilesh Mohite

About the Author

Yuxing Yan graduated from McGill University with a PhD in finance. Over the years, he has been teaching various finance courses at eight universities: McGill University and Wilfrid Laurier University (in Canada), Nanyang Technological University (in Singapore), Loyola University of Maryland, UMUC, Hofstra University, University at Buffalo, and Canisius College (in the US).

His research and teaching areas include: market microstructure, open-source finance and financial data analytics. He has 22 publications including papers published in the Journal of Accounting and Finance, Journal of Banking and Finance, Journal of Empirical Finance, Real Estate Review, Pacific Basin Finance Journal, Applied Financial Economics, and Annals of Operations Research.

He is good at several computer languages, such as SAS, R, Python, Matlab, and C.

His four books are related to applying two pieces of open-source software to finance: *Python for Finance* (2014), *Python for Finance* (2nd ed., expected 2017), Python for Finance (Chinese version, expected 2017), and *Financial Modeling Using R* (2016).

In addition, he is an expert on data, especially on financial databases. From 2003 to 2010, he worked at Wharton School as a consultant, helping researchers with their programs and data issues. In 2007, he published a book titled Financial Databases (with S.W. Zhu). This book is written in Chinese.

Currently, he is writing a new book called Financial Modeling Using Excel — in an R-Assisted Learning Environment. The phrase "R-Assisted" distinguishes it from other similar books related to Excel and financial modeling. New features include using a huge amount of public data related to economics, finance, and accounting; an efficient way to retrieve data: 3 seconds for each time series; a free financial calculator, showing 50 financial formulas instantly, 300 websites, 100 YouTube videos, 80 references, paperless for homework, midterms, and final exams; easy to extend for instructors; and especially, no need to learn R.

I would like to thank Ben Amoako-Adu, Brian Smith (who taught me the first two finance courses and offered unstinting support for many years after my graduation), George Athanassakos (one of his assignments "forced" me to learn C), and Jin-Chun Duan.

I would also like to thank Wei-Hung Mao, Jerome Detemple, Bill Sealey, Chris Jacobs, Mo Chaudhury, Summon Mazumdar (my former professors at McGill), and Lawrence Kryzanowski. (His wonderful teaching inspired me to concentrate on empirical finance and he edited my doctoral thesis word by word even though he was not my supervisor!). There is no doubt that my experience at Wharton has shaped my thinking and enhanced my skill sets. I thank Chris Schull and Michael Boldin for offering me the job; Mark Keintz, Dong Xu, Steven Crispi, and Dave Robinson, my former colleagues, who helped me greatly during my first two years at Wharton; and Eric Zhu, Paul Ratnaraj, Premal Vora, Shuguang Zhang, Michelle Duan, Nicholle Mcniece, Russ Ney, Robin Nussbaum-Gold, and Mireia Gine for all their help. In addition, I'd like to thank Shaobo Ji, Tong Yu, Shaoming Huang, Xing Zhang.

About the Reviewers

Dr. Param Jeet has a Ph.D. in mathematics from one of India's leading engineering institutes, IIT Madras. Dr. Param Jeet has a decade of experience in the data analytics industry. He started his career with Bank of America and since then worked with a few companies as a data scientist. He has also worked across domains such as capital market, education, telecommunication and healthcare. Dr. Param Jeet has expertise in Quantitative finance, Data analytics, machine learning, R, Python, Matlab, SQL, and big data technologies. He has also published a few research papers in reputed international journals, published and reviewed books, and has worked on *Learning Quantitative Finance with R*.

Nabih Ibrahim Bawazir, M.Sc. is a data scientist at an Indonesian financial technology start-up backed by Digital Alpha Group, Pte Ltd., Singapore. Most of his work is research on the development phase, from financial modeling to data-driven underwriting. Previously, he worked as actuary in CIGNA. He holds M.Sc in Financial Mathematics from Gadjah Mada University, Indonesia.

Joran Beasley received his degree in computer science from the University of Idaho. He works has been programming desktop applications in wxPython professionally for monitoring large scale sensor networks for use in agriculture for the last 7 years. He currently lives in Moscow Idaho, and works at Decagon Devices Inc. as a software engineer.

> I would like to thank my wife Nicole, for putting up with my long hours hunched over a keyboard, and her constant support and help in raising our two wonderful children.

www.PacktPub.com

eBooks, discount offers, and more

For support files and downloads related to your book, please visit www.PacktPub.com.

Did you know that Packt offers eBook versions of every book published, with PDF and ePub files available? You can upgrade to the eBook version at www.PacktPub.com and as a print book customer, you are entitled to a discount on the eBook copy. Get in touch with us at customercare@packtpub.com for more details.

At www.PacktPub.com, you can also read a collection of free technical articles, sign up for a range of free newsletters and receive exclusive discounts and offers on Packt books and eBooks.

https://www.packtpub.com/mapt

Get the most in-demand software skills with Mapt. Mapt gives you full access to all Packt books and video courses, as well as industry-leading tools to help you plan your personal development and advance your career.

Why subscribe?

- Fully searchable across every book published by Packt
- Copy and paste, print, and bookmark content
- On demand and accessible via a web browser

Customer Feedback

Thanks for purchasing this Packt book. At Packt, quality is at the heart of our editorial process. To help us improve, please leave us an honest review on this book's Amazon page at https://www.amazon.com/dp/1787125696. If you'd like to join our team of regular reviewers, you can e-mail us at customerreviews@packtpub.com. We award our regular reviewers with free eBooks and videos in exchange for their valuable feedback. Help us be relentless in improving our products!

Table of Contents

Preface

It is our firm belief that an ambitious student major in finance should learn at least one computer language. The basic reason is that we have entered a so-called big data era. In finance, we have a huge amount of data, and most of it is publically available free of charge. To use such rich sources of data efficiently, we need a tool. Among many potential candidates, Python is one of the best choices.

A few words for the second edition

For the second edition, we have reorganized the structure of the book by adding more chapters related to finance. This is recognition and response to the feedbacks from numerous readers. For the second edition, the first two chapters are exclusively devoted to Python. After that, all remaining chapters are associated with finance. Again, Python in this book is used as a tool to help readers learn and understand financial theories better. To meet the demand of using all types of data by various quantitative programs, business analytics programs and financial engineering programs, we add *Chapter 4*, *Sources of Data*. Because of this restructuring, this edition is more suitable for a one-semester course such as Quantitative Finance, Financial Analysis using Python and Business Analytics. Two finance professors, Premal P. Vora, at Penn State University, Sheng Xiao, at Westminister College, have adopted the first edition as their textbook. Hopefully, more finance, accounting professors would find the second edition is more suitable for their students, especially for those students from a financial engineering program, business analytics and other quantitative areas.

Why Python?

There are various reasons that Python should be used. Firstly, Python is free in terms of license. Python is available for all major operating systems, such as Windows, Linux/Unix, OS/2, Mac, and Amiga, among others. Being free has many benefits. When students graduate, they could apply what they have learned wherever they go. This is true for the financial community as well. In contrast, this is not true for SAS and MATLAB. Secondly, Python is powerful, flexible, and easy to learn. It is capable of solving almost all our financial and economic estimations. Thirdly, we could apply Python to big data. Dasgupta (2013) argues that R and Python are two of the most popular open source programming languages for data analysis. Fourthly, there are many useful modules in Python. Each model is developed for a special purpose. In this book, we focus on NumPy, SciPy, Matplotlib, Statsmodels, and Pandas modules.

A programming book written by a finance professor

There is no doubt that the majority of programming books are written by professors from computer science. It seems odd that a finance professor writes a programming book. It is understandable that the focus would be quite different. If an instructor from computer science were writing this book, naturally the focus would be Python, whereas the true focus should be finance. This should be obvious from the title of the book *Python for Finance*. This book intends to change the fact that many programming books serving the finance community have too much for the language itself and too little for finance. Another unique feature of the book is that it uses a huge amount public data related to economics, finance and accounting, see *Chapter 4, Sources of Data* for more details.

What this book covers

Chapter 1, Python Basics, offers a short introduction, and explains how to install Python, how to launch and quit Python, variable assignment, vector, matrix and Tuple, calling embedded functions, write your own functions, input data from an input file, simple data manipulations, output our data and results, and generate a Python dataset with an extension of pickle.

Chapter 2, *Introduction to Python Modules*, discusses the meaning of a module, how to import a module, show all functions contained in an imported module, adopt a short name for an imported module, compare between import math and from math import, delete an imported module, import just a few functions from a module, introduction to NumPy, SciPy, matplotlib, statsmodels, pandas and Pandas_reader, find out all built-in modules and all available (preinstalled) modules, how to find a specific uninstalled module.

Chapter 3, *Time Value of Money*, introduces and discusses various basic concepts and formulae associated with finance, such as present value of one future cash flow, present value of (growing) perpetuity, present and future value of annuity, perpetuity vs. perpetuity due, annuity vs. annuity due, relevant functions contained in SciPy and numpy.lib.financial submodule, a free financial calculator, written in Python, definition of NPV (Net Present Value) and its related rule, definition of IRR (Internal Rate of Return) and its related rule, Python graphical presentation of time value of money, and NPV profile.

Chapter 4, *Sources of Data*, discusses how to retrieve data from various public sources, such as Yahoo!Finance, Google finance, FRED (Federal Reserve Bank's Economics Data Library), Prof. French's Data Library, BLS (Bureau of Labor Statistics) and Census Bureau. In addition, it would discuss various methods to input data, such as files with formats of csv, txt, pkl, Matlab, SAS or Excel.

Chapter 5, *Bond and Stock Valuation*, introduces interest rate and its related concepts, such as APR (Annual Percentage Rate), EAR (Effective Annual Rate), compounding frequency, how to convert one effective rate to another one, the term structure of interest rate, how to estimate the selling price of a regular bond, how to use the so-called discount dividend model to estimate the price of a stock and so on.

Chapter 6, *Capital Asset Pricing Model*, shows how to download data from Yahoo!Finance in order to run a linear regression for CAPM, rolling beta, several Python programs to estimate beta for multiple stocks, adjusted beta and portfolio beat estimation, two beta adjustment methods by Scholes and Williams (1977) Dimson (1979).

Chapter 7, *Multifactor Models and Performance Measures*, shows how to extend the single-factor model, described in *Chapter 6*, *Capital Asset Pricing Model*, to multifactor and complex models such as the Fama-French three-factor model, the Fama-French-Carhart four-factor model, and the Fama-French five-factor model, and performance measures such as the Sharpe ratio, Treynor ratios, Sortino ratio, and Jensen's alpha.

Chapter 8, Time-Series Analysis, shows how to design a good date variable, merge datasets by this date variable, normal distribution, normality tests, term structure of interest rate, 52-week high and low trading strategy, return estimation, convert daily returns to monthly or annual returns, T-test, F-test, Durbin-Watson test for autocorrelation, Fama-MacBeth regression, Roll (1984) spread, Amihud's (2002) illiquidity, Pastor and Stambaugh's (2003) liquidity measure, January effect, weekday effect, retrieving high-frequency data from Google Finance and from Prof. Hasbrouck's TORQ database (Trade, Order, Report and Quotation) and introduction to CRSP (Center for Research in Security Prices) database.

Chapter 9, Portfolio Theory, discusses mean and risk estimation of a 2-stock portfolio, N-stock portfolio, correlation vs. diversification effect, how to generate a return matrix, generating an optimal portfolio based on the Sharpe ratio, the Treynor ratio and the Sortinor ratio; how to construct an efficient frontier; Modigliani and Modigliani performance measure (M2 measure); and how to estimate portfolio returns using value-weighted and equal-weighed methodologies.

Chapter 10, Options and Futures, discusses payoff and profit/loss functions for calls and puts and their graphical representations, European versus American options; normal distribution; standard normal distribution; cumulative normal distribution; the famous Black-Scholes-Merton option model with/without dividend; various trading strategies and their visual presentations, such as covered call, straddle, butterfly, and calendar spread; Greeks; the put-call parity and its graphical representation; a graphical representation of a one-step and a two-step binomial tree model; how to use the binomial tree method to price both European and American options; and implied volatility, volatility smile, and skewness.

Chapter 11, Value at Risk, first reviews the density and cumulative functions of a normal distribution, then discusses the first method to estimate VaR based on the normality assumption, conversion from one day risk to n-day risk, one-day VaR to n-day VaR, normality tests, impact of skewness and kurtosis, modifying the VaR measure by including both skewness and kurtosis, the second method to estimate VaR based on historical returns, how to link two methods by using Monte Carlo simulation, back testing, and stress testing.

Chapter 12, Monte Carlo Simulation, discusses how to estimate the π value by using Monte Carlo simulation; simulating stock price movement with a lognormal distribution; constructing efficient portfolios and an efficient frontier; replicating the Black-Scholes-Merton option model by simulation; pricing several exotic options, such as lookback options with floating strikes; bootstrapping with/without replacements; long term expected return forecast and a related efficiency, quasi Monte Carlo simulation, and Sobol sequence.

Chapter 13, *Credit Risk Analysis*, discusses Moody's, Standard & Poor's, and Fitch's credit ratings, credit spread, 1-year and 5-year migration matrices, term structure of interest rate, Altman's Z-score to predict corporate bankruptcy, the KMV model to estimate total assets and its volatility, default probability and distance to default, and credit default swap.

Chapter 14, *Exotic Options*, first compares European and American options we learned about in *Chapter 9*, *Portfolio Theory* with Bermudan options, then discusses methods to price simple chooser options; shout, rainbow, and binary options; the average price option; barrier options such as the up-and-in option and the up-and-out option; and barrier options such as down-and-in and down-and-out options.

Chapter 15, *Volatility, Implied Volatility, ARCH, and GARCH*, focuses on two issues: volatility measures and ARCH/GARCH.

Small-program oriented

Based on the author's teaching experience at seven schools, McGill and Wilfrid Laurier University (in Canada), NTU (in Singapore), and Loyola University, Maryland, UMUC, Hofstra University, and Canisius College (in the United States), and his eight-year consulting experience at Wharton School, he knows that many finance students like small programs that solve one specific task. Most programming books offer just a few complete and complex programs. The number of programs is far too less than enough few. There are two side effects to such an approach. First, finance students are drowned in programming details, get intimidated, and eventually lose interest in learning a computer language. Second, they don't learn how to apply what they just learned, such as running a capital asset pricing model (CAPM) to estimate IBM's beta from 1990 to 2013. This book offers about 300 complete Python programs around many finance topics.

Using real-world data

Another shortcoming of the majority of books for programming is that they use hypothetical data. In this book, we use real-world data for various financial topics. For example, instead of showing how to run CAPM to estimate the beta (market risk), I show you how to estimate IBM's, Apple's, or Walmart's betas. Rather than just presenting formulae that shows you how to estimate a portfolio's return and risk, the Python programs are given to download real-world data, form various portfolios, and then estimate their returns and risk, including Value at Risk (VaR). When I was a doctoral student, I learned the basic concept of volatility smiles. However, until writing this book, I had a chance to download real-world data to draw IBM's volatility smile.

What you need for this book

Here, we use several concrete examples to show what a reader could achieve after going through this book carefully.

First, after reading the first two chapters, a reader/student should be able to use Python to calculate the present value, future value, present value of annuity, IRR (internal rate of return), and many other financial formulae. In other words, we could use Python as a free ordinary calculator to solve many finance problems. Second, after the first three chapters, a reader/student or a finance instructor could build a free financial calculator, that is, combine a few dozen small Python programs into a big Python program. This big program behaves just like any other module written by others. Third, readers learn how to write Python programs to download and process financial data from various public data sources, such as Yahoo! Finance, Google Finance, Federal Reserve Data Library, and Prof. French's Data Library.

Fourth, readers will understand basic concepts associated with modules, which are packages written by experts, other users, or us, for specific purposes. Fifth, after understanding the Matplotlib module, readers can produce various graphs. For instance, readers could use graphs to demonstrate payoff/profit outcomes based on various trading strategies by combining the underlying stocks and options. Sixth, readers will be able to download IBM's daily price, the S&P 500 index price, and data from Yahoo! Finance and estimate its market risk (beta) by applying CAPM. They will also be able to form a portfolio with different securities, such as risk-free assets, bonds, and stocks. Then, they can optimize their portfolios by applying Markowitz's mean-variance model. In addition, readers will know how to estimate the VaR of their portfolios.

Seventh, a reader should be able to price European and American options by applying both the Black-Scholes-Merton option model for European options only, and the Monte Carlo simulation for both European and American options. Last but not least, readers will learn several ways to measure volatility. In particular, they will learn how to use AutoRegressive Conditional Heteroskedasticity (ARCH) and Generalized AutoRegressive Conditional Heteroskedasticity (GARCH) models.

Who this book is for

If you are a graduate student majoring in finance, especially studying computational finance, financial modeling, financial engineering, or business analytics, this book will benefit you greatly. Here are two examples: Prof. Premal P. Vora at Penn State University has used this book for his course titled *Data Science in Finance*, and Prof. Sheng Xiao at Westminister College has done so for his course titled *Financial Analytics*. If you are a professional, you could learn Python and use it in many financial projects. If you are an individual investor, you could benefit from reading this book as well.

Conventions

In this book, you will find a number of styles of text that distinguish between different kinds of information. Here are some examples of these styles, and an explanation of their meaning.

Code words in text, database table names, folder names, filenames, file extensions, pathnames, dummy URLs, user input, and Twitter handles are shown as follows: "The `sqrt()`, square root, function is contained in the `math` module."

A block of code is set as follows:

```
>>>sqrt(2)
NameError: name 'sqrt' is not defined
>>> Traceback (most recent call last):
  File "<stdin>", line 1, in <module>
math.sqrt(2)
1.4142135623730951
>>>
```

Any command-line input or output is written as follows:

help(pv_f)

New terms and **important words** are shown in bold. Words that you see on the screen, in menus or dialog boxes for example, appear in the text like this: "To write a Python program, we click **File**, then **New File**."

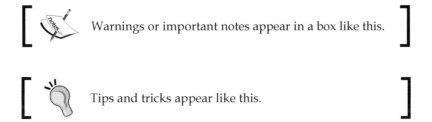

> Warnings or important notes appear in a box like this.

> Tips and tricks appear like this.

Reader feedback

Feedback from our readers is always welcome. Let us know what you think about this book—what you liked or may have disliked. Reader feedback is important for us to develop titles that you really get the most out of.

To send us general feedback, simply send an e-mail to `feedback@packtpub.com`, and mention the book title via the subject of your message.

If there is a topic that you have expertise in and you are interested in either writing or contributing to a book, see our author guide on www.packtpub.com/authors.

Customer support

Now that you are the proud owner of a Packt book, we have a number of things to help you to get the most from your purchase.

Downloading the example code

You can download the example code files for this book from your account at http://www.packtpub.com. If you purchased this book elsewhere, you can visit http://www.packtpub.com/support and register to have the files e-mailed directly to you.

You can download the code files by following these steps:

1. You can download the code files by following these steps:
2. Log in or register to our website using your e-mail address and password.
3. Hover the mouse pointer on the **SUPPORT** tab at the top.
4. Click on **Code Downloads & Errata**.
5. Enter the name of the book in the **Search** box.
6. Select the book for which you're looking to download the code files.
7. Choose from the drop-down menu where you purchased this book from.
8. Click on **Code Download**.

Once the file is downloaded, please make sure that you unzip or extract the folder using the latest version of:

- WinRAR / 7-Zip for Windows
- Zipeg / iZip / UnRarX for Mac
- 7-Zip / PeaZip for Linux

The code bundle for the book is also hosted on GitHub at https://github.com/PacktPublishing/Python-for-Finance-Second-Edition. We also have other code bundles from our rich catalog of books and videos available at https://github.com/PacktPublishing/. Check them out!

Errata

Although we have taken every care to ensure the accuracy of our content, mistakes do happen. If you find a mistake in one of our books—maybe a mistake in the text or the code—we would be grateful if you would report this to us. By doing so, you can save other readers from frustration and help us improve subsequent versions of this book. If you find any errata, please report them by visiting http://www.packtpub.com/submit-errata, selecting your book, clicking on the **errata submission form** link, and entering the details of your errata. Once your errata are verified, your submission will be accepted and the errata will be uploaded on our website, or added to any list of existing errata, under the Errata section of that title. Any existing errata can be viewed by selecting your title from http://www.packtpub.com/support.

Piracy

Piracy of copyright material on the Internet is an ongoing problem across all media. At Packt, we take the protection of our copyright and licenses very seriously. If you come across any illegal copies of our works, in any form, on the Internet, please provide us with the location address or website name immediately so that we can pursue a remedy.

Please contact us at copyright@packtpub.com with a link to the suspected pirated material.

We appreciate your help in protecting our authors, and our ability to bring you valuable content.

Questions

You can contact us at questions@packtpub.com if you are having a problem with any aspect of the book, and we will do our best to address it.

1
Python Basics

In this chapter, we will discuss basic concepts and several widely used functions related to Python. This chapter plus the next one (*Chapter 2, Introduction to Python Modules*) are only the chapters exclusively based on Python techniques. Those two chapters serve as a review for readers who have some basic Python knowledge. There is no way that a beginner, with no prior Python knowledge, could master Python by reading just those two chapters. For a new learner who wants to learn Python in more detail, he/she could find many good books. From *Chapter 3, Time Value of Money* onward, we will use Python, which will help in explaining or demonstrating various finance concepts, running regression, and processing data related to economics, finance, and accounting. Because of this, we will offer more Python-related techniques and usages in each of the upcoming chapters.

In particular, in this chapter, we will discuss the following topics:

- Python installation
- Variable assignment, empty space, and writing our own programs
- Writing a Python function
- Data input
- Data manipulation
- Data output

Python installation

In this section, we will discuss how to install Python. More specifically, we will discuss two methods: installing Python via Anaconda and installing Python directly.

There are several reasons why the first method is preferred:

- First, we can use a Python editor called Spyder, which is quite convenient for writing and editing our Python programs. For example, it has several windows (panels): one for the console, where we can type our commands directly; one for the program editor, where we can write and edit our programs; one for *Variable Explorer*,where we can view our variables and their values; and one for help, where we can seek help.

- Second, different colors for codes or comment lines will help us avoid some obvious typos and mistakes.

- Third, when installing Anaconda, many modules are installed simultaneously. A module is a set of programs written by experts, professionals, or any person around a specific topic. It could be viewed as a toolbox for a specific task. To speed up the process of developing new tools, a new module usually depends on the functions embedded in other, already developed modules. This is called module dependency. One disadvantage of such a module dependency is how to install them at the same time. For more information about this, see *Chapter 2, Introduction to Python Modules*.

Installation of Python via Anaconda

We could install Python in several ways. The consequence is that we will have different environments for writing a Python program and running a Python program.

The following is a simple two-step approach. First, we go to `http://continuum.io/ downloads` and find an appropriate package; see the following screenshot:

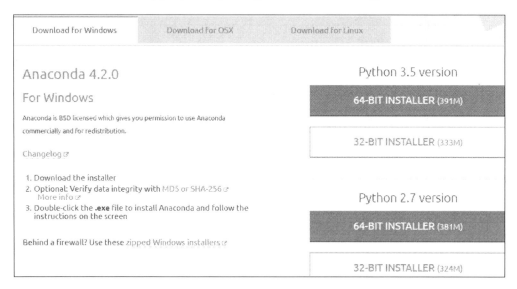

For Python, different versions coexist. From the preceding screenshot, we see that there exist two versions, 3.5 and 2.7.

For this book, the version is not that critical. The old version had fewer problems while the new one usually has new improvements. Again, module dependency could be a big headache; see *Chapter 2, Introduction to Python Modules* for more detail. The version of Anaconda is 4.2.0. Since we will launch Python through Spyder, it might have different versions as well.

Launching Python via Spyder

After Python is installed via Anaconda, we can navigate to **Start** (for a Windows version) | **All Programs** | **Anaconda3(32-bit)**, as shown in the following screenshot:

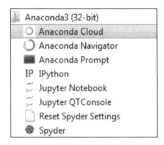

After we click **Spyder**, the last entry in the preceding screenshot, we will see the following four panels:

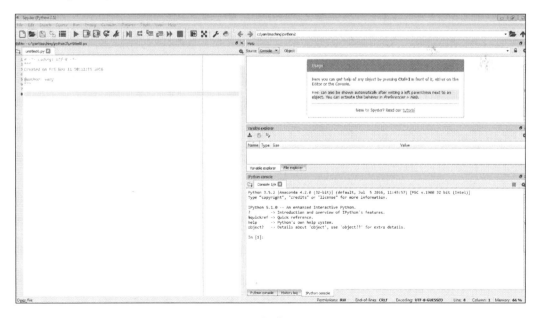

The top-left panel (window) is our program editor, where we write our programs. The bottom-right panel is the IPython console, where we cantype our simple commands. IPython is the default one. To know more about IPython, just type a question mark; see the following screenshot:

```
In [2]: ?

IPython -- An enhanced Interactive Python
==========================================

IPython offers a combination of convenient shell features, special commands
and a history mechanism for both input (command history) and output (results
caching, similar to Mathematica). It is intended to be a fully compatible
replacement for the standard Python interpreter, while offering vastly
improved functionality and flexibility.

At your system command line, type 'ipython -h' to see the command line
options available. This document only describes interactive features.
```

Alternatively, we could launch Python console by clicking **Consoles** on the menu bar and then **Open a Python console**. After that, the following window will appear:

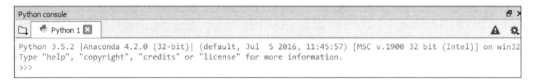

From the image with four panels, the top-right panel is our help window, where we can seek help. The middle one is called *Variable Explorer*, where the names of variables and their values are shown. Depending on personal preference, users willscale those panels or reorganize them.

Direct installation of Python

For most users, knowing how to install Python via Anaconda is more than enough. Just for completeness, here the second way to install Python is presented.

The following steps are involved:

1. First, go to `http://www.python.org/download`:

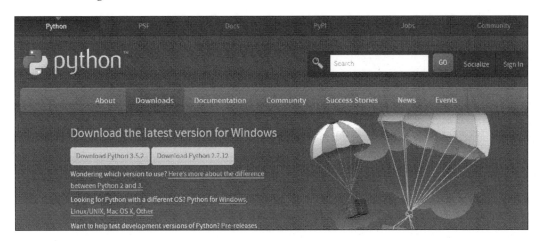

2. Depending on your computer, choose the appropriate package, for example, Python version 3.5.2. For this book, the version of Python is not important. At this stage, a new user could just install Python with the latest version. After installation, we will see the following entries for a Windows version:

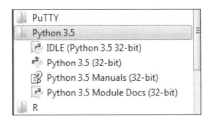

3. To launch Python, we could click `IDLE (Python 3.5. 32 bit)` and get to see the following screen:

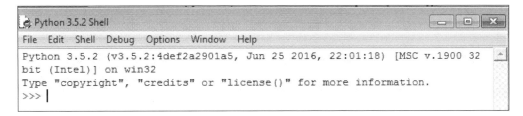

4. From the IPython shown in the screenshotwith four panels, or from the Python console panel or from the previous screenshotsshowing Python Shell, we could type various commands, as shown here:

```
>>>pv=100
>>>pv*(1+0.1)**20
672.7499949325611
>>> import math
>>>math.sqrt(3)
1.7320508075688772
>>>
```

5. To write a Python program, we click **File**, then **New File**:

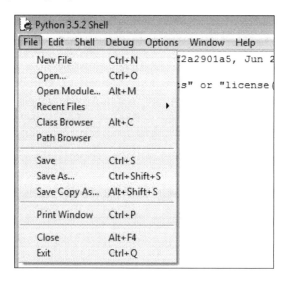

6. Type this program and then save it:

```
File   Edit   Format   Run   Options   Window   Help
def dd(x):
    return 2*x
```

7. Click **Run**, then **Run module**. If no error occurs, we canuse the function just like other embedded functions, as shown here:

```
File  Edit  Shell  Debug  Options  Window  Help
Python 3.5.2 (v3.5.2:4def2a2901a5, Jun 25 2016, 22:01:18) [MSC v.1900 32 bit (In
tel)] on win32
Type "copyright", "credits" or "license()" for more information.
>>>
 RESTART: C:/Users/yany/AppData/Local/Programs/Python/Python35-32/double_f.py
>>> dd(2)
4
>>> dd(2.5)
5.0
>>> |
```

Variable assignment, empty space, and writing our own programs

First, for Python language, an empty space or spaces is very important. For example, if we accidently have a space before typing `pv=100`, we will see the following error message:

```
>>>    pv=100
  File "<stdin>", line 1
    pv=100
    ^
IndentationError: unexpected indent
>>>
```

The name of the error is called `IndentationError`. The reason is that, for Python, indentation is important. Later in the chapter, we will learn that a proper indentation will regulate/define how we write a function or why a group of codes belongs to a specific topic, function, or loop.

Assume that we deposit $100 in the bank today. What will be the value 3 years later if the bank offers us an annual deposit rate of 1.5%? The related codes is shown here:

```
>>>pv=100
>>>pv
    100
>>>pv*(1+0.015)**3
    104.56783749999997
>>>
```

In the preceding codes, $**$ means a power function. For example, $2**3$ has a value of 8. To view the value of a variable, we simply type its name; see the previous example. The formula used is given here:

$$FV = PV(1 + R)^n \quad \ldots\ldots\ldots\ldots\ldots (1)$$

Here, FV is the future value, PV is the present value, R is the period deposit rate while n is the number of periods. In this case, R is the annual rate of 0.015 while n is 3. At the moment, readers should focus on simple Python concepts and operations.

In *Chapter 3, Time Value of Money*, this formula will be explained in detail. Since Python is case-sensitive, an error message will pop up if we type PV instead of pv; see the following code:

```
>>>PV
NameError: name 'PV' is not defined
>>>Traceback (most recent call last):
   File "<stdin>", line 1, in <module>
```

Unlike some languages, such as C and FORTRAN, for Python a new variable does not need to be defined before a value is assigned to it. To show all variables or function, we use the dir() function:

```
>>>dir()
['__builtins__', '__doc__', '__loader__', '__name__', '__package__',
'__spec__', 'pv']
>>>
```

To find out all built-in functions, we type dir(__builtings__). The output is shown here:

```
>>> dir(__builtins__)
['ArithmeticError', 'AssertionError', 'AttributeError', 'BaseException', 'BlockingIOError', 'BrokenPipeErr
or', 'BufferError', 'BytesWarning', 'ChildProcessError', 'ConnectionAbortedError', 'ConnectionError', 'Con
nectionRefusedError', 'ConnectionResetError', 'DeprecationWarning', 'EOFError', 'Ellipsis', 'EnvironmentEr
ror', 'Exception', 'False', 'FileExistsError', 'FileNotFoundError', 'FloatingPointError', 'FutureWarning',
'GeneratorExit', 'IOError', 'ImportError', 'ImportWarning', 'IndentationError', 'IndexError', 'Interrupted
Error', 'IsADirectoryError', 'KeyError', 'KeyboardInterrupt', 'LookupError', 'MemoryError', 'NameError', '
None', 'NotADirectoryError', 'NotImplemented', 'NotImplementedError', 'OSError', 'OverflowError', 'Pending
DeprecationWarning', 'PermissionError', 'ProcessLookupError', 'RecursionError', 'ReferenceError', 'Resourc
eWarning', 'RuntimeError', 'RuntimeWarning', 'StopAsyncIteration', 'StopIteration', 'SyntaxError', 'Syntax
Warning', 'SystemError', 'SystemExit', 'TabError', 'TimeoutError', 'True', 'TypeError', 'UnboundLocalError
', 'UnicodeDecodeError', 'UnicodeEncodeError', 'UnicodeError', 'UnicodeTranslateError', 'UnicodeWarning',
'UserWarning', 'ValueError', 'Warning', 'WindowsError', 'ZeroDivisionError', '_', '__build_class__', '__de
bug__', '__doc__', '__import__', '__loader__', '__name__', '__package__', '__spec__', 'abs', 'all', 'any',
'ascii', 'bin', 'bool', 'bytearray', 'bytes', 'callable', 'chr', 'classmethod', 'compile', 'complex', 'cop
yright', 'credits', 'debugfile', 'delattr', 'dict', 'dir', 'divmod', 'enumerate', 'eval', 'evalsc', 'exec'
, 'exit', 'filter', 'float', 'format', 'frozenset', 'getattr', 'globals', 'hasattr', 'hash', 'help', 'hex'
, 'id', 'input', 'int', 'isinstance', 'issubclass', 'iter', 'len', 'license', 'list', 'locals', 'map', 'ma
x', 'memoryview', 'min', 'next', 'object', 'oct', 'open', 'open_in_spyder', 'ord', 'pow', 'print', 'proper
ty', 'quit', 'range', 'repr', 'reversed', 'round', 'runfile', 'set', 'setattr', 'slice', 'sorted', 'static
method', 'str', 'sum', 'super', 'tuple', 'type', 'vars', 'zip']
>>>
```

Writing a Python function

Assume that we are interested in writing a Python function for equation (1).

After launching Spyder, click **File**, then **New File**. We write the following two lines, as shown in the left panel. The keyword `def` is for function, `fv_f` is the function name, and the three values of `pv`, `r`, and `n` in the pair of parentheses are input variables.

The colon (`:`) indicates the function hasn't finished yet. After we hit the *Enter* key, the next line will be automatically indented.

After we enter return `pv*(1+r)**n` and hit the *Enter* key twice, this simple program is completed. Obviously, for the second line, `**` represents a power function.

Assume that we save it under `c:/temp/temp.py`:

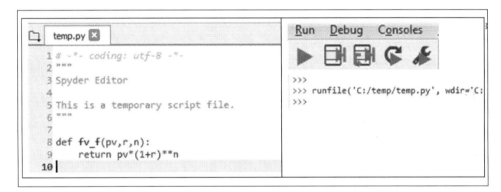

To run or debug the program, click the arrow key under **Run** on the menu bar; see the preceding top-right image. The compiling result is shown by the bottom image right (the second image on top right). Now, we canuse this function easily by calling it with three input values:

```
>>>fv_f(100,0.1,2)
    121.00000000000001
>>>fv_f(100,0.02,20)
   148.59473959783548
```

If some comments are added by explaining the meanings of input variables, the formula used, plus a few examples, it will be extremely helpful for other users or programmers. Check the following program with comments:

```
def pv_f(fv,r,n):
    """Objective: estimate present value
                    fv
    formula  : pv=------------
```

```
                    (1+r)^n
        fv: fture value
        r : discount periodic rate
        n : number of periods

 Example #1   >>>pv_f(100,0.1,1)
                90.9090909090909


 Example #2: >>>pv_f(r=0.1,fv=100,n=1)
                90.9090909090909
    """
    return fv/(1+r)**n
```

The comments or explanations are included in a pair of three double quotation marks (""" and """). The indentation within a comment is not consequential. When compiling, the underlying software will ignore all comments. The beauty of those comments is that we canuse help(pv_f) to see them, as illustrated here:

```
>>> help(pv_f)
>>>
>>>
>>>
Help on function pv_f in module __main__:

pv_f(fv, r, n)
    Objective: estimate present value
                     fv
    formula  : pv=-------------
                  (1+r)^n
        fv: fture value
        r : discount periodic rate
        n : number of periods

    Example #1   >>>pv_f(100,0.1,1)
                90.9090909090909

    Example #2: >>>pv_f(r=0.1,fv=100,n=1)
                90.9090909090909
>> >
```

In *Chapter 2, Introduction to Python Modules*, we will show how to upload a financial calculator written in Python, and in *Chapter 3, Time Value of Money*, we will explain how to generate such a financial calculator.

Python loops

In this section, we discuss a very important concept: loop or loops. A loop is used to repeat the same task with slightly different input or other factors.

Python loops, if...else conditions

Let's look at a simple loop through all the data items in an array:

```
>>>import numpy as np
>>>cashFlows=np.array([-100,50,40,30])
>>>for cash in cashFlows:
...      print(cash)
...
-100
50
40
30
```

One type of data is called a tuple, where we use a pair of parentheses, (), to include all input values. One feature of a tuple variable is that we cannot modify its value. This special property could be valuable if some our variables should never be changed.A tuple is different from a dictionary, which stores data with key-value pairs. It is not ordered and it requires that the keys are hashable. Unlike a tuple, the value for a dictionary canbe modified.

Note that for Python, the subscription for a vector or tuple starts from 0. If x has a length of 3, the subscriptions willbe 0, 1 and 2:

```
>>> x=[1,2,3]
>>>x[0]=2
>>>X
>>>
     [2, 2, 3]
>>> y=(7,8,9)
>>>y[0]=10
>>>
TypeError: 'tuple' object does not support item assignment
>>>Traceback (most recent call last):
  File "<stdin>", line 1, in <module>

>>>type(x)
>>>
<class'list'>
>>>type(y)
>>>
<class'tuple'>
>>>
```

Assuming that we invest $100 today and $30 next year, the future cash inflow will be $10, $40, $50, $45, and $20 at the end of each year for the next 5 years, starting at the end of the second year; see the following timeline and itscorresponding cash flows:

What is the **Net Present Value (NPV)** if the discount rate is 3.5%? NPVis defined as the present values of all benefits minus the present values of all costs. If a cash inflow has a positive sign while a cash outflow has a negative sign, then NPVcanbe defined conveniently as the summation of the present values of all cash flows. The present value of one future value is estimated by applying the following formula:

$$PV = \frac{FV}{(1+R)^n} \quad \dots\dots\dots\dots\dots(2)$$

Here,PV is the present value, FV is the future value,R is the period discount rate and n is the number of periods. In *Chapter 3, Time Value of Money*, the meaning of this formula will be explained in more detail. At the moment, we just want to write annpv_f() function which applies the preceding equation n times, where n is the number of cash flows. The complete NPV program is given here:

```
def npv_f(rate, cashflows):
        total = 0.0
        for i in range(0,len(cashflows)):
                total += cashflows[i] / (1 + rate)**i
        return total
```

In the program, we used a for loop. Again, the correct indentation is important for Python. Lines from 2 to 5 are all indented by one unit, thus they belong to the same function, called npv_f. Similarly, line 4 is indented two units, that is, after the second column (:), it belongs to the forloop. The command of total +=a is equivalent to total=total +a.

For the NPV function, we use a for loop. Note that the subscription of a vector in Python starts from zero, and the intermediate variable i starts from zero as well. We could call this function easily by entering two sets of input values. The output is shown here:

```
>>>r=0.035
>>>cashflows=[-100,-30,10,40,50,45,20]
>>>npv_f(r,cashflows)
14.158224763725372
```

Here is another `npv_f()` function with a function called `enumerate()`. This function willgenerate a pair of indices, starting from 0, and its corresponding value:

```
def npv_f(rate, cashflows):
    total = 0.0
    for i, cashflow in enumerate(cashflows):
        total += cashflow / (1 + rate)**i
    return total
```

Here is an example illustrating the usage of `enumerate()`:

```
x=["a","b","z"]
for i, value in enumerate(x):
    print(i, value)
```

Unlike the `npv_f` function specified previously, the NPV function from Microsoft Excel is actually a PV function, meaning that it canbe applied only to the future values. Its equivalent Python program, which is called `npv_Excel`, is shown here:

```
def npv_Excel(rate, cashflows):
    total = 0.0
    for i, cashflow in enumerate(cashflows):
        total += cashflow / (1 + rate)**(i+1)
    return total
```

The comparisons are shown in the following table. The result from the Python program is shown in the left panel while the result by calling the Excel NPV function is shown in the right panel. Please pay enough attention to the preceding program shown itself and how to call such a function:

>>>r=0.035 >>>cashflows=[-100,-30,10,40,50,45,20] >>>npv_Excel(r,cashflows[1:7])+cashflows[0] 14.158224763725372	f_x =NPV(0.035,D2:D7)+D1		
	C	D	E
	0	-100	14.1582
	1	-30	
	2	10	
	3	40	
	4	50	
	5	45	
	6	20	

By using a loop, we canrepeat the same task with different inputs. For example, we plan to print a set of values. The following is such an example for a `while` loop:

```
i=1
while(i<10):
        print(i)
        i+=1
```

The following programwillreport a discount (or any number of discount rates), making its corresponding NPV equal zero. Assume the cash flow will be `550`, `-500`, `-500`, `-500`, and `1000` at time `0`, at the end of each year of the next 4 years. In *Chapter 3, Time Value of Money*, we will explain the concept of this exercise in more detail.

Write a Python program to find out which discount rate makes NPV equal zero. Since the direction of cash flows changes twice, we might have two different rates making NPV equal zero:

```
cashFlows=(550,-500,-500,-500,1000)
r=0
while(r<1.0):
        r+=0.000001
        npv=npv_f(r,cashFlows)
        if(abs(npv)<=0.0001):
                print(r)
```

The corresponding output is given here:

```
0.07163900000005098
0.33673299999790873
```

Later in the chapter, a `for`loop is used to estimate the NPV of a project.

When we need to use a few math functions, we canimport the `math` module first:

```
>>>import math
>>>dir(math)
['__doc__', '__loader__', '__name__', '__package__', '__spec__',
'acos', 'acosh', 'asin', 'asinh', 'atan', 'atan2', 'atanh', 'ceil',
'copysign', 'cos', 'cosh', 'degrees', 'e', 'erf', 'erfc', 'exp',
'expm1', 'fabs', 'factorial', 'floor', 'fmod', 'frexp', 'fsum',
'gamma', 'gcd', 'hypot', 'inf', 'isclose', 'isfinite', 'isinf',
'isnan', 'ldexp', 'lgamma', 'log', 'log10', 'log1p', 'log2', 'modf',
'nan', 'pi', 'pow', 'radians', 'sin', 'sinh', 'sqrt', 'tan', 'tanh',
'trunc']
>>>math.pi
3.141592653589793
>>>
```

The `sqrt()`, square root, function is contained in the `math` module. Thus, to use the `sqrt()` function, we need to use `math.sqrt()`; see the following code:

```
>>>sqrt(2)
NameError: name 'sqrt' is not defined
>>>Traceback (most recent call last):
  File "<stdin>", line 1, in <module>
math.sqrt(2)
1.4142135623730951
>>>
```

If we want to call those functions directly, we canuse `from math import *`; see the following code:

```
>>>from math import *
>>>sqrt(3)
1.7320508075688772
>>>
```

To learn about individual embedded functions, we canuse the`help()` function;see the following code:

```
>>>help(len)
Help on built-in function len in module builtins:
len(obj, /)
    Return the number of items in a container.
>>>
```

Data input

Let's generate a very simple input dataset first, as shown here. Its name and location is `c:/temp/test.txt`. The format of the dataset is text:

```
a b
1 2
3 4
```

The code is shown here:

```
>>>f=open("c:/temp/test.txt","r")
>>>x=f.read()
>>>f.close()
```

The `print()` function could be used to show the value of x:

```
>>>print(x)
a b
1 2
3 4
>>>
```

For the second example, let's download the daily historical price for IBM from **Yahoo!Finance** first. To do so, we visit `http://finance.yahoo.com`:

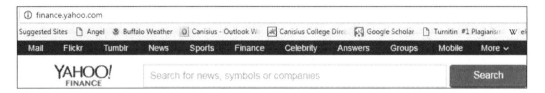

Enter `IBM` to find its related web page. Then click **Historical Data**, then click **Download**:

Assume that we save the daily data as `ibm.csv` under `c:/temp/`. The first five lines are shown here:

```
Date,Open,High,Low,Close,Volume,Adj Close
2016-11-
04,152.399994,153.639999,151.869995,152.429993,2440700,152.429993
2016-11-
03,152.509995,153.740005,151.800003,152.369995,2878800,152.369995
2016-11-
02,152.479996,153.350006,151.669998,151.949997,3074400,151.949997
2016-11-01,153.50,153.910004,151.740005,152.789993,3191900,152.789993
```

The first line shows the variable names: date, open price, high price achieved during the trading day, low price achieved during the trading day, close price of the last transaction during the trading day, trading volume, and adjusted price for the trading day. The delimiter is a comma. There are several ways of loading the text file. Some methods are discussed here:

- **Method I**: We could use `read_csv` from the `pandas` module:

```
>>> import pandas as pd
>>> x=pd.read_csv("c:/temp/ibm.csv")
>>>x[1:3]
          Date        Open        High         Low        Close
Volume   \
1   2016-11-02   152.479996   153.350006   151.669998   151.949997
3074400
2   2016-11-01   153.500000   153.910004   151.740005   152.789993
3191900

Adj.Close
1    151.949997
2    152.789993>>>
```

- **Method II**: We could use `read_table` from the `pandas` module; see the following code:

```
>>> import pandas as pd
>>> x=pd.read_table("c:/temp/ibm.csv",sep=',')
```

Alternatively, we could download the IBM daily price data directly from Yahoo!Finance; see the following code:

```
>>> import pandas as pd
>>>url=url='http://canisius.edu/~yany/data/ibm.csv'
>>> x=pd.read_csv(url)
>>>x[1:5]
          Date        Open        High         Low        Close     Volume
\
1   2016-11-03   152.509995   153.740005   151.800003   152.369995   2843600
2   2016-11-02   152.479996   153.350006   151.669998   151.949997   3074400
3   2016-11-01   153.500000   153.910004   151.740005   152.789993   3191900
4   2016-10-31   152.759995   154.330002   152.759995   153.690002   3553200

Adj Close
1    152.369995
2    151.949997
3    152.789993
4    153.690002>>>
```

We could retrieve data from an Excel file by using theExcelFile() function from thepandas module. First, we generate an Excel file with just a few observations; see the following screenshot:

	A	B	C	
1	date	returnA	returnB	
2	2001	0.1	0.12	
3	2002	0.03	0.05	
4	2003	0.12	0.15	
5	2004	0.2	0.22	

Let's call this Excel file stockReturns.xlxs and assume that it is saved under c:/temp/. The Python code is given here:

```
>>>infile=pd.ExcelFile("c:/temp/stockReturns.xlsx")
>>> x=infile.parse("Sheet1")
>>>x
date   returnAreturnB
0   2001      0.10      0.12
1   2002      0.03      0.05
2   2003      0.12      0.15
3   2004      0.20      0.22
>>>
```

To retrieve Python datasets with an extension of .pkl or .pickle, we canuse the following code. First, we download the Python dataset called ffMonthly.pkl from the author's web page at http://www3.canisius.edu/~yany/python/ffMonthly.pkl.

Assume that the dataset is saved under c:/temp/. The function called read_pickle() included in the pandas module canbe used to load the dataset with an extension of .pkl or .pickle:

```
>>> import pandas as pd
>>> x=pd.read_pickle("c:/temp/ffMonthly.pkl")
>>>x[1:3]
>>>
Mkt_RfSMBHMLRf
196308   0.0507  -0.0085   0.0163   0.0042
196309  -0.0157  -0.0050   0.0019  -0.0080
>>>
```

The following is the simplest `if` function: when our interest rate is negative, print a warning message:

```
if(r<0):
    print("interest rate is less than zero")
```

Conditions related to logicalAND and OR are shown here:

```
>>>if(a>0 and b>0):
  print("both positive")
>>>if(a>0 or b>0):
  print("at least one is positive")
```

For the multiple `if...elif` conditions, the following program illustrates its application by converting a number grade to a letter grade:

```
grade=74
if grade>=90:
    print('A')
elif grade >=85:
    print('A-')
elif grade >=80:
    print('B+')
elif grade >=75:
    print('B')
elif grade >=70:
    print('B-')
elif grade>=65:
    print('C+')
else:
    print('D')
```

Note that it is a good idea for such multiple `if...elif` functions to end with an `else` condition since we know exactly what the result is if none of those conditions are met.

Data manipulation

There are many different types of data, such as integer, real number, or string. The following table offers a list of those data types:

Data types	Description
Bool	Boolean (TRUE or FALSE) stored as a byte
Int	Platform integer (normally either int32 or int64)
int8	Byte (-128 to 127)

Data types	Description
int16	Integer (-32768 to 32767)
int32	Integer (-2147483648 to 2147483647)
int64	Integer (9223372036854775808 to 9223372036854775807)
unit8	Unsigned integer (0 to 255)
unit16	Unsigned integer (0 to 65535)
unit32	Unsigned integer (0 to 4294967295)
unit64	Unsigned integer (0 to 18446744073709551615)
float	Short and for float6
float32	Single precision float: sign bit23 bits mantissa; 8 bits exponent
float64	52 bits mantissa
complex	Shorthand for complex128
complex64	Complex number; represented by two 32-bit floats (real and imaginary components)
complex128	Complex number; represented by two 64-bit floats (real and imaginary components)

Table 1.1 List of different data types

In the following examples, we assign a value to r, which is a scalar, and several values to pv, which is an array (vector).The type() function is used to show their types:

```
>>> import numpy as np
>>> r=0.023
>>>pv=np.array([100,300,500])
>>>type(r)
<class'float'>
>>>type(pv)
<class'numpy.ndarray'>
```

To choose the appropriate decision, we use the round() function; see the following example:

```
>>> 7/3
2.333333333333335
>>>round(7/3,5)
2.33333
>>>
```

For data manipulation, let's look at some simple operations:

```
>>>import numpy as np
>>>a=np.zeros(10)              # array with 10 zeros
>>>b=np.zeros((3,2),dtype=float)   # 3 by 2 with zeros
```

```
>>>c=np.ones((4,3),float)                 # 4 by 3 with all ones
>>>d=np.array(range(10),float)            # 0,1, 2,3 .. up to 9
>>>e1=np.identity(4)                       # identity 4 by 4 matrix
>>>e2=np.eye(4)                            # same as above
>>>e3=np.eye(4,k=1)                        # 1 start from k
>>>f=np.arange(1,20,3,float)               # from 1 to 19 interval 3
>>>g=np.array([[2,2,2],[3,3,3]])           # 2 by 3
>>>h=np.zeros_like(g)                      # all zeros
>>>i=np.ones_like(g)                       # all ones
```

Some so-called `dot` functions are quite handy and useful:

```
>>> import numpy as np
>>> x=np.array([10,20,30])
>>>x.sum()
60
```

Anything after the number sign of # will be a comment. Arrays are another important data type:

```
>>>import numpy as np
>>>x=np.array([[1,2],[5,6],[7,9]])        # a 3 by 2 array
>>>y=x.flatten()
>>>x2=np.reshape(y,[2,3]         ) # a 2 by 3 array
```

We could assign a string to a variable:

```
>>> t="This is great"
>>>t.upper()
'THIS IS GREAT'
>>>
```

To find out all string-related functions, we use `dir('')`; see the following code:

```
>>>dir('')
['__add__', '__class__', '__contains__', '__delattr__', '__dir__',
'__doc__', '__eq__', '__format__', '__ge__', '__getattribute__',
'__getitem__', '__getnewargs__', '__gt__', '__hash__', '__init__',
'__iter__', '__le__', '__len__', '__lt__', '__mod__', '__mul__',
'__ne__', '__new__', '__reduce__', '__reduce_ex__', '__repr__',
'__rmod__', '__rmul__', '__setattr__', '__sizeof__', '__str__',
'__subclasshook__', 'capitalize', 'casefold', 'center', 'count',
'encode', 'endswith', 'expandtabs', 'find', 'format', 'format_
map', 'index', 'isalnum', 'isalpha', 'isdecimal', 'isdigit',
'isidentifier', 'islower', 'isnumeric', 'isprintable', 'isspace',
'istitle', 'isupper', 'join', 'ljust', 'lower', 'lstrip', 'maketrans',
'partition', 'replace', 'rfind', 'rindex', 'rjust', 'rpartition',
'rsplit', 'rstrip', 'split', 'splitlines', 'startswith', 'strip',
'swapcase', 'title', 'translate', 'upper', 'zfill']
>>>
```

For example, from the preceding list we see a function called `split`. After typing `help('' .split)`, we willhave related help information:

```
>>>help('' .split)
Help on built-in function split:

split(...) method of builtins.str instance
S.split(sep=None, maxsplit=-1) -> list of strings

    Return a list of the words in S, using sep as the
delimiter string. If maxsplit is given, at most maxsplit
splits are done. If sep is not specified or is None, any
whitespace string is a separator and empty strings are
removed from the result.
>>>
```

We could try the following example:

```
>>> x="this is great"
>>>x.split()
['this', 'is', 'great']
>>>
```

Matrix manipulation is important when we deal with various matrices:

$$C = A + B \quad\dots\dots\dots\dots\dots\dots(3)$$

The condition for equation (3) is that matrices A and B should have the same dimensions. For the product of two matrices, we have the following equation:

$$C = A * B \dots\dots\dots\dots\dots..(4)$$

Here,A is an n by k matrix (n rows and k columns), while B is a k by m matrix. Remember that the second dimension of the first matrix should be the same as the first dimension of the second matrix. In this case, it is k. If we assume that the individual data items in C, A, and B are $C_{i,j}$ (the *ith* row and the *jth* column), $A_{i,j}$, and $B_{i,j}$, we have the following relationship between them:

$$C_{i,j} = \sum_{i=1}^{n} \sum_{j=1}^{m} \sum_{p=1}^{k} a_{i,p}b_{p,j}\dots\dots\dots\dots\dots\dots\dots\dots(5)$$

The `dot()` function from the NumPy module could be used to carry the preceding matrix multiplication:

```
>>>a=np.array([[1,2,3],[4,5,6]],float)      # 2 by 3
>>>b=np.array([[1,2],[3,3],[4,5]],float)     # 3 by 2
>>>np.dot(a,b)                                # 2 by 2
>>>print(np.dot(a,b))
array([[ 19.,  23.],
 [ 43.,  53.]])
>>>
```

We could manually calculate *c(1,1): 1*1 + 2*3 + 3*4=19.*

After retrieving data or downloading data from the internet, we need to process it. Such a skill to process various types of raw data is vital to finance students and to professionals working in the finance industry. Here we will see how to download price data and then estimate returns.

Assume that we have *n* values of *x1, x2, …* and *xn*. There exist two types of means: arithmetic mean and geometric mean; see their genetic definitions here:

$$Arithmetic\ mean = \frac{\sum_{i=1}^{n} x_i}{n} \quad \dots\dots\dots\dots\dots\dots\dots\dots(6)$$

$$Geometric\ mean = \left(\prod_{i=1}^{n} x_i\right)^{1/n} \quad \dots\dots\dots\dots\dots\dots(7)$$

Assume that there exist three values of 2,3, and 4. Their arithmetic and geometric means are calculated here:

```
>>>(2+3+4)/3.
>>>3.0
>>>geo_mean=(2*3*4)**(1./3)
>>>round(geo_mean,4)
2.8845
```

For returns, the arithmetic mean's definition remains the same, while the geometric mean of returns is defined differently; see the following equations:

$$Arithmetic\ mean = \frac{\sum_{i=1}^{n} R_i}{n} \quad \dots\dots\dots\dots\dots\dots\dots (8)$$

$$Geometric\ mean = \left[\prod_{i=1}^{n}(1 + R_i)\right]^{\frac{1}{n}} - 1 \quad \dots\dots\dots\dots\dots (9)$$

In *Chapter 3, Time Value of Money*, we will discuss both means again.

We could say that NumPy is a basic module while SciPy is a more advanced one. NumPy tries to retain all features supported by either of its predecessors, while most new features belong in SciPy rather than NumPy. On the other hand, NumPy and SciPy have many overlapping features in terms of functions for finance. For those two types of definitions, see the following example:

```
>>> import scipy as sp
>>> ret=sp.array([0.1,0.05,-0.02])
>>>sp.mean(ret)
0.043333333333333342
>>>pow(sp.prod(ret+1),1./len(ret))-1
0.042163887067679262
```

Our second example is related to processing theFama-French 3 factor time series. Since this example is more complex than the previous one, if a user feels it is difficult to understand, he/she could simply skip this example. First, a ZIP file called `F-F_ Research_Data_Factor_TXT.zip` could be downloaded from Prof. French's Data Library. After unzipping and removing the first fewlines and annual datasets, we willhave a monthly Fama-French factor time series. The first fewlines and lastfew lines are shown here:

```
DATE    MKT_RFSMBHMLRF
192607    2.96    -2.30    -2.87    0.22
192608    2.64    -1.40    4.19    0.25
192609    0.36    -1.32    0.01    0.23

201607    3.95    2.90    -0.98    0.02
201608    0.49    0.94    3.18    0.02
201609    0.25    2.00    -1.34    0.02
```

Assume that the final file is called `ffMonthly.txt` under `c:/temp/`. The following program is used to retrieve and process the data:

```
import numpy as np
import pandas as pd
file=open("c:/temp/ffMonthly.txt","r")
data=file.readlines()
f=[]
index=[]
for i in range(1,np.size(data)):
    t=data[i].split()
    index.append(int(t[0]))
    for j in range(1,5):
        k=float(t[j])
        f.append(k/100)
```

```
n=len(f)
f1=np.reshape(f,[n/4,4])
ff=pd.DataFrame(f1,index=index,columns=['Mkt_Rf','SMB','HML','Rf'])
```

To view the first and last few observations for the dataset called `ff`, the functions of `.head()` and `.tail()` canbe used:

```
>>> ff.head()                          >>> ff.tail()
>>>                                    >>>
         Mkt_Rf     SMB      HML            Mkt_Rf     SMB      HML
Rf                                     Rf
192607   0.0296  -0.0230  -0.0287      201605   0.0178  -0.0027  -0.0179
0.0022                                 0.0001
192608   0.0264  -0.0140   0.0419      201606  -0.0004   0.0061  -0.0149
0.0025                                 0.0002
192609   0.0036  -0.0132   0.0001      201607   0.0395   0.0290  -0.0098
0.0023                                 0.0002
192610  -0.0324   0.0004   0.0051      201608   0.0049   0.0094   0.0318
0.0032                                 0.0002
192611   0.0253  -0.0020  -0.0035      201609   0.0025   0.0200  -0.0134
0.0031                                 0.0002
>> >                                   >> >
```

Data output

The simplest example is given here:

```
>>>f=open("c:/temp/out.txt","w")
>>>x="This is great"
>>>f.write(x)
>>>f.close()
```

For the next example, we download historical stock price data first, then write data to an output file:

```
import re
from matplotlib.finance import quotes_historical_yahoo_ochl
ticker='dell'
outfile=open("c:/temp/dell.txt","w")
begdate=(2013,1,1)
enddate=(2016,11,9)
p=quotes_historical_yahoo_ochl
(ticker,begdate,enddate,asobject=True,adjusted=True)
outfile.write(str(p))
outfile.close()
```

To retrieve the file, we have the following code:

```
>>>infile=open("c:/temp/dell.txt","r")
>>>x=infile.read()
```

One issue is that the preceding saved text file contains many unnecessary characters, such as [and]. We could apply a substitution function called `sub()` contained in the Python module;see the simplest example given here:

```
>>> import re
>>>re.sub("a","9","abc")
>>>
'9bc'
>>>
```

In the preceding example, we will replace the letter a with9. Interested readers could try the following two lines of code for the preceding program:

```
p2= re.sub('[\(\)\{\}\.<>a-zA-Z]','', p)
outfile.write(p2)
```

It is a good idea to generate Python datasets with an extension of `.pickle` since we canretrieve such data quite efficiently. The following is the complete Python code to generate `ffMonthly.pickle`. Here, we show how to download price data and then estimate returns:

```
import numpy as np
import pandas as pd
file=open("c:/temp/ffMonthly.txt","r")
data=file.readlines()
f=[]
index=[]
for i in range(1,np.size(data)):
    t=data[i].split()
    index.append(int(t[0]))
    for j in range(1,5):
        k=float(t[j])
        f.append(k/100)
n=len(f)
f1=np.reshape(f,[n/4,4])
ff=pd.DataFrame(f1,index=index,columns=['Mkt_Rf','SMB','HML','Rf'])
ff.to_pickle("c:/temp/ffMonthly.pickle")
```

Exercises

1. Where can youdownload and install Python?

2. Is Python case-sensitive?

3. How do youassign a set of values to *pv* in the format of a tuple. Could we change its values after the assignment?

4. Estimate the area of a circle if the diameter is 9.7 using Python.

5. How do you assign a value to a new variable?

6. How can you find some sample examples related to Python?

7. How do you launch Python's help function?

8. How can you find out more information about a specific function, such as `print()`?

9. What is the definition of built-in functions?

10. Is `pow()` a built-in function? How do we use it?

11. How do we find all built-in functions? How many built-in functions are present?

12. When we estimate the square root of 3, which Python function should we use?

13. Assume that the present value of a perpetuity is $124 and the annual cash flow is $50; what is the corresponding discount rate? The formula is given here:

$$PV = \frac{C}{R}$$

14. Based on the solution of the previous question, what is the corresponding quarterly rate?

15. For a perpetuity, the same cash flow happens at the same interval forever. Agrowing perpetuity is defined as follows: the future cash flow is increased at a constant growth rate forever. If the first cash flow happens at the end of the first period, we have the following formula:

$$PV\,(growing\ perpetuity) = \frac{C}{R - g}$$

Here PV is the present value, C is the cash flow of the next period, g is a growth rate, and R is the discount rate. If the first cash flow is $12.50, the constant growth rate is 2.5 percent, and the discount rate is 8.5 percent. What is the present value of this growing perpetuity?

16. For an *n*-day variance, we have the following formula:

$$\sigma^2_{ndays} = n\sigma^2_{daily}$$

Here σ^2_{ndays} is the daily variance and is σ^2_{days} is the daily standard deviation (volatility). If the volatility (daily standard deviation) of a stock is 0.2, what is its 10-day volatility?

17. We expect to have $25,000 in 5 years. If the annual deposit rate is 4.5 percent, how much do we have to deposit today?

18. The substitution function called `sub()` is from a Python module. Find out how many functions are contained in that module.

19. Write a Python program to convert the standard deviation estimated based on daily data or monthly data to an annual one by using the following formulas:

$$\sigma_{annual} = \sqrt{252}\sigma_{daily}$$

$$\sigma_{annual} = \sqrt{12}\sigma_{monthly}$$

20. The Sharpe ratio is a measure of trade-off between benefit (excess return) and cost (total risk) for an investment such as a portfolio. Write a Python program to estimate the Sharpe ratio by applying the following formula:

$$Sharpe = \frac{\bar{R} - \bar{R}_f}{\sigma}$$

Here $\bar{R}$ is the portfolio mean return, $\bar{R}_f$ is the mean risk-free rate and σ is the risk of the portfolio. Again, at this moment, it is perfectly fine that a reader does not understand the economic meaning of this ratio since the Sharpe ratio will be discussed in more detail in *Chapter 7,Multifactor Models and Performance Measures*.

Summary

In this chapter, many basic concepts and several widely used functions related to Python werediscussed. In *Chapter 2, Introduction to Python Modules*, we will discuss a key component of the Python language: Python modules and theirrelated issues. A module is a set of programs written by experts, professionals, or any person around a specific topic. A module could be viewed as a toolbox for a specific task. The chapter willfocus on the five most important modules: NumPy, SciPy, `matplotlib`, `statsmodels`, and `pandas`.

2
Introduction to Python Modules

In this chapter, we will discuss the most important issues related to Python modules, which are packages written by experts or any individual to serve a special purpose. In this book, we will use about a dozen modules in total. Thus, knowledge related to modules is critical in our understanding of Python and its application to finance. In particular, in this chapter, we will cover the following topics:

- Introduction to Python modules
- Introduction to NumPy
- Introduction to SciPy
- Introduction to `matplotlib`
- Introduction to `statsmodels`
- Introduction to pandas
- Python modules related to finance
- Introduction to the pandas_reader module
- Two financial calculators written in Python
- How to install a Python module
- Module dependency

What is a Python module?

A module is a package or group of programs that is written by an expert, user, or even a beginner who is usually very good in a specific area, to serve a specific purpose.

For example, a Python module called quant is for quantitative financial analysis. quant combines two modules of SciPy and `DomainModel`. The module contains a domain model that has exchanges, symbols, markets, and historical prices, among other things. Modules are very important in Python. In this book, we will discuss about a dozen modules implicitly or explicitly. In particular, we will explain five modules in detail: NumPy, SciPy, `matplotlib`, `statsmodels`, and Pandas.

As of November 16, 2016, there are 92,872 Python modules (packages) with different areas available according to the Python Package Index.

For the financial and insurance industries, there are 384 modules currently available.

Assume that we want to estimate the square root of 3 by using the `sqrt()` function. However, after issuing the following lines of code, we will encounter an error message:

```
>>>sqrt(3)
SyntaxError: invalid syntax
>>>
```

The reason is that the `sqrt()` function is not a built-in function. A built-in function could be viewed as an existing function when Python is launched. To use the `sqrt()` function, we need to import the math module first, as follows:

```
>>>import math
>>>x=math.sqrt(3)
>>>round(x,4)
1.7321
```

To use the `sqrt()` function, we have to type `math.sqrt()` if we use the `import math` command to import or upload the math module. In the preceding code, the `round()` function is used to control the number of decimal places. In addition, after issuing the command of `dir()`, we will see the existence of the math module, which is the last one in the output shown here:

```
>>>dir()
['__builtins__', '__doc__', '__name__', '__package__', 'math']
```

In addition, when a module is preinstalled, we could use `import x_module` to upload it. For instance, the math module is preinstalled. Later in the chapter, we will see how to find all built-in modules. In the preceding output, after issuing the command `dir()`, we also observe `__builtins__`. There are two underscores, before and after `builtin`. This `__builtins__` module is different from other built-in modules, such as the `math` module. It is for all built-in functions and other objects. Again, the command of `dir(__builtins__)` could be issued to list all built-in functions, as shown in the following code:

```
>>> dir(__builtins__)
['ArithmeticError', 'AssertionError', 'AttributeError',
'BaseException', 'BlockingIOError', 'BrokenPipeError', 'BufferError',
'BytesWarning', 'ChildProcessError', 'ConnectionAbortedError',
'ConnectionError', 'ConnectionRefusedError', 'ConnectionResetError',
'DeprecationWarning', 'EOFError', 'Ellipsis', 'EnvironmentError',
'Exception', 'False', 'FileExistsError', 'FileNotFoundError',
'FloatingPointError', 'FutureWarning', 'GeneratorExit',
'IOError', 'ImportError', 'ImportWarning', 'IndentationError',
'IndexError', 'InterruptedError', 'IsADirectoryError', 'KeyError',
'KeyboardInterrupt', 'LookupError', 'MemoryError', 'NameError',
'None', 'NotADirectoryError', 'NotImplemented', 'NotImplementedError',
'OSError', 'OverflowError', 'PendingDeprecationWarning',
'PermissionError', 'ProcessLookupError', 'RecursionError',
'ReferenceError', 'ResourceWarning', 'RuntimeError', 'RuntimeWarning',
'StopAsyncIteration', 'StopIteration', 'SyntaxError', 'SyntaxWarning',
'SystemError', 'SystemExit', 'TabError', 'TimeoutError',
'True', 'TypeError', 'UnboundLocalError', 'UnicodeDecodeError',
'UnicodeEncodeError', 'UnicodeError', 'UnicodeTranslateError',
'UnicodeWarning', 'UserWarning', 'ValueError', 'Warning',
'WindowsError', 'ZeroDivisionError', '_', '__build_class__', '__
debug__', '__doc__', '__import__', '__loader__', '__name__', '__
package__', '__spec__', 'abs', 'all', 'any', 'ascii', 'bin', 'bool',
'bytearray', 'bytes', 'callable', 'chr', 'classmethod', 'compile',
'complex', 'copyright', 'credits', 'debugfile', 'delattr', 'dict',
'dir', 'divmod', 'enumerate', 'eval', 'evalsc', 'exec', 'exit',
'filter', 'float', 'format', 'frozenset', 'getattr', 'globals',
'hasattr', 'hash', 'help', 'hex', 'id', 'input', 'int', 'isinstance',
'issubclass', 'iter', 'len', 'license', 'list', 'locals', 'map',
'max', 'memoryview', 'min', 'next', 'object', 'oct', 'open', 'open_in_
spyder', 'ord', 'pow', 'print', 'property', 'quit', 'range', 'repr',
'reversed', 'round', 'runfile', 'set', 'setattr', 'slice', 'sorted',
'staticmethod', 'str', 'sum', 'super', 'tuple', 'type', 'vars', 'zip']
```

From the preceding output, we find a function called `pow()`. The command of `help(pow)` could be used to find more information about this specific function; see the following:

```
>>> help(pow)
Help on built-in function pow in module builtins:
pow(x, y, z=None, /)
Equivalent to x**y (with two arguments) or x**y % z
(with three arguments)
Some types, such as ints, are able to use a more
efficient algorithm when invoked using the three argument form.
>> >
```

For convenience, it is a good idea to adopt a short name for an imported module. To save some typing effort when programming, we could use the command `import x_module as short_name` as shown in the following lines of code:

```
>>>import sys as s
>>>import time as tt
>>>import numpy as np
>>>import matplotlib as mp
```

When calling a specific function contained in an imported module, we use the module's short name, as shown in the following lines of code:

```
>>> import time as tt
>>> tt.localtime()
time.struct_time(tm_year=2016, tm_mon=11, tm_mday=21, tm_hour=10, tm_
min=58, tm_sec=33, tm_wday=0, tm_yday=326, tm_isdst=0)
>>>
```

Although users are free to choose any short names for an imported module, it is a great idea to respect some conventions, such as using np for NumPy and sp for SciPy. One added advantage of using such commonly used short names is to make our programs more readable to others. To show all functions in an imported module, the `dir(module)` command could be used, as shown in the following lines of code:

```
>>>import math
>>>dir(math)
['__doc__', '__loader__', '__name__', '__package__', 'acos', 'acosh',
'asin', 'asinh', 'atan', 'atan2', 'atanh', 'ceil', 'copysign', 'cos',
'cosh', 'degrees', 'e', 'erf', 'erfc', 'exp', 'expm1', 'fabs',
'factorial', 'floor', 'fmod', 'frexp', 'fsum', 'gamma', 'hypot',
'isfinite', 'isinf', 'isnan', 'ldexp', 'lgamma', 'log', 'log10',
'log1p', 'log2', 'modf', 'pi', 'pow', 'radians', 'sin', 'sinh',
'sqrt', 'tan', 'tanh', 'trunc']
>>>
```

Recall that in *Chapter 1, Python Basics*, `import math` and `from math import *` are compared. Generally speaking, to make your programs simpler, you could use `from math import *`. This is especially true for a beginner who has just started to learn Python programming. Let's take a look at the following lines of code:

```
>>>from math import *
>>>sqrt(3)
   1.7320508075688772
```

Now, all functions contained in the module will be available directly. On the other hand, if we use `import math`, we have to add the module name as a prefix, such as `math.sqrt()` instead of `sqrt()`. After getting more familiar with Python, it is a good idea to use the import module format instead of using `from module import *`. There are two reasons behind such a preference:

- First, users know exactly from which module the function comes from.

- Second, we might have written our own function with the same name as the function contained in another module. A module name ahead of a function will distinguish it from our own function, as shown in the following lines of code:

```
>>>import math
>>>math.sqrt(3)
   1.7320508075688772
```

The `del()` function is used to remove an imported/uploaded module which is deemed unnecessary, as shown in the following lines of code:

```
>>>import math
>>>dir()
['__builtins__', '__doc__', '__loader__', '__name__', '__package__',
'math']
>>>del math
>>>dir()
['__builtins__', '__doc__', '__loader__', '__name__', '__package__']
```

On the other hand, if we use `from math import *`, we cannot remove all functions, just issue `del math`. We have to remove those individual functions separately. The following two commands demonstrate such an effect:

```
>>>from math import *
>>>del math
Traceback (most recent call last):
File "<pyshell#23>", line 1, in <module>
del math NameError: name 'math' is not defined
```

For convenience, we could import only a few needed functions. To price a European call option, several functions are needed, such as `log()`, `exp()`, `sqrt()` and `cdf()`. `cdf()` is the function for cumulative standard normal distribution. To make those four functions available, we specify their names, as shown in the following lines of code:

```
From scipy import log,exp,sqrt,stats
```

The complete codes for pricing Black-Scholes-Merton call options are given here:

```
def bsCall(S,X,T,r,sigma):
    from scipy import log,exp,sqrt,stats
    d1=(log(S/X)+(r+sigma*sigma/2.)*T)/(sigma*sqrt(T))
    d2 = d1-sigma*sqrt(T)
    return S*stats.norm.cdf(d1)-X*exp(-r*T)*stats.norm.cdf(d2)
```

One example of calling the `bsCall` function is given here:

```
>>> bsCall(40,40,0.1,0.05,0.2)
1.1094616585675574
```

To find all available modules, a help window should be activated first. After that, issue modules. The result is shown here:

```
>>> help()
>>>
Welcome to Python 3.5's help utility!
```

If this is your first time using Python, you should definitely check out the tutorial on the internet at `http://docs.python.org/3.5/tutorial/`.

Enter the name of any module, keyword, or topic to get help on writing Python programs and using Python modules. To quit this help utility and return to the interpreter, just type `quit`.

To get a list of available modules, keywords, symbols, or topics, type `modules`, `keywords`, `symbols`, or `topics`. Each module also comes with a one-line summary of what it does; to list the modules whose name or summary contain a given string such as `spam`, type `modules spam`:

```
help>
```

Then, we issue modules under the Python `help>` prompt as shown in the following screenshot (to save space, only the first part of it is shown):

```
help> modules

Please wait a moment while I gather a list of all available modules...

__future__          aifc                html                setuptools
_ast                antigravity         http                shelve
_bisect             argparse            idlelib             shlex
_bootlocale         array               imaplib             shutil
_bz2                ast                 imghdr              signal
_codecs             asynchat            imp                 site
_codecs_cn          asyncio             importlib           smtpd
_codecs_hk          asyncore            inspect             smtplib
_codecs_iso2022     atexit              io                  sndhdr
_codecs_jp          audioop             ipaddress           socket
_codecs_kr          base64              itertools           socketserver
_codecs_tw          bdb                 json                sqlite3
_collections        binascii            keyword             sre_compile
_collections_abc    binhex              lib2to3             sre_constants
_compat_pickle      bisect              linecache           sre_parse
_compression        builtins            locale              ssl
_csv                bz2                 logging             stat
_ctypes             cProfile            lzma                statistics
_ctypes_test        calendar            macpath             string
_datetime           cgi                 macurl2path         stringprep
_decimal            cgitb               mailbox             struct
_dummy_thread       chunk               mailcap             subprocess
_elementtree        cmath               marshal             sunau
_functools          cmd                 math                symbol
```

To find a specific module, we just type `modules` followed by the module's name. Assume that we are interested in the module called `cmd`. Then, we issue `modules cmd` in the help window; see the following screenshot:

```
help> modules cmd

Here is a list of modules whose name or summary contains 'cmd'.
If there are any, enter a module name to get more help.

cmd - A generic class to build line-oriented command interpreters.
distutils.cmd - distutils.cmd
pip._vendor.cachecontrol._cmd
pip.cmdoptions - shared options and groups

help>
```

To get more information on modules, navigate to **All Programs** | Python 3.5 | Python 3.5 Module Docs, as shown in the following screenshot:

After clicking Python 3.5 Module Docs (32-bit), we will get more information.

Introduction to NumPy

In the following examples, the `np.size()` function from NumPy shows the number of data items of an array, and the `np.std()` function is used to calculate standard deviation:

```
>>>import numpy as np
>>>x= np.array([[1,2,3],[3,4,6]])      # 2 by 3 matrix
>>>np.size(x)                          # number of data items
6
>>>np.size(x,1)                        # show number of columns
3
>>>np.std(x)
1.5723301886761005
>>>np.std(x,1)
Array([ 0.81649658, 1.24721913]
>>>total=x.sum()                       # attention to the format
>>>z=np.random.rand(50)                #50 random obs from [0.0, 1)
>>>y=np.random.normal(size=100)        # from standard normal
>>>r=np.array(range(0,100),float)/100  # from 0, .01,to .99
```

Compared with a Python array, a NumPy array is a contiguous piece of memory that is passed directly to LAPACK, which is a software library for numerical linear algebra under the hood, so that matrix manipulation is very fast in Python. An array in NumPy is like a matrix in MATLAB. Unlike lists in Python, an array should contain the same data type, as shown in the following line of code:

```
>>>np.array([100,0.1,2],float)
```

The real data type is `float64`, and the default for numerical values is also `float64`.

In the preceding example, we could view that the `np.array()` function converts a list with the same data type, an integer in this case, to an array. To change the data type, it should be specified with the second input value, `dtype`, as shown in the following lines of code:

```
>>>x=[1,2,3,20]
>>>y=np.array(x1,dtype=float)
>>>y
array([ 1., 2., 3., 20.])
```

In the previous example, `dtype` is the keyword specifying the data type. For a list, different data types could coexist without causing any problems. However, when converting a list containing different data types into an array, an error message will appear, as shown in the following lines of code:

```
>>>x2=[1,2,3,"good"]
>>>x2
[1, 2, 3, 'good']
>>>y3=np.array(x2,float)
Traceback (most recent call last):
File "<pyshell#25>", line 1, in <module>
y3=np.array(x2,float)
ValueError: could not convert string to float: 'good'
. ]])
```

To show all functions contained in Numpy, `dir(np)` is used after the Numpy module is imported.

The following shows the first few lines:

```
>>> import numpy as np
>>> dir(np)
['ALLOW_THREADS', 'BUFSIZE', 'CLIP', 'ComplexWarning', 'DataSource',
'ERR_CALL', 'ERR_DEFAULT', 'ERR_IGNORE', 'ERR_LOG', 'ERR_PRINT',
'ERR_RAISE', 'ERR_WARN', 'FLOATING_POINT_SUPPORT', 'FPE_DIVIDEBYZERO',
'FPE_INVALID', 'FPE_OVERFLOW', 'FPE_UNDERFLOW', 'False_', 'Inf',
'Infinity', 'MAXDIMS', 'MAY_SHARE_BOUNDS', 'MAY_SHARE_EXACT',
'MachAr', 'ModuleDeprecationWarning', 'NAN', 'NINF', 'NZERO', 'NaN',
'PINF', 'PZERO', 'PackageLoader', 'RAISE', 'RankWarning', 'SHIFT_
DIVIDEBYZERO', 'SHIFT_INVALID', 'SHIFT_OVERFLOW', 'SHIFT_UNDERFLOW',
'ScalarType', 'Tester', 'TooHardError', 'True_', 'UFUNC_BUFSIZE_
DEFAULT', 'UFUNC_PYVALS_NAME', 'VisibleDeprecationWarning', 'WRAP', '_
NoValue', '__NUMPY_SETUP__', '__all__', '__builtins__', '__cached__',
'__config__', '__doc__', '__file__', '__git_revision__', '__loader__',
'__mkl_version__', '__name__', '__package__', '__path__', '__spec__',
'__version__', '_import_tools', '_mat', 'abs', 'absolute', 'absolute_
import', 'add', 'add_docstring', 'add_newdoc', 'add_newdoc_ufunc',
'add_newdocs', 'alen', 'all', 'allclose', 'alltrue', 'alterdot',
'amax', 'amin', 'angle', 'any', 'append', 'apply_along_axis', 'apply_
over_axes', 'arange', 'arccos', 'arccosh', 'arcsin', 'arcsinh',
'arctan', 'arctan2', 'arctanh', 'argmax', 'argmin', 'argpartition',
'argsort', 'argwhere', 'around', 'array', 'array2string', 'array_
equal', 'array_equiv', 'array_repr', 'array_split', 'array_str',
'asanyarray',
```

Actually, a better way is to generate an array containing all functions as follows:

```
>>> x=np.array(dir(np))
>>> len(x)
598
```

To show the functions from `200` to `250`, `x[200:250]` is typed; see the following code:

```
>>> x[200:250]
array(['disp', 'divide', 'division', 'dot', 'double', 'dsplit',
'dstack',
       'dtype', 'e', 'ediff1d', 'einsum', 'emath', 'empty', 'empty_
like',
       'equal', 'errstate', 'euler_gamma', 'exp', 'exp2', 'expand_
dims',
       'expm1', 'extract', 'eye', 'fabs', 'fastCopyAndTranspose',
'fft',
       'fill_diagonal', 'find_common_type', 'finfo', 'fix',
'flatiter',
       'flatnonzero', 'flexible', 'fliplr', 'flipud', 'float',
'float16',
       'float32', 'float64', 'float_', 'floating', 'floor', 'floor_
divide',
       'fmax', 'fmin', 'fmod', 'format_parser', 'frexp', 'frombuffer',
       'fromfile'],
      dtype='<U25')
>> >
```

It is easy to find out more information about a specific function. After issuing `dir(np)`, the `std()` function appears, among others. To seek more information about this function, `help(np.std)` is used. The following shows only a few lines of code for brevity:

```
>>>import numpy as np
>>>help(np.std)
Help on function std in module numpy.core.fromnumeric:

std(a, axis=None, dtype=None, out=None, ddof=0, keepdims=False)
    Compute the standard deviation along the specified axis.
```

The function returns the standard deviation, a measure of the spread of a distribution, of the array elements. The standard deviation is computed for the flattened array by default, otherwise over the specified axis:

```
    Parameters
```

```
    - - - - - - - - - -
a : array_like
    Calculate the standard deviation of these values.
axis : None or int or tuple of ints, optional
Axis or axes along which the standard deviation is computed. The
default is to compute the standard deviation of the flattened array.

    .. versionadded: 1.7.0
```

Introduction to SciPy

The following are a few examples based on the functions enclosed in the SciPy module. The `sp.npv()` function estimates the present values for a given set of cash flows with the first cash flow happening at time zero. The first input value is the discount rate, and the second input is an array of all cash flows.

The following is one example. Note that the `sp.npv()` function is different from the Excel `npv()` function. We will explain why this is so in *Chapter 3, Time Value of Money*:

```
>>>import scipy as sp
>>>cashflows=[-100,50,40,20,10,50]
>>>x=sp.npv(0.1,cashflows)
>>>round(x,2)
>>>31.41
```

The `sp.pmt()` function is used to answer the following question.

What is the monthly cash flow to pay off a mortgage of $250,000 over 30 years with an annual percentage rate (APR) of 4.5 percent, compounded monthly? The following code shows the answer:

```
>>>payment=sp.pmt(0.045/12,30*12,250000)
>>>round(payment,2)
-1266.71
```

Based on the preceding result, the monthly payment will be $1,266.71. It might be quite strange that we have a negative value. Actually, this `sp.pmt()` function mimics the equivalent function in Excel, as we will see in the following screenshot:

The input values are: the effective period rate, the number of the period, and the present value. By the way, the number in a pair of parentheses means a negative one.

At the moment, just ignore the negative sign. In *Chapter 3*, *Time Value of Money*, this so-called Excel convention will be discussed in more detail.

Similarly, the `sp.pv()` function replicates the Excel `PV()` function. For the `sp.pv()` function, its input format is `sp.pv(rate, nper, pmt, fv=0.0, when='end')`, where `rate` is the discount rate, `nper` is the number of periods, `pmt` is the period payment, and `fv` is the future value with a default value of zero. The last input variable specifies whether the cash flows are at the end of each time period or at the beginning of each period. By default, it is at the end of each period. The following commands show how to call this function:

```
>>>pv1=sp.pv(0.1,5,0,100) # pv of one future cash flow
>>>round(pv1,2)
-92.09
>>>pv2=sp.pv(0.1,5,100)    # pv of annuity
>>>round(pv2,2)
-379.08
```

The `sp.fv()` function has a setting similar to that of `sp.pv()`. In finance, we estimate both arithmetic and geometric means, which are defined in the following formulas.

For *n* numbers of *x*, that is, *x1*, *x2*, *x3*, and *xn*, we have the following:

$$Arithmetic\ mean = \frac{\sum_{i=1}^{n} x_i}{n} \quad \dots\dots\dots\dots\dots\dots\dots\dots (1)$$

$$Geometric\ mean = \left[\prod_{i=1}^{n} x_i) \right]^{1/n} \quad \dots\dots\dots\dots\dots\dots (2)$$

Here, $\sum_{i=1}^{n} x_i = x_1 + x_2 + \cdots + x_n$ and $\prod_{i=1}^{n} x_i = (x_1 * x_2 * \cdots * x_n)$. Assume that we have three numbers of *a*, *b*, and *c*. Then their arithmetic mean is *(a+b+c)/3*, while their geometric mean is *(a*b*c)^(1/3)*. For three values of 2, 3, and 4, we have the following two means:

```
>>> (2+3+4)/3.
>>>3.0
>>>geo_mean=(2*3*4)**(1./3)
>>>round(geo_mean,4)
2.8845
```

If *n* returns are given, the formula to estimate their arithmetic mean remains the same. However, the geometric mean formula for returns is different, as shown here:

$$Arithmetic\ mean = \frac{\sum_{i=1}^{n} R_i}{n} \quad \dots\dots\dots\dots\dots\dots\dots (3)$$

G

$$Geometric\ mean = [\ \prod_{i=1}^{n}(1 + R_i)\ ]^{\frac{1}{n}} - 1 \quad \dots\dots\dots\dots\dots\dots\dots (4)$$

To estimate a geometric mean, the `sp.prod()` function would be applied. The function gives us the products of all data items; see the following code:

```
>>>import scipy as sp
>>>ret=sp.array([0.1,0.05,-0.02])
>>>sp.mean(ret)                          # arithmetic mean
0.04333
>>>pow(sp.prod(ret+1),1./len(ret))-1 # geometric mean
0.04216
```

Actually, a simple Python function could be written with just two lines to calculate a geometric mean for a set of given returns; see the following code:

```
def geoMeanReturn(ret):
    return pow(sp.prod(ret+1),1./len(ret))-1
```

It is easy to call the preceding function; see the following code:

```
>>> import scipy as sp
>>> ret=sp.array([0.1,0.05,-0.02])
>>> geoMeanReturn(ret)
0.042163887067679262
```

Two other useful functions are `sp.unique()` and `sp.median()`, as shown in the following code:

```
>>>sp.unique([2,3,4,6,6,4,4])
Array([2,3,4,6])
>>>sp.median([1,2,3,4,5])
3.0
```

Python's `sp.pv()`, `sp.fv()`, and `sp.pmt()` functions behave like Excel's `pv()`, `fv()`, and `pmt()` functions, respectively. They have the same sign convention: the sign of the present value is the opposite of the future value.

In the following example, to estimate a present value if we enter a positive future value, we will end up with a negative present value:

```
>>>import scipy as sp
>>>round(sp.pv(0.1,5,0,100),2)
>>>-62.09
>>>round(sp.pv(0.1,5,0,-100),2)
>>>62.09
```

There are several ways to find out all the functions contained in the SciPy module.

Firstly, we can read related manuals. Secondly, we can issue the following lines of code:

```
>>>import numpy as np
>>>dir(np)
```

To save space, only a few lines of the output are shown in the following code:

```
>>> import scipy as sp
>>> dir(sp)
['ALLOW_THREADS', 'BUFSIZE', 'CLIP', 'ComplexWarning', 'DataSource',
'ERR_CALL', 'ERR_DEFAULT', 'ERR_IGNORE', 'ERR_LOG', 'ERR_PRINT',
'ERR_RAISE', 'ERR_WARN', 'FLOATING_POINT_SUPPORT', 'FPE_DIVIDEBYZERO',
'FPE_INVALID', 'FPE_OVERFLOW', 'FPE_UNDERFLOW', 'False_', 'Inf',
'Infinity', 'MAXDIMS', 'MAY_SHARE_BOUNDS', 'MAY_SHARE_EXACT',
'MachAr', 'ModuleDeprecationWarning', 'NAN', 'NINF', 'NZERO', 'NaN',
'PINF', 'PZERO', 'PackageLoader', 'RAISE', 'RankWarning', 'SHIFT_
DIVIDEBYZERO', 'SHIFT_INVALID', 'SHIFT_OVERFLOW', 'SHIFT_UNDERFLOW',
'ScalarType', 'Tester', 'TooHardError', 'True_', 'UFUNC_BUFSIZE_
DEFAULT', 'UFUNC_PYVALS_NAME', 'VisibleDeprecationWarning', 'WRAP',
'__SCIPY_SETUP__', '__all__', '__builtins__', '__cached__', '__
config__', '__doc__', '__file__', '__loader__', '__name__', '__numpy_
version__', '__package__', '__path__', '__spec__', '__version__',
'_lib', 'absolute', 'absolute_import', 'add', 'add_docstring', 'add_
newdoc', 'add_newdoc_ufunc', 'add_newdocs', 'alen', 'all', 'allclose',
'alltrue', 'alterdot', 'amax', 'amin', 'angle', 'any', 'append',
'apply_along_axis', 'apply_over_axes', 'arange', 'arccos', 'arccosh',
'arcsin', 'arcsinh', 'arctan', 'arctan2', 'arctanh', 'argmax',
'argmin', 'argpartition', 'argsort', 'argwhere', 'around', 'array',
'array2string', 'array_equal', 'array_equiv', 'array_repr', 'array_
split', 'array_str', 'asanyarray', 'asarray', 'asarray_chkfinite',
'ascontiguousarray', 'asfarray', 'asfortranarray', 'asmatrix',
'asscalar', 'atleast_1d', 'atleast_2d', 'atleast_3d', 'average',
'bartlett',
```

Similarly, we could save all the functions to a vector (array); see the following code:

```
>>>import scipy as sp
>>> x=dir(sp)
>>> len(x)
588
>>>
```

Introduction to matplotlib

Graphs and other visual representations have become more important in explaining many complex financial concepts, trading strategies, and formulas.

In this section, we discuss the `matplotlib` module, which is used to create various types of graphs. In addition, the module will be used intensively in *Chapter 10, Options and Futures*, when we discuss the famous Black-Scholes-Merton option model and various trading strategies. The `matplotlib` module is designed to produce publication-quality figures and graphs. The `matplotlib` module depends on NumPy and SciPy, which were discussed in the previous sections. To save generated graphs, there are several output formats available, such as PDF, Postscript, SVG, and PNG.

How to install matplotlib

If Python was installed by using the Anaconda super package, then `matplotlib` is preinstalled already. After launching Spyder, type the following line to test. If there is no error, it means that we have imported/uploaded the module successfully. This is the beauty of using a super package such as Anaconda:

```
>>> import matplotlib
```

To install the `matplotlib` module or other modules independently, see the *Module dependency – how to install a module* section.

Several graphical presentations using matplotlib

The best way to understand the usage of the `matplotlib` module is through examples. The following example could be the simplest one since it has just three lines of Python code. The objective is to link several points. By default, the `matplotlib` module assumes that the *x* axis starts at zero and moves by one on every element of the array.

The following screenshot of command lines illustrates this situation:

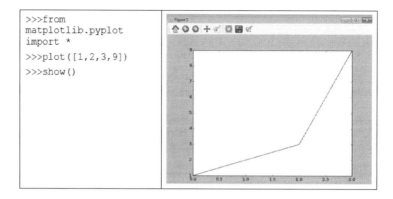

After typing the last command of show() and hitting the *Enter* key, the above-right graph will appear. At the top of the graph, a set of icons (functions) are available. By clicking them, we could adjust our image or save our image. After closing the preceding figure, we could return to the Python prompt. On the other hand, if we issue show() a second time, nothing will happen. To show the preceding graph again, we have to issue both plot([1,2,3,9]) and show(). Two labels could be added for both the *x* axis and *y* axis as follows.

The corresponding graph is shown in the following screenshot on the right:

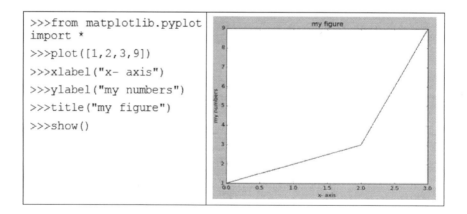

The next example presents two cosine functions:

```
>>>from pylab import *
>>>x=np.linspace(-np.pi,np.pi,256,endpoint=True)
>>>C,S = np.cos(x), np.sin(x)
>>>plot(x,C),plot(x,S)
>>>show()
```

In the preceding code, the `linspace()` function has four input values: `start`, `stop`, `num`, and `endpoint`. In the preceding example, we will start from *-3.1415916* and stop at *3.1415926*, with *256* values between. In addition, the endpoints will be included. By the way, the default value of `num` is *50*. The following example shows the scatter pattern. First, the `np.random.normal()` function is used to generate two sets of random numbers. Since n is `1024`, we have 1,024 observations for both X and Y variables. The key function is `scatter(X,Y)`, as follows:

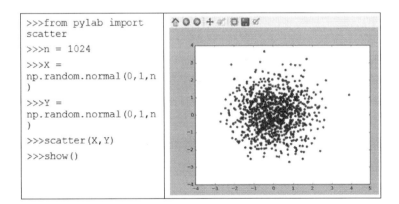

```
>>>from pylab import
scatter
>>>n = 1024
>>>X =
np.random.normal(0,1,n
)
>>>Y =
np.random.normal(0,1,n
)
>>>scatter(X,Y)
>>>show()
```

Here is a more complex graph showing the stock movement. Let's look at the code first:

```
import datetime
import matplotlib.pyplot as plt
from matplotlib.finance import quotes_historical_yahoo_ochl
from matplotlib.dates import MonthLocator,DateFormatter
ticker='AAPL'
begdate= datetime.date( 2012, 1, 2 )
```

```
enddate = datetime.date( 2013, 12,5)
months = MonthLocator(range(1,13), bymonthday=1, interval=3) # every
3rd month
monthsFmt = DateFormatter("%b '%Y")
x = quotes_historical_yahoo_ochl(ticker, begdate, enddate)
if len(x) == 0:
    print ('Found no quotes')
    raise SystemExit
dates = [q[0] for q in x]
closes = [q[4] for q in x]
fig, ax = plt.subplots()
ax.plot_date(dates, closes, '-')
ax.xaxis.set_major_locator(months)
ax.xaxis.set_major_formatter(monthsFmt)
ax.xaxis.set_minor_locator(mondays)
ax.autoscale_view()
ax.grid(True)
fig.autofmt_xdate()
```

The corresponding graph is shown here:

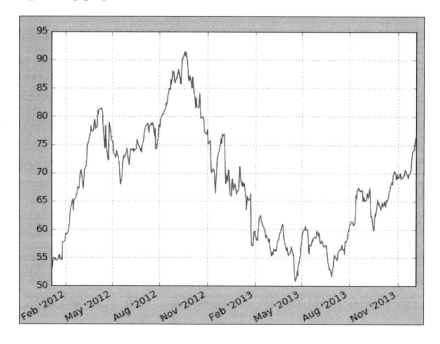

Introduction to statsmodels

`statsmodels` is a powerful Python package for many types of statistical analysis. Again, if Python was installed via Anaconda, then the module was installed at the same time. In statistics, **ordinary least square** (OLS) regression is a method for estimating the unknown parameters in a linear regression model. It minimizes the sum of squared vertical distances between the observed values and the values predicted by the linear approximation. The OLS method is used extensively in finance. Assume that we have the following equation, where y is an n by *1* vector (array), and x is an n by *(m+1)* matrix, a return matrix (n by m), plus a vector that contains *1* only. n is the number of observations, and m is the number of independent variables:

$$y_t = \alpha + \beta * x_t + \varepsilon_t \quad \dots\dots\dots\dots\dots\dots\dots\dots\dots\dots\dots\dots(5)$$

In the following program, after generating the x and y vectors, we run an OLS regression (a linear regression). The x and y are artificial data. The last line prints the parameters only (the intercept is `1.28571420` and the slope is `0.35714286`):

```
>>> import numpy as np
>>> import statsmodels.api as sm
>>> y=[1,2,3,4,2,3,4]
>>> x=range(1,8)
>>> x=sm.add_constant(x)
>>> results=sm.OLS(y,x).fit()
>>> print(results.params)
    [ 1.28571429  0.35714286]
```

To find out more information about this module, the `dir()` function could be used:

```
>>> import statsmodels as sm
>>> dir(sm)
['CacheWriteWarning', 'ConvergenceWarning', 'InvalidTestWarning',
'IterationLimitWarning', 'NoseWrapper', 'Tester', '__builtins__',
'__cached__', '__doc__', '__docformat__', '__file__', '__init__',
'__loader__', '__name__', '__package__', '__path__', '__spec__',
'__version__', 'api', 'base', 'compat', 'datasets', 'discrete',
'distributions', 'duration', 'emplike', 'errstate', 'formula',
'genmod', 'graphics', 'info', 'iolib', 'nonparametric', 'print_
function', 'regression', 'robust', 'sandbox', 'simplefilter', 'stats',
'test', 'tools', 'tsa', 'version']
```

For various submodules, `dir()` could be used as well; see the example shown here:

```
>>> import statsmodels.api as api
>>> dir(api)
['Categorical', 'CategoricalIndex', 'DataFrame', 'DateOffset',
'DatetimeIndex', 'ExcelFile', 'ExcelWriter', 'Expr', 'Float64Index',
'Grouper', 'HDFStore', 'Index', 'IndexSlice', 'Int64Index',
'MultiIndex', 'NaT', 'Panel', 'Panel4D', 'Period', 'PeriodIndex',
'RangeIndex', 'Series', 'SparseArray', 'SparseDataFrame',
'SparseList', 'SparsePanel', 'SparseSeries', 'SparseTimeSeries',
'Term', 'TimeGrouper', 'TimeSeries', 'Timedelta', 'TimedeltaIndex',
'Timestamp', 'WidePanel', '__builtins__', '__cached__', '__doc__',
'__docformat__', '__file__', '__loader__', '__name__', '__package__',
'__path__', '__spec__', '__version__', '_np_version_under1p10',
'_np_version_under1p11', '_np_version_under1p12', '_np_version_
under1p8', '_np_version_under1p9', '_period', '_sparse', '_testing',
'_version', 'algos', 'bdate_range', 'compat', 'computation', 'concat',
'core', 'crosstab', 'cut', 'date_range', 'datetime', 'datetools',
'dependency', 'describe_option', 'eval', 'ewma', 'ewmcorr', 'ewmcov',
'ewmstd', 'ewmvar', 'ewmvol', 'expanding_apply', 'expanding_corr',
'expanding_count', 'expanding_cov', 'expanding_kurt', 'expanding_max',
'expanding_mean', 'expanding_median', 'expanding_min', 'expanding_
quantile', 'expanding_skew', 'expanding_std', 'expanding_sum',
'expanding_var', 'factorize', 'fama_macbeth', 'formats', 'get_
dummies', 'get_option', 'get_store', 'groupby', 'hard_dependencies',
'hashtable', 'index', 'indexes', 'infer_freq', 'info', 'io',
'isnull', 'json', 'lib', 'lreshape', 'match', 'melt', 'merge',
'missing_dependencies', 'msgpack', 'notnull', 'np', 'offsets', 'ols',
'option_context', 'options', 'ordered_merge', 'pandas', 'parser',
'period_range', 'pivot', 'pivot_table', 'plot_params', 'pnow', 'qcut',
'read_clipboard', 'read_csv', 'read_excel', 'read_fwf', 'read_gbq',
'read_hdf', 'read_html', 'read_json', 'read_msgpack', 'read_pickle',
'read_sas', 'read_sql', 'read_sql_query', 'read_sql_table', 'read_
stata', 'read_table', 'reset_option', 'rolling_apply', 'rolling_
corr', 'rolling_count', 'rolling_cov', 'rolling_kurt', 'rolling_max',
'rolling_mean', 'rolling_median', 'rolling_min', 'rolling_quantile',
'rolling_skew', 'rolling_std', 'rolling_sum', 'rolling_var', 'rolling_
window', 'scatter_matrix', 'set_eng_float_format', 'set_option',
'show_versions', 'sparse', 'stats', 'test', 'timedelta_range', 'to_
datetime', 'to_msgpack', 'to_numeric', 'to_pickle', 'to_timedelta',
'tools', 'tseries', 'tslib', 'types', 'unique', 'util', 'value_
counts', 'wide_to_long']
```

From the preceding output, it can be seen that 16 functions start with the word `read`; see the following table:

Name	Description
read_clipboard	Input data from a clipboard
read_csv	Input data from a csv (comma separated value)
read_excel	Input data from an Excel file
read_fwf	Input data with a fixed width
read_gbq	Load data from Google BigQuery
read_hdf	Read HDF5 format data
read_html	Input data from a web page
read_json	Read JSON (JavaScript Object Notation) data
read_msgpack	MessagePack is a fast, compact binary serialization format, suitable for similar data to JSON
read_pickle	Input a Python dataset called pickle
read_sas	Input data from a SAS dataset
read_sql	Input data from SQL database
read_sql_query	Input data from a query
read_sql_table	Read SQL database table into a DataFrame
read_stata	Input data from a Stata dataset
read_table	Input data from a text file

Table 2.1 A list of functions used to input data

Introduction to pandas

The `pandas` module is a powerful tool used to process various types of data, including economics, financial, and accounting data. If Python was installed on your machine via Anaconda, then the `pandas` module was installed already. If you issue the following command without any error, it indicates that the `pandas` module was installed:

```
>>>import pandas as pd
```

In the following example, we generate two time series starting from January 1, 2013. The names of those two time series (columns) are A and B:

```
import numpy as np
import pandas as pd
dates=pd.date_range('20160101',periods=5)
np.random.seed(12345)
x=pd.DataFrame(np.random.rand(5,2),index=dates,columns=('A','B'))
```

First, we import both NumPy and `pandas` modules. The `pd.date_range()` function is used to generate an index array. The `x` variable is a pandas DataFrame with dates as its index. Later in this chapter, we will discuss the `pd.DataFrame()` function. The `columns()` function defines the names of those columns. Because the `seed()` function is used in the program, anyone can generate the same random values. The `describe()` function offers the properties of those two columns, such as mean and standard deviation. Again, we call such a function, as shown in the following code:

```
>>> x
                 A          B
2016-01-01  0.929616   0.316376
2016-01-02  0.183919   0.204560
2016-01-03  0.567725   0.595545
2016-01-04  0.964515   0.653177
2016-01-05  0.748907   0.653570
>>>
>>> x.describe()
              A          B
count  5.000000   5.000000
mean   0.678936   0.484646
std    0.318866   0.209761
min    0.183919   0.204560
25%    0.567725   0.316376
50%    0.748907   0.595545
75%    0.929616   0.653177
max    0.964515   0.653570
>>>
```

To show all functions contained in the `pandas` module, the command of `dir(pd)` is used after importing the module; see the following code and the corresponding output:

```
>>> import pandas as pd
>>> dir(pd)
['Categorical', 'CategoricalIndex', 'DataFrame', 'DateOffset',
'DatetimeIndex', 'ExcelFile', 'ExcelWriter', 'Expr', 'Float64Index',
'Grouper', 'HDFStore', 'Index', 'IndexSlice', 'Int64Index',
'MultiIndex', 'NaT', 'Panel', 'Panel4D', 'Period', 'PeriodIndex',
'RangeIndex', 'Series', 'SparseArray', 'SparseDataFrame',
'SparseList', 'SparsePanel', 'SparseSeries', 'SparseTimeSeries',
'Term', 'TimeGrouper', 'TimeSeries', 'Timedelta', 'TimedeltaIndex',
'Timestamp', 'WidePanel', '__builtins__', '__cached__', '__doc__',
'__docformat__', '__file__', '__loader__', '__name__', '__package__',
'__path__', '__spec__', '__version__', '_np_version_under1p10',
'_np_version_under1p11', '_np_version_under1p12', '_np_version_
under1p8', '_np_version_under1p9', '_period', '_sparse', '_testing',
'_version', 'algos', 'bdate_range', 'compat', 'computation', 'concat',
```

```
'core', 'crosstab', 'cut', 'date_range', 'datetime', 'datetools',
'dependency', 'describe_option', 'eval', 'ewma', 'ewmcorr', 'ewmcov',
'ewmstd', 'ewmvar', 'ewmvol', 'expanding_apply', 'expanding_corr',
'expanding_count', 'expanding_cov', 'expanding_kurt', 'expanding_max',
'expanding_mean', 'expanding_median', 'expanding_min', 'expanding_
quantile', 'expanding_skew', 'expanding_std', 'expanding_sum',
'expanding_var', 'factorize', 'fama_macbeth', 'formats', 'get_
dummies', 'get_option', 'get_store', 'groupby', 'hard_dependencies',
'hashtable', 'index', 'indexes', 'infer_freq', 'info', 'io',
'isnull', 'json', 'lib', 'lreshape', 'match', 'melt', 'merge',
'missing_dependencies', 'msgpack', 'notnull', 'np', 'offsets', 'ols',
'option_context', 'options', 'ordered_merge', 'pandas', 'parser',
'period_range', 'pivot', 'pivot_table', 'plot_params', 'pnow', 'qcut',
'read_clipboard', 'read_csv', 'read_excel', 'read_fwf', 'read_gbq',
'read_hdf', 'read_html', 'read_json', 'read_msgpack', 'read_pickle',
'read_sas', 'read_sql', 'read_sql_query', 'read_sql_table', 'read_
stata', 'read_table', 'reset_option', 'rolling_apply', 'rolling_
corr', 'rolling_count', 'rolling_cov', 'rolling_kurt', 'rolling_max',
'rolling_mean', 'rolling_median', 'rolling_min', 'rolling_quantile',
'rolling_skew', 'rolling_std', 'rolling_sum', 'rolling_var', 'rolling_
window', 'scatter_matrix', 'set_eng_float_format', 'set_option',
'show_versions', 'sparse', 'stats', 'test', 'timedelta_range', 'to_
datetime', 'to_msgpack', 'to_numeric', 'to_pickle', 'to_timedelta',
'tools', 'tseries', 'tslib', 'types', 'unique', 'util', 'value_
counts', 'wide_to_long']
```

If going through the preceding list carefully, we will see the same functions starting with read_, shown in Table 2.1, as those contained in the statsmodels module. This type of duplication makes our program job a little bit easier. Assume that we plan to replace missing values (NaN) with the mean of the time series. The two functions used are mean() and fillna():

```
>>> import pandas as pd
>>> import numpy as np
>>> x=pd.Series([1,4,-3,np.nan,5])
>>> x
0    1.0
1    4.0
2   -3.0
3    NaN
4    5.0
dtype: float64
>>> m=np.mean(x)
>>> m
1.75
>>> x.fillna(m)
0    1.00
```

```
1      4.00
2     -3.00
3      1.75
4      5.00
dtype: float64>> >
```

From the output on the right-hand side, the fourth observation of NaN is replaced with a mean of 1.75. In the following code, we generate a DataFrame by using the dataFrame() function contained in the pandas module:

```
import pandas as pd
import numpy as np
np.random.seed(123)
df = pd.DataFrame(np.random.randn(10, 4))
```

Since, in the program, the numpy.random.seed() function is used, different users will get the same random numbers:

```
>>> df
>>>
            0         1         2         3
0 -1.085631  0.997345  0.282978 -1.506295
1 -0.578600  1.651437 -2.426679 -0.428913
2  1.265936 -0.866740 -0.678886 -0.094709
3  1.491390 -0.638902 -0.443982 -0.434351
4  2.205930  2.186786  1.004054  0.386186
5  0.737369  1.490732 -0.935834  1.175829
6 -1.253881 -0.637752  0.907105 -1.428681
7 -0.140069 -0.861755 -0.255619 -2.798589
8 -1.771533 -0.699877  0.927462 -0.173636
9  0.002846  0.688223 -0.879536  0.283627
>>>
```

At the moment, readers might be confused why we would get the same random values while trying to get a set of random numbers. This topic will be discussed and explained in more detail in *Chapter 12, Monte Carlo Simulation*. In the following code, how to use different ways to interpolate is presented:

```
import pandas as pd
import numpy as np
np.random.seed(123)                     # fix the random numbers
x=np.arange(1, 10.1, .25)**2
n=np.size(x)
y = pd.Series(x + np.random.randn(n))
bad=np.array([4,13,14,15,16,20,30])     # generate a few missing values
```

```
x[bad] = np.nan                          # missing code is np.nan
methods = ['linear', 'quadratic', 'cubic']
df = pd.DataFrame({m: x.interpolate(method=m) for m in methods})
df.plot()
```

The corresponding graph is shown in the following screenshot:

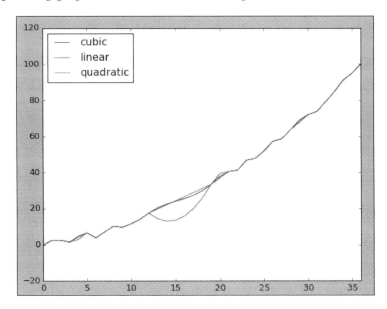

Usually, different languages have their own types of datasets.

For example, SAS has its datasets with an extension of `.sas7bdat`.

For R, its extensions could be `.RData`, `.rda`, or `.rds`. This is true for Python to have its own datasets. One type of dataset is with an extension of `.pickle` or `.pkl`. Let's generate a pickle dataset; see the following code:

```
import numpy as np
import pandas as pd
np.random.seed(123)
df=pd.Series(np.random.randn(100))
df.to_pickle('test.pkl')
```

The last command saves the variable to a pickle dataset called `test.pkl` under the current working directory. To save the pickle dataset to a file under a specific address, that is, an absolute address, we have the following code:

```
df.to_pickle('test.pkl')
```

To read a pickle dataset, the `pd.read_pickle()` function is used:

```
>>>import pandas as pd
>>>x=pd.read_pickle("c:/temp/test.pkl")
>>>x[:5]
>>>
>>>
0    -1.085631
1     0.997345
2     0.282978
3    -1.506295
4    -0.578600
dtype: float64
>>>
```

Merging two different sets is one of the common procedures researchers are routinely doing. The objective of the following program is to merge two datasets based on their common variable called `key`:

```
import numpy as np
import pandas as pd
x = pd.DataFrame({'key':['A','B','C','D'],'value': [0.1,0.2,-
0.5,0.9]})
y = pd.DataFrame({'key':['B','D','D','E'],'value': [2, 3, 4, 6]})
z=pd.merge(x, y, on='key')
```

The initial values for x and y, plus the merged dataset, called z, are shown in the following code:

```
>>> x
  key  value
0   A    0.1
1   B    0.2
2   C   -0.5
3   D    0.9
>>> y
  key  value
0   B    2
1   D    3
2   D    4
3   E    6numpy as np
>>>z
  key  value_x  value_y
0   B      0.2        2
1   D      0.9        3
2   D      0.9        4
>>>
```

For finance, time series occupy a unique position since many datasets are in the form of time series, such as stock prices and returns. Thus, knowing how to define a `date` variable and study related functions is essential for processing economics, financial, and accounting data. Let's look at a few examples:

```
>>> date1=pd.datetime(2010,2,3)
>>> date1
datetime.datetime(2010, 2, 3, 0, 0)
```

The difference between two dates can be easily estimated; see the following code:

```
>>>date1=pd.datetime(2010,2,3)
>>>date2=pd.datetime(2010,3,31)
>>> date2-date1
datetime.timedelta(56)
```

From the `pandas` module, one submodule called `datetools` is quite useful; see the list of functions contained in it:

```
>>> dir(pd.datetools)
>>>
['ABCDataFrame', 'ABCIndexClass', 'ABCSeries', 'AmbiguousTimeError',
'BDay', 'BMonthBegin', 'BMonthEnd', 'BQuarterBegin', 'BQuarterEnd',
'BYearBegin', 'BYearEnd', 'BusinessDay', 'BusinessHour',
'CBMonthBegin', 'CBMonthEnd', 'CDay', 'CustomBusinessDay',
'CustomBusinessHour', 'DAYS', 'D_RESO', 'DateOffset',
'DateParseError', 'Day', 'Easter', 'FY5253', 'FY5253Quarter',
'FreqGroup', 'H_RESO', 'Hour', 'LastWeekOfMonth', 'MONTHS', 'MS_
RESO', 'Micro', 'Milli', 'Minute', 'MonthBegin', 'MonthEnd',
'MutableMapping', 'Nano', 'OLE_TIME_ZERO', 'QuarterBegin',
'QuarterEnd', 'Resolution', 'S_RESO', 'Second', 'T_RESO',
'Timedelta', 'US_RESO', 'Week', 'WeekOfMonth', 'YearBegin',
'YearEnd', '__builtins__', '__cached__', '__doc__', '__file__',
'__loader__', '__name__', '__package__', '__spec__', 'algos',
'bday', 'bmonthBegin', 'bmonthEnd', 'bquarterEnd', 'businessDay',
'byearEnd', 'cache_readonly', 'cbmonthBegin', 'cbmonthEnd', 'cday',
'com', 'compat', 'customBusinessDay', 'customBusinessMonthBegin',
'customBusinessMonthEnd', 'datetime', 'day', 'deprecate_kwarg',
'format', 'getOffset', 'get_base_alias', 'get_freq', 'get_freq_code',
'get_freq_group', 'get_legacy_offset_name', 'get_offset', 'get_offset_
name', 'get_period_alias', 'get_standard_freq', 'get_to_timestamp_
base', 'infer_freq', 'isBMonthEnd', 'isBusinessDay', 'isMonthEnd',
'is_subperiod', 'is_superperiod', 'lib', 'long', 'monthEnd',
'need_suffix', 'normalize_date', 'np', 'offsets', 'ole2datetime',
'opattern', 'parse_time_string', 'prefix_mapping', 'quarterEnd',
'range', 're', 'thisBMonthEnd', 'thisBQuarterEnd', 'thisMonthEnd',
'thisQuarterEnd', 'thisYearBegin', 'thisYearEnd', 'time', 'timedelta',
'to_datetime', 'to_offset', 'to_time', 'tslib', 'unique', 'warnings',
'week', 'yearBegin', 'yearEnd', 'zip']
>>>
```

Here is one example to use the `weekday()` function contained in the `pandas` module. This function will be essential when tests are conducted to test the so-called Weekday-Effect. This test will be explained in detail in *Chapter 4, Sources of Data*. So let's see the following code:

```
>>import pandas as pd
>>>date1=pd.datetime(2010,10,10)
>>>date1.weekday()
6
```

Under certain situations, users might want to stack data together or the other way around; see the following code:

```
import pandas as pd
import numpy as np
np.random.seed(1256)
df=pd.DataFrame(np.random.randn(4,2),columns=['Stock A','Stock B'])
df2=df.stack()
```

The comparison of the original dataset and the stacked datasets is given here. The left-hand side is the original dataset:

```
>>> df
     Stock A    Stock B
0   0.452820  -0.892822
1  -0.476880   0.393239
2   0.961438  -1.797336
3  -1.168289   0.187016
>>>
>>> df2
>>>
0    Stock A     0.452820
     Stock B    -0.892822
1    Stock A    -0.476880
     Stock B     0.393239
2    Stock A     0.961438
     Stock B    -1.797336
3    Stock A    -1.168289
     Stock B     0.187016
dtype: float64>> >
```

The opposite operation of stock is to apply the `unstack()` function; see the following code:

```
>>> k=df2.unstack()
>>> k
```

```
       Stock A    Stock B
0    0.452820  -0.892822
1   -0.476880   0.393239
2    0.961438  -1.797336
3   -1.168289   0.187016
```

This operation could be applied to generate a return matrix if the input dataset is sorted by stock ID and date, that is, a dataset viewed as stacked one stock after another.

Python modules related to finance

Since this book is applying Python to finance, the modules (packages) related to finance will be our first priority.

The following table presents about a dozen Python modules or submodules related to finance:

Name	Description
Numpy.lib.financial	Many functions for corporate finance and financial management.
pandas_datareader	Retrieves data from Google, Yahoo! Finance, FRED, Fama-French factors.
googlefinance	Python module to get real-time (no delay) stock data from Google Finance API.
yahoo-finance	Python module to get stock data from Yahoo! Finance.
Python_finance	Download and analyze Yahoo! Finance data and develop trading strategies.
tstockquote	Retrieves stock quote data from Yahoo! Finance.
finance	Financial risk calculations. Optimized for ease of use through class construction and operator overload.
quant	Enterprise architecture for quantitative analysis in finance.
tradingmachine	A backtester for financial algorithms.
economics	Functions and data manipulation for economics data. Check the following link for better understanding: https://github.com/tryggvib/economics.
FinDates	Deals with dates in finance.

Table 2.2 A list of modules or submodules related to finance

To find out more information about economics, finance or accounting, go to the following web pages:

Name	Location
Python Module Index (v3.5)	`https://docs.python.org/3/py-modindex.html`
PyPI – the Python Package Index	`https://pypi.python.org/pypi`
Python Module Index (v2.7)	`https://docs.python.org/2/py-modindex.html`

Table 2.3 Websites related to Python modules (packages)

Introduction to the pandas_reader module

Via this module, users can download various economics and financial via Yahoo! Finance, Google Finance, **Federal Reserve Economics Data (FRED)**, and Fama-French factors.

Assume that the `pandas_reader` module is installed. For detail on how to install this module, see the *How to install a Python module* section. First, let's look at the simplest example, just two lines to get IBM's trading data; see the following:

```
import pandas_datareader.data as web
df=web.get_data_google("ibm")
```

We could use a dot head and dot tail to show part of the results; see the following code:

```
>>> df.head()
>>>
                 Open        High         Low       Close   Volume
Date
2010-01-04   131.179993  132.970001  130.850006  132.449997  6155300
2010-01-05   131.679993  131.850006  130.100006  130.850006  6841400
2010-01-06   130.679993  131.490005  129.809998  130.000000  5605300
2010-01-07   129.869995  130.250000  128.910004  129.550003  5840600
2010-01-08   129.070007  130.919998  129.050003  130.850006  4197200

             Adj Close
Date
2010-01-04   112.285875
2010-01-05   110.929466
2010-01-06   110.208865
2010-01-07   109.827375
```

```
2010-01-08  110.929466
 >> >df.tail()
>>>
                Open        High         Low       Close    Volume
Date
2016-11-16  158.460007  159.550003  158.029999  159.289993  2244100
2016-11-17  159.220001  159.929993  158.850006  159.800003  2256400
2016-11-18  159.800003  160.720001  159.210007  160.389999  2958700
2016-11-21  160.690002  163.000000  160.369995  162.770004  4601900
2016-11-22  163.000000  163.000000  161.949997  162.669998  2707900

              Adj Close
Date
2016-11-16  159.289993
2016-11-17  159.800003
2016-11-18  160.389999
2016-11-21  162.770004
2016-11-22  162.669998
>>>
```

This module will be explained again in more detail in *Chapter 4, Sources of Data.*

Two financial calculators

In the next chapter, many basic financial concepts and formulas will be introduced and discussed. Usually, when taking corporate finance or financial management, students rely on either Excel or a financial calculator to conduct their estimations. Since Python is the computational tool, a financial calculator written in Python would definitely enhance our understanding of both finance and Python.

Here is the first financial calculator, written in Python, from `Numpy.lib.financial`; see the following code:

```
>>> import numpy.lib.financial as fin
>>> dir(fin)
['__all__', '__builtins__', '__cached__', '__doc__', '__file__', '__
loader__', '__name__', '__package__', '__spec__', '_convert_when',
'_g_div_gp', '_rbl', '_when_to_num', 'absolute_import', 'division',
'fv', 'ipmt', 'irr', 'mirr', 'np', 'nper', 'npv', 'pmt', 'ppmt',
'print_function', 'pv', 'rate']
>>>
```

The functions that will be used and discussed in *Chapter 3, Time Value of Money*, include `fv()`, `irr()`, `nper()`, `npv()`, `pmt()`, `pv()`, and `rate()`. One example of using `pv()` is shown in the following code:

```
>>> import numpy.lib.financial as fin
>>> fin.pv(0.1,1,0,100)
-90.909090909090907
>>>
```

The second financial calculator is supplied by the author. There are many advantages of using this second financial calculator. First, all its functions possess the same format of the formulas from textbooks.

In other words, there is no Excel sign convention.

For example, the `pv_f()` function will depend on the following formula:

$$pv = \frac{fv}{(1+R)^n} \quad \dots\dots\dots\dots\dots\dots\dots\dots\dots(6)$$

The function called `pvAnnuity()` is based on the following formula:

$$pv(annuity) = \frac{pmt}{R}\left[1 - \frac{1}{(1+R)^n}\right] \quad \dots\dots\dots\dots\dots(7)$$

Second, the formula of estimating the present value of one future cash flow is separated from the formula to estimate the present value of an annuity. This would help students, especially beginners, avoid unnecessary confusions.

For a comparison, the `numpy.lib.financial.pv()` function actually combines both equations (6) and (7). We will discuss this in more detail in *Chapter 3, Time Value of Money*. Third, for each function, many examples are offered. It means users spend less time trying to figure out the meaning of individual functions. Fourth, this second financial calculator offers more functions than the `numpy.lib.financial` submodule can offer. Last but not least, users eventually learn to how to write their own financial calculator in Python. For more detail, see the last section in *Chapter 3, Time Value of Money*.

To use such a financial calculator, users should download a file called `fincal.cpython-35.syc` at the author's website (`http://canisius.edu/~yany/fincal.cpython-35.pyc`). Assume that the executable file is saved under `c:/temp/`. To add `c:/temp/` to the Python path, click the rightmost Python logo on the menu bar; see the following screenshot:

After clicking the logo shown in the preceding screenshot, users will see the screen shown on the left in the following screenshot:

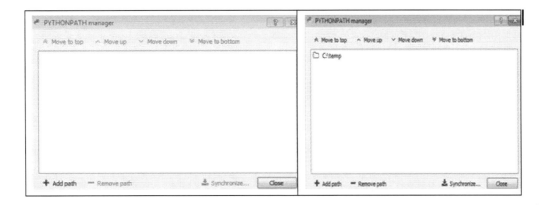

After clicking **Add path**, type `c:/temp/`; see the screen shown on the right in the preceding screenshot. Now, we could use `import fincal` to use all functions contained inside the module. In *Chapter 3, Time Value of Money*, we show how to produce such a `fincal` module:

```
>>>import fincal
>>>dir(fincal)
['CND', 'EBITDA_value', 'IRR_f', 'IRRs_f', 'NPER', 'PMT', 'Rc_f',
'Rm_f', '__builtins__', '__cached__', '__doc__', '__file__', '__
loader__', '__name__', '__package__', '__request', '__spec__',
'bondPrice', 'bsCall', 'convert_B_M', 'duration', 'exp', 'fincalHelp',
'fvAnnuity', 'fv_f', 'get_200day_moving_avg', 'get_50day_moving_
avg', 'get_52week_high', 'get_52week_low', 'get_EBITDA', 'get_all',
'get_avg_daily_volume', 'get_book_value', 'get_change', 'get_
dividend_per_share', 'get_dividend_yield', 'get_earnings_per_share',
'get_historical_prices', 'get_market_cap', 'get_price', 'get_price_
book_ratio', 'get_price_earnings_growth_ratio', 'get_price_earnings_
ratio', 'get_price_sales_ratio', 'get_short_ratio', 'get_stock_
exchange', 'get_volume', 'log', 'market_cap', 'mean', 'modified_
duration', 'n_annuity', 'npv_f', 'payback_', 'payback_period', 'pi',
'pvAnnuity', 'pvAnnuity_k_period_from_today', 'pvGrowPerpetuity',
'pvGrowingAnnuity', 'pvPerpetuity', 'pvPerpetuityDue', 'pv_excel',
'pv_f', 'r_continuous', 're', 'sign', 'sqrt', 'urllib']
```

To find the usage of each function, use the `help()` function; see the following example:

```
>>> import fincal
>>> help(fincal.pv_f)
Help on function pv_f in module fincal:

pv_f(fv, r, n)
    Objective: estimate present value
          fv: fture value
          r : discount period rate
          n : number of periods
    formula : fv/(1+r)**n
        e.g.,
        >>>pv_f(100,0.1,1)
        90.9090909090909
        >>>pv_f(r=0.1,fv=100,n=1)
        90.9090909090909
        >>>pv_f(n=1,fv=100,r=0.1)
        90.9090909090909
>>>
```

From the preceding information, users know the objective of the function, the definitions of three input values, the formula used, plus a few examples.

How to install a Python module

If Python was installed via Anaconda, there is a good chance that many of the modules discussed in this book have been installed together with Python. If Python was installed independently, users could use PyPi to install or update.

For example, we are interested in installing NumPy. On Windows, we have the following code:

```
python -m pip install -U pip numpy
```

If `Python.exe` is on the path, we could open a DOS window first, then issue the preceding line. If `Python.exe` is not on the path, we open a DOS window, then move to the location of the `Python.exe` file; for an example, see the following screenshot:

For a Mac, we have the following codes. Sometimes, after running the preceding command, you might receive the following message asking for an update of PiP:

```
You are using pip version 8.1.1, however version 9.0.1 is available.
You should consider upgrading via the 'python -m pip install --upgrade pip' comm
and.
```

The command line to update `pip` is given here:

```
python -m pip install -upgrade pip
```

See the result shown in the following screenshot:

```
C:\Users\yany\AppData\Local\Programs\Python\Python35-32>python -m pip install --
upgrade pip
Collecting pip
  Downloading pip-9.0.1-py2.py3-none-any.whl (1.3MB)
    100% |################################| 1.3MB 787kB/s
Installing collected packages: pip
  Found existing installation: pip 8.1.1
    Uninstalling pip-8.1.1:
      Successfully uninstalled pip-8.1.1
Successfully installed pip-9.0.1

C:\Users\yany\AppData\Local\Programs\Python\Python35-32>
```

To install NumPy independently, on Linux or OS X, we issue the following command:

```
pip install -U pip numpy
```

To install a new Python module for Anaconda, we have the following list. See the link at http://conda.pydata.org/docs/using/pkgs.html as well:

Command	Description
conda list	Lists all of your packages in the active environment
conda list -n snowflakes	Lists all of your packages installed into a non-active environment named snowflakes
conda search beautiful-soup	Installs a package such as Beautiful Soup into the current environment, using conda install as follows
conda install --name bunnies quant	Installs Python module (package) called quant
conda info	Gets more information

Table 2.4 A list of commands using conda to install a new package

The following screenshot shows what you will see after the command of `conda info` is issued:

```
C:\Users\yany> C:\Users\yany\AppData\Local\Continuum\Anaconda3\Scripts\conda inf
o
Current conda install:

               platform : win-32
          conda version : 4.2.9
      conda is private : False
     conda-env version : 4.2.9
   conda-build version : 2.0.2
         python version : 3.5.2.final.0
       requests version : 2.11.1
       root environment : C:\Users\yany\AppData\Local\Continuum\Anaconda3  (writ
able)
    default environment : C:\Users\yany\AppData\Local\Continuum\Anaconda3
       envs directories : C:\Users\yany\AppData\Local\Continuum\Anaconda3\envs
          package cache : C:\Users\yany\AppData\Local\Continuum\Anaconda3\pkgs
            channel URLs : https://repo.continuum.io/pkgs/free/win-32/
                          https://repo.continuum.io/pkgs/free/noarch/
                          https://repo.continuum.io/pkgs/pro/win-32/
                          https://repo.continuum.io/pkgs/pro/noarch/
                          https://repo.continuum.io/pkgs/msys2/win-32/
                          https://repo.continuum.io/pkgs/msys2/noarch/
            config file : None
           offline mode : False
```

The following example is related to the installation of the Python module called `pandas_datareader`:

```
C:\Users\yany> c:\Users\yany\AppData\local\Continuum\Anaconda3\Scripts\conda.ex
  install pandas-datareader
Fetching package metadata .........
Solving package specifications: ..........

Package plan for installation in environment c:\Users\yany\AppData\local\Contin
um\Anaconda3:

The following packages will be downloaded:

    package                    |            build
    ---------------------------|-----------------
    conda-env-2.6.0            |                0         488 B
    conda-4.2.13              |           py35_0         444 KB
    requests-file-1.4         |           py35_0           5 KB
    pandas-datareader-0.2.1   |           py35_0          49 KB
    ---------------------------|-----------------
                                           Total:         499 KB

The following NEW packages will be INSTALLED:

    conda-env:          2.6.0-0
    pandas-datareader: 0.2.1-py35_0
    requests-file:     1.4-py35_0

The following packages will be UPDATED:

    conda:             4.2.9-py35_0 --> 4.2.13-py35_0

Proceed ([y]/n)?
```

After answering y, the following result will appear after the module is completed:

```
Proceed ([y]/n)? y

Fetching packages ...
conda-env-2.6. 100% |################################| Time: 0:00:00 243.99 kB/s
conda-4.2.13-p 100% |################################| Time: 0:00:00   1.76 MB/s
requests-file- 100% |################################| Time: 0:00:00   2.30 MB/s
pandas-datarea 100% |################################| Time: 0:00:00   1.29 MB/s
Extracting packages ...
[      COMPLETE      ]|###################################################| 100%
Unlinking packages ...
[      COMPLETE      ]|###################################################| 100%
Linking packages ...
[      COMPLETE      ]|###################################################| 100%

C:\Users\yany>
```

To get the versions of various modules, we have the following code:

```
>>>import numpy as np
>>> np.__version__
'1.11.1'
>>> import scipy as sp
>>> sp.__version__
'0.18.1'
>>>import pandas as pd
>>> pd.__version__
'0.18.1'
```

Module dependency

At the very beginning of this book, we argued that one of the advantages of using Python is that it is a rich source of hundreds of special packages called modules.

To avoid duplicated efforts and to save time in developing new modules, later modules choose to use functions developed on early modules; that is, they depend on early modules.

The advantage is obvious because developers can save lots of time and effort when building and testing a new module. However, one disadvantage is that installation becomes difficult.

There are two competing approaches:

- The first approach is to bundle everything together and make sure that all parts play together nicely, thus avoiding the pain of installing *n* packages independently. This is wonderful, assuming that it works. A potential issue is that the updating of individual modules might not be reflected in the super package.

- The second approach is to use minimal dependencies. It causes fewer headaches for the package maintainer, but for users who have to install several components, it can be more of a hassle. Linux has a better way: using the package installer. The publishers of the package can declare dependencies and the system tracks them down, assuming they are in the Linux repository. SciPy, NumPy, and quant are all set up like that, and it works great.

Exercises

1. Do we have to install NumPy independently if our Python was installed via Anaconda?

2. What are the advantages of using a super package to install many modules simultaneously?

3. How do you find all the functions contained in NumPy or SciPy?

4. How many ways are there to import a specific function contained in SciPy?

5. What is wrong with the following operation?

```
>>>x=[1,2,3]
>>>x.sum()
```

6. How can we print all the data items for a given array?

7. What is wrong with the following lines of code?

```
>>>import np
>>>x=np.array([True,false,true,false],bool)
```

8. Find out the meaning of `skewtest` included in the stats submodule (SciPy), and give an example of using this function.

9. What is the difference between an arithmetic mean and a geometric mean?

10. Debug the following lines of code, which are used to estimate a geometric mean for a given set of returns:

```
>>>import scipy as sp
>>>ret=np.array([0.05,0.11,-0.03])
>>>pow(np.prod(ret+1),1/len(ret))-1
```

11. Write a Python program to estimate both arithmetic and geometric means for a given set of returns.

12. Find out the meaning of `zscore()` included in the `stats` submodule (SciPy), and offer a simple example of using this function.

13. What is wrong with the following lines of code?

```
>>>c=20
>>>npv=np.npv(0.1,c)
```

14. What is module dependency and how do you deal with it?

15. What are the advantages and disadvantages of writing a module that depends on other modules?

16. How do you use the financial functions contained in NumPy; for example, the `pv()` or `fv()` functions?

17. For functions contained in `numpy.lib.financial`, are there similar functions contained in SciPy?

18. How do you use the functions contained in the `fincal` module, generated by the author?

19. Where can you find a list of all Python modules?

20. How do you find more information about Python modules related to finance?

Summary

In this chapter, we have discussed one of the most important properties of Python: modules. A module is a package written by an expert or any individual to serve a special purpose. The knowledge related to modules is essential in our understanding of Python and its application to finance. In particular, we have introduced and discussed the most important modules, such as NumPy, SciPy, `matplotlib`, `statsmodels`, `pandas`, and `pandas_reader`. In addition, we have briefly mentioned module dependency and other issues. Two financial calculators written in Python were also presented. In *Chapter 3*, *Time Value of Money*, we will discuss many basic concepts associated with finance, such as the present value of one future cash flow, present value of perpetuity, present value of growing perpetuity, present value of annuity, and formulas related to future values. In addition, we will discuss definitions of **Net Present Value (NPV)**, **Internal Rate of Return (IRR)**, and Payback period. After that, several investment decision rules will be explained.

3
Time Value of Money

In terms of finance per se, this chapter does not depend on the first two chapters. Since, in this book, Python is used as a computational tool to solve various finance problems, the minimum requirement is that readers should have installed Python plus NumPy and SciPy. In a sense, if a reader has installed Python via Anaconda, he/she will be fine without reading the first two chapters. Alternatively, readers could read Appendix A on how to install Python.

In this chapter, various concepts and formulae associated with finance will be introduced and discussed in detail. Since those concepts and formulae are so basic, readers who have taken one finance course, or professionals with a few years' working experience in the financial industry, could go through this chapter quickly. Again, one feature of this book, quite different from a typical finance textbook, is that Python is used as the computational tool. In particular, the following topics will be covered:

- Present value of one future cash flow and the present value of perpetuity
- Present value of growing perpetuity
- Present and future value of annuity
- Perpetuity versus perpetuity due, annuity versus annuity due
- Relevant functions contained in SciPy and the `numpy.lib.financial` submodule
- A free financial calculator, written in Python, called `fincal`
- Definition of NPV and NPV rule
- Definition of IRR and IRR rule
- Python graphical presentation of time value of money, and NPV profile
- Definition of payback period and payback period rule
- How to write your own financial calculator using Python

Introduction to time value of money

Let's use a very simple example to illustrate. Assume that $100 is deposited in a bank today with an annual interest rate of 10%. What is the value of the deposit one year later? Here is the timeline with the dates and cash flows:

```
     $100        10%            FV=?
     |-------------------------------------|
     0                                     1
```

Obviously, our annual interest payment will be $10, that is, *100*0.1=10*. Thus, the total value will be *110*, that is, *100 + 10*. The original $100 is principal. Alternatively, we have the following result:

$$100 + 100*0.1 = 100*(1+0.1)$$

Assume that $100 will be kept in the bank for two years with the same 10% annual interest rate for two years. What will be the future value at the end of year two?

```
     $100    10%            10%    FV=?
     |----------------|----------------|
     0                1                2
```

Since at the end of the first year, we have $110 and by applying the same logic, the future value at the end of year two should be:

$$110 + 110*0.1 = 110*(1+0.1) = 121$$

Since *110 = 100*(1+0.1)*, then we have the following expression:

$$FV(at\ the\ end\ of\ year\ 2) = 100 * (1 + 0.1)^2$$

If $100 is deposited for five years with an annual interest rate of 10%, what is the future value at the end of year five? Based on the preceding logic, we could have the following formula:

$$FV(at\ the\ end\ of\ year\ 5) = 100 * (1 + 0.1)^5$$

Generalization leads to our first formula to estimate the future value for one given present value:

$$FV = PV(1 + R)^n \qquad \ldots\ldots\ldots(1)$$

Here, FV is the future value, PV is the present value, R is the period rate and n is the number of periods. In the preceding example, R is the annual interest rate and n is the number of years. The frequencies of R and n should be the same. This means that if R is the annual (monthly/quarterly/daily) rate then n must be number of years (months/quarters/days). The corresponding function, called `fv()` in the SciPy module, could be used to estimate the future value; see the following code. To estimate the future value at the end of year two with a 10% annual interest rate, we have the following code:

```
>>>import scipy as sp
>>> sp.fv(0.1,2,0,100)
-121.00000000000001
```

For the function, the input format is `sp.fv(rate,nper,pmt,pv=0,when='end')`. At the moment, just ignore the last variable called when. For Equation (1), there is no pmt, thus the third input should be zero. Please pay attention to the negative sign of the previous result. The reason is that `scipy.fv()` function follows the Excel sign convention: a positive future value leads to a negative present value, and vice versa. To find more information about this function, we type `help(sp.fv)`, see the following first several lines:

```
>>> help(sp.fv)
```
Help on function fv in module `numpy.lib.financial`:

```
fv(rate, nper, pmt, pv, when='end')
```

Compute the future value.

If we accidentally enter `sp.fv(0.1,2,100,0)`, the result and corresponding cash flows are shown here:

```
>>>import scipy as sp
>>> sp.fv(0.1,2,100,0)
    -210.0000000000002
    >>>
```

Later in this chapter, it will be shown that `sp.fv(0.1,2,100,0)` corresponds to the present value of two equal $100 occur at the end of the first and second years. From Equation (1), we could easily derive our second formula:

$$PV = \frac{FV}{(1+R)^n} \qquad \ldots\ldots(2)$$

The notations of *PV*, *FV*, *R*, and *n* remain the same as those in *Equation (1)*. If we plan to have $234 at the end of year five and the interest rate is 1.45% per year, how much we have to deposit today? The result is shown here on the left after applying Equation (2) manually:

```
>>> 234/(1+0.0145)**5
   217.74871488824184
>>> sp.pv(0.0145,5,0,234)
    -217.74871488824184
```

Alternatively, the `sp.pv()` function could be used, see the following right result. To find out more information about the `sp.pv()` function, we use `help(sp.pv)`, see the part of the following output:

```
>>>import scipy as sp
>>> help(sp.pv)
```

```
Help on function pv in module numpy.lib.financial:

pv(rate, nper, pmt, fv=0.0, when='end')
    Compute the present value.

    Given:
     * a future value, `fv`
     * an interest `rate` compounded once per period, of which
       there are
     * `nper` total
     * a (fixed) payment, `pmt`, paid either
     * at the beginning (`when` = {'begin', 1}) or the end
       (`when` = {'end', 0}) of each period

    Return:
       the value now

    Parameters
    ----------
    rate : array_like
        Rate of interest (per period)
    nper : array_like
        Number of compounding periods
    pmt : array_like
        Payment
    fv : array_like, optional
        Future value
    when : {{'begin', 1}, {'end', 0}}, {string, int}, optional
        When payments are due ('begin' (1) or 'end' (0))

    Returns
    -------
    out : ndarray, float
        Present value of a series of payments or investments.
```

Note that for the fourth input variable of a set of inputs, the `scipy.fv()` and `scipy.pv()` functions behave differently: `spicy.fv(0.1,1,100)` would give us an error message while `scipy.pv(0.1,1,100)` would work perfectly. The reason is that the default value of the fourth input variable in `scipy.pv()` function is zero while there is no default value for the fourth input variable in the `scipy.fv()` function. This is one type of inconsistency in terms of Python programming.

In finance, it is well known that $100 received today is more valuable than $100 received one year later, which in turn is more valuable than $100 received in year two. If different sizes are used to represent relative values, we will get the following figure. The first blue circle is the present value of $100 today, while the second one is the present value of $100 at the end of the first year and so on. The Python program to generate such an image is given in *Appendix B*:

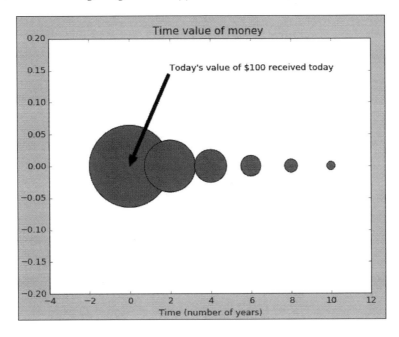

The next concept is perpetuity, which is defined as *the same constant cash flows, at the same intervals forever*. Here is the timeline and those constant cash flows:

Note that in the previous case, the first cash flow happens at the end of the first period. We could have other perpetuity with its first cash flow at the end of other period. Let's study this case first, and later in the chapter, we will have a simple extension. What is the present value of such perpetuity when the period discount rate is R?

First, Equation (2) could be applied to each of those future cash flows. Thus, the summation of all those present values will be the solution:

$$PV(\text{perpeturity}) = \frac{c}{(1+R)} + \frac{c}{(1+R)^2} + \frac{c}{(1+R)^3} + \cdots$$

To make our derivation simpler, *PV(Perpetuity)* is replaced by *PV*. Let's call it Equation (I):

$$PV = \frac{c}{(1+R)} + \frac{c}{(1+R)^2} + \frac{c}{(1+R)^3} + \cdots. \quad \dots (I)$$

To derive the formula, both sides of *Equation (I)* are multiplied by *1/(1+R)*; see the following equation. Let's call it *Equation (II)*:

$$PV(\frac{1}{(1+R)}) = \frac{c}{(1+R)^2} + \frac{c}{(1+R)^3} + \cdots. \quad \dots (II)$$

Equation (I) minus Equation (II) leads to the next equation:

$$PV - PV(\frac{1}{(1+R)}) = \frac{C}{(1+R)}$$

Both sides time *(1+R)*, we have:

$$PV(1+R) - PV = C$$

Reorganizing the preceding result, finally we have the formula to estimate the present value of perpetuity:

$$PV(\text{perpeturity}) = \frac{C}{R} \quad \dots (3)$$

Here is one example. John plans to donate $3,000 per year to his alma mater to have a welcoming party for the forthcoming MBA students at the end of the year forever. If the annual discount rate is 2.5% and the first party will occur at the end of the first year, how much he should donate today? By applying the preceding formula, the answer is $120,000:

```
>>> 3000/0.025
    120000.0
```

Assume that the first cash flow is C and the following cash flows enjoy a constant growth rate of g; see the following timeline and cash flows:

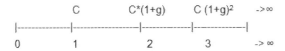

If the discount rate is R, then the formula to estimate the present value of a growing perpetuity has the following form:

$$PV\,(growing\,perpeturity) = \frac{C}{R-g} \qquad \dots\, (4)$$

Again, the frequencies of C, R, and g should be consistent, that is, have the same frequencies. One of the end-of-chapter problems asks readers to prove *Equation (4)*. For the previous example of John's MBA welcoming party donation, the cost of $3,000 needed every year is based on zero inflation. Assume that the annual inflation is 1%, how much does he have to denote today? The amount needed each year is shown here:

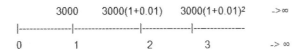

The following result indicates that he needs $200,000 today:

```
>>> 3000/(0.025-0.01)
199999.99999999997
```

For perpetuity, if the first cash flow happens at the end of kth period, we have the following formula:

$$PV(perpeturity, 1st\ cash\ flow\ @\ end\ of\ k^{th}) = \frac{1}{(1+R)^{k-1}}\frac{C}{R-g} \qquad \dots (5)$$

Obviously, when the first cash flow happens at the end of the first period, *Equation (5)* collapses to *Equation (3)*. An annuity is defined as *the same cash flows at the same intervals for n periods*. If the first cash flow occurs at the end of the first period, the present value of an annuity is estimated by the following formula:

$$PV(annuity) = \frac{C}{R}\left[1 - \frac{1}{(1+R)^n}\right] \qquad \dots (6)$$

Here, C is a recursive cash flow that happens at the end of each period, R is the period discount rate, and n is the number of periods. *Equation (5)* is quite complex than other equations. However, with a little bit imagination, *Equation (6)* could be derived by combining Equations (2) and (3); see *Appendix C* for more detail.

To estimate the future value of annuity, we have the following formula:

$$FV(annuity) = \frac{C}{R}\left[(1 + R)^n - 1\right] \qquad \dots (7)$$

Conceptually, we could view *Equation (7)* as the combination of *Equations (6)* and (1). In the previous formulae related to perpetuity or annuity, all cash flows are assumed to happen at the end of periods. For annuity or perpetuity, when the cash flows happen at the beginning of each time period, they are called annuity due or perpetuity due. There are three ways to calculate their present values.

For the first method, the last input value in `scipy.pv()` or `numpy.lib.financial.pv()` will take a value of one.

Assume that the discount rate is 1% per year. The annual cash flow is $20 for the next 10 years. The first cash flow will be paid today. What is the present value of those cash flows? The result is shown here:

```
>>>import numpy.lib.financial as fin
>>> fin.pv(0.01,10,20,0,1)
-191.32035152017377
```

Note that the input format for the `numpy.lib.financial.pv()` function is `rate`, `nper`, `pmt`, `fv`, and `when`. The default value of the last variable called `when` is zero, that is, at the end of the period. When the variable called `when` takes a value of one, it means it is annuity due.

For the second method , the following formulae could be applied:

$$PV(annuity\ due) = \frac{C}{R}\left[1 - \frac{1}{(1+R)^n}\right] * (1+R) \qquad ... \ (8)$$

$$FV(annuity\ due) = \frac{C}{R}\left[(1+R)^n - 1\right] * (1+R) \qquad ... \ (9)$$

Here is the methodology: treat annuity due as normal annuity, then multiply the result by *(1+R)*. The application is shown here:

```
>>>import numpy.lib.financial as fin
>>> fin.pv(0.01,10,20,0)*(1+0.01)
-191.3203515201738
```

For the third method , we use the function called `fincal.pvAnnuityDue()` contained in the `fincal` package, a financial calculator written in Python; see the following result:

```
>>> import fincal
>>> fincal.pvAnnuityDue(0.01,10,20)
191.32035152017383
```

For how to download this `fincal` module, see *Appendix D – how to download a free financial calculator written in Python*. To get more information about this function, the `help()` function is applied; see the following code:

```
>>>import fincal
>>>help(fincal.pvAnnuityDue)
Help on function pvAnnuityDue in module __main__:

pvAnnuityDue(r, n, c)
     Objective : estimate present value of annuity due
            r      : period rate
            n      : number of periods
            c      : constant cash flow

                              c               1
     formula    : pvAnnuityDue = -- *[ 1 -  -------  ] * (1+r)
                              r            (1+r)**n
```

```
Example 1: >>>pvAnnuityDue(0.1,10,20)
              135.1804763255031

    Example #2:>>> pvAnnuityDue(c=20,n=10,r=0.1)
              135.1804763255031
>>>
```

For more detail about such a financial calculator called `fincal`, see the next section. If cash flows will increase at a constant rate of g, we have the following formulae for a growing annuity:

$$PV(growing\ annuity) = \frac{c}{R-g}\left[1 - \frac{(1+g)^n}{(1+R)^n}\right] \qquad \dots (10)$$

$$FV(growing\ annuity) = \frac{c}{R-g}\left[(1+R)^n - (1+g)^n\right] \qquad \dots (11)$$

There are no corresponding functions from SciPy nor from `numpy.lib.financial`. Fortunately, we have the functions called `pvGrowingAnnuity()` and `fvGrowingAnnuity()` functions from the financial calculator called `fincal`; for more detail, see the following code:

```
>>> import fincal
>>> fincal.pvGrowingAnnuity(0.1,10,20,0.03)
137.67487382555464
>>>
```

To find more information about this function, issue `help(fincal.pvGrowingAnnuity)`; see the following code:

```
>>> import fincal
>>> help(fincal.pvGrowingAnnuity)
Help on function pvGrowingAnnuity in module fincal:
pvGrowingAnnuity(r, n, c, g)
    Objective: estimate present value of a growting annuity
        r     : period discount rate
        n     : number of periods
        c     : period payment
        g     : period growth rate   (g<r)


                                          c             (1+g)**n
        formula   : pv(growing annuity) = ----- *[ 1 -  ------------  ]
                                          R             (1+r)**n
```

```
Example #1 >>>pvGrowingAnnuity(0.1,30,10000,0.05)
               150463.14700582038


   Example #2: >>> pvGrowingAnnuity(g=0.05,r=0.1,c=10000,n=30)
               150463.14700582038
>> >
```

Writing a financial calculator in Python

When discussing the various concepts of the time value of money, learners need a financial calculator or Excel to solve various related problems.

From the preceding illustrations, it is clear that several functions, such as `scipy.pv()`, could be used to estimate the present value of one future cash flow or present value of annuity. Actually, the functions related to finance contained in the SciPy module came from the `numpy.lib.financial` submodule:

```
>>> import numpy.lib.financial as fin
>>> dir(fin)
['__all__', '__builtins__', '__cached__', '__doc__', '__file__', '__
loader__', '__name__', '__package__', '__spec__', '_convert_when',
'_g_div_gp', '_rbl', '_when_to_num', 'absolute_import', 'division',
'fv', 'ipmt', 'irr', 'mirr', 'np', 'nper', 'npv', 'pmt', 'ppmt',
'print_function', 'pv', 'rate']
>>>
Below are a few examples, below.
>>>import numpy.lib.financial as fin
>>> fin.pv(0.1,3,0,100)        # pv of one future cash flow
-75.131480090157751
>>> fin.pv(0.1,5,100)          # pv of annuity
-379.07867694084507
>>> fin.pv(0.1,3,100,100)      # pv of annuity plus pv of one fv
-323.81667918858022
>>>
```

First, we import two modules related to various finance functions.

```
>>>import scipy as sp
>>>import numpy.lib.financial as fin
```

The following table summarizes those functions:

Function		Input format
sp.fv()	fin.fv()	fv(rate, nper, pmt, pv, when='end')
sp.pv()	fin.pv()	pv(rate, nper, pmt, fv=0.0, when='end')
sp.pmt()	fin.pmt()	pmt(rate, nper, pv, fv=0, when='end')
sp.npv()	fin.npv()	npv(rate, values)
sp.rate()	fin.rate()	rate(nper, pmt, pv, fv, when='end', guess=0.1, tol=1e-06, maxiter=100)
sp.nper()	fin.nper()	nper(rate, pmt, pv, fv=0, when='end')
sp.irr()	fin.irr()	irr(values)
sp.mirr()	fin.mirr()	mirr(values, finance_rate, reinvest_rate)
sp.ipmt()	fin.ipmt()	ipmt(rate, per, nper, pv, fv=0.0, when='end')
sp.ppmt()	fin.ppmt()	ppmt(rate, per, nper, pv, fv=0.0, when='end')

Table 3.1 A list of functions contained in Scipy and numpy.lib.financial

The other financial calculator was written by the author of this book. *Appendix B* shows how to download it. Here is a list of functions:

```
>>> import fincal
>>> dir(fincal)
 ['CND', 'EBITDA_value', 'IRR_f', 'IRRs_f', 'NPER', 'PMT', 'Rc_f',
'Rm_f', '__builtins__', '__cached__', '__doc__', '__file__', '__
loader__', '__name__', '__package__', '__request', '__spec__',
'bondPrice', 'bsCall', 'convert_B_M', 'duration', 'exp', 'fincalHelp',
'fvAnnuity', 'fv_f', 'get_200day_moving_avg', 'get_50day_moving_avg',
'get_52week_high', 'get_52week_low', 'get_EBITDA', 'get_all', 'get_
avg_daily_volume', 'get_book_value', 'get_change', 'get_dividend_
per_share', 'get_dividend_yield', 'get_earnings_per_share', 'get_
historical_prices', 'get_market_cap', 'get_price', 'get_price_book_
ratio', 'get_price_earnings_growth_ratio', 'get_price_earnings_ratio',
'get_price_sales_ratio', 'get_short_ratio', 'get_stock_exchange',
'get_volume', 'log', 'market_cap', 'mean', 'modified_duration', 'n_
annuity', 'npv_f', 'payback_', 'payback_period', 'pi', 'pvAnnuity',
'pvAnnuityDue', 'pvAnnuity_k_period_from_today', 'pvGrowingAnnuity',
'pvGrowingPerpetuity', 'pvPerpetuity', 'pvPerpetuityDue', 'pv_excel',
'pv_f', 'r_continuous', 're', 'sign', 'sqrt', 'urllib']
```

There are several advantages of using this financial calculator over the functions contained in both the SciPy module and `numpy.lib.financial` submodule. First, for three present values, `pv` (one cash flow), `pv` (annuity), and `pv` (annuity due), there exist three corresponding functions called `pv_f()`, `pvAnnuity()` and `pvAnnuityDue()`. Thus, a new learner who has little knowledge about finance would have a much smaller chance to get confused. Second, for each function such as present value of one future cash flow, the output is exactly the same as the formula shown on a typical textbook; see the following formula:

$$PV = \frac{FV}{(1+R)^n}$$

In other words, there is no Excel sign convention. For *fv=100, r=0.1,* and *n=1,* from the preceding formula, we are supposed to get a value of 90.91. With the following code, we show the results without and with the sign convention:

```
>>>import fincal
>>> fincal.pv_f(0.1,1100)
90.9090909090909
>>> import scipy as sp
>>> sp.pv(0.1,1,0,100)
   -90.909090909090907
```

Third, for each function contained in `fincal`, we could find out which formula is used plus a few examples:

```
>>>import fincal
>>> help(fincal.pv_f)
Help on function pv_f in module __main__:

pv_f(r, n, fv)
    Objective: estimate present value
            r : period rate
            n : number of periods
           fv : future value


                                    fv
        formula used : pv = --------
                            (1+r)**n
```

```
Example 1: >>>pv_f(0.1,1,100)        # meanings of input variables
            90.9090909090909          # based on their input order

    Example #2 >>>pv_f(r=0.1,fv=100,n=1) # meanings based on keywords
            90.9090909090909
>>>
```

Last but not least, a new learner could write his/her own financial calculator! For more detail, see the *Writing your own financial calculator written in Python* section and *Appendix H*.

From the preceding discussion, it is known that for the present value of annuity, the following formula could be used:

$$PV(annuity) = \frac{c}{R}[1 - \frac{1}{(1+R)^n}]$$

In the preceding formula, we have four variables of *pv, c, R,* and *n*. To estimate a present value, we are given *c, R,* and *n*. Actually, for any set of three values, we could estimate the number 4. Let's use the same notations in SciPy and NumPy:

$$PV(annuity) = \frac{pmt}{rate}[1 - \frac{1}{(1+rate)^{nper}}]$$

The four corresponding functions are: sp.pv(), sp.pmt(), sp.rate(), and sp.nper(). Here is an example. John is planning to buy a used car with a price tag of $5,000. Assume that he would pay $1,000 as the download payment and borrow the rest. The annual interest rate for a car load is 1.9% compounded monthly. What is his monthly payment if he plans to retire his load in three years? We could calculate the monthly payment manually; see the following code:

```
>>> r=0.019/12
>>> pv=4000
>>> n=3*12
>>> pv*r/(1-1/(1+r)**n)
114.39577546409993
```

Since the annual interest rate is compounded monthly, the effective monthly rate is 0.019/12. In *Chapter 5, Bond and Stock Valuation*, how to convert different effective rates will be discussed in more detail. Based on the preceding result, John's monthly payment is $114.40. Alternatively, we could use the `scipy.pmt()` function; see the following code:

```
>>import scipy as sp
>>> sp.pmt(0.019/12,3*12,4000)
-114.39577546409993
```

Similarly, for the rate in the preceding function, the `scipy.rate()` and `numpy.lib.rate()` functions could be applied. Here is one example. A company plans to lease a limousine for its CEO. If the monthly payment is $2,000 for the next three years and the present value of the car is $50,000, what is the implied annual rate?

```
>>>import scipy as sp
>>>r=sp.rate(3*12,2000,-50000,0)    # monthly effective rate
>>>r
  0.021211141641636025
>>> r*12
  0.2545336996996323               # annual percentage rate
```

The monthly effective rate is 2.12% while the annual rate is 25.45%.

With the same logic, for the nper in the preceding function, the `scipy.nper()` and `numpy.lib.financial.nper()` functions could be applied.

Here is one example. Peter borrows $5,000 to pay the cost to get a Python certificate. If the monthly rate is 0.25% and he plans to pay back $200 per month, how many months will he need to repay his loan?

```
>>>import scipy as sp
>>> sp.nper(0.012,200,-5000,0)
29.900894915842475
```

Based on the preceding result, he needs about 30 months to repay his whole loan. In the preceding two examples, the future value is zero. Following the same logic, for a future value annuity, we have the following function:

$$FV(annuity) = \frac{C}{R}\left[(1+R)^n - 1\right]$$

If using the same notations as SciPy and `numpy.lib.financial`, we have the following formula:

$$fv(annuity) = \frac{pmt}{rate}\left[(1 + rate)^{nper} - 1\right]$$

The `scipy.pmt()`, `scipy.rate()`, `scipy.nper()`, `numy.lib.financial.pmt()`, `numpy.lib.financial.rate()`, and `numpy.lib.financial.nper()` functions could be used to estimate those values. We will discuss those formulae further in the *The general formulae for many functions* section used in Scipy and `numpy.lib.financial`.

Definition of NPV and NPV rule

The **Net Present Value (NPV)** is defined by the following formula:

$$NPV = PV(all\ benefits) - PV(all\ costs)$$

Here is an example. The initial investment is $100. The cash inflows in the next five years are $50, $60, $70, $100, and $20, starting from year one. If the discount rate is 11.2%, what is the project's NPV value? Since only six cash flows are involved, we could do the calculation manually:

```
>>> r=0.112
>>> -100+50/(1+r)+60/(1+r)**2+70/(1+r)**3+100/(1+r)**4+20/(1+r)**5
121.55722687966407
Using the scipy.npv() function, the estimation process could be
simplified dramatically:
>>> import scipy as sp
>>> cashflows=[-100,50,60,70,100,20]
>>> sp.npv(0.112,cashflows)
121.55722687966407
```

Based on the preceding result, the NPV of this project is $121.56. A normal project is defined as follows: *cash outflows first, then cash inflows*. Anything else is an abnormal project. For a normal project, its NPV is negatively correlated with the discount rate; see the following graph. The reason is that when the discount rate increases, the present value of the future cash flows (most of times benefits) will decrease more than the current or the earliest cash flows (most of times costs). The NPV profile describes the relationship between NPV and discount rate as shown in the following graph. See *Appendix E* for the Python program to generate the graph. The y-axis is NPV while the x-axis is the discount rate:

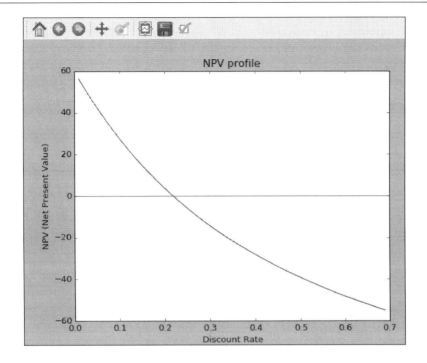

To estimate the NPV of a project, we could call the npv() function contained either in SciPy or numpy.lib.financial; see the following code:

```
>>>import scipy as sp
>>>cashflows=[-100,50,60,70]
>>>rate=0.1
>>>npv=sp.npv(rate,cashflows)
>>>round(npv,2)
47.62
```

The scipy.npv() function estimates the present values for a given set of cash flows. The first input variable is the discount rate, while the second input is an array of cash flows. Note that the first cash flow in this cash flow array happens at time zero. This scipy.npv() function is different from the Excel's NPV function, which is not a true NPV function. Actually, the Excel NPV is a PV function. It estimates the present value of future cash flows by assuming the first cash flow happens at the end of the first period. An example of using an Excel npv() function is as follows:

D2			*fx*	=NPV(0.1,B1:D1)+A1	
	A	B	C	D	E	F
1	-100	50	60	70		
2				47.63		

While using just one future cash flow, the meaning of the `scipy.npv()` function is clearer as shown in the following lines of code:

```
>>>c=[100]
>>>x=np.npv(0.1,c)
>>>round(x,2)
>>>100.0
```

The related Excel function and its output is shown here:

For just one future cash flow, the result based on Excel's `npv()` function is shown in the preceding right image. For the `numpy.lib.financial.npv()` function, the only cash flows of $100 would happen today, while for the Excel `npv()` function, the only cash flow of $100 would happen one period later. Thus, *100/(1+0.1)* leads to 90.91.

The NPV rule is given here:

$$\begin{cases} if\ NPV\ > 0 & accept \\ if\ NPV < 0 & reject \end{cases} \quad \dots (12)$$

Definition of IRR and IRR rule

The **Internal Rate of Return (IRR)** is defined as the discount rate that makes NPV equal zero. Assume that we invest $100 today and the future cash flows will be $30, $40, $40, and $50 for the next four years. Assuming that all cash flows happen at the end of the year, what is the IRR for this investment? In the following program, the `scipy.irr()` function is applied:

```
>>>import scipy as sp
>>> cashflows=[-100,30,40,40,50]
>>> sp.irr(cashflows)
        0.2001879105140867
```

We could verify whether such a rate does make NPV equal zero. Since the NPV is zero, 20.02% is indeed an IRR:

```
>>> r=sp.irr(cashflows)
>>> sp.npv(r,cashflows)
    1.7763568394002505e-14
>>>
```

For a normal project, the IRR rule is given here:

$$\begin{cases} if\ IRR > R_c & accept \\ if\ IRR < R_c & reject \end{cases} \quad \dots (13)$$

Here, Rc is the cost of capital. This IRR rule holds only for a normal project. Let's look at the following investment opportunity. The initial investment is $100 today and $50 next year. The cash inflows for the next five years will be $50, $70, $100, $90, and $20. If the cost of capital is 10%, should we take the project? The time line and corresponding cash flows are shown here:

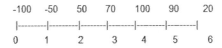

The Python codes are given here:

```
>>>import scipy as sp
>>> cashflows=[-100,-50,50,70,100,90,20]
>>> sp.irr(cashflows)
0.25949919326073245
```

Since the IRR is 25.9%, which is higher than the cost of capital of 10%, we should accept the project based on the IRR rule. In the preceding example, it is a normal project. For abnormal projects or projects with multiple IRRs, we could not apply the IRR rule. When the cash flows change direction more than once, we might have multiple IRRs. Assume that our cash flows will be 504, -432,-432, -432, and 843, starting today:

```
>>>import scipy as sp
>>> cashflows=[504, -432,-432, -432,843]
>>> sp.irr(cashflows)
    0.14277225152187745
```

The related graph is shown here:

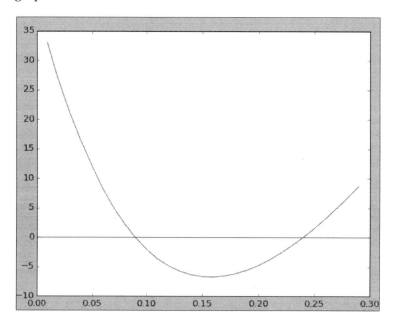

Since the direction of our cash flows changes twice, the project might have two different IRRs. The preceding right image shows that this is the case. For the Python program to draw the preceding NPV profile, see *Appendix F*. Using the `spicy.npv()` function, we only got one IRR. From the `fincal.IRRs_f()` function, we could get both IRRs; see the following code:

```
>>>import fincal
>>> cashflows=[504, -432,-432, -432,843]
>>> fincal.IRRs_f(cashflows)
 [0.143, 0.192]
```

Definition of payback period and payback period rule

A payback period is defined as the number of years needed to recover the initial investment. Assume that the initial investment is $100. If every year the firm could recover $30, then the payback period is 3.3 years:

```
>>import fincal
>>>cashflows=[-100,30,30,30,30,30]
>>> fincal.payback_period(cashflows)
    3.3333333333333335
```

The decision rule for the payback rule is given here:

$$\begin{cases} if\ T < T_c & accept \\ if\ T > T_c & reject \end{cases} \quad \dots (14)$$

Here, T is the payback period for a project while Tc is the maximum number of years required to recover the initial investment. Thus, if Tc is four, the preceding project with a payback period of 3.3 should be accepted.

The major advantage of the payback period rule is its simplicity. However, there are many shortcomings for such a rule. First, it does not consider the time value of money. In the previous case, $30 received at the end of the first year is the same as $30 received today. Second, any cash flows after the payback period is ignored. This bias would be against the project with a long period of future cash flows. Last but not least, there is no theoretical foundation to define a good cut-off point of Tc. In other words, there is no viable reason to argue why a cut-off of four years is better than five.

Writing your own financial calculator in Python

It could be viewed as a great achievement when a new Python learner could write his/her own financial calculator. The basic knowledge to do so includes the following:

* Knowledge on how to write a function
* What are the related finance formulae?

For the latter, we have learnt from the preceding sections, such as the formula to calculate the present value of one future cash flow. Let's write the simplest Python function to double an input value:

```
def dd(x):
    return 2*x
```

Here, `def` is the keyword for writing a function, `dd` is the function name, and `x` in the parentheses is an input variable. For Python, the indentation is critical. The preceding indentation indicates that the second line is the part of the `dd` function. Calling this function is the same as calling other built-in Python functions:

```
>>>dd(5)
 10
>>>dd(3.42)
 6.84
```

Now, let's write our simplest financial calculator. First, launch Python and use its editor to enter the following codes:

```
def pvFunction(fv,r,n):
    return fv/(1+r)**n
def pvPerpetuity(c,r):
    return c/r
def pvPerpetuityDue(c,r):
    return c/r*(1+r)
```

For simplicity, each function of the preceding three functions has just two lines. After activating those functions by running the whole program, the `dir()` function could be used to show their existence:

```
>>> dir()
['__builtins__', '__doc__', '__loader__', '__name__', '__package__',
'__spec__', 'pvFunction', 'pvPerpetuity','pvPerpetuityDue']
>>>
```

Calling this self-generated financial calculator is trivial; see the following code:

```
>>> pvFunction(100,0.1,1)
90.9090909090909
>>> pvFunction(n=1,r=0.1,fv=100)
90.9090909090909
>>> pvFunction(n=1,fv=100,r=0.1)
90.9090909090909
>>>
```

Again, when entering input values, two methods could be used: the meaning of input variables depend on their order, see the first call, and with a keyword, see the last two preceding examples.

A more elegant method to write one's own financial calculator is shown in *Appendix G*.

Two general formulae for many functions

This section is optional since it is quite complex in terms of mathematical expression. Skipping this section would not have any impact on the understanding of the other chapters. Thus, this section is for advanced learners. Up to now in this chapter, we have learnt the usage of several functions, such as `pv()`, `fv()`, `nper()`, `pmt()`, and `rate()` included in the SciPy module or `numpy.lib.financial` submodule. The first general formula is related to the present value:

$$pv = -\left\{ \frac{fv}{(1+R)^n} + \frac{c}{R}\left[1 - \frac{1}{(1+R)^n}\right] * (1 + R * type) \right\} \quad \dots (15)$$

On the right-hand side of the preceding equation, the first one is the present value of one future cash flow, while the second part is the present value of annuity. The variable *type* takes a value of zero (default value); it is the present value of a normal annuity, while it is an annuity due if *type* takes a value of 1. The negative sign is for the sign convention. If using the same notation as that used for the functions contained in SciPy and `numpy.lib.financial`, we have the following formula:

$$pv = -\left\{ \frac{fv}{(1+rate)^{nper}} + \frac{pmt}{rate}\left[1 - \frac{1}{(1+rate)^{nper}}\right] * (1 + rate * when) \right\} \quad \dots (16)$$

Here are several examples using both Equation (14) and the `pv()` function from SciPy. James intends to invest x dollars today for the next 10 years. His annual rate of return is 5%. During the next 10 years, he will withdraw $5,000 at the beginning of each year. In addition, he hopes that he will have $7,000 at the end of his investment horizon. How much must he invest today, that is, what is the value of x? By applying the preceding equation manually, we have the following result. Please pay attention to the negative sign:

```
>>> -(7000/(1+0.05)**10 + 5000/0.05*(1-1/(1+0.05)**10)*(1+0.05))
-44836.501153005614
```

The result is the same as when the `scipy.pv()` function is called; see the following code:

>>> import scipy as sp

```
>>> sp.pv(0.05,10,5000,7000,1)
-44836.5011530056
```

To separate normal annuity from annuity due, we have the following two equations. For a normal annuity, we have the following equation:

$$pv = -\left\{ \frac{fv}{(1+rate)^{nper}} + \frac{pmt}{rate}\left[1 - \frac{1}{(1+rate)^{nper}}\right] \right\} \quad \dots (16B)$$

For annuity due, we have the following equation:

$$pv = -\{\frac{fv}{(1+rate)^{nper}} + \frac{pmt}{rate}\left[1 - \frac{1}{(1+rate)^{nper}}\right] * (1+rate)\} \quad \dots \text{(16C)}$$

Similarly, for the future value, we have the following general formula:

$$fv = -\{pv(1+R)^n + \frac{c}{R}[(1+R)^n - 1] * (1+R*type)\} \quad \dots \text{(17)}$$

If using the same notations used in SciPy and `numpy.lib.financial`, we have the following formula:

$$fv = -\{pv(1+rate)^{nper} + \frac{pmt}{rate}[(1+rate)^{nper} - 1] * (1+rate*when)\} \quad \dots \text{(18)}$$

Similarly, we could separate annuity from annuity due. For a normal annuity, we have the following formula:

$$fv = -\{pv(1+rate)^{nper} + \frac{pmt}{rate}[(1+rate)^{nperm} - 1]\} \dots \text{(18B)}$$

For an annuity due, we have the following formula:

$$fv = -\{pv(1+rate)^{nper} + \frac{pmt}{rate}[(1+rate)^{nper} - 1] * (1+rate)\} \dots \text{(18C)}$$

In the following equations, **present value (pv)** appears twice. However, they have quite different meanings. Similarly, future value appears twice with different meanings as well:

$$pv = -\{\frac{fv}{(1+R)^n} + \frac{c}{R}\left[1 - \frac{1}{(1+R)^n}\right] * (1+R*type)\}$$

$$fv = -\{pv(1+R)^n + \frac{c}{R}[(1+R)^n - 1] * (1+R*type)\}$$

Let's use a simple example to explain the links between those two equations. First, let's simplify our functions by dropping the sign convention and assume normal annuity, that is, it is not annuity due:

$$pv = \frac{fv}{(1+R)^n} + \frac{C}{R}\left[1 - \frac{1}{(1+R)^n}\right] \quad \cdots (19)$$

$$fv = pv(1+R)^n + \frac{C}{R}\left[(1+R)^n - 1\right] \quad \cdots (20)$$

Actually, we would have three *pv* (present value) and three *fv* (future value). We invest $100 for three years. In addition, at the end of each year for the next three years, we invest $20. If the rate of return is 4% per year, what is the future value of our investment?

Obviously, we could apply the last equation to get our answer:

```
>>> 100*(1+0.04)**3+20/0.04*((1+0.04)**3-1)
    174.91840000000005
>>> import scipy as sp
>>> sp.fv(0.04,3,20,100)
    -174.91840000000005
```

Actually, we have three future values. Let's call them **FV(total)**, **FV(annuity)** and **FV(one PV)**. The relationship between them is given here:

FV(total) = FV(annuity) + FV(one PV)

The following code shows how to calculate the future value of annuity and the future value of one present value:

```
>>> fv_annuity=20/0.04*((1+0.04)**3-1)
>>> fv_annuity
62.432000000000045
>>>fv_one_PV=100*(1+0.04)**3
>>> fv_one_PV
112.4864
```

The total future value is the summation of those two future values: *62.4320+ 112.4864=174.92.* Now, let's see how to get three corresponding present values. Let's call them **PV(total)**, **PV(annuity)**, and **PV(one PV)**. The relationship between them will be as follows:

$$PV(total) = PV(annuity) + PV(one\ FV)$$

Let's use the same cash flows shown previously. Obviously, the first $100 is itself the present value. The present value of three $20s could be calculated manually; see the following code:

```
>>>20/0.04*(1-1/(1+0.04)**3)
55.501820664542564
```

Thus, the total present value will be *100 + 55.51=155.51*. Alternatively, we could apply `scipy.pv()` to estimate the present value of annuity; see the following code:

```
>>>import scipy as sp
>>> sp.pv(0.04,3,20)
  -55.501820664542592
>>>import fincal
>>> fincal.pvAnnuity(0.04,3,20)
  55.501820664542564
```

The relationship between total future value (`174.92`) and total present value (`155.51`), has the following relationship:

```
>>>174.92/(1+0.04)**3
155.5032430587164
```

In summary, when calling the `scipy.pv()` and `scipy.fv()` functions, the meaning of `fv` in the `scipy.pv()` function is different from the final value of `scipy.fv()`. Readers have to understand the difference between a total future, the future value of one present value, and the future value of annuity. This is true for the `pv` variable in the `scipy.fv()` function and the final result after calling the `scipy.pv()` function.

Appendix A – Installation of Python, NumPy, and SciPy

To install Python via Anaconda, we have the following steps:

1. Go to `http://continuum.io/downloads`.

2. Find an appropriate package; see the following screenshot:

For Python, different versions coexist. From the preceding screenshot, we see that there exist two versions of **3.5** and **2.7**. For this book, the version is not that critical. The old version has fewer problems while the new one usually has new improvements. After Python is installed via Anaconda, NumPy and SciPy will be installed at the same time. After launching Python through Spyder, issue the following two lines. If there is no error, then those two modules were pre-installed:

```
>>> import numpy as np
>>> import scipy as sp
```

The other method is to install Python directly.

Go to `http://www.python.org/download`. Depending on your computer, choose the appropriate package, for example, Python 3.5.2 version. In terms of installing a module, find the Python documentation. The following command will install the latest version of a module and its dependencies from the **Python Packaging Index (PIP)**:

```
python -m pip install SomePackage
```

For POSIX users (including Mac OS X and Linux users), the examples in this guide assume the use of a virtual environment. To install a specific version, see the following code:

```
python -m pip install SomePackage==1.0.4    # specific version
python -m pip install "SomePackage>=1.0.4"  # minimum version
```

Normally, if a suitable module is already installed, attempting to install it again will have no effect. Upgrading existing modules must be requested explicitly:

```
python -m pip install --upgrade SomePackage
```

Appendix B – visual presentation of time value of money

If a reader has difficulty understanding the following code, she/he could just ignore this part. In finance, we know that $100 received today is more valuable than $100 received one year later. If we use size to represent the difference, we could have the following Python program to represent the same concept:

```
from matplotlib.pyplot import *
fig1 = figure(facecolor='white')
ax1 = axes(frameon=False)
ax1.set_frame_on(False)
ax1.get_xaxis().tick_bottom()
ax1.axes.get_yaxis().set_visible(False)
x=range(0,11,2)
x1=range(len(x),0,-1)
y = [0]*len(x);
name="Today's value of $100 received today"
annotate(name,xy=(0,0),xytext=(2,0.001),arrowprops=dict(facecolor='bla
ck',shrink=0.02))
s = [50*2.5**n for n in x1];
title("Time value of money ")
xlabel("Time (number of years)")
scatter(x,y,s=s);
show()
```

The graph is shown here. The first blue circle is the present value, while the second one is the present value of the same $100 at the end of the second year:

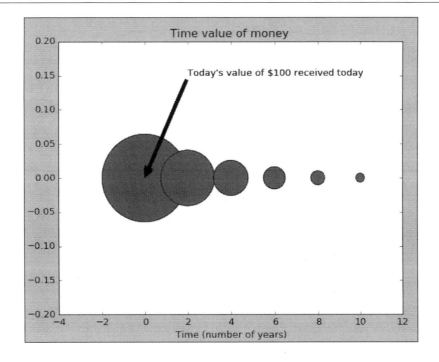

Appendix C – Derivation of present value of annuity from present value of one future cash flow and present value of perpetuity

First, we have the following two formulae:

$$PV = \frac{FV}{(1+R)^n} \quad \ldots(1)$$

$$PV(\text{perpeturity}) = \frac{C}{R} \quad \ldots(2)$$

Here, FV is the future value, R is the discount period rate, n is the number of periods, and C is the same cash flow happening at the end of each period with the first cash flow happening at the end of the first period.

An annuity is defined as *a set of equivalent cash flows occurring in the future*. If the first cash flow occurs at the end of the first period, the present value of an annuity is by the following formula:

$$PV(annuity) = \frac{C}{R}\left[1 - \frac{1}{(1+R)^n}\right] \quad \cdots \quad (3)$$

Here, C is a recursive cash flow happening at the end of each period, R is period discount rate, and n is the number of periods. *Equation (3)* is quite complex. However, with a little bit of imagination, we could combine equations (1) and (2) to derive Equation (3). This can be done by decomposing an annuity into two perpetuities:

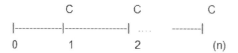

This is equivalent to the following two perpetuities:

Conceptually, we could think this way: Mary would receive $20 per year for the next 10 years. This is equivalent to two perpetuities: she would receive $20 every year forever and at the same time PAY $20 every year forever, starting at year 11. Thus, the present value of her annuity will be the present value of the first perpetuity minus the present value of her second perpetuity:

$$pv(annuity) = pv(1st\ perpetuity) - pv(2nd\ perpeturity)$$

If the same cash flow happens at the same interval forever, it is called perpetuity. If the discount rate is a constant and the first cash flows happens at the end of the first period, its present value has the following.

Appendix D – How to download a free financial calculator written in Python

Download an executable file at `http://canisius.edu/~yany/fincal.pyc`. Assume that it was saved under `c:/temp/`. Change your path; see the following screenshot:

Here is an example:

```
>>>import fincal
>>> fincal.pv_f(0.1,1,100)
90.9090909090909
```

To find out all contained functions, the `dir()` function is used; see the following code:

```
>>> import fincal
>>> dir(fincal)
['CND', 'EBITDA_value', 'IRR_f', 'IRRs_f', 'NPER', 'PMT', 'Rc_f',
'Rm_f', '__builtins__', '__cached__', '__doc__', '__file__', '__
loader__', '__name__', '__package__', '__request', '__spec__',
'bondPrice', 'bsCall', 'convert_B_M', 'duration', 'exp', 'fincalHelp',
'fvAnnuity', 'fvAnnuityDue', 'fv_f', 'get_200day_moving_avg',
'get_50day_moving_avg', 'get_52week_high', 'get_52week_low', 'get_
EBITDA', 'get_all', 'get_avg_daily_volume', 'get_book_value',
'get_change', 'get_dividend_per_share', 'get_dividend_yield', 'get_
earnings_per_share', 'get_historical_prices', 'get_market_cap',
'get_price', 'get_price_book_ratio', 'get_price_earnings_growth_
ratio', 'get_price_earnings_ratio', 'get_price_sales_ratio', 'get_
short_ratio', 'get_stock_exchange', 'get_volume', 'log', 'market_
cap', 'mean', 'modified_duration', 'n_annuity', 'npv_f', 'payback_',
'payback_period', 'pi', 'pvAnnuity', 'pvAnnuityDue', 'pvAnnuity_k_
period_from_today', 'pvGrowingAnnuity', 'pvGrowingPerpetuity',
'pvPerpetuity', 'pvPerpetuityDue', 'pv_excel', 'pv_f', 'r_continuous',
're', 'sign', 'sqrt', 'urllib']
```

To find out the usage of each function, the `help()` function could be used:

```
>>> help(fincal.pv_f)
Help on function pv_f in module fincal:
pv_f(r, n, fv)
    Objective: estimate present value
          r : period rate
          n : number of periods
         fv : future value
```

$$\text{formula used} : pv = \frac{fv}{(1+r)^{**}n}$$

```
Example 1: >>>pv_f(0.1,1,100)        # meanings of input variables
              90.9090909090909         # based on their input order

    Example #2 >>>pv_f(r=0.1,fv=100,n=1) # meanings based on keywords
              90.9090909090909
>> >
```

Appendix E – The graphical presentation of the relationship between NPV and R

An NPV profile is the relationship between a project's NPV and its discount rate (cost of capital). For a normal project, where cash outflows first then cash inflows, its NPV will be a decreasing function of the discount rate; see the following code:

```
import scipy as sp
from matplotlib.pyplot import *
cashflows=[-120,50,60,70]
rate=[]
npv =[]
for i in range(1,70):
    rate.append(0.01*i)
    npv.append(sp.npv(0.01*i,cashflows))

plot(rate,npv)
show()
```

The associated graph is shown here:

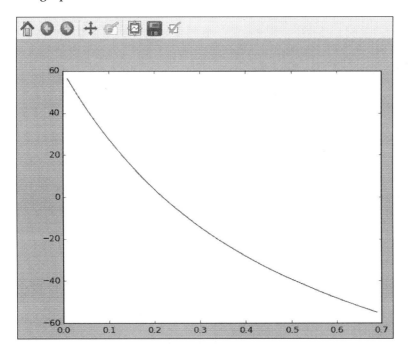

To make our graph better, we could add a title, both labels, and one horizon line; see the following code:

```
import scipy as sp
from matplotlib.pyplot import *
cashflows=[-120,50,60,70]
rate=[]
npv=[]
x=(0,0.7)
y=(0,0)
for i in range(1,70):
    rate.append(0.01*i)
    npv.append(sp.npv(0.01*i,cashflows))

title("NPV profile")
xlabel("Discount Rate")
ylabel("NPV (Net Present Value)")
plot(rate,npv)
plot(x,y)
show()
```

The output is shown here:

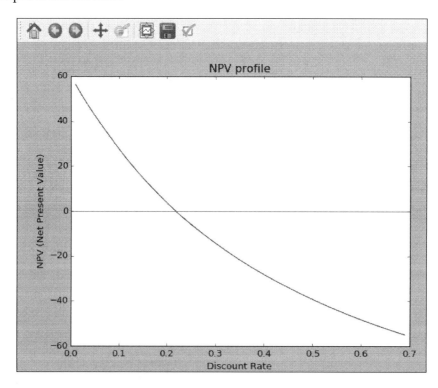

Appendix F – graphical presentation of NPV profile with two IRRs

Since the direction of cash flow changes twice, we might have two IRRs:

```
import scipy as sp
import matplotlib.pyplot as plt
cashflows=[504,-432,-432,-432,832]
rate=[]
npv=[]
x=[0,0.3]
y=[0,0]
for i in range(1,30):
    rate.append(0.01*i)
    npv.append(sp.npv(0.01*i,cashflows))

plt.plot(x,y),plt.plot(rate,npv)
plt.show()
```

The corresponding graph is shown here:

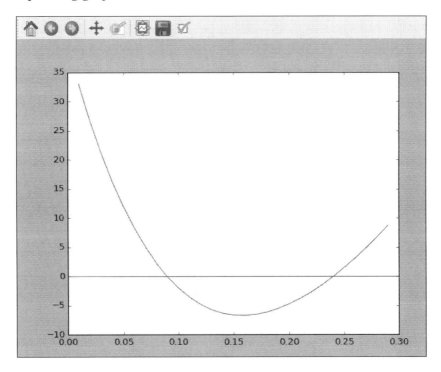

Appendix G – Writing your own financial calculator in Python

Now, let's write our simplest financial calculator. First, launch Python and use the editor to enter the following codes. For simplicity, each function of preceding 10 functions has just two lines. Again, a proper indentation is critical. Thus, the second line of each function should be indented:

```
def pvFunction(fv,r,n):
    return fv/(1+r)**n
def pvPerpetuity(c,r):
    return c/r
def pvPerpetuityDue(c,r):
    return c/r*(1+r)
def pvAnnuity(c,r,n):
    return c/r*(1-1/(1+r)**n)
def pvAnnuityDue(c,r,n):
    return c/r*(1-1/(1+r)**n)*(1+r)
```

```
def pvGrowingAnnuity(c,r,n,g):
    return c/(r-g)*(1-(1+g)**n/(1+r)**n)
def fvFunction(pv,r,n):
    return pv*(1+r)**n
def fvAnnuity(cv,r,n):
    return c/r*((1+r)**n-1)
def fvAnnuityDue(cv,r,n):
    return c/r*((1+r)**n-1)*(1+r)
def fvGrowingAnnuity(cv,r,n):
    return c/(r-g)*((1+r)**n-(1+g)*n)
```

Assume that the preceding program is called `myCalculator`.

The following program would generate an executable filed called `myCalculator.cpython-35.pyc`:

```
>>> import py_compile
>>> py_compile.compile('myCalculator.py')
'__pycache__\\myCalculator.cpython-35.pyc'
>>> __pycache__
py_compile.compile('c:/temp/myCalculator.py')
```

Exercises

1. What is the present value of $206 received in 10 years with an annual discount rate of 2.5%?

2. What is the future value of perpetuity with a periodic annual payment of $1 and a 2.4% annual discount rate?

3. For a normal project, its NPV is negatively correlated with the discount rate. Why?

4. John deposits $5,000 in the bank for 25 years. If the annual rate is 0.25% per year, what is the future value?

5. If the annual payment is $55 with 20 years remaining, what is the present value if the annual discount rate is 5.41%, compounded semi-annually?

6. If Mary plans to have $2,400 by the end of year 5, how much does she have to save each year if the corresponding annual rate is 3.12%?

7. Why have we got a negative number of periods in the following code?

```
>>>import scipy as sp
>>> sp.nper(0.012,200,5000,0)
-21.99461003591637
```

8. If a firm's earnings per share grows from $2 to $4 over a 9-year period (the total growth is 100%), what is its annual growth rate?

9. In this chapter, while writing a present value function, we use `pv_f()`. Why not use `pv()`, the same as the following formula?

$$PV = \frac{FV}{(1+R)^n}$$

Here PV is the present value, FV is the future value, R is the periodic discount rate, and n is the number of periods.

10. A project contributes cash inflows of $5,000 and $8,000 at the end of the first and second years. The initial cost is $3,000. The appropriate discount rates are 10% and 12% for the first and the second years respectively. What is the NPV of the project?

11. Firm A will issue new bonds with annual coupon payment of $80 and a face value of $1,000. Interest payments are made semi-annually, and the bond matures in 2 years. The spot interest rate for the first year is 10%. At the end of the first year, the 1-year spot rate is expected to be 12%:

    ◦ What is the present value of the bond?

    ◦ What is the lump sum you are willing to accept at the end of the second year?

12. Peter's rich uncle has promised him a payment of $4,000 if he completes college in four years. Richard has just finished a very difficult sophomore (second) year, including taking several finance courses. Richard would very much like to take a long vacation. The appropriate discount rate is 10% compounded semi-annually. What is value that Peter would be giving up today if he took his vacation?

13. Today, you have $5,000 to invest and your investment horizon is 25 years. You are offered an investment plan that will pay you 6 percent per year for the next 10 years and 9 percent per year for the last 15 years. How much will you have at the end of the 25 years? What is your average annual percentage return?

14. What are the advantages and disadvantages of using a default input value or values?

15. We know that the present value of growing perpetuity has the following formula:

$$PV(growing\ perpeturity) = \frac{C}{R-g}$$

Prove it.

16. Today, Jane is 32 years old. She plans to retire at the age of 65 with $2.5 million savings. If she could get a 3.41%, compounded monthly, return every year, what will be her monthly contribution?

17. Assume that we have a set of small programs put together called `fin101.py`. What is the difference between the two Python commands, `import fin101` and `from fin101 import *`?

18. How can you prevent erroneous inputs such as negative interest rate?

19. Write a Python program to estimate payback period. For example, the initial investment is $256, and the expected future cash inflows in the next 7 years will be $34, $44, $55, $67, $92, $70, and $50. What is the project's payback period in years?

20. In the preceding exercise, if the discount rate is 7.7 percent per year, what is the discounted payback period? Note: The discount payback period looks at how to recover our initial investment by checking the summation of present values of future cash flows.

Summary

In this chapter, many basic concepts related to finance were introduced, such as present value of one future cash flow, present value of perpetuity, present value of annuity, future value of one cash flow/annuity, and the concept of present of annuity due. The several decision rules were discussed in detail, such as the NPV rule, IRR rule, and payback period rule. For the next chapter, we will discuss how to retrieve data associated with economics, finance, and accounting from several open sources such as Yahoo!Finance, Google finance, Prof. French's data library, and Federal Research's economic data library.

4
Sources of Data

Since our society entered a so-called information era, we have been engulfed by a huge amount ofinformation or data. For this very reason, there is an increasing demand for persons armed with data handling skills, such as data scientists or graduates from business analytics programs. Kane (2006) proposed an opensourcefinance concept which consists of three components:

- The use of open source software in testing hypotheses and implementing investment strategies
- Cheap access to financial data
- Replication to confirm published research results

In this book, these three components are simply called: open software, open data, and open codes. Python is one of the best-known pieces of open source software. At the moment, usage of public data is quite inconsistent with the current environment. In this book, we use a huge amount of data, especially public data. In this chapter, the following topics will be covered:

- Open source finance
- Source of macro-economic data
- Source of accounting data
- Source of finance data
- Other data sources

Diving into deeper concepts

The focus of this chapter will be on how to retrieve economic, finance, and accounting related data, especially public data. For example, Yahoo Finance offers rich data, such as historical trading price, current price, option data, annual and quarterly financial statements, and bond data. Such publicly available data could be used to estimate β (market risk), volatility (total risk), Sharpe ratio, Jensen's alpha, Treynor ratio, liquidity, transaction costs, and conduct financial statement analysis (ratio analysis) and performance evaluation. In future chapters, the topics mentioned would be discussed in more detail. For the public data related to economics, finance, and accounting, many wonderful sources are available, see the following table:

Name	Data types
Yahoo Finance	Historical price, annual and quarterly financial statements, and so on
Google Finance	Current, historical trading prices
Federal Reserve Economic Data	Interest rates, rates for AAA, AA rated bonds
Prof. French's Data Library	Fama-French factor time series, market index returns, risk-free rate, industry classification
Census Bureau	Census data
US. Department of Treasury	US. Treasure yield
Bureau of Labor Statistics	Inflation, employment, unemployment, pay and benefits
Bureau of Economic Analysis	Gross Domestic Product (GDP) and so on
National Bureau of Economic Research	Business cycles, vital statistics, report of presidents

Table 4.1: A list of open data sources

Usually, there are two ways to retrieve data:

- Manually download data from a specific location and then write a Python program to retrieve and process it

- Use the functions contained in various Python modules, such as the function called `quotes_historical_yahoo_ohlc()` in the `matplotlib.finance` submodule

For both methods, there are some advantages and disadvantages. The main advantage of the first method is that we know where to get our data. In addition, since we write our own programs to download and process data, the logic of those programs is clearer. The advantage of the second method is that it is quick and convenient to retrieve data. In a sense, users don't even have to know from where to retrievethe data and the structure of the original datasets. The disadvantage is that the functions used might change. This might cause certain problems. For example, the old version of `quotes_historical_yahoo_ohlc()` is `quotes_historical_yahoo()`.

In order to retrieve useful information from the preceding sources, two submodules could be used: `pandas_datareader.data` and `matplotlib.financial`. To find out functions included in `pandas_datareader.data`, the `dir()` function is applied:

```
>>> import pandas_datareader.data as pddata
>>> dir(pddata)
['DataReader', 'EurostatReader', 'FamaFrenchReader', 'FredReader', 'GoogleDailyReader', 'OECDReader', 'Options', 'YahooActionReader', 'YahooDailyReader', 'YahooOptions', 'YahooQuotesReader', '__builtins__', '__cached__', '__doc__', '__file__', '__loader__', '__name__', '__package__', '__spec__', 'get_components_yahoo', 'get_data_famafrench', 'get_data_fred', 'get_data_google', 'get_data_yahoo', 'get_data_yahoo_actions', 'get_quote_google', 'get_quote_yahoo', 'warnings']
>>>
```

From the preceding output, it seems that we have eight functions related to YahooFinance, such as `YahooDailyReader()`, `YahooActionReader()`, `YahooOptions()`, `YahooQuotesReader()`, `get_components_yahoo()`, `get_data_yahoo()`, `get_data_yahoo_actions()`, and `get_quote_yahoo()`. Actually, we could use `theDataReader()` function as well.Similarly, a few functions are available for retrieving data from Google, FRED, and from Prof. French's Data Library.

To find the usage of individual functions, the `help()` function could be applied. In the following, the first function called `DataReader()` from the preceding output, is used as an example:

```
>>> import pandas_datareader.data as pddata
>>> help(pddata.DataReader)
Help on function DataReader in module pandas_datareader.data:

DataReader(name, data_source=None, start=None, end=None, retry_count=3, pause=0.001, session=None)
    Imports data from a number of online sources.

    Currently supports Yahoo! Finance, Google Finance, St. Louis FED (FRED)
    and Kenneth French's data library.

    Parameters
    ----------
    name : str or list of strs
        the name of the dataset. Some data sources (yahoo, google, fred) will
        accept a list of names.
    data_source: {str, None}
        the data source ("yahoo", "yahoo-actions", "google", "fred", or "ff")
    start : {datetime, None}
        left boundary for range (defaults to 1/1/2010)
    end : {datetime, None}
        right boundary for range (defaults to today)
    retry_count : {int, 3}
        Number of times to retry query request.
    pause : {numeric, 0.001}
        Time, in seconds, to pause between consecutive queries of chunks. If
        single value given for symbol, represents the pause between retries.
    session : Session, default None
            requests.sessions.Session instance to be used
```

From the output, it can be seen that the function could be used to retrieve data from YahooFinance, Google Finance, St. Louis FED (FRED), and Prof. French's data library. To find out all the functions contained in the `matplotlib.finance` submodules, see the following codes:

```
>>> import matplotlib.finance as fin
>>> dir(fin)
['Affine2D', 'Line2D', 'LineCollection', 'PolyCollection', 'Rectangle', 'TICKLEFT', 'TICKRIGHT', '__builti
ns__', '__cached__', '__doc__', '__file__', '__loader__', '__name__', '__package__', '__spec__', '__warnin
gregistry__', '_candlestick', '_check_input', '_parse_yahoo_historical', '_plot_day_summary', '_quotes_his
torical_yahoo', 'absolute_import', 'cachedir', 'candlestick2_ochl', 'candlestick2_ohlc', 'candlestick_ochl
', 'candlestick_ohlc', 'colorConverter', 'contextlib', 'date2num', 'datetime', 'division', 'fetch_historic
al_yahoo', 'get_cachedir', 'hashlib', 'index_bar', 'iterable', 'md5', 'mkdirs', 'np', 'os', 'parse_yahoo_h
istorical_ochl', 'parse_yahoo_historical_ohlc', 'plot_day_summary2_ochl', 'plot_day_summary2_ohlc', 'plot_
day_summary_oclh', 'plot_day_summary_ohlc', 'print_function', 'quotes_historical_yahoo_ochl', 'quotes_hist
orical_yahoo_ohlc', 'six', 'stock_dt_ochl', 'stock_dt_ohlc', 'unicode_literals', 'urlopen', 'verbose', 'vo
lume_overlay', 'volume_overlay2', 'volume_overlay3', 'warnings', 'xrange', 'zip']
>>>
```

A careful reader would find some inconsistency for the definitions of those names; see the last four letters of some functions, that is, `ochl`, `ohlc`, and `oclh`.

Retrieving data from Yahoo!Finance

Yahoo!Finance offers historical market data, recent, several years' financial statements, current quotes, analyst recommendations, options data, and more. The historical trading data include daily, weekly, monthly, and dividends. The historical data has several variables: open price, high price achieved, lowest price achieved, trading volume, close price, and adjusted-close price (which is adjusted for splits and dividends). Historical quotes typically do not go back further than 1960.Here, we show how to manually retrieve the monthly data for IBM:

1. Go to `http://finance.yahoo.com/`.

2. Enter `IBM` in the search box.

3. Click on **Historical Price** in the middle.

4. Choose the monthly data, then click **Apply**.

5. Click **Download data** under **Apply**.

A few lines at the beginning and at the end are shown here:

```
Date,Open,High,Low,Close,Volume,Adj.Close
2017-03-09,179.149994,179.25,175.880005,177.179993,5413100,177.179993
2017-03-08,180.75,180.949997,179.300003,179.449997,3520000,179.449997
2017-03-07,180.710007,181.289993,180.199997,180.380005,2930800,180.380005
2017-03-06,179.720001,180.990005,179.570007,180.470001,3180900,180.470001
2017-03-03,180.529999,181.320007,179.759995,180.050003,1822000,180.050003
2017-03-02,181.880005,181.880005,180.429993,180.529999,2913600,180.529999
2017-03-01,180.479996,182.550003,180.029999,181.949997,2960000,181.949997
2017-02-28,179.380005,180.630005,179.350006,179.820007,3272500,179.820007



1962-01-17,558.000004,558.000004,550.000012,551.50001,419200,2.162375
1962-01-16,565.999997,565.999997,560.500002,560.500002,251200,2.197663
1962-01-15,565.999997,567.750013,565.999997,566.499996,251200,2.221188
1962-01-12,563.999999,567.999995,563.999999,563.999999,435200,2.211386
1962-01-11,558.500004,563,558.500004,563,315200,2.207465
1962-01-10,557.000005,559.500003,557.000005,557.000005,299200,2.18394
1962-01-09,552.00001,563,552.00001,556.000006,491200,2.180019
1962-01-08,559.500003,559.500003,545.000017,549.500012,544000,2.154533
1962-01-05,570.499992,570.499992,559.000003,560.000002,363200,2.195703
1962-01-04,576.999986,576.999986,570.999992,571.25001,256000,2.239813
1962-01-03,571.999991,576.999986,571.999991,576.999986,288000,2.262358
1962-01-02,578.499985,578.499985,571.999991,571.999991,387200,2.242753
```

Assume that the above downloaded data is saved under `c:/temp`, the following codes could be used to retrieve it:

```
>>>import pandas as pd
>>>x=pd.read_csv("c:/temp/ibm.csv")
```

To view the first and the last few observations, the `.head()` and `.tail()` functions could be used. The default values of those two functions are 5. In the following, the command of `x.head()` will output the first five lines, while `x.tail(2)` will output the last two lines:

```
In [2]: x.head()
Out[2]:
         Date       Open        High         Low       Close   Volume  \
0  2017-03-09  179.149994  179.250000  175.880005  177.179993  5413100
1  2017-03-08  180.750000  180.949997  179.300003  179.449997  3520000
2  2017-03-07  180.710007  181.289993  180.199997  180.380005  2930800
3  2017-03-06  179.720001  180.990005  179.570007  180.470001  3180900
4  2017-03-03  180.529999  181.320007  179.759995  180.050003  1822000

    Adj.Close
0   177.179993
1   179.449997
2   180.380005
3   180.470001
4   180.050003

In [3]: x.tail(2)
Out[3]:
             Date        Open        High         Low       Close  Volume  \
13890  1962-01-03  571.999991  576.999986  571.999991  576.999986  288000
13891  1962-01-02  578.499985  578.499985  571.999991  571.999991  387200

       Adj.Close
13890   2.262358
13891   2.242753
```

A better way is to use certain functions contained in various modules or submodules. Here is one of the simplest examples, just two lines to get IBM's trading data, see the following code:

```
>>>import pandas_datareader.data as getData
df = getData.get_data_google("IBM")
```

Again, the `.head()` and `.tail()` functions could be used to show the part of the result, see the following code:

```
>>>df.head(2)
>>>
                  Open        High         Low       Close   Volume  \
Date
2010-01-04  131.179993  132.970001  130.850006  132.449997  6155300
2010-01-05  131.679993  131.850006  130.100006  130.850006  6841400
Adj Close
Date
2010-01-04  112.285875
2010-01-05  110.929466
>>>df.tail(2)
                  Open        High         Low       Close   Volume  \
```

```
Date
2016-12-08  164.869995  166.000000  164.220001  165.360001  3259700
2016-12-09  165.179993  166.720001  164.600006  166.520004  3143900
Adj Close
Date
2016-12-08  165.360001
2016-12-09  166.520004
>>>
```

If a longer time period is desired, the start and ending input variables should be specified, see the following code:

```
>>>import pandas_datareader.data as getData
>>>import datetime
>>>begdate = datetime.datetime(1962, 11, 1)
>>>enddate = datetime.datetime(2016, 11, 7)
df = getData.get_data_google("IBM",begdate, enddate)
```

In the preceding code, the function called `datetime.datetime()` defines a true date variable. Later in the chapter, it is shown how to retrieve year and month from such a variable. The first two observations are given here:

```
>>>df[0:2]
                Open        High        Low        Close    Volume
AdjClose
Date
1962-11-01  345.999992  351.999986  341.999996  351.999986  1992000
1.391752
1962-11-02 351.999986369.875014 346.999991 357.249999  3131200
1.412510
>>>
```

A careful reader should find that the order of data is different. When downloading data manually, the order is from the latest (such as yesterday) going back in history. However, when retrieving data via a function, we would have the oldest date first. Most financial databases adopt the same sorting order: from the oldest to the latest.

The following program uses another function called `quotes_historical_yahoo_ochl`. The program is the simplest one with just two lines:

```
>>>from matplotlib.finance import quotes_historical_yahoo_ochl as
getData
>>>p=getData("IBM", (2015,1,1),(2015,12,31),asobject=True,adjusted=Tr
ue)
```

In the preceding program, the first line imports a function called `quotes_historical_yahoo_ochl()` contained in the `matplotlib.finance`. In addition, to make our typing easier, the long function name is renamed `getData`. Users could use other more convenient names. The second line retrieves data from the Yahoo!Finance web page with a specific ticker symbol over a fixed period defined by beginning and ending dates. To show the first several lines, we type `p[0:4]`:

```
>>>p[0:4]
rec.array([ (datetime.date(2015, 1, 2), 2015, 1, 2, 735600.0,
150.47501253708967, 151.174636, 152.34067510485053, 150.1858367047493,
5525500.0, 151.174636),
 (datetime.date(2015, 1, 5), 2015, 1, 5, 735603.0, 150.43770546142676,
148.795914, 150.43770546142676, 148.497414517829, 4880400.0,
148.795914),
 (datetime.date(2015, 1, 6), 2015, 1, 6, 735604.0, 148.9451702494383,
145.586986, 149.215699719094, 144.7474294432884, 6146700.0,
145.586986),
 (datetime.date(2015, 1, 7), 2015, 1, 7, 735605.0, 146.64107567217212,
144.635494, 146.64107567217212, 143.68400235493388, 4701800.0,
144.635494),
dtype=[('date', 'O'), ('year', '<i2'), ('month', 'i1'), ('day', 'i1'),
('d', '<f8'), ('open', '<f8'), ('close', '<f8'), ('high', '<f8'),
('low', '<f8'), ('volume', '<f8'), ('aclose', '<f8')])>>>
```

The last several lines indicate the structure of the dataset. For example, `O` is for Python objects, `i2` is for integer, and `f8` is for floating. At the moment, it is not that critical to fully understand the meanings of those data types.

To understand how to estimate returns from a price array, let's look at a simple illustration. Assume that we have five prices and their time line is t, t+1, t+2, t+3 and t+4:

```
>>> import numpy as np
>>>price=np.array([10,10.2,10.1,10.22,9])
>>>price[1:]
array([ 10.2 ,  10.1 ,  10.22,   9.  ])
>>>price[:-1]
array([ 10.  ,  10.2 ,  10.1 ,  10.22])
>>> (price[1:]-price[:-1])/price[:-1]
array([ 0.02      , -0.00980392,  0.01188119, -0.11937378])
>>>
```

For a NumPy array, defined by `np.array()`, such as price defined previously, we use `price[1:]` for the second item to the last one, that is, all the data items except the first one. Recall that the subscript of a NumPy array starts from 0. For `price[:-1]`, it represents all data items except the last one. We could manually verify those return numbers; see the following code for the first two returns:

```
>>> (10.2-10)/10
0.019999999999999928
>>>
>>> (10.1-10.2)/10.2
-0.009803921568627416
```

Here is another example:

```
>>>import scipy as sp
>>>sp.random.seed(123)
>>>price=sp.random.random_sample(10)*15
>>>price
array([ 10.44703778,   4.29209002,   3.4027718 ,   8.26972154,
        10.79203455,   6.3465969 ,  14.71146298,  10.27244608,
         7.21397852,   5.88176277])
>>>price[1:]/price[:-1]-1
array([-0.58915722, -0.20719934,  1.43028978,  0.3050058 , -0.4119184
,
         1.31800809, -0.30173864, -0.29773508, -0.18467143])
>>>
```

Note that if the price array is sorted the other way around: from the newest to the oldest, then the return estimation should be `price[:-1]/price[1:]-1`. With the preceding logic, the following program calculates returns:

```
from matplotlib.finance import quotes_historical_yahoo_ochl as getData
ticker='IBM'
begdate=(2015,1,1)
enddate=(2015,11,9)
p = getData(ticker, begdate, enddate,asobject=True, adjusted=True)
ret = p.aclose[1:]/p.aclose[:-1]-1
```

To make our programs more general, in the preceding program, three new variables called `begdate`, `enddate`, and `ticker`are added. Please pay attention to the last line of commands. For a given pair of two prices, p1 and p2, assume that p2 is after p1. We could use two ways to estimate a return: `(p2-p1)/p1` or `p2/p1-1`. The former is conceptually clearer while the latter makes our program less prone to error. Again, we could verify a few returns manually:

```
>>>p.aclose[0:4]
array([ 151.174636,  148.795914,  145.586986,  144.635494])>>>
```

```
>>>ret[0:3]
array([-0.01573493, -0.02122663, -0.00629399])
>>> (p.aclose[1]-p.aclose[0])/p.aclose[0]
-0.01573492791475934
```

For the following example, daily price data for IBM from January 1, 2011 to December 31, 2015 is downloaded first. Then, daily returns are calculated. The mean daily return is 0.011%:

```
from scipy import stats
import numpy as np
from matplotlib.finance import quotes_historical_yahoo_ochl as getData
ticker='ibm'
begdate=(2011,1,1)
enddate=(2015,12,31)
p=getData(ticker,begdate,enddate,asobject=True, adjusted=True)
ret=p.aclose[1:]/p.aclose[:-1]-1
mean=np.mean(ret)
print('   Mean '  )
print(round(mean,5))
>>>
    Mean
>>>
0.00011
```

To answer the question whether this mean daily return of `0.00011` is statistically different from zero, the function called `ttest_1samp()` contained in the stats module could be applied:

```
0.00011
print(' T-test result: T-value and P-value'  )
print(stats.ttest_1samp(ret,0))
>>>
 T-test result: T-value and P-value
>>>
Ttest_1sampResult(statistic=0.3082333300938474,
pvalue=0.75795590301241988)
>>>
```

Since the T-value is 0.31 and the P-value is 0.76, we accept the null hypothesis. In other words, the daily mean return for IBM from 2011 to 2015 is statistically the same as zero. To get more information about this function, the `help()` function would be applied. To save space, only the first several lines are shown here:

```
>>>import scipy.stats
>>>help(stats.ttest_1samp)
Help on function ttest_1samp in module scipy.stats.stats:

ttest_1samp(a, popmean, axis=0, nan_policy='propagate')
```

It calculates the T-test for the mean of ONE group of scores.

This is a two-sided test for the null hypothesis that the expected value (mean) of a sample of independent observations, `a`, is equal to the given population mean, `popmean`.

The following program tests the equal means for two stocks: `IBM` vs. `MSFT`:

```
import scipy.stats as stats
from matplotlib.finance import quotes_historical_yahoo_ochl as getData
begdate=(2013,1,1)
enddate=(2016,12,9)

def ret_f(ticker,begdate,enddate):
    p = getData(ticker,begdate,
enddate,asobject=True,adjusted=True)
    ret=p.aclose[1:]/p.aclose[:-1]-1
    return(ret)

a=ret_f('IBM',begdate,enddate)
b=ret_f('MSFT',begdate,enddate)
```

The means of those two returns are shown here:

```
>>>a.mean()*100
0.0022164073263915601
>>>b.mean()*100
0.10399096829827408
>>>
```

Note that in the preceding code, the `.mean()` is used instead of `scipy.mean()`. To conduct a T-test for equal means, the function called `ttest_ind()` is called; see the following code:

```
>>>print(stats.ttest_ind(a,b))
Ttest_indResult(statistic=-1.652826053660396,
pvalue=0.09852448906883747)
```

Assume that two prices exist, *p1* and *p2*. The following equation defines a percentage return (R) and a log return:

$$R = \frac{p_2 - p_1}{p_1}$$ ....(1)

$$R^{log} = \ln(\frac{p_2}{p_1})$$ ....(2)

The relation between those two are shown here:

$$R^{log} = \ln(R + 1)$$ ....(3)

$$R = e^{R^{log}} - 1$$ ....(4)

One of the beauties of a log return is that the return of a longer period is the summation of a short period. This means that annual log return is the summation of log quarterly returns. A log quarterly return is the summation of log monthly returns. This property makes our programming better. Here is a more general formula:

$$R^{log}_{long\_period} = \Sigma R^{log}_{short\_period}$$ ....(5)

For a log annual return, we could apply the following formula:

$$R^{log}_{annual} = \Sigma R^{log}_{monthly} = \Sigma R^{log}_{daily}$$ ....(6)

The following code is used to convert daily returns into monthly ones:

```
from matplotlib.finance import quotes_historical_yahoo_ochl as getData
import numpy as np
import pandas as pd
ticker='IBM'
begdate=(2015,1,1)
enddate=(2015,12,31)
x = getData(ticker, begdate, enddate,asobject=True, adjusted=True)
logret = np.log(x.aclose[1:]/x.aclose[:-1])

date=[]
```

```
d0=x.date
for i in range(0,np.size(logret)):
    date.append(''.join([d0[i].strftime("%Y"),d0[i].strftime("%m")]))

y=pd.DataFrame(logret,date,columns=['retMonthly'])
retMonthly=y.groupby(y.index).sum()
```

In the preceding program, the command of `strftime("%Y")` is used to extract the string of a year, such as `2016`. A much simpler example is shown here:

```
>>>import pandas as pd
>>> x=pd.datetime(2016,1,1)
>>>x
datetime.datetime(2016, 1, 1, 0, 0)
>>>x.strftime("%Y")
'2016'
```

Similarly, the command of `strftime("%m")` would extract the string for a month. To find the first and last two monthly returns, the `.head()` and `.tail()` functions could be used; see the following code:

```
>>>retMonthly.head(2)
>>>
retMonthly
201501    -0.046737
201502     0.043930
>>>
>>>retMonthly.tail(2)
>>>
retMonthly
201511     0.015798
201512    -0.026248
>>>
```

Along the same line, the following code converts daily returns into annual ones:

```
from matplotlib.finance import quotes_historical_yahoo_ochl as getData
import numpy as np
import pandas as pd
ticker='IBM'
begdate=(1980,1,1)
enddate=(2012,12,31)
x=getData(ticker,begdate,enddate,asobject=True,adjusted=True)
logret = np.log(x.aclose[1:]/x.aclose[:-1])

date=[]
```

```
d0=x.date
for i in range(0,np.size(logret)):
    date.append(d0[i].strftime("%Y"))
#
y=pd.DataFrame(logret,date,columns=['retAnnual'])
ret_annual=exp(y.groupby(y.index).sum())-1
```

A few annual returns are shown here:

```
>>>ret_annual[0:5]
retAnnual
1980   0.167561
1981  -0.105577
1982   0.679136
1983   0.352488
1984   0.028644
>>>
>>>ret_annual.tail(2)
>>>
retAnnual
2011   0.284586
2012   0.045489
>>>
```

In finance, standard deviation and variance are used to measure risk. To tell which stock is riskier, their variances or standard deviations could be compared. The following program tests whether IBM and Microsoft have equal variances:

```
import scipy as sp
from matplotlib.finance import quotes_historical_yahoo_ochl as getData
begdate=(2013,1,1)
enddate=(2015,12,31)
def ret_f(ticker,begdate,enddate):
    p = getData(ticker,begdate,
enddate,asobject=True,adjusted=True)
    return(p.aclose[1:]/p.aclose[:-1]-1)
y=ret_f('IBM',begdate,enddate)
x=ret_f('MSFT',begdate,enddate)
```

The function called `bartlett()` contained in `scipy.stats` is used. The following output shown suggests that those two companies have different variance since the F-value is 44.39 while the P-value is almost zero:

```
>>>print(sp.stats.bartlett(x,y))
BartlettResult(statistic=44.392308291526497,
pvalue=2.6874090005526671e-11)
```

To find out more information about this function, the `help()` function could be used.

To save space, only the first few lines are shown here:

1. Help on function `bartlett` in module `scipy.stats.morestats`:

    ```
    bartlett(*args)
    ```

2. Perform Bartlett's test for equal variances.

> Bartlett's test tests the null hypothesis that all input samples are from populations with equal variances.
>
> For samples from significantly non-normal populations, Levene's test, `levene`, is more robust.

For finance, we have a very important assumption: stock returns follow a normal distribution. Thus, it is a good idea to graphically show how the stock returns are distributed; see the following image. The code in Appendix A is relatively complex. In this chapter, it is not required to understand the program. This is true for the several programs described as well.

The following graph shows how IBM's returns distributed plus a normal distribution. The price moment is shown on the right and its Python program is included in Appendix A:

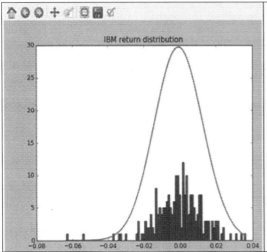

The so-called candle-stick picture could be used to vividly present a stock price or trading volume, as shown in the following screenshot. The corresponding Python program is in Appendix C:

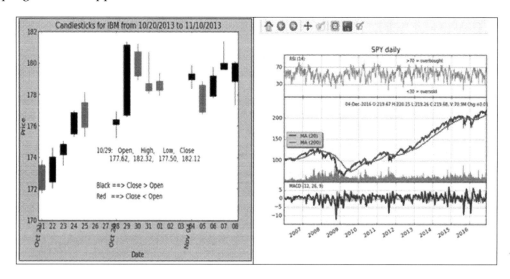

The upper-right picture is extremely sophisticated. Since beginners don't need to understand it, the program is not included in this book. If a reader is interested, the complete program canbe found at two locations. Here are the links:
http://matplotlib.org/examples/pylab_examples/finance_work2.html
and http://canisius.edu/~yany/python/finance_work2.txt.

The following is another example to retrieve IBM daily data from Yahoo! Financeby calling the DataReader() function contained in the pandas_datareader. datasubmodule:

```
>>>import pandas_datareader.data as getData
>>>x = getData.DataReader('IBM', data_source='yahoo',
start='2004/1/30')
>>>x[1:5]
               Open        High          Low         Close     Volume
Adj Close
Date
2004-02-02   99.150002    99.940002    98.500000    99.389999   6200000
77.666352
2004-02-03   99.000000   100.000000    98.949997   100.000000   5604300
78.143024
2004-02-04   99.379997   100.430000    99.300003   100.190002   8387500
78.291498
2004-02-05  100.000000   100.089996    98.260002    98.860001   5975000
77.252194
>>>
```

Retrieving data from Google Finance

Like Yahoo Finance, Google Finance offers a significant amount of public information, such as news, option chains, related companies (good for competitor and industry analysis), historical prices, and financials (income statement, balance sheet, and cash flow statements). We could manually download data by going to Google Finance directly. Alternatively, to retrieve data from Google finance, the DataReader() function contained in the pandas_datareader submodule could be applied:

```
>>>import pandas_datareader.data as getData
>>>aapl =getData.DataReader("AAPL", "google")
>>>aapl.head(2)
>>>
            Open    High    Low   Close     Volume
Date
2010-01-04  30.49   30.64   30.34  30.57    123432050
2010-01-05  30.66   30.80   30.46  30.63    150476004
>>>aapl.tail(2)
            Open    High     Low    Close     Volume
Date
2016-12-08  110.86  112.43  110.60  112.12   27068316
2016-12-09  112.31  114.70  112.31  113.95   34402627
>>>
```

The following screenshot shows a stock's intraday moment. The related Python program is included in Appendix C:

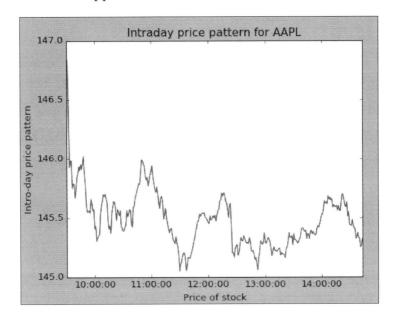

Retrieving data from FRED

The Federal Reserve has many datasets related to current economics and historical time series. For instance, they have data related to interest rates, such as Euro-dollar deposit rates. There are two ways to retrieve such interest rate data. First, we could use their Data Download Program, as seen in the following steps:

1. Go to the Federal Reserve Bank's web link at `https://www.federalreserve.gov/econresdata/default.html`.

2. Click the **Data Download Program** at `https://www.federalreserve.gov/data.htm`.

3. Choose an appropriate data item.

4. Click **Go to download**.

For example, we choose Fed fund rate. The first couple of lines are given here:

```
"Series Description","Federal funds effective rate"
"Unit:","Percent:_Per_Year"
"Multiplier:","1"
"Currency:","NA"
"Unique Identifier: ","H15/H15/RIFSPFF_N.D"
"Time Period","RIFSPFF_N.D"
1954-07-01,1.13
1954-07-02,1.25
1954-07-03,1.25
1954-07-04,1.25
1954-07-05,0.88
1954-07-06,0.25
1954-07-07,1.00
1954-07-08,1.25
```

The following program could be used to retrieve the downloaded data. Here the dataset is assumed to be saved under the `c:/temp/` directory:

```
import pandas as pd
importnumpy as np
file=open("c:/temp/fedFundRate.csv","r")
data=pd.read_csv(file,skiprows=6)
```

Alternatively, the function called `DataReader()` contained in the`pandas_datareader` module could be used. One example is given here:

```
>>>import pandas_datareader.data as getData
>>>vix = DataReader("VIXCLS", "fred")
>>>vis.head()
VIXCLS
DATE
2010-01-01     NaN
2010-01-04    20.04
2010-01-05    19.35
2010-01-06    19.16
2010-01-07    19.06
>>>
```

Retrieving data from Prof. French's data library

Prof. French has a very good and widely used data library.You can visit this link at `http://mba.tuck.dartmouth.edu/pages/faculty/ken.french/data_library.html` for more information. It contains the daily, weekly, and monthly Fama-French factors and other useful datasets. After clicking *Fama-French Factors*, a ZIPfile called `F-F_Research_Data_Factors.zip` can be downloaded. Unzip it, and we will have a text file called `F_F_Research_Data_Factors.txt` which includes both monthly and annual Fama-French factors starting from July 1926 onward. The first several lines are shown here. For more detail, see *Chapter 7*, *Multifactor Models and Performance Measures*, Sharpe ratio, Treynor ratio, and Jensen's α.

This file was created by `CMPT_ME_BEME_RETS` using the `201012 CRSP` database:

```
The 1-month TBill return is from Ibbotson and Associates, Inc.
Mkt-RFSMBHMLRF
192607     2.62    -2.16    -2.92    0.22
192608     2.56    -1.49     4.88    0.25
192609     0.36    -1.38    -0.01    0.23
192610    -3.43     0.04     0.71    0.32
192611     2.44    -0.24    -0.31    0.31
```

Assume that the data is saved under `C:/temp/`. Remember to remove the annual data at the bottom of the file before running the following code:

```
>>>import pandas as pd
>>>file=open("c:/temp/ffMonthly.txt","r")
>>>data=file.readlines()
```

The first 10 observations are shown here:

```
>>>data[0:10]
['DATE    MKT_RFSMBHMLRF\n', '192607    2.96   -2.30   -2.87
0.22\n', '192608   2.64   -1.40    4.19    0.25\n', '192609    0.36
-1.32    0.01    0.23\n', '192610   -3.24    0.04    0.51    0.32\n',
'192611   2.53   -0.20   -0.35    0.31\n', '192612    2.62   -0.04
-0.02    0.28\n', '192701   -0.06   -0.56    4.83    0.25\n', '192702
4.18   -0.10    3.17    0.26\n', '192703    0.13   -1.60   -2.67
0.30\n']
>>>
```

Alternatively, we could write a Python program to retrieve the monthly Fama-French time series:

```
import pandas_datareader.data as getData
ff =getData.DataReader("F-F_Research_Data_Factors", "famafrench")
```

Again, the beauty of using the `pandas_datareader()` module is that we could use the `.head()` and `.tail()` function to view the retrieved datasets. Several more examples are given now:

```
import pandas_datareader.data as pdata
ff2=web.DataReader("F-F_Research_Data_Factors_weekly", "famafrench")
ff3 =web.DataReader("6_Portfolios_2x3", "famafrench")
ff4=web.DataReader("F-F_ST_Reversal_Factor", "famafrench")
```

Retrieving data from the Census Bureau, Treasury, and BLS

In this section, we briefly show how to retrieve data from the US Census Bureau. You can learn more about it at http://www.census.gov/compendia/statab/ hist_stats.html. After we go to the census's historical data, the following window will pop up. This is the link: http://www.census.gov/econ/census/data/ historical_data.html. The following screenshot shows what kind of historical data we can download:

Historical Data

[Tweet] [Share]

2007 Economic Census Data in American FactFinder

00 Core Reports
21 Mining, quarrying, and oil and gas extraction
22 Utilities
23 Construction
31-33 Manufacturing
42 Wholesale Trade
44-45 Retail Trade
48-49 Transportation and Warehousing
51 Information
52 Finance and Insurance

53 Real Estate and Rental and Leasing
54 Professional, Scientific, and Technology Services
55 Management of Companies and Enterprises
56 Administrative and Support and Waste Management and Remediation Services
61 Educational Services
62 Health Care and Social Assistance
71 Arts, Entertainment, and Recreation
72 Accommodation and Food Services
81 Other Services (except Public Administration)

2002 Economic Census Data in American FactFinder

00 Core Reports
21 Mining, quarrying, and oil and gas extraction
22 Utilities
23 Construction
31-33 Manufacturing
42 Wholesale Trade
44-45 Retail Trade
48-49 Transportation and Warehousing
51 Information
52 Finance and Insurance

53 Real Estate and Rental and Leasing
54 Professional, Scientific, and Technology Services
55 Management of Companies and Enterprises
56 Administrative and Support and Waste Management and Remediation Services
61 Educational Services
62 Health Care and Social Assistance
71 Arts, Entertainment, and Recreation
72 Accommodation and Food Services
81 Other Services (except Public Administration)

Assume that we are interested in **61Educational Services**. After clicking the link, we could choose one time series to download. After clicking the **Download** icon, a ZIP file which contains four files will be downloaded.

The next example shows how to get data from the Bureau of Labor Statistics web page. First, go to the related web page at `http://www.bls.gov/`and click **Data Tools** on the menu bar:

On This Page:

» **Inflation & Prices**
» **Employment**
» **Unemployment**
» **Employment Projections**
» **Pay & Benefits**

» **Spending & Time Use**
» **Productivity**
» **Workplace Injuries**
» **Occupational Requirements**
» **Regional Resources**

» **International**
» **Historical News Release Tables**
» **Maps**
» **Calculators**
» **Public Data API**

Click **Inflation & Prices**, and **CPI**; we will be led to a location where we candownload related datasets, as you can see at this link: `http://download.bls.gov/pub/time.series/cu/`

Generating two dozen datasets

To help readers of this book, many datasets are generated. First, let's look at a simple example of a download and load a Python dataset called `ffMonthly.pkl`. For more information on the mentioned dataset, visit the following link:`http://canisius.edu/~yany/python/ffMonthly.pkl`.

This dataset was generated based on the monthly Fama-French 3 factor time series. Assuming that the dataset is saved under `c:/temp/`, then we could use the following Python program to load it:

```
>>>import pandas as pd
>>>ff=pd.read_pickle("c:/temp/ffMonthly.pkl")
```

We could view the first and last several lines:

```
>>>import pandas as pd
>>>ff=pd.read_pickle("c:/temp/ffMonthly.pkl")
```

A better way is to use the `.head()` and `.tail()` functions; see the following code:

```
>>>import pandas as pd
>>>ff=pd.read_pickle("c:/temp/ffMonthly.pkl")
>>>ff.head(5)
DATE   MKT_RFSMBHMLRF
1    1926-10-01 -0.0324   0.0004   0.0051   0.0032
2    1926-11-01  0.0253  -0.002  -0.0035   0.0031
3    1926-12-01  0.0262 -0.0004 -0.0002   0.0028
4    1927-01-01 -0.0006 -0.0056   0.0483   0.0025
5    1927-02-01  0.0418  -0.001   0.0317   0.0026
>>>ff.tail(3)
DATE   MKT_RFSMBHMLRF
1078  2016-07-01  0.0395   0.029 -0.0098   0.0002
1079  2016-08-01  0.0049  0.0094  0.0318   0.0002
1080  2016-09-01  0.0025    0.02 -0.0134   0.0002
>>>
```

The command of `ff.head(5)` would show the first five lines while `ff.tail(3)` would show the last three lines. The `date` variable is vitally important for time series. The major reason is that we are dealing with time series. When merging different datasets, one of the most common variables used to merge them is the `date` variable. The following example shows how to define such a `date` variable:

```
>>>import pandas as pd
>>>from datetime import timedelta
>>>a=pd.to_datetime('12/2/2016', format='%m/%d/%Y')
```

```
>>>a+timedelta(40)
>>>
Timestamp('2017-01-11 00:00:00')
>>> b=a+timedelta(40)
>>>b.date()
datetime.date(2017, 1, 11)
```

To help readers of this book, the author has generated about two dozen Python datasets with an extension of `.pkl`. Those datasets are from the previously mentioned public sources, such as from the Prof. French data library, and Prof. Hasbrouck's TORQ, which contains transactions, quotes, order processing data, and audit trail data for a sample of 144 NYSE stocks for the 3 months, November 1990 through January 1991. To facilitate an easy downloading, a Python program called `loadYan.py` is available. You will find more information on that at: `http://caniisus.edu/~yany/loadYan.py`.

After you run the program, the `help(loadYan)` could be issued to find out all datasets generated; see the following code:

```
>>>help(loadYan)
Help on function loadYan in module __main__:

loadYan(i, loc='c:/temp/temp.pkl')
    Objective: download datasets with an extension of .pkl
i     : an integer
loc   : a temporary location, such as c:/temp/temp.pkl

i  dataset            description
   --- -------        ------------------
1  ffMonthlyFama-French 3 factors monthly
2  ffDailyFama-French 3 factors daily
3  ffMonthly5Fama-French 5 factors monthly
4  ffDaily5Fama-French 5 factors daily
5  sp500listsCurrent S&P 500 constituents
6  tradingDaysMonthly trading days monthly
7  tradingDaysDaily   trading days daily
8  usGDPannual        US GDP annual
9  usGDPmonthly       US GDP monthly
10 usCPI              US Consumer Price Index
11 dollarIndex        US dollar index
12 goldPriceMonthly   gold price monthly
13 goldPriceDaily     gold price daily
14 spreadAAA          Moody's spread for AAA rated bonds
```

```
15   spreadBBB          Moody's spread for BBB rated bonds
16   spreadCCC          Moody's spread for CCC rated bonds
17   TORQctTORQ Consolidated Trade
18   TORQcqTORQ Consolidated Quote
19   TORQcodTORQ Consolidated Order
20   DTAQibmCTTAQ Consolidated Trade for IBM (one day)
21   DTAQibmCQDTAQ Consolidated Quote for IBM (one day)
22   DTAQ50CTDTAQ Consolidated Trade for 50  (one day)
23   DTAQ50CQDTAQ Consolidated Quote for 50  (one day)
24   spreadCredit   Spreads based on credit ratings
25journalRankings  A list of journals


    Example 1:
>>>x=loadYan(1)
>>>x.head(2)
DATE   MKT_RFSMBHMLRF
1   1926-10-01 -0.0324  0.0004  0.0051  0.0032
2   1926-11-01  0.0253  -0.002 -0.0035  0.0031


>>>x.tail(2)
DATE   MKT_RFSMBHMLRF
1079  2016-08-01  0.0049  0.0094  0.0318  0.0002
1080  2016-09-01  0.0025    0.02 -0.0134  0.0002
>>>
```

Several datasets related to CRSP and Compustat

The Center for Research in Security Prices (CRSP) contains all trading data, such as closing price, trading volume, shares outstanding, for all listed stocks in the US from 1926 onward. Because of its quality and long history, it has been used extensively by academic researchers and practitioners. The database is generated and maintained by the University of Chicago, and is available at: http://www.crsp.com/. About 100 Python datasets are generated; see the following table:

Name	Description
crspInfo.pkl	Contains PERMNO, header cusip, stock exchange, and starting and ending trading dates
stockMonthly.pkl	Monthly stock file, contains PERMNO, date, return, price, trading volume, and shares outstanding
indexMonthly.pkl	Index file with a monthly frequency

Name	Description
`indexDaily.pkl`	Index file with a monthly frequency
`tradingDaysMonthly.pkl`	Trading days from 1926 to 12/31/2015 for monthly data
`tradingDaysDaily.pkl`	Trading days from 1926 to 12/31/2015 for daily data
`sp500add.pkl`	S&P500 constituents, that is, for each stock when it was added to the index and when it was removed from it
`sp500daily.pkl`	S&P500 daily index level and return
`sp500monthly.pkl`	S&P500 monthly index level and return
`d1925.pkl`	Daily stock price file for 1925
`d1926.pkl`	Daily stock price file for 1926
...	[more here between 1926 and 2014]
`d2014.pkl`	Daily stock price file for 2014
`d2015.pkl`	Daily stock price file for 2015

Table 4.2: A list of Python datasets related CRSP

To load data is quite straightforward by using the `pandas.read_pickle()` function:

```
>>>import pandas as pd
>>>crspInfo=pd.read_pickle("c:/temp/crspInfo.pkl")
```

To view the first and last couple of observations, the `.head()` and `.tail()` functions could be applied:

```
>>>crspInfo.shape
    (31218, 8)
>>>crspInfo.head()
PERMNOPERMCOCUSIP                         NAME TICKER EX    BEGDATE   \
0    10001    7953  6720410          AS NATURAL INCEGAS    2
19860131
1    10002    7954  5978R10ANCTRUST FINANCIAL GROUP IN    BTFG    3
19860131
2    10003    7957  9031810REAT COUNTRY BKASONIA CT      GCBK    3
19860131
3    10005    7961  5815510ESTERN ENERGY RESOURCES INCWERC    3
19860131
4    10006   22156  0080010          C F INDUSTRIES INCACF    1
19251231
ENDDATE
```

```
0   20151231
1   20130228
2   19951229
3   19910731
4   19840629
>>>crspInfo.tail(3)
PERMNOPERMCOCUSIP             NAME TICKER  EX   BEGDATE  \
31215   93434   53427  8513510& W SEED CO   SANW   3  20100630
31216   93435   53452  2936G20INO CLEAN ENERGY INCSCEI   3   20100630
31217   93436   53453  8160R10ESLA MOTORS INCTSLA   3   20100630
ENDDATE
31215   20151231
31216   20120531
31217   20151231>>>
```

The PERMNO is the CRSP's stock ID, PERMCO is the firm ID, Name is the company's current name, Ticker is the header ticker, that is, the current ticker symbol, EX is the exchange code (1 for New York Stock Exchange, 2 for American Stock Exchange, 3 for Nasdaq), BEGDATE is the first trading day while the ENDDATE is the last trading day for one given PERMNO. For the pandas module, column selection is done by passing a list of column names to our DataFrame.

For example, to choose just three columns of PERMNO, BEGDATE, and ENDDATE, we have the following code:

```
>>>myColumn=['PERMNO','BEGDATE','ENDDATE']
>>>crspInfo[myColumn].head(6)
>>>
PERMNOBEGDATEENDDATE
0   10001  19860131  20151231
1   10002  19860131  20130228
2   10003  19860131  19951229
3   10005  19860131  19910731
4   10006  19251231  19840629
5   10007  19860131  19901031
>>>
```

The Compustat(CapitalIQ) database offers financial statements such as balance sheet, income statement, and cash flows for public firms in the US from 1960 to today. The database is generated by Standard &Poor's. You can find more about it at http://marketintelligence.spglobal.com/our-capabilities/our-capabilities.html?product=compustat-research-insight. The following table lists a few related Python datasets:

Name	Description
compInfo.pkl	Key header file for all firms
varDefinitions.pkl	Definitions of all variables used in the datasets
deletionCodes.pkl	Shows when a firm was deleted from the database and why
acc1950.pkl	Annual financial statements for 1950
acc1951.pkl	Annual financial statements for 1951
acc2014.pkl	Annual financial statements for 2014
acc2015.pkl	Annual financial statements for 2015

Table 4.3: A list of Python datasets related Compustat

Note that since both CRSP and Compustat are proprietary databases, related datasets willnot be available on the author's website. If an instructor is interested in thatdata, please contact the author directly. A few datasets for high frequency data are listed in the following table:

Name	Description
TORQct.pkl	TORQ database for Consolidated Trade
TORQcq.pkl	TORQ database for Consolidated Quote
TORQcod.pkl	TORQ database for COD
DTAQibmCT	DTAQ stands for Daily Trade and Quote, millisecond-by-millisecond trading data, one-day data for IBM
DTAQibmCQ	One-day data for IBM, Consolidated Quote
DTAQ50CT	One-day data for 50 stocks (Consolidated Trade)
DTAQ50CQ	One-day data for 50 stocks (Consolidated Quote)

Table 4.4: A list of Python datasets related high-frequency trading data

Assume that `TORQcq.pkl` is saved under `c:/temp/`. We could view its first and last several observations:

```
>>>import pandas as pd
>>>x=pd.read_pickle("c:/temp/TORQcq.pkl")
>>>x.head()
>>>
     SYMBOL      DATE      TIME      BID      OFRBIDSIZOFRSIZ   MODE   QSEQ
EX
0       AC  19901101   9:30:44   12.875   13.125            32      5     10
1586  N
1       AC  19901101   9:30:47   12.750   13.250             1      1     12
0   M
2       AC  19901101   9:30:51   12.750   13.250             1      1     12
0   B
3       AC  19901101   9:30:52   12.750   13.250             1      1     12
0   X
4       AC  19901101  10:40:13   12.750   13.125             2      2     12
0
>>>x.tail()
          SYMBOL      DATE      TIME      BID     OFRBIDSIZOFRSIZ   MODE
\
1111220      ZNT  19910131  13:31:06   12.375   12.875            1      1
12
1111221      ZNT  19910131  13:31:06   12.375   12.875            1      1
12
1111222      ZNT  19910131  16:08:44   12.500   12.750            1      1
3
1111223      ZNT  19910131  16:08:49   12.375   12.875            1      1
12
1111224      ZNT  19910131  16:16:54   12.375   12.875            1      1
3
         QSEQ EX
1111220       0  B
1111221       0  X
1111222  237893  N
1111223       0  X
1111224       0  X
>>>M
```

The following table shows a few examples of retrieving data for different formats, such as SAS, Matlab, and Excel:

Format	Code
	`>>>import pandas as pd`
CSV	`>>>a=pd.read_csv("c:/temp/ffMonthly.csv",skip=4)`
Text	`>>>b=pd.read_table("c:/temp/ffMonthly.txt",skip=4)`
Pickle	`>>>c=pd.read_pickle("c:/temp/ffMonthly.pkl")`
SAS	`>>>d= sp.read_sas('c:/temp/ffMonthly.sas7bdat')`
Matlab	`>>>import scipy.io as sio`
	`>>>e= sio.loadmat('c:/temp/ffMonthly.mat')`
Excel	`>>>infile=pd.ExcelFile("c:/temp/ffMonthly.xlsx")`
	`>>>f=infile.parse("ffMonthly",header=T)`

Table 4.5: Retrieving data with different formats

To help readers of this chapter, all input files for the preceding table are available. Please refer to this link for more information: `http://canisius.edu/~yany/ffMonthly.zip`.

Reference:
Kane, David, 2006, Open Source Finance, working paper, Harvard University, SSRN link is at`http://papers.ssrn.com/sol3/papers.cfm?abstract_id=966354`

Appendix A – Python program for return distribution versus a normal distribution

```
from matplotlib.pyplot import *
from matplotlib.finance import quotes_historical_yahoo_ochl as getData
import numpy as np
import matplotlib.mlab as mlab

ticker='IBM'
begdate=(2015,1,1)
enddate=(2015,11,9)
p = getData(ticker, begdate, enddate,asobject=True, adjusted=True)
ret = (p.aclose[1:] - p.aclose[:-1])/p.aclose[:1]
[n,bins,patches] = hist(ret, 100)
mu = np.mean(ret)
```

```
sigma = np.std(ret)
x = mlab.normpdf(bins, mu, sigma)
plot(bins, x, color='red', lw=2)
title("IBM return distribution")
xlabel("Returns")
ylabel("Frequency")
show()
```

The corresponding graph is shown here:

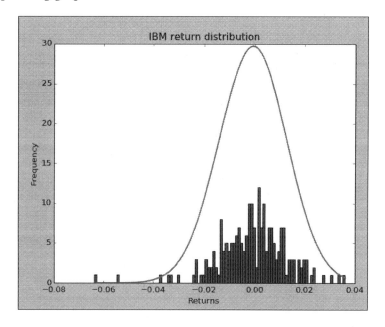

Appendix B – Python program to a draw candle-stick picture

```
import numpy as np
import matplotlib.pyplot as plt
from matplotlib.dates import DateFormatter, WeekdayLocator
from matplotlib.dates import HourLocator,DayLocator, MONDAY
from matplotlib.finance import candlestick_ohlc,plot_day_summary_oclh
from matplotlib.finance import quotes_historical_yahoo_ochl as getData
#
date1 = ( 2013, 10, 20)
date2 = ( 2013, 11, 10 )
ticker='IBM'
mondays = WeekdayLocator(MONDAY)        # major ticks on the mondays
alldays = DayLocator()                  # minor ticks on the days
```

```
weekFormatter = DateFormatter('%b %d') # e.g., Jan 12
dayFormatter = DateFormatter('%d')     # e.g., 12
quotes = getData(ticker, date1, date2)
if len(quotes) == 0:
    raiseSystemExit
fig, ax = plt.subplots()
fig.subplots_adjust(bottom=0.2)
ax.xaxis.set_major_locator(mondays)
ax.xaxis.set_minor_locator(alldays)
ax.xaxis.set_major_formatter(weekFormatter)
ax.xaxis.set_minor_formatter(dayFormatter)
plot_day_summary_oclh(ax, quotes, ticksize=3)
candlestick_ohlc(ax, quotes, width=0.6)
ax.xaxis_date()
ax.autoscale_view()
plt.setp(plt.gca().get_xticklabels(), rotation=80,horizontalalignment
='right')
plt.figtext(0.35,0.45, '10/29: Open, High, Low, Close')
plt.figtext(0.35,0.42, ' 177.62, 182.32, 177.50, 182.12')
plt.figtext(0.35,0.32, 'Black ==> Close > Open ')
plt.figtext(0.35,0.28, 'Red ==> Close < Open ')
plt.title('Candlesticks for IBM from 10/20/2013 to 11/10/2013')
plt.ylabel('Price')
plt.xlabel('Date')
plt.show()
```

The picture is shown here:

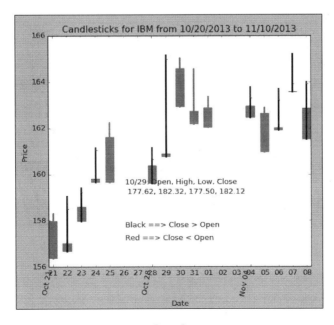

Appendix C – Python program for price movement

```
import datetime
import matplotlib.pyplot as plt
from matplotlib.finance import quotes_historical_yahoo_ochl
from matplotlib.dates import MonthLocator,DateFormatter
ticker='AAPL'
begdate= datetime.date( 2012, 1, 2 )
enddate = datetime.date( 2013, 12,4)

months= MonthLocator(range(1,13), bymonthday=1, interval=3)# 3rd month
monthsFmt = DateFormatter("%b '%Y")
x = quotes_historical_yahoo_ochl(ticker, begdate, enddate)
if len(x) == 0:
    print ('Found no quotes')
    raiseSystemExit
dates = [q[0] for q in x]
closes = [q[4] for q in x]
fig, ax = plt.subplots()
ax.plot_date(dates, closes, '-')
ax.xaxis.set_major_locator(months)
ax.xaxis.set_major_formatter(monthsFmt)
ax.autoscale_view()
ax.grid(True)
fig.autofmt_xdate()
plt.show()
```

The corresponding graph is given here:

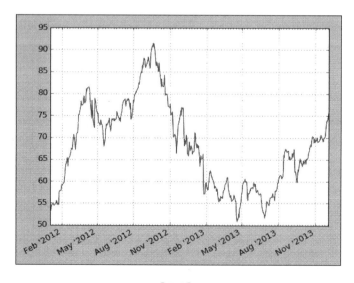

Appendix D – Python program to show a picture of a stock's intra-day movement

```
import numpy as np
import pandas as pd
import datetime as datetime
import matplotlib.pyplot as plt
ticker='AAPL'
path='http://www.google.com/finance/getprices?q=ttt&i=60&p=1d&f=d,o,h
,l,c,v'
p=np.array(pd.read_csv(path.replace('ttt',ticker),skiprows=7,header=N
one))
#
date=[]
for i in np.arange(0,len(p)):
    if p[i][0][0]=='a':
        t= datetime.datetime.fromtimestamp(int(p[i][0].
replace('a','')))
        date.append(t)
    else:
        date.append(t+datetime.timedelta(minutes =int(p[i][0])))
#
final=pd.DataFrame(p,index=date)
final.columns=['a','Open','High','Low','Close','Vol']
del final['a']
#
x=final.index
y=final.Close
#
plt.title('Intraday price pattern for ttt'.replace('ttt',ticker))
plt.xlabel('Price of stock')
plt.ylabel('Intro-day price pattern')
plt.plot(x,y)
plt.show()
```

The corresponding graph is shown here:

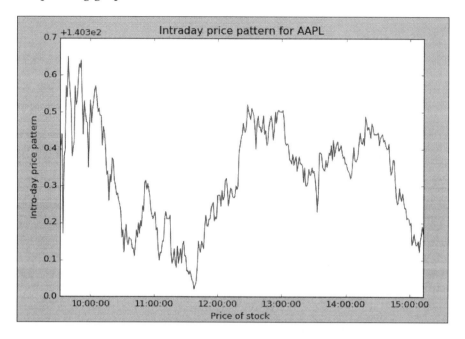

Appendix E –properties for a pandas DataFrame

First, let's download a Python dataset called `ffMonthly.pickle` from `http://canisius.edu/~yany/python/ffMonthly.pickle`. Assume that the dataset is saved under `c:/temp`:

```
>>>
>>>import pandas as pd
>>>ff=pd.read_pickle("c:/temp/ffMonthly.pickle")
>>>type(ff)
<class'pandas.core.frame.DataFrame'>
>>>
```

The last result shows that the type of `ff` dataset is a panda DataFrame. Because of this, it might be a good idea to get more information about this type of data. After we type `ff.`, we cansee a drop-down list; see the following screenshot:

```
>>>
>>>    abs
>>>    add
>>>    add_prefix
>>>    add_suffix
>>>    align
>>>    all
>>>    any
>>>    append
>>>    apply
>>>    applymap
>>>
>>> ff.
```

We can find a function called `hist()`; see its usage in the following code:

```
>>>import pandas as pd
>>>infile=("c:/temp/ffMonthly.pickle")
>>>ff=pd.read_pickle(infile)
>>>ff.hist()
```

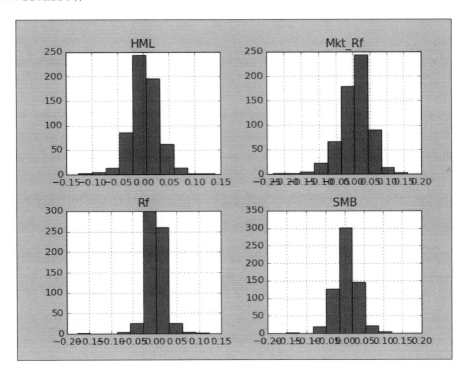

For more detail, see the related link at: `http://pandas.pydata.org/pandas-docs/stable/generated/pandas.DataFrame.html`.

Appendix F –how to generate a Python dataset with an extension of .pkl or .pickle

First, let look at the simplest dataset:

```
>>>import pandas as pd
>>>import numpy.ranom  as random
>>>x=random.randn(10)
>>>y=pd.DataFrame(x)
>>>y.to_pickle("c:/temp/test.pkl")
```

Reading a Python dataset with an extension of .pkl or .pickle, we use thepd.read_pickle() function:

```
>>> import pandas as pd
>>>kk=pd.read_pickle("c:/temp/test.pkl")
```

Next, the Python program is shown to generate theffMonthly.pkl dataset:

```
import pandas as pd
import numpy as np
file=open("c:/temp/ffMonthly.txt","r")
data=file.readlines()
dd=mkt=smb=hml=rf=[]
n=len(data)
index=range(1,n-3)
#
for i in range(4,n):
    t=data[i].split()
    dd.append(pd.to_datetime(t[0]+'01', format='%Y%m%d').date())
    mkt.append(float(t[1])/100)
    smb.append(float(t[2])/100)
    hml.append(float(t[3])/100)
     rf.append(float(t[4])/100)
#
d=np.transpose([dd,mkt,smb,hml,rf])
ff=pd.DataFrame(d,index=index,columns=['DATE','MKT_
RF','SMB','HML','RF'])
ff.to_pickle("c:/temp/ffMonthly.pkl")
```

The first and last several observations are shown here:

```
>>>ff.head(2)
DATE   MKT_RFSMBHML
1   1926-10-01 -0.0324   0.0004   0.0051
2   1926-11-01  0.0253   -0.002 -0.0035
```

```
>>>ff.tail(2)
DATE   MKT_RFSMBHML
1079   2016-08-01   0.0049   0.0094   0.0318
1080   2016-09-01   0.0025     0.02  -0.0134
```

Appendix G – data case #1 -generating several Python datasets

For this data case, students are required to generate about five Python datasets with an extension of .pkl:

```
>>import pandas as pd
>>>a = pd.Series(['12/1/2014', '1/1/2015'])
>>>b= pd.to_datetime(a, format='%m/%d/%Y')
>>>b
0    2014-12-01
1    2015-01-01
dtype: datetime64[ns]
>>>
```

Please generate the following datasets with a Python format of .pickle (.pkl or .pickle):

#	Dataset name	Description
1	ffDaily	Daily Fama and French 3 factor time series
2	ffMonthly5	Monthly Fama and French 5 factor time series
3	usGDPannual	US annual GDP (Gross Domestic Product)
4	usGDPquarterly	US quarterly GDP (Gross Domestic Product)
5	dollarIndex	US dollar index
6	goldPriceMonthly	Monthly gold price
7	goldPriceDaily	Daily Gold price
8	tradingDaysMonthly	Trading days for monthly time series
9	tradingDaysDaily	Trading days for daily data
10	spreadAAA	Moody's AAA rated bond's spread

Exercises

1. From where could we get daily stock price data?
2. Could we download returns data directly?

3. Manually download monthly and daily price data for CitiGroup.

4. Convert daily price data for the CitiGroup to daily returns.

5. Convert monthly prices to monthly returns and convert daily returns to monthly returns. Are they the same?

6. Are the following two lines equivalent?

```
>>>ret = p.aclose[1:]/p.aclose[:-1]-1
>>>ret = (p.aclose[1:]-p.aclose[:-1]/p.aclose[1:]
```

7. What are advantages and disadvantages of using public stock data versus private stock data, for example, from some financial databases?

8. Find the annual cost of subscribing Compustat, related to accounting information and CRSP, related to trading data.

9. Download IBM monthly data from Yahoo Finance. Estimate its standard deviation and Sharpe ratio from January 2000 to December 2004.

10. What is the annual beta for IBM, DELL, and MSFT from 2001 to 2010?

11. What is the correlation between IBM and DELL from 2006 to 2010?

12. Estimate the mean weekday returns for IBM. Do you observe a weekday effect?

13. Does the volatility decline over the years? For example, you could select IBM, DELL, and MSFT to investigate this hypothesis.

14. What is the correlation between S&P500 and DJI (Dow Jones Industrial average)?Note: S&P500 Index ticker in Yahoo Finance is ^GSPC and for DJIit's^DJI.

15. How do youdownload data for *n* given tickers?

16. Write an R program to input *n* tickers from an input file.

17. What is the correlation coefficient between the US stock market (S&P500) and the Hong Kong market (Hang Seng Index)?

18. Is it true that the Singaporean equity market is more strongly correlated with the Japanese equitymarket than with the American equity market?

19. How would youdownload daily price data for 50 stocks and save to just one text file?

20. After downloading data from Yahoo!Finance,assume that *p* vector contains all the daily price data. What is the meaning of the following two lines of code? When should we apply them?

```
>>> ret = p.aclose[1:]/p.aclose[:-1]-1
>>> ret = p.aclose[:-1]/p.aclose[1:]-1
```

Summary

In this chapter, we have discussed various public data sources for economics, finance and accounting. For economics, we could go to Federal Reserve Bank's data library, Prof. French's Data library to retrieve many useful time series. For finance, we could use Yahoo!Finance and Google finance to download historical price data. For accounting information, such as latest several years' balance sheets and income statements, we could use Yahoo!Finance, Google finance, and SEC filings. For the next chapter, we explain many concepts related to interest rate. After that, we explain how to price bonds and stocks.

5

Bond and Stock Valuation

Bond or fixed income securities and stock are two widely used investment vehicles. Thus, they deserve a thorough discussion. Before touching upon bond or stock valuation, we have to discuss interest rate and its related concepts, such as **Annual Percentage Rate (APR)**, **Effective Annual Rate (EAR)**, compounding frequency, how to convert one effective rate to another one, the term structure of interest rate, how to estimate the selling price of a regular bond, how to use the so-called discount dividend model to estimate the price of a stock, and so on. In particular, this chapter will cover the following topics:

- Introduction to interest rates
- Conversion between various effective rates, APR
- The term structure of interest rates
- Bond evaluation and YTM
- Credit rating versus default spread
- Definition of duration and modified duration
- Stock evaluation, total returns, capital gain yield, and dividend yield
- A new data type – dictionary

Introduction to interest rates

There is no doubt that interest rates play an important role in our economy. When the economy is expanding, interest rates tend to go high since the high demand of capital would push up borrowing rates. In addition, inflation might go up as well. When this is happening, central banks will do their best to control the inflation at an appropriate level. One tool to fight the potential inflation hike is to increase banks' lending rates. On the other hand, the bond price is negatively correlated with interest rates.

There is a good chance that many readers of this book are confused with the difference between simple interest and compound interest. Simple interest does not consider interest on interest while compound interest rate does. Assume that we borrow $1,000 today for 10 years. What are the future values at the end of each year if the annual rate is 8%? Assume that this annual rate is both the simple and compounded interest rates. Their corresponding formulae are shown here:

$$FV(simple\ interest) = PV(1 + R * n) .... (1)$$

$$FV(compounded\ interest) = PV(1 + R)^n .... (2)$$

Here, PV is the loan today, R is the period rate, and n is the number of periods. The graphic representation of the principal, the future values with a simple interest rate, and the future values with a compound interest rate are shown in the diagram which follows. The related Python program is in *Appendix A*. The difference between the top red line (future values with a compounded interest rate) and the middle one (future values with a simple interest rate) is interest on interest:

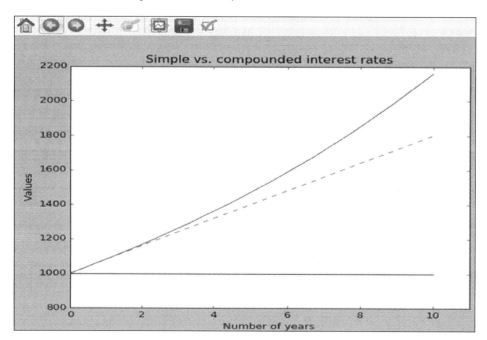

In *Chapter 3, Time Value of Money* we have learnt the time value of money. Let's use the same simple example to start.

Today, $100 is deposited in a bank with a 10% annual interest rate. How much is it at the end of one year? We know that it will be $110. $100 is our principal while $10 will be the interest payment. Alternatively, the following formula could be applied:

$$FV = PV * (1 + R)^n$$

..........(3)

Here, *FV* is the future value, *PV* is the present value, *R* is the period effective rate and *n* is the number of periods. Here is the result: *100*(1+0.1)=110*. Compared with *Chapter 3,Time Value of Money*, a careful reader would find that *R* is here defined as *effective period rate* instead of *period rate*. The keyword of *effective* was added. In previous chapters, there is an *R* in all formulae, such as in *FV*(of one *PV*), *PV*(one *FV*), *PV*(annuity), *PV*(annuity due), *PV*(growing annuity), *FV*(annuity), *FV*(annuity due) and *FV*(growing annuity). The *R* in those formulae is actually an effective rate. Here, we explain this important concept.

First, let's see the conversional way to estimate an effective rate for a given **Annual Percentage Rate** (**APR**) and a compounding frequency (*m*):

$$R_m^{effective} = \frac{APR}{m}$$

......(4)

Here, $R_m^{effective}$ is an effective period rate with respect to a certain period (identified by *m*), *APR* is Annual Percentage Rate and *m* is the compounding frequency. The values of m could be 1 for annual, 2 for semi-annual, 4 for quarterly, 12 for monthly, and 365 for daily. If APR is 10% compounded semi-annually, then the effective semi-annual rate is 5% (=0.10/2). On the other hand, if APR is 0.08 compounded quarterly, then the effective quarterly rate is 2% (=0.08/4).

Here is an example related to house mortgage. John Doe intends to buy a house in Buffalo, New York, with a price tag of $240,000. He plans to pay 20% of the price of the house as a down payment and borrow the rest from M&T Bank. For a 30-year mortgage, the bank offers an annual rate of 4.25%. How much is his monthly mortgage payment? As discussed in *Chapter 3,Time Value of Money*, the `scipy.pmt()` function could be applied here:

```
>>> import scipy as sp
>>>sp.pmt(0.045/12,30*12,240000*0.8)
-972.83579486570068
```

In the preceding code, the effective monthly rate is 0.045/12. The reason behind this calculation is that the compounding frequency is assumed to be monthly since this is a mortgage with a regular monthly payment. Based on this result, every month John has to pay $972.84.

To compare two rates with different compounding frequencies, we have to convert them into the same rates before we could compare. One such effective rate is called **Effective Annual Rate** (**EAR**). For a given APR with a compounding frequency of m, its *EAR* is calculated here:

$$EAR = (1 + \frac{APR}{m})^m - 1$$

.......(5)

Assume that a company plans to borrow $10m for a long-term investment project. Bank A offers an annual rate of 8% compounded semi-annually, while bank B offers a rate of 7.9% compounded quarterly. For the company, which borrowing rate is cheaper? By applying the preceding formula, we have the following results. Since 8.137% is lower than 8.160%, the offer from bank B is better:

```
>>> (1+0.08/2)**2-1
0.08160000000000012
>>> (1+0.079/4)**4-1
0.08137134208625363
```

Obviously, we could have other benchmarks. For example, we know that the effective semi-annual rate from bank A's offer is 4% (=0.08/2). Then we would ask: what is the equivalent effective quarterly rate from bank B? In other words, we compare two effective semi-annual rates. In order to convert one effective rate to another one, a so-called **2-Step Approach** is introduced:

1. Which effective rate is given? To answer this question, we simply apply equation (4). There is no rationality behind this since it is quoted this way by financial institutions. Assume that the annual rate is 10%, compounded semi-annually. The effective semi-annual rate is given, and its value is 5%, that is, *0.1/2=0.05*.If APR is 8%, compounded monthly, then it means that the effective monthly rate is 0.833%, that is,*0.08/12=0.006666667*.

2. How to convert one given effective rate to another target effective rate? If the given effective semi-annual rate is 5%, what is the equivalent effective quarterly rate? We draw a time line of one year, with two frequencies. On top, we have the given effective rate and its corresponding compounding frequency. In this case, 5% and 2 periods (Rsemi=5% and n1=2):

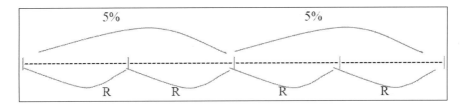

On the bottom, we have the effective rate we intend to estimate and its corresponding frequency (R and $n2=4$). Then, we apply the future formula of $FV = PV(1 + R)^n$ by using $PV=1$ twice with different input values:

$$FV_1 = 1 * (1 + R_1)^{n_1} = (1 + 0.05)^2$$

$$FV_2 = 1 * (1 + R_2)^{n_2} = (1 + R)^4$$

Set them equal, that is, $(1 + 0.05)^2 = (1 + R)^4$ Solve for R, we have $R=(1+0.05)**(2/4)-1$. The result is shown here:

```
>>> (1+0.05)**(2/4)-1
   0.02469508
```

The effective quarterly rate is 2.469508%. The beauty of this approach is that we don't have to remember other formula except $FV=PV(1+R)n$. By the way, there is no link between this step and step 1.

Alternatively, we could apply certain formula directly. Here, we show how to derive two formula: from *APR* to *Rm* and from *APR1* to *APR2*. For formula between two annual rates of *APR1(m1)* and *APR2(m2)* is given here:

$$(1 + \frac{APR_2}{m_2})^{m_2} = (1 + \frac{APR_1}{m_1})^{m_1}$$

........(6)

Here, *APR1* (*APR2*) is the first (second) APR Annual Percentage Rate, while *m1* (*m2*) is its corresponding compounding frequency per year. Based on the preceding equation, we have the following formula to calculate the effective rate with a new compounding frequency (*m2*) for a given APR (*APR1*) and its corresponding frequency (*m1*):

$$R_{m_2}^{effective} = (1 + \frac{APR_1}{m_1})^{\frac{m_1}{m_2}} - 1$$

......(7)

For the same example, a bank offers10% annual rate compounding semi-annually. What is its equivalent effective quarterly rate? By applying *Equation (7)* with a set of input values of *APR1=0.10, m1=2*, and *m2=4*, see the following code:

```
>>> (1+0.10/2)**(2/4)-1
>>>
0.02469507659595993
```

We have the same results as that from the 2-step approach. Actually, we could write a simple Python function based on equation (7), see the following code:

```
def APR2Rm(APR1,m1,m2):
        return (1+APR1/m1)**(m1/m2)-1
```

Calling the function is simple, as we can see in the following code:

```
>>> APR2Rm(0.1,2,4)
       0.02469507659595993
>>> APR2Rm(0.08,2,12)
0.008164846051901042
```

With a few comments, such as the definitions of those three inputs, a formula used to estimate our target effective rate, plus a few examples, could be added. The program should be clearer see the following code:

```
def APR2Rm(APR1,m1,m2):
    """
```

Objective: convert one APR to another effective rate Rm:

```
        APR1: annual percentage rate
          m1: compounding frequency for APR1
          m2: effective period rate of our target effective rate
```

Formula used: *Rm=(1+APR1/m1)**(m1/m2)-1*

```
        Example #1>>>APR2Rm(0.1,2,4)
                0.02469507659595993
    """
        return (1+APR1/m1)**(m1/m2)-1
```

To get the second APR(*APR2*) for a given APR and its corresponding frequency, we have the following formula:

$$APR_2 = m_{2*}\left[\left(1 + \frac{APR_1}{m_1}\right)^{\frac{m_1}{m_2}} - 1\right] \quad ....(8)$$

By applying *equation (8)*, we have a result for APR2:

```
>>>Rs=(1+0.05/2)**(2/12)-1
>>>Rs*2
0.008247830930288469
>>>
```

The corresponding -line Python program is shown here. To save space, the program has no additional explanation or comments:

```
def APR2APR(APR1,m1,m2):
    return m2*((1+APR1/m1)**(m1/m2)-1)
```

For a continuously compounded interest rate, different ways could be used to explain this confusion concept. First, we apply the formula of **Effective Annual Rate (EAR)** by increasing the compounding frequency of *m*:

$$EAR = (1 + \frac{APR}{m})^m - 1$$

For example, if APR is 10% and compounded semi-annually, EAR will be 10.25%:

```
>>> (1+0.1/2)**2-1
>>>
0.10250000000000004
```

Since this function is quite simple, we could write a Python function instead, see the following program:

```
def EAR_f(APR,m):
    return (1+APR/m)**m-1
```

Next, assume that the APR is 10% and let's increase the compounding frequency, see the following program:

```
import numpy as np
d=365
h=d*24
m=h*60
s=m*60
ms=s*1000
x=np.array([1,2,4,12,d,h,m,s,ms])
APR=0.1
for i in x:
    print(EAR_f(APR,i))
```

The following is the output image:

```
0.1
0.1025
0.103812890625
0.104713067441
0.105155781616
0.105170287275
0.10517090754
0.105170919942
0.105172305371
```

Actually, when the compounding frequency approaches an infinity, the limit will be our continuously compounded rate with a formula of *EAR=exp(Rc)-1*, see the following code:

```
>>>exp(0.1)-1
    0.10517091807564771
```

The second method to explain the formula of a continuously compounded rate, is to remember another way to calculate the future value of one present cash flow. Recall in *Chapter 3,Time Value of Money*, we have the following formula to calculate the future value for a given present value:

$$FV = PV(1 + R)^n$$

Here, *FV* is the future value, *PV* is the present value, *R* is the effective period rate and *n* is the number of periods. Another way to calculate the future value of one present value is using a continuously compounded rate, *Rc*. Its formula is given here:

$$FV = PV * e^{R_c T} \quad ....(9)$$

Here, *Rc* is the continuously compounded rate, *T* is time when the future value is calculated (in years). If we choose one year as *T* and \$1 as *PV*, equaling the preceding two equations would lead to the following one:

$$e^{R_c} = (1 + \frac{APR}{m})^m$$

Note that *Rm=APR/m* is from *Equation (4)*. Then solve the preceding equation for *Rc*. Finally, for a given APR and *m* (compounding frequency), we have the following formula to estimate *Rc*:

$$R_c = m * \ln(1 + \frac{APR}{m})$$

......(10)

Here, `log()` is the natural logarithm function. Assume that the APR is 2.34% compounded semi-annually. What is its equivalent Rc?

```
>>>from math import log
>>>2*log(1+0.0234/2)
0.023264168459415393
```

Alternatively, we could write a 2-line Python function based on the preceding formula to convert an APR to Rc:

```
def APR2Rc(APR,m):
        return m*log(1+APR/m)
```

The output would be as follows:

```
>>> APR2Rc(0.0234,2)
0.023264168459415393
```

Similarly, for a given *Rc*, we have the following formula to calculate its corresponding *APR*:

$$APR = m * (e^{\frac{R_C}{m}} - 1)$$

......(11)

The related Python function is shown here:

```
def Rc2APR(Rc,m):
        return m*(exp(Rc/m)-1)
```

The output is as shown:

```
>>> Rc2APR(0.02,2)
0.020100334168335898
```

For an effective period rate, we have the following equation:

$$R_m = e^{\frac{R_C}{m}} - 1$$

..........(12)

The function and an example are shown in the following code:

```
def Rc2Rm(Rc,m):
        return exp(Rc/m)-1
```

The output can be seen here:

```
>>> Rc2Rm(0.02,2)
0.010050167084167949
```

Here, an analogy of withdrawing $100 from a bank is compared with the concept of effective rates. Assume that we go to a bank to withdraw $100. The following seven combinations are all equal:

Denomination of bills	Number of bills
100	1
50	2
20	5
10	10
5	20
2	50
1	100

Table 5.1 Denominations and number of bills for withdrawing $100

Now, let's look at the similar situation related to effective rates with different combinations of APRs and compounding frequencies (m). APR is 10% and compounded semi-annually. The following 11 interest rates are all equal, where **NA** is not applicable:

Interest rate quotation	M
APR is 10%, compounded semi-annually	2
APR is 10.25%, compounded annually	1
APR is 9.87803063838397%,compounded quarterly	4
APR is 9.79781526228125%,compounded monthly	12
APR is 9.75933732280154%. compounded daily	365
Effective annual rate is 0.1025	NA
Effective semi-annually rate is 0.05	NA

Interest rate quotation	M
Effective quarterly rate is 0.0246950765959599	NA
Effective monthly rate is 0.00816484605190104	NA
Effective daily rate is 0.000267379104734289	NA
Continuously compounded rate is 0.0975803283388641	NA

Table 5.2 Even with different APRs and compounding frequencies, they are all equal

Let's look at another analogy. Mary's monthly salary is $5,000. Thus, her annual salary would be *$60,000 (=50,000 * 12)*. This is our conventional way to calculate monthly salary versus the annual one. Now, let's make a simple twist. The company tells Mary that she would get just one lump sum at the end of the year. At the same time, she could borrow her original monthly salary from their company's accounting department and the company would cover the related cost. Literately, there is no difference between those two scenarios. Assume that the monthly effective rate is 0.25%. This means that in January, Mary would borrow $5,000 for 11 months because she would pay it back at the end of the year. This is true for February and other months. Recall from *Chapter 3,Time Value of Money*, this represents the future value of an annuity. For this case, the `scipy.fv()` function could be used:

```
>>> import scipy as sp
>>>sp.fv(0.0025,12,5000,0)
>>>
-60831.913827013472
```

The result suggests that receiving $5,000 every month for 12 months is the same as receiving $60,831.91 at the end of the year just once. Obviously, compared with the original $60,000 annual salary, the extra money of $831.91is for the interest payments.

Term structure of interest rates

The term structure of interest rates is defined as the relationship between risk-free rate and time. A risk-free rate is usually defined as the default-free treasury rate. From many sources, we could get the current term structure of interest rates. For example, on 12/21/2016, from Yahoo!Finance at `http://finance.yahoo.com/bonds`, we could get the following information.

The plotted term structure of interest rates could be more eye catching; see the following image:

US Treasury Bonds Rates				
Maturity	Yield	Yesterday	Last Week	Last Month
3 Month	0.47	0.46	0.48	0.40
6 Month	0.60	0.58	0.60	0.55
2 Year	1.18	1.20	1.24	1.05
3 Year	1.53	1.54	1.54	1.32
5 Year	2.00	2.02	2.03	1.74
10 Year	2.53	2.54	2.55	2.29
30 Year	3.12	3.12	3.16	2.97

Based on the information supplied by the preceding image, we have the following code to draw a so-called yield curve:

```
from matplotlib.pyplot import *
time=[3/12,6/12,2,3,5,10,30]
rate=[0.47,0.6,1.18,1.53,2,2.53,3.12]
title("Term Structure of Interest Rate ")
xlabel("Time ")
ylabel("Risk-free rate (%)")
plot(time,rate)
show()
```

The related graph is given in the following image:

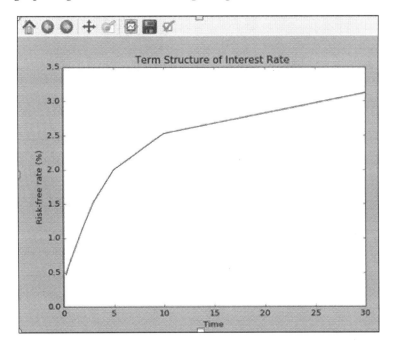

The upward sloping's term structure means the long-term rates are higher than the short-term rates. Since the term structure of interest rates has many missing numbers, the function called .interpolate() from the pandas module could be used to interpolate those values, see the following example where we have two missing values between 2 and 6:

```
>>>import pandas as pd
>>>import numpy as np
>>>x=pd.Series([1,2,np.nan,np.nan,6])
>>>x.interpolate()
```

The related output is shown here:

```
>>>
01.000000
12.000000
23.333333
34.666667
46.000000
```

We could manually calculate those missing values. First, a Δ is estimated:

$$\Delta = \frac{v_2 - v_1}{n}$$
........(13)

Here, Δ is the incremental value between $v2$ (the ending value) and $v1$ (the beginning value), and n is the number of internals between those two values. The Δ for the above case is *(6-2)/3=1.33333*. Thus, the next value will be *v1+Δ=2+1.33333=3.33333*.

For the preceding example, related to the term structure of interest rates, from years 6 to 9, there is no data. The code and output are shown here:

```
>>> import pandas as pd
>>> import numpy as np
>>> nan=np.nan
>>> x=pd.Series([2,nan,nan,nan,nan,2.53])
>>>x.interpolate()
```

The output is shown here:

```
>>>
0      2.000
1      2.106
2      2.212
3      2.318
4      2.424
5      2.530
dtype: float64
>>>
```

The term structure of interest rates is very important since it serves as a benchmark to estimate **Yield to Maturity (YTM)** for corporate bonds. YTM is the period return if the bond holder holds until the bond expires. Technically speaking, YTM is the same as **Internal Rate of Return (IRR)**. In the financial industry, the spread, defined as the difference between YTM of a corporate bond over the risk-free rate, is used to estimate the discount rate for corporate bonds. The spread is a measure of the default risk. Thus, it should be closely correlated with the credit rating of the company and of the bond.

For this reason, a Python dataset called `spreadBasedOnCreditRating.pkl` is used to explain the relationship between the default spread and credit rating. The dataset could be downloaded from the author's web page at `http://canisius.edu/~yany/python/spreadBasedOnCreditRating.pkl`. The following program retrieves and prints the data. The dataset is assumed to be in the `c:/temp/` directory:

```
>>>import pandas as pd
>>>spread=pd.read_pickle("c:/temp/spreadBasedOnCreditRating.pkl")
>>> spread
```

	1	2	3	5	7	10	30
Rating							
Aaa/AAA	5.00	8.00	12.00	18.00	28.00	42.00	65.00
Aa1/AA+	10.00	18.00	25.00	34.00	42.00	54.00	77.00
Aa2/AA	14.00	29.00	38.00	50.00	57.00	65.00	89.00
Aa3/AA-	19.00	34.00	43.00	54.00	61.00	69.00	92.00
A1/A+	23.00	39.00	47.00	58.00	65.00	72.00	95.00
A2/A	24.00	39.00	49.00	61.00	69.00	77.00	103.00
A3/A-	32.00	49.00	59.00	72.00	80.00	89.00	117.00
Baa1/BBB+	38.00	61.00	75.00	92.00	103.00	115.00	151.00
Baa2/BBB	47.00	75.00	89.00	107.00	119.00	132.00	170.00
Baa3/BBB-	83.00	108.00	122.00	140.00	152.00	165.00	204.00
Ba1/BB+	157.00	182.00	198.00	217.00	232.00	248.00	286.00
Ba2/BB	231.00	256.00	274.00	295.00	312.00	330.00	367.00
Ba3/BB-	305.00	330.00	350.00	372.00	392.00	413.00	449.00
B1/B+	378.00	404.00	426.00	450.00	472.00	495.00	530.00
B2/B	452.00	478.00	502.00	527.00	552.00	578.00	612.00
B3/B-	526.00	552.00	578.00	604.00	632.00	660.00	693.00
Caa/CCC+	600.00	626.00	653.00	682.00	712.00	743.00	775.00
Treasury-Yield	0.13	0.45	0.93	1.74	2.31	2.73	3.55

```
>>>
```

The index column is the credit rating based on both Moody's and Standard& Poor's credit rating scales. Except for the last row, US Treasury Yield, the values in the dataset have a unit of basis point which is worth one hundredth of 1%. In other words, each value should be divided by 100 twice. For example, for an AA rated bond, its spread on year 5 is 50 basis points, that is, *0.005 (=50/10000)*. If the risk-free rate for a 5-year zero-coupon bond is 2%, the corresponding rate for a corporate bond, rated as AA, would be *2.5% (2.5%+ 0.5%)*.

The duration is a very important concept for risk analysis and hedging. The duration is defined as: the number of years needed to recover our initial investment. Let's look at the simple case: a zero-coupon bond. Today, we buy a 1-year zero-coupon bond. One year later, we would receive its face value of $100. Its timeline and cash flow are shown here:

```
        investment              $100
        |--------------------------|
        0                       1 year
```

Obviously, we have to wait for one year to recover our initial investment. Thus, the duration of this 1-year bond is 1. For a zero-coupon bond, the duration of the bond is the same as its maturity:

$$D = T \qquad ....(14)$$

Here, D is duration and T is the maturity of a zero-coupon bond (in years). Let's look at our second example that we would have two equal cash flows of $100 at the end of the first two years:

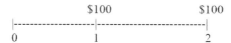

```
                     $100                    $100
      |--------------------|--------------------|
      0                    1                    2
```

How many years do we have to wait to recover our initial investment? The fact is that we have to wait for one year to receive the first $100 and wait for two years to receive the second $100. Thus, the first guess would be 1.5 years. However, after reading *Chapter 3,Time Value of Money*, we know that $100 received in year 2 is not equivalent to $100 received in year 1. If using the end of year 1 as our benchmark, the equivalent value of the second $100 is shown here:

```
>>> 100/(1+0.05)
95.23809523809524
```

Now, we would say that we have to wait 1 year to receive $100 and wait two years to receive $95.24. On average, how many years would we wait? The solution should be a weighted average. The weights of those two $100s are given here:

```
> pv2<-100/(1+0.05)
>w1=100/(100+pv2)
>>>w1
 0.5121951
>>>w2= pv2/(100+pv2)
```

```
>>>w2
 0.4878049
>>>w1*1 + w2*2
   1.487281
```

Finally, we have $D=w1*T1+w2*T2=w1*1+w2*2=0.5122*1 + 0.487805*2=1.487$. The answer is that we have to wait 1.487 years to recover our initial investment. In the above reasoning, we discount the second $100 to the end of year 1 to get our answer.

Alternatively, we could compound the first $100 to the end of year2, then compare, see the following code:

```
>>>fv=100*(1+0.05)
>>>fv
   105
```

The corresponding weights are given here:

```
> w1=105/(100+105)
> w1
[1] 0.5121951
> w2=100/(100+105)
> w2
[1] 0.4878049
>
```

The solution should be the same since the weights are the same as before. This suggests that we could use any point of time to estimate the weights of those cash flows happening at different points in time. Conventionally, the present value is used as the benchmark, see the following code:

```
>>> pv1=100/(1+0.05)
>>> pv2=100/(1+0.05)**2
>>>w1= pv1/(pv1+pv2)
>>>w1
0.5121951219512195
>>>1-w1
0.4878048780487805
```

Again, both weights remain the same. Another advantage of using the present value as our benchmark is that we could estimate the total present value as well. The total value is given here. We could argue that if we invested $185.94 today, we would recover 51.2% in year 1 and the rest by the end of year 2. Thus, on average we have to wait for 1.487 years:

```
> pv1+pv2
[1] 185.941
```

The general formula to estimate the duration for *n* given future cash flows is given in the following formula:

$$D = \sum_{i=1}^{n} w_i * T_i$$

.........(15)

D is duration, n is the number of cash flows, wi is the weight of the ith cash flow, and wi is defined as the present value of ith cash flow over the present values of all cash flows, Ti is the timing (in years) of the ith cash flow. Here, a Python function called `duration` is written:

```
def duration(t,cash_flow,y):
    n=len(t)
B,D=0,0
for i in range(n):
        B+=cash_flow[i]*exp(-y*t[i])
for i in range(n):
        D+=t[i]*cash_flow[i]*exp(-y*t[i])/B
    return D
```

If we add a header, the program would be more helpful, see the following code:

```
def duration(t,cash_flow,y):
    n=len(t)
    B=0     # B is the bond's present value
    for i in range(n):
        B+=cash_flow[i]*exp(-y*t[i])

    D=0     # D is the duration
    for i in range(n):
        D+=t[i]*cash_flow[i]*exp(-y*t[i])/B
    return D
```

Bond evaluation

Bond is also called fixed income security. There are different types of categories. Based on maturity, bonds could be classified into short-term, median-term, and long-term. For US Treasury securities, T-bills are the securities issued by the Department of Treasury with a maturity less than 1 year, T-notes are for government bonds beyond 1 year but less than 10 years. T-bonds are treasury securities with a maturity beyond 10 years. Based on coupon payments, there are zero-coupon bonds and coupon bonds. When it is a central government's bond, we call them risk-free bonds since the central government usually has a right to print money, that is by default, free.

If a bond holder could convert his/her bond into the underlying common stock with a predetermined number of shares before maturity, it is called a convertible bond. If a bond issuer could retire or buy back a bond before its maturity, it is named a **callable bond**. On the other hands, if the bond buyers could sell the bond back to the original issuers before maturity, it is balled a **puttable bond**. The cashflow for a zero-coupon bond is shown here:

Here, FV is the face value and n is the maturity (in years). To estimate the price of such a zero-coupon bond, we could apply the present value of one future cash flow easily. In other words, we could apply the `scipy.pv()` function.

For a coupon bond, we expect a set of regular coupon payments. The periodic coupon payment is estimated by the following formula:

$$coupon\ payment = \frac{coupon\ rate * FV}{freq}$$

Here,FV is the face value of the bond and frequency is the number of coupon payments each year. Let's look at a 3-year coupon bond. The face value is $100 with an annual coupon rate of 8%. The coupon payment is annual. The annual coupon payment is $8 for the next three years and the investors would also receive the face value of $100 on the maturity date. The timeline of this coupon bond and related future cash flows are shown here:

Recall that for the present value of one future cash flow and the present value of annuity, we have the following two formulae:

$$PV = \frac{FV}{(1+R)^n}$$

$$PV(annuity) = \frac{C}{R}\left[1 - \frac{1}{(1+R)^n}\right]$$

Here, C is a constant cash flow and n is the number of periods. The price of a coupon bond is the combination of these two types of payments:

$$PV(bond) = \frac{C}{R}\left[1 - \frac{1}{(1+R)^n}\right] + \frac{FV}{(1+R)^n} \quad \dots \dots \dots (16)$$

The `scipy.pv()` function could be used to calculate the price of bond. Assume that the effective annual rate is 2.4%:

```
>>> import scipy as sp
>>>sp.pv(0.024,3,0.08*100,100)
-116.02473258972169
```

Based on the above result, the price of this 3-year coupon bond is $116.02.

Since the price of a bond is the present value of its all future cash flows, its price should be negatively correlated with the discount rate. In other words, should the interest rate increase, the price of bonds would fall, and vice versa.

Yield to Maturity (YTM) is the same concept as **International Rate of Return (IRR)**. Assume that we bought a zero-coupon bond for $717.25. The face value of the bond is $1,000 and it would mature in 10 years. What is its YTM? For a zero-coupon bond, we have the following formula for YTM:

$$YTM = \left(\frac{FV}{PV}\right)^{\frac{1}{n}} \quad \dots \dots \dots (17)$$

Here, FV is the face value, PV is the price of the zero-coupon bond and n is the number of years (maturity). By applying the formula, we have $717.25*(1+YTM)^{10}=1000$. Thus, we have the following result:

```
>>> (1000/717.25)**(1/10)-1
>>>
0.033791469771228044
```

Assume that we bought a bond for $825 today. It has a maturity term of 5 years. The coupon rate is 3% and coupon payments are annual. If the face value is $1,000, what is the YTM? The `scipy.rate()` function could be used to estimate the YTM:

```
>>> import scipy as sp
>>> sp.rate(5,0.03*1000,-818,1000)
0.074981804314870726
```

Based on this result, the YTM is 7.498%. The relationship between bond price, coupon rate, and face value is shown in the following table:

Condition	Bond price versus face value	Premium, par, and discount
Coupon rate> YTM	Price of bond> FV	At a premium
Coupon rate =YTM	Price of bond=FV	At par
Coupon rate <YTM	Price of bond<FV	At a discount

Table 5.3: Relationship between bond price, coupon rate, and face value

Obviously, for two zero-coupon bonds, the longer the maturity, the riskier the bond. The reason is that for a zero-coupon bond with a longer maturity, we have to wait longer to recoup our initial investment. For the coupon bond with the same maturity, the higher the coupon rates, the safer the bond is since we could receive more payments early for the bond with a higher coupon rate. How about zero-coupon bonds and a coupon bond with different maturity dates?

Here is one example, we have a 15-year zero coupon bond with a face value of $100 and a coupon bond of 30years. The coupon rate is 9% with an annual coupon payment. Which bond is riskier? If the current yield jumps from 4% to 5%, what are the percentages for both of them? The riskier bond would have a much higher percentage change when the yield jumps or falls:

```
# for zero-coupon bond
>> p0=sp.pv(0.04,15,0,-100)
>>> p1=sp.pv(0.05,15,0,-100)
>>> (p1-p0)/p0
-0.1337153811552842
```

The related output is shown here:

```
>>> p0
>>> 55.526450271327484
>>> p1
48.101709809096995
```

For the coupon bond, we have the following result:

```
>>> p0
>>> p0=sp.pv(0.04,30,-0.09*100,-100)
>>> p1=sp.pv(0.05,30,-0.09*100,-100)
>>> (p1-p0)/p0
>>>
```

```
    -0.13391794539315816
>>> p0
    186.46016650332245
>>> p1
    161.48980410753134
```

Based on the preceding results, the 30-year coupon bond is riskier than the 15-year zero coupon bond since it has a bigger percentage change. For the 15-year zero coupon bond, its duration is 15 years. How about the aforementioned 30-year coupon bonds? The following result shows it is 17 years. Note that `p4f` is a set of Python programs written by the author:

```
>>>import p4f
>>>p4f.durationBond(0.04,0.09,30)
>>>
17.036402239014734
```

Note, in order to use the model called `p4f`, readers of this book can download it at `http://canisius.edu/~yany/python/p4f.cpython-35.pyc`. The relationship between the percentage change of a bond price and the change of YTM is given here:

$$\frac{\Delta B}{B} = D \frac{1}{1+\frac{y}{m}} \Delta y \qquad ....(18)$$

Here, B is the bond price, ΔB is the change in bond price, y is YTM, m is the corresponding compounding frequency. The modified duration is defined here:

$$D_{modified} = D \frac{1}{1+\frac{y}{m}} \qquad ....(19)$$

$$\frac{\Delta B}{B} = D' \Delta y \qquad ....(20)$$

For banks, their deposits usually are short-term while their loans (lending) are usually long-term. Thus, banks face an interest rate risk. One hedging strategy is called *duration matching*, that is, match the duration of liabilities with the duration of assets.

Stock valuation

There are several ways to estimate the price of a stock. One method is called the *dividend discount model*. The logic is that the price of a stock today is simply the summation of the present value of all its future dividends. Let's use the simplest one period model to illustrate. We expect a $1 dividend at the end of one year and its selling price is expected to be $50. If the appropriate cost of equity is 12%, what is the price of stock today? The timeline and future cash flows are shown here:

<pre>
        R=12%   D=1
                           FV=50

       |------------------------------|
</pre>

The price of stock is simply the present values of those two future cash flows, $45.54:

```
>> (1+50)/(1+0.12)
>>>
        45.535714285714285
>>> import scipy as sp
>>>sp.pv(0.12,1,1+50)
        -45.53571428571432
```

Let's look at a two-period model. We expect two dividends of $1.5 and $2 at the end of the next 2 years. In addition, the selling price is expected to be $78. What is the price today?

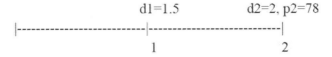

<pre>
              d1=1.5   d2=2, p2=78
       |--------------------------|--------------------------|
                    1   2
</pre>

Assume that for this stock, the appropriate discount rate is 14%. Then the present value of the stock is $62.87:

```
>>>1.5/(1+0.14)+(2+78)/(1+0.14)**2
62.873191751308084
```

Along the same lines, we could estimate the cost of equity if both the present value and futures values are given. If the current price is $30 and the expected selling price at the end of one year is $35:

<pre>
                              d=1
         P0=30   FV=35

         |------------------------------|
</pre>

Then we could estimate the total return:

```
>>> (35-30+1)/30
0.2
```

The total return, cost of equity (Re), has two components: capital gain yield and dividend yield:

$$R_e = \frac{P_1 - P_0 + D_1}{P_0} = \underbrace{\frac{P_1 - P_0}{P_0}}_{capital\ gain\ yield} + \underbrace{\frac{D_1}{P_0}}_{divident\ yield} \quad ....(21)$$

The capital gain yield is 16.667% while the dividend yield is 3.333%. Another possible scenario is that a stock might enjoy a constant dividend growth rate. Company A is expected to issue a $4 dividend next year and enjoys a constant dividend growth rate of 2% afterward. If the cost of equity is 18%, what will be the stock price today? From *Chapter 3, Time Value of Money*, we know that the present value of growing perpetuity formula could be applied:

$$PV(growing\ perpetuiry) = \frac{c}{R-g}$$

By using the correct notation, that is, *P0* as today's stock price, *d1* as the first expected dividend, we could have the following equivalent pricing formula:

$$P_0 = \frac{d_1}{R-g} \quad ....(22)$$

From the following results, we know that today's price should be $25:

```
>>> 4/(0.18-0.02)
>>>
25.0
```

Many young and small firms would not issue any dividends since they might need capital greatly after they came into existence. After a successful period, those firms might enjoy a super growth. After that, firms usually enter a long-term normal growth. For those cases, we could apply an n-period model. For an n-period model, we have $n+1$ future cash flows: n dividend plus 1 selling price. Thus, we could have the following general formula for an n period model:

$$P_0 = \frac{d_1}{(1+R_e)} + \frac{d_1}{(1+R_e)^2} + \cdots + \frac{d_n}{(1+R_e)^n} + \frac{P_n}{(1+R_e)^n}$$

......(23)

The selling price at the end of the n period is given here:

$$P_n = \frac{d_{n+1}}{R-g}$$

........(24)

Let's use an example to explain how to apply this n-period model. Assume that a company had issued a $1.5 dividend last year. The dividend would enjoy grammatical growth in the next 5 years with growth rates of 20%, 15%, 10%, 9%, and 8%. After that, the growth rate would be reduced to a long-term growth rate of 3% forever. If the rate of return for such types of stocks is 18.2%, what is the stock price today? The following table shows the time periods and the growth rates:

Period=>	1	2	3	4	5	6
Growth rate	0.2	0.15	0.1	0.09	0.08	0.04

As our first step, it should be asked how many periods for the n-period model? The rule of thumb is *one period less than the year when the dividend enjoys a long-term growth rate*. For this case, we could choose 5:

Period=>	1	2	3	4	5	6
Growth rate	0.2	0.15	0.1	0.09	0.08	0.04
dividend	1.80	2.07	2.277	2.48193	2.680	2.7877

The first dividend of 1.8 is from *1.5*(1+0.2)*. To solve this problem, we have the following codes:

```
>>>import scipy as sp
>>>dividends=[1.80,2.07,2.277,2.48193,2.680,2.7877]
>>>R=0.182
>>>g=0.03
>>>sp.npv(R,dividends[:-1])*(1+R)
>>>
9.5233173204508681
>>>sp.pv(R,5,0,2.7877/(R-g))
>>>
-7.949046992374841
```

In the preceding codes, we drop the last cash flow since it is used to calculate the selling price of P5. Because the `scipy.npv()` treats the first cash flow happening at time zero, we have to adjust the result by timing it by `(1+R)`. Calculating the present of five future dividends separated with the calculation of the present value of the selling price is to remind readers of the existence of so-called Excel sign convention. The stock price is `17.47` (=9.52+7.95). Alternatively, we could use the `p4f.pvPriceNperiodModel()` function, see the following code. The Python program is included in *Appendix D*:

```
>>>import p4f
>>> r=0.182
>>> g=0.03
>>> d=[1.8,2.07,2.277,2.48193,2.68,2.7877]
>>> p4f.pvValueNperiodModel(r,g,d)
        17.472364312825711
```

The preceding model depends on an important assumption, the number of shares is constant. Thus, if a company uses a part of its earnings to buy back shares, this assumption is violated. Thus, we could not use the *dividend discount model*. For those cases, we could apply a so-called share repurchase and the total payout model. Here is the formula. The present value of all of the firm's equity, rather than a single share, is calculated first:

$$P_0 = \frac{PV(Future\ dividens\ \&\ shares\ repurchase)}{\#\ of\ shares\ outstanding} \quad \dotsb \quad (25)$$

Logic Solution expects its total earnings at the end of the year to be about $400 million. The company plans to payout 45% of its total earnings: 30% for dividends and 15% for shares repurchases. If the company's long-term growth rate is 3%, the cost of equity is 18%, and the number of shares outstanding is 50 million, what is its stock price today? The solution is shown here:

```
>>> 400*0.45/(0.18-0.03)/50
>>>
24.0
```

The third method is to estimate the total value of the firm, that is, the enterprise value. Then we estimate the total value of the equity. Finally, we divide the total value of equity by the number of shares outstanding to reach the price. The enterprise value is defined here:

$$Enterprise\ value = Equity + Debt - Cash \dotsb (26)$$

Here, *Equity* is the market value of equity, *Debt* is the total book value of debt and Cash is the cash holding. The enterprise value could be viewed as the total capital we need to buy a whole company. Let's look at a simple example. Assume that the market value of a company is $6 million, the total debt is $4 million and the cash holding is $1 million. It seems that an investor needs $10 million to buy the whole company since she needs $6 million to buy all the shares and assume the debt burden of $4 million. Actually, since $1 million cash is available for the new owner, she needs to raise just $9 million. After we have the enterprise value, the following formula is used to find out the price of one share:

$$P_0 = \frac{V_0 - Debt + Cash}{\# \ shares \ outstanding} \quad \text{............ (27)}$$

Here $V0$ is the enterprise value, *Debt* is the debt today, and *Cash* is the cash today. $V0$ could be viewed as the total value of the firm owned by both equity holders and debt (bond) holders:

$$V_0 = PV(all \ future \ Free \ cash \ flows) \quad \text{.........(28)}$$

Free cash flow at time *t* is defined as:

$$FCF_t = NI_t - D_t - CapEx_t + \Delta NWC_t \quad \text{.........(29)}$$

FCFt is free cash flow for year *t*, NIt is the net income or year *t*, Dt is the depreciation for year *t*, CapExt is the capital expenditure for year *t* and $+\Delta NWC_t$ is the change in net working capital for year *t*. Net working capital is the difference between current assets and current liability. The generated formula is given here:

$$V_0 = \frac{FCF_1}{(1+WACC)} + \frac{FCF_1}{(1+WACC)^2} + \cdots + \frac{FCF_n}{(1+WACC)^n} + \frac{V_n}{(1+WACC)^n} \quad \text{......(30)}$$

WACC is the weighted average cost of capital. The reason is that we estimate the total value of the whole company, thus it is not appropriate to use the cost of equity as our discount rate:

$$WACC = W_e R_e + W_d R_d (1 - T_c) \quad \text{...............(31)}$$

Where *We (Re)* is the weight (cost) for equity, *Wd (Rd)* is the weight (before-tax cost) for debt, and *Tc* is the corporate tax rate. Since Re is after-tax cost of equity, we have to convert *Rd* (before tax of equity) into the after-tax cost of debt by timing (1-Tc). *Vn* could be viewed as the selling price of the whole company:

$$V_n = \frac{FCF_{n+1}}{WACC-g} \quad \text{.............(32)}$$

Another way to estimate a current stock price is based on certain multiples, such as industry P/E ratio. The method is straightforward. Assume that a company's next year's expected EPS is $4. If the industry average P/E ratio is 10, what is the stock price today? It is $40 today.

A new data type – dictionary

Dictionaries are unordered datasets and are accessed via keys and not via their position. A dictionary is an associative array (also known as hashes). Any key of the dictionary is associated (or mapped) to a value. The first variable is the `key`, while the second one is the `value`; see the following example. The curly parentheses are used. The second value could be any data type such as a string, an integer, or a real number:

```
>>>houseHold={"father":"John","mother":"Mary","daughter":"Jane"}
>>> household
{'father': 'John', 'daughter': 'Jane','mother': 'Mary'}
>>> type(houseHold)
<class 'dict'>
>>>houseHold['father']
'John'
```

Appendix A – simple interest rate versus compounding interest rate

The formula for payment of a simple interest rate is as follows:

$$FV(simple\ interest) = PV(1 + R * n)\text{.........}(1)$$

The future value for compounded interest is as follows:

$$FV(compounded\ interest) = PV(1 + R)^n\text{..........}(2)$$

Here, *PV* is the present value, *R* is the period rate, and *n* is the number of periods. Thus, those two future values will be $1,800 and $2,158.93.

The following program offers a graphic representation of a principal, simple interest payment, and the future values:

```
import numpy as np
from matplotlib.pyplot import *
from pylab import *
pv=1000
r=0.08
n=10
t=linspace(0,n,n)
y1=np.ones(len(t))*pv # a horizontal line
y2=pv*(1+r*t)
y3=pv*(1+r)**t
title('Simple vs. compounded interest rates')
xlabel('Number of years')
ylabel('Values')
xlim(0,11)
ylim(800,2200)
plot(t, y1, 'b-')
plot(t, y2, 'g--')
plot(t, y3, 'r-')
show()
```

The related graph is shown here:

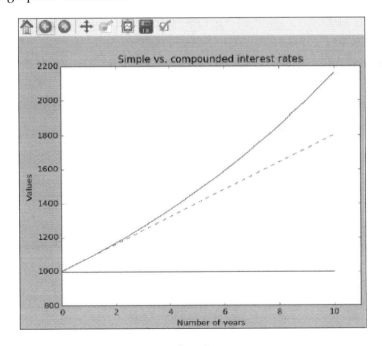

In the preceding program, the `xlim()` function would set the range of the x axis. This is true for the `ylim()` function. The third input variable for both the `xlim()` and `ylim()` functions are for the color and the line. The letter `b` is for black, `g` is for green, and `r` is for red.

Appendix B – several Python functions related to interest conversion

```python
def APR2Rm(APR1,m1,m2):
    """

    Objective: convert one APR to another Rm
        APR1: annual percentage rate
        m1:   compounding frequency
        m2:   effective period rate with this compounding

    Formula used:  Rm=(1+APR1/m1)**(m1/m2)-1

    Example #1>>>APR2Rm(0.1,2,4)
             0.02469507659595993
    """
    return (1+APR/m1)**(m1/m2)-1

def APR2APR(APR1,m1,m2):
    """

    Objective: convert one APR to another Rm
        APR1: annual percentage rate
        m1:   compounding frequency
        m2:   effective period rate with this compounding

    Formula used:  Rm=(1+APR1/m1)**(m1/m2)-1

    Example #1>>>APR2APR(0.1,2,4)
             0.09878030638383972
    """
    return m2*((1+APR/m1)**(m1/m2)-1)

def APR2Rc(APR,m):
    return m*log(1+APR/m)

def Rc2Rm(Rc,m):
    return exp(Rc/m)-1

def Rc2APR(Rc,m):
    return m*(exp(Rc/m)-1)
```

Appendix C – Python program for rateYan.py

```python
def rateYan(APR,type):
"""Objective: from one APR to another effective rate and APR2
        APR : value of the given Annual Percentage Rate
        type : Converting method, e.g., 's2a', 's2q', 's2c'
's2a' means from semi-annual to annual
a for annual
                s for semi-annual
                q for quarterly
                m for monthly
                d for daily
                c for continuously
    Example #1>>>rateYan(0.1,'s2a')
                [0.10250000000000004, 0.10250000000000004]
    Example #2>>>rateYan(0.1,'q2c')
                0.098770450361485657
"""
    import scipy as sp
    rate=[]
    if(type[0]=='a'):
        n1=1
elif(type[0]=='s'):
        n1=2
elif(type[0]=='q'):
        n1=4
elif(type[0]=='m'):
        n1=12
elif(type[0]=='d'):
        n1=365
    else:
        n1=-9
    if(type[2]=='a'):
        n2=1
elif(type[2]=='s'):
        n2=2
elif(type[2]=='q'):
        n2=4
elif(type[2]=='m'):
        n2=12
elif(type[2]=='d'):
        n2=365
    else:
        n2=-9
```

```
        if(n1==-9 and n2==-9):
            return APR
    elif(n1==-9 and not(n2==-9)):
    effectiveRate=sp.exp(APR/n2)-1
            APR2=n2*effectiveRate
    rate.append(effectiveRate)
    rate.append(APR2)
            return rate
    elif(n2==-9 and not(n1==-9)):
    Rc=n1*sp.log(1+APR/n1)
            return Rc
        else:
    effectiveRate=(1+APR/n1)**(n1/n2)-1
            APR2=n2*effectiveRate
    rate.append(effectiveRate)
    rate.append(APR2)
            return rate
```

Appendix D – Python program to estimate stock price based on an n-period model

For an n-period model, we have n+1 future cash flows: n dividends plus one selling price:

$$P_0 = \frac{d_1}{(1+R_e)} + \frac{d_1}{(1+R_e)^2} + \cdots + \frac{d_n}{(1+R_e)^n} + \frac{P_n}{(1+R_e)^n} \quad \text{......(1)}$$

The selling price at the end of the n-period is given here:

$$P_n = \frac{d_{n+1}}{R-g} \quad \text{.................(2)}$$

See the following code for estimating the present value for a growing perpetuity with the first cash flow *n+1* from today:

```
def pvValueNperiodModel(r,longTermGrowthRate,dividendNplus1):
"""Objective: estimate stock price based on an n-period model
                    r: discount rate
LongTermGrowhRate: long term dividend growth rate
        dividendsNpus1    : a dividend vector n + 1

        PV     = d1/(1+R) + d2/(1+R)**2 +  ....  + dn/(1+R)**n +
```

```
sellingPrice/(1+R)**n
sellingPrice= d(n+1)/(r-g)
            where g is long term growth rate


    Example #1: >>> r=0.182
>>> g=0.03
>>> d=[1.8,2.07,2.277,2.48193,2.68,2.7877]
>>>pvValueNperiodModel(r,g,d)
                    17.472364312825711
"""
    import scipy as sp
    d=dividendNplus1
    n=len(d)-1
    g=longTermGrowthRate
pv=sp.npv(r,d[:-1])*(1+r)
sellingPrice=d[n]/(r-g)
pv+=sp.pv(r,n,0,-sellingPrice)
    return pv
```

Appendix E – Python program to estimate the duration for a bond

```
def durationBond(rate,couponRate,maturity):
"""Objective : estimte the durtion for a given bond
      rate      : discount rate
couponRate: coupon rate
      maturity  : number of years


      Example 1: >>>discountRate=0.1
>>>couponRate=0.04
>>> n=4
>>>durationBond(rate,couponRate,n)
                    3.5616941835365492


      Example #2>>>durationBond(0.1,0.04,4)
                    3.7465335177625576
"""
    import scipy as sp
    d=0
    n=maturity
    for i in sp.arange(n):
        d+=(i+1)*sp.pv(rate,i+1,0,-couponRate)
    d+=n*sp.pv(rate,nper,0,-1)
    return d/sp.pv(rate,n,-couponRate,-1)
```

Appendix F – data case #2 – fund raised from a new bond issue

Currently, you are working as a financial analyst at **International Business Machine Corporation** (IBM). The firm plans to issue 30-year corporate bonds with a total face value of $60 million in the United States. Each bond has a face value of $1,000. The annual coupon rate is 3.5%. The firm plans to pay coupons once every year at the end of each year. Answer the following three questions:

1. How much would your company receive today by issuing the 30-year bonds?

2. What is the YTM (Yield to Maturity) of the bond?

3. How much extra money could your company receive if your company manages to increase its credit rating by one notch?

The price of a bond is the summation of all its discounted future cash flows:

$$PV(bond) = price = \frac{C_1}{(1+R_1)^1} + \frac{C_2}{(1+R_2)^2} + \cdots + \frac{C_{n-1}}{(1+R_{n-1})^{n-1}} + \frac{C_n+FV}{(1+R_n)^n} \quad \text{......(1)}$$

Find out the appropriate discount rate for each future cash flow:

$$R_i = R_{f,i} + S_i \quad \text{..........(2)}$$

Here, R_i is the discount rate for year i, $R_{f,i}$ is the risk-free rate, from the Government Treasury term structure of interest (yield curve) for year i, and S_i is the credit spread which depends on the credit rating of your firm. The spread is based on the Python dataset called spreadBasedOnCreditRating.pkl. The Python dataset is available at the website of: http://canisius.edu/~yany/python/spreadBasedOnCreditRating.pkl:

```
>>>import pandas as pd
>>>spread=pd.read_pickle("c:/temp/spreadBasedOnCreditRating.pkl")
>>> spread
```

Rating	1	2	3	5	7	10	30
Aaa/AAA	5.00	8.00	12.00	18.00	28.00	42.00	65.00
Aa1/AA+	10.00	18.00	25.00	34.00	42.00	54.00	77.00
Aa2/AA	14.00	29.00	38.00	50.00	57.00	65.00	89.00
Aa3/AA-	19.00	34.00	43.00	54.00	61.00	69.00	92.00
A1/A+	23.00	39.00	47.00	58.00	65.00	72.00	95.00
A2/A	24.00	39.00	49.00	61.00	69.00	77.00	103.00

A3/A-	32.00	49.00	59.00	72.00	80.00	89.00	117.00
Baa1/BBB+	38.00	61.00	75.00	92.00	103.00	115.00	151.00
Baa2/BBB	47.00	75.00	89.00	107.00	119.00	132.00	170.00
Baa3/BBB-	83.00	108.00	122.00	140.00	152.00	165.00	204.00
Ba1/BB+	157.00	182.00	198.00	217.00	232.00	248.00	286.00
Ba2/BB	231.00	256.00	274.00	295.00	312.00	330.00	367.00
Ba3/BB-	305.00	330.00	350.00	372.00	392.00	413.00	449.00
B1/B+	378.00	404.00	426.00	450.00	472.00	495.00	530.00
B2/B	452.00	478.00	502.00	527.00	552.00	578.00	612.00
B3/B-	526.00	552.00	578.00	604.00	632.00	660.00	693.00
Caa/CCC+	600.00	626.00	653.00	682.00	712.00	743.00	775.00
US Treasury Yield	0.13	0.45	0.93	1.74	2.31	2.73	3.55

>>>

For year 5 and double AA rating, the spread is 55 basis-points. For each base point, it is 100th of 1%. In other words, we should divide 55 by 100 twice, that is, *55/10000=0.0055*.

The procedure of a linear interpolation is shown here:

1. First, let me use a simple example. Assume that the YTM for 5years is 5%, the YTM for a 10-year bond is 10%. What are the YTMs for 6, 7, 8, and 9-year bonds?

2. A quick answer is 6% for a 6-year bond, 7% for a 7-year bond, 8% for an 8-year bond, and 9% for a 9-year bond. The basic idea is an equal incremental value.

3. Assume that YTM for a 5-year bond is *R5*, the YTM for a 10-year bond is *R10*. There are five intervals between year 5 and year 10. Thus, the incremental value between each year is $\Delta=\frac{R_{10}-R_5}{5}$:
   - For a 6-year bond, its value will be $R_5 + \Delta$
   - For a 7-year bond, its value will be $R_5 + 2\Delta$
   - For an 8-year bond, its value will be $R_5 + 3\Delta$
   - For a 9-year bond, its value will be $R_5 + 4\Delta$

Here is a more detailed explanation. If the two known points are given by the coordinates (x_0,y_0) and (x_1,y_1), the linear interpolation is the straight line between these points. For a value x in the interval (x_0,x_1), the value y along the straight line is given in the equation:

$$\frac{y-y_0}{x-x_0} = \frac{y_1-y_0}{x_1-x_0} \quad ....(4)$$

This can be derived geometrically from the figure on the right. It is a special case of polynomial interpolation with *n=1*.

Solving this equation for y, which is the unknown value at x, gives:

$$y = y_0 + (x - x_0)\frac{y_1 - y_0}{x_1 - x_0} = y_0 + \frac{(x - x_0)y_1 - (x - x_0)y_0}{x_1 - x_0}$$ ......(5)

This is the formula for linear interpolation in the interval of *(x0, x1)*.

Summary

In this chapter, we cover various concepts related to interest rates, such as **Annual Percentage Rate (APR)**, **Effective Annual Rate (EAR)**, compounding frequency, how to convert one interest rate to another one with different compounding frequencies, and the term structure of interest rates. Then we discussed how to estimate the selling price of a regular bond and how to estimate the **Yield to Maturity (YTM)** and duration. To get a stock price, the so-called discount dividend model could be applied.

In the next chapter, we will discuss CAPM which is probably the most widely used model in assets pricing. After discussing its basic forms, we show how to download historical price data for a listed company and market index data. We illustrate how to estimate returns and run a linear regression to calculate the market risk for the stock.

6
Capital Asset Pricing Model

Capital Asset Pricing Model (CAPM) is probably the most widely used model in assets pricing. There are several reasons behind its popularity. First, it is quite simple since it is a one-factor linear model. Second, it is quite easy to implement this one-factor model. Any interested reader could download historical price data for a listed company and market index data to calculate return first, and then estimate the market risk for the stock. Third, this simplest one-factor asset pricing model could be served as the first model for other more advanced ones, such as Fama-French 3-factor, Fama-French-Carhart 4-factor, and Fama-French 5-factor models introduced in the next chapter (*Chapter 7, Multifactor Models and Performance Measures*). In this chapter, the following topics will be covered:

- Introduction to CAPM
- How to download data from Yahoo Finance
- Rolling beta
- Several Python programs to estimate beta for multiple stocks
- Adjusted beta and portfolio beta estimation
- Scholes and Williams (1977) adjustment for beta
- Dimson (1979) adjustment for beta
- Output data to various types of external files
- Simple string manipulation
- Python via Canopy

Introduction to CAPM

According to the famous CAPM, the expected returns of a stock are linearly correlated with expected market returns. Here, we use the international business machine with a ticker of IBM as an example and this linear one-factor asset pricing model could be applied to any other stocks or portfolios. The formula is given here:

$$E(R_{IBM}) = R_f + \beta_{IBM}(E(R_{mkt}) - R_f) \quad \dots \quad (1)$$

Here, $E()$ is the expectation, $E(R_{IBM})$ is the expected return for IBM, R_f is the risk-free rate, and $E(R_{mkt})$ is the expected market return. For instance, the S&P500 index could be served as a market index. The slope of the preceding equation or β_{IBM} is a measure of IBM's market risk. To make our notation simpler, the expectation could be dropped:

$$R_{IBM} = R_f + \beta_{IBM}\left(R_{mkt} - R_f\right) \quad \dots(2)$$

Actually, we could consider the relationship between the excess stock returns and the excess market returns. The following formula is essentially the same as the preceding formula, but it has a better and clearer interpretation:

$$R_{IBM} - R_f = a + \beta_{IBM}\left(R_{mkt} - R_f\right) \quad \dots(3)$$

Recall that in *Chapter 3, Time Value of Money,* we learnt that the difference between a stock's expected return and the risk free rate is called risk premium. This is true for both individual stocks and for a market index. Thus, the meaning of the *Equation (3)* is quite easy to interpret: the risk premium of individual stock depends on two components: its market risk and the market risk-premium.

Mathematically, the slop of the preceding linear regression could be written as follows:

$$\beta_{IBM} = \frac{\sigma_{IBM,MKT}}{\sigma^2_{MKT}} \quad \dots(4)$$

Here $\sigma_{IBM,MKT}$ is the covariance between IBM's returns and the market index returns and σ_{MKT}^2 is the variance of the market returns. Since $\sigma_{IBM,MKT} = \rho_{IBM,MKT}\sigma_{IBM}\sigma_{MKT}$, where $\rho_{IBM,MKT}$ is the correlation between IBM's return and the index returns, the preceding equation could be written as the following one:

$$\beta_{IBM} = \frac{\rho_{IBM,MKT} * \sigma_{IBM}}{\sigma_{MKT}} \quad \dots (5)$$

The meaning of beta is that when the expected market risk-premium increases by 1%, the individual stock's expected return would increase by β%, vice versa. Thus, beta (market risk) could be viewed as an amplifier. The average beta of all stocks is one. Thus, if a stock's beta is higher than 1, it means that its market risk is higher than that of an average stock.

The following lines of code are an example of this:

```
>>> import numpy as np
>>> import statsmodels.api as sm
>>> y=[1,2,3,4,2,3,4]
>>> x=range(1,8)
>>> x=sm.add_constant(x)
>>> results=sm.OLS(y,x).fit()
>>> print(results.params)
    [ 1.28571429  0.35714286]
```

To see all information about the OLS results, we will use the command of `print(results.summary())`, see the following screenshot:

```
[ 1.28571429  0.35714286]
                            OLS Regression Results
==============================================================================
Dep. Variable:                      y   R-squared:                       0.481
Model:                            OLS   Adj. R-squared:                  0.377
Method:                 Least Squares   F-statistic:                     4.630
Date:                Mon, 05 Jun 2017   Prob (F-statistic):             0.0841
Time:                        14:34:15   Log-Likelihood:                -7.8466
No. Observations:                   7   AIC:                             19.69
Df Residuals:                       5   BIC:                             19.59
Df Model:                           1
Covariance Type:            nonrobust
==============================================================================
                 coef    std err          t      P>|t|      [95.0% Conf. Int.]
------------------------------------------------------------------------------
const          1.2857      0.742      1.732      0.144      -0.622       3.194
x1             0.3571      0.166      2.152      0.084      -0.070       0.784
==============================================================================
Omnibus:                          nan   Durbin-Watson:                   1.976
Prob(Omnibus):                    nan   Jarque-Bera (JB):                0.342
Skew:                           0.289   Prob(JB):                        0.843
Kurtosis:                       2.083   Cond. No.                         10.4
==============================================================================
```

At the moment, readers could just pay attention to the values of two coefficients and their corresponding T-values and P-values. We would discuss other results, such as Durbin-Watson statistics and the Jarque-Bera normality test in *Chapter 8, Time-Series Analysis*. The beta is 0.3571, which has a T-value of 2.152. Since it is bigger than 2, we could claim that it is significantly different from zero. Alternatively, based on the P-value of 0.084, we would have the same conclusion if we choose a 10% as our cut-off point. Here is the second example:

```
>>> from scipy import stats
>>> ret = [0.065, 0.0265, -0.0593, -0.001,0.0346]
>>> mktRet = [0.055, -0.09, -0.041,0.045,0.022]
>>>(beta, alpha, r_value,p_value,std_err)=stats.linregress(ret,mktRet)
```

The corresponding result is shown here:

```
>>> print(beta, alpha)
0.507743187877 -0.00848190035246
>>> print("R-squared=", r_value**2)
R-squared= 0.147885662966
>>> print("p-value =", p_value)
p-value = 0.522715523909
```

Again, the `help()` function could be used to get more information about this function, see the following first few lines:

```
>>>help(stats.linregress)
```

Help on the `linregress` function in the `scipy.stats._stats_mstats_common` module:

```
linregress(x, y=None)
```

Calculate a linear least-squares regression for two sets of measurements.

Parameters x, y: array like two sets of measurements. Both arrays should have the same length. If only x is given (and y=None), then it must be a two- dimensional array where one dimension has length 2. The two sets of measurements are then found by splitting the array along the length-2 dimension.

For the third example, we generate a known set of y and x observations with known intercept and slop, such as *alpha=1* and *beta=0.8*, see the following formula:

$$y_i = 1 + 0.8x_i + \varepsilon_i$$

Here, *yi* is the *ith* observation for dependent variable y, 1 is the intercept, 0.8 is the slope (beta), *xi* is the *ith* observation for an independent variable of *x*, and ϵ_i is the random value. For the preceding equation, after we have generated a set of y and x, we could run a linear regression. For this purpose, a set of random numbers are used:

```
from scipy import stats
import scipy as sp
sp.random.seed(12456)
alpha=1
beta=0.8
n=100
x=sp.arange(n)
y=alpha+beta*x+sp.random.rand(n)
(beta,alpha,r_value,p_value,std_err)=stats.linregress(y,x)
print(alpha,beta)
print("R-squared=", r_value**2)
print("p-value =", p_value)
```

In the preceding code, the `sp.random.rand()` function would call a set of random numbers. In order to get the same set of random numbers, the `sp.random.seed()` function is applied. In other words, whenever the same seed is used, any programmers would get the same set of random numbers. This will be discussed in more detail in *Chapter 12, Monte Carlo Simulation*. The result is shown here:

```
%run "C:/yan/teaching/Python2/codes/c6_02_random_OLS.py"
(-1.9648401142472594,1.2521836174247121,)
('R-squared=', 0.99987143193925765)
('p-value =', 1.7896498998980323e-192)
```

Now let's look at how to estimate the beta (market risk) for Microsoft. Assume that we are interested in the period from 1/1/2012 to 12/31/2016, for a total of five year's data. The complete Python program is shown here:

```
from scipy import stats
from matplotlib.finance import quotes_historical_yahoo_ochl as getData
begdate=(2012,1,1)
enddate=(2016,12,31)

ticker='MSFT'
p =getData(ticker, begdate, enddate,asobject=True,adjusted=True)
retIBM = p.aclose[1:]/p.aclose[:1]-1

ticker='^GSPC'
```

```
p2 = getData(ticker, begdate, enddate,asobject=True,adjusted=True)
retMkt = p2.aclose[1:]/p2.aclose[:1]-1
(beta,alpha,r_value,p_value,std_err)=stats.linregress(retMkt,retIBM)
print(alpha,beta)
print("R-squared=", r_value**2)
print("p-value =", p_value)
```

To estimate the beta of IBM using five year data, the main function used to download historical price data in the preceding Python program is `matplotlib.finance.quotes_historical_yahoo_ochl`. Here is the related link `https://matplotlib.org/api/finance_api.html`. The ticker symbol of ^GSPC stands for the S&P500 market index. The result is shown here:

```
(-0.14096610663371933, 1.9090742294915726)
('R-squared=', 0.82187242796817805)
('p-value =', 0.0)
```

Based the preceding results, the beta for IBM is 0.41, while the intercept is 0.004. In addition, the R2 is 0.36 and P-value is almost zero. In the preceding program, the risk-free rate is ignored. The impact of its omission on beta (slop) is small. In the next chapter, we will show how to include the risk free rate when discussing the Fama-French 3-factor model. To get more information about the `quotes_historical_yahoo_ochl`, the help function could be used:

```
help(quotes_historical_yahoo_ochl)
Help on function quotes_historical_yahoo_ochl in
module matplotlib.finance:
quotes_historical_yahoo_ochl(ticker, date1, date2, asobject=False,
adjusted=True, cachename=None)
 Get historical data for ticker between date1 and date2.

See :func:`parse_yahoo_historical` for explanation of
output formats and the *asobject* and *adjusted* kwargs.
Parameters
    ----------
ticker : str    stock ticker
date1 : sequence of form (year, month, day), `datetime`,
        or `date` start date
date2 : sequence of form (year, month, day), `datetime`, or
             `date`  end date
  cachename : str or `None`
             is the name of the local file cache.  If None, will
```

```
           default to the md5 hash or the url (which incorporates
           the ticker and date range)
    Examples
    --------
     sp=f.quotes_historical_yahoo_ochl('^GSPC',d1,d2,asobject=True,
         adjusted=True)
      returns = (sp.open[1:] - sp.open[:-1])/sp.open[1:]
     [n,bins,patches] = hist(returns, 100)
     mu = mean(returns)
     sigma = std(returns)
     x = normpdf(bins, mu, sigma)
     plot(bins, x, color='red', lw=2)
```

Obviously, it is a good idea to write a function to get data with just three import values: ticker, beginning, and ending dates, see the following code:

```
from scipy import stats
from matplotlib.finance import quotes_historical_yahoo_ochl as aa
#
def dailyReturn(ticker,begdate,enddate):
    p = aa(ticker, begdate,enddate,asobject=True,adjusted=True)
    return p.aclose[1:]/p.aclose[:-1]-1
#
begdate=(2012,1,1)
enddate=(2017,1,9)
retIBM=dailyReturn("wmt",begdate,enddate)
retMkt=dailyReturn("^GSPC",begdate,enddate)
outputs=stats.linregress(retMkt,retIBM)
print(outputs)
```

The output for Walmart's beta (market risk) is as follows:

```
LinregressResult(slope=0.55353541278814211, intercept=-9.1964731487727638e-06,
rvalue=0.42520665972337468, pvalue=1.4353326986553025e-56, stderr=0.033193638902038199)
```

Alternatively, we could call the `p4f.dailyReturnYahoo()` function, see the following code:

```
import p4f
x=dailyReturn("ibm",(2016,1,1),(2016,1,10))
print(x)
Out[51]: array([-0.0007355 , -0.00500558, -0.01708957, -0.00925784])
```

Moving beta

Sometimes, researchers need to generate a beta time series based on, for example, a three-year moving window. In such cases, we could write a loop or double loops. Let's look at a simpler case: estimating the annual beta for IBM over several years. First, let's look at two ways of getting years from a date variable:

```
import datetime
today=datetime.date.today()
year=today.year                    # Method I
print(year)
2017
print(today.strftime("%Y"))        # Method II
 '2017'
```

The Python program used to estimate the annual beta is shown here:

```
import numpy as np
import scipy as sp
import pandas as pd
from scipy import stats
from matplotlib.finance import quotes_historical_yahoo_ochl

def ret_f(ticker,begdate, enddate):
    p = quotes_historical_yahoo_ochl(ticker, begdate,
    enddate,asobject=True,adjusted=True)
    return((p.aclose[1:] - p.aclose[:-1])/p.aclose[:-1])
#
begdate=(2010,1,1)
enddate=(2016,12,31)
#
y0=pd.Series(ret_f('IBM',begdate,enddate))
x0=pd.Series(ret_f('^GSPC',begdate,enddate))
#
d=quotes_historical_yahoo_ochl('^GSPC', begdate, enddate,asobject=True
,adjusted=True).date[0:-1]
lag_year=d[0].strftime("%Y")
y1=[]
x1=[]
beta=[]
index0=[]
for i in sp.arange(1,len(d)):
    year=d[i].strftime("%Y")
    if(year==lag_year):
        x1.append(x0[i])
        y1.append(y0[i])
    else:
```

```
(beta,alpha,r_value,p_value,std_err)=stats.linregress(y1,x1)
alpha=round(alpha,8)
beta=round(beta,3)
r_value=round(r_value,3)
p_vaue=round(p_value,3)
print(year,alpha,beta,r_value,p_value)
x1=[]
y1=[]
lag_year=year
```

The corresponding output is shown here:

```
('2011', 2.135e-05, 0.8, 0.786, 6.9128248064735092e-54)
('2012', -0.00075952, 0.813, 0.782, 4.96325795230486995e-53)
('2013', 0.00039118, 0.535, 0.674, 2.73527380292002755e-34)
('2014', 0.00094466, 0.258, 0.441, 2.2535628936863174e-13)
('2015', 0.00062177, 0.321, 0.486, 2.847815548680024e-16)
('2016', 0.00025991, 0.544, 0.743, 3.0643358991245905e-45)
```

Adjusted beta

Many researchers and professionals find that beta has a mean-reverting tendency. It means that if this period's beta is less than 1, there is a good chance that the next beta would be higher. On the other hand, if the current beta is higher than 1, the next beta might be smaller. The adjusted beta has the following formula:

$$\beta_{adj} = \frac{2}{3}\beta + \frac{1}{3}1.0 \quad \ldots (6)$$

Here, βadj is the adjusted beta and β is our estimated beta. The beta of a portfolio is the weighted beta of individual stocks within the portfolio:

$$\beta_{port} = \sum_{i=1}^{n} w_i \beta_i \quad \ldots (7)$$

Here β_{port} is the beta of a portfolio, wi (βi) is the weight (beta) of its stock, and n is the number of stocks in the portfolio. The weight of wi is calculated according to the following equation:

$$w_i = \frac{v_i}{\sum_{i}^{n} v_i} \quad \ldots (8)$$

Here vi is the value of stock i, and summation of all vi, the denominator in the preceding equation is the value of the portfolio.

Scholes and William adjusted beta

Many researchers find that β would have an upward bias for frequently traded stocks and a downward bias for infrequently traded stocks. To overcome this, Sholes and Williams recommend the following adjustment:

$$\beta = \frac{\beta^{-1} + \beta^0 + \beta^{+1}}{1 + 2\rho_m} \qquad \ldots (9)$$

Here, β is the stock or portfolio beta and ρm is the autocorrelation for the market return. The three betas in the preceding formula are defined by the following three equations:

$$\begin{cases} R_t = a + \beta^{-1} R_{m,t-1} + \varepsilon_t \\ R_t = a + \beta^0 R_{m,t} + \varepsilon_t \qquad \ldots (10) \\ R_t = a + \beta^{+1} R_{m,t+1} + \varepsilon_t \end{cases}$$

Here, let's look at how to add a lag to an array. The program is in the left panel, while the output is shown in the right one:

```
import pandas as pd
import scipy as sp
x=sp.arange(1,5,0.5)
y=pd.DataFrame(x,columns=['Ret'])
y['Lag']=y.shift(1)
print(y)
```

In the preceding program the `.shift()` function is applied. Since we need the market return one period ahead, we could specify a negative value of `-1` in the `.shift()` function, see the following code:

```
import pandas as pd
import scipy as sp
x=sp.arange(1,5,0.5)
y=pd.DataFrame(x,columns=['Ret'])
y['Lag']=y.shift(1)
y['Forward']=y['Ret'].shift(-1)
print(y)
```

```
    Ret Lag  Forward
```

```
0    1.0   NaN       1.5
1    1.5   1.0       2.0
2    2.0   1.5       2.5
3    2.5   2.0       3.0
4    3.0   2.5       3.5
5    3.5   3.0       4.0
6    4.0   3.5       4.5
7    4.5   4.0       NaN
```

The output is as follows:

```
     Ret   Lag
0    1.0   NaN
1    1.5   1.0
2    2.0   1.5
3    2.5   2.0
4    3.0   2.5
5    3.5   3.0
6    4.0   3.5
7    4.5   4.0
```

First, let's look at a Python dataset related to monthly data with a name of yanMonthly.pkl, http://canisius.edu/~yany/python/yanMonthly.pkl. The following code would read in the dataset:

```
import pandas as pd
x=pd.read_pickle("c:/temp/yanMonthly.pkl")
print(x[0:10])
```

The related output is shown here:

```
                 DATE    VALUE
NAME
000001.SS    19901231   127.61
000001.SS    19910131   129.97
000001.SS    19910228   133.01
000001.SS    19910329   120.19
000001.SS    19910430   113.94
000001.SS    19910531   114.83
000001.SS    19910628   137.56
000001.SS    19910731   143.80
000001.SS    19910830   178.43
000001.SS    19910930   180.92
```

Let's look at what kind of securities are included in this monthly dataset, see the following output:

```
import pandas as pd
import numpy as np
df=pd.read_pickle("c:/temp/yanMonthly.pkl")
unique=np.unique(df.index)
print(len(unique))
print(unique)
```

From the output shown here, we can see that there are 129 securities:

```
129
['000001.SS' 'A' 'AA' 'AAPL' 'BC' 'BCF' 'C' 'CNC' 'COH' 'CPI' 'DELL' 'GE'
 'GOLDPRICE' 'GV' 'GVT' 'HI' 'HML' 'HPS' 'HY' 'IBM' 'ID' 'IL' 'IN' 'INF'
 'ING' 'INY' 'IO' 'ISL' 'IT' 'J' 'JKD' 'JKE' 'JPC' 'KB' 'KCC' 'KFT' 'KIE'
 'KO' 'KOF' 'LBY' 'LCC' 'LCM' 'LF' 'LG' 'LM' 'M' 'MA' 'MAA' 'MD' 'MFL' 'MM'
 'MPV' 'MY' 'Mkt_Rf' 'NEV' 'NIO' 'NP' 'NU' 'NYF' 'OI' 'OPK' 'PAF' 'PFO'
 'PSJ' 'PZZA' 'Q' 'RH' 'RLV' 'Rf' 'Russ3000E_D' 'Russ3000E_X' 'S' 'SBR'
 'SCD' 'SEF' 'SI' 'SKK' 'SMB' 'STC' 'T' 'TA' 'TBAC' 'TEN' 'TK' 'TLT' 'TOK'
 'TR' 'TZE' 'UHS' 'UIS' 'URZ' 'US_DEBT' 'US_GDP2009dollar'
 'US_GDP2013dollar' 'V' 'VC' 'VG' 'VGI' 'VO' 'VV' 'WG' 'WIFI' 'WMT' 'WR'
 'XLI' 'XON' 'Y' 'YANG' 'Z' '^AORD' '^BSESN' '^CCSI' '^CSE' '^FCHI' '^FTSE'
 '^GSPC' '^GSPTSE' '^HSI' '^IBEX' '^ISEQ' '^JKSE' '^KLSE' '^KS11' '^MXX'
 '^NZ50' '^OMX' '^STI' '^STOXX50E' '^TWII']
```

To get S&P500 data, we would use ^GSPC since this is the ticker symbol used by Yahoo!Finance:

```
import pandas as pd
import numpy as np
df=pd.read_pickle("c:/temp/yanMonthly.pkl")
sp500=df[df.index=='^GSPC']
print(sp500[0:5])
ret=sp500['VALUE'].diff()/sp500['VALUE'].shift(1)
print(ret[0:5])
```

The first 10 lines are shown here:

```
                DATE   VALUE
NAME
^GSPC   19500131   17.05
^GSPC   19500228   17.22
^GSPC   19500331   17.29
^GSPC   19500428   17.96
^GSPC   19500531   18.78
NAME
^GSPC              NaN
^GSPC       0.009971
^GSPC       0.004065
^GSPC       0.038751
^GSPC       0.045657
```

After estimating returns, we could estimate their lag and lead, and then three different regressions to estimate those three betas.

Along the same line, Dimson (1979) suggests the following method to adjust beta:

$$\begin{cases} R_t = a + \sum_{i=-k}^{k} \beta_i R_{m.t+i} + \varepsilon_t \\ \beta = \sum_{i=-k}^{k} \beta_i \end{cases} \quad \ldots(11)$$

The most frequently used k value is 1. Thus, we have the following equation:

$$\begin{cases} R_t = a + \beta^{-1} R_{m,t-1} + \beta^0 R_{m,t} + \beta^{+1} R_{m,t+1} + \varepsilon_t \\ \beta = \beta^{-1} + \beta^0 + \beta^{+1} \end{cases} \quad \ldots(12)$$

Since this is equivalent to running a three-factor linear model, we will leave it to the next chapter (*Chapter 7, Multifactor Models and Performance Measures*).

Extracting output data

In this section, we'll be discussing different ways to extract our output data to different file formats.

Outputting data to text files

The following code will download the daily price data for Microsoft and save it to a text file:

```
import pandas_datareader.data as getData
import re
ticker='msft'
f=open("c:/temp/msft.txt","w")
p = getData.DataReader(ticker, "google")
f.write(str(p))
f.close()
```

The first several saved observations are shown in the following screenshot:

```
msft.txt - Notepad
File  Edit  Format  View  Help
            Open    High     Low   Close      Volume
Date
2010-01-04  30.62   31.10   30.59   30.95    38414185
2010-01-05  30.85   31.10   30.64   30.96    49758862
2010-01-06  30.88   31.08   30.52   30.77    58182332
2010-01-07  30.63   30.70   30.19   30.45    50564285
2010-01-08  30.28   30.88   30.24   30.66    51201289
2010-01-11  30.71   30.76   30.12   30.27    68754648
2010-01-12  30.15   30.40   29.91   30.07    65913228
```

Saving our data to a .csv file

The following program first retrieves IBM price data, and then saves it as a `.csv` file under `c:/temp`:

```
from matplotlib.finance import quotes_historical_yahoo_ochl as getData
import csv
f=open("c:/temp/c.csv","w")

ticker='c'
begdate=(2016,1,1)
enddate=(2017,1,9)
p = getData(ticker, begdate, enddate,asobject=True,adjusted=True)

writer = csv.writer(f)
writer.writerows(p)
f.close()
```

In the preceding code, we rename the `quotes_historical_yahoo_ochl()` function as `getData` for convenience. A reader could use their own name.

Saving our data to an Excel file

The following program first retrieves IBM price data, and then saves it as a `.csv` file under `c:/temp`:

```
import pandas as pd
df=pd.read_csv("http://chart.yahoo.com/table.csv?s=IBM")
f= pd.ExcelWriter('c:/temp/ibm.xlsx')
df.to_excel(f, sheet_name='IBM')
f.save()
```

Note that, if readers find an error message of `No module named openpyxl`, it means that you have to install that module first. A few observations are shown in the following screenshot:

	A	B	C	D	E	F	G	H
1		Date	Open	High	Low	Close	Volume	Adj Close
2	0	2017-01-09	169.470001	169.800003	167.619995	167.649994	3184700	167.649994
3	1	2017-01-06	168.690002	169.919998	167.520004	169.529999	2814900	169.529999
4	2	2017-01-05	169.25	169.389999	167.259995	168.699997	2681000	168.699997
5	3	2017-01-04	167.770004	169.869995	167.360001	169.259995	3357000	169.259995
6	4	2017-01-03	167	167.869995	166.009995	167.190002	2927900	167.190002

Obviously, there is a good change that we don't link the first columns since it is just the irrelevant row column indicator:

```
import pandas as pd
df=pd.read_csv("http://chart.yahoo.com/table.csv?s=IBM")
f= pd.ExcelWriter('c:/temp/ibm.xlsx')
df.to_excel(f,index=False,sheet_name='IBM')
f.save()
```

Saving our data to a pickle dataset

The following program first generates a simple array that has just three values. We save them to a binary file named `tmp.bin` at `C:\temp\`:

```
>>>import pandas as pd
>>>import numpy as np
>>>np.random.seed(1234)
>>> a = pd.DataFrame(np.random.randn(6,5))
>>>a.to_pickle('c:/temp/a.pickle')
```

The dataset of named `a` is shown here:

```
In [155]: a
Out[155]:
          0         1         2         3         4
0  0.471435 -1.190976  1.432707 -0.312652 -0.720589
1  0.887163  0.859588 -0.636524  0.015696 -2.242685
2  1.150036  0.991946  0.953324 -2.021255 -0.334077
3  0.002118  0.405453  0.289092  1.321158 -1.546906
4 -0.202646 -0.655969  0.193421  0.553439  1.318152
5 -0.469305  0.675554 -1.817027 -0.183109  1.058969
```

Saving our data to a binary file

The following program first generates a simple array that has just three values. We save them to a binary file named `tmp.bin` at `C:\temp\`:

```
>>>import array
>>>import numpy as np
>>>outfile = "c:/temp/tmp.bin"
>>>fileobj = open(outfile, mode='wb')
>>>outvalues = array.array('f')
>>>data=np.array([1,2,3])
>>>outvalues.fromlist(data.tolist())
>>>outvalues.tofile(fileobj)
>>>fileobj.close()
```

Reading data from a binary file

Assume that we have generated a binary file called `C:\temp\tmp.bin` from the previous discussion. The file has just three numbers: 1, 2, and 3. The following Python code is used to read them:

```
>>>import array
>>>infile=open("c:/temp/tmp.bin", "rb")
>>>s=infile.read() # read all bytes into a string
>>>d=array.array("f", s) # "f" for float
>>>print(d)
>>>infile.close()
```

The contents of `d` are as follows:

```
array('f', [1.0, 2.0, 3.0])
```

Simple string manipulation

For Python, we could assign a string to a variable without defining it in the first place:

```
>>> x="This is great"
>>> type(x)
<class 'str'>
```

For the formula to convert an effective rate to another one, the second input value is a string. For example, `'s2a'`:

```
>>> type='s2a'
>>> type[0]
's'
>>> len(type)
3
```

The `len()` function shows the length of a string, see the following code:

```
>>>x='Hello World!'
>>>len(x)
13
```

Here are several widely used ways to select substring:

```
string='Hello World!'

# find the length of the string
n_length=len(string)
print(n_length)

# the number of appearance of letter l
n=string.count('l')
print(n)

# find teh locatoin of work of 'World'
loc=string.index("World")
print(loc)

# number of spaces
n2=string.count(' ')
print(n2)

print(string[0]) # print the first letter
print(string[0:1]) # print the first letter (same as above)
```

```
print(string[0:3]) # print the first three letters
print(string[:3]) # same as above
print(string[-3:]) # print the last three letters
print(string[3:]) # ignore the first three
print(string[:-3]) # except the last three
```

The corresponding output is shown here:

```
12
3
6
1
H
H
Hel
Hel
ld!
lo World!
Hello Wor
```

Many times, we want to remove the prevailing or trailing spaces. For those cases, three functions, called `strip()`, `lstrip()`, and `rstrip()` could be applied:

```
string='Hello World!'

print(string.lower())
print(string.title())
print(string.capitalize())
print(string.swapcase())

string2=string.replace("World", "John")
print(string2)

# strip() would remove spaces before and the end of string
# lstrip() would remove spaces before and the end of string
# rstrip() would remove spaces before and the end of string
string3=' Hello World! '
print(string3)
print(string3.strip())
print(string3.lstrip())
print(string3.rstrip())
```

The output is shown here:

```
hello world!
Hello World!
Hello world!
hELLO wORLD!
Hello John!
 Hello World!
Hello World!
Hello World!
 Hello World!
```

The following Python program generates the frequency table for all words used in the bible:

```python
from string import maketrans
import pandas as pd
word_freq = {}
infile="c:/temp/AV1611.txt"
word_list = open(infile, "r").read().split()
ttt='!"#$%&()*+,./:;<=>?@[\\]^_`{|}~0123456789'
for word in word_list:
    word = word.translate(maketrans("",""),ttt )
    if word.startswith('-'):
        word = word.replace('-','')
    if len(word):
        word_freq[word] = word_freq.get(word, 0) + 1
keys = sorted(word_freq.keys())
x=pd.DataFrame(keys)
x.to_pickle('c:/temp/uniqueWordsBible.pkl')
```

An interested reader would download the pickle file from the author's web page at http://canisius.edu/~yany/python/uniqueWordsBible.pkl. After typeing x[0:10], we can see the first 10 words, see the following screenshot:

```
In [163]: x[0:10]
Out[163]:
              0
0             A
1   ABOMINATIONS
2      ACCORDING
3          ACTS
4           AIN
5         ALEPH
6            AM
7          AMOS
8           AND
9        APOSTLE
```

Python via Canopy

This section is optional, especially for readers who have no issues with Python or Python via Anaconda. It is a good idea to have another super package to make our programming in Python easier. In this section, we will discuss two simple tasks: how to install Python via Canopy and how to check and install various Python modules. To install Python, go to the related web page at `https://store.enthought.com/downloads/#default`. After that, you will see the following screen:

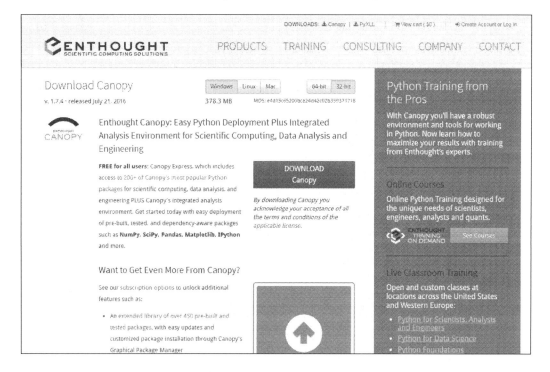

Depending on the operating system; you could download Canopy, such as winders 32-bit. After launching Canopy, the following screen will appear:

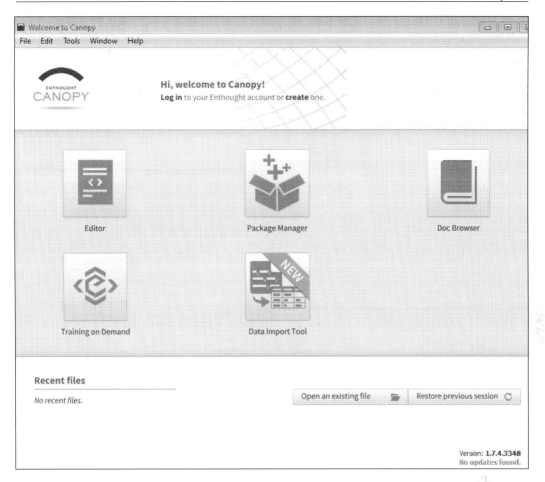

The two most used panels are **Editor** and **Package Manager**. After clicking **Editor**, the following panel will pop up:

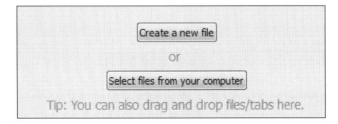

Obviously, we could create a new file or select files from our existing programs. Let's try the simplest one; see the following screenshot. After clicking the green bottom, we can run the program:

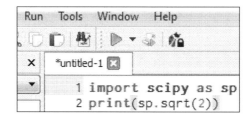

Alternatively, we could click **Run** on the menu bar and then choose the appropriate action. The most important advantage that Canopy could offer is that it is extremely easy to install various Python modules. After clicking **Package Manager**, we will see the following screen:

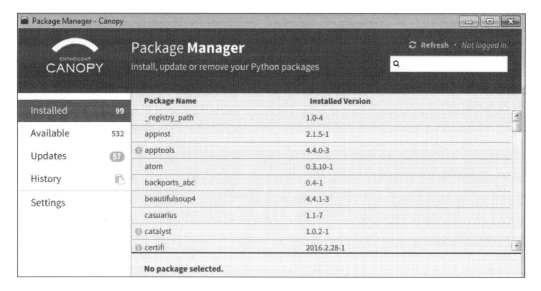

From the left-hand side, we see that there are 99 packages installed and 532 are available. Assume that the Python model called statsmodels is not pre-installed. After clicking **Available** on the left-hand side, we search for this model by typing the keyword. After finding the module, we can decide whether we should install it. Quite often, multiple versions exist; see the following screenshot:

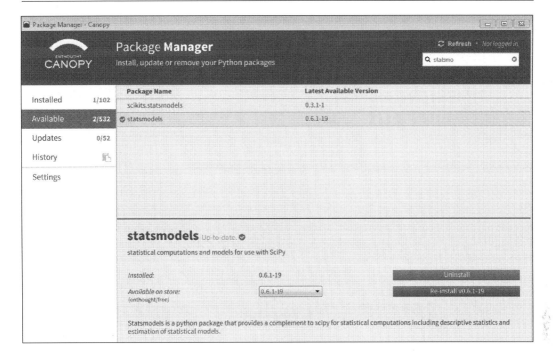

References

Please refer to the following articles:

- Carhart, Mark M., 1997, On Persistence in Mutual Fund Performance, Journal of Finance 52, 57-82.

- Fama, Eugene and Kenneth R. French, 1993, Common risk factors in the returns on stocks and bonds, Journal of Financial Economics 33, 3056.

- Fama, Eugene and Kenneth R. French, 1992, The cross-section of expected stock returns, Journal of Finance 47, 427-465.

- String manipulation: `http://www.pythonforbeginners.com/basics/string-manipulation-in-python`

Appendix A – data case #3 - beta estimation

Objective: hands-on experience to estimate the market risk for a given set of companies:

1. What are alpha and beta for those companies?
2. Comment on your results.

3. Based on your monthly returns, what are the means of annual returns for S&P500 and risk-free rate?

4. If the expected market return is 12.5% per year and the expected risk-free rate is 0.25% per year, what are the costs of equity for those companies?

5. What is the portfolio beta?

Computational tool: Python

Period: From 1/2/ 2011 to 12/31/2016 (the last five years).

Technical details:

$$y = a + \beta * x \qquad \ldots(1)$$

$$R_i - R_f = a + \beta_i \left(R_{mkt} - R_f \right) \ldots(2)$$

i	Company name	Ticker	Industry	Shares
1	Wal-Mart Stores Inc.	WMT	Superstore	1000
2	Apple Inc.	AAPL	Computer	2000
3	International Business Machine	IBM	Computer	1500
4	General Electric Company	GE	Technology	3000
5	Citigroup	C	Banking	1800

Procedure for data downloading and manipulation:

1. Stock monthly price data is from Yahoo finance (`http://finance.yahoo.com`).
2. Calculate monthly returns from monthly prices.
3. S&P500 is used as the market index and its ticker is `^GSPC`.
4. Risk-free rate from Prof. French monthly dataset is used as our risk-free rate.
5. When merging those datasets, please pay attention to the order of their dates.

Note 1 – how to download data? Here we use S&P500 as an example (ticker is ^GSPC):

1. Go to Yahoo Finance (`http://finance.yahoo.com`).
2. Enter `^GSPC`.
3. Click **Historical Prices**.
4. Choose starting date and ending dates. Click **Get Prices**.
5. Go to the bottom of the page and click **Download to spreadsheet**.
6. Give a name, such as `sp500.csv`.

Note 2 – how to download a monthly risk-free rate?

1. Go to the Prof. French Data library at `http://mba.tuck.dartmouth.edu/pages/faculty/ken.french/data_library.html`.

2. Choose Fama-French 3 factors, see the following screenshot:

Fama/French 3 Factors TXT CSV Details
Fama/French 3 Factors [Weekly] TXT CSV Details
Fama/French 3 Factors [Daily] TXT CSV Details

The first several lines and the last several lines are given in the following screenshot:

F-F_Research_Data_Factors.txt - Notepad

File   Edit   Format   View   Help

This file was created by CMPT_ME_BEME_RETS using the 201704 CRSP database
The 1-month TBill return is from Ibbotson and Associates, Inc.

	Mkt-RF	SMB	HML	RF
192607	2.96	-2.30	-2.87	0.22
192608	2.64	-1.40	4.19	0.25
192609	0.36	-1.32	0.01	0.23
192610	-3.24	0.04	0.51	0.32
192611	2.53	-0.20	-0.35	0.31
192612	2.62	-0.04	-0.02	0.28

Exercises

1. What is the meaning of CAPM? Is it a linear model?

2. What are the features of a one-factor linear model?

3. What are the definitions of total risk and market risk and do you measure them?

4. Explain the similarity and difference between the following two equations:

$$R_{IBM} = R_f + \beta_{IBM}\left(R_{mkt} - R_f\right) \quad \dots(1)$$

$$R_{IBM} - R_f = a + \beta_{IBM}\left(R_{mkt} - R_f\right) \quad \dots(2)$$

5. What is the relationship between total risk and market risk for a stock?

6. Who should care about CAPM or what are the usages of the model?

7. If stock A has a higher market risk than stock B, does it mean that A has a higher expected return as well? Explain.

8. How do you measure different types of risk?

9. How do you predict the expected market returns?

10. If we know the expected market risk premium, how do you predict the cost of equity of a firm?

11. What is the logic behind the following beta adjustment formula?

$$\beta_{adj} = \frac{2}{3}\beta + \frac{1}{3}1.0$$

12. Construct a portfolio with unequal weight of 20%, 10%, 30%, 10%, 10%, and 20%. The list of stocks are Walmart (WMT), International Business Machine (IBM), Citi Group (C), Microsoft (MSFT), Google (GOOG), and Dell (DELL). Estimate their monthly portfolio returns from 2001 to 2016.

13. Find the beta of IBM from Yahoo Finance. Go to Yahoo Finance, then IBM, and then click Key Statistics on the left-hand side. `http://finance.yahoo.com/q/ks?s=IBM+Key+Statistics`

    Download IBM's historical price data and estimate its beta and compare.

14. What is the total risk and market risk for DELL, IBM, GOOG, and C if you are using five-year monthly data?

15. Write a Python program to estimate a and β for the following 10 stocks. The time period covered should be the last five years (1/2/2012-1/10/2017) by using monthly data from the Yahoo Finance and the Federal Reserve Web site (for risk-free rate):

	Company name	Ticker	Industry
1	Family Dollar Stores	FDO	Retail
2	Wal-Mart Stores	WMT	Superstore
3	McDonald's	MCD	Restaurants
4	Dell	DELL	Computer hardware
5	International Business Machine	IBM	Computer
6	Microsoft	MSFT	Software
7	General Electric	GE	Conglomerates
8	Google	GOOG	Internet services
9	Apple	AAPL	Computer hardware
10	eBay	EBAY	Internet services

16. From this chapter, we know that we could call the `p4f.dailyReturn` function to download the historical data for a given ticker plus a designed time period; see the following code:

```
import p4f
x=dailyReturn("ibm",(2016,1,1),(2016,1,10))
```

The function is shown in the following code:

```
def dailyReturn(ticker,begdate,enddate):
    from scipy import stats
    from matplotlib.finance import quotes_historical_yahoo_ochl
    p = quotes_historical_yahoo_ochl(ticker, begdate,
        enddate,asobject=True,adjusted=True)
    return p.aclose[1:]/p.aclose[:-1]-1
```

Obviously, the second and the third input formats of beginning dates and ending dates are not user-friendly; see `dailyReturn("ibm",(2016,1,1),(2016,1,10))`. Modify the program to make it more user-friendly, such as `dailyReturn2("ibm", 20160101, 20160110)`.

17. Download price data, as long as it's possible, from Yahoo Finance for a few stocks such as DELL, IBM, and MSFT. Then calculate their volatilities over several decades. For example, estimate volatilities for IBM over several five-year periods. What is the trend of the volatility?

18. What is the correlation between (among) market indices? For example, you can download price data for S&P500 (its Yahoo ticker is `^GSPC`), and Dow Jones Industrial Average (`^DJI`) over the last 10 years. Then estimate their returns and calculate the corresponding correlation. Comment on your result.

19. Which five stocks are most strongly correlated with IBM from 2006 to 2010? (Hint: there is not a unique answer. You can try a dozen stocks).

20. On January 2nd 2017, your portfolio consists of 2,000 shares of IBM, 1,500 shares of Citigroup, and 500 shares of Microsoft (MSFT). What is the portfolio's beta? You can use past five-year historical to run CAPM.

21. What is the correlation between IBM stock returns and Microsoft (MSFT)?

 You can use the past 10 years' historical data to estimate the correlation.

22. Find the issue and correct it for the following code:

```
from scipy import stats
from matplotlib.finance import quotes_historical_yahoo_ochl

def dailyReturn(ticker,begdate=(1962,1,1),enddate=(2017,1,10)):
    p = quotes_historical_yahoo_ochl(ticker, begdate, enddate,asobject
=True,adjusted=True)
    return p.aclose[1:]/p.aclose[:-1]-1

retIBM=dailyReturn("wmt")
retMkt=dailyReturn("^GSPC")

outputs=stats.linregress(retIBM,retMkt)
print(outputs)
```

23. Write a Python function called `beta()` to offer a beta value, its significance value such as T-vale or P-value by using the last five years of historical data, plus S&P500 as the index.

Summary

Capital Asset Pricing Model (CAPM) is probably the most widely used model in assets pricing. There are several reasons behind its popularity. First, it is quite simple. It is just a one-factor linear model. Second, it is quite easy to implement this one-factor model. Any interested reader could download historical price data for a listed company and a market index data to calculate their return, and then estimate the market risk for the stock. Third, this simplest one-factor asset pricing model could be served as the first model for other more advanced ones, such as Fama-French 3-factor, Fama-French-Carhart 4-factor models, and Fama-French 5 factor models, which will be introduced in the next chapter.

7
Multifactor Models and Performance Measures

In *Chapter 6*, *Capital Asset Pricing Model*, we discussed the simplest one-factor linear model: CAPM. As mentioned, this one-factor linear model serve as a benchmark for more advanced and complex models. In this chapter, we will focus on the famous Fama-French three-factor model, Fama-French-Carhart four-factor model, and Fama-French five-factor model. After understanding those models, readers should be able to develop their own multifactor linear models, such as by adding **Gross Domestic Product (GDP)**, **Consumer Price Index (CPI)**, a business cycle indicator or other variables as an extra factor(s). In addition, we will discuss performance measures, such as the Sharpe ratio, Treynor ratio, and Jensen's alpha. In particular, the following topics will be covered in this chapter:

- Introduction to the Fama-French three-factor model
- Fama-French-Carhart four-factor model
- Fama-French five-factor model
- Other multiplefactor models
- Sharpe ratio and Treynor ratio
- Lower partial standard deviation and Sortino ratio
- Jensen's alpha
- How to merge different datasets

Introduction to the Fama-French three-factor model

Before discussing the Fama-French three-factor model and other models, let's look at a general equation for a three-factor linear model:

$$y = \alpha + \beta_1 x_1 + \beta_2 x_2 + \beta_3 x_3 + \varepsilon \qquad \dots (1)$$

Here, y is the dependent variable, a is the intercept, $x1$, $x2$, and $x3$ are three independent variables, $\beta1$, $\beta2$ and $\beta3$ are three coefficients, and ε is a random factor. In other words, we try to use three independent variables to explain one dependent variable. The same as a one-factor linear model, the graphical presentation of this three-factor linear model is a straight line, in a four-dimensional space, and the power of each independent variable is a unit as well. Here, we will use two simple examples to show how to run multifactor linear regression. For the first example, we have the following code. The values have no specific meaning and readers could enter their own values as well:

```
from pandas.stats.api import ols
import pandas as pd
y = [0.065, 0.0265, -0.0593, -0.001,0.0346]
x1 = [0.055, -0.09, -0.041,0.045,0.022]
x2 = [0.025, 0.10, 0.021,0.145,0.012]
x3= [0.015, -0.08, 0.341,0.245,-0.022]
df=pd.DataFrame({"y":y,"x1":x1, 'x2':x2,'x3':x3})
result=ols(y=df['y'],x=df[['x1','x2','x3']])
print(result)
```

In the preceding program, the `pandas.stats.api.ols()` function is applied. **OLS** stands for **Ordinary Least Squares**. For more information about the OLS model, we could use the `help()` function; see the following two lines of code. For brevity, the output is not shown here:

```
from pandas.stats.api import ols
help(ols)
```

The pandas DataFrame is used to construct our dataset. Readers should pay attention to the structure of {"y":y, "x1":x1, 'x2':x2, 'x3':x3}. It has the data format of a dictionary. The result of running the regression is shown here:

```
------------------------Summary of Regression Analysis------------------------

Formula: Y ~ <x1> + <x2> + <x3> + <intercept>

Number of Observations:        5
Number of Degrees of Freedom:  4

R-squared:         0.9603
Adj R-squared:     0.8414

Rmse:              0.0187

F-stat (3, 1):     8.0725, p-value:      0.2519

Degrees of Freedom: model 3, resid 1

----------------------Summary of Estimated Coefficients----------------------
     Variable      Coef    Std Err    t-stat    p-value    CI 2.5%    CI 97.5%
-----------------------------------------------------------------------------
           x1    0.3796     0.1526      2.49     0.2433     0.0805      0.6787
           x2    0.0589     0.1600      0.37     0.7755    -0.2547      0.3724
           x3   -0.2342     0.0518     -4.52     0.1385    -0.3356     -0.1327
    intercept    0.0336     0.0134      2.52     0.2407     0.0075      0.0598
------------------------------End of Summary---------------------------------
```

From the output, the three-factor model is listed first: y is against three independent or explainable variables of x1, x2, and x3. The number of observations is 5, while the degree of freedom is 4. The value of R^2 is 0.96 while the adjusted R^2 is 0.84. The R^2 value reflects the percentage of variations in y could be explained by x1, x2, and x3. Since the adjusted R^2 considers the impact of the number of independent variables, it is more meaningful. **RMSE** stands for **Mean Standard Square Error**. The smaller this value, the better our model. The F-stat and the p-value reflect the goodness of our linear model. The F-value reflects the quality of the whole model. The F-value should be compared with its critical F-value, which in turn depends on three input variables: confidence level, degree of freedom for the numerator, and degree of freedom for the denominator. The scipy.stats.f.ppf() function could be applied to find out the critical F-value; see the following code:

```
import scipy.stats as stats
alpha=0.05
dfNumerator=3
dfDenominator=1
f=stats.f.ppf(q=1-alpha, dfn=dfNumerator, dfd=dfDenominator)
print(f)
215.70734537
```

The confidence level is equal to 1 minus alpha, that is, 95% in this case. The higher the confidence level, the more reliable the result, such as 99% instead of 95%. The most-used confidence levels are 90%, 95%, and 99%. `dfNumeratro` (`dfDenominator`) is the degree of freedom for the numerator (denominator), which depends on the simple sizes. From the preceding result of OLS regression, we know that those two values are 3 and 1.

From the preceding values, *F=8.1 < 215.7* (critical F-value), we should accept the null hypothesis that all coefficients are zero, that is, the quality of the model is not good. On the other hand, a P-value of 0.25 is way higher the critical value of 0.05. It also means that we should accept the null hypothesis. This makes sense since we have entered those values without any meanings.

For the second example, one CSV file related to IBM, downloaded from Yahoo! Finance, is used and the dataset can be downloaded at `http://canisius.edu/~yany/data/ibm.csv`. Alternatively, readers can go to `http://finance.yahoo.com/` to download IBM's historical data. The first several lines are shown here:

```
Date,Open,High,Low,Close,Volume,Adj.Close
2017-05-11,151.050003,151.149994,149.789993,150.649994,5627900,150.649994
2017-05-10,151.649994,152.369995,151.130005,151.25,4999900,151.25
2017-05-09,152.600006,153.100006,151.559998,152.110001,6853000,152.110001
2017-05-08,152.800003,153.470001,152.199997,153.029999,7492000,153.029999
2017-05-05,153.520004,155.779999,153,155.050003,12521300,153.550001
2017-05-04,158.889999,159.139999,158.360001,159.050003,4280600,157.511304
2017-05-03,158.740005,159.449997,158.520004,158.630005,3993300,157.095369
2017-05-02,159.440002,159.490005,158.639999,159.100006,3208200,157.560823
2017-05-01,160.050003,160.419998,158.699997,158.839996,4935300,157.303329
2017-04-28,160.5,160.589996,159.699997,160.289993,4154100,158.739298
```

`Date` is the date variable, `Open` is the opening price, `High` (`Low`) is the highest (lowest) price achieved during the period, `Close` is the closing price, `Volume` is the trading volume and `Adj.Close` is the adjusted closing price, adjusted for stock split and dividend distributions. In the following Python program, we try to use three variables of `Open`, `High`, and `Volume` to explain `Adj.Close`; see the following equation:

$$Adj.Close = \alpha + \beta_1 * Open + \beta_2 * High + \beta_3 * Volume + \varepsilon \qquad \dots (2)$$

Again, this OLS regression just serves as an illustration showing how to run a three-factor model. It might have no economic meaning at all. The beauty of such an example is that we could easily get data and test our Python program:

```python
import pandas as pd
import numpy as np
```

```
import statsmodels.api as sm
inFile='http://canisius.edu/~yany/data/ibm.csv'
df = pd.read_csv(inFile, index_col=0)
x = df[['Open', 'High', 'Volume']]
y = df['Adj.Close']
x = sm.add_constant(x)
result = sm.OLS(y, x).fit()
print(result.summary())
```

The first three commands import three Python modules. The command line of x=sm.
add_constant(x) will add a column of 1s. If the line is missing, we would force a
zero intercept. To enrich our experience of running a three-factor linear model, this
time, a different OLS function is applied. The advantage of using the statsmodels.
apilsm.OLS() function is that we could find more information about our results,
such as **Akaike Information Criterion (AIC)**, **Bayesian Information Criterion (BIC)**,
skew, and kurtosis. The discussion of their definitions will be postponed to the next
chapter (*Chapter 8, Time-Series Analysis*). The corresponding output after running the
preceding Python program is given here:

```
                            OLS Regression Results
==============================================================================
Dep. Variable:            Adj.Close   R-squared:                       0.090
Model:                          OLS   Adj. R-squared:                  0.090
Method:               Least Squares   F-statistic:                     455.1
Date:              Mon, 12 Jun 2017   Prob (F-statistic):           5.22e-282
Time:                      14:21:45   Log-Likelihood:                -73371.
No. Observations:             13807   AIC:                         1.468e+05
Df Residuals:                 13803   BIC:                         1.468e+05
Df Model:                         3
Covariance Type:          nonrobust
==============================================================================
                 coef    std err          t      P>|t|      [95.0% Conf. Int.]
------------------------------------------------------------------------------
const         55.1657      1.171     47.115      0.000      52.871     57.461
Open           0.7044      0.242      2.909      0.004       0.230      1.179
High          -0.7926      0.240     -3.297      0.001      -1.264     -0.321
Volume      1.081e-06     1.1e-07      9.850      0.000    8.66e-07     1.3e-06
==============================================================================
Omnibus:                     3214.259   Durbin-Watson:                   0.005
Prob(Omnibus):                  0.000   Jarque-Bera (JB):             6047.952
Skew:                           1.475   Prob(JB):                         0.00
Kurtosis:                       4.345   Cond. No.                     1.87e+07
==============================================================================

Warnings:
[1] Standard Errors assume that the covariance matrix of the errors is correctly specified.
[2] The condition number is large, 1.87e+07. This might indicate that there are
strong multicollinearity or other numerical problems.
```

Again, we will refrain from spending time interpreting the result since our objective
at the moment is to show how to run a three-factor regression.

Fama-French three-factor model

Recall that the CAPM has the following form:

$$E(R_i) = R_f + \beta_i(E(R_{mkt}) - R_t) \qquad \dots (3)$$

Here, $E()$ is the expectation, $E(Ri)$ is the expected return for stock i, Rf is the risk-free rate, and $E(Rmkt)$ is the expected market return. For instance, the S&P500 index could serve as a market index. The slope of the preceding equation (β_i) is a measure of the stock's market risk. To find out the value of β_i, we run a linear regression. The Fama-French three-factor model could be viewed as a natural extension of CAPM, see here:

$$R_i = R_f + \beta_{mkt}(R_{mkt} - R_f) + \beta_{SMB} * SMB + \beta_{HML} * HML + \varepsilon \qquad \dots (4)$$

The definitions of Ri, Rf, and $Rmkt$ remain the same. SMB is the portfolio returns of small stocks minus the portfolio returns of big stocks; HML is the portfolio returns for high book-to-market value minus returns of low book-to-market value stocks. The Fama/French factors are constructed using the six value-weight portfolios formed on size and book-to-market. **Small Minus Big (SMB)** is the average return on the three small portfolios minus the average return on the three big portfolios. Based on the size, measured by the market capitalization (numbers of shares outstanding times the end of year price), they classify all stocks into two categories, **S** (small) and **H** (high). Similarly, based on the ratio of book value of equity to the market value of equity, all stocks are classified into three groups of **H** (high), **M** (Median), and **L** (Low). Eventually, we could have the following six groups:

		Sorted by size into two groups	
Sorted by book/market ratio into three groups		SH	BH
		SM	BM
		SL	BL

The SMB is constructed by the following six portfolios:

$$MB = \frac{1}{3}(SH + SM + SL) - \frac{1}{3}(BH + BM + BL) \qquad \dots (5)$$

When ratios of equity book value over market value are low (high), those stocks are called growth (value stocks) stocks. Thus, we could use another formula; see here:

$$SMB = \frac{1}{3}(Small\ value + Small\ neutral + Samall\ growth) - \frac{1}{3}(Big\ value + Big\ neutral + Big\ growth) \quad \dots (6)$$

High Minus Low (HML) is the average return on the two value portfolios minus the average return on the two growth portfolios; see the following equation:

$$HML = \frac{1}{2}(Small\ value + Big\ value) - \frac{1}{2}(Small\ growth + Big\ growth) \quad \dots (7)$$

Rm-Rf, the excess return on the market, value-weight return of all CRSP firms incorporated in the US and listed on the NYSE, AMEX, or NASDAQ that have a CRSP share code of 10 or 11 at the beginning of month t, good shares and price data at the beginning of t, and good return data for t minus the 1-month Treasury bill rate (from Ibbotson Associates). The following program retrieves the Fama-French monthly factors and generates a dataset with the .pickle format. The dataset for the Fama-French monthly dataset in the pandas .pickle format can be downloaded from http://www.canisius.edu/~yany/python/ffMonthly.pkl:

```
import pandas as pd
x=pd.read_pickle("c:/temp/ffMonthly.pkl")
print(x.head())
print(x.tail())
```

The corresponding output is show here:

	DATE	MKT_RF	SMB	HML	RF
1	1926-07-01	0.0296	-0.023	-0.0287	0.0022
2	1926-08-01	0.0264	-0.014	0.0419	0.0025
3	1926-09-01	0.0036	-0.0132	0.0001	0.0023
4	1926-10-01	-0.0324	0.0004	0.0051	0.0032
5	1926-11-01	0.0253	-0.002	-0.0035	0.0031
	DATE	MKT_RF	SMB	HML	RF
1081	2016-07-01	0.0395	0.029	-0.0098	0.0002
1082	2016-08-01	0.005	0.0094	0.0318	0.0002
1083	2016-09-01	0.0025	0.02	-0.0134	0.0002
1084	2016-10-01	-0.0202	-0.044	0.0415	0.0002
1085	2016-11-01	0.0486	0.0569	0.0844	0.0001

Next, we show how to run a Fama-French three-factor regression using 5-year monthly data. The added twist is that the historical price data is downloaded first. Then we calculate monthly returns and convert them to monthly ones before merging with the monthly Fama-French three-factor time series:

```
from matplotlib.finance import quotes_historical_yahoo_ochl as getData
import numpy as np
import pandas as pd
import scipy as sp
import statsmodels.api as sm

ticker='IBM'
begdate=(2012,1,1)
enddate=(2016,12,31)

p= getData(ticker, begdate, enddate,asobject=True, adjusted=True)
logret = sp.log(p.aclose[1:]/p.aclose[:-1])

ddate=[]
d0=p.date

for i in range(0,sp.size(logret)):
    x=''.join([d0[i].strftime("%Y"),d0[i].strftime("%m"),"01"])
    ddate.append(pd.to_datetime(x, format='%Y%m%d').date())

t=pd.DataFrame(logret,np.array(ddate),columns=[''RET''])
ret=sp.exp(t.groupby(t.index).sum())-1
ff=pd.read_pickle('c:/temp/ffMonthly.pkl')
final=pd.merge(ret,ff,left_index=True,right_index=True)
y=final[''RET'']
x=final[[''MKT_RF'',''SMB'',''HML'']]
x=sm.add_constant(x)
results=sm.OLS(y,x).fit()
print(results.summary())
```

In the preceding program, the start date is January 1, 2012, and the end date is December 31, 2016. After retrieving the daily price data, we estimate the daily returns and then convert them to monthly ones. The Fama-French monthly three-factor time series with the pandas `.pickle` format is uploaded. In the preceding program, the usage of `np.array(date,dtype=int64)` is to make both indices have the same data types. The corresponding output is as follows:

```
                         OLS Regression Results
==============================================================================
Dep. Variable:                     RET   R-squared:                       0.382
Model:                             OLS   Adj. R-squared:                  0.348
Method:                  Least Squares   F-statistic:                     11.31
Date:                 Mon, 12 Jun 2017   Prob (F-statistic):           6.94e-06
Time:                         14:56:20   Log-Likelihood:                 105.72
No. Observations:                   59   AIC:                            -203.4
Df Residuals:                       55   BIC:                            -195.1
Df Model:                            3
Covariance Type:             nonrobust
==============================================================================
                 coef     std err          t      P>|t|      [95.0% Conf. Int.]
------------------------------------------------------------------------------
const         -0.0119       0.006     -2.017      0.049      -0.024 -7.78e-05
MKT_RF         0.9886       0.182      5.429      0.000       0.624     1.354
SMB           -0.1253       0.253     -0.495      0.623      -0.633     0.382
HML            0.4232       0.253      1.673      0.100      -0.084     0.930
==============================================================================
Omnibus:                         3.511   Durbin-Watson:                   2.253
Prob(Omnibus):                   0.173   Jarque-Bera (JB):                2.966
Skew:                           -0.242   Prob(JB):                        0.227
Kurtosis:                        3.986   Cond. No.                         49.3
==============================================================================

Warnings:
[1] Standard Errors assume that the covariance matrix of the errors is correctly specified.
```

To save space, we will not discuss the result.

Fama-French-Carhart four-factor model and Fama-French five-factor model

Jegadeesh and Titman (1993) show a profitable momentum trading strategy: buy winners and sell losers. The basic assumption is that within a short time period, such as 6 months, a winner will remain as a winner, while a loser will remain as a loser. For example, we could classify winners from losers based on the last 6-month cumulative total returns. Assume we are in January 1965. The total returns over the last 6 months are estimated first. Then sort them into 10 portfolios according to their total returns from the highest to the lowest. The top (bottom) 10% are labeled as winners (losers). We long winner portfolio and short loser portfolio with a 6-month holding period. The next month, February 1965, we repeat the same procedure. Over January 1965 to December 1989, Jegadeesh and Titman's (1993) empirical results suggest that such a trading strategy would generate a return of 0.95% per month. Based on this result, Carhart (2000) adds the momentum as the 4th to the Fama-French three-factor model:

$$R_i = R_f + \beta_{mkt}(R_{mkt} - R_f) + \beta_{SMB}SMB + \beta_{HML}HML + \beta_{MOM}MOM + \varepsilon \qquad \dots (8)$$

Here, *MOM* is the momentum factor. The following codes could upload `ffcMonthly.pkl` and print the first and last several lines. The Python dataset can be downloaded from the author's website at `http://www.canisius.edu/~yany/python/ffcMonthly.pkl`:

```python
import pandas as pd
x=pd.read_pickle("c:/temp/ffcMonthly.pkl")
print(x.head())
print(x.tail())
```

The output is shown here:

	MKT_RF	SMB	HML	RF	MOM
1927-01-01	-0.0006	-0.0056	0.0483	0.0025	0.0044
1927-02-01	0.0418	-0.0010	0.0317	0.0026	-0.0201
1927-03-01	0.0013	-0.0160	-0.0267	0.0030	0.0359
1927-04-01	0.0046	0.0043	0.0060	0.0025	0.0419
1927-05-01	0.0544	0.0141	0.0493	0.0030	0.0301
	MKT_RF	SMB	HML	RF	MOM
2016-06-01	-0.0005	0.0061	-0.0149	0.0002	0.0428
2016-07-01	0.0395	0.0290	-0.0098	0.0002	-0.0317
2016-08-01	0.0050	0.0094	0.0318	0.0002	-0.0316
2016-09-01	0.0025	0.0200	-0.0134	0.0002	-0.0052
2016-10-01	-0.0202	-0.0440	0.0415	0.0002	0.0058

In 2015, Fama and French developed a so-called five-factor model; see the following formula:

$$R_i = R_f + \beta_{mkt}(R_{mkt} - R_f) + \beta_{SMB}SMB + \beta_{HML}HML + \beta_{MOM}RMW + \beta_{MOM}CMA \quad \dots (9)$$

In the preceding equation, *RMW* is the difference between the returns on diversified portfolio of stocks with robust and weak profitability, *CMA* is the difference between the returns of diversified portfolios of the stocks of low and high investment firms, which Fama and French call conservative and aggressive. If the exposures to the five factors capture all variation in expected returns, the intercept for all securities and portfolio *i* should be zero. Again, we would not show how to run a Fama-French five-factor model since it is quite similar to running a Fama-French three-factor model. Instead, the following code shows the first and last several lines of a Python dataset called `ffMonthly5.pkl`. The Python dataset can be downloaded from the author's website at `http://www.canisius.edu/~yany/python/ffMonthly5.pkl`:

```python
import pandas as pd
x=pd.read_pickle("c:/temp/ffMonthly5.pkl")
print(x.head())
print(x.tail())
```

The corresponding output is shown here:

	MKT_RF	SMB	HML	RMW	CMA	RF
1963-07-01	-0.0039	-0.0046	-0.0082	0.0072	-0.0116	0.0027
1963-08-01	0.0507	-0.0081	0.0163	0.0042	-0.0040	0.0025
1963-09-01	-0.0157	-0.0048	0.0019	-0.0080	0.0023	0.0027
1963-10-01	0.0253	-0.0129	-0.0011	0.0275	-0.0226	0.0029
1963-11-01	-0.0085	-0.0084	0.0166	-0.0034	0.0222	0.0027
	MKT_RF	SMB	HML	RMW	CMA	RF
2016-07-01	0.0395	0.0291	-0.0098	0.0143	-0.0102	0.0002
2016-08-01	0.0050	0.0152	0.0318	-0.0124	-0.0056	0.0002
2016-09-01	0.0025	0.0172	-0.0134	-0.0185	-0.0005	0.0002
2016-10-01	-0.0202	-0.0397	0.0415	0.0136	0.0022	0.0002
2016-11-01	0.0486	0.0704	0.0844	-0.0068	0.0384	0.0001

Along the same lines, for the daily frequency, we have several datasets called `ffDaily`, `ffcDaily`, and `ffDaily5`; see *Appendix A – list of related Python datasets* for more detail.

Implementation of Dimson (1979) adjustment for beta

Dimson (1979) suggests the following method:

$$\begin{cases} R_t = \alpha + \sum_{i=-k}^{k} \beta_i R_{m,t+i} + \epsilon_t \\ \beta = \sum_{i=-k}^{k} \beta_i \end{cases} \qquad \dots (10)$$

The most frequently used *k* value is *1*. Thus, we have the next equation:

$$\begin{cases} R_t = \alpha + \beta^{-1} R_{m,t-1} + \beta^0 R_{m,t} + \beta^{+1} R_{m,t+1} + \varepsilon_t \\ \beta = \beta^{-1} + \beta^0 + \beta^{+1} \end{cases} \qquad \dots (11)$$

Before we run the regression based on the preceding equation, two functions called `.diff()` and `.shift()` are explained. Here, we randomly choose five prices. Then we estimate their price difference returns and add lag and forward returns:

```
import pandas as pd
import scipy as sp

price=[10,11,12.2,14.0,12]
```

```
x=pd.DataFrame({'Price':price})
x['diff']=x.diff()
x['Ret']=x['Price'].diff()/x['Price'].shift(1)
x['RetLag']=x['Ret'].shift(1)
x['RetLead']=x['Ret'].shift(-1)
print(x)
```

The output is shown here:

```
    Price  diff        Ret      RetLag    RetLead
0   10.0   NaN         NaN         NaN   0.100000
1   11.0   1.0    0.100000         NaN   0.109091
2   12.2   1.2    0.109091    0.100000   0.147541
3   14.0   1.8    0.147541    0.109091  -0.142857
4   12.0  -2.0   -0.142857    0.147541        NaN
```

Obviously, the price time series is assumed from the oldest to the newest. The difference is defined as *p(i) – p(i-1)*. Thus, the first difference is NaN, that is, a missing value. Let's look at period 4, that is, index=3. The difference is *1.8 (14-12.2)*, return is *(14-12.2)/12.2= 0.147541*. The lag ret will be the return before this period, that is, *0.109091*, while the lead return will be the next period return, that is, *-0.142857*. In the following Python program, we illustrate how to run the previous program for IBM stocks:

```
import pandas as pd
import numpy as np
from pandas.stats.api import ols

df=pd.read_pickle("c:/temp/yanMonthly.pkl")
sp500=df[df.index=='^GSPC']
sp500['retMkt']=sp500['VALUE'].diff()/sp500['VALUE'].shift(1)
sp500['retMktLag']=sp500['retMkt'].shift(1)
sp500['retMktLead']=sp500['retMkt'].shift(-1)

ibm=df[df.index=='IBM']
ibm['RET']=ibm['VALUE'].diff()/ibm['VALUE'].shift(1)
y=pd.DataFrame(ibm[['DATE','RET']])
x=pd.DataFrame(sp500[['DATE','retMkt','retMktLag','retMktLead']])
data=pd.merge(x,y)

result=ols(y=data['RET'],x=data[['retMkt','retMktLag','retMktLead']])
print(result)
```

The output is shown here:

```
-----------------------Summary of Regression Analysis------------------------

Formula: Y ~ <retMkt> + <retMktLag> + <retMktLead> + <intercept>

Number of Observations:        621
Number of Degrees of Freedom:  4

R-squared:          0.3608
Adj R-squared:      0.3577

Rmse:               0.0562

F-stat (3, 617):    116.1098, p-value:     0.0000

Degrees of Freedom: model 3, resid 617

----------------------Summary of Estimated Coefficients----------------------
    Variable      Coef    Std Err    t-stat    p-value    CI 2.5%   CI 97.5%
-----------------------------------------------------------------------------
      retMkt     0.9714    0.0521     18.64     0.0000     0.8693     1.0736
   retMktLag     0.0012    0.0521      0.02     0.9813    -0.1009     0.1033
  retMktLead    -0.0408    0.0521     -0.78     0.4339    -0.1429     0.0613
   intercept     0.0037    0.0023      1.58     0.1142    -0.0009     0.0082
----------------------------End of Summary-----------------------------------
```

Performance measures

To compare the performance of mutual functions or individual stocks, we need a performance measure. In finance, we know that investors should seek a trade-off between risk and returns. It might not be a good idea to say that portfolio A is better than portfolio B since the former offered us a 30% return last year while the latter offered just 8%. The obvious reason is that we should not ignore risk factors. Because of this, we often hear the phrase "risk-adjusted return". In this section, the Sharpe ratio, Treynor ratio, Sortino ratio, and Jensen's alpha will be discussed. The Sharpe ratio is a widely used performance measure and it is defined as follows:

$$\text{Sharpe} = \frac{\bar{R}-\bar{R}_f}{\sigma} = \frac{\overline{R-R_f}}{\sqrt{\text{var}(R-R_f)}} \quad \dots (12)$$

Here, $\bar{R}$ is the mean return for a portfolio or a stock, $\bar{R}_f$ is the mean return for a risk-free security, σ is the variance of the excess portfolio (stock) return, and VaR is the variance of the excess portfolio (stock) return. The following code is used to estimate the Sharpe ratio with a hypothetical risk-free rate:

```
import pandas as pd
import scipy as sp
df=pd.read_pickle("c:/temp/yanMonthly.pkl")
rf=0.01
ibm=df[df.index=='IBM']
ibm['RET']=ibm['VALUE'].diff()/ibm['VALUE'].shift(1)
ret=ibm['RET']
sharpe=sp.mean((ret)-rf)/sp.std(ret)
print(sharpe)
```

The Sharpe ratio is -0.00826559763423. The following code will download daily data directly from Yahoo! Finance, then estimate the Sharpe ratio without considering the impact of the risk-free rate:

```
import scipy as sp
from matplotlib.finance import quotes_historical_yahoo_ochl as getData
begdate=(2012,1,1)
enddate=(2016,12,31)
def ret_f(ticker,begdate,enddate):
    p = getData(ticker,begdate, enddate,asobject=True,adjusted=True)
    return(p.aclose[1:]/p.aclose[:-1]-1)
y=ret_f('IBM',begdate,enddate)
sharpe=sp.mean(y)/sp.std(y)
print(sharpe)
```

The result is `0.00686555838073`. Based on the preceding code, a Python program is developed with more explanation plus two examples; see *Appendix C* for more detail. The Sharpe ratio looks at the total risk since the standard deviation is used as the denominator. This measure is appropriate when the portfolio in consideration is all the wealth for a company or individual owner. In *Chapter 6, Capital Asset Pricing Model*, we argued that a rational investor should consider only the market risk instead of the total risk when he/she estimates the expected returns. Thus, when the portfolio under consideration is only part of the wealth, using total risk is not appropriate. Because of this, Treynor suggests using beta as the denominator:

$$Treynor\ Ratio = \frac{\bar{R}-\bar{R}_f}{\beta} \qquad \dots (13)$$

The only modification is that the sigma (total risk) is replaced by beta (market risk). Another argument against using standard deviation in the Sharpe ratio is that it considers the deviations in both directions, below and above the mean. However, we know that investors are worried more about the downside risk (deviation below mean return). The second issue for the Sharpe ratio is that for the numerator, we compare mean returns with a risk-free rate. Nevertheless, for the denominator, the deviations are from the mean return instead for the same risk-free rate. To overcome those two shortcomings, a so-called **Lower Partial Standard Deviation (LPSD)** is developed. Assume we have n returns and one **risk-free rate (Rf)**. Assume further that there are m returns are less than this risk-free rate. LPSD is defined here:

$$LPSD = \frac{\sum_{i=1}^{n}(R_i - R_f)^2}{m-1} \qquad when\ R_i < R_f \qquad \dots (14A)$$

Alternatively, we have the following equivalent formula:

$$LPSD = \frac{\sum_{i=1}^{m}(R_i - R_f)^2}{m-1} \qquad \dots (14B)$$

The Sortino ratio is defined here:

$$Sortino\ Ratio = \frac{\bar{R} - \bar{R}_f}{LPSD} \qquad \dots (15)$$

We could write a Python program to estimate the Sortino ratio; see the following code. To guarantee getting the same set of random numbers, the same seed should be used in the `sp.random.seed()` function:

```
import scipy as sp
import numpy as np

mean=0.10;
Rf=0.02
std=0.20
n=100
sp.random.seed(12456)
x=sp.random.normal(loc=mean,scale=std,size=n)
```

```
print("std=", sp.std(x))

y=x[x-Rf<0]
m=len(y)
total=0.0
for i in sp.arange(m):
    total+=(y[i]-Rf)**2

LPSD=total/(m-1)
print("y=",y)
print("LPSD=",LPSD)
```

The corresponding output is shown here:

```
('std=', 0.22390046079419465)
('y=', array([-0.03617864, -0.24779587, -0.17175758, -0.07237123, -0.15030091,
       -0.18118841, -0.36155805, -0.13719439,  0.0157449 , -0.13539236,
        0.00846964, -0.05233665, -0.05640252, -0.18031585, -0.25526014,
       -0.17721833, -0.08142896, -0.13402592,  0.00374025, -0.58408627,
       -0.17609145, -0.15373335, -0.35146788, -0.04982488, -0.09724399,
       -0.27940142, -0.17744838, -0.10056407,  0.00294057, -0.24376592,
       -0.02807728, -0.17468942, -0.21132712,  0.01173588, -0.30696174,
        0.0024149 ]))
('LPSD=', 0.045388122899450663)
```

From the output, the standard deviation is `0.22` while the LPSD value is `0.045`. For mutual fund managers, getting a positive alpha is quite important. Thus, alpha or Jensen's alpha is a performance measure. Jensen's alpha is defined as the difference between the realized returns and the expected returns. It has the following form:

$$\alpha_p = \bar{R}_p - \bar{R}_{predicted} = \bar{R}_p - [\bar{R}_f + \hat{\beta}_p(\bar{R}_m - \bar{R}_f)] \qquad \dots (16)$$

How to merge different datasets

It is a common task to merge different datasets, such as merging index data with stock data and the like. Thus, it is quite important to understand the mechanism of merging different datasets. Here, the `pandas.merge()` function is discussed:

```
import pandas as pd
import scipy as s
x= pd.DataFrame({'key': ['K0', 'K1', 'K2', 'K3'],
                 'A': ['A0', 'A1', 'A2', 'A3'],
                 'B': ['B0', 'B1', 'B2', 'B3']})
```

```
y = pd.DataFrame({'key': ['K0', 'K1', 'K2', 'K6'],
                  'C': ['C0', 'C1', 'C2', 'C3'],
                  'D': ['D0', 'D1', 'D2', 'D3']})
```

The sizes of both x and y are 4 by 3, that is, four rows and three columns; see the following code:

```
print(sp.shape(x))
print(x)
```

The output is shown here:

```
(4, 3)
    A   B  key
0  A0  B0   K0
1  A1  B1   K1
2  A2  B2   K2
3  A3  B3   K3
```

```
print(sp.shape(y))
print(y)
```

```
(4, 3)
    C   D  key
0  C0  D0   K0
1  C1  D1   K1
2  C2  D2   K2
3  C3  D3   K6
```

Assume that we intend to merge them based on the variable called key, a common variable shared by both datasets. Since the common values of this variable are K0, K1 and K2. The final result should have three rows and five columns since K3 and K6 are not the common values by the two datasets; see the result shown here:

```
result = pd.merge(x,y, on='key')
print(result)
```

The output is shown here:

```
    A   B  key   C   D
0  A0  B0   K0  C0  D0
1  A1  B1   K1  C1  D1
2  A2  B2   K2  C2  D2
```

Since `key` is shared by both datasets, we could simply ignore it; see the following code. In other words, `result` and `result2` are the same:

```
result2 = pd.merge(x,y)
print(result2)
```

The complete meaning of the `pandas.merge()` function is given here:

```
pd.merge(left, right, how='inner', on=None, left_on=None, right_on =
None,left_index=False, right_index=False, sort=True,suffixes=('_x',
'_y'), copy=True, indicator=False)
```

For the first two input variables, `left` is for the first input dataset while `right` is the second input dataset. For the `how=` condition, we have the following four possible scenarios:

how='inner'	Meaning	Description
Inner	INNER JOIN	Use intersection of keys from both frames
Outer	FULL OUTER JOIN	Use union of keys from both frames
Left	LEFT OUTER JOIN	Use keys from left frame only
Right	RIGHT OUTER JOIN	Use keys from right frame only

Table 7.1 Meanings of the four join conditions: inner, outer, left, and right

The format of an inner join demands both datasets have the same items. An analogy is students from a family with both parents. The left join is based on the left dataset. In other words, our benchmark is the first dataset (`left`). An analogy is choosing students from families with a mum. The right is the opposite of the left, that is, the benchmark is the second dataset (`right`). The outer is the full dataset which contain both datasets, the same as students from all families: with both parents, with mum only, and with dad only.

In the following example, the first dataset has 4 years of data. Those values are entered with no specific meanings. Readers could use their own values. Our common variable is YEAR. For the first dataset, we have 4 years of data: 2010, 2011, 2012, and 2013. For the second dataset, we have 2011, 2013, 2014, and 2015. Obviously, only 2 years overlap. In total, we have 6 years of data:

```
import pandas as pd
import scipy as sp
x= pd.DataFrame({'YEAR': [2010,2011, 2012, 2013],
'IBM': [0.2, -0.3, 0.13, -0.2],
'WMT': [0.1, 0, 0.05, 0.23]})
y = pd.DataFrame({'YEAR': [2011,2013,2014, 2015],
'C': [0.12, 0.23, 0.11, -0.1],
```

```
              'SP500': [0.1,0.17, -0.05, 0.13]})

print(pd.merge(x,y, on='YEAR'))
print(pd.merge(x,y, on='YEAR',how='outer'))
print(pd.merge(x,y, on='YEAR',how='left'))
print(pd.merge(x,y, on='YEAR',how='right'))
```

The four outputs are shown here:

```
     IBM   WMT  YEAR     C  SP500
0  -0.3  0.00  2011  0.12   0.10
1  -0.2  0.23  2013  0.23   0.17
     IBM   WMT  YEAR     C  SP500
0   0.20  0.10  2010   NaN    NaN
1  -0.30  0.00  2011  0.12   0.10
2   0.13  0.05  2012   NaN    NaN
3  -0.20  0.23  2013  0.23   0.17
4    NaN   NaN  2014  0.11  -0.05
5    NaN   NaN  2015 -0.10   0.13
     IBM   WMT  YEAR     C  SP500
0   0.20  0.10  2010   NaN    NaN
1  -0.30  0.00  2011  0.12   0.10
2   0.13  0.05  2012   NaN    NaN
3  -0.20  0.23  2013  0.23   0.17
     IBM   WMT  YEAR     C  SP500
0  -0.3  0.00  2011  0.12   0.10
1  -0.2  0.23  2013  0.23   0.17
2   NaN   NaN  2014  0.11  -0.05
3   NaN   NaN  2015 -0.10   0.13
```

When the common variable has different names in those two datasets, we should specify their names by using `left_on='left_name'` and `right_on='another_name'`; see the following code:

```
import pandas as pd
import scipy as sp
x= pd.DataFrame({'YEAR': [2010,2011, 2012, 2013],
               'IBM': [0.2, -0.3, 0.13, -0.2],
               'WMT': [0.1, 0, 0.05, 0.23]})
y = pd.DataFrame({'date': [2011,2013,2014, 2015],
               'C': [0.12, 0.23, 0.11, -0.1],
               'SP500': [0.1,0.17, -0.05, 0.13]})
print(pd.merge(x,y, left_on='YEAR',right_on='date'))
```

If we intend to merge based on the index (row numbers), we specify that `left_index='True'`, and `right_index='True'`; see the following code. In a sense, since both datasets have four rows, we simply put them together, row by row. The true reason is that for those two datasets, there is no specific index. For a comparison, the `ffMonthly.pkl` data has the date as its index:

```
import pandas as pd
import scipy as sp
x= pd.DataFrame({'YEAR': [2010,2011, 2012, 2013],
                 'IBM': [0.2, -0.3, 0.13, -0.2],
                 'WMT': [0.1, 0, 0.05, 0.23]})
y = pd.DataFrame({'date': [2011,2013,2014, 2015],
                  'C': [0.12, 0.23, 0.11, -0.1],
                  'SP500': [0.1,0.17, -0.05, 0.13]})
print(pd.merge(x,y, right_index=True,left_index=True))
```

The output is shown here. Again, we simply illustrate the outcome without considering the economic meaning by merging different years' data together:

```
    IBM   WMT  YEAR     C  SP500  date
0  0.20  0.10  2010  0.12   0.10  2011
1 -0.30  0.00  2011  0.23   0.17  2013
2  0.13  0.05  2012  0.11  -0.05  2014
3 -0.20  0.23  2013 -0.10   0.13  2015
```

Here is another example of merging on index where `date` is used as the index for both datasets:

```
import pandas as pd
ff=pd.read_pickle("c:/temp/ffMonthly.pkl")
print(ff.head(2))
mom=pd.read_pickle("c:/temp/ffMomMonthly.pkl")
print(mom.head(3))
x=pd.merge(ff,mom,left_index=True,right_index=True)
print(x.head(2))
```

Both datasets are available, for example, `http://canisius.edu/~yany/python/ffMonthly.pkl`. The output is shown here:

```
             MKT_RF     SMB      HML      Rf
1926-07-01   0.0296  -0.023  -0.0287   0.0022
1926-08-01   0.0264  -0.014   0.0419   0.0025
                MOM
1927-01-01   0.0044
1927-02-01  -0.0201
1927-03-01   0.0359
             MKT_RF     SMB      HML      Rf     MOM
1927-01-01  -0.0006  -0.0056   0.0483  0.0025  0.0044
1927-02-01   0.0418  -0.0010   0.0317  0.0026 -0.0201
```

Sometimes, we need to merge two datasets based on two keys, such as stock `ID` and `date`; see the format here:

```
result = pd.merge(left, right, how='left', on=['key1', 'key2'])
```

Let's use the following hypothetical example by typing some values:

```
import pandas as pd
x= pd.DataFrame({'ID': ['IBM', 'IBM', 'WMT', 'WMT'],
'date': [2010, 2011, 2010, 2011],
'SharesOut': [100, 40, 60, 90],
'Asset': [20, 30, 10, 30]})

y = pd.DataFrame({'ID': ['IBM', 'IBM', 'C', 'WMT'],
'date': [2010, 2014, 2010, 2010],
'Ret': [0.1, 0.2, -0.1,0.2],
'ROA': [0.04,-0.02,0.03,0.1]})

z= pd.merge(x,y, on=['ID', 'date'])
```

For the first dataset, we have shares outstanding data for two stocks over the years `2010` and `2011`. The second dataset has data for annual returns and ROA for three stocks over 2 years (`2010` and `2014`). Our objective is to merge those two datasets by stock `ID` and `date` (year). The output is shown here:

```
   Asset   ID  SharesOut  date
0     20  IBM        100  2010
1     30  IBM         40  2011
2     10  WMT         60  2010
3     30  WMT         90  2011
    ID   ROA  Ret  date
0  IBM  0.04  0.1  2010
1  IBM -0.02  0.2  2014
2    C  0.03 -0.1  2010
3  WMT  0.10  0.2  2010
   Asset   ID  SharesOut  date   ROA  Ret
0     20  IBM        100  2010  0.04  0.1
1     10  WMT         60  2010  0.10  0.2
```

After understanding how to run a multifactor regression and how to merge different datasets, readers will be able to add their own factor or factors. One issue is that some factors might have a different frequency, such as quarterly GDP instead of monthly ones. For those cases, we could use various ways to fill in those missing values; see the following example:

```
import pandas as pd
GDP=pd.read_pickle("c:/temp/usGDPquarterly.pkl")
ff=pd.read_pickle("c:/temp/ffMonthly.pkl")
final=pd.merge(ff,GDP,left_index=True,right_index=True,how='left')
tt=final['AdjustedGDPannualBillion']
GDP2=pd.Series(tt).interpolate()
final['GDP2']=GDP2

print(GDP.head())
print(ff.head())
print(final.tail(10))
```

The output is shown here:

```
            AdjustedGDPannualBillion
1947-01-01                     243.1
1947-04-01                     246.3
1947-07-01                     250.1
1947-10-01                     260.3
1948-01-01                     266.2
            MKT_RF      SMB      HML      Rf
1926-07-01  0.0296  -0.0230  -0.0287  0.0022
1926-08-01  0.0264  -0.0140   0.0419  0.0025
1926-09-01  0.0036  -0.0132   0.0001  0.0023
1926-10-01 -0.0324   0.0004   0.0051  0.0032
1926-11-01  0.0253  -0.0020  -0.0035  0.0031
            MKT_RF      SMB      HML      Rf  AdjustedGDPannualBillion  \
2016-02-01 -0.0007   0.0083  -0.0048  0.0002                       NaN
2016-03-01  0.0696   0.0086   0.0111  0.0002                       NaN
2016-04-01  0.0092   0.0068   0.0325  0.0001                   18450.1
2016-05-01  0.0178  -0.0027  -0.0179  0.0001                       NaN
2016-06-01 -0.0005   0.0061  -0.0149  0.0002                       NaN
2016-07-01  0.0395   0.0290  -0.0098  0.0002                   18675.3
2016-08-01  0.0050   0.0094   0.0318  0.0002                       NaN
2016-09-01  0.0025   0.0200  -0.0134  0.0002                       NaN
2016-10-01 -0.0202  -0.0440   0.0415  0.0002                       NaN
2016-11-01  0.0486   0.0569   0.0844  0.0001                       NaN

                    GDP2
2016-02-01  18337.766667
2016-03-01  18393.933333
2016-04-01  18450.100000
2016-05-01  18525.166667
2016-06-01  18600.233333
2016-07-01  18675.300000
2016-08-01  18675.300000
2016-09-01  18675.300000
2016-10-01  18675.300000
2016-11-01  18675.300000
```

Readers should compare those two GDP time series to the impact.

Appendix A – list of related Python datasets

The prefix for these datasets is `http://canisius.edu/~yany/python/`. For example, for `ffMonthly.pkl`, we would have `http://canisius.edu/~yany/python/ffMonthly.pkl`:

Filename	Description
ibm3factor.pkl	A simple dataset for the FF three-factor model for IBM
ffMonthly.pkl	Fama-French monthly three factors
ffMomMonthly.pkl	Monthly momentum factor
ffcMonthly.pkl	Fama-French-Carhart monthly four factors
ffMonthly5.pkl	Fama-French monthly five factors
yanMonthly.pkl	A monthly dataset generated by the author
ffDaily.pkl	Fama-French-Carhart daily four factors
ffcDaily.pkl	Fama-French daily five factors
ffDaily5.pkl	Fama-French monthly four factors
usGDPquarterly.pkl	Quarterly US GDP data
usDebt.pkl	US national debt level
usCPImonthly.pkl	Consumer Price Index (CPI) data
tradingDaysMonthly.pkl	Trading days for monthly data
tradingDaysDaily.pkl	Trading days for daily data
businessCycleIndicator.pkl	A business cycle indicator
businessCycleIndicator2.pkl	Another business cycle indicator
uniqueWordsBible.pkl	All unique words from the Bible

One example of the code is shown here:

```
import pandas as pd
x=pd.read_pickle("c:/temp/ffMonthly.pkl")
print(x.head())
print(x.tail())
```

The output is shown here:

```
            MKT_RF     SMB     HML      Rf
1926-07-01  0.0296 -0.0230 -0.0287  0.0022
1926-08-01  0.0264 -0.0140  0.0419  0.0025
1926-09-01  0.0036 -0.0132  0.0001  0.0023
1926-10-01 -0.0324  0.0004  0.0051  0.0032
1926-11-01  0.0253 -0.0020 -0.0035  0.0031
            MKT_RF     SMB     HML      Rf
2016-07-01  0.0395  0.0290 -0.0098  0.0002
2016-08-01  0.0050  0.0094  0.0318  0.0002
2016-09-01  0.0025  0.0200 -0.0134  0.0002
2016-10-01 -0.0202 -0.0440  0.0415  0.0002
2016-11-01  0.0486  0.0569  0.0844  0.0001
```

Appendix B – Python program to generate ffMonthly.pkl

The following program is used to generate the dataset called `ffMonthly.pkl`:

```python
import scipy as sp
import numpy as np
import pandas as pd
file=open("c:/temp/ffMonthly.txt","r")
data=file.readlines()
f=[]
index=[]
for i in range(4,sp.size(data)):
print(data[i].split())
t=data[i].split()
index.append(pd.to_datetime(t[0]+'01', format='%Y%m%d').date())
#index.append(int(t[0]))
for j in range(1,5):
k=float(t[j])
f.append(k/100)
n=len(f)
f1=np.reshape(f, [n/4,4])
ff=pd.DataFrame(f1,index=index,columns=['MKT_RF','SMB','HML','Rf'])
ff.to_pickle("c:/temp/ffMonthly.pkl")
```

The first and last several lines are shown here:

```
In [179]: ff.head()
Out[179]:
            MKT_RF      SMB      HML      Rf
1926-07-01   0.0296  -0.0230  -0.0287   0.0022
1926-08-01   0.0264  -0.0140   0.0419   0.0025
1926-09-01   0.0036  -0.0132   0.0001   0.0023
1926-10-01  -0.0324   0.0004   0.0051   0.0032
1926-11-01   0.0253  -0.0020  -0.0035   0.0031

In [180]: ff.tail()
Out[180]:
            MKT_RF      SMB      HML      Rf
2016-07-01   0.0395   0.0290  -0.0098   0.0002
2016-08-01   0.0050   0.0094   0.0318   0.0002
2016-09-01   0.0025   0.0200  -0.0134   0.0002
2016-10-01  -0.0202  -0.0440   0.0415   0.0002
2016-11-01   0.0486   0.0569   0.0844   0.0001
```

Appendix C – Python program for Sharpe ratio

```
def sharpeRatio(ticker,begdate=(2012,1,1),enddate=(2016,12,31)):
    Objective: estimate Sharpe ratio for stock
         ticker   : stock symbol
         begdate  : beginning date
         enddate  : ending date

    Example #1: sharpeRatio("ibm")
                  0.0068655583807256159

    Example #2: date1=(1990,1,1)
                date2=(2015,12,23)
                sharpeRatio("ibm",date1,date2)
                0.027831010497755326

    import scipy as sp
    from matplotlib.finance import quotes_historical_yahoo_ochl as
getData
    p = getData(ticker,begdate, enddate,asobject=True,adjusted=True)
    ret=p.aclose[1:]/p.aclose[:-1]-1
    return sp.mean(ret)/sp.std(ret)
```

Appendix D – data case #4 – which model is the best, CAPM, FF3, FFC4, or FF5, or others?

Currently, we have many asset pricing models. Among them, the most important ones are CAPM, Fama-French three-factor model, Fama-French-Carhart four-factor model, or Fama-French five-factor model. The objectives of this data case include the following:

- Becoming familiar with the method to download data
- Understanding the T-value, F-values, and adjusted R2
- Writing various Python programs to conduct the test

Definitions of those four models CAPM:

$$E(R_i) = R_f + \beta_i(E(R_{mkt}) - R_t) \qquad \dots (1)$$

Fama-French three-factor model:

$$R_i = R_f + \beta_{mkt}(R_{mkt} - R_f) + \beta_{SMB} * SMB + \beta_{HML} * HML \qquad \dots (2)$$

Fama-French-Carhart four-factor model:

$$R_i = R_f + \beta_{mkt}(R_{mkt} - R_f) + \beta_{SMB} * SMB + \beta_{HML} * HML + \beta_{MOM}MOM \qquad \dots (3)$$

Fama-French five-factor model:

$$R_i = R_f + \beta_{mkt}(R_{mkt} - R_f) + \beta_{SMB}SMB + \beta_{HML}HML + \beta_{MOM}RMW + \beta_{MOM}CMA$$
$$\dots (4)$$

In the preceding equation, RMV is the difference between the returns on diversified portfolio of stocks with robust and weak profitability, and CMA is the difference between the returns of diversified portfolios of the stocks of low and high investment firms, which Fama and French call conservative and aggressive. If the exposures to the five factors capture all variation in expected returns, the intercept for all securities and portfolio should be zero. The source of the data is as follows:

- http://mba.tuck.dartmouth.edu/pages/faculty/ken.french/data_library.html

- `http://canisius.edu/~yany/python/ffMonthly.pkl`

`ffMonthly.pkl`	Fama-French monthly three factors
`ffcMonthly.pkl`	Fama-French-Carhart monthly four factors
`ffMonthly5.pkl`	Fama-French monthly five factors
`yanMonthly.pkl`	Fama-French daily three factors
`yanMonthly.pkl`	A monthly dataset generated by the author
`usGDPannual.pkl`	US GDP annual
`usCPImonthly.pkl`	Consumer Price Index (CPI) monthly

Several questions:

- Which criterion?
- Is the performance time-period independent?
- In-sample estimation versus out-sample prediction

References

Please refer to the following articles:

- *Carhart, Mark M., 1997, On Persistence in Mutual Fund Performance, Journal of Finance 52, 57-82*

- *Fama, Eugene and Kenneth R. French, 2015, A five-factor asset pricing model, Journal of Financial Economics 116, 1, 1-22*

- *Fama, Eugene and Kenneth R. French, 1993, Common risk factors in the returns on stocks and bonds, Journal of Financial Economics 33, 3056*

- *Fama, Eugene and Kenneth R. French, 1992, The cross-section of expected stock returns, Journal of Finance 47, 427-465*

- *Jegadeesh, N., & Titman, S., 1993, Returns to buying winners and selling losers: Implications for stock market efficiency, Journal of Finance 48(1): 65–91*

- *Sharpe, W. F., 1966, Mutual Fund Performance, Journal of Business 39 (S1), 119–138*

- *Sharpe, William F., 1994, The Sharpe Ratio, The Journal of Portfolio Management 21 (1), 49–58*

- *Sortino, F.A., Price, L.N.,1994, Performance measurement in a downside risk framework, Journal of Investing 3, 50–8*

- *Treynor, Jack L., 1965, How to Rate Management of Investment Funds, Harvard Business Review 43, pp. 63–75*

Exercises

1. What are the differences between the CAPM and Fama-French 3three-factor models?

2. What are the meanings of SMB and HML in the Fama-French three-factor model?

3. What is the meaning of MOM in the Fama-French-Carhart four-factor model?

4. What are the meanings of RMW and CMA in the Fama-French five-factor model?

5. What is the difference between R2 and adjusted R2 when running multifactor models?

6. How many OLS functions we could use? Please offer at least two functions from different Python modules.

7. Which module contains the function called `rolling_kurt`? How can you use the function?

8. Based on daily data downloaded from Yahoo! Finance, find the results for IBM based on the last 5 years by running both the CAPM and Fama-French three-factor models. Which model is better?

9. What is the momentum factor? How do you run a Fama-French-Carhart four-factor model? Please use a few tickers as an illustration.

10. What is the definition of the Fama-French 5 factor model? How do you run it for Citi Group? The ticker of the financial institution is C.

11. For the following stock tickers, IBM, DELL, WMT, ^GSPC, C, A, AA, and MOFT, run regression based on CAPM, FF3, FFC4, and FF5. Which one is the best? Discuss your benchmark or criteria to compare.

12. Write a Python program to estimate rolling beta on a yearly basis based on the Fama-French three-factor model. Use it to show the annual beta for IBM from 1962 to 2016.

13. Update the following Python datasets. The original datasets can be downloaded from the author's web page. For example, in order to download the first dataset, called `ffMonthly.pkl`, go to `http://canisius.edu/~yany/python/ffMonthly.pkl`:

`ffMonthly.pkl`	Fama-French monthly three factors
`ffcMonthly.pkl`	Fama-French-Carhart monthly four factors
`ffMonthly5.pkl`	Fama-French monthly five factors

14. Data source: `http://mba.tuck.dartmouth.edu/pages/faculty/ken. french/data_library.html`.

15. Update the following Python datasets:

`usGDPannual.pkl`	US GDP annual
`usCPImonthly.pkl`	CPI (Consumer price index) monthly

16. The Fama-French SMH could be viewed as a portfolio. Download both daily and monthly SMB. Then estimate the total returns over 10-, 20-, and 30-year periods. Compare the differences between each pair of total returns. For example, compare total returns from 1980 to 2000 based on both daily SML and monthly SML. Why they are different?

17. Do the same thing for the market return and compare with SML. Why is the difference for market much smaller than the difference for SML portfolio?

18. Do the same thing for HML and explain.

19. How many ways are there to merge two datasets?

20. If we have two datasets, sorted by ticker and date, how do you merge them?

21. Write a function to estimate the Treynor ratio. The format of the function is `treynorRatio(ticker, rf, begdate, enddate)`, where ticker is a stock symbol, such as IBM, `rf` is the risk-free rate, `begdate` is the beginning date, and `enddate` is the end date.

22. Randomly choose 10 stocks, such as stocks with tickers of IBM, C, WMT, MSFT, and so on, and run CAPM to test whether their intercepts are zero or not.

23. Write a Python program to calculate the Sortino ratio. The format of the program will be `sortinoRatio(ticker,rf,begdate,enddate)`.

24. How can you replicate the Jagadeesh and Tidman (1993) momentum strategy using Python and CRSP data? (Assume that your school has a CRSP subscription.)

25. When using the `statsodels.api.ols()` function to run a linear regression, what is the consequence when the following line is omitted?

```
x = sm.add_constant(x)
```

26. Debug the following program used to estimate LPSD:

```
import scipy as sp
import numpy as np
mean=0.08;Rf=0.01;std=0.12;n=100
x=sp.random.normal(loc=mean,scale=std,size=n)
y=x[x-Rf<0]
m=len(y)
for i in sp.arange(m):
    total=0.0
    total+=(y[i]-Rf)**2
LPSD=total/(m-1)
```

Summary

In this chapter, we have discussed multiple-factor linear models. Those models could be viewed as a simple extension of the CAPM, a single one-factor linear model. These multifactor models include the Fama-French three-factor, Fama-French-Carhart four-factor, and Fama-French five-factor models.

In the next chapter, we will discuss various properties for time series. In finance and economics, a huge amount of our data is in the format of time series, such as stock price and **Gross Domestic Product (GDP)**, or stocks' monthly or daily historical prices. For time series, there exist many issues, such as how to estimate returns from historical price data, how to merge datasets with the same or different frequencies, seasonality, and detection of auto-correlation. Understanding those properties is vitally important for our knowledge development.

8
Time-Series Analysis

In finance and economics, a huge amount of our data is in the format of time-series, such as stock prices and **Gross Domestic Products** (**GDP**). From *Chapter 4*, *Sources of Data*, it is shown that from Yahoo!Finance, we could download daily, weekly, and monthly historical price time-series. From **Federal Reserve Bank's Economics Data Library** (**FRED**), we could retrieve many historical time-series such as GDP. For time-series, there exist many issues, such as how to estimate returns from historical price data, how to merge datasets with the same or different frequencies, seasonality, and detect auto-correlation. Understanding those properties is vitally important for our knowledge development.

In this chapter, the following topics will be covered:

- Introduction to time-series analysis
- Design a good date variable, and merging different datasets by date
- Normal distribution and normality test
- Term structure of interest rates, 52-week high, and low trading strategy
- Return estimation and converting daily returns to monthly or annual returns
- T-test, F-test, and Durbin-Watson test for autocorrelation
- Fama-MacBeth regression
- Roll (1984) spread, Amihud's (2002) illiquidity, and Pastor and Stambaugh's (2003) liquidity measure
- January effect and weekday effect
- Retrieving high-frequency data from Google Finance and Prof. Hasbrouck's TORQ database (Trade, Order, Report, and Quotation)
- Introduction to CRSP (Center for Research in Security Prices) database

Introduction to time-series analysis

Most finance data is in the format of time-series, see the following several examples. The first one shows how to download historical, daily stock price data from Yahoo!Finance for a given ticker's beginning and ending dates:

```
from matplotlib.finance import quotes_historical_yahoo_ochl as getData
x = getData("IBM",(2016,1,1),(2016,1,21),asobject=True, adjusted=True)
print(x[0:4])
```

The output is shown here:

```
[ (datetime.date(2016, 1, 4), 2016, 1, 4, 735967.0, 130.62253911309833, 130.959683,
130.97895271354574, 129.31245964439717, 5229400.0, 130.959683)
 (datetime.date(2016, 1, 5), 2016, 1, 5, 735968.0, 131.73994804831432, 130.863362,
131.86517999356315, 129.9000689840247, 3924800.0, 130.863362)
 (datetime.date(2016, 1, 6), 2016, 1, 6, 735969.0, 129.44732026068075, 130.208315,
130.60326898959215, 128.71520793584997, 4310900.0, 130.208315)
 (datetime.date(2016, 1, 7), 2016, 1, 7, 735970.0, 128.79227327983133, 127.983111,
130.06382680331637, 127.56888729699934, 7025800.0, 127.983111)]
```

The type of the data is `numpy.recarray` as the `type(x)` would show. The second example prints the first several observations from two datasets called `ffMonthly.pkl` and `usGDPquarterly.pkl`, and both are available from the author's website, such as `http://canisius.edu/~yany/python/ffMonthly.pkl`:

```
import pandas as pd
GDP=pd.read_pickle("c:/temp/usGDPquarterly.pkl")
ff=pd.read_pickle("c:/temp/ffMonthly.pkl")
print(GDP.head())
print(ff.head())
```

The related output is shown here:

```
            AdjustedGDPannualBillion
1947-01-01              243.1
1947-04-01              246.3
1947-07-01              250.1
1947-10-01              260.3
1948-01-01              266.2
        DATE   MKT_RF     SMB     HML      RF
1  1926-07-01   0.0296  -0.023 -0.0287  0.0022
2  1926-08-01   0.0264  -0.014  0.0419  0.0025
3  1926-09-01   0.0036 -0.0132  0.0001  0.0023
4  1926-10-01  -0.0324  0.0004  0.0051  0.0032
5  1926-11-01   0.0253  -0.002 -0.0035  0.0031
```

There is one end of chapter problem which is designed to *merge* discrete data with the daily data. The following program retrieves the daily price data from Google finance:

```
import pandas_datareader.data as web
import datetime
ticker='MSFT'
begdate = datetime.datetime(2012, 1, 2)
enddate = datetime.datetime(2017, 1, 10)
a = web.DataReader(ticker, 'google',begdate,enddate)
print(a.head(3))
print(a.tail(2))
```

The corresponding output is shown here:

	Open	High	Low	Close	Volume
Date					
2012-01-03	26.55	26.96	26.39	26.76	64735391
2012-01-04	26.82	27.47	26.78	27.40	80519402
2012-01-05	27.38	27.73	27.29	27.68	56082205
	Open	High	Low	Close	Volume
Date					
2017-01-09	62.76	63.08	62.54	62.64	20382730
2017-01-10	62.73	63.07	62.28	62.62	18593004

To get the current stock quote, we have the following program. Note that the output is for January 21, 2017:

```
import pandas_datareader.data as web
ticker='AMZN'
print(web.get_quote_yahoo(ticker))
```

	PE	change_pct	last	short_ratio	time
AMZN	189.78	-0.23%	1007.73	2.09	9:59am

By using the next Python program, the **Gross Domestic Product (GDP)** data from January 1947 to June 2016 would be retrieved:

```
import pandas_datareader.data as web
import datetime
begdate = datetime.datetime(1900, 1, 1)
enddate = datetime.datetime(2017, 1, 27)
x= web.DataReader("GDP", "fred", begdate,enddate)
print(x.head(2))
print(x.tail(3))
```

The output is shown here:

```
                    GDP
DATE
1947-01-01   243.1
1947-04-01   246.3
                    GDP
DATE
2016-07-01   18675.3
2016-10-01   18869.4
2017-01-01   19027.6
```

Merging datasets based on a date variable

To make our time-series more manageable, it is a great idea to generate a date variable. When talking about such a variable, readers could think about year (YYYY), year and month (YYYYMM) or year, month, and day (YYYYMMDD). For just the year, month, and day combination, we could have many forms. Using January 20, 2017 as an example, we could have 2017-1-20, 1/20/2017, 20Jan2017, 20-1-2017, and the like. In a sense, a true date variable, in our mind, could be easily manipulated. Usually, the true date variable takes a form of *year-month-day* or other forms of its variants. Assume the date variable has a value of 2000-12-31. After adding one day to its value, the result should be 2001-1-1.

Using pandas.date_range() to generate one dimensional time-series

We could easily use the pandas.date_range() function to generate our time-series; refer to the following example:

```python
import pandas as pd
import scipy as sp
sp.random.seed(1257)
mean=0.10
std=0.2
ddate = pd.date_range('1/1/2016', periods=252)
n=len(ddate)
rets=sp.random.normal(mean,std,n)
data = pd.DataFrame(rets, index=ddate,columns=['RET'])
print(data.head())
```

In the preceding program, since the `sp.random.seed()` function is applied, readers should get the same output if he/she uses the same seed. The output is shown here:

```
                RET
2016-01-01  0.431031
2016-01-02  0.279193
2016-01-03  0.002549
2016-01-04  0.109546
2016-01-05  0.068252
```

To better facilitate working with time-series data, in the following program, the `pandas.read_csv()` function is used, see the following code:

```
import pandas as pd
url='http://canisius.edu/~yany/data/ibm.csv'
x=pd.read_csv(url,index_
col=0,parse_dates=True)
print(x.head())
```

The output is shown here:

```
                Open        High        Low         Close     Volume
Date
2016-11-03  152.509995  153.740005  151.800003  152.369995  2843600
2016-11-02  152.479996  153.350006  151.669998  151.949997  3074400
2016-11-01  153.500000  153.910004  151.740005  152.789993  3191900
2016-10-31  152.759995  154.330002  152.759995  153.690002  3553200
2016-10-28  154.050003  154.440002  152.179993  152.610001  3654500

                Adj.Close
Date
2016-11-03  152.369995
2016-11-02  151.949997
2016-11-01  152.789993
2016-10-31  153.690002
2016-10-28  152.610001
```

To see the format of date, we have the following code:

```
>>>x[0:1]
```

```
                Open        High        Low         Close     Volume  \
Date
2016-11-03  152.509995  153.740005  151.800003  152.369995  2843600

                Adj.Close
Date
2016-11-03  152.369995
```

```
>>>x[0:1].index
```

```
In [17]: x[0:1].index
Out[17]: DatetimeIndex(['2016-11-03'], dtype='datetime64[ns]', name=u'Date', freq=None)
```

In the following program, the `matplotlib.finance.quotes_historical_yahoo_ochl()` function is applied:

```
from matplotlib.finance import quotes_historical_yahoo_ochl as getData
x = getData("IBM",(2016,1,1),(2016,1,21),asobject=True, adjusted=True)
print(x[0:4])
```

The output is shown here:

```
[ (datetime.date(2016, 1, 4), 2016, 1, 4, 735967.0, 130.62253911309833, 130.959683,
130.97895271354574, 129.31245964439717, 5229400.0, 130.959683)
 (datetime.date(2016, 1, 5), 2016, 1, 5, 735968.0, 131.73994804831432, 130.863362,
131.86517999356315, 129.9000689840247, 3924800.0, 130.863362)
 (datetime.date(2016, 1, 6), 2016, 1, 6, 735969.0, 129.44732026068075, 130.208315,
130.60326898959215, 128.71520793584997, 4310900.0, 130.208315)
 (datetime.date(2016, 1, 7), 2016, 1, 7, 735970.0, 128.79227327983133, 127.983111,
130.06382680331637, 127.56888729699934, 7025800.0, 127.983111)]
```

Note that the index is in a form of date format, see the following code. For the meaning of `.strftime("%Y")`, see *Table 8.2*:

```
>>>x[0][0]
   datetime.date(2016, 1, 4)
>>>x[0][0].strftime("%Y")
 '2016'
```

Here are several ways to define a `date` variable:

Function	Description	Examples
pandas.date_range	1. For a range of dates	pd.date_range('1/1/2017', periods=252)
datetime.date	2. One day	>>>from datetime import datetime >>>datetime.date(2017,1,20)
datetime.date.today()	3. Get today's value	>>>datetime.date.today() datetime.date(2017, 1, 26)
datetime.now()	4. Get the current time	>>>from datetime import datetime >>>datetime.now() datetime.datetime(2017, 1, 26, 8, 58, 6, 420000)

Function	Description	Examples

`relativedelta()`	5. Add certain numbers of days, months, or years to a date variable	`>>>from datetime import datetime`
		`>>>today=datetime.today().date()`
		`>>>print(today)`
		`2017-01-26`
		`>>>print(today+relativedelta(days=31))`
		`2017-02-26`

Table 8.1 A few ways to define a date variable

Retrieving the year, month, and day from a `date` variable is used quite frequently when dealing with time-series—see the following Python program by using the `strftime()` function. The corresponding output is in the following right panel. The format of those results of year, month, and day, is string:

```
import datetime
today=datetime.date.today()
year=today.strftime("%Y")
year2=today.strftime("%y")
month=today.strftime("%m")
day=today.strftime("%d")
print(year,month,day,year2)
('2017', '01', '24', '17')
```

The following table summarizes its usages. For more details, see the link at:
`http://strftime.org/`:

Function	Description	Examples
`.strftime("%Y")`	1. 4-digit year string	`a=datetime.date(2017,1,2)` `a.strftime("%Y")`
`.strftime("%y")`	2. 2-digit year string	`a.strftime("%y")`
`.strftime("%m")`	3. Month string	`a.strftime("%m")`
`.strftime("%d")`	4. Day string	`a.strftime("%d")`

Table 8.2 Retrieving year, month, and day

Return estimation

With price data, we could calculate returns. In addition, sometimes we have to convert daily returns to weekly or monthly, or convert monthly returns to quarterly or annual ones. Thus, understanding how to estimate returns and their conversion is vital. Assume that we have the following four prices:

```
>>>p=[1,1.1,0.9,1.05]
```

It is important to know how these prices are sorted. If the first price happened before the second price, then the first return should be *(1.1-1)/1=10%*. Next, we learn how to retrieve the first *n-1* and the last *n-1* records from an *n* record array. To list the first *n-1* price, we use p[:-1], while for the last three prices we use p[1:] as shown in the following code:

```
>>>print(p[:-1])
>>>print(p[1:])
[ 1.  1.1 0.9]
[ 1.1 0.9 1.05]
```

To estimate returns, we could use the following code:

```
>>>ret=(p[1:]-p[:-1])/p[:-1]
>>>print(ret )
[ 0.1 -0.18181818 0.16666667]
```

When given two prices of *x1* and *x2* and assume that *x2* is behind *x1*, we could use *ret=(x2-x1)/x1*. Alternatively, we could use *ret=x2/x1-1*. Thus, for the preceding example, we could use ret=p[1:]/p[:-1]-1. Obviously, this second method would avoid certain typing errors. On the other hand, if the prices are arranged in the reverse order, for example, the first one is the latest price and the last one is the oldest price, then we have to estimate returns in the following way:

```
>>>ret=p[:-1]/p[1:]-1
>>>print(ret )
[-0.09090909 0.22222222 -0.14285714]
>>>
```

As it is mentioned in *Chapter 7, Multifactor Models and Performance Measures* we could use .diff() and .shift() functions to estimate returns. See the following code:

```
import pandas as pd
import scipy as sp
p=[1,1.1,0.9,1.05]
a=pd.DataFrame({'Price':p})
a['Ret']=a['Price'].diff()/a['Price'].shift(1)
print(a)
```

The output is shown here:

```
Price        Ret
0    1.00          NaN
1    1.10    0.100000
2    0.90   -0.181818
3    1.05    0.166667
```

The following code shows how to download daily price data from Yahoo!Finance and estimate daily returns:

```
>>>from matplotlib.finance import quotes_historical_yahoo_ochl as
getData
>>>ticker='IBM'
>>>begdate=(2013,1,1)
>>>enddate=(2013,11,9)
>>>x =getData(ticker, begdate, enddate,asobject=True, adjusted=True)
>>>ret=x.aclose[1:]/x.aclose[:-1]-1
```

The first line uploads a function from `matplotlib.finance`. We define the beginning and ending dates using a `tuple` data type. The downloaded historical daily price data is assigned to x. To verify that our returns are correctly estimated, we can print a few prices to our screen. Then, we could manually verify one or two return values as shown in the following code:

```
>>>x.date[0:3]
array([datetime.date(2013, 1, 2), datetime.date(2013, 1, 3),
datetime.date(2013, 1, 4)], dtype=object)
>>>x.aclose[0:3]
array([ 192.61, 191.55, 190.3 ])
>>>ret[0:2]
array([-0.00550335, -0.00652571])
>>> (191.55-192.61)/192.61
-0.005503348735787354
>>>
```

Yes, the last result confirms that our first return is correctly estimated.

Converting daily returns to monthly ones

Sometimes, we need to convert daily returns to monthly or annual ones. Here is our procedure. First, we estimate the daily log returns. We then take a summation of all daily log returns within each month to find out the corresponding monthly log returns. The final step is to convert a log monthly return to a monthly percentage return. Assume that we have the price data of *p0, p1, p2, ..., p20*, where *p0* is the last trading price of the last month, *p1* is the first price of this month, and *p20* is the last price of this month. Thus, this month's percentage return is given as follows:

$$R_{monthly} = \frac{p_{20} - p_0}{p_0} \qquad \dots (1)$$

The monthly log return is defined as follows:

$$log\_return_{monthly} = \log\left(\frac{p_{20}}{p_0}\right) \qquad \dots (2)$$

The relationship between a monthly percentage and a log monthly return is given as follows:

$$R_{monthly} = \exp(log\_return) - 1 \qquad \dots (3)$$

The daily log return is defined similarly, as follows:

$$log\_return_i^{daily} = \log\left(\frac{p_i}{p_{i-1}}\right) \qquad \dots (4)$$

Let's look at the following summation of log returns:

$$log\_return_{monthly} = \log\left(\frac{p_{20}}{p_0}\right) = \sum_{i=1}^{20} log\_return_i^{daily} \dots (5)$$

Based on the previous procedure, the following Python program converts daily returns into monthly returns:

```
from matplotlib.finance import quotes_historical_yahoo_ochl as getData
import numpy as np
import pandas as pd
#
```

```
ticker='IBM'
begdate=(2013,1,1)
enddate=(2013,11,9)
#
x = getData(ticker, begdate, enddate,asobject=True, adjusted=True)
logret = np.log(x.aclose[1:]/x.aclose[:-1])
yyyymm=[]
d0=x.date
#
for i in range(0,np.size(logret)):
    yyyymm.append(''.join([d0[i].strftime("%Y"),d0[i].
strftime("%m")]))

y=pd.DataFrame(logret,yyyymm,columns=['retMonthly'])
retMonthly=y.groupby(y.index).sum()


print(retMonthly.head())
```

The output is shown here:

```
          retMonthly
201301      0.043989
201302     -0.006925
201303      0.045615
201304     -0.061911
201305      0.050305
```

Merging datasets by date

The following program merges the daily adjusted closing price of IBM with the
daily Fama-French 3-factor time-series. The ffMonthly.pkl is available at:
http://canisius.edu/~yany/python/ffDaily.pkl:

```
from matplotlib.finance import quotes_historical_yahoo_ochl as getData
import numpy as np
import pandas as pd
ticker='IBM'
begdate=(2016,1,2)
enddate=(2017,1,9)
x =getData(ticker, begdate, enddate,asobject=True, adjusted=True)
myName=ticker+'_adjClose'
x2=pd.DataFrame(x['aclose'],x.date,columns=[myName])
ff=pd.read_pickle('c:/temp/ffDaily.pkl')
final=pd.merge(x2,ff,left_index=True,right_index=True)
print(final.head())
```

The output is given as follows:

```
              IBM_adjClose  MKT_RF      SMB      HML    RF
2016-01-04     130.959683  -0.0159  -0.0083   0.0053   0.0
2016-01-05     130.863362   0.0012  -0.0021   0.0000   0.0
2016-01-06     130.208315  -0.0135  -0.0013   0.0001   0.0
2016-01-07     127.983111  -0.0244  -0.0028   0.0012   0.0
2016-01-08     126.798264  -0.0111  -0.0047  -0.0004   0.0
```

Understanding the interpolation technique

Interpolation is a technique used quite frequently in finance. In the following example, we have to replace two missing values, NaN, between 2 and 6. The pandas.interpolate() function, for a linear interpolation, is used to fill in the two missing values:

```
import pandas as pd
import numpy as np
nn=np.nan
x=pd.Series([1,2,nn,nn,6])
print(x.interpolate())
```

The output is shown here:

```
0    1.000000
1    2.000000
2    3.333333
3    4.666667
4    6.000000
dtype: float64
```

The preceding method is a linear interpolation. Actually, we could estimate a Δ and calculate those missing values manually:

$$\Delta = \frac{v_2 - v_1}{n} \qquad \dots (6)$$

Here, *v2(v1)* is the second (first) value and *n* is the number of intervals between those two values. For the preceding case, Δ is *(6-2)/3=1.33333*. Thus, the next value will be *v1+Δ=2+1.33333=3.33333*. This way, we could continually estimate all missing values. Note that if we have several periods with missing values, then the delta for each period has to be calculated manually to verify the methodology. From the Yahoo!Finance bond page at `http://finance.yahoo.com/bonds`, we could get the following information:

Maturity	Yield	Yesterday	Last week	Last month
3 Month	0.05	0.05	0.04	0.03
6 Month	0.08	0.07	0.07	0.06
2 Year	0.29	0.29	0.31	0.33
3 Year	0.57	0.54	0.59	0.61
5 Year	1.34	1.32	1.41	1.39
10 Year	2.7	2.66	2.75	2.66
30 Year	3.8	3.78	3.85	3.72

Table 8.3 Term structure interest rate

Based on the tabular data, we have the following code:

```
>>>import numpy as np
>>>import pandas as pd
>>>nn=np.nan
>>>x=pd.Series([0.29,0.57,nn,1.34,nn,nn,nn,nn,2.7])
>>>y=x.interpolate()
>>>print(y)
0 0.290
1 0.570
2 0.955
3 1.340
4 1.612
5 1.884
6 2.156
7 2.428
8 2.700
dtype: float64
>>>
```

Merging data with different frequencies

The following Python program merges two datasets: US **Gross Domestic Product (GDP)** data with a quarterly frequency and ffMonthly, http://canisius.edu/~yany/python/ffMonthly.pkl with a monthly frequency.

The interpolation methodology discussed previously is applied to the missing months in terms of GDP data. The ffMonthly dataset is assumed to be saved in the c:/temp/ directory:

```
import pandas as pd
import pandas_datareader.data as web
import datetime
begdate = datetime.datetime(1900, 1, 1)
enddate = datetime.datetime(2017, 1, 27)
GDP= web.DataReader("GDP", "fred", begdate,enddate)
ff=pd.read_pickle("c:/temp/ffMonthly.pkl")
final=pd.merge(ff,GDP,left_index=True,right_index=True,how='left')
tt=final['GDP']
GDP2=pd.Series(tt).interpolate()
final['GDP2']=GDP2
```

The outputs are shown here. Since there is no data for GDP before 1947 and the ffMonthly time-series starts from July 1926, the last several observations of the merged data are more informative:

```
print(final.head())
print(final.tail(10))
            MKT_RF     SMB      HML      RF      GDP     GDP2
1926-07-01  0.0296  -0.0230  -0.0287  0.0022   NaN      NaN
1926-08-01  0.0264  -0.0140   0.0419  0.0025   NaN      NaN
1926-09-01  0.0036  -0.0132   0.0001  0.0023   NaN      NaN
1926-10-01 -0.0324   0.0004   0.0051  0.0032   NaN      NaN
1926-11-01  0.0253  -0.0020  -0.0035  0.0031   NaN      NaN
            MKT_RF     SMB      HML       RF      GDP           GDP2
2016-02-01 -0.0007   0.0083  -0.0048  0.0002      NaN    18337.766667
2016-03-01  0.0696   0.0086   0.0111  0.0002      NaN    18393.933333
2016-04-01  0.0092   0.0068   0.0325  0.0001  18450.1    18450.100000
2016-05-01  0.0178  -0.0027  -0.0179  0.0001      NaN    18525.166667
2016-06-01 -0.0005   0.0061  -0.0149  0.0002      NaN    18600.233333
2016-07-01  0.0395   0.0290  -0.0098  0.0002  18675.3    18675.300000
2016-08-01  0.0050   0.0094   0.0318  0.0002      NaN    18675.300000
2016-09-01  0.0025   0.0200  -0.0134  0.0002      NaN    18675.300000
2016-10-01 -0.0202  -0.0440   0.0415  0.0002      NaN    18675.300000
2016-11-01  0.0486   0.0569   0.0844  0.0001      NaN    18675.300000
2016-07-01  0.0395   0.0290  -0.0098  0.0002  18675.3    18675.300000
2016-08-01  0.0050   0.0094   0.0318  0.0002      NaN    18675.300000
```

```
2016-09-01  0.0025  0.0200 -0.0134  0.0002     NaN  18675.300000
2016-10-01 -0.0202 -0.0440  0.0415  0.0002     NaN  18675.300000
2016-11-01  0.0486  0.0569  0.0844  0.0001     NaN  18675.300000
```

For the second example, we merge a business cycle indicator, called `businessCycle.pkl`, available at `http://canisius.edu/~yany/python/businessCycle.pkl`, with a monthly frequency and GDP (quarterly frequency). See the following code:

```python
import pandas as pd
import pandas_datareader.data as web
import datetime
import scipy as sp
import numpy as np
cycle=pd.read_pickle("c:/temp/businessCycle.pkl")
begdate = datetime.datetime(1947, 1, 1)
enddate = datetime.datetime(2017, 1, 27)
GDP= web.DataReader("GDP", "fred", begdate,enddate)
final=pd.merge(cycle,GDP,left_index=True,right_index=True,how='right')
```

We could print a few lines to see the results:

```
print(cycle.head())
print(GDP.head())
print(final.head())
            cycle
date
1926-10-01  1.000
1926-11-01  0.846
1926-12-01  0.692
1927-01-01  0.538
1927-02-01  0.385
1947-07-01  0.135   250.1
1947-10-01  0.297   260.3
1948-01-01  0.459   266.2
            GDP
DATE
1947-01-01  243.1
1947-04-01  246.3
1947-07-01  250.1
1947-10-01  260.3
1948-01-01  266.2
            cycle    GDP
DATE
1947-01-01 -0.189   243.1
1947-04-01 -0.027   246.3
```

Tests of normality

In finance, knowledge about normal distribution is very important for two reasons. First, stock returns are assumed to follow a normal distribution. Second, the error terms from a good econometric model should follow a normal distribution with a zero mean. However, in the real world, this might not be true for stocks. On the other hand, whether stocks or portfolios follow a normal distribution could be tested by various so-called normality tests. The Shapiro-Wilk test is one of them. For the first example, random numbers are drawn from a normal distribution. As a consequence, the test should confirm that those observations follow a normal distribution:

```
from scipy import stats
import scipy as sp
sp.random.seed(12345)
mean=0.1
std=0.2
n=5000
ret=sp.random.normal(loc=0,scale=std,size=n)
print 'W-test, and P-value'
print(stats.shapiro(ret))
W-test, and P-value
(0.9995986223220825, 0.4129064679145813)
```

Assume that our confidence level is 95%, that is, alpha=0.05. The first value of the result is the test statistic, and the second one is its corresponding P-value. Since the P-value is so big, much bigger than 0.05, we accept the null hypothesis that the returns follow a normal distribution. For the second example, random numbers are drawn from a uniform distribution:

```
from scipy import stats
import scipy as sp
sp.random.seed(12345)
n=5000
ret=sp.random.uniform(size=n)
print 'W-test, and P-value'
print(stats.shapiro(ret))
W-test, and P-value
(0.9537619352340698, 4.078975800593137e-37)
```

Since the P-value is close to zero, we reject the null hypothesis. In other words, those observations do not follow a normal distribution. The third example verifies whether IBM's returns follow a normal distribution. The last five year's daily data from Yahoo! Finance is used for the test. The null hypothesis is that IBM's daily returns are drawn from a normal distribution:

```
from scipy import stats
from matplotlib.finance import quotes_historical_yahoo_ochl as getData
```

```
import numpy as np

ticker='IBM'
begdate=(2012,1,1)
enddate=(2016,12,31)

p =getData(ticker, begdate, enddate,asobject=True, adjusted=True)
ret = (p.aclose[1:] - p.aclose[:-1])/p.aclose[1:]
print 'ticker=',ticker,'W-test, and P-value'
print(stats.shapiro(ret))
ticker= IBM W-test, and P-value
(0.9213278889656067, 4.387053202198418e-25)
```

Since this P-value is so close to zero, we reject the null hypothesis. In other words, we conclude that IBM's daily returns do not follow a normal distribution. For a normality test, we could also apply the Anderson-Darling test, which is a modification of the Kolmogorov-Smirnov test, to verify whether the observations follow a particular distribution. See the following code:

```
print( stats.anderson(ret) )
AndersonResult(statistic=12.613658863646833, critical_values=array([
0.574,  0.654,  0.785,  0.915,  1.089]), significance_level=array([
15. ,   10. ,    5. ,    2.5,    1. ]))
```

Here, we have three sets of values: the Anderson-Darling test statistic, a set of critical values, and a set of corresponding confidence levels, such as 15 percent, 10 percent, 5 percent, 2.5 percent, and 1 percent, as shown in the previous output. If we choose a 1 percent confidence level — the last value of the third set — the critical value is 1.089, the last value of the second set. Since our testing statistic is 12.61, which is much higher than the critical value of 1.089, we reject the null hypothesis. Thus, our Anderson-Darling test leads to the same conclusion as our Shapiro-Wilk test. One of the beauties of the `scipy.stats.anderson()` test is that we can test for other distributions. After applying the `help()` function, we would get the following list. The default distribution is for the normality test:

```
>>>from scipy import stats
>>>help(stats.anderson)
anderson(x, dist='norm')
Anderson-Darling test for data coming from a particular distribution
dist : {'norm','expon','logistic','gumbel','extreme1'}, optional the
type of distribution to test against.  The default is 'norm'  and
'extreme1' is a synonym for 'gumbel'
```

Estimating fat tails

One of the important properties of a normal distribution is that we could use mean and standard deviation, the first two moments, to fully define the whole distribution. For n returns of a security, its first four moments are defined in equation (1). The mean or average is defined as follows:

$$\bar{R} = \mu = \frac{\sum_{i=1}^{n} R_i}{n} \quad \dots (7)$$

Its (sample) variance is defined by the following equation. The standard deviation, that is, σ, is the square root of the variance:

$$\sigma^2 = \frac{\sum_{i=1}^{n}(R_i - \bar{R})^2}{n-1} \quad \dots (8)$$

The skewness defined by the following formula indicates whether the distribution is skewed to the left or to the right. For a symmetric distribution, its skewness is zero:

$$skew = \frac{\sum_{i=1}^{n}(R_i - \bar{R})^3}{(n-1)\sigma^3} \quad \dots (9)$$

The kurtosis reflects the impact of extreme values because of its power of four. There are two types of definitions with and without minus three; refer to the following two equations. The reason behind the deduction of three in equation (10B), is that for a normal distribution, its kurtosis based on equation (10A) is three:

$$kurtosis = \frac{\sum_{i=1}^{n}(R_i - \bar{R})^4}{(n-1)\sigma^4} \quad \dots (10A)$$

$$kurtosis = \frac{\sum_{i=1}^{n}(R_i - \bar{R})^4}{(n-1)\sigma^4} - 3 \quad \dots (10B)$$

Some books distinguish these two equations by calling equation (10B) excess kurtosis. However, many functions based on equation (10B) are still named kurtosis. We know that a standard normal distribution has a zero mean, unit standard deviation, zero skewness, and zero kurtosis (based on equation 10B). The following output confirms these facts:

```
from scipy import stats,random
import numpy as np
np.random.seed(12345)
ret = random.normal(0,1,500000)
print('mean     =', np.mean(ret))
print('std      =',np.std(ret))
print('skewness=',stats.skew(ret))
print('kurtosis=',stats.kurtosis(ret))
```

The related output is shown here. Note that since the `scipy.random.seed()` function is applied, readers should get the same results if the same seed of 12345 is used:

```
('mean     =', 0.0008226651714714 18)
('std      =', 0.99898956586553034)
('skewness=', 0.006299066118437377)
('kurtosis=', 0.0015439776051819898)
```

The mean, skewness, and kurtosis are all close to zero, while the standard deviation is close to one. Next, we estimate the four moments for S&P500 based on its daily returns as follows:

```
from scipy import stats
from matplotlib.finance import quotes_historical_yahoo_ochl as getData
import numpy as np
ticker='^GSPC'
begdate=(1926,1,1)
enddate=(2016,12,31)
p = getData(ticker, begdate, enddate,asobject=True, adjusted=True)
ret = p.aclose[1:]/p.aclose[:-1]-1
print( 'S&P500   n       =',len(ret))
print( 'S&P500   mean    =',round(np.mean(ret),8))
print('S&P500   std      =',round(np.std(ret),8))
print('S&P500   skewness=',round(stats.skew(ret),8))
print('S&P500   kurtosis=',round(stats.kurtosis(ret),8))
```

The output for those five values, including the number of observations, is given here:

```
('S&P500   n        =',  16858)
('S&P500   mean     =',  0.00033769)
('S&P500   std      =',  0.00966536)
('S&P500   skewness=',  -0.64035588)
('S&P500   kurtosis=',  20.81432822)
```

This result is very close to the result in the paper titled *Study of Fat Tail Risk* by Cook Pine Capital (2008). Using the same argument, we conclude that the SP500 daily returns are skewed to the left, that is, a negative skewness, and have fat tails (kurtosis is 20.81 instead of zero).

T-test and F-test

In finance, a T-test could be viewed as one of the most widely used statistical hypothesis tests in which the test statistic follows a student's t distribution if the null hypothesis is supported. We know that the mean for a standard normal distribution is zero. In the following program, we generate 1,000 random numbers from a standard normal distribution. Then, we conduct two tests: test whether the mean is 0.5, and test whether the mean is zero:

```
>>>from scipy import stats
>>>import numpy as np
>>>np.random.seed(1235)
>>>x = stats.norm.rvs(size=10000)
>>>print("T-value P-value (two-tail)")
>>>print(stats.ttest_1samp(x,0.5))
>>>print(stats.ttest_1samp(x,0))
T-value P-value (two-tail)
Ttest_1sampResult(statistic=-49.763471231428966, pvalue=0.0)
Ttest_1sampResult(statistic=-0.26310321925083019,
pvalue=0.79247644375164861)
```

For the first test, in which we test whether the time-series has a mean of *0.5*, we reject the null hypothesis since the T-value is *49.76* and the P-value is 0. For the second test, we accept the null hypothesis since the T-value is close to -0.26 and the P-value is 0.79. In the following program, we test whether the mean of the daily returns from IBM in 2013 is zero:

```
from scipy import stats
import scipy as sp
from matplotlib.finance import quotes_historical_yahoo_ochl as getData
```

```
ticker='ibm'
begdate=(2013,1,1)
enddate=(2013,12,31)
p=getData(ticker,begdate,enddate,asobject=True, adjusted=True)
ret=p.aclose[1:]/p.aclose[:-1]-1
print(' Mean T-value P-value ' )
print(round(sp.mean(ret),5), stats.ttest_1samp(ret,0))
Mean T-value P-value
(-4e-05, Ttest_1sampResult(statistic=-0.049698422671935881,
pvalue=0.96040239593479948))
```

From the previous results, we know that the average daily returns for IBM is 0.00004 percent. The T-value is -0.049 while the P-value is 0.96. Thus, we accept the null hypothesis, that is, the daily mean return is statistically the same as zero.

Tests of equal variances

Next, we test whether two variances for IBM and DELL are the same or not over a five-year period from 2012 to 2016. The function called `sp.stats.bartlet()` performs Bartlett's test for equal variances with a null hypothesis that all input samples are from populations with equal variances. The outputs are the T-value and P-value:

```
import scipy as sp
from matplotlib.finance import quotes_historical_yahoo_ochl as getData
begdate=(2012,1,1)
enddate=(2016,12,31)
def ret_f(ticker,begdate,enddate):
    p = getData(ticker,begdate, enddate,asobject=True,adjusted=True)
    return p.aclose[1:]/p.aclose[:-1]-1
y=ret_f('IBM',begdate,enddate)
x=ret_f('DELL',begdate,enddate)
print(sp.stats.bartlett(x,y))
BartlettResult(statistic=108.07747537504794,
pvalue=2.5847436899908763e-25)
```

With a T-value of 108 and a P-value of 0, we conclude that these two stocks will have different variances for their daily stock returns from 2012 to 2016 for any significance level.

Testing the January effect

In this section, we use IBM's data to test the existence of the so-called **January** effect, which states that stock returns in January are statistically different from those in other months. First, we collect the daily price for IBM from Yahoo! Finance. Then, we convert daily returns to monthly ones. After that, we classify all monthly returns into two groups: returns in January versus returns in other months.

Finally, we test the equality of group means as shown in the following code:

```
from matplotlib.finance import quotes_historical_yahoo_ochl as getData
import numpy as np
import scipy as sp
import pandas as pd
from datetime import datetime
ticker='IBM'
begdate=(1962,1,1)
enddate=(2016,12,31)
x =getData(ticker, begdate, enddate,asobject=True, adjusted=True)
logret = sp.log(x.aclose[1:]/x.aclose[:-1])
date=[]
d0=x.date
for i in range(0,sp.size(logret)):
    t1=''.join([d0[i].strftime("%Y"),d0[i].strftime("%m"),"01"])
    date.append(datetime.strptime(t1,"%Y%m%d"))

y=pd.DataFrame(logret,date,columns=['logret'])
retM=y.groupby(y.index).sum()
ret_Jan=retM[retM.index.month==1]
ret_others=retM[retM.index.month!=1]
print(sp.stats.ttest_ind(ret_Jan.values,ret_others.values))
Ttest_indResult(statistic=array([ 1.89876245]), pvalue=array([
0.05803291]))
>>>
```

Since the T-value is 1.89 and P-value is 0.058, we conclude that there is no January effect if we use IBM as an example and choose a 5 percent significance level. A word of caution: we should not generalize this result since it is based on just one stock. In terms of the weekday effect, we could apply the same procedure to test its existence. One end of chapter problems is designed to test the weekday effect based on the same logic.

52-week high and low trading strategy

Some investors/researchers argue that we could adopt a 52-week high and low trading strategy by taking a long position if today's price is close to the maximum price achieved in the past 52 weeks and taking an opposite position if today's price is close to its 52-week low. Let's randomly choose a day of 12/31/2016. The following Python program presents this 52-week's range and today's position:

```
import numpy as np
from datetime import datetime
from dateutil.relativedelta import relativedelta
from matplotlib.finance import quotes_historical_yahoo_ochl as getData
#
ticker='IBM'
enddate=datetime(2016,12,31)
#
begdate=enddate-relativedelta(years=1)
p =getData(ticker, begdate, enddate,asobject=True, adjusted=True)
x=p[-1]
y=np.array(p.tolist())[:,-1]
high=max(y)
low=min(y)
print(" Today, Price High Low, % from low ")
print(x[0], x[-1], high, low, round((x[-1]-low)/(high-low)*100,2))
```

The corresponding output is shown as follows:

```
Today, Price High Low, % from low
(datetime.date(2016, 12, 30), 165.990005, 168.509995, 114.68367, 95.32)
```

According to the 52-week high and low trading strategy, we have more incentive to buy IBM's stock today. This example is just an illustration on how to make a decision. There is nothing done to test whether this is a profitable trading strategy. If a reader is interested in testing this 52-week high and low trading strategy, he/she should use all stocks to form two portfolios. For more details, see George and Huang (2004).

Estimating Roll's spread

Liquidity is defined as how quickly we can dispose of our asset without losing its intrinsic value. Usually, we use spread to represent liquidity. However, we need high-frequency data to estimate spread. Later in the chapter, we show how to estimate spread directly by using high-frequency data. To measure spread indirectly based on daily observations, Roll (1984) shows that we can estimate it based on the serial covariance in price changes, as follows:

$$S = 2\sqrt{-cov(\Delta P_t, \Delta p_{t-1})} \qquad \dots (11)$$

$$\%spread = \frac{S}{\bar{P}} \qquad \dots (11B)$$

Here, S is the Roll spread, Pt is the closing price of a stock on day, ΔP_t is Pt-Pt-1, and $\bar{P}$, t is the average share price in the estimation period. The following Python code estimates Roll's spread for IBM, using one year's daily price data from Yahoo! Finance:

```
from matplotlib.finance import quotes_historical_yahoo_ochl as getData
import scipy as sp
ticker='IBM'
begdate=(2013,9,1)
enddate=(2013,11,11)
data= getData(ticker, begdate, enddate,asobject=True, adjusted=True)
p=data.aclose
d=sp.diff(p)
cov_=sp.cov(d[:-1],d[1:])
if cov_[0,1]<0:
    print("Roll spread for ", ticker, 'is', round(2*sp.sqrt(-cov_
[0,1]),3))
else:
    print("Cov is positive for ",ticker, 'positive', round(cov_
[0,1],3))
```

The corresponding output is shown as follows:

```
('Roll spread for ', 'IBM', 'is', 1.136)
```

Thus, during that period, Roll's spread for IBM is $1.136. See the following for the major assumption for Roll's model, ΔP_t and ΔP_{t-1}.

The covariance between them is negative. When its value is positive, Roll's model would fail. In a real world, it could occur for many cases. Usually, practitioners adopt two approaches: when the spread is negative, we just ignore those cases or use other methods to estimate spread. The second approach is to add a negative sign in front of a positive covariance.

Estimating Amihud's illiquidity

According to Amihud (2002), liquidity reflects the impact of order flow on price. His illiquidity measure is defined as follows:

$$illiq(t) = \frac{1}{n}\sum_{i=1}^{n}\frac{|R_i|}{P_i * v_i} \qquad \dots (12)$$

Here, *illiq(t)* is the Amihud's illiquidity measure for month *t*, *Ri* is the daily return at day *i*, *Pi* is the closing price at *i*, and *Vi* is the daily dollar trading volume at *i*. Since the illiquidity is the reciprocal of liquidity, the lower the illiquidity value, the higher the liquidity of the underlying security. First, let's look at an item-by-item division:

```
>>>x=np.array([1,2,3],dtype='float')
>>>y=np.array([2,2,4],dtype='float')
>>>np.divide(x,y)
array([ 0.5 , 1. , 0.75])
>>>
```

In the following code, we estimate Amihud's illiquidity for IBM based on trading data in October 2013. The value is *1.21*10-11*. It seems that this value is quite small. Actually, the absolute value is not important; the relative value matters. If we estimate the illiquidity for WMT over the same period, we would find a value of *1.52*10-11*. Since 1.21 is less than 1.52, we conclude that IBM is more liquid than WMT. This correlation is represented in the following code:

```
import numpy as np
import statsmodels.api as sm
from matplotlib.finance import quotes_historical_yahoo_ochl as getData
begdate=(2013,10,1)
enddate=(2013,10,30)
ticker='IBM'                    # or WMT
data= getData(ticker, begdate, enddate,asobject=True, adjusted=True)
p=np.array(data.aclose)
dollar_vol=np.array(data.volume*p)
ret=np.array((p[1:] - p[:-1])/p[1:])
illiq=np.mean(np.divide(abs(ret),dollar_vol[1:]))
```

```
print("Aminud illiq for =",ticker,illiq)
'Aminud illiq for =', 'IBM', 1.2117639237103875e-11)
  ('Aminud illiq for =', 'WMT', 1.5185471291382207e-11)
```

Estimating Pastor and Stambaugh (2003) liquidity measure

Based on the methodology and empirical evidence in Campbell, Grossman, and Wang (1993), Pastor and Stambaugh (2003) designed the following model to measure individual stock's liquidity and the market liquidity:

$$y_t = \alpha + \beta_1 x_{1,t-1} + \beta_2 x_{2,t-1} + \varepsilon \qquad \dots (13)$$

Here, y_t is the excess stock return, $R_t\text{-}Rf$, t, on day t, R_t is the return for the stock, $R_{f,t}$ is the risk-free rate, x_1,t is the market return, and x_2,t is the signed dollar trading volume:

$$(x_{2,t} = sign(R_t - R_{f,t}) * P_t * volume)$$

p_t is the stock price, and volume, t is the trading volume. The regression is run based on daily data for each month. In other words, for each month, we get one β_2 that is defined as the liquidity measure for individual stock. The following code estimates the liquidity for IBM. First, we download the IBM and S&P500 daily price data, estimate their daily returns, and merge them as follows:

```
import numpy as np
from matplotlib.finance import quotes_historical_yahoo_ochl as getData
import numpy as np
import pandas as pd
import statsmodels.api as sm
ticker='IBM'
begdate=(2013,1,1)
enddate=(2013,1,31)

data =getData(ticker, begdate, enddate,asobject=True, adjusted=True)
ret = data.aclose[1:]/data.aclose[:-1]-1
dollar_vol=np.array(data.aclose[1:])*np.array(data.volume[1:])
d0=data.date

tt=pd.DataFrame(ret,index=d0[1:],columns=['ret'])
tt2=pd.DataFrame(dollar_vol,index=d0[1:],columns=['dollar_vol'])
```

```
ff=pd.read_pickle('c:/temp/ffDaily.pkl')
tt3=pd.merge(tt,tt2,left_index=True,right_index=True)
final=pd.merge(tt3,ff,left_index=True,right_index=True)
y=final.ret[1:]-final.RF[1:]
x1=final.MKT_RF[:-1]
x2=np.sign(np.array(final.ret[:-1]-final.RF[:-1]))*np.array(final.
dollar_vol[:-1])
x3=[x1,x2]
n=np.size(x3)
x=np.reshape(x3,[n/2,2])
x=sm.add_constant(x)
results=sm.OLS(y,x).fit()
print(results.params)
```

In the previous program, *y* is IBM's excess return at time *t+1*, *x1* is the market excess return at time *t*, and *x2* is the signed dollar trading volume at time *t*. The coefficient before *x2* is Pastor and Stambaugh's liquidity measure. The corresponding output is given as follows:

```
const    2.702020e-03
x1      -1.484492e-13
x2       6.390822e-12
dtype: float64
```

Fama-MacBeth regression

First, let's look at the OLS regression by using the `pandas.ols` function as follows:

```
from datetime import datetime
import numpy as np
import pandas as pd
n = 252
np.random.seed(12345)
begdate=datetime(2013, 1, 2)
dateRange = pd.date_range(begdate, periods=n)
x0= pd.DataFrame(np.random.randn(n, 1),columns=['ret'],index=dateRan
ge)
y0=pd.Series(np.random.randn(n), index=dateRange)
print pd.ols(y=y0, x=x0)
```

For the Fama-MacBeth regression, we have the following code:

```
import numpy as np
import pandas as pd
import statsmodels.api as sm
```

```
from datetime import datetime
#
n = 252
np.random.seed(12345)
begdate=datetime(2013, 1, 2)
dateRange = pd.date_range(begdate, periods=n)
def makeDataFrame():
    data=pd.DataFrame(np.random.randn(n,7),columns=['A','B','C','D',
'E',' F','G'],
    index=dateRange)
    return data
#
data = { 'A': makeDataFrame(), 'B': makeDataFrame(), 'C':
makeDataFrame() }
Y = makeDataFrame()
print(pd.fama_macbeth(y=Y,x=data))
```

Durbin-Watson

Durbin-Watson statistic is related auto-correlation. After we run a regression, the error term should have no correlation, with a mean zero. Durbin-Watson statistic is defined as:

$$DW = \frac{\sum_{t=2}^{T}((e_t - e_{t-1})^2}{\sum_{t=1}^{T} e_t^2} \qquad \cdots (14)$$

Here, et is the error term at time t, T is the total number of error term. The Durbin-Watson statistic tests the null hypothesis that the residuals from an ordinary least-squares regression are not auto-correlated against the alternative that the residuals follow an AR1 process. The Durbin-Watson statistic ranges in value from 0 to 4. A value near 2 indicates non-autocorrelation; a value toward 0 indicates positive autocorrelation; a value toward 4 indicates negative autocorrelation, see the following table:

Durbin-Watson Test	Description
≈ 2	No autocorrelation
Towards 0	Positive auto-correlation
Towards 4	Negative auto-correlation

Table 8.3 Durbin-Watson Test

The following Python program runs a CAPM first by using daily data for IBM. The S&P500 is used as the index. The time period is from 1/1/2012 to 12/31/2016, a 5-year window. The risk-free rate is ignored in this case. For the residual from the regression, a Durbin-Watson test is run to test its autocorrelation:

```python
import pandas as pd
from scipy import stats
import statsmodels.formula.api as sm
import statsmodels.stats.stattools as tools
from matplotlib.finance import quotes_historical_yahoo_ochl as getData
#
begdate=(2012,1,1)
enddate=(2016,12,31)
#
def dailyRet(ticker,begdate,enddate):
    p =getData(ticker, begdate, enddate,asobject=True,adjusted=True)
    return p.aclose[1:]/p.aclose[:-1]-1

retIBM=dailyRet('IBM',begdate,enddate)
retMkt=dailyRet('^GSPC',begdate,enddate)

df = pd.DataFrame({"Y":retIBM, "X": retMkt})
result = sm.ols(formula="Y ~X", data=df).fit()
print(result.params)
residuals=result.resid
print("Durbin Watson")
print(tools.durbin_watson(residuals))
```

The output is shown here:

```
Intercept    -0.000342
X             0.881215
dtype: float64
Durbin Watson
1.82117707154
```

A positive of 1.82 close to 2 indicates the autocorrelation might be zero for the residuals from the CAPM for IBM. We would have a more definitive answer. Alternatively, we simply type the command of `print(result.summary())`, see the following screenshot:

```
In [73]: print(result.summary())
                            OLS Regression Results
==============================================================================
Dep. Variable:                      Y   R-squared:                       0.367
Model:                            OLS   Adj. R-squared:                  0.367
Method:                 Least Squares   F-statistic:                     728.4
Date:                Thu, 08 Jun 2017   Prob (F-statistic):           6.95e-127
Time:                        15:45:34   Log-Likelihood:                 4089.9
No. Observations:                1257   AIC:                            -8176.
Df Residuals:                    1255   BIC:                            -8166.
Df Model:                           1
Covariance Type:            nonrobust
==============================================================================
                 coef    std err          t      P>|t|      [95.0% Conf. Int.]
------------------------------------------------------------------------------
Intercept     -0.0003      0.000     -1.293      0.196      -0.001      0.000
X              0.8812      0.033     26.989      0.000       0.817      0.945
==============================================================================
Omnibus:                      709.941   Durbin-Watson:                   1.821
Prob(Omnibus):                  0.000   Jarque-Bera (JB):            20762.632
Skew:                          -2.059   Prob(JB):                         0.00
Kurtosis:                      22.480   Cond. No.                         124.
==============================================================================

Warnings:
[1] Standard Errors assume that the covariance matrix of the errors is correctly specified.
```

The preceding result shows the number of observations is 1,257 and Durbin-Watson test is 1.82. Based on lower (upper) bounds (dL and dU) at: `https://web.stanford.edu/~clint/bench/dwcrit.htm`, we conclude that 1.82 is not close enough to 2. Thus, the residuals are still positively correlated. The **Akaike Information Criterion (AIC)** is a measure of the relative quality of statistical models for a given set of data. It has the following formula:

$$AIC = 2 * k - 2 * L \quad \dots (15)$$

Here, k is the number of coefficients to be estimated in the model and L is the value of the log-likelihood. In the preceding example, $k=1$ and $L=4089.0$. Thus, AIC will be $2*1-2*4089.9=8177.8$. AIC would test whether this is a good model in an absolute term. However, given several candidate models, the preferred model is the one with the minimum AIC value. AIC rewards goodness of fit (as assessed by the likelihood function), but it also includes a penalty that is an increasing function of the number of estimated parameters (k). BIC stands for Bayesian Information Criterion and it is defined here:

$$BIC = \ln(n) * k - \ln(L) \qquad \dots (16)$$

Here, n is the number of observations and k is the number of parameters to be estimated including the intercept. The Jarque–Bera test is a goodness-of-fit test of whether our data has the skewness and kurtosis matching a normal distribution:

$$JB = \frac{n-k+1}{6}\left(S^2 + \frac{1}{4}(C-3)^2\right) \qquad \dots (17)$$

Here, S is the skewness and C is the kurtosis. The null hypothesis is a joint hypothesis of the skewness being zero and the excess kurtosis being zero. From the preceding result, since Prob. (*JB*) is zero, we reject the null hypothesis.

Python for high-frequency data

High-frequency data is referred to as second-by-second or millisecond-by-millisecond transaction and quotation data. The New York Stock Exchange's **Trade and Quotation (TAQ)** database is a typical example (`http://www.nyxdata.com/data-products/daily-taq`). The following program can be used to retrieve high-frequency data from Google Finance:

```
import tempfile
import re, string
import pandas as pd
ticker='AAPL'                   # input a ticker
f1="c:/temp/ttt.txt"            # ttt will be replace with above
sticker
f2=f1.replace("ttt",ticker)
outfile=open(f2,"w")
#path="http://www.google.com/finance/getprices?q=ttt&i=300&p=10d&f=d
,o, h,l,c,v"
path="https://www.google.com/finance/getprices?q=ttt&i=300&p=10d&f=d
,o,%20h,l,c,v"
path2=path.replace("ttt",ticker)
df=pd.read_csv(path2,skiprows=8,header=None)
fp = tempfile.TemporaryFile()
df.to_csv(fp)
print(df.head())
fp.close()
```

In the preceding program, we have two input variables: `ticker` and `path`. After we choose `path` with an embedded variable called `ttt`, we replace it with our `ticker` using the `string.replace()` function. The first and last five lines are shown as follows using the `.head()` and `.tail()` functions:

```
In [44]: df.head()
Out[44]:
     0        1        2        3       4
0    1   153.1500   153.05   153.7800   618967
1    2   153.3650   153.16   153.1600   547612
2    3   153.2000   153.10   153.3600   327123
3    4   153.2300   153.13   153.1800   241701
4    5   153.2048   153.06   153.2299   342035

In [45]: df.tail()
Out[45]:
       0         1         2         3        4
772  926   154.7458   154.6500   154.6800   110489
773  927   154.7257   154.6825   154.7500    98470
774  928   154.6600   154.5747   154.7200   123185
775  929   154.6000   154.6000   154.6850    91887
776  930   154.6275   154.5400   154.6082   138256
```

The related web page for the intra-day high-frequency data from Google is located at `https://www.google.com/finance/getprices?q=AAPL&i=300&p=10d&f=d,o,%20 h,l,c,v` and its header (first 10) lines are given as follows:

```
EXCHANGE%3DNASDAQ
MARKET_OPEN_MINUTE=570
MARKET_CLOSE_MINUTE=960
INTERVAL=300
COLUMNS=DATE,CLOSE,LOW,OPEN,VOLUME
DATA=
TIMEZONE_OFFSET=-300
a1484145000,118.75,118.7,118.74,415095
1,119.1975,118.63,118.73,1000362
2,119.22,119.05,119.2,661651
3,118.96,118.91,119.225,487105
4,118.91,118.84,118.97,399730
5,118.985,118.82,118.91,334648
```

The objective of the following program is to add a timestamp:

```
import tempfile
import pandas as pd, numpy as np, datetime
ticker='AAPL'
path="https://www.google.com/finance/getprices?q=ttt&i=300&p=10d&f=d
,o,%20h,l,c,v"
```

```
x=np.array(pd.read_csv(path.replace('ttt',ticker),skiprows=7,header=N
one))
#
date=[]
for i in np.arange(0,len(x)):
    if x[i][0][0]=='a':
        t= datetime.datetime.fromtimestamp(int(x[i][0].
replace('a','')))
        print ticker, t, x[i][1:]
        date.append(t)
    else:
        date.append(t+datetime.timedelta(minutes =int(x[i][0])))

final=pd.DataFrame(x,index=date)
final.columns=['a','CLOSE','LOW','OPEN','VOL']
del final['a']
fp = tempfile.TemporaryFile()
#final.to_csv('c:/temp/abc.csv'.replace('abc',ticker))
final.to_csv(fp)
print(final.head())
```

After running the program, we can observe the following output:

```
%run "c:\users\yany\appdata\local\temp\tmppuuqpb.py"
AAPL 2017-01-11 09:30:00 [118.75 118.7 118.74 415095L]
AAPL 2017-01-17 09:30:00 [118.27 118.22 118.34 665157L]
AAPL 2017-01-23 09:30:00 [119.96 119.95 120.0 506837L]
```

To view the first and last several lines, we could use the `.head()` and `.tail()` functions as follows:

```
>>>final.head()
                      CLOSE      LOW      OPEN      VOL
2017-01-11 09:30:00   118.75    118.7    118.74    415095
2017-01-11 09:31:00   119.198   118.63   118.73    1000362
2017-01-11 09:32:00   119.22    119.05   119.2     661651
2017-01-11 09:33:00   118.96    118.91   119.225   487105
2017-01-11 09:34:00   118.91    118.84   118.97    399730
>>>final.tail()
                      CLOSE      LOW      OPEN      VOL
2017-01-23 20:05:00   121.86    121.78   121.79    343711
2017-01- 23 20:06:00  121.84    121.815  121.86    162673
2017-01-23 20:07:00   121.77    121.75   121.84    166523
2017-01-23 20:08:00   121.7     121.69   121.78    68754
2017-01-23 20:09:00   121.82    121.704  121.707   103578
```

Since the TAQ database is quite expensive, potentially, most readers might not be able to access the data. Fortunately, we have a database called **Trade, Order, Report, and Quotation (TORQ)**. Thanks to Prof. Hasbrouck, the database can be downloaded from `http://people.stern.nyu.edu/jhasbrou/Research/`.

From the same web page, we could download the TORQ manual as well. Based on Prof. Hasbrouck's binary datasets, we generate a few corresponding datasets in the pickle format of pandas. The **Consolidated Trade (CT)** dataset can be downloaded from `http://canisius.edu/~yany/python/TORQct.pkl`. After saving this dataset in `C:\temp`, we can issue the following two lines of Python code to retrieve it:

```
import pandas as pd
import pandas as pd
import scipy as sp
x=pd.read_pickle("c:/temp/TORQct.pkl")
print(x.head())
print(x.tail())
print(sp.shape(x))
```

To view the first and last couple of lines, we use the `.head()` and `.tail()` functions as follows:

```
date        time  price  siz   g127  tseq cond ex
symbol
AC        19901101  10:39:06   13.0   100      0  1587        N
AC        19901101  10:39:36   13.0   100      0     0        M
AC        19901101  10:39:38   13.0   100      0     0        M
AC        19901101  10:39:41   13.0   100      0     0        M
AC        19901101  10:41:38   13.0   300      0  1591        N
               date      time    price     siz   g127    tseq cond ex
symbol
ZNT       19910131  11:03:31  12.375    1000      0  237884        N
ZNT       19910131  12:47:21  12.500    6800      0  237887        N
ZNT       19910131  13:16:59  12.500   10000      0  237889        N
ZNT       19910131  14:51:52  12.500     100      0  237891        N
ZNT       19910131  14:52:27  12.500    3600      0       0   Z   T
(728849, 8)
```

Since the `ticker` is used as an index, we could list all unique index values to find out the names of stocks contained in the dataset as follows:

```
import numpy as np
import pandas as pd
ct=pd.read_pickle("c:/temp/TORQct.pkl")
print(np.unique(np.array(ct.index)))
```

The output is shown here:

```
['AC' 'ACN' 'ACS' 'ADU' 'AL' 'ALL' 'ALX' 'AMD' 'AMN' 'AMO' 'AR' 'ARX'
'ATE'
 'AYD' 'BA' 'BG' 'BMC' 'BRT' 'BZF' 'CAL' 'CL' 'CLE' 'CLF' 'CMH' 'CMI'
'CMY'
 'COA' 'CP' 'CPC' 'CPY' 'CU' 'CUC' 'CUE' 'CYM' 'CYR' 'DBD' 'DCN' 'DI'
'DLT'
 'DP' 'DSI' 'EFG' 'EHP' 'EKO' 'EMC' 'FBO' 'FDX' 'FFB' 'FLP' 'FMI'
'FNM'
 'FOE' 'FPC' 'FPL' 'GBE' 'GE' 'GFB' 'GLX' 'GMH' 'GPI' 'GRH' 'HAN'
'HAT'
 'HE' 'HF' 'HFI' 'HTR' 'IBM' 'ICM' 'IEI' 'IPT' 'IS' 'ITG' 'KFV' 'KR'
'KWD'
 'LOG' 'LPX' 'LUK' 'MBK' 'MC' 'MCC' 'MCN' 'MDP' 'MNY' 'MO' 'MON' 'MRT'
 'MTR' 'MX' 'NI' 'NIC' 'NNP' 'NSI' 'NSO' 'NSP' 'NT' 'OCQ' 'OEH' 'PCO'
'PEO'
 'PH' 'PIM' 'PIR' 'PLP' 'PMI' 'POM' 'PPL' 'PRI' 'RDA' 'REC' 'RPS'
'SAH'
 'SJI' 'SLB' 'SLT' 'SNT' 'SPF' 'SWY' 'T' 'TCI' 'TEK' 'TUG' 'TXI' 'UAM'
 'UEP' 'UMG' 'URS' 'USH' 'UTD' 'UWR' 'VCC' 'VRC' 'W' 'WAE' 'WBN' 'WCS'
 'WDG' 'WHX' 'WIN' 'XON' 'Y' 'ZIF' 'ZNT']
```

Spread estimated based on high-frequency data

Based on the **Consolidated Quote (CQ)** dataset supplied by Prof. Hasbrouck, we generate a dataset with the pickle format of pandas, that can be downloaded from http://canisius.edu/~yany/python/TORQcq.pkl. Assume that the following data is located under C:\temp:

```
import pandas as pd
cq=pd.read_pickle("c:/temp/TORQcq.pkl")
print(cq.head() )
```

The output is shown here:

	date	time	bid	ofr	bidsiz	ofrsiz	mode	qseq
symbol								
AC	19901101	9:30:44	12.875	13.125	32	5	10	50
AC	19901101	9:30:47	12.750	13.250	1	1	12	0
AC	19901101	9:30:51	12.750	13.250	1	1	12	0
AC	19901101	9:30:52	12.750	13.250	1	1	12	0
AC	19901101	10:40:13	12.750	13.125	2	2	12	0

```
>>>cq.tail()
```

	date	time	bid	ofr	bidsiz	ofrsiz	mode	qseq

```
symbol
ZNT      19910131  13:31:06  12.375  12.875      1      1    12      0
ZNT      1 9910131  13:31:06  12.375  12.875      1      1    12
0
ZNT      19910131  16:08:44  12.500  12.750      1      1     3     69
ZNT      19910131  16:08:49  12.375  12.875      1      1    12      0
ZNT      19910131  16:16:54  12.375  12.875      1      1     3      0
```

Again, we could use the unique() function to find out all tickers. Assume that we are interested in a stock with an MO ticker as shown in the following code:

```
>>>x=cq[cq.index=='MO']
>>>x.head()
            date       time       bid      ofr   bidsiz   ofrsiz   mode   qseq
symbol
MO        19901101   9:30:33   47.000   47.125      100        4     10     50
MO        19901101   9:30:35   46.750   47.375        1        1     12      0
MO        19901101   9:30:38   46.875   47.750        1        1     12      0
MO        19901101   9:30:40   46.875   47.250        1        1     12      0
MO        19901101   9:30:47   47.000   47.125      100        3     12     51
```

It is a good idea to check a few observations. From the first line of the following output, we know that spread should be 0.125 (47.125-47.000):

```
>>>x.head().ofr-x.head().bid
symbol
MO 0.125
MO 0.625
MO 0.875
MO 0.375
MO 0.125
dtype: float64
>>>
```

To find the mean spread and the mean relative spread, we have the following code. The complete program is given as follows:

```
import pandas as pd
import scipy as sp
cq=pd.read_pickle('c:/temp/TORQcq.pkl')
x=cq[cq.index=='MO']
spread=sp.mean(x.ofr-x.bid)
rel_spread=sp.mean(2*(x.ofr-x.bid)/(x.ofr+x.bid))
print(round(spread,5) )
print(round(rel_spread,5) )
0.39671
0.00788
```

In the preceding example, we didn't process or clean the data. Usually, we have to process data by adding various filters, such as delete quotes with negative spread, `bidsiz` is zero, or `ofrsiz` is zero, before we estimate spread and do other estimates.

Introduction to CRSP

For this book, our focus is free public data. Thus, we only discuss a few financial databases since some readers might from schools with valid subscription. CRSP is the one. In this chapter, we mention just three Python datasets.

Center for Research in Security Prices (CRSP). It contains all trading data, such as closing price, trading volume, and shares outstanding for all listed stocks in the US from 1926 onward. Because of its quality and long history, it has been used intensively by academic researchers and practitioners. The first dataset is called `crspInfo.pkl`, see the following code:

```
import pandas as pd
x=pd.read_pickle("c:/temp/crspInfo.pkl")
print(x.head(3))
print(x.tail(2))
```

The related output is shown here:

```
     PERMNO  PERMCO     CUSIP                    FIRMNAME TICKER
EXCHANGE  \
0    10001    7953  36720410             GAS NATURAL INC   EGAS
2
1    10002    7954  05978R10  BANCTRUST FINANCIAL GROUP INC   BTFG
3
2    10003    7957  39031810    GREAT COUNTRY BK ASONIA CT   GCBK
3
     BEGDATE   ENDDATE
0  19860131  20151231
1  19860131  20130228
2  19860131  19951229


       PERMNO  PERMCO     CUSIP              FIRMNAME TICKER
EXCHANGE  \
31216   93435   53452  82936G20  SINO CLEAN ENERGY INC   SCEI
3
31217   93436   53453  88160R10       TESLA MOTORS INC   TSLA
3
       BEGDATE   ENDDATE
31216  20100630  20120531
31217  20100630  20151231
```

The `PERMNO` is the stock ID, `PERMCO` is the company ID, `CUSIP` is security ID, `FIRMNAME` is the company header name, that is, today's name, `EXCHANGE` is the exchange code, `BEGDATE` (`ENDDATE`) is when the data is available. The second dataset is for market indices, see the following code:

```
import pandas as pd
x=pd.read_pickle("c:/temp/indexMonthly.pkl")
print(x.head())
     DATE    VWRETD    VWRETX    EWRETD    EWRETX  SP500RET  SP500INDEX
\
0  19251231       NaN       NaN       NaN       NaN       NaN
12.46
1  19260130  0.000561 -0.001390  0.023174  0.021395  0.022472
12.74
2  19260227 -0.033040 -0.036580 -0.053510 -0.055540 -0.043950
12.18
3  19260331 -0.064000 -0.070020 -0.096820 -0.101400 -0.059110
11.46
4  19260430  0.037019  0.034031  0.032946  0.030121  0.022688
11.72
    TOTALVAL  TOTALN      USEDVAL   USEDN
0  27487487     503          NaN     NaN
1  27624240     506   27412916.0   496.0
2  26752064     514   27600952.0   500.0
3  25083173     519   26683758.0   507.0
4  25886743     521   24899755.0   512.0
```

The last dataset is for monthly stocks.

References

Please refer to the following articles:

- *Amihud and Yakov, 2002, Illiquidity and stock returns: cross-section and time-series effects, Journal of Financial Markets, 5, 31–56,* `http://citeseerx.ist.psu.edu/viewdoc/download?doi=10.1.1.145.9505&rep=rep1&type=pdf`

- *Bali, T. G., Cakici, N., and Whitelaw, R. F., 2011, Maxing out: Stocks as lotteries and the cross-section of expected returns, Journal of Financial Economics, 99(2), 427–446* `http://www.sciencedirect.com/science/article/pii/S0304405X1000190X`

- *Cook Pine Capital LLC, November 26, 2008, Study of Fat-tail Risk,* `http://www.cookpinecapital.com/pdf/Study%20of%20Fat-tail%20Risk.pdf`

- CRSP web site, `http://crsp.com/`

- CRSP user manual, `http://www.crsp.com/documentation`

- *George, T.J., and Hwang, C., 2004, The 52-Week High and Momentum Investing, Journal of Finance 54(5), 2145–2176,* `http://www.bauer.uh.edu/tgeorge/papers/gh4-paper.pdf`

- *Hasbrouck, Joel, 1992, Using the TORQ database, New York University,* `http://people.stern.nyu.edu/jhasbrou/Research/Working%20Papers/TORQDOC3.PDF`

- *Jegadeesh, N., and Titman, S., 1993, Returns to Buying Winners and Selling Losers: Implications for Stock Market Efficiency, Journal of Finance 48(1), 65–91,* `http://www.e-m-h.org/JeTi93.pdf`

- *Moskowitz, T., and Grinblatt, M., 1999, Do industries explain momentum? Journal of Finance 54(4), 2017–2069,* `http://faculty.som.yale.edu/Tobiasmoskowitz/documents/DoIndustriesExplainMomentum.pdf`

- *Pastor and Stambaugh, 2003, Liqudity measure and expected stock returns, Journal of Political Economy, 642-685,* `http://people.stern.nyu.edu/lpederse/courses/LAP/papers/TransactionCosts/PastorStam.pdf`

- *Roll. R., 1984, A Simple Measure of the Effective Bid-Ask Spread in an Efficient Market, Journal of Finance, 39, 1127-1139,* `http://onlinelibrary.wiley.com/doi/10.1111/j.1540-6261.1984.tb03897.x/pdf`

Appendix A – Python program to generate GDP dataset usGDPquarterly2.pkl

The first program generates a Python dataset with a `.pkl` extension:

```
import pandas_datareader.data as web
import datetime
begdate = datetime.datetime(1900, 1, 1)
enddate = datetime.datetime(2017, 1, 27)

x= web.DataReader("GDP", "fred", begdate,enddate)
x.to_pickle("c:/temp/ugGDPquarterly2.pkl")
```

To retrieve the dataset, we use the `pandas.read_pickle()` function. See the following code:

```
import pandas as pd
a=pd.read_pickle("c:/temp/usGDPquarterly2.pkl")
print(a.head())
print(a.tail())


            GDP
DATE
1947-01-01  243.1
1947-04-01  246.3
```

```
1947-07-01   250.1
1947-10-01   260.3
1948-01-01   266.2
                  GDP
DATE
2015-07-01   18141.9
2015-10-01   18222.8
2016-01-01   18281.6
2016-04-01   18450.1
2016-07-01   18675.3
```

Appendix B – critical values of F for the 0.05 significance level

The first row is for the degree of freedom for the denominator while the first column is for the degree of freedom for the numerator:

	A	B	C	D	E	F	G	H	I	J	K
1		1	2	3	4	5	6	7	8	9	10
2	1	161.45	199.5	215.71	224.58	230.16	233.99	236.77	238.88	240.54	241.88
3	2	18.51	19	19.16	19.25	19.3	19.33	19.35	19.37	19.38	19.4
4	3	10.13	9.55	9.28	9.12	9.01	8.94	8.89	8.85	8.81	8.79
5	4	7.71	6.94	6.59	6.39	6.26	6.16	6.09	6.04	6	5.96
6	5	6.61	5.79	5.41	5.19	5.05	4.95	4.88	4.82	4.77	4.74
7	6	5.99	5.14	4.76	4.53	4.39	4.28	4.21	4.15	4.1	4.06
8	7	5.59	4.74	4.35	4.12	3.97	3.87	3.79	3.73	3.68	3.64
9	8	5.32	4.46	4.07	3.84	3.69	3.58	3.5	3.44	3.39	3.35
10	9	5.12	4.26	3.86	3.63	3.48	3.37	3.29	3.23	3.18	3.14
11	10	4.96	4.1	3.71	3.48	3.33	3.22	3.14	3.07	3.02	2.98
12	11	4.84	3.98	3.59	3.36	3.2	3.09	3.01	2.95	2.9	2.85
13	12	4.75	3.89	3.49	3.26	3.11	3	2.91	2.85	2.8	2.75
14	13	4.67	3.81	3.41	3.18	3.03	2.92	2.83	2.77	2.71	2.67
15	14	4.6	3.74	3.34	3.11	2.96	2.85	2.76	2.7	2.65	2.6
16	15	4.54	3.68	3.29	3.06	2.9	2.79	2.71	2.64	2.59	2.54
17	16	4.49	3.63	3.24	3.01	2.85	2.74	2.66	2.59	2.54	2.49
18	17	4.45	3.59	3.2	2.96	2.81	2.7	2.61	2.55	2.49	2.45
19	18	4.41	3.55	3.16	2.93	2.77	2.66	2.58	2.51	2.46	2.41
20	19	4.38	3.52	3.13	2.9	2.74	2.63	2.54	2.48	2.42	2.38
21	20	4.35	3.49	3.1	2.87	2.71	2.6	2.51	2.45	2.39	2.35
22	21	4.32	3.47	3.07	2.84	2.68	2.57	2.49	2.42	2.37	2.32
23	22	4.3	3.44	3.05	2.82	2.66	2.55	2.46	2.4	2.34	2.3
24	23	4.28	3.42	3.03	2.8	2.64	2.53	2.44	2.37	2.32	2.27
25	24	4.26	3.4	3.01	2.78	2.62	2.51	2.42	2.36	2.3	2.25
26	25	4.24	3.39	2.99	2.76	2.6	2.49	2.4	2.34	2.28	2.24
27	26	4.23	3.37	2.98	2.74	2.59	2.47	2.39	2.32	2.27	2.22
28	27	4.21	3.35	2.96	2.73	2.57	2.46	2.37	2.31	2.25	2.2
29	28	4.2	3.34	2.95	2.71	2.56	2.45	2.36	2.29	2.24	2.19
30	29	4.18	3.33	2.93	2.7	2.55	2.43	2.35	2.28	2.22	2.18
31	30	4.17	3.32	2.92	2.69	2.53	2.42	2.33	2.27	2.21	2.16
32	31	4.16	3.3	2.91	2.68	2.52	2.41	2.32	2.25	2.2	2.15
33	32	4.15	3.29	2.9	2.67	2.51	2.4	2.31	2.24	2.19	2.14
34	33	4.14	3.28	2.89	2.66	2.5	2.39	2.3	2.23	2.18	2.13
35	34	4.13	3.28	2.88	2.65	2.49	2.38	2.29	2.23	2.17	2.12
36	35	4.12	3.27	2.87	2.64	2.49	2.37	2.29	2.22	2.16	2.11

The key part of the program used to generate the preceding table is given here:

```
import scipy.stats as stats
alpha=0.05
dfNumerator=5
dfDenominator=10
f=stats.f.ppf(q=1-alpha, dfn=dfNumerator, dfd=dfDenominator)
print(f)
3.32583453041
```

Appendix C – data case #4 - which political party manages the economy better?

In the US, people have been seeing many presidential debates among potential presidential nominees for the Republican and Democratic parties. One question a potential voter likes to ask is, which party could manage the economy better? With this term project, we try to ask this question: which party could manage the economy better in terms of the performance of the stock market? According to the web page of `http://www.enchantedlearning.com/history/us/pres/list.shtml`, we could find which party a US president belongs to:

President	which party	time period
30. Calvin Coolidge (1872-1933)	Republican	1923-1929
31. Herbert C. Hoover (1874-1964)	Republican	1929-1933
32. Franklin Delano Roosevelt (1882-1945)	Democrat	1933-1945
33. Harry S Truman (1884-1972)	Democrat	1945-1953
34. Dwight David Eisenhower (1890-1969)	Republican	1953-1961
35. John Fitzgerald Kennedy (1917-1963)	Democrat	1961-1963
36. Lyndon Baines Johnson (1908-1973)	Democrat	1963-1969
37. Richard Milhous Nixon (1913-1994)	Republican	1969-1974
38. Gerald R. Ford (1913- 2006)	Republican	1974-1977
39. James (Jimmy) Earl Carter, Jr. (1924-)	Democrat	1977-1981
40. Ronald Wilson Reagan (1911- 2004)	Republican	1981-1989
41. George H. W. Bush (1924-)	Republican	1989-1993
42. William (Bill) Jefferson Clinton (1946-)	Democrat	1993-2001
43. George W. Bush (1946-)	Republican	2001-2009
44. Barack Obama (1961-)	Democrat	2009-

Thus, we could generate the following table. The PARTY and RANGE variables are from the web page. YEAR2 is the second number of RANGE minus 1, except for the last row:

PARTY	RANGE	YEAR1	YEAR2
Republican	1923-1929	1923	1928
Republican	1929-1933	1929	1932
Democrat	1933-1945	1933	1944
Democrat	1945-1953	1945	1952
Republican	1953-1961	1953	1960
Democrat	1961-1963	1961	1962
Democrat	1963-1969	1963	1968
Republican	1969-1974	1969	1973
Republican	1974-1977	1974	1976
Democrat	1977-1981	1977	1980
Republican	1981-1989	1981	1988
Republican	1989-1993	1989	1992
Democrat	1993-2001	1993	2000
Republican	2001-2009	2001	2008
Democrat	2009-2017	2009	2016

Table 1: Parties and Presidents since 1923

1. Retrieve monthly stock data.
2. Classify returns into two groups according to YEAR1 and YEAR2: under Republican and under Democratic.
3. Test the null hypothesis: two group means are equal:

$$\bar{R}_{Democratic} = \bar{R}_{Republican} \qquad \cdots (1)$$

4. Discuss your results and answer the following question: are the monthly mean returns under both parties equal? Based on the preceding table, readers could sort all monthly mean returns into two categories: under Democratic Party and under the Republican Party.

For readers from schools without CRSP subscription, they could download the S&P500 market index from Yahoo! Finance. On the other hand, for readers from schools with CRSP subscriptions, they could use both **value-weighted market returns (VWRETD)** and **equal-weighted market index (EWRETD)**.

Exercises

1. Which module contains the function called rolling_kurt? How can you use the function?

2. Based on daily data downloaded from Yahoo! Finance, find whether Wal-Mart's daily returns follow a normal distribution.

3. Based on daily returns in 2016, are the mean returns for IBM and DELL the same?

 You can use Yahoo! Finance as your source of data

4. How many dividends distributed or stock splits happened over the past 10 years for IBM and DELL based on the historical data?

5. Write a Python program to estimate rolling beta on a 3-year window for a few stocks such as IBM, WMT, C and MSFT.

6. Assume that we just downloaded the prime rate from the Federal Banks' data library from: `http://www.federalreserve.gov/releases/h15/data.htm`. We downloaded the time-series for Financial 1-month business day. Write a Python program to merge them using:

    ○ Go to the web page: `http://mba.tuck.dartmouth.edu/pages/faculty/ken.french/data_library.html`.

    ○ Click on Fama-French Factor, and download their monthly factors named `F-F_Research_Data_Factors.zip`. Unzip the `.zip` file and estimate market monthly returns.

    ○ For example, for July 1926, *market return = 2.65/100+0.22/100*. This file was created by `CMPT_ME_BEME_RETS` using the 201212 CRSP database.

7. Download the monthly and daily Fama-French factors from Prof. French's data library at: `http://mba.tuck.dartmouth.edu/pages/faculty/ken.french/data_library.html`. Assume that you are holding an SMB portfolio. Answer the following three questions:

    ○ What is the total return from January 1, 1989 to December 31, 2016 using daily data?

    ○ What is the total return from January 1, 1989, to December 31, 2016, using monthly data?

    ○ Are they the same? If they are different, explain some reasons that lead to their differences.

8. How to replicate Jagadeech and Tidman (1993) momentum strategy by using Python and CRSP data? [Assume that your school has CRSP subscription].

9. Write a Python program to estimate returns. The format of your function could be `dailyRet(data,sorted=0)`. Then sorted is for how the price is sorted. For example, the default value could be from the oldest to the newest, while `sorted=1` for the opposite. One related Python program is given here:

```
import pandas as pd
import scipy as sp
p=[1,1.1,0.9,1.05]
a=pd.DataFrame({'Price':p})
a['Ret']=a['Price'].diff()/a['Price'].shift(1)
print(a)
    Price       Ret
0   1.00        NaN
1   1.10   0.100000
2   0.90  -0.181818
3   1.05   0.166667
```

 Note that there are two sorting: p1 is before p2 or p1 is after p2.

10. Replicate the table for the critical values of F for the `0.05` significant level in Appendix B. The following Python program is offered:

```
import scipy.stats as stats
alpha=0.05
dfNumerator=5
dfDenominator=10
stats.f.ppf(q=1-alpha, dfn=dfNumerator, dfd=dfDenominator)
```

11. In addition, generate the similar tables for 0.01 and 0.10 significant levels.

12. Based on the program to test the January effect, write a Python program to test week-day effect.

13. Generate a business cycle indicator. The business cycle data is from the National Bureau of Economic Research center. The original starting date is June 1854, http://www.nber.org/cycles/cyclesmain.html. Since stock data starts from 1926, we could remove data before 1923. For a peak, we assign a positive 1, while for a trough, we assign a negative 1. Any months between those peaks and troughs, we linearly interpolate, see the following Panel B. *P* for peak and *T* for trough. *T(t-1)* is for the previous trough and *P(t-1)* is for the previous peak:

Peak (P)	Trough (T)	Contraction P to T	Expansion T(t-1) to P	Cycle T(-1) to T	P(t-1) to P
May 1923(II)	July 1924 (III)	14	22	36	40
October 1926(III)	November 1927 (IV)	13	27	40	41
August 1929(III)	March 1933 (I)	43	21	64	34
May 1937(II)	June 1938 (II)	13	50	63	93
February 1945(I)	October 1945 (IV)	8	80	88	93
November 1948(IV)	October 1949 (IV)	11	37	48	45
July 1953(II)	May 1954 (II)	10	45	55	56
August 1957(III)	April 1958 (II)	8	39	47	49
April 1960(II)	February 1961 (I)	10	24	34	32
December 1969(IV)	November 1970 (IV)	11	106	117	116
November 1973(IV)	March 1975 (I)	16	36	52	47
January 1980(I)	July 1980 (III)	6	58	64	74
July 1981(III)	November 1982 (IV)	16	12	28	18
July 1990(III)	March 1991(I)	8	92	100	108
March 2001(I)	November 2001 (IV)	8	120	128	128
December 2007 (IV)	June 2009 (II)	18	73	91	81

14. Write a Python program to download daily price and estimate daily returns. Then convert daily returns into monthly ones. The date variable for the monthly returns should be the last trading days of the month. A Python dataset at: http://canisius.edu/~yany/python/tradingDaysMonthly.pkl, could be used, see the following code:

```
>>>import pandas as pd
>>>x=pd.read_pickle("c:/temp/tradingDaysMonthly.pk")
```

```
>>>print(x.head())
   tradingDays
0   1925-12-31
1   1926-01-30
2   1926-02-27
3   1926-03-31
4   1926-04-30
```

15. Write a Python program to generate quarterly returns from historical daily price or historical monthly price data.

Summary

In this chapter, many concepts and issues associated with time-series are discussed in detail. Topics include how to design a true date variable, how to merge datasets with different frequencies, how to download historical prices from Yahoo! Finance; also, different ways to estimate returns, estimate the Roll (1984) spread, Amihud's (2002) illiquidity, Pastor and Stambaugh's (2003) liquidity, and how to retrieve high-frequency data from Prof. Hasbrouck's TORQ database (Trade, Oder, Report and Quotation). In addition, two datasets from CRSP are shown. Since this book is focusing on open and publicly available finance, economics, and accounting data, we could mention a few financial databases superficially.

In the next chapter, we discuss many concepts and theories related to portfolio theory such as how to measure portfolio risk, how to estimate the risk of 2-stock and n-stock portfolio, the trade-off between risk and return by using various measures of Sharpe ratio, Treynor ratio, and Sortino ratio, how to minimize portfolio risk based on those measures (ratios), how to set up an objective function, how to choose an efficient portfolio for a given set of stocks, and how to construct an efficient frontier.

9
Portfolio Theory

Understanding portfolio theory is very important in learning finance. It is well known that *don't put all your eggs in one basket*, that is, it is a great idea to diversify away your risk. However, very few know the implied assumption behind such a famous idiom. In this chapter, we will discuss various risk measures for individual stocks or portfolios, such as Sharpe ratio, Treynor ratio, Sortino ratio, how to minimize portfolio risk based on those measures (ratios), how to set up an objective function, how to choose an efficient portfolio for a given set of stocks, and how to construct an efficient frontier. Our focus is on how to apply portfolio theory by using real-world data. For instance, today we have $2 million cash and plan to purchase IBM and Walmart stocks. If we have 30% invested in the first one and the rest in the second, what is our portfolio risk? What is the least risky portfolio that we could form based on those two stocks? How about 10 or 500 stocks? In this chapter, the following topics will be covered:

- Introduction to portfolio theory
- A 2-stock portfolio
- N-stock portfolio
- Correlation versus diversification effect
- Producing a return matrix
- Generating an optimal portfolio based on Sharpe ratio, Treynor ratio, and Sortinor ratio
- Constructing an efficient frontier
- Modigliani and Modigliani performance measure (M2 measure)

Introduction to portfolio theory

The keyword for the portfolio theory is diversification, while the keyword for diversification is correlation. In other words, correlation is used to measure how closely two stocks or portfolios are moving together. The objective of portfolio theory is to allocate our assets optimally with respect to risk and return. Markowitz (1952) argues that we should consider only the first two moments of a security's return distribution: mean and variance. For financial markets, several important assumptions are made, such as stock markets are inefficient, a typical investor is rational, and an arbitrage opportunity would not last long. For the preferences between two stocks, for a given risk, a rational investor would prefer stock with a higher expected return; for a given return, a rational investor prefers stock with a lower risk level. Sometimes, a single period portfolio optimization is called *Markowitz Portfolio Optimization*. The input includes a return matrix, and a variance and covariance matrix, while the output is an efficient portfolio. By connecting numerous efficient portfolios, an efficient frontier is formed. Here, we start with the simplest scenario: a two-stock portfolio.

A 2-stock portfolio

Clearly, a 2-stock portfolio is the simplest one. Let's assume that the weights of those two stocks are *w1* and *w2*. The portfolio returns are given here:

$$R_{p,t} = w_1 R_{1,t} + w_2 R_{1,t} \ldots\ldots\ldots\ldots (1)$$

Here, *Rp,t*, is the portfolio return at time *t*, *w1* (*w2*) is the weight for stock 1 (2), and *R1,t* (*R2,t*) is return at time *t* for stock 1 (2). When talking about expected return or mean, we have a quite similar formula:

$$\bar{R}_p = w_1 \bar{R}_1 + w_2 \bar{R}_1 \ldots\ldots\ldots (2)$$

Here, $\bar{R}_p$ is the mean or expected portfolio returns and $\bar{R}_1$ $(\bar{R}_2)$ is the mean or expected returns for stock 1 (2). The variance of such a 2-stock portfolio is given here:

$$\sigma_p^2 = w_1^2 \sigma_1^2 + w_2^2 \sigma_2^2 + 2w_1 w_2 \sigma_{1,2} = w_1^2 \sigma_1^2 + w_2^2 \sigma_2^2 + 2w_1 w_2 \rho_{1,2} \sigma_1 \sigma_2, \qquad (3)$$

Here, σ_p^2 is the portfolio variance and σ_1 (σ_2) is the standard deviation for stock 1 (2). The definitions of variance and standard for stock 1 are shown here:

$$\begin{cases} \sigma_1^2 = \frac{\sum_{i=1}^{n}(R_{1,i}-\bar{R}_1)^2}{n-1}, \\ \sigma_1 = \sqrt{\sigma_1^2} \end{cases} \quad (4)$$

$\sigma_{1,2}$ ($\rho_{1,2}$) is the covariance (correlation) between stocks 1 and 2. They are defined here:

$$\begin{cases} \sigma_{1,2} = \frac{\sum_{i=1}^{n}(R_{1,i}-\bar{R}_1)(R_{2,i}-\bar{R}_2)}{n-1} \\ \rho_{1,2} = \frac{\sigma_{1,2}}{\sigma_1 * \sigma_2} \end{cases} \quad (5)$$

For covariance, if it is positive, then those two stocks usually would move together. On the other hand, if it is negative, they would move in the opposite way most of times. If the covariance is zero, then they are not related. However, if we know that $\sigma_{A,B} > \sigma_{A,C}$, we could not claim whether A is strongly correlated with B than C, or the other way around. On the other hand, if $\rho_{A,B} > \rho_{A,B}$, we would claim that A is strongly correlated with B than A. This suggests that correlation is more useful than covariance. The range of a correlation is from -1 to 1. The lower the value of correlation, the higher is the effectiveness of the diversification effect. When the correlation is -1 (1), it is called perfectively negatively (positively) correlated. When two stocks (or portfolios) are perfectively positively correlated there is no diversification.

Assume that the volatilities (standard deviations) of two stocks are 0.06 and 0.24 and they are perfectively negatively correlated. What are two weights in order to form a zero-risk portfolio? There exist several methods to find a solution.

Method 1: we could manually find a solution: plug in given values into Equation (3) and set it equal to zero where $x=x1$ and $x2=1-x$:

$$x*0.06^2 + (1-x)*0.24^2-2*x*(1-x)*0.06*0.24=0$$

After expanding and collecting terms, we would end up with the following general equation:

$$ax^2 + bx - c = 0$$

For such a general form, we have the following two solutions if the term inside the square root is positive, that is, $b^2 - 4ac > 0$:

$$x = \frac{b \pm \sqrt{b^2 - 4ac}}{2a} \qquad (6)$$

Based on a set of *a*, *b*, and *c*, we have a solution of x=80%, that is, when *w1=0.80* and *w2=0.2*, the preceding 2-stock portfolio will be risk-free. Assume that we have an equation of *x2+6x+3=0*, the following Python program offers two solutions:

```
import scipy as sp
a=1
b=6
c=3
inside=b**2-4*a*c
if inside>0:
    squared=sp.sqrt(inside)
print("x1=",(b+squared)/(2*a))
print("x2=",(b-squared)/(2*a))
('x1=', 5.4494897427831779)
('x2=', 0.55051025721682212)
```

Method 2: For a given pair of standard deviations (or a pair of variances) plus a correlation between those two stocks, we generate many weights for stock 1, such as 0, 0.001, 0.002, 0.003, and the like. Remember that *w2=1-w1*. By applying Equation (3), we estimate the variances of this 2-stock portfolio. Our final solution will be the pair of *w1* and *w2* achieving the minimum portfolio variance, see the following code:

```
import scipy as sp
sigma1=0.06
sigma2=0.24
var1=sigma1**2
var2=sigma2**2
rho=-1
n=1000
portVar=10    # assign a big number
tiny=1.0/n

for i in sp.arange(n):
    w1=i*tiny
    w2=1-w1
```

```
    var=w1**2*var1 +w2**2*var2+2*w1*w2*rho*sigma1*sigma2
    if(var<portVar):
        portVar=var
        finalW1=w1
    #print(vol)
print("min vol=",sp.sqrt(portVar), "w1=",finalW1) ('min vol=',
('min vol=', ('min vol=', 9.3132257461547852e-10, 'w1=',
0.80000000000000004)
```

First, the result confirms our previous result with *w1=0.8* and *w2=0.2*. In the program, we have 1000 pairs of *w1* and *w2*. A small value, called `tiny`, is *1/1000=0.001*. The first pair of two weights is 0.1% and 99.9%. A very big number is assigned to our solution variable, that is, as an initial value. In this program, `portVar=10`. Other big numbers would work perfectly, such as 100. Here is the logic: based on the first pair of *w1* and *w2*, we estimate the portfolio variance. If this new portfolio variance is less than `portVar`, we replace `portVar` with this new value and record *w1* as well. If the new portfolio variance is bigger than `portVar`, we do nothing. Repeat the same procedure until we finish the loop. Here is an analogy. Assume that we want to find the tallest person among 1,000 persons. Assume that we have a variable call `tallestPerson` and its initial vale is 0.1 inch. Since every person will be taller than this value, the first person's height will replace this value. If the next person's height is higher than this variable, we replace it. Otherwise, we go to the next one. The procedure is repeated until the last person. In terms of efficiency, one small trick is to estimate `var1` and `var2` just once.

In finance, it is a convention to use both variance and standard deviation to represent risk, since they describe uncertainty. Usually, we use standard deviation of returns to represent the volatility. It is a good idea to look at the impact of correlation on the efficient frontier. First, let's learn how to generate a set of correlated random numbers. There are two steps involved:

1. Generate two random time series, *x1* and *x2*, with a zero-correlation.
2. Apply the following formula:

$$\begin{cases} y_1 = x_1 \\ y_2 = \rho x_1 + \sqrt{1-\rho^2} * x_2 \end{cases} \tag{7}$$

Here ρ is the predetermined correlation between those two time series. Now, *y1* and *y2* are correlated with a predetermined correlation. The following Python program would implement the preceding approach:

```
import scipy as sp
sp.random.seed(123)
n=1000
rho=0.3
x1=sp.random.normal(size=n)
x2=sp.random.normal(size=n)
y1=x1
y2=rho*x1+sp.sqrt(1-rho**2)*x2
print(sp.corrcoef(y1,y2))
[[ 1.         0.28505213]
 [ 0.28505213  1.         ]]
```

Optimization – minimization

Before discussing how to generate an optimal portfolio, it is necessary to study a few optimization functions. In the following example, we minimize our objective function of y:

$$y = 3.2 + 5x^2 \qquad (8)$$

First, let's look at the graph of this objective function, see the following code:

```
import scipy as sp
import matplotlib.pyplot as plt
x=sp.arange(-5,5,0.01)
a=3.2
b=5.0
y=a+b*x**2
plt.plot(x,y)
plt.title("y= "+str(a)+"+"+str(b)+"x^2")
plt.ylabel("y")
plt.xlabel("x")
plt.show()
```

The graph is shown here:

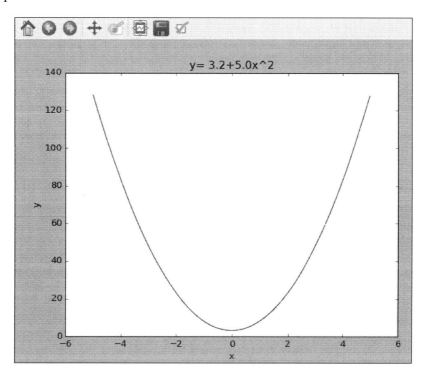

To make the program more general, two coefficients of a and b are generated. Apparently, since the power of x is 2, y is minimized only when x is 0. The Python code for minimization is as follows:

```
from scipy.optimize import minimize
def myFunction(x):
    return (3.2+5*x**2)
x0=100
res = minimize(myFunction,x0,method='nelder-mead',options={'xtol':1e-
8,'disp': True})
```

In the preceding program, the major function used is called the `scipy.optimize.minimize()` function. The first input is our objective function. In this case, it is our y function. The second value is our input value, that is, initial value. Since there is only one independent variable of x for the y function, x0 is a scalar. For the third input value, method, we have several choices: `NelderMead`. The following table lists 11 choices for the variable:

Method	Description
NelderMead	Uses the Simplex algorithm. This algorithm is robust in many applications. However, if numerical computation of derivative can be trusted, other algorithms using the first and/or second derivatives information might be preferred for their better performance in general.
Powell	It is a modification of Powell's method, which is a conjugate direction method. It performs sequential one-dimensional minimizations along each vector of the directions set, which is updated at each iteration of the main minimization loop. The function need not be differentiable, and no derivatives are taken.
CG	Uses a nonlinear conjugate gradient algorithm by Polak and Ribiere, a variant of the Fletcher-Reeves method. Only the first derivatives are used.
BFGS	Uses the quasi-Newton method of Broyden, Fletcher, Goldfarb, and Shanno (BFGS). It uses the first derivatives only. BFGS has proven good performance even for non-smooth optimizations. This method also returns an approximation of the Hessian inverse, stored as hess_inv in the OptimizeResult object.
NewtonCG	Uses a Newton-CG algorithm (also known as the truncated Newton method). It uses a CG method to compute the search direction.
LBFGSB	Uses the help() function to find more information.
TNC	[ibid]
COBYLA	[ibid]
SLSQP	[ibid]
dogleg	[ibid]
trustncg	[ibid]

Table 9.1 Types of solver

The output shows that the function value is 3.2, and it is achieved by assigning 0 to x.

Optimization terminated successfully:

```
Optimization terminated successfully.
        Current function value: 3.200000
        Iterations: 37
        Function evaluations: 74
```

The next example is using the `scipy.optimize.brent()` function on an exponential function minimization, see the code followed by the objective function:

$$y = 3.4 - 2e^{-(x-0.8)^2} \tag{9}$$

The following program tries to minimize the objective function, that is, y:

```python
from scipy import optimize
import numpy as np
import matplotlib.pyplot as plt
# define a function
a=3.4
b=2.0
c=0.8
def f(x):
    return a-b*np.exp(-(x - c)**2)

x=np.arange(-3,3,0.1)
y=f(x)
plt.title("y=a-b*exp(-(x-c)^2)")
plt.xlabel("x")
plt.ylabel("y")
plt.plot(x,y)
plt.show()

# find the minimum
solution= optimize.brent(f)
print(solution)
```

The solution is 0.799999999528 and the related graph is shown here:

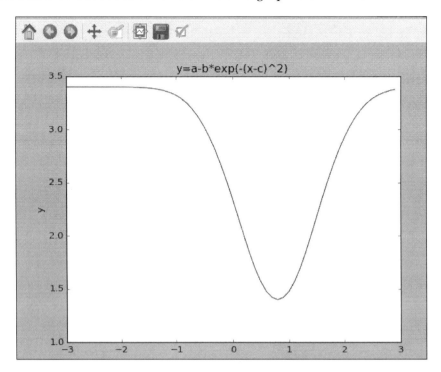

In economics and finance, there is an important concept called utility. One of the major reasons to design such a concept is that for many situations, we could not quantify certain effects, such as happiness, willingness, risk preference, wellness, emotion, and the like. For example, your boss asks you to work extra hours on Friday and promises you a bonus. Assume that its value is x dollar per hour and you are happy with it. If the task is urgent, your boss might ask for more hours. Assume that you have to work on Saturday. Do you think the same x dollar per hour would make your happy? For most workers the extra bonus should be higher than x since they would think that they have sacrificed more now than just a Friday evening. Usually, a utility function could be defined as the different between benefits and costs. The marginal benefit is a decreasing function of our input. It means the extra dollar received is not as valuable of the previous dollar. On the other hand, the marginal cost will be an increasing function of your input. When you asked to contribute extra work, the appropriate monetary incentive would go higher. Here is one utility function:

$$U = E(R) - \frac{1}{2}A * \sigma^2 , \qquad (10)$$

Here, U is the utility function, $E(R)$ is the expected portfolio return and we could use its mean to approximate, A is the risk-averse coefficient, and $\sigma2$ is the variance of the portfolio. When the expected return is higher, our utility is higher. The opposite is true: when the risk of our portfolio is higher the utility is lower. The key is A, which represents the risk-tolerance. With the same expected return and risk level, a more risk-reverse investor (a higher A) would experience a lower utility. Generally speaking, the objective is to balance the benefits (expected returns) with risk (variance).

Assume that we have a set of stocks, such as **International Business Machine (IBM)**, **Walmart (WMT)**, and **Citi Group (C)**. Based on the preceding utility function, which stock should we choose for different given risk preference? The code is given here:

```
from matplotlib.finance import quotes_historical_yahoo_ochl as getData
import numpy as np
import pandas as pd
import scipy as sp

tickers=('IBM','WMT','C')   # tickers
begdate=(2012,1,1)          # beginning date
enddate=(2016,12,31)        # ending date
n=len(tickers)              # number of observations
A=1                         # risk preference

def ret_f(ticker,begdate,enddte):
    x=getData(ticker,begdate,enddate,asobject=True,adjusted=True)
    ret =x.aclose[1:]/x.aclose[:-1]-1
    return ret

def myUtilityFunction(ret,A=1):
    meanDaily=sp.mean(ret)
    varDaily=sp.var(ret)
    meanAnnual=(1+meanDaily)**252
    varAnnual=varDaily*252
    return meanAnnual- 0.5*A*varAnnual

for i in sp.arange(n):
    ret=ret_f(tickers[i],begdate,enddate)
    print(myUtilityFunction(ret,A))
```

In the preceding program, the mean and standard deviation are both annualized. The value of 252 represents the number of trading days per year. The time period used is from 1/1/2012 to 12/31/2016, that is, a five-year period. The output is shown here. Again, the result is for the investor with a risk preference with A=1:

```
1.00313882726
1.05555982644
1.17072799785
```

Based on the concept of utility, investors prefer stock with the highest utility. Thus, we should choose the last stock. In other words, if we have to choose one stock as our investment, we should choose City Group. On the other hand, when A=10, that is, extremely risk-averse, we have the following utility values for those three stocks:

```
0.846544319839
0.930158828132
0.829073166372
```

The result suggests that such an investor should choose the second stock, that is, Walmart as our sole investment. This is consistent with our common sense, see their corresponding mean returns and risk levels:

```python
from matplotlib.finance import quotes_historical_yahoo_ochl as getData
import numpy as np
import pandas as pd
import scipy as sp

tickers=('IBM','WMT','C')    # tickers
begdate=(2012,1,1)           # beginning date
enddate=(2016,12,31)         # ending date
n=len(tickers)               # number of observations

def ret_f(ticker,begdate,enddte):
    x=getData(ticker,begdate,enddate,asobject=True,adjusted=True)
    ret =x.aclose[1:]/x.aclose[:-1]-1
    return ret

def meanVarAnnual(ret):
    meanDaily=sp.mean(ret)
    varDaily=sp.var(ret)
    meanAnnual=(1+meanDaily)**252
    varAnnual=varDaily*252
return meanAnnual, varAnnual
```

```
print("meanAnnual,      varAnnjal")
for i in sp.arange(n):
    ret=ret_f(tickers[i],begdate,enddate)
    print(meanVarAnnual(ret))
```

The output is shown here:

```
meanAnnual,varAnnjal
(1.0205382169700783, 0.034798779426166895)
(1.0694932706963931, 0.027866888512792672)
(1.2086896457878877, 0.075923295883153247)
```

In the preceding program, a function called meanVarAnnual() is generated that delivers annualized mean return and annualized volatility. Let's compare the last two stocks. The second stock is less risky than the third one at the same time; it has a higher risk than the third stock. The mean annual return of the second stock decreases by 12%, however, its variance decreases by 63%. The consequence is that utility increased.

For portfolio optimization, or Markowitz Portfolio Optimization, our input datasets include: expected returns, standard deviations, and correlation matrix. The output will be an optimal portfolio. By connecting those efficient portfolios, an efficient frontier could be constructed. In the rest of this chapter, we use historical returns to represent expected returns and use the historical correlation in the place of expected correlation.

Forming an n-stock portfolio

The following program generates a return matrix with three stocks plus S&P500:

```
import statsimport numpy as np
import pandas as pd
tickers=['IBM','dell','wmt']
path1='http://chart.yahoo.com/table.csv?s=^GSPC'
final=pd.read_csv(path1,usecols=[0,6],index_col=0)
final.columns=['^GSPC']
path2='http://chart.yahoo.com/table.csv?s=ttt'
for ticker in tickers:
    print ticker
    x = pd.read_csv(path2.replace('ttt',ticker),usecols=[0,6],index_col=0)
    x.columns=[ticker]
    final=pd.merge(final,x,left_index=True,right_index=True)
```

To show the first and last few lines, we use the `.head()` and `.tail()` functions as follows:

```
>>>final.head()
             ^GSPC      IBM     dell      wmt
Date
2013-10-18  1744.50   172.85   13.83    75.71
2013-10-17  1733.15   173.90   13.85    75.78
2013-10-16  1721.54   185.73   13.85    75.60
2013-10-15  1698.06   183.67   13.83    74.37
2013-10-14  1710.14   185.97   13.85    74.68
>>>final.tail()
             ^GSPC     IBM    dell    wmt
Date
1988-08-23   257.09   17.38   0.08   2.83
1988-08-22   256.98   17.36   0.08   2.87
1988-08-19   260.24   17.67   0.09   2.94
1988-08-18   261.03   17.97   0.09   2.98
1988-08-17   260.77   17.97   0.09   2.98
>>>
```

In the preceding program, we retrieve S&P500 data first. Then stock data is merged with the market index. The major function used is `pandas.merge()`. Please pay attention to the meanings of two input parameters: `left_index=True` and `right_index=True`. They indicate that those two datasets are merged by their indices. In the program, the daily frequency is retrieved. It is quite often that academic researchers and professionals prefer monthly frequency. One of the reasons is that monthly data has little so-called micro-structure effect compared with daily data. The following program uses monthly data. The Python data used is `yanMonthly.pkl`, `http://canisius. edu/~yany/python/yanMonthly.pkl`. First, we print a list of securities included:

```
import pandas as pd
import scipy as sp
df=pd.read_pickle("c:/temp/yanMonthly.pkl")
print(sp.unique(df.index))
['000001.SS' 'A' 'AA' 'AAPL' 'BC' 'BCF' 'C' 'CNC' 'COH' 'CPI' 'DELL'
'GE'
 'GOLDPRICE' 'GV' 'GVT' 'HI' 'HML' 'HPS' 'HY' 'IBM' 'ID' 'IL' 'IN'
'INF'
 'ING' 'INY' 'IO' 'ISL' 'IT' 'J' 'JKD' 'JKE' 'JPC' 'KB' 'KCC' 'KFT'
'KIE'
 'KO' 'KOF' 'LBY' 'LCC' 'LCM' 'LF' 'LG' 'LM' 'M' 'MA' 'MAA' 'MD' 'MFL'
'MM'
 'MPV' 'MY' 'Mkt_Rf' 'NEV' 'NIO' 'NP' 'NU' 'NYF' 'OI' 'OPK' 'PAF'
'PFO'
 'PSJ' 'PZZA' 'Q' 'RH' 'RLV' 'Rf' 'Russ3000E_D' 'Russ3000E_X' 'S'
'SBR'
```

```
'SCD' 'SEF' 'SI' 'SKK' 'SMB' 'STC' 'T' 'TA' 'TBAC' 'TEN' 'TK' 'TLT'
'TOK'
'TR' 'TZE' 'UHS' 'UIS' 'URZ' 'US_DEBT' 'US_GDP2009dollar'
'US_GDP2013dollar' 'V' 'VC' 'VG' 'VGI' 'VO' 'VV' 'WG' 'WIFI' 'WMT'
'WR'
'XLI' 'XON' 'Y' 'YANG' 'Z' '^AORD' '^BSESN' '^CCSI' '^CSE' '^FCHI'
'^FTSE'
'^GSPC' '^GSPTSE' '^HSI' '^IBEX' '^ISEQ' '^JKSE' '^KLSE' '^KS11'
'^MXX'
'^NZ50' '^OMX' '^STI' '^STOXX50E' '^TWII']
```

To choose a specific security, the index of the dataset is compared with the ticker; see the following code for choosing IBM's monthly price data:

```python
import scipy as sp
import pandas as pd
import numpy as np
n_stocks=10
x=pd.read_pickle('c:/temp/yanMonthly.pkl')
ibm=x[x.index=='IBM']
print(ibm.head(3))
print(ibm.tail(3))
          DATE    VALUE
NAME
IBM    19620131   2.36
IBM    19620228   2.34
          DATE    VALUE
NAME
IBM    20130930  185.18
IBM    20131031  179.21
IBM    20131104  180.27
```

The following program generates returns first, and then use ticker name as its corresponding column name instead of using a generate term, such as `return`. The reason is that we intend to choose several stocks and put them together side-by-side, that is, arranged by date:

```python
import scipy as sp
import pandas as pd
import numpy as np
n_stocks=10
x=pd.read_pickle('c:/temp/yanMonthly.pkl')
def ret_f(ticker):
    a=x[x.index==ticker]
    p=sp.array(a['VALUE'])
    ddate=a['DATE']
    ret=p[1:]/p[:-1]-1
```

```
          output=pd.DataFrame(ret,index=ddate[1:])
          output.columns=[ticker]
          return output
ret=ret_f('IBM')
print(ret.head())
                    IBM
DATE
19620228 -0.008475
19620330 -0.008547
19620430 -0.146552
19620531 -0.136364
19620629 -0.134503
```

Finally, we could construct an n-stock return matrix from yanMonthly.pkl:

```
import scipy as sp
import pandas as pd
import numpy as np
n_stocks=10
x=pd.read_pickle('c:/temp/yanMonthly.pkl')
x2=sp.unique(np.array(x.index))
x3=x2[x2<'ZZZZ']                        # remove all indices
sp.random.seed(1234567)
nonStocks=['GOLDPRICE','HML','SMB','Mkt_Rf','Rf','Russ3000E_D','US_
DEBT','Russ3000E_X','US_GDP2009dollar','US_GDP2013dollar']
x4=list(x3)

for i in range(len(nonStocks)):
    x4.remove(nonStocks[i])
k=sp.random.uniform(low=1,high=len(x4),size=n_stocks)
y,s=[],[]

for i in range(n_stocks):
    index=int(k[i])
    y.append(index)
    s.append(x4[index])
final=sp.unique(y)
print(s)

def ret_f(ticker):
    a=x[x.index==ticker]
    p=sp.array(a['VALUE'])
    ddate=a['DATE']
    ret=p[1:]/p[:-1]-1
    output=pd.DataFrame(ret,index=ddate[1:])
```

```
        output.columns=[ticker]
        return output
final=ret_f(s[0])
for i in sp.arange(1,n_stocks):
    ret=ret_f(s[i])
    final=pd.merge(final,ret,left_index=True, right_index=True)
```

To randomly choose m stocks from a set of existing available stocks (n of them), see the command of `scipy.random.uniform(low=1,high=len(x4),size=n_stocks)`. Since `n_stocks` has a value of 10, we choose 10 stocks from `len(x4)`. The output is shown here:

```
                   IO         A        AA        KB       DELL        IN
\
DATE
20110930  -0.330976 -0.152402 -0.252006 -0.206395 -0.048679 -0.115332
20111031   0.610994  0.185993  0.124464  0.192002  0.117690  0.237730
20111130  -0.237533  0.011535 -0.066794 -0.106274 -0.002616 -0.090458
20111230   0.055077 -0.068422 -0.135992 -0.102006 -0.072131 -0.065395
20120131   0.212072  0.215972  0.173964  0.209317  0.178092  0.230321


                  INF       IBM       SKK        BC
DATE
20110930  -0.228456  0.017222  0.227586 -0.116382
20111031   0.142429  0.055822 -0.305243  0.257695
20111130  -0.038058  0.022314 -0.022372  0.057484
20111230   0.059345 -0.021882 -0.024262 -0.030140
20120131   0.079202  0.047379 -0.142131  0.182020
```

In finance, constructing an efficient frontier is always a challenging job. This is especially true with real-world data. In this section, we discuss the estimation of a variance-covariance matrix and its optimization, finding an optimal portfolio, and constructing an efficient frontier with stock data downloaded from Yahoo! Finance. When a return matrix is given, we could estimate its variance-covariance matrix. For a given set of weights, we could further estimate the portfolio variance. The formula to estimate the variance and standard deviation for returns from a single stock are given as follows:

$$\bar{R} = \frac{\sum_{i=1}^{n} R_i}{n}, \qquad (11)$$

$$\sigma^2 = \frac{\sum_{i=1}^{n}(R_i - \bar{R})^2}{n-1} \qquad (12)$$

Here, $\bar{R}$ is the mean, R_i is the stock return for period i, and n is the number of returns. For an n-stock portfolio, we have the following formula to estimate its portfolio return:

$$R_p = \sum_{i=1}^{n} w_i R_i, \qquad (13)$$

Here, R_p is the portfolio return, w_i is the weight for stock i, and R_i is the stock i's return. This is true for the portfolio mean or expected portfolio return, see here:

$$\bar{R}_p = \sum_{i=1}^{n} w_i \bar{R}_i, \qquad (14A)$$

$$E(R_p) = \sum_{i=1}^{n} w_i E(R_i), \qquad (14B)$$

The portfolio variance for an n-stock portfolio is defined here:

$$\sigma_p^2 = \sum_{i=1}^{n} \sum_{j=1}^{n} w_i \, w_i \sigma_{i,j} \qquad (15)$$

Here, σ_p^2 is the portfolio variance, n is the number of stocks in the portfolio, w_i is the weight of stock i, and $\sigma_{i,j}$ is the covariance between stocks i and j. Note that when i is the same as j, $\sigma_{i,j}$ is the variance, that is:

$$\sigma_{i,i} = \sigma_i^2 \qquad (16)$$

Understandably, a 2-stock portfolio is just a special case of an n-stock portfolio. Again, when the values of the return matrix and the weight vector are given, we can estimate their variance-covariance matrix and portfolio variance as follows:

```
import numpy as np
ret=np.matrix(np.
array([[0.1,0.2],[0.10,0.1071],[-0.02,0.25],[0.012,0.028],[0.06,0.
262],[0.14,0.115]]))
print("return matrix")
print(ret)
covar=ret.T*ret
print("covar")
print(covar)
weight=np.matrix(np.array([0.4,0.6]))
print("weight ")
print(weight)
print("mean return")
print(weight*covar*weight.T)
```

The key command used is `ret.T*ret`. `ret.T` is the transpose of a return matrix. Since the return matrix is 6 by 2 matrix, its transpose will be a 2 by 6 matrix. Thus, the result of a matrix multiplication of *(2*6)* and *(6*2)* will be *(2*2)*. The corresponding outputs, such as return matrix, covariance matrix, weights, and portfolio variance, are given as follows:

```
return matrix
[[ 0.1      0.2    ]
 [ 0.1      0.1071]
 [-0.02     0.25   ]
 [ 0.012    0.028 ]
 [ 0.06     0.262 ]
 [ 0.14     0.115 ]]
covar
[[ 0.043744     0.057866   ]
 [ 0.057866     0.19662341]]
weight
[[ 0.4   0.6]]
mean return
[[ 0.10555915]]
```

The second way to conduct a matrix multiplication is by using the `spcipy.dot()` function, see the following code:

```
import numpy as np
ret=np.matrix(np.
array([[0.1,0.2],[0.10,0.1071],[-0.02,0.25],[0.012,0.028],[0.06,
0.262],[0.14,0.115]]))
covar=np.dot(ret.T,ret)
print("covar")
print(covar)
```

Constructing an optimal portfolio

In finance, we are dealing with a trade-off between risk and return. One of the widely used criteria is Sharpe ratio, which is defined as follows:

$$sharpe = \frac{E(R_p)-R_f}{\sigma_p} \qquad (17)$$

The following program would maximize the Sharpe ratio by changing the weights of the stocks in the portfolio. The whole program could be divided into several parts. The input area is very simple, just several tickers in addition to the beginning and ending dates. Then, we define four functions, convert daily returns into annual ones, estimate a portfolio variance, estimate the Sharpe ratio, and estimate the last (that is, nth) weight when *n-1* weights are estimated from our optimization procedure:

```
from matplotlib.finance import quotes_historical_yahoo_ochl as getData
import numpy as np
import pandas as pd
import scipy as sp
from scipy.optimize import fmin
```

1. Code for input area:

```
ticker=('IBM','WMT','C')    # tickers
begdate=(1990,1,1)          # beginning date
enddate=(2012,12,31)        # ending date
rf=0.0003                   # annual risk-free rate
```

2. Code for defining a few functions:

```
# function 1:
def ret_annual(ticker,begdate,enddte):
    x=getData(ticker,begdate,enddate,asobject=True,adjusted=True)
    logret =sp.log(x.aclose[1:]/x.aclose[:-1])
    date=[]
    d0=x.date
    for i in range(0,sp.size(logret)):
        date.append(d0[i].strftime("%Y"))
    y=pd.DataFrame(logret,date,columns=[ticker])
    return sp.exp(y.groupby(y.index).sum())-1


# function 2: estimate portfolio variance
def portfolio_var(R,w):
    cor = sp.corrcoef(R.T)
    std_dev=sp.std(R,axis=0)
    var = 0.0
    for i in xrange(n):
        for j in xrange(n):
            var += w[i]*w[j]*std_dev[i]*std_dev[j]*cor[i, j]
    return var


# function 3: estimate Sharpe ratio
```

```
def sharpe(R,w):
    var = portfolio_var(R,w)
    mean_return=sp.mean(R,axis=0)
    ret = sp.array(mean_return)
    return (sp.dot(w,ret) - rf)/sp.sqrt(var)

# function 4: for given n-1 weights, return a negative sharpe
ratio
def negative_sharpe_n_minus_1_stock(w):
    w2=sp.append(w,1-sum(w))
    return -sharpe(R,w2)        # using a return matrix here!!!!!!
```

3. Code for generating a return matrix (annul return):

```
n=len(ticker)                # number of stocks
x2=ret_annual(*ticker[0],begdate,enddate)
for i in range(1,n):
    x_=ret_annual(ticker[i],begdate,enddate)
    x2=pd.merge(x2,x_,left_index=True,right_index=True)

# using scipy array format
R = sp.array(x2)
print('Efficient porfolio (mean-variance) :ticker used')
print(ticker)
print('Sharpe ratio for an equal-weighted portfolio')
equal_w=sp.ones(n, dtype=float) * 1.0 /n
print(equal_w)
print(sharpe(R,equal_w))

# for n stocks, we could only choose n-1 weights
w0= sp.ones(n-1, dtype=float) * 1.0 /n
w1 = fmin(negative_sharpe_n_minus_1_stock,w0)
final_w = sp.append(w1, 1 - sum(w1))
final_sharpe = sharpe(R,final_w)
print ('Optimal weights are ')
print (final_w)
print ('final Sharpe ratio is ')
print(final_sharpe)
```

In step 2, we estimate annual returns from daily returns. For the optimization, the most important function is the `scipy.optimize.fmin()` function. The first input for this minimization function is our objective function, `negative_sharpe_n_minus_1`. Our objective is to maximize a Sharpe Ratio. Since this is a minimization function, it is equivalent to minimize a negative Sharpe ratio. Another issue is that we need n weights to calculate a Sharpe ratio. However, since the summation of *n* weights is 1, we have only n-1 weights as our choice variables. From the following output, we know that if we use a naïve equal-weighted strategy, the Sharpe ratio is 0.63. On the other hand, the Sharpe ratio for our optimal portfolio is 0.67:

```
Efficient porfolio (mean-variance) :ticker used
('IBM', 'WMT', 'C')
Sharpe ratio for an equal-weighted portfolio
[ 0.33333333  0.33333333  0.33333333]
0.634728319263
Optimization terminated successfully.
        Current function value: -0.669758
        Iterations: 31
        Function evaluations: 60
Optimal weights are
[ 0.49703463  0.31044168  0.19252369]
final Sharpe ratio is
0.66975823926
```

Constructing an efficient frontier with n stocks

Constructing an efficient frontier is always one of the most difficult tasks for finance instructors since the task involves matrix manipulation and a constrained optimization procedure. One efficient frontier could vividly explain the Markowitz Portfolio theory. The following Python program uses five stocks to construct an efficient frontier:

```
from matplotlib.finance import quotes_historical_yahoo_ochl as getData
import matplotlib.pyplot as plt
import numpy as np
import pandas as pd
import scipy as sp
from numpy.linalg import inv, pinv
```

1. Code for input area:

```
begYear,endYear = 2001,2013
stocks=['IBM','WMT','AAPL','C','MSFT']
```

2. Code for defining two functions:

```
def ret_monthly(ticker):  #  function 1
    x = getData(ticker,(begYear,1,1),(endYear,12,31),asobject=True
,adjusted=True)
    logret=np.log(x.aclose[1:]/x.aclose[:-1])
    date=[]
    d0=x.date
    for i in range(0,np.size(logret)):
        date.append(''.join([d0[i].strftime("%Y"),d0[i].
strftime("%m")]))
    y=pd.DataFrame(logret,date,columns=[ticker])
    return y.groupby(y.index).sum()


# function 2: objective function
def objFunction(W, R, target_ret):
    stock_mean=np.mean(R,axis=0)
    port_mean=np.dot(W,stock_mean)          # portfolio mean
    cov=np.cov(R.T)                         # var-cov matrix
    port_var=np.dot(np.dot(W,cov),W.T)    # portfolio variance
    penalty = 2000*abs(port_mean-target_ret)# penalty 4 deviation
    return np.sqrt(port_var) + penalty     # objective function
```

3. Code for generating a return matrix R:

```
R0=ret_monthly(stocks[0])                  # starting from 1st
stock
n_stock=len(stocks)                        # number of stocks
for i in xrange(1,n_stock):                # merge with other
stocks
    x=ret_monthly(stocks[i])
    R0=pd.merge(R0,x,left_index=True,right_index=True)
    R=np.array(R0)
```

4. Code for estimating optimal portfolios for a given return:

```
out_mean,out_std,out_weight=[],[],[]
stockMean=np.mean(R,axis=0)
for r in np.linspace(np.min(stockMean),np.max(stockMean),num=100):
    W = np.ones([n_stock])/n_stock    # starting from equal
weights
    b_ = [(0,1)
    for i in range(n_stock)]                # bounds, here no short
    c_ = ({'type':'eq', 'fun': lambda W: sum(W)-1. })#constraint
    result=sp.optimize.minimize(objFunction,W,(R,r),method='SLSQP'
,constraints=c_, bounds=b_)
    if not result.success:                # handle error raise
```

```
        BaseException(result.message)
  out_mean.append(round(r,4))          # 4 decimal places
  std_=round(np.std(np.sum(R*result.x,axis=1)),6)
  out_std.append(std_)
  out_weight.append(result.x)
```

5. Code for plotting the efficient frontier:

```
plt.title('Efficient Frontier')
plt.xlabel('Standard Deviation of the porfolio (Risk))')
plt.ylabel('Return of the portfolio')
plt.figtext(0.5,0.75,str(n_stock)+' stock are used: ')
plt.figtext(0.5,0.7,' '+str(stocks))
plt.figtext(0.5,0.65,'Time period: '+str(begYear)+' ------
'+str(endYear))
plt.plot(out_std,out_mean,'--')
plt.show()
```

The key to understanding this program is its objective function under the title of
function 2: objective function. Our objective is for a given target portfolio mean or
expected value, we would minimize our portfolio risk. The first part of the command
line of return `np.sqrt(port_var) + penalty`, is the portfolio variance. There is
no ambiguity about the first term. Now, let's turn to the second term called penalty,
which is defined as the absolute deviation of the portfolio mean from our target mean
times a big number. This is a quite popular way to define our objective function by
using an unconstrained optimization procedure. An alternative way is to apply an
optimization procedure with constraints. The output graph is presented as follows:

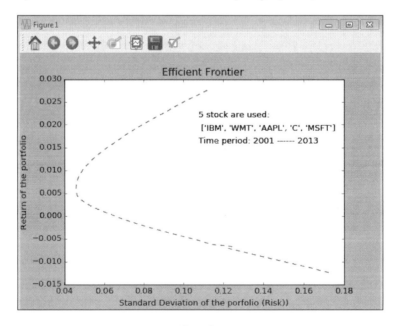

In one of the previous programs, our objective function is to maximize a Sharpe ratio. From the previous chapter, we know that when the portfolio under consideration is not all our wealth, Sharpe ratio might not be a good measure. Viewed as a modification to the Sharpe ratio, the Treynor ratio is defined here:

$$Treynor\ Ratio = \frac{\bar{R}_p - \bar{R}_f}{\beta_p} \qquad (18)$$

Here, the left-hand side is Treynor ratio, $\bar{R}_p$ is the mean portfolio return, R_f is the risk-free rate, and β_p is the portfolio beta. The only modification is that the sigma (total risk) is replaced by beta (market risk).

In the following program, Treynor ratio will be our objective function:

```
import matplotlib.pyplot as plt
from matplotlib.finance import quotes_historical_yahoo_ochl as getData
import numpy as np
import pandas as pd
import scipy as sp
from scipy.optimize import fmin


# Step 1: input area
ticker=('IBM','WMT','C')     # tickers
begdate=(1990,1,1)           # beginning date
enddate=(2012,12,31)         # ending date
rf=0.0003                    # annual risk-free rate
betaGiven=(0.8,0.4,0.3)      # given beta's


# Step 2: define a few functions

# function 1:
def ret_annual(ticker,begdate,enddte):
    x=getData(ticker,begdate,enddate,asobject=True,adjusted=True)
    logret =sp.log(x.aclose[1:]/x.aclose[:-1])
    date=[]
    d0=x.date
    for i in range(0,sp.size(logret)):
        date.append(d0[i].strftime("%Y"))
    y=pd.DataFrame(logret,date,columns=[ticker])
    return sp.exp(y.groupby(y.index).sum())-1


# function 2: estimate portfolio beta
```

```
def portfolioBeta(betaGiven,w):
    #print("betaGiven=",betaGiven,"w=",w)
    return sp.dot(betaGiven,w)
# function 3: estimate Treynor
def treynor(R,w):
    betaP=portfolioBeta(betaGiven,w)
    mean_return=sp.mean(R,axis=0)
    ret = sp.array(mean_return)
    return (sp.dot(w,ret) - rf)/betaP


# function 4: for given n-1 weights, return a negative Sharpe ratio
def negative_treynor_n_minus_1_stock(w):
    w2=sp.append(w,1-sum(w))
    return -treynor(R,w2)        # using a return matrix here!!!!!!


# Step 3: generate a return matrix (annul return)
n=len(ticker)                      # number of stocks
x2=ret_annual(ticker[0],begdate,enddate)
for i in range(1,n):
    x_=ret_annual(ticker[i],begdate,enddate)
    x2=pd.merge(x2,x_,left_index=True,right_index=True)
# using scipy array format
R = sp.array(x2)
print('Efficient porfolio (Treynor ratio) :ticker used')
print(ticker)
print('Treynor ratio for an equal-weighted portfolio')
equal_w=sp.ones(n, dtype=float) * 1.0 /n
print(equal_w)
print(treynor(R,equal_w))


# for n stocks, we could only choose n-1 weights
w0= sp.ones(n-1, dtype=float) * 1.0 /n
w1 = fmin(negative_treynor_n_minus_1_stock,w0)
final_w = sp.append(w1, 1 - sum(w1))
final_treynor = treynor(R,final_w)
print ('Optimal weights are ')
print (final_w)
print ('final Sharpe ratio is ')
print(final_treynor)
```

The output is shown here:

```
Efficient porfolio (Treynor ratio) :ticker used
('IBM', 'WMT', 'C')
Treynor ratio for an equal-weighted portfolio
[ 0.33333333  0.33333333  0.33333333]
0.313034361254
Warning: Maximum number of function evaluations has been exceeded.
Optimal weights are
[-0.69742062  0.48710308  1.21031754]
final Sharpe ratio is
inf
c:\users\yany\appdata\local\temp\tmpmq8xp9.py:37: RuntimeWarning: divide by zero encountered in double_scalars
  return (sp.dot(w,ret) - rf)/betaP
C:\Users\yany\AppData\Local\Enthought\Canopy32\User\lib\site-packages\scipy\optimize\optimize.py:528: RuntimeWarning: invalid
value encountered in subtract
  numpy.max(numpy.abs(fsim[0] - fsim[1:])) <= fatol):
```

Another argument against using standard deviation in the Sharpe ratio is that it considers the deviations in both directions, below and above the mean. Nevertheless, we know that investors worry more about the downside risk (deviation below mean return). The second issue for the Sharpe ratio is that for the numerator, we compare mean returns with a risk-free rate. Nevertheless, for the denominator, the deviations are from the mean return instead of the same risk-free rate. To overcome those two shortcomings, a so-called **Lower Partial Standard Deviation (LPSD)** is developed. Assume we have n returns and one **risk-free rate (Rf)**. Assume further that there are m returns that are less than this risk-free rate. We estimate LPSP by using only those m returns and it is defined here:

$$LPSD = \frac{\sum_{i=1}^{m}(R_i - R_f)^2}{m-1} \qquad where \ R_i < R_f \qquad (19)$$

The following program shows how to estimate LPSD for a given set of returns:

```python
import scipy as sp
import numpy as np
mean=0.15;
Rf=0.01
std=0.20
n=200
sp.random.seed(3412)
x=sp.random.normal(loc=mean,scale=std,size=n)
def LPSD_f(returns, Rf):
    y=returns[returns-Rf<0]
    m=len(y)
    total=0.0
    for i in sp.arange(m):
        total+=(y[i]-Rf)**2
    return total/(m-1)
answer=LPSD_f(x,Rf)
print("LPSD=",answer)
('LPSD=', 0.022416749724544906)
```

Similar to Sharpe ratio and Treynor ratio, the Sortino ratio is defined as follows:

$$Sortino\ Ratio = \frac{\bar{R}_p - \bar{R}_f}{LPSD} \qquad (20)$$

The following program would maximize Sortino ratio for a few given stocks:

```
import scipy as sp
import numpy as np
import pandas as pd
from scipy.optimize import fmin
from matplotlib.finance import quotes_historical_yahoo_ochl as getData
#
# Step 1: input area
ticker=('IBM','WMT','C')    # tickers
begdate=(1990,1,1)          # beginning date
enddate=(2012,12,31)        # ending date
rf=0.0003                   # annual risk-free rate
#
# Step 2: define a few functions
# function 1:
def ret_annual(ticker,begdate,enddte):
    x=getData(ticker,begdate,enddate,asobject=True,adjusted=True)
    logret =sp.log(x.aclose[1:]/x.aclose[:-1])
    date=[]
    d0=x.date
    for i in range(0,sp.size(logret)):
        date.append(d0[i].strftime("%Y"))
    y=pd.DataFrame(logret,date,columns=[ticker])
    return sp.exp(y.groupby(y.index).sum())-1

# function 2: estimate LPSD
def LPSD_f(returns, Rf):
    y=returns[returns-Rf<0]
    m=len(y)
    total=0.0
    for i in sp.arange(m):
        total+=(y[i]-Rf)**2
    return total/(m-1)

# function 3: estimate Sortino
def sortino(R,w):
    mean_return=sp.mean(R,axis=0)
```

```
        ret = sp.array(mean_return)
        LPSD=LPSD_f(R,rf)
        return (sp.dot(w,ret) - rf)/LPSD


# function 4: for given n-1 weights, return a negative sharpe ratio
def negative_sortino_n_minus_1_stock(w):
        w2=sp.append(w,1-sum(w))
        return -sortino(R,w2)            # using a return matrix here!!!!!!


# Step 3: generate a return matrix (annul return)
n=len(ticker)                    # number of stocks
x2=ret_annual(ticker[0],begdate,enddate)
for i in range(1,n):
        x_=ret_annual(ticker[i],begdate,enddate)
        x2=pd.merge(x2,x_,left_index=True,right_index=True)


# using scipy array format
R = sp.array(x2)
print('Efficient porfolio (mean-variance) :ticker used')
print(ticker)
print('Sortino ratio for an equal-weighted portfolio')
equal_w=sp.ones(n, dtype=float) * 1.0 /n
print(equal_w)
print(sortino(R,equal_w))
# for n stocks, we could only choose n-1 weights
w0= sp.ones(n-1, dtype=float) * 1.0 /n
w1 = fmin(negative_sortino_n_minus_1_stock,w0)
final_w = sp.append(w1, 1 - sum(w1))
final_sortino = sortino(R,final_w)
print ('Optimal weights are ')
print (final_w)
print ('final Sortino ratio is ')
print(final_sortino)
```

Here is the corresponding output:

```
Efficient porfolio (mean-variance) :ticker used
('IBM', 'WMT', 'C')
Sortino ratio for an equal-weighted portfolio
[ 0.33333333  0.33333333  0.33333333]
1.66860012089
Warning: Maximum number of function evaluations has been exceeded.
Optimal weights are
[  6.34898056e+42   3.41085097e+43  -4.04574902e+43]
final Sortino ratio is
6.18154566459e+42
```

Modigliani and Modigliani (1997) propose another performance measure. Their benchmark is a specified market index. Let's use S&P500 index as an example. Assume that our portfolio has a higher risk and a higher return compared with the S&P500 market index:

$$\begin{cases} \bar{R}_p > \bar{R}_{sp500} \\ \sigma_p < \sigma_{sp500} \end{cases} \qquad (21)$$

Here is their two-step approach:

1. Form a new portfolio with two weights w for our original portfolio and (1-w) for a risk-free investment. The new portfolio would have the risk as the SP500 market index:

$$w^2 \sigma_p^2 = \sigma_{sp500}^2 \qquad (22)$$

Actually, the weight of w will be given by the following formula:

$$w = \frac{\sigma_p}{\sigma_{S\&P500}} \qquad (23)$$

2. Calculate the portfolio mean returns by applying the following formula:

$$\bar{R}_p^{new} = w_1 R_p + (1 - w_1) R_f \qquad (24)$$

The final judgment is whether this new risk-adjusted portfolio is bigger or less than S&P500 mean return. The following Python program achieves this:

```
from matplotlib.finance import quotes_historical_yahoo_ochl as getData
import matplotlib.pyplot as plt
import pandas as pd
import numpy as np
import scipy as sp

begdate=(2012,1,1)
enddate=(2016,12,31)
ticker='IBM'

def ret_f(ticker):   #  function 1
```

```
x = getData(ticker,begdate,enddate,asobject=True,adjusted=True)
ret=x.aclose[1:]/x.aclose[:-1]-1
ddate=x['date'][1:]
y=pd.DataFrame(ret,columns=[ticker],index=ddate)
return y.groupby(y.index).sum()

a=ret_f(ticker)
b=ret_f("^GSPC")
c=pd.merge(a,b,left_index=True, right_index=True)
print(c.head())
mean=sp.mean(c)
print(mean)
cov=sp.dot(c.T,c)
print(cov)
```

The output is shown here:

```
                  IBM      ^GSPC
2012-01-04 -0.004079   0.000188
2012-01-05 -0.004743   0.002944
2012-01-06 -0.011481  -0.002537
2012-01-09 -0.005204   0.002262
2012-01-10 -0.001542   0.008886
IBM        0.000081
^GSPC      0.000479
dtype: float64
[[ 0.17358781   0.07238903]
 [ 0.07238903   0.08238055]]
```

There are different weighting schemes to estimate the portfolio returns. The commonly used ones are value-weighed, equal-weighted, and price-weighted. When estimating certain indices, the value-weighted is also called market capitalization weighted. For example, S&P500 returns are value-weighted and Dow Jones Industrial Average is price-weighed. The equal-weighted is the simplest one:

$$R_{p,t} = \frac{\sum_{i=1}^{n} R_{i,t}}{n} \qquad (25)$$

Here, $R_{p,t}$ is the portfolio return at time t, $R_{i,t}$ is the stock i's return at time t, and n is the number of stocks in the portfolio. Here is a very simple example, assume that we have two stocks in our portfolio. Last year stock A had a return of 20% while stock B had a -10%, what is an equal-weighted return based on those two values? The answer is 5%. For a value-weighted index, the key is the weight w_i, see the following formula:

$$\begin{cases} R_{p,t} = \sum_{i=1}^{n} w_i R_{i,t} \\ \quad w_i = \frac{v_i}{\sum_{i=1}^{n} v_i} \end{cases} \qquad (26)$$

Here vi is the value of our investment for ith stock, $\sum_{i=1}^{n} v_i$ is the total value of our portfolio. Assume that we have a 2-stock portfolio. Last year, stock A (B) has a return of 20% (-10%). If our investment for stocks A and B are 90% versus 10%, what is their value-weighted return last year? The answer is *17% (0.9*0.2+0.1*(-0.1))*. For a market index, such as S&P5000, vi will be the market capitalization of stock i and the summation of all 500 stocks' market capitalizations will be the market value of the index portfolio. When estimating the value-weighed market index, the small stocks would have little impact since their weights are so tiny. Here is a simple example by using yanMonthly.pkl, downloadable at http://canisius.edu/~yany/python/yanMonthly.pkl:

```
import scipy as sp
import pandas as pd
x=pd.read_pickle("c:/temp/yanMonthly.pkl")
def ret_f(ticker):
    a=x[x.index==ticker]
    p=sp.array(a['VALUE'])
    ddate=a['DATE'][1:]
    ret=p[1:]/p[:-1]-1
    out1=pd.DataFrame(p[1:],index=ddate)
    out2=pd.DataFrame(ret,index=ddate)
    output=pd.merge(out1,out2,left_index=True, right_index=True)
    output.columns=['Price_'+ticker,'Ret_'+ticker]
    return output
a=ret_f("IBM")
b=ret_f('WMT')
c=pd.merge(a,b,left_index=True, right_index=True)
print(c.head())
```

```
              Price_IBM    Ret_IBM  Price_WMT   Ret_WMT
DATE
19720929           7.09  -0.005610       0.04      0.00
19721031           6.73  -0.050776       0.04      0.00
19721130           6.85   0.017831       0.04      0.00
19721229           7.04   0.027737       0.05      0.25
19730131           7.63   0.083807       0.04     -0.20
```

Since there are just two stocks, we could manually calculate a few days for several weighting schemes. Let's use the last observation, January 1973, as an example and assume that we have 100 shares of IBM and 200 shares of Walmart. The equal-weighted monthly return is *-0.08 (0.04-0.2)/2)*. For a value-weighted one, we estimate two weights and assume that we use the previous price to estimate those weights. The total value is *100*7.04 + 200*0.05= 714*. Thus *w1= 0.9859944 (704/714)* and *w2=0.0140056*. The value-weighted return is 0.0366, that is, *0.9859944*0.04 + 0.0140056*(-0.2)*. For a price-weighted portfolio, we have the same format as a value-weighted one. The major difference is how to define its weights:

$$\begin{cases} R_{p,t} = \sum_{i=1}^{n} w_i R_{i,t} \\ w_i = \frac{p_i}{\sum_{i=1}^{n} p_i} \end{cases} \qquad (27)$$

Here, p_i is the price of ith stock. In a sense, a price-weighted portfolio could be viewed as we only have one share for each stock in our portfolio for the same 2-stock portfolio. Last year, stock A (B) has a return of 20% (-10%). If the price of stock A (B) is \$10 (\$90), then the price-weighted portfolio return would be -7%, that is, *0.2*(10/100)-0.1*(90/100)*. It is obvious that stocks with a higher unit price command a higher weight. Based on the preceding results for IBM and Walmart, the two weights for the price-weighted scheme are *0.9929478*; that is, *7.04/(7.04+0.05)* and *0.007052186*. Thus, the price-weighted portfolio return in that month is *0.03830747* and *0.9929478*0.04+0.007052186*(-0.2)*.

There are a few twists when estimating portfolio or index returns. The first one is whether returns include dividends and other distributions. For example, the CRSP database has EWRETD and EWRETX. EWRETD is defined as equal-weighed market returns based on stock returns including dividend, that is, total return. EWRETX is defined as equal-weighted market returns without dividends or other distributions. Similarly, for value-weighed returns, there exists VWRETD and VWRETX. The second twist is that it is common practice to use previous period's market capitalizations as weights instead of the current ones.

References

Please refer to the following articles:

- *Markowitz, Harry, 1952, Portfolio Selection, Journal of Finance 8,77-91,* http://onlinelibrary.wiley.com/doi/10.1111/j.1540-6261.1952.tb01525.x/full

- *Modigliani, Franco, 1997, Risk-Adjusted Performance, Journal of Portfolio Managemen, 45–54*

- *Sharpe, William F., 1994, the Sharpe Ratio, the Journal of Portfolio Management 21 (1), 49–58*

- *Sharpe, W. F., 1966, Mutual Fund Performance, Journal of Business 39 (S1), 119–138*

- *Scipy manual, Mathematical optimization: finding minima of functions,* http://www.scipy-lectures.org/advanced/mathematical_optimization/

- *Sortino, F.A., Price, L.N.,1994, Performance measurement in a downside risk framework, Journal of Investing 3, 50–8*

- *Treynor, Jack L., 1965, How to Rate Management of Investment Funds, Harvard Business Review 43, pp. 63–75*

Appendix A – data case #5 - which industry portfolio do you prefer?

Please go through the following objectives:

1. Understand the definitions of 49 industries.
2. Learn how to download data from Prof. French's Data Library.
3. Understand the utility function, see here.
4. Find out which industry is optimal for different types of investors.
5. Learn how to draw an indifference curve (for just one optimal portfolio).
   Procedure:
6. Go to *Professor French's Data Library* at:http://mba.tuck.dartmouth.edu/pages/faculty/ken.french/data_library.html.

7. Click CSV on the right-hand side of **49 Industry Portfolios**, see the following screenshot:

> **49 Industry Portfolios** TXT CSV Details
> **49 Industry Portfolios [ex. Dividends]** TXT CSV Details
> **49 Industry Portfolios [Daily]** TXT CSV Details

8. Estimate returns and variances for both value-weighted and equal-weighed industry portfolios.

9. Estimate the utility function for three types of investors with A=1, 2, and 4:

$$U = E(R) - \frac{1}{2}A * \sigma^2, \qquad (1)$$

Here U is the utility function, $E(R)$ is the expected portfolio return and we could use its mean to approximate, A is the risk-averse coefficient, and $\sigma2$ is the variance of the portfolio.

10. Choose one result, for example, the optimal value-weighted portfolio for an investor who has a value of 1 for A, draw an indifference curve.

11. Comment on your results.

From `http://mba.tuck.dartmouth.edu/pages/faculty/ken.french/Data_Library/det_49_ind_port.html`, we could find the definition of those 49 industries.

Appendix B – data case #6 - replicate S&P500 monthly returns

To finish this data case, your school has subscribed to the CRSP database.

Objectives:

1. Understand the concepts of equal-weighted and value weighed market index.

2. Write a Python program to replicate sp500 monthly returns.

3. Comment on your results.

Source of data: CRSP
sp500monthly.pkl
sp500add.pkl
stockMonthly.pkl

For the `sp500monthly.pkl`, see the following few observations:

```
import pandas as pd
x=pd.read_pickle("c:/temp/sp500monthly.pkl")
print(x.head())
print(x.tail())
      DATE     VWRETD    EWRETD     VWRETX     EWRETX  SP500INDEX
SP500RET   N
0  19251231       NaN       NaN        NaN        NaN       12.46
NaN   89
1  19260130 -0.001780  0.006457  -0.003980   0.003250       12.74
0.022472   89
2  19260227 -0.033290 -0.039970  -0.037870  -0.042450       12.18
-0.043950   89
3  19260331 -0.057700 -0.067910  -0.062000  -0.073270       11.46
-0.059110   89
4  19260430  0.038522  0.031441   0.034856   0.027121       11.72
0.022688   89
          DATE     VWRETD    EWRETD     VWRETX     EWRETX  SP500INDEX
SP500RET \
1076  20150831 -0.059940 -0.052900  -0.062280  -0.054850     1972.18
-0.062580
1077  20150930 -0.024530 -0.033490  -0.026240  -0.035550     1920.03
-0.026440
1078  20151030  0.083284  0.073199   0.081880   0.071983     2079.36
0.082983
1079  20151130  0.003317  0.002952   0.000771   0.000438     2080.41
0.000505
1080  20151231 -0.015180 -0.025550  -0.017010  -0.027650     2043.94
-0.017530
```

For `sp500add.pkl`, see the following few observations:

```
import pandas as pd
x=pd.read_pickle("c:/temp/sp500add.pkl")
print(x.head())
print(x.tail())
   PERMNO  DATEADDED  DAYDELETED
```

```
0     10006     19570301     19840718
1     10030     19570301     19690108
2     10049     19251231     19321001
3     10057     19570301     19920702
4     10078     19920820     20100128
        PERMNO    DATEADDED    DAYDELETED
1847    93002     20140508     20151231
1848    93089     20151008     20151231
1849    93096     20121203     20151231
1850    93159     20120731     20151231
1851    93422     20100701     20150630
```

For the last dataset called `stockMonthly.pkl`, see a few observations from it:

```
import pandas as pd
x=pd.read_pickle("c:/temp/stockMonthly.pkl")
print(x.head())
print(x.tail())
```

The output is shown here:

```
          Date      Return   Volume     Price   SharesOutStanding
permno
10000    1985-12-31      NaN      NaN      NaN                 NaN
10000    1986-01-31      NaN   1771.0  -4.3750              3680.0
10000    1986-02-28  -0.257140   828.0  -3.2500              3680.0
10000    1986-03-31   0.365385  1078.0  -4.4375              3680.0
10000    1986-04-30  -0.098590   957.0  -4.0000              3793.0
             Date      Return     Volume      Price   SharesOutStanding
permno
93436    2014-08-29   0.207792  1149281.0  269.7000           124630.0
93436    2014-09-30  -0.100180  1329469.0  242.6799           125366.0
93436    2014-10-31  -0.004030  1521398.0  241.7000           125382.0
93436    2014-11-28   0.011667  1077170.0  244.5200           125382.0
93436    2014-12-31  -0.090420  1271222.0  222.4100           125382.0
```

Exercises

1. What is the assumption behind *don't put all your eggs in one basket*?

2. What are the measures of risk?

3. How do you measure the co-moment between two stock returns?

4. Why it is argued that correlation is a better measure than covariance when we evaluate the co-movements between two stocks?

5. For two stocks A and B, with two pairs of (σA, σB) and (βA,βB), which pair is important when comparing their expected returns?

6. Is it true that variance and correlation of historical returns possess the same sign?

7. Find some inefficiency with the following code:

```
import scipy as sp
sigma1=0.02
sigma2=0.05
rho=-1
n=1000
portVar=10    # assign a big number
tiny=1.0/n
for i in sp.arange(n):
    w1=i*tiny
    w2=1-w1
    var=w1**2*sigma1**2 +w2**2*sigma2**2+2*w1*w2*rho*sigma1*sigma2
    if(var<portVar):
        portVar=var
        finalW1=w1
    #print(vol)
print("min vol=",sp.sqrt(portVar), "w1=",finalW1)
```

8. For a given set of σA, σB, and correlation (ρ), write a Python program to test whether we have a solution or not.

$$\left[\quad \text{ Test the equation of } \quad ax^2 + bx - c = 0 \quad \right]$$

$$x = \frac{b \pm \sqrt{b^2 - 4ac}}{2a}$$

9. What are the differences between covariance and correlation? Write a Python program to find out results for a given set of returns.

10. The portfolio risk is defined here. What is the impact of correlation on a portfolio's risk?

$$\sigma_p^2 = \sum_{i=1}^{n} \sum_{j=1}^{n} w_i \, w_i \sigma_{i,j}$$

11. For several stocks such as MSFT, IBM, WMT, ^GSPC, C, A, and AA, estimate their variance-covariance and correlation matrices based on the last five-year monthly returns data, for example, over the last five years. Which two stocks are most strongly correlated?

12. Based on the latest five-year monthly data and daily data, what are the correlations between IBM and WMT? Are they the same?

13. Generate a variance-covariance matrix for a market index and several stocks. Their tickers are C, MSFT, IBM, WMT, AAPL, AF, AIG, AP, and ^GSPC.

14. Is correlation constant between stocks over time?

[You could pick up a couple of stocks and then estimate correlations among them for several five-year windows.]

15. Are larger stocks, measured by their market capitalization, more strongly correlated among themselves than the correlation of small stocks among themselves?

16. To form a portfolio, we have the following three stocks to choose from:

    ○   Is it possible to form a 2-stock portfolio with zero portfolio risk?

    ○   What are the weights of those two stocks (to form a risk-free portfolio)?

Stock	Variance	Stock	Variance	Stock	Variance
A	0.0026	B	0.0418	C	0.0296

The corresponding correlation (coefficient) matrix is given here:

	A	B	C
A	1.0	-1.0	0.0
B	-1.0	1.0	0.7
C	0.0	0.7	1.0

1. When calculating variance or standard deviation, usually there are two definitions, based on population or based on a sample. The difference is the denominator. If based on population, we have the following formula:

$$\begin{cases} var = \sigma^2 = \dfrac{\sum_{i=1}^{n}(R_i - \bar{R})^2}{n} \\ \sigma = \sqrt{\sigma^2} \end{cases},$$

If based on a sample, we have the following formula:

$$\begin{cases} var = \sigma^2 = \dfrac{\sum_{i=1}^{n}(R_i - \bar{R})^2}{n-1} \\ \sigma = \sqrt{\sigma^2} \end{cases},$$

1. Find out whether `scipy.var()` and `spcipy.std()` functions are based on a sample or based on population.

2. Write a Python program to estimate the expected portfolio returns for 20 stocks by using your own weights and the latest 10 year data.

3. For 50 stocks, select at least five years of data. Estimate volatility for each stock, their average will be $\bar{\sigma}_1$. Then form several equal-weighted 2-stock portfolios and estimate their volatilities. Their average will be our $\bar{\sigma}_2$. Continue this way and $\bar{\sigma}_n$ will be the average volatility for n-stock equal-weighted portfolios. Draw a graph with n, the number of n-stock portfolios, as the x axis and the volatility of the n-stock portfolio $\bar{\sigma}_n$ as the y axis. Comment on it.

4. Find an appropriate definition for industry. Choosing seven stocks from each industry, estimate their correlation matrix. Then do the same thing on another industry. Comment on your results.

5. Write a Python program to estimate the optimal portfolio construction by using 10 stocks.

6. Find the average of correlations for five industries, at least 10 stocks in each industry.

7. To estimate the volatility of a portfolio, we have two formulae: for a 2-stock portfolio and for an n-stock portfolio. Show that when n equals 2, we expand the formula to estimate the volatility of an n-stock portfolio; we end up with the same formula for a 2-stock portfolio.

8. Is the following statement correct? Prove or disapprove it.

$$\Bigg[\quad \quad \text{Stock returns are uncorrelated.} \qquad \Bigg]$$

9. Downloading one year IBM daily data and estimate its Sharpe ratio by using two methods: its definition, and write a `sharpe()` function in Python.

10. Update yanMonthly.pkl, http://canisius.edu/~yany/python/
    yanMonthly.pkl, see the following first and last several lines. Note that for
    stock, VALUE is monthly stock price, for Fama-French factors, VALUE is their
    factor, that is, their monthly portfolio returns:

```
import pandas as pd
x=pd.read_pickle('c:/temp/yanMonthly.pkl')
print(x.head(2))
print(x.tail(3))
              DATE    VALUE
NAME
000001.SS  19901231  127.61
000001.SS  19910131  129.97
              DATE    VALUE
NAME
^TWII  20130930  8173.87
^TWII  20131031  8450.06
^TWII  20131122  8116.78
```

11. For the Markowitz's optimization, only the first two moments are used.
    Why? What are the definitions of the third and fourth moments? What is the
    impact when those two moments are ignored? How do you include them?

12. Write a Python program to estimate equal-weighed and value-weighted
    monthly returns for 10 stocks from January 2nd, 2012 to December 31st, 2013.
    The data used is yanMonthly.pkl, http://canisius.edu/~yany/python/
    yanMonthly.pkl. For value-weighed returns, the weight is the number of
    shares invested times the price of the previous month.

13. For this question, assume that your school has subscribed to the **Center
    for Research in Security Prices (CRSP)** database. Replicate VWRETD and
    EWRETD in CRSP. Note that the monthly CRSP dataset should be used. A few
    observations from a dataset called stockMonthly.pkl are shown here:

```
import pandas as pd
x=pd.read_pickle("c:/temp/stockMonthly.pkl")
print(x.head())
print(x.tail())
```

The output is shown here:

```
         Date    Return  Volume   Price  SharesOutStanding
permno
10000  1985-12-31     NaN    NaN     NaN               NaN
10000  1986-01-31     NaN  1771.0  -4.3750            3680.0
10000  1986-02-28  -0.257140   828.0  -3.2500            3680.0
10000  1986-03-31   0.365385  1078.0  -4.4375            3680.0
```

```
10000   1986-04-30  -0.098590    957.0  -4.0000              3793.0
              Date      Return     Volume      Price
SharesOutStanding
permno
93436   2014-08-29   0.207792  1149281.0  269.7000
124630.0
93436   2014-09-30  -0.100180  1329469.0  242.6799
125366.0
93436   2014-10-31  -0.004030  1521398.0  241.7000
125382.0
93436   2014-11-28   0.011667  1077170.0  244.5200
125382.0
93436   2014-12-31  -0.090420  1271222.0  222.4100
125382.0
```

14. Write a Python program to complete Modigliani and Modigliani (1997) performance test.

15. For several performance measures such as Sharpe ratio, Treynor ratio, and Sortino ratio, see here, the benefits and costs are compared by dividing them:

$$sharpe = \frac{E(R_p) - R_f}{\sigma_p} \qquad (1)$$

$$Treynor\ Ratio = \frac{\bar{R}_p - \bar{R}_f}{\beta_p} \qquad (2)$$

$$Sortino\ Ratio = \frac{\bar{R}_p - \bar{R}_f}{LPSD} \qquad (3)$$

On the other hand, the utility function, see the following formula, also balances the benefits with the costs by choosing their difference:

$$U = E(R) - \frac{1}{2} A * \sigma^2, \qquad (4)$$

Compare those two approaches. Could we have a more general form to combine those two ways?

16. Estimating the Sharpe ratio, Treynor, and Sortino ratio for the Fama-French 49 industries. The risk-free rate could be found at http://finance.yahoo.com/bonds. Alternatively, the risk-free rate from ffMonthly.pkl, http://canisius.edu/~yany/python/ffMonthly.pkl, could be used. The dataset used is ff49industries.pkl, which is downloadable at http://canisius.edu/~yany/python/ff49industries.pkl. A few lines are shown here:

```
import pandas as pd
x=pd.read_pickle("c:/temp/ff49industries.pkl")
print(x.head(2))
        Agric    Food     Soda     Beer    Smoke     Toys
Fun       \
192607    2.37    0.12   -99.99    -5.19    1.29     8.65
2.50
192608    2.23    2.68   -99.99    27.03    6.50    16.81
-0.76
        Books    Hshld    Clths    ...      Boxes    Trans
Whlsl     \
192607   50.21   -0.48     8.08    ...       7.70     1.94
-23.79
192608   42.98   -3.58    -2.51    ...      -2.38     4.88
5.39
        Rtail    Meals    Banks    Insur    RlEst     Fin
Other
192607    0.07    1.87     4.61    -0.54     2.89    -4.85
5.20
192608   -0.75   -0.13    11.83     2.57     5.30    -0.57
6.76
[2 rows x 49 columns]
```

Summary

In this chapter, we first explained various concepts related to portfolio theory, such as covariance and correlation for a pair of stocks and for a portfolio. After that, we discussed various risk measures for individual stocks or portfolios, such as the Sharpe ratio, Treynor ratio, and Sortino ratio, how to minimize portfolio risks based on those measures (ratios), how to set up an objective function, how to choose an efficient portfolio for a given set of stocks, and how to construct an efficient frontier.

For the next chapter, *Chapter 10*, *Options and Futures*, we will explain some basic concepts first. Then, we will discuss the famous Black-Scholes-Merton options model. In addition, various trading strategies involving options will be discussed in detail.

10
Options and Futures

In modern finance, the option theory (including futures and forwards) and its applications play an important role. Many trading strategies, corporate incentive plans, and hedging strategies include various types of options. For example, many executive incentive plans are based on stock options. Assume that an importer located in the US has just ordered a piece of machinery from England with a payment of £10 million in three months. The importer has a currency risk (or exchange rate risk). If the pound depreciates against the US dollar, the importer would be better off since he/she pays less US dollars to buy £10 million. On the contrary, if the pound appreciates against the US dollar, then the importer would suffer a loss. There are several ways that the importer could avoid or reduce such a risk: buy pounds right now, enter a futures market to buy pounds with a fixed exchange rate determined today, or long a call option with a fixed exercise price. In this chapter, we will explain the option theory and its related applications. In particular, the following topics will be covered:

- How to hedge currency risk, a market-wide short-term downturn
- Payoff and profit/loss functions for calls and puts and their graphical representations
- European versus American options
- Normal distribution, standard normal distribution, and cumulative normal distribution
- Black-Scholes-Merton option model with/without dividend
- Various trading strategies and their visual presentations, such as covered call, straddle, butterfly, and calendar spread
- Delta, gamma, and other Greeks
- The put-call parity and its graphical representation
- Graphical representation for a one-step and a two-step binomial tree model

- Using the binomial tree method to price both European and American options
- Implied volatility, volatility smile and skewness

Options theory is an integral part of finance theory. It is difficult to image that a finance student would not understand it. However, it is quite demanding to comprehend the theory thoroughly. Many finance-major students view options theory as rocket science, since it involves how to solve various differential equations. In order to satisfy as many readers as possible, in this chapter we avoid complex mathematical derivations.

An option would give the option buyer a right to buy or sell something in the future with a fixed price determined today. If the buyer has a right to buy something in the future, it is called a call option. If the option buyer is entitled to sell something, it is called a put option. Since there are two persons (sides) for each transaction, the buyer pays to acquire a right, while the seller receives cash inflow today to bear an obligation. Unlike options, a futures contract would give the buyer and seller both rights and obligations. Unlike options with an initial cash flow from buyer to seller, for a futures contract, usually there is no initial cash flow. Forward contracts are quite similar to future contracts with a few exceptions. In this chapter, these two types of contracts (futures and forwards) are not distinguished. A forward contract is easier to analyze than a future contract. If a reader wants a more in-depth analysis, he/she should consult other related textbooks.

Introducing futures

Before discussing the basic concepts and formulas related to futures, let's review the concept of continuously compounded interest rates. In *Chapter 3*, *Time Value of Money*, we learned that the following formula could be applied to estimate the future value of a given present value:

$$FV = PV(1 + R)^n \qquad \dots (1)$$

Here, FV is the future value, PV is the present value, R is the effective period rate and n is the number of periods. For example, assume that the **Annual Percentage Rate (APR)** is 8%, compounded semiannually. If we deposit $100 today, what is its future value in two years? The following code shows the result:

```
import scipy as ps
pv=100
APR=0.08
rate=APR/2.0
```

```
n=2
nper=n*2
fv=ps.fv(rate,nper,0,pv)
print(fv)
```

The output is shown here:

```
-116.985856
```

The future value is $116.99. In the preceding program, the effective semiannual rate is 4% since the APR is 8% compounded semiannually. In options theory, risk-free rates and dividend yields are defined as continuously compounded. It is easy to derive the relationship between an effective (or APR) rate and a continuously compounded rate. The second way to estimate a future value for a given present value is shown here:

$$FV = PV e^{R_c T} \quad \ldots (2)$$

Here, R_c is the continuously compounded rate and T is the number of years. In other words, when applying Equation (1), we could have many combinations, such as annual effective rate and the number of years, effective monthly rate and number of months, and the like. However, this is not true for Equation (2), which has only one pair: continuously compounded rate and the number of years. To derive the relationship between one effective rate and its corresponding continuously compounded rate, we recommend the following simple approach: choose $1 as our present value and 1 year as our investment horizon. Then apply the previous two equations and set them equal. Assume that we know that the effective semiannual rate is given, 4% in the preceding case. What is its equivalent R_c?

$$FV = (1 + R_{semiannual})^n$$
$$FV = e^{R_c}$$

We equate them to have the following equation:

$$e^{R_c} = (1 + R_{semiannual})^2$$

Taking the natural log on both sides of the previous equation, we have the following solution:

$$R_c = 2 * \ln(1 + R_{semiannual}) = 2 * \ln(1 + 0.04) = 0.078441426306562659$$

With a simple generalization of the preceding approach, we end up with the following formula to convert an effective rate to its corresponding continuously compounded rate:

$$R_c = m * \ln\left(1 + R_{effective}\right) \quad \dots (3)$$

Here, m is the compounding frequency per year: $m=1, 2, 4, 12, 52, 365$ for annual, semiannual, quarterly, monthly, weekly, and daily, respectively. *Reffective* is APR divided by m. If an APR with related compounding frequency is given, we have the following equivalent converting formula:

$$R_c = m * \ln\left(1 + \frac{APR}{m}\right) \quad \dots (3B)$$

On the other hand, it is quite easy to derive the formula to estimate an effective rate from a given continuous rate:

$$R_{effective} = e^{\frac{R_c}{m}} \quad \dots (4)$$

To verify the preceding equation, see the following codes:

```
import scipy as sp
Rc=2*log(1+0.04)
print(sp.exp(Rc/2)-1
0.040000000000000036
```

Similarly, we have the following formula to estimate the APR from an Rc:

$$APR = m * e^{\frac{R_c}{m}} \quad \dots (4B)$$

For a futures contract, let's use the preceding example of an importer in the US who is going to pay £10 million in three months. Usually, there are two ways to present an exchange rate: value of the first currency per unit of the second currency, and the opposite. Let's treat US as domestic and England as foreign, and the exchange rate is quoted in dollars per pound. Assume that today the exchange rate is £1 = 1.25 USD, the domestic interest rate is 1% and the foreign interest rate (in England) is 2%. The following codes show how much we need today in terms of pounds and US dollars:

```
import scipy as sp
amount=5
r_foreign=0.02
T=3./12.
exchangeRateToday=1.25
poundToday=5*sp.exp(-r_foreign*T)
print("Pound needed today=", poundToday)
usToday=exchangeRateToday*poundToday
print("US dollar needed today", usToday)
('Pound needed today=', 4.9750623959634117)
('US dollar needed today', 6.2188279949542649)
```

The result shows that we would need £4.975 million today to satisfy the payment of £5 million in three months, since we could deposit £4.975 million in a bank to earn extra interest (at 1%). If the importer has no pounds, they could spend $6.2188 million US dollars to purchase the amount of pounds today. Alternatively, the importer could long a future contract (or a few future contracts) to purchase pounds in three months with a fixed exchange rate determined today. The forward rate (future exchange rate) is given here:

$$F = S_0 e^{(R_d - R_f)T} \qquad \dots (5)$$

Here, F is the future price (in this case future exchange rate determined today), $S0$ is the spot price (in this case today's exchange rate), Rd is the domestic risk-free rate compounded continuously, Rf is the foreign deposit rate compounded continuously and T is the maturity in years. The following Python program shows the future price today:

```
import scipy as sp
def futuresExchangeRate(s0,rateDomestic,rateForeign,T):
    futureEx=s0*sp.exp((rateDomestic-rateForeign)*T)
return futureEx

# input area
```

```
s0=1.25
rHome=0.01
rForeigh=0.02
T=3./12.
#
futures=futuresExchangeRate(s0,rHome,rForeigh,T)
print("futures=",futures)
```

The output is shown here:

```
('futures=', 1.246878902996825)
```

Based on the result, the exchange rate in three months should be 1.2468789 US dollars per pound. In other words, US dollars should have depreciated against the British pound. The reason is based on the two interest rates. Here is the logic based on the no arbitrage principle. Assume that we have $1.25 USD today. We have two choices: deposit in a US bank to enjoy 2%, or exchange it for 1 pound and deposit it in a foreign bank, enjoying 1%. Assume further, if the future exchange rate is not 1.246879, we would have an arbitrate opportunity. Just assume that the futures price (for exchange rate) is $1.26 indicating that the pound is overvalued relative to the US dollar. An arbitrator would buy low and sell high, that is, short futures. Assume that we have one pound obligation in three months. Here is the arbitrage strategy: borrow $1.25 (USD) and sell one pound in three months with a future price of $1.26. At the end of three months, here is the profit of our arbitrage:

```
import scipy as sp
obligationForeign=1.0              # how much to pay in 3 months
f=1.26                             # future price
s0=1.25                            # today's exchange rate
rHome=0.01
rForeign=0.02
T=3./12.
todayObligationForeign=obligationForeign*sp.exp(-rForeign*T)
usBorrow=todayObligationForeign*s0
costDollarBorrow=usBorrow*sp.exp(rHome*T)
profit=f*obligationForeign-costDollarBorrow
print("profit in USD =", profit)
```

The output is shown here:

```
('profit in USD =', 0.013121097003174764)
```

The profit is 0.15 USD. If the future price is lower than 1.246878902996825, an arbitrager would take an opposite position, that is, long a future contract. For stocks with no dividend payment before the expiry date, we have the following future price:

$$F = S_0 e^{(R_f - yield)T} \quad \dots (6)$$

Here F is the futures price, $S0$ is the current stock price, Rf is the continuously compounded risk-free rate, yield is the dividend yield continuously compounded. For known discrete dividends before a maturity date, we have the following formula:

$$F = [S_0 - PV(D)]e^{R_f T} \quad \dots (7)$$

Here, $PV(D)$ is the present value of all dividends before the expiry date. Futures could be used as a hedging tool or for speculation. Assume that a mutual fund manager is worried about the market's potential negative movement in a short term. Assume further that his/her portfolio is positively correlated with the market portfolio, such as S&P500 index. Thus, he/she should short futures on S&P500. Here is a related formula:

$$n = \left(\beta_{target} - \beta_p\right) * \frac{V_p}{V_F} \quad \dots (8)$$

Here, n is the number of futures contracts to long or short, $\beta target$ is the target beta, βp is the beta of our current portfolio, Vp is the value of the portfolio, and VF is the value of one futures contract. If n is less (bigger) than zero, it means a short (long) position. Here is an example. Assume John Doe is managing a portfolio worth $50 million today and his portfolio has a beta of 1.10 with S&P500. He is worried that the market might go down in the next six months. It is not feasible to sell his portfolio or part of it because of the transaction costs. Assume that in the short term, his target beta is zero. For each point of S&P500, the price is $250. Since today's S&P500 is 2297.41, the value of one futures contract is $5,743,550. The number of contracts John should short (or long) is given here:

```
import scipy as ps
# input area
todaySP500index=2297.42
valuePortfolio=50e6
betaPortfolio=1.1
betaTarget=0
#
priceEachPoint=250
```

```
contractFuturesSP500=todaySP500index*priceEachPoint
n=(betaTarget-betaPortfolio)*valuePortfolio/contractFuturesSP500
print("number of contracts SP500 futures=",n)
```

The output is shown here:

```
('number of contracts SP500 futures=', -95.75959119359979)
```

A negative value indicates a short position. John Doe should short 96 S&P500 futures contracts. This is consistent with common sense, since the portfolio is positively correlated with the S&P500 index. The following program shows the profit or loss with and without hedging when the S&P500 index level falls 97 points:

```
# input area

import scipy as sp
sp500indexToday=2297.42
valuePortfolio=50e6
betaPortfolio=1.1
betaTarget=0
sp500indexNmonthsLater=2200.0
#
priceEachPoint=250
contractFuturesSP500=sp500indexToday*priceEachPoint
n=(betaTarget-betaPortfolio)*valuePortfolio/contractFuturesSP500
mySign=sp.sign(n)
n2=mySign*sp.ceil(abs(n))
print("number of contracts=",n2)
# hedging result
v1=sp500indexToday
v2=sp500indexNmonthsLater
lossFromPortfolio=valuePortfolio*(v2-v1)/v1
gainFromFutures=n2*(v2-v1)*priceEachPoint
net=gainFromFutures+lossFromPortfolio
print("loss from portfolio=", lossFromPortfolio)
print("gain from futures contract=", gainFromFutures)
print("net=", net)
```

The related output is shown here:

```
('number of contracts=', -96.0)
('loss from portfolio=', -2120204.403200113)
('gain from futures contract=', 2338080.0000000019)
('net=', 217875.59679988865)
```

From the last three lines, we know that without hedging, the loss in portfolio value would be $2.12 million. On the other hand, after shorting 96 S&P500 futures contracts, the net loss is only $217,876 after the S&P500 index falls 98 points in six months. With a few different potential S&P500 index levels, we could find out their related hedging and no-hedging results. Such a hedging strategy is usually called portfolio insurance.

Payoff and profit/loss functions for call and put options

An option gives its buyer the right to buy (call option) or sell (put option) something in the future to the option seller at a predetermined price (exercise price). For example, if we buy a European call option to acquire a stock for X dollars, such as $30, at the end of three months our payoff on maturity day will be the one calculated using the following formula:

$$payoff(call) = Max(S_T - X, 0) \quad \dots (9)$$

Here, S_T is the stock price at the maturity date (T), the exercise price is X (X=30 in this case). Assume that three months later the stock price is $25. We would not exercise our call option to pay $30 in exchange for the stock since we could buy the same stock with $25 in the open market. On the other hand, if the stock price is $40, we will exercise our right to reap a payoff of $10, that is, buy the stock at $30 and sell it at $40. The following program presents the payoff function for a call:

```
>>>def payoff_call(sT,x):
        return (sT-x+abs(sT-x))/2
```

Applying the `payoff` function is straightforward:

```
>>> payoff_call(25,30)
0
>>> payoff_call(40,30)
10
```

The first input variable, stock price at the maturity T, could be an array as well:

```
>> import numpy as np
>> x=20
>> sT=np.arange(10,50,10)
>>> sT
array([10, 20, 30, 40])
>>> payoff_call(s,x)
array([ 0.,   0.,   10.,   20.])
>>>
```

To create a graphic presentation, we have the following codes:

```
import numpy as np
import matplotlib.pyplot as plt
s = np.arange(10,80,5)
x=30
payoff=(abs(s-x)+s-x)/2
plt.ylim(-10,50)
plt.plot(s,payoff)
plt.title("Payoff for a call (x=30)")
plt.xlabel("stock price")
plt.ylabel("Payoff of a call")
plt.show()
```

The graph is shown here:

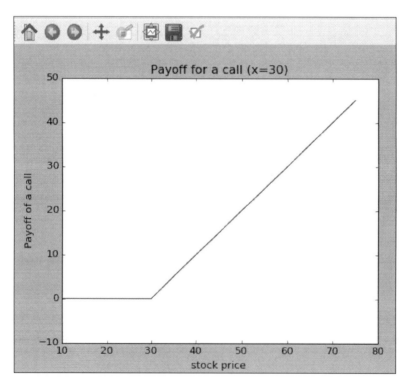

The payoff for a call option seller is the opposite of its buyer. It is important to remember that this is a zero-sum game: you win, I lose. For example, an investor sold three call options with an exercise price of $10. When the stock price is $15 on the maturity, the option buyer's payoff is $15, while the total loss to the option writer is $15 as well. If the call premium (option price) is c, the profit/loss function for a call option buyer is the difference between her payoff and her initial investment (c). Obviously, the timing of cash-flows of paying an option premium upfront and its payoff at maturity day is different. Here, we ignore the time value of money since maturities are usually quite short.

For a call option buyer:

$$Profit/loss(call) = Max(S_T - X, 0) - c \qquad \dots (10)$$

For a call option seller:

$$Profit/loss(call) = c - Max(S_T - X, 0) \qquad \dots (11)$$

The following graph shows the profit/loss functions for call option buyer and seller:

```
import scipy as sp
import matplotlib.pyplot as plt
s = sp.arange(30,70,5)
x=45;c=2.5
y=(abs(s-x)+s-x)/2 -c
y2=sp.zeros(len(s))
plt.ylim(-30,50)
plt.plot(s,y)
plt.plot(s,y2,'-.')
plt.plot(s,-y)
plt.title("Profit/Loss function")
plt.xlabel('Stock price')
plt.ylabel('Profit (loss)')
plt.annotate('Call option buyer', xy=(55,15), xytext=(35,20),
            arrowprops=dict(facecolor='blue',shrink=0.01),)
plt.annotate('Call option seller', xy=(55,-10), xytext=(40,-20),
            arrowprops=dict(facecolor='red',shrink=0.01),)
plt.show()
```

A graphical representation is shown here:

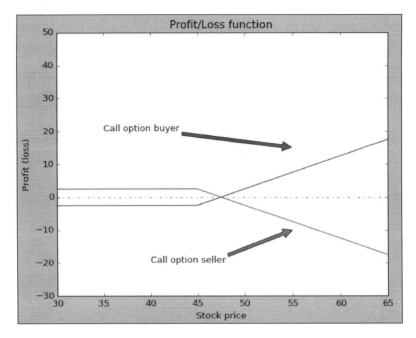

A put option gives its buyer a right to sell a security (commodity) to the put option buyer in the future at a predetermined price, X. Here is its payoff function:

$$Payoff(put) = Max(X - S_T, 0) \quad \dots (12)$$

Here, ST is the stock price at maturity and X is the exercise price (strike price). For a put option buyer, the profit/loss function is given here:

$$Profit/loss(put) = Max(X - S_T, 0) - p \quad \dots (13)$$

The profit/loss function for a put option seller is just the opposite:

$$Profit/loss(put) = p - Max(X - S_T, 0) \quad \dots (14)$$

The related program and graph for the profit and loss functions for a put option buyer and a seller are shown here:

```
import scipy as sp
import matplotlib.pyplot as plt
s = sp.arange(30,70,5)
```

```
x=45;p=2;c=2.5
y=c-(abs(x-s)+x-s)/2
y2=sp.zeros(len(s))
x3=[x, x]
y3=[-30,10]
plt.ylim(-30,50)
plt.plot(s,y)
plt.plot(s,y2,'-.')
plt.plot(s,-y)
plt.plot(x3,y3)
plt.title("Profit/Loss function for a put option")
plt.xlabel('Stock price')
plt.ylabel('Profit (loss)')
plt.annotate('Put option buyer', xy=(35,12), xytext=(35,45), arrowprop
s=dict(facecolor='red',shrink=0.01),)
plt.annotate('Put option seller', xy=(35,-10), xytext=(35,-25), arrowp
rops=dict(facecolor='blue',shrink=0.01),)
plt.annotate('Exercise price', xy=(45,-30), xytext=(50,-20), arrowprop
s=dict(facecolor='black',shrink=0.01),)
plt.show()
```

The graph is shown here:

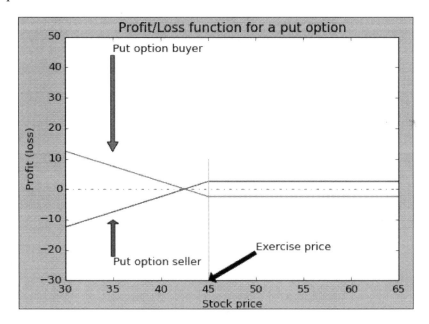

European versus American options

A European option can be exercised only on maturity day, while an American option can be exercised any time before or on its maturity day. Since an American option could be held until it matures, its price (option premium) should be higher than or equal to its European counterpart:

$$\begin{cases} C_{American} \geq C_{European} \\ P_{American} \geq P_{European} \end{cases} \quad \dots (15)$$

An import difference is that for a European option, we have a close form solution, that is, the Black-Scholes-Merton option model. However, we don't have a close-form solution for an American option. Fortunately, we have several ways to price an American option. Later in the chapter, we show how to use the Binomial-tree method, also called the CRR method, to price an American option.

Understanding cash flows, types of options, rights and obligations

We know that for each business contract, we have two sides: buyer versus seller. This is true for an option contract as well. A call buyer will pay upfront (cash output) to acquire a right. Since this is a zero-sum game, a call option seller would enjoy an upfront cash inflow and assumes an obligation.

The following table presents those positions (buyer or seller), directions of the initial cash flows (inflow or outflow), the option buyer's rights (buy or sell) and the option seller's obligations (that is, to satisfy the option seller's desires):

	Buyer (long position)	Seller (short position)	European Options	American Options
Call	A right to buy a security (commodity) at a pre-fixed price	An obligation to sell a security (commodity) at a pre-fixed price	Can be exercised on maturity day only	Can be exercised any time before or on maturity day
Put	A right to sell a security with a pre-fixed price	An obligation to buy		
Cash Flow	Upfront cash outflow	Upfront cash inflow		

Table 10.1 Long, short positions, initial cash flows, and right versus obligation

Black-Scholes-Merton option model on non-dividend paying stocks

The **Black-Scholes-Merton option** model is a closed-form solution to price a European option on a stock which does not pay any dividends before its maturity date. If we use S_0 or the price today, X for the exercise price, r for the continuously compounded risk-free rate, T for the maturity in years, σ for the volatility of the stock, the closed-form formulae for a European call (c) and put (p) are:

$$
\left\{
\begin{array}{l}
d_1 = \dfrac{\ln\left(\frac{S_0}{X}\right)+\left(r+\frac{1}{2}\sigma^2\right)T}{\sigma\sqrt{T}} \\[2ex]
d_2 = d_1 - \sigma\sqrt{T} \\[1ex]
c = S_0 N(d_1) - X e^{-rT} N(d_2) \\[1ex]
p = X e^{-rT} N(-d_2) - S_0 N(-d_1) d_2
\end{array}
\right. \qquad \ldots (18)
$$

Here, N() is the cumulative standard normal distribution. The following Python codes represent the preceding equations to evaluate a European call:

```
from scipy import log,exp,sqrt,stats
def bs_call(S,X,T,r,sigma):
    d1=(log(S/X)+(r+sigma*sigma/2.)*T)/(sigma*sqrt(T))
    d2 = d1-sigma*sqrt(T)
return S*stats.norm.cdf(d1)-X*exp(-r*T)*stats.norm.cdf(d2)
```

In the preceding program, the stats.norm.cdf() is the cumulative normal distribution, that is, N() in the Black-Scholes-Merton option model. The current stock price is $40, the strike price is $42, the time to maturity is six months, the risk-free rate is 1.5% compounded continuously, and the volatility of the underlying stock is 20% (compounded continuously). Based on the preceding codes, the European call is worth $1.56:

```
>>>c=bs_call(40.,42.,0.5,0.015,0.2)
>>>round(c,2)
1.56
```

Generating our own module p4f

We could combine many small Python progams as one program, such as `p4f.py`. For instance, the preceding Python program called `bs_call()` function is included. Such a collection of programs offers several benefits. First, when we use the `bs_call()` function, we don't have to type those five lines. To save space, we only show a few functions included in `p4f.py`. For brevity, we remove all comments included for each function. Those comments are designed to help future users when issuing the `help()` function, such as `help(bs_call())`:

```python
def bs_call(S,X,T,rf,sigma):
    from scipy import log,exp,sqrt,stats
    d1=(log(S/X)+(rf+sigma*sigma/2.)*T)/(sigma*sqrt(T))
    d2 = d1-sigma*sqrt(T)
    return S*stats.norm.cdf(d1)-X*exp(-rf*T)*stats.norm.cdf(d2)

def binomial_grid(n):
    import networkx as nx
    import matplotlib.pyplot as plt
    G=nx.Graph()
    for i in range(0,n+1):
        for j in range(1,i+2):
            if i<n:
                G.add_edge((i,j),(i+1,j))
                G.add_edge((i,j),(i+1,j+1))
    posG={}    #dictionary with nodes position
    for node in G.nodes():
        posG[node]=(node[0],n+2+node[0]-2*node[1])
    nx.draw(G,pos=posG)

def delta_call(S,X,T,rf,sigma):
    from scipy import log,exp,sqrt,stats
    d1=(log(S/X)+(rf+sigma*sigma/2.)*T)/(sigma*sqrt(T))
    return(stats.norm.cdf(d1))

def delta_put(S,X,T,rf,sigma):
    from scipy import log,exp,sqrt,stats
    d1=(log(S/X)+(rf+sigma*sigma/2.)*T)/(sigma*sqrt(T))
    return(stats.norm.cdf(d1)-1)
```

To apply the Black-Scholes-Merton call option model, we simply use the following codes:

```python
>>>import p4f
>>>c=p4f.bs_call(40,42,0.5,0.015,0.2)
>>>round(c,2)
1.56
```

The second advantage is to save space and make our programming simpler. Later in the chapter, this point will become clearer when we use a function called `binomial_ grid()`. From now onward, when a function is discussed the first time, we will offer the complete codes. However, when the program is used again and the program is quite complex, we will call it indirectly via `p4f`. To find out our working directory, use the following codes:

```
>>>import os
>>>print os.getcwd()
```

European options with known dividends

Assume that we have a known dividend $d1$ distributed at time T1, T1<T, where T is our maturity date. We can modify the original Black-Scholes-Merton option model by replacing *S0* with *S*, where $S = S_0 - PV(d_1) = S_0 - e^{-rT_1}d_1$:

$$S = S_0 - e^{-rT_1}d_1 \qquad \dots (19)$$

$$d_1 = \frac{\ln\left(\frac{S}{X}\right)+(r+\frac{1}{2}\sigma^2)T}{\sigma\sqrt{T}} \qquad \dots (20)$$

$$d_2 = \frac{\ln\left(\frac{S}{X}\right)+(r-\frac{1}{2}\sigma^2)T}{\sigma\sqrt{T}} = d_1 - \sigma\sqrt{T} \qquad \dots (21)$$

$$c = S * N(d_1) - X * e^{-rT}N(d_2) \qquad \dots (22)$$

$$p = X * e^{-rT}N(-d_2) - S * N(-d_1) \qquad \dots (23)$$

In the preceding example, if we have a known dividend of \$1.5 delivered in one month, what is the price of the call?

```
>>>import p4f
>>>s0=40
>>>d1=1.5
>>>r=0.015
>>>T=6/12
>>>s=s0-exp(-r*T*d1)
>>>x=42
>>>sigma=0.2
>>>round(p4f.bs_call(s,x,T,r,sigma),2)
1.18
```

The first line of the program imports the module called `p4f` which contains the call option model. The result shows that the price of the call is $1.18, which is lower than the previous value ($1.56). It is understandable since the price of the underlying stock would drop roughly by $1.5 in one month. Because of this, the chance that we could exercise our call option will be smaller, that is, less likely to go beyond $42. The preceding argument is true for multiple known dividends distributed before T, that is, $= S_0 - \sum e^{-rT_i} d_i$.

Various trading strategies

In the following table, we summarize several commonly used trading strategies involving various types of options:

Names	Description	Direction of initial cash-flow	Expectation of future price movement
Bull spread with calls	Buy a call (x1) sell a call (x2) [x1< x2]	Outflow	Rise
Bull spread with puts	Buy a put (x1), sell a put (x2) [x1< x2]	Inflow	Rise
Bear spread with puts	Buy a put (x2), sell a put (x1) [x1 < x2]	Outflow	Fall
Bear spread with calls	Buy a call (x2), sell a call (x1) [x1 < x2]	Inflow	Fall
Straddle	Buy a call & sell a put with the same x	Outflow	Rise or fall
Strip	Buy two puts and a call (with the same x)	Outflow	Prob (fall) > prob (rise)
Strap	Buy two calls and one put (with the same x)	Outflow	Prob (rise)> prob(fall)
Strangle	Buy a call (x2) and buy a put (x1) [x1 < x2]	Outflow	Rise or fall
Butterfly with calls	Buy two calls (x1,x3) and sell two calls (x2) [x2=(x1+x3)/2]	Outflow	Stay around x2
Butterfly with puts	Buy two puts (x1,x3) and sell two puts (x2) [x2=(x1+x3)/2]		Stay around x2
Calendar spread	Sell a call (T1) and buy a call (T2) with the same strike price and T1<T2	Outflow	

Table 10.2 Various trading strategies

Covered-call – long a stock and short a call

Assume that we purchase 100 shares of stock A, with a price of $10 each. Thus, the total cost is $1,000. If at the same time we write a call contract, one contract is worth 100 shares, at a price of $20. Thus, our total cost will be reduced by $20. Assume further that the exercise price is $12. The graphic presentation of our profit and loss function is given here:

```python
import matplotlib.pyplot as plt
import numpy as np
sT = np.arange(0,40,5)
k=15;s0=10;c=2
y0=np.zeros(len(sT))
y1=sT-s0                    # stock only
y2=(abs(sT-k)+sT-k)/2-c     # long a call
y3=y1-y2                    # covered-call
plt.ylim(-10,30)
plt.plot(sT,y1)
plt.plot(sT,y2)
plt.plot(sT,y3,'red')
plt.plot(sT,y0,'b-.')
plt.plot([k,k],[-10,10],'black')
plt.title('Covered call (long one share and short one call)')
plt.xlabel('Stock price')
plt.ylabel('Profit (loss)')
plt.annotate('Stock only (long one share)', xy=(24,15),xytext=(15,20),
arrowprops=dict(facecolor='blue',shrink=0.01),)
plt.annotate('Long one share, short a call', xy=(10,4), xytext=(9,25),
arrowprops=dict(facecolor='red',shrink=0.01),)
plt.annotate('Exercise price= '+str(k), xy=(k+0.2,-10+0.5))
plt.show()
```

The related graph showing the positions of a stock only, call, and covered-call is given here. Obviously, when the stock price is under $17 (15 +2), the covered-call is better than long a share:

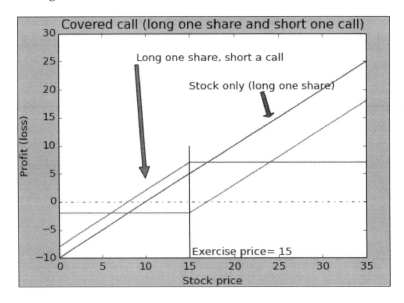

Straddle – buy a call and a put with the same exercise prices

Let's look at the simplest scenario. A firm faces an uncertain event next month. The issue is that we are not sure about its direction, that is, a good event or bad one. To take advantage of such an opportunity, we could u a call and buy a put with the same exercise prices. This means that we will benefit either way: the stock moves up or down. Assume further that the exercise price is $30. The payoff of such a strategy is given here:

```
import matplotlib.pyplot as plt
import numpy as np
sT = np.arange(30,80,5)
x=50;    c=2; p=1
straddle= (abs(sT-x)+sT-x)/2-c + (abs(x-sT)+x-sT)/2-p
y0=np.zeros(len(sT))
plt.ylim(-6,20)
plt.xlim(40,70)
plt.plot(sT,y0)
plt.plot(sT,straddle,'r')
plt.plot([x,x],[-6,4],'g-.')
```

```
plt.title("Profit-loss for a Straddle")
plt.xlabel('Stock price')
plt.ylabel('Profit (loss)')
plt.annotate('Point 1='+str(x-c-p), xy=(x-p-c,0), xytext=(x-p-c,10),
arrowprops=dict(facecolor='red',shrink=0.01),)
plt.annotate('Point 2='+str(x+c+p), xy=(x+p+c,0), xytext=(x+p+c,13),
arrowprops=dict(facecolor='blue',shrink=0.01),)
plt.annotate('exercise price', xy=(x+1,-5))
plt.annotate('Buy a call and buy a put with the same exercise
price',xy=(45,16))
plt.show()
```

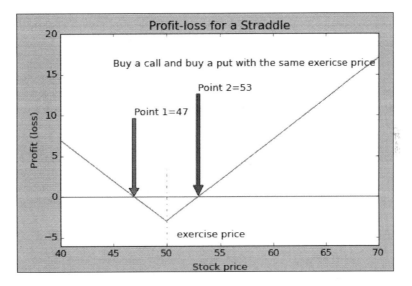

The preceding graph shows whichever way the stock goes, we would profit. Could we lose? Obviously, when the stock does not change much, our expectation fails to materialize.

Butterfly with calls

When buying two calls with the exercises price of $x1$ and $x3$ and selling two calls with the exercise price of $x2$, where $x2=(x1+x2)/2$, with the same maturity for the same stock, we call it a butterfly. Its profit-loss function is shown here:

```
import matplotlib.pyplot as plt
import numpy as np
sT = np.arange(30,80,5)
x1=50;    c1=10
x2=55;    c2=7
```

```
x3=60;      c3=5
y1=(abs(sT-x1)+sT-x1)/2-c1
y2=(abs(sT-x2)+sT-x2)/2-c2
y3=(abs(sT-x3)+sT-x3)/2-c3
butter_fly=y1+y3-2*y2
y0=np.zeros(len(sT))
plt.ylim(-20,20)
plt.xlim(40,70)
plt.plot(sT,y0)
plt.plot(sT,y1)
plt.plot(sT,-y2,'-.')
plt.plot(sT,y3)
plt.plot(sT,butter_fly,'r')
plt.title("Profit-loss for a Butterfly")
plt.xlabel('Stock price')
plt.ylabel('Profit (loss)')
plt.annotate('Butterfly', xy=(53,3), xytext=(42,4), arrowprops=dict(fa
cecolor='red',shrink=0.01),)
plt.annotate('Buy 2 calls with x1, x3 and sell 2 calls with x2',
xy=(45,16))
plt.annotate('    x2=(x1+x3)/2', xy=(45,14))
plt.annotate('    x1=50, x2=55, x3=60',xy=(45,12))
plt.annotate('    c1=10,c2=7, c3=5', xy=(45,10))
plt.show()
```

The related graph is shown here:

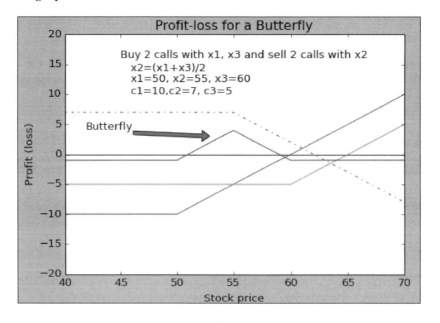

The relationship between input values and option values

When the volatility of an underlying stock increases, both its call and put values increase. The logic is that when a stock becomes more volatile, we have a better chance to observe extreme values, that is, we have a better chance to exercise our option. The following Python program shows this relationship:

```python
import numpy as np
import p4f as pf
import matplotlib.pyplot as plt
s0=30
T0=0.5
sigma0=0.2
r0=0.05
x0=30
sigma=np.arange(0.05,0.8,0.05)
T=np.arange(0.5,2.0,0.5)
call_0=pf.bs_call(s0,x0,T0,r0,sigma0)
call_sigma=pf.bs_call(s0,x0,T0,r0,sigma)
call_T=pf.bs_call(s0,x0,T,r0,sigma0)
plt.title("Relationship between sigma and call, T and call")
plt.plot(sigma,call_sigma,'b')
plt.plot(T,call_T,'r')
plt.annotate('x=Sigma, y=call price', xy=(0.6,5), xytext=(1,6), arrowp
rops=dict(facecolor='blue',shrink=0.01),)
plt.annotate('x=T(maturity), y=call price', xy=(1,3), xytext=(0.8,1),
arrowprops=dict(facecolor='red',shrink=0.01),)
plt.ylabel("Call premium")
plt.xlabel("Sigma (volatility) or T(maturity) ")
plt.show()
```

The corresponding graph is shown here:

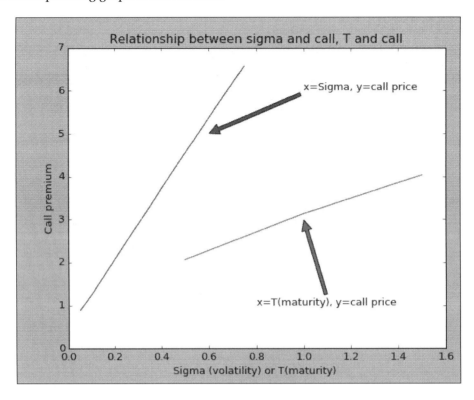

Greeks

Delta (Δ) is defined as the derivative of the option to its underlying security price. The delta of a call is defined here:

$$\Delta = \frac{\partial c}{\partial s} \quad \dots (24)$$

The delta of a European call on a non-dividend-paying stock is defined as:

$$\Delta_{call} = N(d_1) \quad \dots (25)$$

The program of `delta_call()` is quite simple. Since it is included in the `p4f.py`, we could call it easily:

```
>>>>from p4f import *
>>> round(delta_call(40,40,1,0.1,0.2),4)
0.7257
```

The delta for a European put on a non-dividend-paying stock is:

$$\Delta_{put} = N(d_1) - 1 \qquad \dots (26)$$

```
>>>>from p4f import *
>>> round(delta_put(40,40,1,0.1,0.2),4)
-0.2743
```

Gamma is the rate of change of delta with respect to price, as shown in this formula:

$$\Gamma = \frac{\partial \Delta}{\partial S} \qquad \dots (27)$$

For a European call (or put), its gamma is shown here, where $N'(x) = \frac{1}{\sqrt{2\pi}} e^{-\frac{x^2}{2}}$:

$$\Gamma = \frac{N'(d_1)}{S_0 \sigma \sqrt{T}} \qquad \dots (28)$$

The mathematical definitions of Greek letters for a European call and put are given in the following table:

Greek	A European call	A European put
Delta	$\Delta = N(d_1)$	$\Delta = N(d_1) - 1$
Gamma	$\Gamma = \frac{N'(d_1)}{S_0 \sigma \sqrt{T}}$	← same as the formula for the call
Theta	$\theta = -\frac{S_0 N'(d_1)\sigma}{2\sqrt{T}} - rKe^{-rT}N(d_2)$	$\theta = -\frac{S_0 N'(d_1)\sigma}{2\sqrt{T}} + rKe^{-rT}N(-d_2)$
Vega	$v = S_0\sqrt{T}N'(d_1)$	← same as the formula for the call
Rho	$rho = KTe^{-rT}N(d_2)$	$rho = -KTe^{-rT}N(-d_2)$

Table 10.1 Mathematical definitions of Greek letters

Note that in the table, $N'(x) = \dfrac{1}{\sqrt{2\pi}} e^{-\frac{x^2}{2}}$

Obviously, very few people can remember these formulae. Here is a very simple approach, based on their definition:

Greek	Description	Using call as an example
Delta	the change in an option value divided by the change in the underlying stock's price	$\Delta = \dfrac{C_2 - C_1}{S_2 - S_1}$
Gamma	the change in Delta divided by the change in the stock's price	$\Gamma = \dfrac{\Delta_2 - \Delta_1}{S_2 - S_1}$
Theta	the change in the option value divided by the change in the time	$\Theta = \dfrac{C_2 - C_1}{T_2 - T_1}$
Vega	the change in the option value divided by the change in the volatility	$\upsilon = \dfrac{C_2 - C_1}{\sigma_2 - \sigma_1}$
Rho	the change in the option value divided the by the change in the interest rate	$rho = \dfrac{C_2 - C_1}{r_2 - r_1}$

Table 10.2 A simple approach to estimating Greek letters

How to remember?

- **Delta**: First order derivative
- **Gamma**: Second order derivative
- **Theta**: Time (T)
- **Vega**: Volatility (V)
- **Rho**: Rate (R)

For example, based on delta's definition, we know that it is the ratio of `c2 - c1` and `s2 - s1`. Thus, we could generate a small number to generate those two pairs; see the following codes:

```
from scipy import log,exp,sqrt,stats
tiny=1e-9
S=40
X=40
T=0.5
r=0.01
sigma=0.2

def bsCall(S,X,T,r,sigma):
```

```
    d1=(log(S/X)+(r+sigma*sigma/2.)*T)/(sigma*sqrt(T))
    d2 = d1-sigma*sqrt(T)
    return S*stats.norm.cdf(d1)-X*exp(-r*T)*stats.norm.cdf(d2)

def delta1(S,X,T,r,sigma):
    d1=(log(S/X)+(r+sigma*sigma/2.)*T)/(sigma*sqrt(T))
    return stats.norm.cdf(d1)

def delta2(S,X,T,r,sigma):
    s1=S
    s2=S+tiny
    c1=bsCall(s1,X,T,r,sigma)
    c2=bsCall(s2,X,T,r,sigma)
    delta=(c2-c1)/(s2-s1)
    return delta

print("delta (close form)=", delta1(S,X,T,r,sigma))
print("delta (tiny number)=", delta2(S,X,T,r,sigma))
('delta (close form)=', 0.54223501331161406)
('delta (tiny number)=', 0.54223835949323917)
```

Based on the last two values, the difference is quite small. We could apply this method to other Greek letters, see one end of chapter problems.

Put-call parity and its graphic presentation

Let's look at a call with an exercise price of $20, a maturity of three months and a risk-free rate of 5%. The present value of this future $20 is given here:

```
>>>x=20*exp(-0.05*3/12)
>>>round(x,2)
19.75
>>>
```

In three months, what will be the wealth of our portfolio which consists of a call on the same stock plus $19.75 cash today? If the stock price is below $20, we don't exercise the call and keep the cash. If the stock price is above $20, we use our cash of $20 to exercise our call option to own the stock. Thus, our portfolio value will be the maximum of those two values: stock price in three months or $20, that is, *max(s,20)*.

On the other hand, how about a portfolio with a stock plus a put option with an exercise price of $20? If the stock price falls by $20, we exercise the put option and get $20. If the stock price is above $20, we simply keep the stock. Thus, our portfolio value will be the maximum of those two values: stock price in three months or $20, that is, *max(s,20)*.

Thus, for both portfolios we have the same terminal wealth of *max(s,20)*. Based on the no-arbitrage principle, the present values of those two portfolios should be equal. We call this put-call parity:

$$C + Xe^{-r_f T} = P + S_o \quad \dots (29)$$

When the stock has known dividend payments before its maturity date, we have the following equality:

$$C + PV(D) + Xe^{-r_f T} = P + S_o \quad \dots (30)$$

Here, D is the present value of all dividends before their maturity date (T). The following Python program offers a graphic presentation of the put-call parity:

```
import pylab as pl
import numpy as np
x=10
sT=np.arange(0,30,5)
payoff_call=(abs(sT-x)+sT-x)/2
payoff_put=(abs(x-sT)+x-sT)/2
cash=np.zeros(len(sT))+x

def graph(text,text2=''):
    pl.xticks(())
    pl.yticks(())
    pl.xlim(0,30)
    pl.ylim(0,20)
    pl.plot([x,x],[0,3])
    pl.text(x,-2,"X");
    pl.text(0,x,"X")
    pl.text(x,x*1.7, text, ha='center', va='center',size=10, alpha=.5)
    pl.text(-5,10,text2,size=25)

pl.figure(figsize=(6, 4))
pl.subplot(2, 3, 1); graph('Payoff of call');        pl.plot(sT,payoff_
call)
```

```
pl.subplot(2, 3, 2); graph('cash','+');                  pl.plot(sT,cash)
pl.subplot(2, 3, 3); graph('Porfolio A ','=');
pl.plot(sT,cash+payoff_call)
pl.subplot(2, 3, 4); graph('Payoff of put ');           pl.plot(sT,payoff_
put)
pl.subplot(2, 3, 5); graph('Stock','+');        pl.plot(sT,sT)
pl.subplot(2, 3, 6); graph('Portfolio B','=');   pl.plot(sT,sT+payoff_
put)
pl.show()
```

The output is shown here:

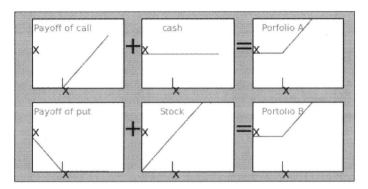

The put-call ratio represents the perception of investors jointly towards the future. If there is no obvious trend, that is, we expect a normal future, then the put-call ratio should be close to one. On the other hand, if we expect a much brighter future, the ratio should be lower than one.

The following code shows a ratio of this type over the years. First, we have to download the data from CBOE.

Perform the following steps:

1. Go to `http://www.cboe.com/`.
2. Click on **Quotes & Data** in the menu bar.
3. Find `put call ratio`, that is, `http://www.cboe.com/data/putcallratio.aspx`.
4. Click on **CBOE Total Exchange Volume and Put/Call Ratios (11-01-2006 to present)** under **Current**.

For the data, readers can download it at `http://canisius.edu/~yany/data/totalpc.csv`.

The following codes shows the trends of a call-put ratio:

```
import pandas as pd
import scipy as sp
from matplotlib.pyplot import *
infile='c:/temp/totalpc.csv'
data=pd.read_csv(infile,skiprows=2,index_col=0,parse_dates=True)
data.columns=('Calls','Puts','Total','Ratio')
x=data.index
y=data.Ratio
y2=sp.ones(len(y))
title('Put-call ratio')
xlabel('Date')
ylabel('Put-call ratio')
ylim(0,1.5)
plot(x, y, 'b-')
plot(x, y2,'r')
show()
```

The related graph is shown here:

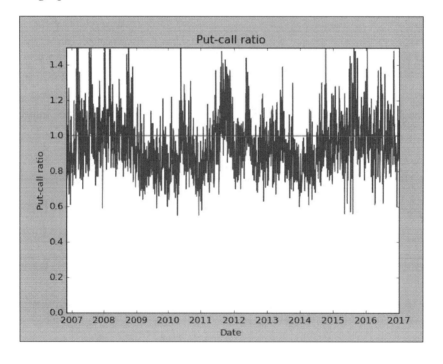

The put-call ratio for a short period with a trend

Based on the preceding program, we could choose a shorter period with a trend, as shown in the following code:

```
import scipy as sp
import pandas as pd
from matplotlib.pyplot import *
import matplotlib.pyplot as plt
from datetime import datetime
import statsmodels.api as sm

data=pd.read_csv('c:/temp/totalpc.csv',skiprows=2,index_col=0,parse_
dates=True)
data.columns=('Calls','Puts','Total','Ratio')
begdate=datetime(2013,6, 1)
enddate=datetime(2013,12,31)
data2=data[(data.index>=begdate) & (data.index<=enddate)]
x=data2.index
y=data2.Ratio
x2=range(len(x))
x3=sm.add_constant(x2)
model=sm.OLS(y,x3)
results=model.fit()

#print results.summary()
alpha=round(results.params[0],3)
slope=round(results.params[1],3)
y3=alpha+sp.dot(slope,x2)
y2=sp.ones(len(y))
title('Put-call ratio with a trend')
xlabel('Date')
ylabel('Put-call ratio')
ylim(0,1.5)
plot(x, y, 'b-')
plt.plot(x, y2,'r-.')
plot(x,y3,'y+')
plt.figtext(0.3,0.35,'Trend: intercept='+str(alpha)+',slope='+str(slo
pe))
show()
```

The corresponding graph is shown here:

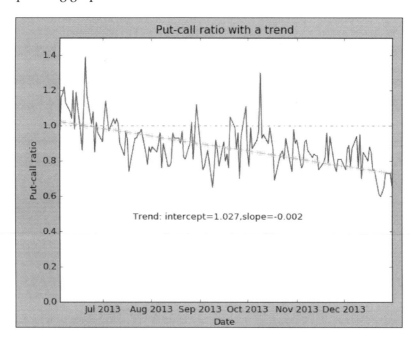

Binomial tree and its graphic presentation

The binomial tree method was proposed by Cox, Ross, and Robinstein in 1979. Because of this, it is also called the CRR method. Based on the CRR method, we have the following two-step approach. First, we draw a tree, such as the following one-step tree. Assume that our current stock value is S. Then, there are two outcomes of su and sd, where *u>1* and *d<1*, see the following code:

```
import matplotlib.pyplot as plt
plt.xlim(0,1)
plt.figtext(0.18,0.5,'S')
plt.figtext(0.6,0.5+0.25,'Su')
plt.figtext(0.6,0.5-0.25,'Sd')

plt.annotate('',xy=(0.6,0.5+0.25), xytext=(0.1,0.5), arrowprops=dict(f
acecolor='b',shrink=0.01))
plt.annotate('',xy=(0.6,0.5-0.25), xytext=(0.1,0.5), arrowprops=dict(f
acecolor='b',shrink=0.01))
plt.axis('off')
plt.show()
```

The graph is shown here:

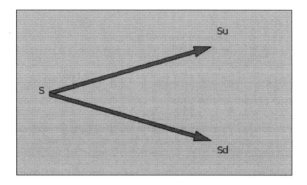

Obviously, the simplest tree is a one-step tree. Assume that today's price is $10, the exercise price is $11, and a call option will mature in six months. In addition, assume that we know that the price will have two outcomes: moving up (*u=1.15*) or moving down (d=0.9). In other words, the final values are either $11 or $9. Based on such information, we have the following graph showing the prices for such a one-step binomial tree:

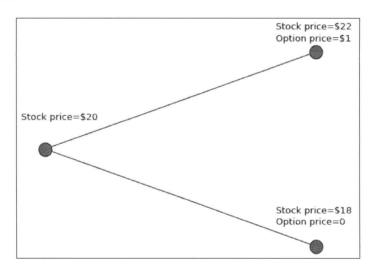

The codes to generate the preceding graph are shown here.

The codes are based on the codes at `https://pypi.python.org/pypi/PyFi`:

```
import networkx as nx
import matplotlib.pyplot as plt
plt.figtext(0.08,0.6,"Stock price=$20")
plt.figtext(0.75,0.91,"Stock price=$22")
```

```
plt.figtext(0.75,0.87,"Option price=$1")
plt.figtext(0.75,0.28,"Stock price=$18")
plt.figtext(0.75,0.24,"Option price=0")
n=1
def binomial_grid(n):
    G=nx.Graph()
    for i in range(0,n+1):
        for j in range(1,i+2):
            if i<n:
                G.add_edge((i,j),(i+1,j))
                G.add_edge((i,j),(i+1,j+1))
    posG={}
    for node in G.nodes():
        posG[node]=(node[0],n+2+node[0]-2*node[1])
    nx.draw(G,pos=posG)
binomial_grid(n)
plt.show()
```

In the preceding program, we generate a function called `binomial_grid()` since we will call this function many times later in the chapter. Since we know beforehand that we will have two outcomes, we can choose an appropriate combination of stock and call options to make our final outcome with certainty, that is, the same terminal values. Assume that we choose an appropriate delta shares of underlying security plus one call to have the same terminal value at the end of one period, that is, $\Delta * me\ terminal$.

Thus, $\Delta \frac{1}{11.5-9} = 0.4$. This means that if we long 0.4 shares and short one call option, our final wealth will be the same, $0.4*11.5-1 =3.6$ when stock moves up or $0.4*9=3.6$ when the stock moves down. Assume further that if the continuously compounded risk-free is 0.12%, then the value of today's portfolio will be equivalent to the discounted future certain value of 4.5, that is, $0.4*10 – c=pv(3.6)$. That is, $c = 0.4 * 10 - e^{-0.012*0.5} * .012 * 0.5$. If using Python, we have the following result:

```
>>>round(0.4*10-exp(-0.012*0.5)*3.6,2)
0.42
>>>
```

For a two-step binomial tree, we have the following codes:

```
import p4f
plt.figtext(0.08,0.6,"Stock price=$20")
plt.figtext(0.08,0.56,"call =7.43")
plt.figtext(0.33,0.76,"Stock price=$67.49")
plt.figtext(0.33,0.70,"Option price=0.93")
plt.figtext(0.33,0.27,"Stock price=$37.40")
plt.figtext(0.33,0.23,"Option price=14.96")
plt.figtext(0.75,0.91,"Stock price=$91.11")
plt.figtext(0.75,0.87,"Option price=0")
plt.figtext(0.75,0.6,"Stock price=$50")
plt.figtext(0.75,0.57,"Option price=2")
plt.figtext(0.75,0.28,"Stock price=$27.44")
plt.figtext(0.75,0.24,"Option price=24.56")
n=2
p4f.binomial_grid(n)
```

Based on the CRR method, we have the following procedure:

1. Draw a *n*-step tree.
2. At the end of *n*-step, estimate terminal prices.
3. Calculate the option value at each node based on the terminal price, exercise, call or put.
4. Discount it back one step, that is, from nth to nth-1, according to the risk-neutral probability.
5. Repeat the previous step until we find the final value at step 0. The formulas for u, d, p are given here:

$$u = e^{\sigma\sqrt{\Delta t}} \qquad \dots (31)$$

$$d = \frac{1}{u} = e^{-\sigma\sqrt{\Delta t}} \qquad \dots (32)$$

$$a = e^{(r-q)\Delta t} \qquad \dots (33)$$

$$p = \frac{a-d}{u-d} \qquad \dots (34)$$

$$v_i = pv_{i+1}^u + (1-p)v_{i+1}^d \qquad \dots (35)$$

Here, u is the up movement, d is the down movement, σ is the volatility of the underlying security, r is the risk-free rate, Δt is the step, that is, $\Delta t = \frac{T}{n}$, T is the maturity in years, n is the number of steps, q is the dividend yield, and p is the risk-neutral probability of an up movement. The `binomial_grid()` function is based on the functions shown under the one-step binomial tree graphic presentation. Again, as we mentioned before, this function is included in the grand master file called `p4fy.py`. The output graph is shown here. One obvious result is that the preceding Python program is very simple and straight forward. Here, let us use a two-step binomial tree to explain the whole process. Assume that the current stock price is $10, the exercise price is $10, the maturity is three months, the number of steps is two, the risk-free rate is 2%, and the volatility of the underlying security is 0.2. The following Python codes would generate a two-step tree:

```
import p4f
from math import sqrt,exp
import matplotlib.pyplot as plt
s=10
r=0.02
sigma=0.2
T=3./12
x=10
n=2
deltaT=T/n
q=0
u=exp(sigma*sqrt(deltaT))
d=1/u
a=exp((r-q)*deltaT)
p=(a-d)/(u-d)
su=round(s*u,2);
suu=round(s*u*u,2)
sd=round(s*d,2)
sdd=round(s*d*d,2)
sud=s

plt.figtext(0.08,0.6,'Stock '+str(s))
plt.figtext(0.33,0.76,"Stock price=$"+str(su))
plt.figtext(0.33,0.27,'Stock price='+str(sd))
plt.figtext(0.75,0.91,'Stock price=$'+str(suu))
plt.figtext(0.75,0.6,'Stock price=$'+str(sud))
plt.figtext(0.75,0.28,"Stock price="+str(sdd))
p4f.binomial_grid(n)
plt.show()
```

The tree is shown here:

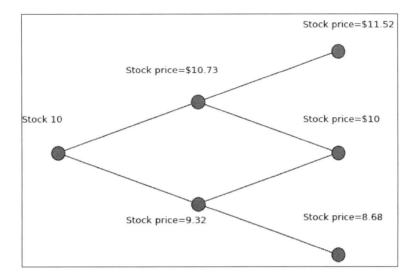

Now, we use the risk-neutral probability to discount each value one step backward. The codes and the graph are given here:

```
import p4f
import scipy as sp
import matplotlib.pyplot as plt
s=10;x=10;r=0.05;sigma=0.2;T=3./12.;n=2;q=0     # q is dividend yield
deltaT=T/n     # step
u=sp.exp(sigma*sp.sqrt(deltaT))
d=1/u
a=sp.exp((r-q)*deltaT)
p=(a-d)/(u-d)
s_dollar='S=$'
c_dollar='c=$'
p2=round(p,2)
plt.figtext(0.15,0.91,'Note: x='+str(x)+', r='+str(r)+', deltaT='+str(
deltaT)+',p='+str(p2))
plt.figtext(0.35,0.61,'p')
plt.figtext(0.65,0.76,'p')
plt.figtext(0.65,0.43,'p')
plt.figtext(0.35,0.36,'1-p')
plt.figtext(0.65,0.53,'1-p')
plt.figtext(0.65,0.21,'1-p')
```

```python
# at level 2
su=round(s*u,2);
suu=round(s*u*u,2)
sd=round(s*d,2);
sdd=round(s*d*d,2)
sud=s
c_suu=round(max(suu-x,0),2)
c_s=round(max(s-x,0),2)
c_sdd=round(max(sdd-x,0),2)
plt.figtext(0.8,0.94,'s*u*u')
plt.figtext(0.8,0.91,s_dollar+str(suu))
plt.figtext(0.8,0.87,c_dollar+str(c_suu))
plt.figtext(0.8,0.6,s_dollar+str(sud))
plt.figtext(0.8,0.64,'s*u*d=s')
plt.figtext(0.8,0.57,c_dollar+str(c_s))
plt.figtext(0.8,0.32,'s*d*d')
plt.figtext(0.8,0.28,s_dollar+str(sdd))
plt.figtext(0.8,0.24,c_dollar+str(c_sdd))

# at level 1
c_01=round((p*c_suu+(1-p)*c_s)*sp.exp(-r*deltaT),2)
c_02=round((p*c_s+(1-p)*c_sdd)*sp.exp(-r*deltaT),2)

plt.figtext(0.43,0.78,'s*u')
plt.figtext(0.43,0.74,s_dollar+str(su))
plt.figtext(0.43,0.71,c_dollar+str(c_01))
plt.figtext(0.43,0.32,'s*d')
plt.figtext(0.43,0.27,s_dollar+str(sd))
plt.figtext(0.43,0.23,c_dollar+str(c_02))
# at level 0 (today)

c_00=round(p*sp.exp(-r*deltaT)*c_01+(1-p)*sp.exp(-r*deltaT)*c_02,2)
plt.figtext(0.09,0.6,s_dollar+str(s))
plt.figtext(0.09,0.56,c_dollar+str(c_00))
p4f.binomial_grid(n)
```

The tree is shown here:

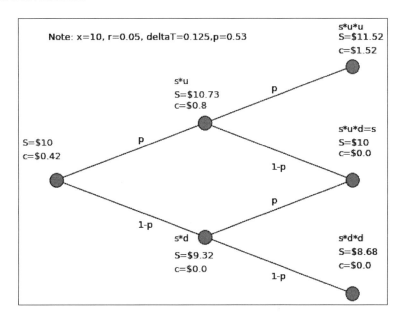

Here, we explain a few values shown in the preceding graph. At the highest node (**s*u*u**), since the terminal stock price is 11.52 and the exercise price is 10, the call value is 1.52 (11.52-10). Similarly, at node **s*u*d=s** the call value is 0 since 10-10=0. For a call value of 0.8, we have the following verification:

```
>>>p
0.5266253390068362
>>>deltaT
0.125
>>>v=(p*1.52+(1-p)*0)*exp(-r*deltaT)
>>>round(v,2)
0.80
>>>
```

Binomial tree (CRR) method for European options

The following codes are for the binomial-tree method to price a European option:

```
def binomialCallEuropean(s,x,T,r,sigma,n=100):
    from math import exp,sqrt
    deltaT = T /n
    u = exp(sigma * sqrt(deltaT))
```

```
        d = 1.0 / u
        a = exp(r * deltaT)
        p = (a - d) / (u - d)
        v = [[0.0 for j in xrange(i + 1)]  for i in xrange(n + 1)]
        for j in xrange(i+1):
            v[n][j] = max(s * u**j * d**(n - j) - x, 0.0)
        for i in xrange(n-1, -1, -1):
            for j in xrange(i + 1):
                v[i][j]=exp(-r*deltaT)*(p*v[i+1][j+1]+(1.0-p)*v[i+1][j])
        return v[0][0]
```

To apply the function, we give it a set of input values. For comparison, the result
based on the *Black-Scholes-Merton option* model is shown here as well:

```
>>> binomialCallEuropean(40,42,0.5,0.1,0.2,1000)
2.278194404573134
>>> bs_call(40,42,0.5,0.1,0.2)
2.2777803294555348
>>>
```

Binomial tree (CRR) method for American options

Unlike the Black-Scholes-Merton option model, which can only be applied to
European options, the binomial tree (CRR method) can be used to price American
options. The only difference is that we have to consider the early exercise:

```
def binomialCallAmerican(s,x,T,r,sigma,n=100):
    from math import exp,sqrt
    import numpy as np
    deltaT = T /n
    u = exp(sigma * sqrt(deltaT))
    d = 1.0 / u
    a = exp(r * deltaT)
    p = (a - d) / (u - d)
    v = [[0.0 for j in np.arange(i + 1)] for i in np.arange(n + 1)]
    for j in np.arange(n+1):
        v[n][j] = max(s * u**j * d**(n - j) - x, 0.0)
    for i in np.arange(n-1, -1, -1):
        for j in np.arange(i + 1):
            v1=exp(-r*deltaT)*(p*v[i+1][j+1]+(1.0-p)*v[i+1][j])
            v2=max(v[i][j]-x,0)              # early exercise
            v[i][j]=max(v1,v2)
    return v[0][0]
```

The key difference between pricing an American call option and pricing a European is its early exercise opportunity. In the preceding program, the last several lines reflect this. For each node, we estimate two values: `v1` is for the discounted value and `v2` is the payoff from an early exercise. We choose a higher value, `max(v1, v2)`. If using the same set of values to apply this binomial tree to price an American call, we have the following value. It is understandable the final result is higher than a European call counterpart:

```
>>> call=binomialCallAmerican(40,42,0.5,0.1,0.2,1000)
>>> round(call,2)
2.28
>>>
```

Hedging strategies

After selling a European call, we could hold Δ shares of the same stock to hedge our position. This is named a delta hedge. Since the delta (Δ) is a function of the underlying stock (S), to maintain an effective hedge we have to rebalance our holding constantly. This is called dynamic hedging. The delta of a portfolio is the weighted deltas of individual securities in the portfolio. Note that when we short a security, its weight will be negative:

$$\Delta_{port} = \sum_{i=1}^{n} w_i \Delta_i \qquad \dots (36)$$

Assume that a US importer will pay £10 million in three months. He or she is concerned with a potential depreciation of the US dollar against the pound. There are several ways to hedge such a risk: buy pounds now, enter a futures contract to buy £10 million in three months with a fixed exchange rate, or buy call options with a fixed exchange rate as its exercise price. The first choice is costly since the importer does not need pounds today. Entering a future contract is risky as well since an appreciation of the US dollar would cost the importer extra money. On the other hand, entering a call option will guarantee a maximum exchange rate today. At the same time, if the pound depreciates, the importer will reap the benefits. Such activities are called hedging since we take the opposite position of our risks.

For the currency options, we have the following equations:

$$d_1 = \frac{\ln\left(\frac{S_0}{X}\right) + (r_d - r_f + \frac{1}{2}\sigma^2)T}{\sigma\sqrt{T}}$$

$$d_2 = \frac{\ln\left(\frac{S_0}{X}\right) + (r_d - r_f - \frac{1}{2}\sigma^2)T}{\sigma\sqrt{T}} = d_1 - \sigma\sqrt{T}$$

$$c = S_0 * N(d_1) - X * e^{-rT}N(d_2)$$

$$p = X * e^{-rT}N(-d_2) - S_0 * N(-d_1)$$

Here, S_0 is the exchange rate in US dollars per foreign currency, r_d is the domestic risk-free, rate and r_f is the foreign country's risk-free rate.

Implied volatility

From the previous sections, we know that for a set of input variables — s (the present stock price), x (the exercise price), T (the maturity date in years), r (the continuously compounded risk-free rate), and sigma (the volatility of the stock, that is, the annualized standard deviation of its returns) — we could estimate the price of a call option based on the Black-Scholes-Merton option model. Recall that to price a European call option, we have the following Python code of five lines:

```
def bs_call(S,X,T,r,sigma):
    from scipy import log,exp,sqrt,stats
    d1=(log(S/X)+(r+sigma*sigma/2.)*T)/(sigma*sqrt(T))
    d2 = d1-sigma*sqrt(T)
    return S*stats.norm.cdf(d1)-X*exp(-r*T)*stats.norm.cdf(d2)
```

After entering a set of five values, we can estimate the call price as follows:

```
>>>bs_call(40,40,0.5,0.05,0.25)
3.3040017284767735
```

On the other hand, if we know S, X, T, r, and c, how can we estimate sigma? Here, sigma is our implied volatility. In other words, if we are given a set values such as S=40, X=40, T=0.5, r=0.05, and c=3.30, we should find out the value of sigma, and it should be equal to 0.25. In this chapter, we will learn how to estimate the implied volatility. Actually, the underlying logic to figure out the implied volatility is very simple: trial and error. Let's use the previous example as an illustration. We have five values— *S=40, X=40, T=0.5, r=0.05, and c=3.30.* The basic design is that after inputting 100 different sigmas, plus the first four input values shown earlier, we have 100 call prices. The implied volatility is the sigma that achieves the smallest absolute difference between the estimated call price and 3.30. Of course, we could increase the number of trials to achieve a higher precision, that is, more decimal places.

Alternatively, we could adopt another conversion criterion: we stop when the absolute difference between our estimated call price and the given call value is less than a critical value, such as 1 cent, that is, |c-3.30|<0.01. Since it is not a good idea to randomly pick up 100 or 1,000 different sigmas, we systematically choose those values, that is, use a loop by selecting those sigmas systematically. Next, we will discuss two types of loops: a for loop and a while loop. Implied volatility function based on a European call. Ultimately, we could write a function to estimate the implied volatility based on a European call. To save space, we remove all comments and examples from the program as shown:

```
def implied_vol_call(S,X,T,r,c):
    from scipy import log,exp,sqrt,stats
    for i in range(200):
        sigma=0.005*(i+1)
        d1=(log(S/X)+(r+sigma*sigma/2.)*T)/(sigma*sqrt(T))
        d2 = d1-sigma*sqrt(T)
        diff=c-(S*stats.norm.cdf(d1)-X*exp(-r*T)*stats.norm.cdf(d2))
        if abs(diff)<=0.01:
            return i,sigma, diff
```

With a set of input values, we could apply the previous program easily as follows:

```
>>>implied_vol_call(40,40,0.5,0.05,3.3)
(49, 0.25, -0.0040060797372882817)
```

Similarly, we could estimate an implied volatility based on a European put option model. In the following program, we design a function named `implied_vol_put_min()`. There are several differences between this function and the previous one. First, the current function depends on a put option instead of a call. Thus, the last input value is a put premium instead of a call premium. Second, the conversion criterion is that an estimated price and the given put price have the smallest difference. In the previous function, the conversion criterion is when the absolute difference is less than 0.01. In a sense, the current program will guarantee an implied volatility while the previous program does not guarantee an output:

```
def implied_vol_put_min(S,X,T,r,p):
    from scipy import log,exp,sqrt,stats
    implied_vol=1.0
    min_value=100.0
    for i in xrange(1,10000):
        sigma=0.0001*(i+1)
        d1=(log(S/X)+(r+sigma*sigma/2.)*T)/(sigma*sqrt(T))
        d2 = d1-sigma*sqrt(T)
        put=X*exp(-r*T)*stats.norm.cdf(-d2)-S*stats.norm.cdf(-d1)
        abs_diff=abs(put-p)
        if abs_diff<min_value:
            min_value=abs_diff
            implied_vol=sigma
            k=i
        put_out=put
    print ('k, implied_vol, put, abs_diff')
    return k,implied_vol, put_out,min_value
```

Let's use a set of input values to estimate the implied volatility. After that, we will explain the logic behind the previous program. Assume *S=40*, *X=40*, *T=12* months, *r=0.1*, and the put price is $1.50, as shown in the following code:

```
>>>implied_vol_put_min(40,40,1.,0.1,1.501)
k, implied_vol, put, abs_diff
(1999, 0.2, 12.751879946129757, 0.00036735530273501737)
```

The implied volatility is 20 percent. The logic is that we assign a big value, such as 100, to a variable called `min_value`. For the first sigma with a value of 0.0002, we have an almost zero put value. Thus, the absolute difference is 1.50, which is smaller than 100. Because of this, our `min_value` variable will be replaced with the value 1.50. We continue this way until we go through the loop. For the recorded minimum value, its corresponding sigma will be our implied volatility. We could optimize the previous program by defining some intermediate values. For example, in the previous program, we estimate *ln(S/X)* 10,000 times. Actually, we define a new variable such as `log_S_over_X`, estimate its value just once, and use it 10,000 times. This is true for `sigma*sigma/2.`, and `sigman*sqrt(T)`:

Binary-search

To estimate the implied volatility, the logic underlying the earlier methods is to run the Black-Scholes-Merton option model 100 times and choose the sigma value that achieves the smallest difference between the estimated option price and the observed price. Although the logic is easy to understand, such an approach is not efficient since we need to call the Black-Scholes-Merton option model a few hundred times. To estimate a few implied volatilities, such an approach would not pose any problems. However, under two scenarios, such an approach is problematic. First, if we need higher precision, such as *sigma=0.25333*, or we have to estimate several million implied volatilities, we need to optimize our approach. Let's look at a simple example. Assume that we randomly pick up a value between one and 5,000. How many steps do we need to match this value if we sequentially run a loop from one to 5,000? A binomial search is the *log(n)* worst-case scenario when linear search is the n worst case scenario. Thus, to search a value from one to 5,000, a linear search would need 5,000 steps (average 2,050) in a worst-case scenario, while a binary search would need 12 steps (average six) in a worst-case scenario. The following Python program performs a binary search:

```
def binary_search(x, target, my_min=1, my_max=None):
    if my_max is None:
        my_max = len(x) - 1
    while my_min <= my_max:
      mid = (my_min + my_max)//2
      midval = x[mid]
      if midval < target:
          my_min = my_mid + 1
      elif midval > target:
          my_max = mid - 1
      else:
          return mid
    raise ValueError
```

The following program shows its application for searching an implied volatility:

```
from scipy import log,exp,sqrt,stats
S=42;X=40;T=0.5;r=0.01;c=3.0
def bsCall(S,X,T,r,sigma):
    d1=(log(S/X)+(r+sigma*sigma/2.)*T)/(sigma*sqrt(T))
    d2 = d1-sigma*sqrt(T)
    return S*stats.norm.cdf(d1)-X*exp(-r*T)*stats.norm.cdf(d2)
#
def impliedVolBinary(S,X,T,r,c):
    k=1
    volLow=0.001
```

```
        volHigh=1.0
        cLow=bsCall(S,X,T,r,volLow)
        cHigh=bsCall(S,X,T,r,volHigh)
        if cLow>c or cHigh<c:
            raise ValueError
        while k ==1:
            cLow=bsCall(S,X,T,r,volLow)
            cHigh=bsCall(S,X,T,r,volHigh)
            volMid=(volLow+volHigh)/2.0
            cMid=bsCall(S,X,T,r,volMid)
            if abs(cHigh-cLow)<0.01:
                k=2
            elif cMid>c:
                volHigh=volMid
            else:
                volLow=volMid
        return volMid, cLow, cHigh
#
print("Vol,      cLow,       cHigh")
print(impliedVolBinary(S,X,T,r,c))
Vol,      cLow,       cHigh
(0.16172778320312498, 2.998464657758511, 3.0039730848624977)
```

Based on the result, the implied volatility is 16.17%. In the preceding program, the conversion condition, when the program should stop, is the difference between two call options. Readers could set up other conversion conditions. To avoid an infinitive loop, we have a screen condition of:

```
        if cLow>c or cHigh<c:
            raise ValueError
```

Retrieving option data from Yahoo! Finance

There are many sources of option data that we can use for our investments, research or teaching. One of them is Yahoo! Finance.

To retrieve option data for IBM, we have the following procedure:

1. Go to http://finance.yahoo.com.

2. Type IBM in the search box.

3. Click on **Options** in the navigation bar.

The related page is `http://finance.yahoo.com/quote/IBM/options?p=IBM`. A screenshot of this web page is as follows:

February 10, 2017 ▼	In The Money	Show: **List** Straddle			Lookup Option			🔍
Calls For February 10, 2017								
∧ Strike	Contract Name	Last Price	Bid	Ask	Change	% Change	Volume	Open Interest	Implied Volatility
149.00	IBM170210C00149000	19.21	19.10	22.30	0.00	0.00%	7	7	0.00%
150.00	IBM170210C00150000	26.40	25.30	26.00	-1.33	-4.80%	1	8	0.00%
157.50	IBM170210C00157500	10.90	10.65	14.20	0.00	0.00%	5	5	0.00%
160.00	IBM170210C00160000	15.14	13.70	17.60	4.64	44.19%	3	6	67.14%
162.50	IBM170210C00162500	16.15	14.50	16.70	8.75	118.24%	6	80	74.41%

Volatility smile and skewness

Obviously, each stock should possess one value for its volatility. However, when estimating implied volatility, different strike prices might offer us different implied volatilities. More specifically, the implied volatility based on out-of-the-money options, at-the-money options, and in-the-money options might be quite different. Volatility smile is the shape going down then up with the exercise prices, while the volatility skewness is downward or upward sloping. The key is that investors' sentiments and the supply and demand relationship have a fundamental impact on the volatility skewness. Thus, such a smile or skewness provides information on whether investors, such as fund managers, prefer to write calls or puts, as shown in the following code:

```
import datetime
import pandas as pd
import matplotlib.pyplot as plt
from matplotlib.finance import quotes_historical_yahoo_ochl as getData

# Step 1: input area
infile="c:/temp/callsFeb2014.pkl"
ticker='IBM'
r=0.0003                          # estimate
begdate=datetime.date(2010,1,1)   # this is arbitrary
enddate=datetime.date(2014,2,1)   # February 2014

# Step 2: define a function
def implied_vol_call_min(S,X,T,r,c):
    from scipy import log,exp,sqrt,stats
    implied_vol=1.0
```

```
            min_value=1000
            for i in range(10000):
                sigma=0.0001*(i+1)
                d1=(log(S/X)+(r+sigma*sigma/2.)*T)/(sigma*sqrt(T))
                d2 = d1-sigma*sqrt(T)
                c2=S*stats.norm.cdf(d1)-X*exp(-r*T)*stats.norm.cdf(d2)
                abs_diff=abs(c2-c)
                if abs_diff<min_value:
                    min_value=abs_diff
                    implied_vol=sigma
                    k=i
            return implied_vol


    # Step 3: get call option data
    calls=pd.read_pickle(infile)
    exp_date0=int('20'+calls.Symbol[0][len(ticker):9])  # find expiring
    date
    p = getData(ticker, begdate,enddate,asobject=True, adjusted=True)
    s=p.close[-1]                    # get current stock price
    y=int(exp_date0/10000)
    m=int(exp_date0/100)-y*100
    d=exp_date0-y*10000-m*100
    exp_date=datetime.date(y,m,d)    # get exact expiring date
    T=(exp_date-enddate).days/252.0  # T in years


    # Step 4: run a loop to estimate the implied volatility
    n=len(calls.Strike)    # number of strike
    strike=[]              # initialization
    implied_vol=[]         # initialization
    call2=[]               # initialization
    x_old=0                # used when we choose the first strike


    for i in range(n):
        x=calls.Strike[i]
        c=(calls.Bid[i]+calls.Ask[i])/2.0
        if c >0:
            print ('i=',i,'',    c='',c)
            if x!=x_old:
                vol=implied_vol_call_min(s,x,T,r,c)
                strike.append(x)
                implied_vol.append(vol)
                call2.append(c)
                print x,c,vol
                x_old=x


    # Step 5: draw a smile
    plt.title('Skewness smile (skew)')
```

```
plt.xlabel('Exercise Price')
plt.ylabel('Implied Volatility')
plt.plot(strike,implied_vol,'o')
plt.show()
```

 Note that the `.pickle` dataset can be downloaded at
`http://canisus.edu/~yan/python/callsFeb2014.pkl`.

The graph related to volatility smile is shown here:

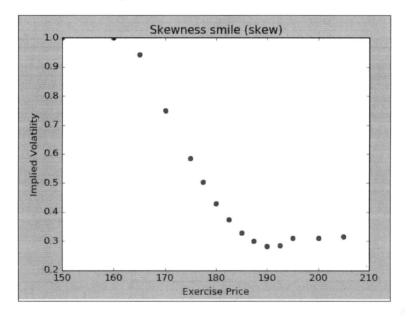

References

Please refer to the following articles:

- *Black, F., M. Scholes, 1973, The pricing of options and corporate liabilities, Journal of Political Economy 81,3,637-654,* `https://www.cs.princeton.edu/courses/archive/fall09/cos323/papers/black_scholes73.pdf`

- *Cox, J. C., Ross, S. A., Rubinstein, M, 1979, Option pricing: A simplified approach, Journal of Financial Economics, 7(3), 229-263,* `http://www.sciencedirect.com/science/article/pii/0304405X79900151`

Appendix A – data case 6: portfolio insurance

Portfolio insurance is a method of hedging a portfolio of stocks against market risk by short selling stock index futures. This hedging technique is frequently used by institutional investors when the market direction is uncertain or volatile. Assume that you manage one of the industry portfolios with a current value of $50 million. If you expect the whole market to be quite volatile in next three months--in other words, the market might go down significantly--what might be our choices at the moment?

- **Alternative #1**: Sell stocks right now and buy them back in a few months
- **Alternative #2**: Sell S&P500 index futures

Obviously, the first alternative is costly because of the transaction cost:

1. Get five industry portfolios:

    1. To retrieve Fama-French five-industry portfolio, go to Prof. French's Data Library.

    2. Go to `http://mba.tuck.dartmouth.edu/pages/faculty/ken.french/data_library.html`.

    3. Search for the keyword `Industry`; see the following screenshot:

    > ### Industry Portfolios
    >
    > **5 Industry Portfolios** TXT CSV Details
    > **5 Industry Portfolios [ex. Dividends]** TXT CSV Details
    > **5 Industry Portfolios [Daily]** TXT CSV Details

    4. Download the data and estimate beta for those five industries. Let's see what happens when the market is down one point. Here is today's S&P500 level:

    5. If the market goes down one point, the long position (S&P500 futures contract) would lose $250, while the short position would gain $250. The size of one futures contract on S&P500 is index level *250.

6. If we want to hedge our $5 portfolio, we should short n futures contracts. For the specification, see `http://www3.canisius.edu/~yany/doc/sp500futures.pdf`:

$$n = \frac{V_p \beta_p}{index\ level * 250} \quad \ldots (1)$$

Here, Vp is the portfolio value, βp is the portfolio beta, and the index level is the S&P500 index level. Applying the preceding formula, we should short ten futures contracts. Assume, in three months, it is 2090.4, that is, ten points down. Since we know that beta is a measure of market risk, assume that annul risk-free rate is 1%, that is, 0.25% for three months.

2. Estimate the portfolio beta by applying the following linear regression:

$$R_i = R_f - \beta_i (R_{mkt} - R_f) \quad \ldots (2)$$

3. Identify several moments when the market falls dramatically.

    You can use a business cycle Python dataset called:

```
import pandas as pd
x=pd.read_pickle("c:/temp/businessCycle.pkl")
print(x.head())
print(x.tail())
date
1926-10-01   1.000
1926-11-01   0.846
1926-12-01   0.692
1927-01-01   0.538
1927-02-01   0.385
   cycle
date
2009-02-01  -0.556
2009-03-01  -0.667
2009-04-01  -0.778
2009-05-01  -0.889
2009-06-01  -1.000
```

[Note that -1 means deep in recession, while 1 means the economy is expanding.]

4. Estimate the loss with and without a hedging strategy. What is the loss of your portfolio? What is the gain if you short one future contract of S&P500 future?

5. Repeat the whole processing that we have 1,000 shares of IBM, 2,000 shares of DELL, and 5,000 shares of Citi Group, and 7,000 shares of IBM.

    ○   What is the total market value today?

    ○   What is the portfolio beta? [note: you can use the latest five-year monthly data to estimate beta]

    ○   If we want to hedge our portfolio by using S&P500 futures contracts, how many contracts should we long (short)?

    ○   If the market down by 5%, what is our portfolio loss and what is the gain in terms of our hedging position?

The following formula is a general one:

$$n = (\beta^* - \beta_p)\frac{V_p}{V_F} \quad \dots (3)$$

Here, n is the number of contracts, β^* is our target beta, VF is the value of one futures contract. Vp and βp are defined previously. If n is positive (negative), it means a long (short) position. In the preceding case for using S&P500 futures, VF=S&P500 index level *250.

[Think about market timing by using S&P500 futures to change your portfolio beta for bad times.]

Exercises

1. If the APR is 5% compounded quarterly, what is its equivalent continuously compounded rate?

2. The value of a portfolio is $4.77 million today with a beta of 0.88. If the portfolio manager explains the market will surge in the next three months and s/he intends to increase her/ his portfolio beta from 0.88 to 1.20 in just three months by using S&P500 futures, how many contracts should s/he long or short? If the S&P500 index increases by 70 points what will be her/ his gain or loss? How about if the S&P500 falls by 50 points instead?

3. Write a Python program to price a call option.

4. Explain the empty shell method when writing a complex Python program.

5. Explain the logic behind the so-called comment-all-out method when writing a complex Python program.

6. Explain the usage of the return value when we debug a program.

7. When we write the CND (cumulative standard normal distribution), we could define a1, a2, a3, a4, and a5 separately. What are the differences between the following two approaches?

    ° Current approach: (a1,a2,a3,a4 ,a5)=(0.31938153,-0.356563782,1.781477937,-1.821255978,1.330274429)

8. An alternative approach:

    ° a1=0.31938153

    ° a2=-0.356563782

    ° a3=1.781477937

    ° a4=-1.821255978

    ° a5=1.330274429

9. What is the difference between an American call and a European call?

10. What is the unit of rf in the Black-Scholes-Merton option model?

11. If we are given an annual rate of 3.4% compounded semi-annually, what is the value of rf we should use for the Black-Scholes-Merton option model?

12. How do you use options to hedge?

13. How do you treat predetermined cash dividends to price a European call?

14. Why is an American call worth more than a European call?

15. Assume you are a mutual manager and your portfolio's β is strongly correlated with the market. You are worried about the short-term fall of the market. What could you do to protect your portfolio?

16. The current price of stock A is $38.5, the strike prices for a call and a put are both $37. If the continuously compounded risk-free rate is 3.2%, maturity is three months, and the volatility of stock A is 0.25, what are the prices for a European call and put?

17. Use the put-call parity to verify the preceding solutions.

18. When the strike prices for call and put in 9.11) are different, can we apply the put-call parity?

19. For a set of input values, such as S=40, X=40, T=3/12=0.25, r=0.05 and sigma=0.20, using the Black-Scholes-Merton option model, we can estimate the value of the call. Now keep all parameters constant except S (current price of a stocks); show the relationship, a graph is better, between calls and S.

20. What are the definitions of effective annual rate, effect semi annual rate, and risk-free rate for the call option model? Assume the current annual risk-free rate is 5 percent, compounded semi annually, which value should we use as our input value for the Black-Scholes-Merton call option model?

21. What is the call premium when the stock is traded at $39, the exercise price is $40, the maturity date is three months, the risk-free rate is 3.5 percent, compounding continuously, and the volatility is 0.15 per year?

22. Repeat the previous exercise for when the risk-free rate is still 3.5 percent per year but compounded semi annually.

23. What are the advantages and disadvantages of using others' programs?

24. How do you debug others' programs?

25. Write a Python program to convert any given APR compounded m times per year, to a continuously compounded interest rate.

26. How do you improve the accuracy of the cumulative normal distribution?

27. What is the relationship between APR and Rc, a continuously compounded rate?

28. For a stock with the current stock price of $52.34, what is its call price if the exercise price is the same as its current stock price, matures in six months with a 0.16 annual volatility, and the risk-free rate is 3.1 percent, compounded continuously?

29. For a set of S, X, T, r, and sigma, we could estimate a European call option by using those 13 lines of Python codes. When the current stock price, S, increases while other input values are the same, will the call price increase or decrease? Why?

30. Show the preceding result graphically.

31. When the exercise price, *X*, increases, the value of a call will fall. Is this true? Why?

    ° If other input values are constant, the value of the call premium will increase if the sigma of the stock increases. Is this true? Why?

32. For a set of input values of *S*, *X*, *T*, *r*, and sigma, we could use the codes in this chapter to price a European call option, that is, *C*. On the other hand, if we observe a real-world price of a call premium (Cobs) with a set of values *S*, *X*, *T*, and *r*, we could estimate an implied volatility (sigma). Specify a trial-and-error method to roughly estimate the implied volatility (if a new learner does not get this question, it is perfectly fine since we will devote a whole chapter to discussing how to do it).

33. According to so-called put-call parity, which holds that a call option with enough cash at maturity (X dollar) is equivalent to holding a put option with a share of the underlying stock in hand--here, both call and put options have the same exercise price (X) with the same maturity (T) and both are European options--if the stock price is $10, exercise price is $11, maturity is six months, and risk-free rate is 2.9 percent, compounded semi annually, what is the price of a European put option?

Summary

In this chapter, first we have explained many basic concepts related to portfolio theory, such as covariance, correlation, the formulas on how to calculate variance of a 2-stock portfolio and variance of an n-stock portfolio. After that, we have discussed various risk measures for individual stocks or portfolios, such as Sharpe ratio, Treynor ratio, Sortino ratio, how to minimize portfolio risk based on those measures (ratios), how to setup an objective function, how to choose an efficient portfolio for a given set of stocks, and how to construct an efficient frontier.

In the next chapter, we will discuss one of the most important theory in modern finance: options and futures. We will start from the basic concepts such as payoff functions for a call and for a put. Then we explain the related applications such as various trading strategies, corporate incentive plans, and hedging strategies including different types of options and futures.

11
Value at Risk

In finance, implicitly or explicitly, rational investors always consider a trade-off between risk and returns. Usually, there is no ambiguity to measure returns. However, in terms of risk, we have numerous different measures such as using variance and standard deviation of returns to measure the total risk, individual stocks' beta, or portfolio beta to measure market risk. In the previous chapters, we know that the total risk has two components: market risk and firm-specific risks. To balance between the benefit of return and the cost of risk, many measures can be applied, such as the Sharpe ratio, Treynor ratio, Sortino ratio, and M2 performance measure (Modigliani and Modigliani performance measure). All of those risk measures or ratios have a common format: a trade-off between benefits expressed as risk-premium and risk expressed as a standard deviation, or beta, or **Lower Partial Standard Deviation (LPSD)**. On the other hand, those measures do not consider a probability distribution. In this chapter, a new risk measure called **Value at Risk (VaR)** will be introduced and applied by using real-world data. In particular, the following topics will be covered:

- Introduction to VaR
- Review of density and cumulative functions of a normal distribution
- Method I—Estimating VaR based on the normality assumption
- Conversion from 1-day risk to n-day risk, one-day VaR versus n-day VaR
- Normality tests
- Impact of skewness and kurtosis
- Modified VaR measure by using including skewness and kurtosis
- Method II—Estimating a VaR based on historical returns
- Linking two methods by using Monte Carlo simulation
- Backtesting and stress testing

Introduction to VaR

Up to now, we have several ways to evaluate risk for an individual stock or a portfolio, such as variance, standard deviation of returns to measure the total risk, or beta to measure the market risk of a portfolio or individual stocks. On the other hand, many CEOs prefer a simple measure called **Value at Risk (VaR)**, which has the simple definition given here:

> *"The maximum loss with a confidence level over a predetermined period."*

From the preceding definition, it has three explicit factors plus one implied one. The implied factor or variable is our current position, or the value of our current portfolio or individual stock(s). The preceding statement offers the maximum possible loss in the future and this is the first factor. The second one is over a specific time period. Those two factors are quite common. However, the last factor is quite unique: with a confidence level or probability. Here are a few examples:

- **Example #1**: On February 7, 2017, we own 300 shares of International Business Machine's stocks worth $52,911. The maximum loss tomorrow, that is, February 8, 2017, is $ 1,951 with a 99% confidence level.

- **Example #2**: Our mutual fund has a value of $10 million today. The maximum loss over the next 3 months is $0.5 million at a 95% confidence level.

- **Example #3**: The value of our bank is $200 million. The VaR of our bank is $10m with a 1% probability over the next 6 months.

Usually, there are two methods to estimate a VaR. The first method is based on the assumption that our security or portfolio returns follow a normal distribution, while the second method depends on the ranking of the historical returns. Before discussing the first method, let's review the concepts with respect to a normal distribution. The density of a normal distribution is defined here:

$$f(x) = \frac{1}{\sqrt{2\pi\sigma^2}} e^{-\frac{(x-\mu)^2}{2\sigma^2}} \qquad \dots (1)$$

Here, $f(x)$ is the density function, x is an input variable, μ is the mean and σ is the standard deviation. One function called `spicy.stats.norm.pdf()` could be used to estimate the density. The function has three input values: x, μ, and σ. The following code calls this function and verifies the results manually according to the preceding formula:

```
import scipy.stats as stats
from scipy import sqrt, exp,pi
```

```
d1=stats.norm.pdf(0,0.1,0.05)
print("d1=",d1)
d2=1/sqrt(2*pi*0.05**2)*exp(-(0-0.1)**2/0.05**2/2)  # verify manually
print("d2=",d2)
('d1=', 1.0798193302637611)
('d2=', 1.0798193302637611)
```

In the preceding code, we import the `sqrt()`, `exp()` functions plus pi to make our code simpler. Setting μ=0, and σ=1, the preceding general normal distribution density function collapses to a standard normal distribution; see its corresponding density function:

$$f(x) = \frac{1}{\sqrt{2\pi}} e^{-\frac{x^2}{2}} \qquad \dots (2)$$

The default values for the second and third input values for the `spicy.stats.norm.pdf()` function are zero and 1, respectively. In other words, with just one input value, it represents a standard normal distribution; see the following code and how to manually verify it:

```
from scipy import exp,sqrt,stats,pi
d1=stats.norm.pdf(0)
print("d1=",d1)
d2=1/sqrt(2*pi)               # verify manually
print("d2=",d2)
('d1=', 0.3989422804014327)
('d2=', 0.3989422804014327)
```

The following code generates a graph for a standard normal distribution where the `spicy.stats.norm.pdf()` function takes just one input:

```
import scipy as sp
import matplotlib.pyplot as plt
x = sp.arange(-3,3,0.1)
y=sp.stats.norm.pdf(x)
plt.title("Standard Normal Distribution")
plt.xlabel("X")
plt.ylabel("Y")
plt.plot(x,y)
plt.show()
```

The graph is shown here:

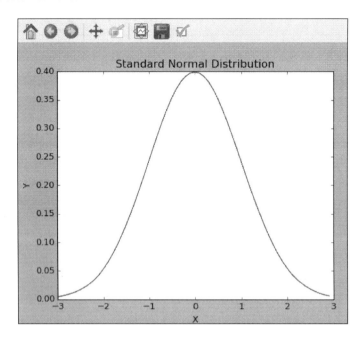

For the VaR estimation, usually we would choose two confidence levels of 95% and 99%. For the 95% (99%) confidence level, we actually look at the left tail with a 5% (1%) probability. The following graph illustrates the concept of VaR based on a standard normal distribution with a 95% confidence level:

```
import scipy as sp
from matplotlib import pyplot as plt
z=-2.325          # user can change this number
xStart=-3.8      # arrow line start x
yStart=0.2       # arrow line start x
xEnd=-2.5        # arrow line start x
yEnd=0.05        # arrow line start x
def f(t):
    return sp.stats.norm.pdf(t)

plt.ylim(0,0.45)
x = sp.arange(-3,3,0.1)
y1=f(x)
plt.plot(x,y1)
x2= sp.arange(-4,z,1/40.)
sum=0
delta=0.05
```

```
s=sp.arange(-10,z,delta)
for i in s:
    sum+=f(i)*delta

plt.annotate('area is '+str(round(sum,4)),xy=(xEnd,yEnd),xytext=(xStar
t,yStart), arrowprops=dict(facecolor='red',shrink=0.01))
plt.annotate('z= '+str(z),xy=(z,0.01))
plt.fill_between(x2,f(x2))
plt.show()
```

To generate a graph, three functions are applied. The purpose of the `matplotlib.pyplot.annotate()` function is used to generate a text or an arrow with a text description at the end of the arrow. The `str()` function will convert a number into a string. `matplotlib.pyplot.fill_between()` will fill the specified area. The output graph is shown here:

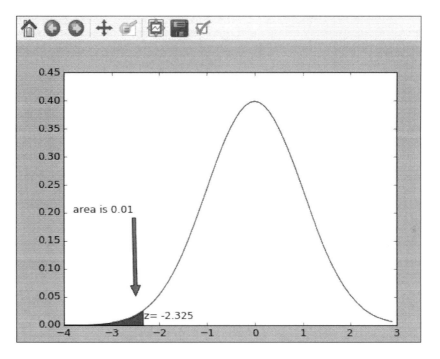

Based on the assumption of normality, we have the following general form to estimate VaR:

$$VaR = position * (\mu_{period} - z * \sigma_p) \quad \dots (3)$$

Here, *VaR* is our value at risk, *position* is the current market value of our portfolio, *μperiod* is the expected period return, *z* is a cut-off point depending on the confidence level, and σ is the volatility of our portfolio. For a normal distribution, *z*=2.33 for a 99% confidence level, and *z*=1.64 for a 95% confidence level. Since we could use `scipy.stats.norm.ppf()` to get the z value, the preceding equation could be rewritten as follows:

$$\begin{cases} z = scipy.\,stats.\,norm.\,ppf\,(1 - confidence) \\ \qquad VaR = position * (\mu_{period} + z * \sigma_p) \end{cases} \quad \dots (4)$$

Compare the preceding two equations. A careful reader should notice that the signs in front of z are different. For the preceding equation, it has a positive sign instead of the negative one shown in the previous equation. The reason is that the z value estimated by applying `scipy.stats.norm.ppf()` would be negative; see the following code:

```
from scipy.stats import norm
confidence_level=0.99
z=norm.ppf(1-confidence_level)
print(z)
-2.32634787404
```

When the time period is short, such as 1 day, we could ignore the impact of *μperiod*. Therefore, we have the following simplest form:

$$VaR = p * z * \sigma \qquad \dots (5)$$

The following program shows the 5% VaR of a hypothetical profit-and-loss probability density function:

```
import scipy as sp
import scipy as sp
from scipy.stats import norm
from matplotlib import pyplot as plt

confidence_level=0.95    # input
z=norm.ppf(1-confidence_level)
def f(t):
    return sp.stats.norm.pdf(t)
#
plt.ylim(0,0.5)
x = sp.arange(-7,7,0.1)
```

```
ret=f(x)
plt.plot(x,ret)
x2= sp.arange(-4,z,1/40.)
x3=sp.arange(z,4,1/40.)
sum=0
delta=0.05
s=sp.arange(-3,z,delta)
for i in s:
    sum+=f(i)*delta
note1='Red area to the left of the'
note2='dotted red line reprsesents'
note3='5% of the total area'
#
note4='The curve represents a hypothesis'
note5='profit/loss density function. The'
note6='5% VaR is 1.64 standard deviation'
note7='from the mean, i.e.,zero'
#
note8='The blue area to the righ of the'
note9='red dotted line represents 95%'
note10='of the returns space'
# this is for the vertical line
plt.axvline(x=z, ymin=0.1, ymax = 1, linewidth=2,ls='dotted',
color='r')
plt.figtext(0.14,0.5,note1)
plt.figtext(0.14,0.47,note2)
plt.figtext(0.14,0.44,note3)
#
plt.figtext(0.5,0.85,note4)
plt.figtext(0.5,0.82,note5)
plt.figtext(0.5,0.79,note6)
plt.figtext(0.5,0.76,note7)
plt.annotate("",xy=(-2.5,0.08),xytext=(-2.5,0.18), arrowprops=dict(fac
ecolor='red',shrink=0.001))
#
plt.figtext(0.57,0.5,note8)
plt.figtext(0.57,0.47,note9)
plt.figtext(0.57,0.44,note10)
plt.annotate("",xy=(1.5,0.28),xytext=(4.5,0.28), arrowprops=dict(facec
olor='blue',shrink=0.001))
#
plt.annotate('z= '+str(z),xy=(2.,0.1))
plt.fill_between(x2,f(x2), color='red')
plt.fill_between(x3,f(x3), color='blue')
plt.title("Visual presentation of VaR, 5% vs. 95%")
plt.show()
```

The related graph is shown here:

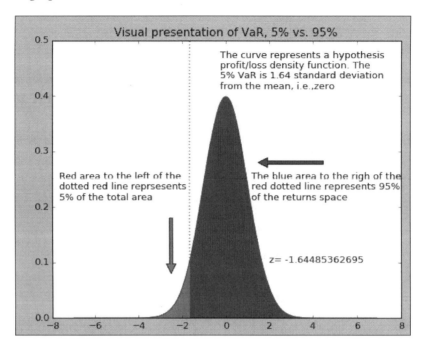

Here is the simplest example to estimate the maximum loss tomorrow. Assume that we have 1,000 shares of IBM's stock on February 7, 2017. What is the maximum loss tomorrow with a confidence level of 99%? To estimate the standard deviation of daily returns, we use the last 5 years' data. Actually, this is a decision variable. We could use 1-year data or multiple-year data. Each approach has its advantages and disadvantages. The standard deviation estimated based on a longer period would be more stable because we have a much larger sample size. However, some information in the remote past would definitely be outdated:

```
import numpy as np
import pandas as pd
from scipy.stats import norm
from matplotlib.finance import quotes_historical_yahoo_ochl as getData
#
# input area
ticker='IBM'                # input 1
n_shares=1000               # input 2
confidence_level=0.99       # input 3
begdate=(2012,2,7)          # input 4
enddate=(2017,2,7)          # input 5
#
```

```
z=norm.ppf(1-confidence_level)
x=getData(ticker,begdate,enddate,asobject=True,adjusted=True)
print(x[0])
ret = x.aclose[1:]/x.aclose[:-1]-1
#
position=n_shares*x.close[0]
std=np.std(ret)
#
VaR=position*z*std
print("Holding=",position, "VaR=", round(VaR,4), "tomorrow")
(datetime.date(2012, 2, 7), 2012, 2, 7, 734540.0, 167.75861437920275,
168.543152, 169.23178870104016, 167.34020198573538, 3433000.0,
168.543152)
('Holding=', 168543.152, 'VaR=', -4603.5087, 'tomorrow')
```

The objective of printing the first line of the data is to show the closing price is indeed on 2/7/2017. The value of our holding is $168,543 and its 1-day VaR is $4,604. The second example is about the VaR over a 10-day period. To convert a variance (standard deviation) on daily returns to an n-day variance (standard deviation), we have the following formulas:

$$\begin{cases} \sigma^2_{n\_day} = n * \sigma^2_{daily} \\ \sigma_{n\_day} = \sqrt{n} * \sigma_{daily} \end{cases} \quad \dots (6)$$

For example, the annual volatility is equal to the daily volatility times the square root of 252 ($\sigma_{annual} = \sigma_{daily}\sqrt{252}$). In order to convert a daily mean return to an n-day mean return, we have the following formula:

$$\mu_{n\_day} = (\mu_{daily} + 1)^n - 1 \quad \dots (7)$$

Based on daily returns, we have the following general formulas for VaR with a confidence level to estimate an n-day VaR:

$$\begin{cases} \mu_{n\_day} = (\mu_{daily} + 1)^n - 1 \\ \sigma_{n_{day}} = \sigma_{daily}\sqrt{n} \\ z = scipy.stats.norm.ppf(1 - confidence) \\ VaR = position * (\mu_{period} + z * \sigma_p) \end{cases} \quad \dots (8)$$

The following code shows the VaR for holding 50 shares of Wal-Mart stocks, on the last day of 2016, over a 10-day period with a confidence level of 99%:

```
import numpy as np
import pandas as pd
from scipy.stats import norm
from matplotlib.finance import quotes_historical_yahoo_ochl as getData
ticker='WMT'              # input 1
n_shares=50               # input 2
confidence_level=0.99     # input 3
n_days=10                 # input 4
begdate=(2012,1,1)        # input 5
enddate=(2016,12,31)      # input 6


z=norm.ppf(confidence_level)


x=getData(ticker,begdate,enddate,asobject=True,adjusted=True)
ret = x.aclose[1:]/x.aclose[:-1]-1
position=n_shares*x.close[0]
VaR=position*z*np.std(ret)*np.sqrt(n_days)
print("Holding=",position, "VaR=", round(VaR,4), "in ", n_days,
"Days")
('Holding=', 2650.3070499999999, 'VaR=', 205.0288, 'in ', 10, 'Days')
```

On December 31, 2016, the value of our holding is $2,650. Our maximum loss is $205 in the next 10 days with a confidence level of 99%. In the preceding program, based on daily returns, we estimate both daily mean return and the standard deviation. Then we convert them into a 10-day mean return and 10-day volatility. On the other hand, actually we could calculate a 10-day return directly. After 10-day returns available, the `scipy.mean()` and `scipy.std()` functions could be applied directly. In other words, we don't need to convert a daily mean and daily standard deviation into a 10-day mean and 10-day standard deviation. The related code is given here. To save space, the first 11 lines are not repeated:

```
x = getData(ticker, begdate, enddate,asobject=True, adjusted=True)
logret = np.log(x.aclose[1:]/x.aclose[:-1])


# method 2: calculate 10 day returns
ddate=[]
d0=x.date
for i in range(0,np.size(logret)):
    ddate.append(int(i/nDays))
y=pd.DataFrame(logret,ddate,columns=['retNdays'])
retNdays=y.groupby(y.index).sum()
```

```
#print(retNdays.head())
position=n_shares*x.close[0]
VaR=position*z*np.std(retNdays)
print("Holding=",position, "VaR=", round(VaR,4), "in ", nDays, "Days")
('Holding=', 2650.3070499999999, 'VaR=', 209.1118, 'in ', 10, 'Days')
```

Our new result shows that the VaR is $209.11 compared with $205.03. The percentage of the underestimation is -0.01951126, about -2%. The following code estimate the VaR for the Fama-French five value-weighted industry portfolios with a monthly frequency. The dataset is available at the author's website, http://canisius.edu/~yany/python/ff5VWindustryMonthly.pkl. Those five industries are Consumer, Manufacture, High Tech, Health, and Other. The first and last several lines are shown here:

```
import pandas as pd
x=pd.read_pickle("c:/temp/ff5VWindustryMonthly.pkl")
print(x.head())
print(x.tail())
         CNSMR    MANUF    HITEC    HLTH     OTHER
192607   0.0543   0.0273   0.0183   0.0177   0.0216
192608   0.0276   0.0233   0.0241   0.0425   0.0438
192609   0.0216  -0.0044   0.0106   0.0069   0.0029
192610  -0.0390  -0.0242  -0.0226  -0.0057  -0.0285
192611   0.0370   0.0250   0.0307   0.0542   0.0211
         CNSMR    MANUF    HITEC    HLTH     OTHER
201608  -0.0101   0.0040   0.0068  -0.0323   0.0326
201609  -0.0143   0.0107   0.0202   0.0036  -0.0121
201610  -0.0252  -0.0231  -0.0141  -0.0743   0.0059
201611   0.0154   0.0539   0.0165   0.0137   0.1083
201612   0.0132   0.0158   0.0163   0.0084   0.0293
```

The following program estimates their VaR with $1,000 invested in each industry portfolio with a 99% confidence level over the next period. Since the frequency is monthly, the fixed period will be the next month:

```
import pandas as pd
import scipy as sp
from scipy.stats import norm
#
confidence_level=0.99    # input
position=([1000,1000,1000,1000,1000])
z=norm.ppf(1-confidence_level)
x=pd.read_pickle("c:/temp/ff5VWindustryMonthly.pkl")
#
```

```
std=sp.std(x,axis=0)
mean=sp.mean(x,axis=0)
#
t=sp.dot(position,z)
VaR=t*std
#
# output area
print(sp.shape(x))
print("Position=",position)
print("VaR=")
print(VaR)
1086, 5)
('Position=', [1000, 1000, 1000, 1000, 1000])
VaR=
CNSMR    -122.952735
MANUF    -128.582446
HITEC    -129.918893
HLTH     -130.020356
OTHER    -149.851230
dtype: float64
```

The VaR for those five industries are $122.95, $128.58, $129.92, $130.02, and $149.85, respectively, for an equal holding of $1,000 invested in each industry. Comparing those values, we could see that the Consumer industry has the lowest risk while the industry defined as Other would have the highest maximum possible loss.

Normality tests

The first method to estimate VaR is based on a vital assumption that individual stock or portfolio returns follow a normal distribution. However, in the real world, we know that stock returns or portfolio returns do not necessarily follow a normal distribution. The following program tests whether Microsoft returns satisfy this assumption by using 5-year daily data:

```
from scipy import stats
from matplotlib.finance import quotes_historical_yahoo_ochl as getData
import numpy as np
#
ticker='MSFT'
begdate=(2012,1,1)
enddate=(2016,12,31)
#
```

```
p =getData(ticker, begdate, enddate,asobject=True, adjusted=True)
ret = (p.aclose[1:] - p.aclose[:-1])/p.aclose[1:]
print 'ticker=',ticker,'W-test, and P-value'
print(stats.shapiro(ret))
print( stats.anderson(ret))
ticker= MSFT W-test, and P-value
(0.9130843877792358, 3.2116320877511604e-26)
AndersonResult(statistic=14.629260310763584, critical_values=array([
0.574,  0.654,  0.785,  0.915,  1.089]), significance_level=array([
15. ,  10. ,   5. ,   2.5,   1. ]))
```

Our null hypothesis is that Microsoft stock daily returns following a normal distribution. Based on the preceding result, the null hypothesis is rejected since the F-value is much higher than the critical value of 1.089 if we choose a 1% significance level. Even if we reject the hypothesis based on just one stock, some might argue that portfolio returns might satisfy this assumption. The next program tests whether S&P500 daily returns follow a normal distribution. The ticker symbol for S&P500 from Yahoo!Finance is ^GSPC:

```
import numpy as np
from scipy import stats
from matplotlib.finance import quotes_historical_yahoo_ochl as getData
#
ticker='^GSPC'    # ^GSPC is for S&P500
begdate=(2012,1,1)
enddate=(2016,12,31)
#
p =getData(ticker, begdate, enddate,asobject=True, adjusted=True)
ret = (p.aclose[1:] - p.aclose[:-1])/p.aclose[1:]
print 'ticker=',ticker,'W-test, and P-value'
print(stats.shapiro(ret))
print( stats.anderson(ret) )
ticker= ^GSPC W-test, and P-value
(0.9743353128433228, 3.7362179458122827e-14)
AndersonResult(statistic=8.6962226557502618, critical_values=array([
0.574,  0.654,  0.785,  0.915,  1.089]), significance_level=array([
15. ,  10. ,   5. ,   2.5,   1. ]))
```

From the preceding results, we reject the normality assumption for S&P500. In other words, the market index, represented by S&P500 daily returns, does not follow a normal distribution.

Skewness and kurtosis

Based on the normality assumption, a VaR estimation considers only the first two moments: mean and variance. If stock returns truly follow a normal distribution, those two moments would fully define their probability distribution. From the preceding sections, we know that this is not true. The first remedy is to include other higher moments in addition to the first two moments. The third and fourth moments are called skewness and kurtosis. For a stock or portfolio with n returns, skewness is estimated by the following formula:

$$skewness = \frac{\sum_{i=1}^{n}(R_i - \bar{R})^3}{(n-1)\sigma^3} \qquad \dots (9)$$

Here, *skewness* is the skewness, R_i is the ith return, $\bar{R}$ is the mean return, n is the number of returns, and σ is the standard deviation of returns. The kurtosis reflects the impact of extreme values because a power of 4 is very high. The kurtosis is usually estimated by the following formula is:

$$kurtosis = \frac{\sum_{i=1}^{n}(R_i - \bar{R})^4}{(n-1)\sigma^4} \qquad \dots (10)$$

For a standard moral distribution, it has a zero mean, unit variance, zero skewness, and its kurtosis is 3. Because of this, sometimes kurtosis is defined as the preceding equation minus 3:

$$kurtosis = \frac{\sum_{i=1}^{n}(R_i - \bar{R})^4}{(n-1)\sigma^4} - 3 \qquad \dots (11)$$

Some textbooks distinguish those two definitions as kurtosis and excess kurtosis. However, others simply label the preceding formula as kurtosis as well. Thus, when we conduct a test to see whether the kurtosis of a time series is zero, we have to know which benchmark is used. The following program generates 5 million random numbers from a standard deviation and applies four functions to estimate those four moments, that is, mean, standard deviation, skewness, and kurtosis:

```
from scipy import stats,random
import numpy as np
np.random.seed(12345)
```

```
n=5000000
#
ret = random.normal(0,1,n)
print('mean      =', np.mean(ret))
print('std       =',np.std(ret))
print('skewness=',stats.skew(ret))
print('kurtosis=',stats.kurtosis(ret))
('mean      =', 0.00035852273706422504)
('std       =', 0.99983435063933623)
('skewness=', -0.00040545999711941665)
('kurtosis=', -0.001162270913658947)
```

Since the kurtosis is close to zero for random numbers drawn from a standard normal distribution, the `scipy.stats.kurtosis()` function should be based on *Equation (11)* instead of *Equation (10)*.

Modified VaR

From the previous discussion, we know that based on the assumption, that stock returns follow a normal distribution. Because of this, the skewness and kurtosis of returns are both assumed to be zero. However, in the real world, skewness and excess kurtosis of many stock returns are not zero. As a consequence, the modified VaR was developed to utilize those four moments instead of just two; see the following definition:

$$\begin{cases} z = abs(scipy.stats.ppf(1 - confidence)) \\ S = scipy.stats.skewness(ret) \\ K = scipy.stats.kurtosis(ret) \\ t = z + \frac{1}{6}(z^2 - 1)S + \frac{1}{24}(z^3 - 3z)K - \frac{1}{36}(2z^3 - 5z)S^2 \\ mVaR = position * (\mu - t * \sigma) \end{cases} \quad \dots (12)$$

Here, z is the value based on a normal distribution, S is the skewness, K is kurtosis, t is an intermediate variable, and the `scipy.stats.ppf()` function would offer a z-value for a given confidence level. The following program offers two VaRs based on the normality assumption and based on the preceding formula, that is, using all four moments. The number of shares is 500 at the end of year 2016. The stock tested is **Walmart (WMT)**. The confidence level is 99% for a 1-day VaR:

```
import numpy as np
import pandas as pd
from scipy.stats import stats,norm
```

```
from matplotlib.finance import quotes_historical_yahoo_ochl as getData
#
ticker='WMT'              # input 1
n_shares=500              # input 2
confidence_level=0.99     # input 3
begdate=(2000,1,1)        # input 4
enddate=(2016,12,31)      # input 5
#
# Method I: based on the first two moments
z=abs(norm.ppf(1-confidence_level)) x=getData(ticker,begdate,enddate,a
sobject=True,adjusted=True)
ret = x.aclose[1:]/x.aclose[:-1]-1
position=n_shares*x.close[0]
mean=np.mean(ret)
std=np.std(ret)
VaR1=position*(mean-z*std)
print("Holding=",round(position,2), "VaR1=", round(VaR1,2), "for 1 day
")
#
# Modified VaR: based on 4 moments
s=stats.skew(ret)
k=stats.kurtosis(ret)
t=z+1/6.*(z**2-1)*s+1/24.*(z**3-3*z)*k-1/36.*(2*z**3-5*z)*s**2
mVaR=position*(mean-t*std)
print("Holding=",round(position,2), "modified VaR=", round(mVaR,2),
"for 1 day ")
('Holding=', 24853.46, 'VaR1=', -876.84, 'for 1 day ')
('Holding=', 24853.46, 'modified VaR=', -1500.41, 'for 1 day ')
```

Based on the last two lines, we have a VaR of $876.84 based on the normality and the modified VaR has a value of $1,500. The percentage difference of those two is 42%. This result suggests that ignoring the skewness and kurtosis would understate VaR enormously.

VaR based on sorted historical returns

We know that stock returns do not necessarily follow a normal distribution. An alternative is to use sorted returns to evaluate a VaR. This method is called VaR based on historical returns. Assume that we have a daily return vector called *ret*. We sort it from the smallest to the highest. Let's call the sorted return vector *sorted_ret*. For a given confidence level, the one-period VaR is given here:

$$\begin{cases} n = len(ret) \\ t = int((1 - confidence) * n) \qquad \dots (13) \\ VaR = position * sorted\_ret[t] \end{cases}$$

Here, *position* is our wealth (value of our portfolio), *confidence* is the confidence level and n is the number of returns. The `len()` function shows the number of observations and the `int()` function takes the integer part of an input value. For example, if the length of the return vector is 200 and the confidence level is 99%, then the second value (200*0.01) of the sorted returns, from the smallest to the highest, times our wealth, will be our VaR. Obviously, if we have a longer time series, that is, more return observations, our final VaR would be more accurate. For owning 500 shares of Walmart, what is the maximum loss with a 99% confidence level the next day? First, let's look at several ways to sort our data. The first one uses the `numpy.sort()` function:

```
import numpy as np
a = np.array([[1,-4],[9,10]])
b=np.sort(a)
print("a=",a)
print("b=",b)
('a=', array([[ 1,  -4],
        [ 9,  10]]))
('b=', array([[-4,   1],
        [ 9,  10]]))
```

Here is the second way to sort by using Python's `pandas` module:

```
import pandas as pd
a = pd.DataFrame([[9,4],[9,2],[1,-1]],columns=['A','B'])
print(a)
# sort by A ascedning, then B descending
b= a.sort_values(['A', 'B'], ascending=[1, 0])
print(b)
# sort by A and B, both ascedning
c= a.sort_values(['A', 'B'], ascending=[1, 1])
print(c)
```

For an easy comparison, those three datasets are put side by side. The left panel shows the original dataset. The middle one shows the result sorted by column A first in ascending order, then by column B in descending order. The right panel shows the result sorted by columns A then B, both in ascending order:

```
In [199]: print(a)
     A  B
0    9  4
1    9  2
2    1 -1

In [200]: print(b)
     A  B
2    1 -1
0    9  4
1    9  2

In [201]: print(c)
     A  B
2    1 -1
1    9  2
0    9  4
```

The next two programs compare two methods used to estimate VaR: based on the normality and based on sorting. To make our programs easier to understand, the time period is just 1 day:

```
#
z=norm.ppf(confidence_level)
x=getData(ticker,begdate,enddate,asobject=True,adjusted=True)
ret = x.aclose[1:]/x.aclose[:-1]-1
#
position=n_shares*x.close[0]
std=np.std(ret)
#
VaR=position*z*std
print("Holding=",position, "VaR=", round(VaR,4), "tomorrow")
('Holding=', 26503.070499999998, 'VaR=', 648.3579, 'tomorrow')
```

The formula used in the preceding program is *VaR=position*z*sigma*. The result tells us that the holding is $26,503 and its 1-day VaR is $648 with a 99% confidence level. The following program estimates the VaR for the same stock based on sorting:

```
ret = np.array(x.aclose[1:]/x.aclose[:-1]-1)
ret2=np.sort(ret)
#
position=n_shares*x.close[0]
n=np.size(ret2)
```

```
leftTail=int(n*(1-confidence_level))
print(leftTail)
#
VaR2=position*ret2[leftTail]
print("Holding=",position, "VaR=", round(VaR2,4), "tomorrow")
('Holding=', 26503.070499999998, 'VaR=', -816.7344, 'tomorrow')
```

The result shows that the 1-day VaR is $817. Recall that the VaR based on the normality is $648. If the second method is more accurate, the first method underestimates our potential loss by 20%. This is a huge number in terms of risk evaluation! The following codes are for an n-day period based on sorting:

```
ret = x.aclose[1:]/x.aclose[:-1]-1
position=n_shares*x.close[0]
#
# Method 1: based on normality
mean=np.mean(ret)
std=np.std(ret)
meanNdays=(1+mean)**nDays-1
stdNdays=std*np.sqrt(nDays)
z=norm.ppf(confidence_level)
VaR1=position*z*stdNdays
print("Holding=",position, "VaR1=", round(VaR1,0), "in ", nDays,
"Days")
#
# method 2: calculate 10 day returns
ddate=[]
d0=x.date
for i in range(0,np.size(logret)):
    ddate.append(int(i/nDays))
y=pd.DataFrame(logret,index=ddate,columns=['retNdays'])
logRet=y.groupby(y.index).sum()
retNdays=np.exp(logRet)-1
#
VaR2=position*z*np.std(retNdays)
print("Holding=",position, "VaR2=", round(VaR2,0), "in ", nDays,
"Days")
#
# Method III
ret2=np.sort(retNdays)
n=np.size(ret2)
leftTail=int(n*(1-confidence_level))
print(leftTail)
#
VaR3=position*ret2[leftTail]
print("Holding=",position, "VaR=", round(VaR3,0), "in ",nDays, "Days")
('Holding=', 24853.456000000002, 'VaR1=', 2788.0, 'in ', 10, 'Days')
```

```
('Holding=', 24853.456000000002, 'VaR2=', 2223.0, 'in ', 10, 'Days')
4
('Holding=', 24853.456000000002, 'VaR=', 1301.0, 'in ', 10, 'Days')
```

There are two tricks in the preceding program. The first one is the summation of a daily log return will be a 10-day log return. Then we convert a log return to a percentage return. The second trick is how to generate a 10-day return. First, we generate groups by using the int() function, that is, int(i/nDays). Since nDays has a value of 10, int(i/10) would generate 10 zeros, ten ones, ten twos, and so on. The VaRs based on the three methods are $2,788, $2,223, and $1,301, respectively. Obviously, there are some issues with method 3. One of the concerns is that for n-day periods, we have only 428 observations, that is, the size of our sample might be too small. If we choose a 99% confidence interval, we have to choose the fourth lowest return in our calculation. This would definitely cause some issues here.

Simulation and VaR

In the previous sections, we have learned that there are two ways to estimate VaR for an individual stock or for a portfolio. The first method depends on the assumption that stock returns follow a normal distribution. The second one uses the sorted historical returns. What is the link between those two methods? Actually, Monte Carlo simulation could be served as a link. First, let's look at the first method based on the normality assumption. We have 500 Walmart shares on the last day of 2016. What is the VaR tomorrow if the confidence level is 99%?

```
#
position=n_shares*x.close[0]
mean=np.mean(ret)
std=np.std(ret)
#
VaR=position*(mean+z*std)
print("Holding=",position, "VaR=", round(VaR,4), "tomorrow")
('Holding=', 26503.070499999998, 'VaR=', -641.2911, 'tomorrow')
```

The VaR is $641.29 for tomorrow with a confidence level of 99%. Here is how Monte Carlo simulation works. First, we calculate the mean and standard deviation based on daily returns. Since stock returns are assumed to follow a normal distribution, we could generate 5,000 returns with the same mean and standard deviation. If our confidence level is 99%, then the 50th return from the lowest sorted returns would be our cut-off point, *5000*0.01=50*. The code is shown here:

```
#
position=n_shares*x.close[0]
mean=np.mean(ret)
```

```
std=np.std(ret)
#
n_simulation=5000
sp.random.seed(12345)
ret2=sp.random.normal(mean,std,n_simulation)
ret3=np.sort(ret2)
m=int(n_simulation*(1-confidence_level))
VaR=position*(ret3[m])
print("Holding=",position, "VaR=", round(VaR,4), "tomorrow")
('Holding=', 26503.070499999998, 'VaR=', -627.3443, 'tomorrow')
```

Monte Carlo Simulation offers a quite similar value of $627.34 compared with $641.29 based on the formula.

VaR for portfolios

In *Chapter 9, Portfolio Theory*, it was shown that when putting many stocks in our portfolio, we could reduce or eliminate firm-specific risk. The formula to estimate an n-stock portfolio return is given here:

$$R_{p,t} = \sum_{i=1}^{n} w_i R_{i,t} \qquad \dots (14)$$

Here $R_{p,t}$ is the portfolio return at time t, wi is the weight for stock i, and Ri, t is the return at time t for stock i. When talking about the expected return or mean, we have a quite similar formula:

$$\bar{R}_p = \sum_{i=1}^{n} w_i \bar{R}_i \qquad \dots (15)$$

Here, $\bar{R}_p$ is the mean or expected portfolio return, $\bar{R}_i$ is the mean or expected return for stock i. The variance of such an n-stock portfolio is given here:

$$\sigma_p^2 = \sum_{i=1}^{n} \sum_{j=1}^{n} w_i w_i \sigma_{i,j} \qquad \dots (16)$$

Here, σ_p^2 is the portfolio variance, $\sigma i,j$ is covariance between stocks i and j; see the following formula:

$$\sigma_{i,j} = \frac{\sum_{k=1}^{n} (R_{i,k}-\bar{R}_i)*(R_{j,k}-\bar{R}_j)}{n-1} \qquad \dots (17)$$

The correlation between stocks i and j, $\rho_{i,j}$, is defined here:

$$\rho_{i,j} = \frac{\sigma_{i,j}}{\sigma_i \sigma_j} \quad \dots (18)$$

When stocks are not positively perfectively correlated, combining stocks would reduce our portfolio risk. The following program shows that the VaR of the portfolio is not simply the summation or weighted VaR of individual stocks within the portfolio:

```
from matplotlib.finance import quotes_historical_yahoo_ochl as getData

# Step 1: input area
tickers=('IBM','WMT','C')   # tickers
begdate=(2012,1,1)          # beginning date
enddate=(2016,12,31)        # ending date
weight=(0.2,0.5,0.3)        # weights
confidence_level=0.99       # confidence level
position=5e6                # total value
#
z=norm.ppf(confidence_level)
# Step 2: define a function
def ret_f(ticker,begdate,enddte):
    x=getData(ticker,begdate,enddate,asobject=True,adjusted=True)
    ret=x.aclose[1:]/x.aclose[:-1]-1
    d0=x.date[1:]
    return pd.DataFrame(ret,index=d0,columns=[ticker])
# Step 3
n=np.size(tickers)
final=ret_f(tickers[0],begdate,enddate)
for i in np.arange(1,n):
    a=ret_f(tickers[i],begdate,enddate)
    if i>0:
        final=pd.merge(final,a,left_index=True,right_index=True)
#
# Step 4: get porfolio returns
portRet=sp.dot(final,weight)
portStd=sp.std(portRet)
portMean=sp.mean(portRet)
VaR=position*(portMean-z*portStd)
print("Holding=",position, "VaR=", round(VaR,2), "tomorrow")

# compare
total2=0.0
```

```
for i in np.arange(n):
    stock=tickers[i]
    ret=final[stock]
    position2=position*weight[i]
    mean=sp.mean(ret)
    std=sp.std(ret)
    VaR=position2*(mean-z*std)
    total2+=VaR
    print("For ", stock, "with a value of ", position2, "VaR=",
round(VaR,2))
print("Sum of three VaR=",round(total2,2))
('Holding=', 5000000.0, 'VaR=', -109356.22, 'tomorrow')
('For ', 'IBM', 'with a value of ', 1000000.0, 'VaR=', -27256.67)
('For ', 'WMT', 'with a value of ', 2500000.0, 'VaR=', -60492.15)
('For ', 'C', 'with a value of ', 1500000.0, 'VaR=', -59440.77)
('Sum of three VaR=', -147189.59)
```

The VaR for our current portfolio of $5 million is $109,356. However, the summation of the VaR for those three stocks based on our weights is $147,190. This result verifies the diversification effect by choosing different stocks.

Backtesting and stress testing

In finance, a stress test could be viewed as an analysis or simulation designed to determine the ability of a given financial instrument, such as a VaR to deal with an economic crisis. Since the first method to estimate a VaR is based on the assumption that stock returns following a normal distribution, its accuracy depends how far, in the real world, stock returns deviate from this assumption. A key component to the implementation of model-based risk management is model validation. That is, we need some way to determine whether the model chosen is accurate and performs consistently. This step is quite important both to firms and their regulators. According to Lopez (2000), we have the following table:

Name	Objectives	Methods
Backtesting	Compare observed outcomes with a model's expected output	Forecast evaluation established empirical issue with a large academic literature
Stress testing	Examples a model's expected outcomes under extreme conditions	• Projection analysis • Outlier analysis • Scenario analysis and case studies

Table 11.1 Backtesting versus stress testing

Assume that we use just 1 year's data to estimate 1-day VaR with a 99% confidence level for holding 1,000 shares of IBM on February 7, 2017. The program is shown here:

```
#
position=n_shares*x.close[0]
mean=np.mean(ret)
z=norm.ppf(1-confidence_level)
std=np.std(ret)
#
VaR=position*(mean+z*std)
print("Holding=",position, "VaR=", round(VaR,4), "tomorrow")
print("VaR/holding=",VaR/position)
 (datetime.date(2016, 2, 8), 2016, 2, 8, 736002.0, 121.65280462310274,
 122.598996, 123.11070921267809, 119.84731962624865, 7364000.0,
 122.598996)
 ('Holding=', 122598.996, 'VaR=', -3186.5054, 'tomorrow')
 ('VaR/holding=', -0.025991284652254254)
```

Based on the preceding result, our holding is $122,599 and the maximum loss next day is $3,187. Remember that the confidence level is 99% and it means that during this 1-year period, we should expect about 2.5 violations (0.01*252). The value of 252 is the number of trading days within 1 year. The following program shows the number of violations:

```
VaR=-3186.5054              # from the previous program
position=122598.996         # from the previous program
#('Holding=', 122598.996, 'VaR=', -3186.5054, 'tomorrow')
#('VaR/holding=', -0.025991284652254254)
#
z=norm.ppf(1-confidence_level)
x=getData(ticker,begdate,enddate,asobject=True,adjusted=True)
print("first day=",x[0])
ret = x.aclose[1:]/x.aclose[:-1]-1
#
cutOff=VaR/position
n=len(ret)
ret2=ret[ret<=cutOff]
n2=len(ret2)
print("n2=",n2)
ratio=n2*1./(n*1.)
print("Ratio=", ratio)
 ('first day=', (datetime.date(2016, 2, 8), 2016, 2, 8,
 736002.0, 121.65280462310274, 122.598996, 123.11070921267809,
 119.84731962624865, 7364000.0, 122.598996))
 ('n2=', 4)
 ('Ratio=', 0.015873015873015872)
```

Again, we expect to see 2.5 violations based on our model. However, we have four. Based on a 99% confidence level, we expected that returns worse than -2.599% should be around 1%. Unfortunately, based on 1 year's data, this ratio is 1.58%. If based on 55 years' historical data for this specific stock, the frequency of worse returns than this ratio is more than double, 3.66% versus 1%. This indicates that the underlying model underestimates the potential maximum loss.

Expected shortfall

In the previous sections, we have discussed many issues related to VaR, such as its definition and how to estimate it. However, one major concern with VaR is that it depends on the shape of the distribution of the underlying security or portfolio. If the assumption of normality is close to hold, then VaR is a reasonable measure. Otherwise, we might underestimate the maximum loss (risk) if we observe a fat tail. Another problem is that the shape of the distribution after a VaR is hit is ignored. If we have a fatter left tail than a normal distribution describes, then our VaR would underestimate the true risk. The opposite is true: if the left tail is thinner than the normal distribution, our VaR would overestimate the true risk. **Expected shortfall (ES)** is the expected loss if a VaR is hit, and it is defined here:

$$ES = (loss|z < -\alpha) = \frac{\int_{-\infty}^{-\alpha} x f(x)dx}{\int_{-\infty}^{-\alpha} f(x)dx} = \frac{-\emptyset(\alpha)}{F(\alpha)} \quad \dots (19)$$

Here, ES is the expected shortfall and α is our significant level, such as 1% or 5%. Based on the assumption of normality, for our Python presentation, we have the following formula:

$$zES = (loss|z < -\alpha) = \frac{-norm.pdf(norm.ppf(1-dividence))}{1-confidence} \quad \dots (20)$$

The expected shortfall could be estimated in the following way:

$$ES = position * zES * \sigma \quad \dots (21)$$

The following program shows how to generate returns from a normal distribution, then estimates both the VaR and ES:

```
import scipy as sp
import scipy.stats as stats
x = sp.arange(-3,3,0.01)
```

```
ret=stats.norm.pdf(x)
confidence=0.99
position=10000
z=stats.norm.ppf(1-confidence)
print("z=",z)
zES=-stats.norm.pdf(z)/(1-confidence)
print("zES=", zES)
std=sp.std(ret)
VaR=position*z*std
print("VaR=",VaR)
ES=position*zES*std
print("ES=",ES)
```

Similarly, we could derive the formula to estimate the expected shortfall based on historical returns. In a sense, the expected shortfall is the average loss based on returns with a lower value than the VaR threshold. Assume that we have n return observations. The expected shortfall could be defined as follows:

$$ES = Position * \frac{1}{m}\sum_{i=1}^{n} R_i I_i [R_i < R_{cutoff}] \qquad \dots (22)$$

Here, *ES* is the expected shortfall, *position* is the value of our portfolio, *m* is the number of observations which are worse than our cut-off point specified by the given confidence level, *Ii* is a dummy variable which takes a value of 1 for returns less than *Rcutoff* and zero otherwise, *Ri* is the *i*th return, *Rcutoff* is the cutoff return determined by a given confidence level, n is the number of total return observations, m is the number of returns less than the cutoff return. For example, if we have 1,000 observations and the confidence level is 99%, then the cutoff return will be the 10th observation of the returns sorted from the lowest to the highest. The expected shortfall will be the average loss of those 10 worst scenarios.

Assume that on the last day of 2016, we own 500 shares of Walmart stocks. Assume that we care about the next day's maximum loss with a confidence level of 99%. Based on the ranking of historical returns, what is the VaR and the expected shortfall? The following code offers an answer:

```
x=getData(ticker,begdate,enddate,asobject=True,adjusted=True)
ret = np.array(x.aclose[1:]/x.aclose[:-1]-1)
ret2=np.sort(ret)
#
position=n_shares*x.close[0]
n=np.size(ret2)
m=int(n*(1-confidence_level))
print("m=",m)
```

```
#
sum=0.0
for i in np.arange(m):
    sum+=ret2[i]
ret3=sum/m
ES=position*ret3
print("Holding=",position, "Expected Shortfall=", round(ES,4),
"tomorrow")
('m=', 12)
('Holding=', 26503.070499999998, 'Expected Shortfall=', -1105.1574,
'tomorrow')
```

Since there are 11 returns are less the 12th returns, the expected shortfall will be the average of those 12 returns times our portfolio market value on the evaluation day:

Appendix A – data case 7 – VaR estimation for individual stocks and a portfolio

There are three objectives of this dataset:

- Understand the concepts and methodology related to a VaR
- Estimate a VaR for individual stocks
- Estimate a VaR for a portfolio

The question is: What are your VaRs for each stock and for an equal-weighted portfolio over 10 days for a 99% confidence interval? Assume that the data period is from February 7, 2012 to February 7, 2017 and you have a $1m investment (position in Equation 1):

i	Company name	Ticker	Industry
1	Microsoft Corporation	MSFT	Application software
2	Apple Inc.	AAPL	Personal computer
3	Home Depot, Inc.	HD	Home improvement services
4	Citigroup Inc.	C	Money Center Banks
5	Wal-Mart Stores, Inc.	WMT	Discount, variety stores
6	General Electric Corporation	GE	Technology

The concrete steps are given here:

1. Retrieve the daily data from Yahoo! Finance.
2. Estimate the daily returns.

3. Apply the following formula to estimate the VaR:

$$VaR_{period} = position * \left(\mu_{period} - z * \sigma_{period}\right) \quad \dots (1)$$

4. Estimate the VaR based on sorted historical returns.
5. If possible, use VBA, R, SAS, or Matlab to automate the process.

The most commonly used parameters for the VaR are 1% and 5% probabilities (99% and 95% confidence levels) and 1-day and 2-week horizons. Based on the assumption of normality, we have the following general form:

$$VaR_{period} = position * \left(\mu_{period} - z * \sigma_{period}\right)$$

Here, *position* is the current market value of our portfolio, *μperiod* is the expected period return, z is the cut-off point depending on a confidence level, and σ is the volatility. For a normal distribution, z=2.33 for a 99% confidence level and z=1.64 for a 95% confidence level. When the time period is short, such as 1 day, we could ignore the impact of *μperiod*. Thus, we have the simplest form:

$$VaR = p * z * \sigma \quad \dots (2)$$

Estimate the VaR based on the normality assumption.

If the underlying security follows a normal distribution, the VaR formula will be as follows:

$$VaR_{period} = position * [\mu_{period} + qnorm(1 - confident)\sigma_{period}] \quad \dots (3)$$

For 99% and 95% confidence levels, *Equation (5)* becomes the following formulas:

Confidence level	Formula
99%	$VaR_{period} = position\left(\mu_{period} - 2.33\sigma_{period}\right)$
95%	$VaR_{period} = position\left(\mu_{period} - 1.64\sigma_{period}\right)$

Estimation of an n-day VaR depends on how to calculate the n-day return and standard deviation. Transformations are based on the following equation between the variances of different frequencies:

$$\begin{cases} \sigma^2_{n\_day} = n * \sigma^2_{daily} \\ \sigma_{n\_day} = \sqrt{n} * \sigma_{daily} \end{cases} \quad \dots (4)$$

For example, the annual volatility is equal to the daily volatility times the square root of 252 ($\sigma_{annual} = \sigma_{daily}\sqrt{252}$). Based on the daily return, we have the following general formulas for the VaR with a 99% or a 95% confidence level:

$$\begin{cases} \mu_{n\_day} = (\mu_{daily} + 1)^n - 1 \\ \sigma_{n\_day} = \sigma_{daily}\sqrt{n} \\ VaR_{n\_day} = p * [\mu_{n\_day} + qnorm(1 - confident)\sigma_{n\_day}] \end{cases} \quad \dots (5A)$$

Here, μ_{daily} is the expected daily returns, n is the number of days, σ_{daily} is the daily volatility, σ_{n_day} is an n-day volatility, confident is the confidence level, such as 99% or 95%, and p is the position. If we don't know the expected returns and we assume the expected mean return is the same as the realized mean return, then we have the following formulas instead:

$$\begin{cases} \bar{R}_{n\_day} = (\bar{R}_{daily} + 1)^n - 1 \\ \sigma_{n\_day} = \sigma_{daily}\sqrt{n} \\ VaR_{n\_day} = p * [\bar{R}_{n\_day} + qnorm(1 - confident)\sigma_{n\_day}] \end{cases} \quad \dots (5B)$$

For the confidence levels of 99% and 95%, we have the following:

$$\begin{cases} VaR_{n\_day} = p * [(\mu_{daily} + 1)^n - 1 - 2.33\sigma_{daily}\sqrt{n}] \\ VaR_{n\_day} = p * [(\mu_{daily} + 1)^n - 1 - 1.64\sigma_{daily}\sqrt{n}] \end{cases} \quad \dots (5C)$$

References

Please refer to the following articles:

- *Jorion, Philippe, Value at Risk, 2nd edition, McGraw-Hill, 2001*

- *Lopez, Jose A., 2000, An Academic Perspective on Backtesting and Stress-Testing Presentation for Credit Risk Models and the Future of Capital Management, Federal Reserve Bank of San Francisco,* `http://www.frbsf.org/economic-research/files/lopezbktesting.pdf`

- *Wikiperia, Value at Risk,* `https://en.wikipedia.org/wiki/Value_at_risk`

Exercises

1. What is the simplest definition of a VaR? What are the differences between a VaR and variance and standard deviation and beta?

2. Assume that we have a plan to form a two-stock portfolio. The confidence level is 99% and number of period is 10 days. If the VaR for the first stock is x while the VaR for the second stock is y, is the portfolio VaR the weighted individual stock's VaR, that is, $VaR(portfolio) = wA*x + wB*y$, where WA is the weight for stock A while wB is the weight for stock B? Explain.

3. Do IBM's returns follow a normal distribution? Are their skewness and kurtosis zero and 3 (excess kurtosis is zero)?

4. What are the values of skewness and kurtosis for a normal distribution? Generate n random numbers by using `rnorm()` to support your conclusion.

5. Write a Python function to estimate mean, standard deviation, skewness, and kurtosis of a given ticker; for example, `moments4("ticker",begdate,enddate)`.

6. Assuming that we own 134 shares of Microsoft; what is the total value today? What is the maximum loss tomorrow with a 95% confidence level? What is the value if our holding period is 1 month instead of 1 day?

7. Repeating the last question of 11.4 by using a monthly return instead of a daily return, is the answer different from that in 11.4?

8. Our portfolio has 100 shares of IBM, and 300 shares of Microsoft. What is the VaR with a 99% confidence level for our 1-day holding period?

9. To estimate a VaR for Dell over 1 month, we could convert the daily VaR to a monthly VaR or calculate the VaR from the monthly data directly. Are they different?

10. When we estimate a VaR, we could use different time periods, such as over the past year or past 5 years. Does this make a difference? Use a few tickers to explore and comment on your results.

11. Comment on the different VaR approaches, such as those based on the normality assumption, historical returns, and the modified VaR.

12. If a fund has a 10% invested in IBM, 12% with Google, and the rest with Walmart, what is the volatility of the portfolio?

13. If the weights are 10% for IBM stocks, 12% for Dell, 20% for Walmart, and the rest of them for a long-term Treasury 10-year bond, what is the volatility of the portfolio?

14. Based on 11.11, if the portfolio value is $10 million, what is the VaR with a 99% confidence level over the next 6 months?

15. Use a 99% confidence level and 10 trading days as your holding period to estimate a VaR based on the historical returns method: 100 shares IBM, 200 shares Citigroup, 200 shares Microsoft, and 400 shares Walmart.

16. Is it true that a VaR based on a normality assumption is usually less than a VaR based on historical returns?

 You could use a rolling window to a stock to show your result (answer). Alternatively, you could use several stocks.

17. Based on the code for the skewness, write a Python function for kurtosis. Compare your function with the function of `scipy.stats.kurtosis()`.

18. If our holding period is not 1 day, what is the format (formulas) to estimate a VaR based on our historical returns?

19. If the holding period is 2 weeks (10 trading days), how do you estimate a VaR based on the historical return data?

20. What is the maximum possible loss (VaR) if our holdings for IBM, Dell, and Walmart stocks are 100, 200, and 500 shares, respectively? The confidence level is 99% and the holding period is 2 weeks.

21. Write a Python program to generate a VaR using historical value. The structure of the function will be `VaR_historical(ticker, confidence_level, n_days)`.

Summary

In this chapter, an important risk measure called the **Value at Risk (VaR)** was discussed in detail. To estimate the VaR for individual stocks or portfolios, the two most popular methods are explained: based on the normality assumption and based on the sorting of historical returns. In addition, we have discussed the modified VaR method which considers the third and fourth moments in addition to the first two moments of returns. In *Chapter 12*, *Monte Carlo Simulation*, we explain how to apply simulation to finance, such as simulating stock price movements and returns, replicating the Black-Scholes-Merton options model, and pricing some exotic options.

12
Monte Carlo Simulation

Monte Carlo Simulation is an extremely useful tool in finance. For example, because we can simulate stock price by drawing random numbers from a lognormal distribution, the famous **Black-Scholes-Merton option** model can be replicated. From *Chapter 9, Portfolio Theory*, we have learnt that by adding more stocks into a portfolio, the firm specific risk could be reduced or eliminated. Via simulation, we can see the diversification effect much clearly since we can randomly select 50 stocks from 5,000 stocks repeatedly. For capital budgeting, we can simulate over several dozen variables with uncertain future values. For those cases, simulation can be applied to generate many possible future outcomes, events, and various types of combinations. In this chapter, the following topics will be covered:

- Generating random numbers drawn from a normal, uniform, and Poisson distributions
- Estimating π value by using Monte Carlo simulation
- Simulate stock price movement with a lognormal distribution
- Constructing efficient portfolios and an efficient frontier
- Replicating the Black-Scholes-Merton option model by simulation
- Pricing several exotic options, such as lookback options with floating strikes
- Bootstrapping with/without replacements
- Long term expected return forecast
- Efficiency, Quasi Monte Carlo simulation, and Sobol sequence

Importance of Monte Carlo Simulation

Monte Carlo Simulation, or simulation, plays a quite important role in finance with many applications. Assume that we intend to estimate **Net Present Value (NPV)** of a project. There are many uncertainties in the future, such as borrowing cost, price of our final products, raw materials, and so on. For just a few variables, we still could manage the task easily. However, if we face two dozen variables with uncertain future values, it is a headache to find a solution. Fortunately, Monte Carlo Simulation can be applied here. In *Chapter 10, Options and Futures*, we have learnt that the logic behind the Black-Scholes-Merton option models is the normality assumption for stock returns. Because of this, their closed-firm solution could be replicated by simulation. Another example is to randomly choose 50 stocks from 4,500 available stocks. Unlike vanilla options, such as the Black-Scholes-Merton model, there are no closed-form solutions for exotic options. Fortunately, we can use simulation to price some of them.

Generating random numbers from a standard normal distribution

Normal distributions play a central role in finance. A major reason is that many finance theories, such as option theory and their related applications, are based on the assumption that stock returns follow a normal distribution. The second reason is that if our econometric models are well designed, the error terms from the models should follow a zero-mean normal distribution. It is a common task that we need to generate n random numbers from a standard normal distribution. For this purpose, we have the following three lines of code:

```
import scipy as sp
x=sp.random.standard_normal(size=10)
print(x)
[-0.98350472  0.93094376 -0.81167564 -1.83015626 -0.13873015
0.33408835
   0.48867499 -0.17809823  2.1223147   0.06119195]
```

The basic random numbers in SciPy/NumPy are created by Mersenne Twister PRNG in the `numpy.random` function. The random numbers for distributions in `numpy.random` are in cython/pyrex and are pretty fast. There is no chance that readers would get the same `10` random numbers shown here. We will explain how to generate the same set of random numbers pretty soon. Alternatively, we can use the following code:

```
>>>import scipy as sp
>>>x=sp.random.normal(size=10)
```

This program is equivalent to the following one:

```
>>>import scipy as sp
>>>x=sp.random.normal(0,1,10)
```

The first input is for mean, the second input is for standard deviation, and the last one is for the number of random numbers, that is, the size of our desired dataset. Comparing the previous two programs, obviously the default settings for mean and standard deviations are 0 and 1. We can use the `help()` function to find out the names of those three input variables. To save space, only the first few lines are shown here:

```
>>>help(sp.random.normal)
Help on built-in function normal:
normal(...)
normal(loc=0.0, scale=1.0, size=None)
```

Drawing random samples from a normal distribution

The probability density function of the normal distribution, first derived by De Moivre and 200 years later by both Gauss and Laplace independently, is often called the bell curve because of its characteristic shape; refer to the following graph:

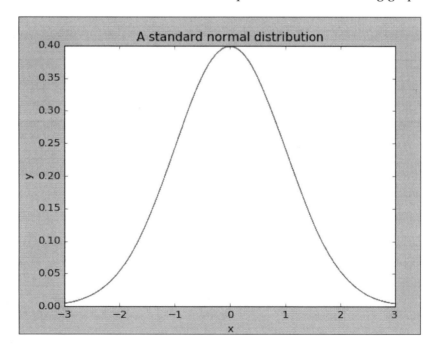

The density function for a standard normal distribution is given here:

$$f(x) = \frac{1}{\sqrt{2\pi}} e^{-\frac{x^2}{2}} \qquad \dots (1)$$

Here, *f(x)* is the density function for a standard normal distribution, *x* is an input value, *e* is the exponential function, and *π* is *3.1415926*. Here is the code to generate the preceding bell curve:

```
import scipy as sp
import scipy.stats as stats
import matplotlib.pyplot as plt
x = sp.arange(-3,3,0.01)
y=stats.norm.pdf(x)
plt.plot(x,y)
plt.title("A standard normal distribution")
plt.xlabel('x')
plt.ylabel('y')
plt.show()
```

Generating random numbers with a seed

Quite often, users want to produce the same set of random numbers repeatedly. For example, when a professor is explaining how to estimate the mean, standard deviation, skewness, and kurtosis of a set of random numbers, it is a good idea that students could generate exactly the same values as their instructor. Another example would be that when we are debugging our Python program to simulate a stock's movements, we might prefer to have the same intermediate results. For such cases, we use the `scipy.random.seed()` function as follows:

```
>>>import scipy as sp
>>>sp.random.seed(12345)
>>>x=sp.random.normal(0,1,20)
>>>print x[0:5]
[-0.20470766 0.47894334 -0.51943872 -0.5557303 1.96578057]
>>>
```

Here, `12345` is a seed. The value of the seed is not important. The key is that the same seed leads to the same set of random values. The formula for a more general normal distribution is shown here:

$$f(x) = \frac{1}{\sqrt{2\pi\sigma^2}} e^{-\frac{(x-\mu)^2}{2\sigma^2}} \qquad \dots (2)$$

Here, $f(x)$ is the density function for a normal distribution, x is an input value, e is the exponential function, μ is the mean, σ is the standard deviation.

Random numbers from a normal distribution

To generate n random numbers from a normal distribution, we have the following code:

```
>>>impimport scipy as sp
>>>sp.random.seed(12345)
>>>mean=0.05
>>>std=0.1
>>>n=50
>>>x=sp.random.normal(mean,std,n)
>>>print(x[0:5])
[ 0.02952923 0.09789433 -0.00194387 -0.00557303 0.24657806]
>>>
```

The difference between this program and the previous one is that the mean is `0.05` instead of `0`, while the standard deviation is `0.1` instead of `1`.

Histogram for a normal distribution

A histogram is used intensively in the process of analyzing the properties of datasets. To generate a histogram for a set of random values drawn from a normal distribution with specified mean and standard deviation, we have the following code:

```
import scipy as sp
import matplotlib.pyplot as plt
sp.random.seed(12345)
mean=0.1
std=0.2
n=1000
x=sp.random.normal(mean,std,n)
plt.hist(x, 15, normed=True)
plt.title("Histogram for random numbers drawn from a normal
distribution")
```

```
plt.annotate("mean="+str(mean),xy=(0.6,1.5))
plt.annotate("std="+str(std),xy=(0.6,1.4))
plt.show()
```

The resultant graph is presented as follows:

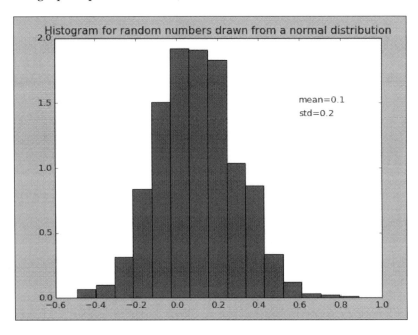

Graphical presentation of a lognormal distribution

When stock returns follow a normal distribution, then its prices should follow a lognormal distribution. The definition of a lognormal distribution is as follows:

$$f(x; \mu, \sigma) = \frac{1}{x\sigma\sqrt{2\pi}} e^{-\frac{(\ln(x)-\mu)^2}{2\sigma^2}} \qquad \ldots (3)$$

Here, $f(x;\mu,\sigma)$ is the density of a lognormal distribution, ln() is the natural log function. The following code shows three different lognormal distributions with three pairs of parameters, such as (0, 0.25), (0, 0.5), and (0, 1.0). The first parameter is for mean (μ), while the second one is for standard deviation, see the following code:

```
import scipy as sp
import numpy as np
```

```
import matplotlib.pyplot as plt
from scipy import sqrt,exp,log,pi
#
x=np.linspace(0.001,3,200)
mu=0
sigma0=[0.25,0.5,1]
color=['blue','red','green']
target=[(1.2,1.3),(1.7,0.4),(0.18,0.7)]
start=[(1.8,1.4),(1.9,0.6),(0.18,1.6)]
#
for i in sp.arange(len(sigma0)):
    sigma=sigma0[i]
    y=1/(x*sigma*sqrt(2*pi))*exp(-(log(x)-mu)**2/(2*sigma*sigma))
    plt.annotate('mu='+str(mu)+', sigma='+str(sigma),xy=target[i],xyte
xt=start[i],arrowprops=dict(facecolor=color[i],shrink=0.01),)
    plt.plot(x,y,color[i])
    plt.title('Lognormal distribution')
    plt.xlabel('x')
    plt.ylabel('lognormal density distribution')
#
plt.show()
```

The graph is shown here. Obviously, unlike a density of a normal distribution, the density function of a lognormal distribution is not symmetric:

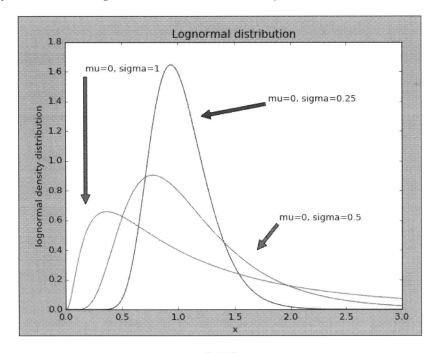

Generating random numbers from a uniform distribution

When randomly choosing m stocks from *n* available stocks, we can draw a set of random numbers from a uniform distribution. To generate 10 random numbers between 1 and 100 from a uniform distribution, we have the following code. To guarantee for the same set of numbers, the `seed()` function is used:

```
>>>import scipy as sp
>>>sp.random.seed(123345)
>>>x=sp.random.uniform(low=1,high=100,size=10)
```

Again, low, high, and size are the three input names. The first one specifies the minimum, the second one specifies the high end, while the size gives the number of the random numbers we intend to generate. The first five numbers are shown as follows:

```
>>>print(x[0:5])
[ 30.32749021 20.58006409 2.43703988 76.15661293 75.06929084]
>>>
```

Next program randomly roll a dice with a value from 1, 2, and up to 6:

```
import random
def rollDice():
    roll = random.randint(1,6)
    return roll
i =1
n=10
result=[]
random.seed(123)
while i<n:
    result.append(rollDice())
    i+=1
print(result)
[1, 1, 3, 1, 6, 1, 4, 2, 6]
```

In the previous program, the `random.seed()` function is applied. Thus, any reader should get the same results shown by the last line.

Using simulation to estimate the pi value

It is a good exercise to estimate π value by simulation. Let's draw a square with 2R as its side. If putting the largest circle inside the square, its radius will be R, described by the following equation:

$$S_{circle} = \pi * R^2 \quad \dots (4)$$

On the other hand, the square is the product of its sides:

$$S_{square} = (2R) * (2R) = 4R^2 \quad \dots (5)$$

Dividing *Equation (4)* by *Equation (5)*, we have the following result:

$$\frac{S_{circle}}{S_{square}} = \frac{\pi}{4}$$

Reorganize it; we end up with the following equation:

$$\pi = 4 * \frac{S_{circle}}{S_{quare}} \quad \dots (6)$$

In other words, the value of π will be 4* *Scircle/Square*. When running the simulation, we generate *n* pairs of *x* and *y* from a uniform distribution with a range of zero and 0.5. Then we estimate a distance that is the square root of the summation of the squared *x* and *y*, that is, $d = \sqrt{x^2 + y^2}$.

Obviously, when *d* is less than 0.5 (value of R), it will fall into the circle. We can imagine throwing a dart that falls into the circle. The value of the pi will take the following form:

$$pi = 4 * \frac{numbers\ of\ darts\ in\ circle}{numbers\ of\ darts\ in\ square, i.e., number\ of\ sumualations} \quad \dots (7)$$

The following graph illustrates these random points within a circle and within a square:

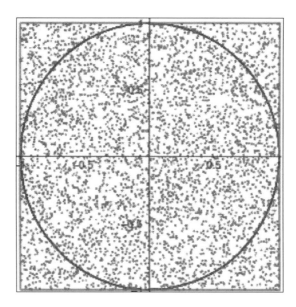

The Python program to estimate the value of pi is presented as follows:

```
import scipy as sp
n=100000
x=sp.random.uniform(low=0,high=1,size=n)
y=sp.random.uniform(low=0,high=1,size=n)
dist=sp.sqrt(x**2+y**2)
in_circle=dist[dist<=1]
our_pi=len(in_circle)*4./n
print ('pi=',our_pi)
print('error (%)=', (our_pi-sp.pi)/sp.pi)
```

The estimated pi value would change whenever we run the previous code, as shown in the following code, and the accuracy of its estimation depends on the number of trials, that is, *n*:

```
('pi=', 3.14168)
('error (%)=', 2.7803225891524895e-05)
```

Generating random numbers from a Poisson distribution

To investigate the impact of private information, Easley, Kiefer, O'Hara, and Paperman (1996) designed a **Probability of informed (PIN)** trading measure that is derived based on the daily number of buyer-initiated trades and the number of seller-initiated trades. The fundamental aspect of their model is to assume that order arrivals follow a Poisson distribution. The following code shows how to generate *n* random numbers from a Poisson distribution:

```
import numpy as np
import scipy as sp
import matplotlib.pyplot as plt
x=sp.random.poisson(lam=1, size=100)
#plt.plot(x,'o')
a = 5. # shape
n = 1000
s = np.random.power(a, n)
count, bins, ignored = plt.hist(s, bins=30)
x = np.linspace(0, 1, 100)
y = a*x**(a-1.)
normed_y = n*np.diff(bins)[0]*y
plt.title("Poisson distribution")
plt.ylabel("y")
plt.xlabel("x")
plt.plot(x, normed_y)
plt.show()
```

The graph is shown here:

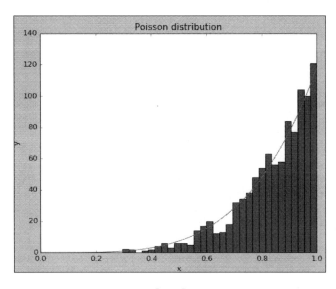

Selecting m stocks randomly from n given stocks

Based on the preceding program, we could easily choose 20 stocks from 500 available securities. This is an important step if we intend to investigate the impact of the number of randomly selected stocks on the portfolio volatility, as shown in the following code:

```python
import scipy as sp
n_stocks_available=500
n_stocks=20
sp.random.seed(123345)
x=sp.random.uniform(low=1,high=n_stocks_available,size=n_stocks)
y=[]
for i in range(n_stocks):
    y.append(int(x[i]))
#print y
final=sp.unique(y)
print(final)
print(len(final))
[  8   31   61   99 124 148 155 172 185 205 226 275 301 334 356 360 374
379
 401 449]
20
```

In the preceding program, we select 20 numbers from 500 numbers. Since we have to choose integers, we might end up with less than 20 values, that is, some integers appear more than once after we convert real numbers into integers. One solution is to pick more than we need. Then choose the first 20 integers. An alternative is to use the randrange() and randint() functions. In the next program, we choose *n* stocks from all available stocks. First, we download a dataset from http://canisius.edu/~yany/python/yanMonthly.pkl. Assume that the dataset is located under C:/temp/:

```python
import scipy as sp
import numpy as np
import pandas as pd
#
n_stocks=10
x=pd.read_pickle('c:/temp/yanMonthly.pkl')
x2=sp.unique(np.array(x.index))
x3=x2[x2<'ZZZZ']                          # remove all indices
sp.random.seed(1234567)
nonStocks=['GOLDPRICE','HML','SMB','Mkt_Rf','Rf','Russ3000E_D','US_
DEBT','Russ3000E_X','US_GDP2009dollar','US_GDP2013dollar']
x4=list(x3)
```

```
#
for i in range(len(nonStocks)):
    x4.remove(nonStocks[i])
#
k=sp.random.uniform(low=1,high=len(x4),size=n_stocks)
y,s=[],[]
for i in range(n_stocks):
    index=int(k[i])
    y.append(index)
    s.append(x4[index])
#
final=sp.unique(y)
print(final)
print(s)
```

In the preceding program, we remove non-stock data items. These non-stock items are a part of data items. First, we load a dataset called `yanMonthly.pickle` that includes over 200 stocks, gold price, GDP, unemployment rate, **Small Minus Big (SMB)**, **High Minus Low (HML)**, risk-free rate, price rate, market excess rate, and Russell indices.

One type of output formats from pandas is with a `.pkl .png`. Since `x.index` would present all indices for each observation, we need to use the `unique()` function to select all unique IDs. Since we only consider stocks to form our portfolio, we have to move all market indices and other non-stock securities, such as HML and `US_DEBT`. Because all stock market indices start with a carat (^), we use less than ZZZZ to remove them. For other IDs that are between A and Z, we have to remove them one after another. For this purpose, we use the `.remove()` function available for a list variable. The final output is shown as follows:

```
[ 1  2  4 10 17 20 21 24 31 70]
['IO', 'A', 'AA', 'KB', 'DELL', 'IN', 'INF', 'IBM', 'SKK', 'BC']
```

With/without replacements

Assume that we have the historical data, such as price and return, for a stock. Obviously, we could estimate their mean, standard deviation, and other related statistics. What are their expected annual mean and risk next year? The simplest, maybe naïve way is to use the historical mean and standard deviation. A better way is to construct the distribution of annual return and risk. This means that we have to find a way to use historical data more effectively to predict the future. In such cases, we could apply the bootstrapping methodology. For example, for one stock, we have its last 20-year monthly returns, that is, 240 observations.

To estimate next year's 12 monthly returns, we need to construct a return distribution. First, we choose 12 returns randomly from the historical return set without replacements and estimate their mean and standard deviations. We repeat this procedure 5,000 times. The final output will be our return-standard distribution. Based on such a distribution, we can estimate other properties as well. Similarly, we can do so with replacements. One of the useful functions present in NumPy is called `numpy.random.permutation()`. Assume that we have 10 numbers from one to 10 (inclusive of one and 10). We can call the `numpy.random.permutation()` function to reshuffle them as follows:

```
import numpy as np
x=range(1,11)
print(x)
for i in range(5):
    y=np.random.permutation(x)
#
print(y)
```

The output of this code is shown as follows:

```
[1, 2, 3, 4, 5, 6, 7, 8, 9, 10]
[ 7  3  9  5 10  4  8  6  2  1]
```

Based on the `numpy.random.permutation()` function, we can define a function with three input variables: data, number of observations we plan to choose from the data randomly, and whether we choose to bootstrap with or without replacement, as shown in the following code:

```
import numpy as np
def boots_f(data,n_obs,replacement=None):
    n=len(data)
    if (n<n_obs):
        print "n is less than n_obs"
    else:
        if replacement==None:
            y=np.random.permutation(data)
            return y[0:n_obs]
        else:
            y=[]
    #
    for i in range(n_obs):
        k=np.random.permutation(data)
        y.append(k[0])
    return y
```

The constraint specified in the previous program is that the number of given observations should be larger than the number of random returns we plan to pick up. This is true for the bootstrapping without the replacement method. For the bootstrapping with the replacement method, we could relax this constraint; refer to the related exercise.

Distribution of annual returns

It is a good application to estimate annualized return distribution and represent it as a graph. To make our exercise more meaningful, we download Microsoft's daily price data. Then, we estimate its daily returns and convert them into annual ones. Based on those annual returns, we generate its distribution by applying bootstrapping with replacements 5,000 times, as shown in the following code:

```
import numpy as np
import scipy as sp
import pandas as pd
import matplotlib.pyplot as plt
from matplotlib.finance import quotes_historical_yahoo_ochl as getData
# Step 1: input area
ticker='MSFT'            # input value 1
begdate=(1926,1,1)       # input value 2
enddate=(2013,12,31)     # input value 3
n_simulation=5000        # input value 4
# Step 2: retrieve price data and estimate log returns
x=getData(ticker,begdate,enddate,asobject=True)
logret = sp.log(x.aclose[1:]/x.aclose[:-1])
# Step 3: estimate annual returns
date=[]
d0=x.date
for i in range(0,sp.size(logret)):
    date.append(d0[i].strftime("%Y"))
y=pd.DataFrame(logret,date,columns=['logret'])
ret_annual=sp.exp(y.groupby(y.index).sum())-1
ret_annual.columns=['ret_annual']
n_obs=len(ret_annual)
# Step 4: estimate distribution with replacement
sp.random.seed(123577)
final=sp.zeros(n_obs,dtype=float)
for i in range(0,n_obs):
    x=sp.random.uniform(low=0,high=n_obs,size=n_obs)
    y=[]
```

```
        for j in range(n_obs):
            y.append(int(x[j]))
            z=np.array(ret_annual)[y]
        final[i]=sp.mean(z)
# step 5: graph
plt.title('Mean return distribution: number of simulations ='+str(n_
simulation))
plt.xlabel('Mean return')
plt.ylabel('Frequency')
mean_annual=round(np.mean(np.array(ret_annual)),4)
plt.figtext(0.63,0.8,'mean annual='+str(mean_annual))
plt.hist(final, 50, normed=True)
plt.show()
```

The corresponding graph is shown as follows:

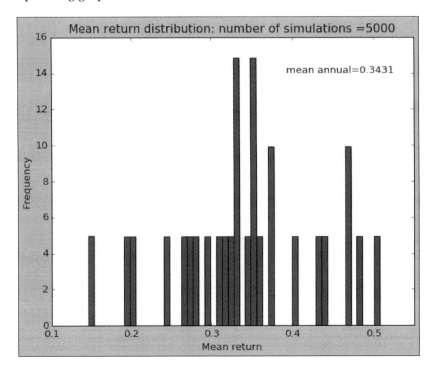

Simulation of stock price movements

We mentioned in the previous sections that in finance, returns are assumed to follow a normal distribution, whereas prices follow a lognormal distribution. The stock price at time *t+1* is a function of the stock price at *t*, mean, standard deviation, and the time interval, as shown in the following formula:

$$S_{t+1} = S_t + \hat{\mu}S_t\Delta t + \sigma S_t \epsilon\sqrt{\Delta t} \qquad \text{... (8)}$$

In this formula, *St + 1* is the stock price at *t+1*, ˆμ is the expected stock return, *t _* is the time interval (*T t n_=*), *T* is the time (in years), *n* is the number of steps, *ε* is the distribution term with a zero mean, and *σ* is the volatility of the underlying stock. With a simple manipulation, equation (4) can lead to the following equation that we will use in our programs:

$$S_{t+1} = S_t \exp((\hat{\mu} - \frac{1}{2}\sigma^2)\Delta t + \sigma\epsilon\sqrt{\Delta t}) \quad \text{... (9)}$$

In a risk-neutral work, no investors require compensation for bearing risk. In other words, in such a world, the expected return on any security (investment) is the risk-free rate. Thus, in a risk-neutral world, the previous equation becomes the following equation:

$$S_{t+1} = S_t \exp((r - \frac{1}{2}\sigma^2)\Delta t + \sigma\epsilon\sqrt{\Delta t}) \qquad \text{... (10)}$$

If you want to learn more about the risk-neutral probability, refer to *Options, Futures and Other Derivatives, 7th edition, John Hull, Pearson, 2009*. The Python code to simulate a stock's movement (path) is as follows:

```
import scipy as sp
import matplotlib.pyplot as plt
# input area
stock_price_today = 9.15 # stock price at time zero
T =1.                    # maturity date (in years)
n_steps=100.             # number of steps
mu =0.15                 # expected annual return
sigma = 0.2              # annualized volatility
sp.random.seed(12345)    # fixed our seed
n_simulation = 5         # number of simulations
dt =T/n_steps
```

```
#
S = sp.zeros([n_steps], dtype=float)
x = range(0, int(n_steps), 1)
for j in range(0, n_simulation):
    S[0]= stock_price_today
    for i in x[:-1]:
        e=sp.random.normal()
        S[i+1]=S[i]+S[i]*(mu-0.5*pow(sigma,2))*dt+sigma*S[i]*sp.
sqrt(dt)*e;
    plt.plot(x, S)
#
plt.figtext(0.2,0.8,'S0='+str(S[0])+',mu='+str(mu)+',sigma='+str(sig
ma))
plt.figtext(0.2,0.76,'T='+str(T)+', steps='+str(int(n_steps)))
plt.title('Stock price (number of simulations = %d ' % n_simulation
+')')
plt.xlabel('Total number of steps ='+str(int(n_steps)))
plt.ylabel('stock price')
plt.show()
```

To make our graph more readable, we deliberately choose just five simulations. Since the `scipy.random.seed()` function is applied, you can replicate the following graph by running the previous code. The graph is shown here:

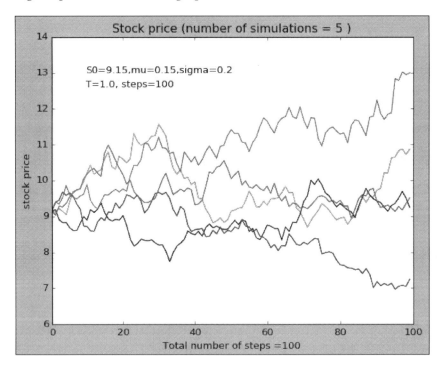

Graphical presentation of stock prices at options' maturity dates

Up to now, we have discussed that options are really path-independent, which means the option prices depend on terminal values. Thus, before pricing such an option, we need to know the terminal stock prices. To extend the previous program, we have the following code to estimate the terminal stock prices for a given set of values: S0 (initial stock price), n_simulation (number of terminal prices), T (maturity date in years), n_steps (number of steps), mu (expected annual stock returns), and sigma (volatility):

```python
import scipy as sp
import matplotlib.pyplot as plt
from scipy import zeros, sqrt, shape
#input area
S0 = 9.15               # stock price at time zero
T =1.                   # years
n_steps=100.            # number of steps
mu =0.15                # expected annual return
sigma = 0.2             # volatility (annual)
sp.random.seed(12345)   # fix those random numbers
n_simulation = 1000     # number of simulation
dt =T/n_steps
#
S = zeros([n_simulation], dtype=float)
x = range(0, int(n_steps), 1)
for j in range(0, n_simulation):
    tt=S0
    for i in x[:-1]:
        e=sp.random.normal()
        tt+=tt*(mu-0.5*pow(sigma,2))*dt+sigma*tt*sqrt(dt)*e;
        S[j]=tt
#
plt.title('Histogram of terminal price')
plt.ylabel('Number of frequencies')
plt.xlabel('Terminal price')
plt.figtext(0.5,0.8,'S0='+str(S0)+',mu='+str(mu)+',sigma='+str(sigma))
plt.figtext(0.5,0.76,'T='+str(T)+', steps='+str(int(n_steps)))
plt.figtext(0.5,0.72,'Number of terminal prices='+str(int(n_
simulation)))
plt.hist(S)
plt.show()
```

The histogram of our simulated terminal prices is shown as follows:

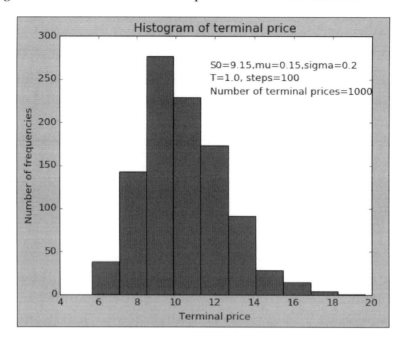

As we mentioned in *Chapter 9*, *Portfolio Theory*, in order to generate two correlated random number time series, there are two step involved: generate two random time series *x1* and *x2* with a zero-correlation; and then apply the following formulae:

$$\begin{cases} y_1 = x_1 \\ y_2 = \rho x_1 + \sqrt{1 - \rho^2} * x_2 \end{cases} \quad \cdots \text{ (11)}$$

Here, ρ is the predetermined correlation between those two time series. Now, y1 and y2 are correlated with a predetermined correlation. The following Python program will implement the preceding approach:

```
import scipy as sp
sp.random.seed(123)
n=1000
rho=0.3
x1=sp.random.normal(size=n)
x2=sp.random.normal(size=n)
y1=x1
```

```
y2=rho*x1+sp.sqrt(1-rho**2)*x2
print(sp.corrcoef(y1,y2))
[[ 1.          0.28505213]
 [ 0.28505213  1.         ]]
```

Replicating a Black-Scholes-Merton call using simulation

After knowing the terminal prices, we can estimate the payoff for a call if the exercise price is given. The mean of those discounted payoffs using the risk-free rate as our discount rate will be our call price. The following code helps us estimate the call price:

```
import scipy as sp
from scipy import zeros, sqrt, shape
#
S0 = 40.                # stock price at time zero
X= 40.                  # exercise price
T =0.5                  # years
r =0.05                 # risk-free rate
sigma = 0.2             # annualized volatility
n_steps=100             # number of steps
#
sp.random.seed(12345) # fix those random numbers
n_simulation = 5000    # number of simulation
dt =T/n_steps
call = sp.zeros([n_simulation], dtype=float)
x = range(0, int(n_steps), 1)
for j in range(0, n_simulation):
    sT=S0
    for i in x[:-1]:
        e=sp.random.normal()
        sT*=sp.exp((r-0.5*sigma*sigma)*dt+sigma*e*sqrt(dt))
        call[j]=max(sT-X,0)
#
call_price=sp.mean(call)*sp.exp(-r*T)
print('call price = ', round(call_price,3))
```

The estimated call price is $2.748. The same logic applies to pricing a put option.

Exotic option #1 – using the Monte Carlo Simulation to price average

Up to now, we have discussed European and American options in *Chapter 9*, *Portfolio Theory*. The Black-Scholes-Merton Option Model, which is also called a vanilla option. One of the characters is path independent. On the other hand, exotic options are more complex since they might have several triggers relating to the determination of their payoffs. For example, a refinery is worried about the oil, its major raw material, and price movement in the next three months. They plan to hedge the potential price jumps in crude oil. The company could buy a call option. However, since the firm consumes a huge amount of crude oil every day, naturally it cares more about the average price instead of just the terminal price on which a vanilla call option depends. For such cases, average options will be more effective. Average options are a type of Asian options. For an average option, its payoff is determined by the average underlying prices over some preset period of time. There are two types of averages: arithmetic average and geometric average. The payoff function of an Asian call (average price) is given as follows:

$$payoff\ (call) = Max(P_{average} - X, 0) \quad \dots (12)$$

The payoff function of an Asian put (average price) is given here:

$$payoff\ (put) = Max(X - P_{average}, 0) \quad \dots (13)$$

Asian options are one of the basic forms of exotic options. Another advantage of Asian options is that their costs are cheaper compared to European and American vanilla options since the variation of an average will be much smaller than a terminal price. The following Python program is for an Asian option with an arithmetic average price:

```
import scipy as sp
s0=40.                   # today stock price
x=40.                    # exercise price
T=0.5                    # maturity in years
r=0.05                   # risk-free rate
sigma=0.2                # volatility (annualized)
sp.random.seed(123)      # fix a seed here
n_simulation=100         # number of simulations
n_steps=100.             # number of steps
#
```

```
dt=T/n_steps
call=sp.zeros([n_simulation], dtype=float)
for j in range(0, n_simulation):
    sT=s0
    total=0
    for i in range(0,int(n_steps)):
        e=sp.random.normal()
        sT*=sp.exp((r-0.5*sigma*sigma)*dt+sigma*e*sp.sqrt(dt))
        total+=sT
        price_average=total/n_steps
    call[j]=max(price_average-x,0)
#
call_price=sp.mean(call)*sp.exp(-r*T)
print('call price based on average price = ', round(call_price,3))
('call price based on average price = ', 1.699)
```

Based on the preceding result, the call premium for this average price call is $1.70.

Exotic option #2 – pricing barrier options using the Monte Carlo Simulation

Unlike the Black-Scholes-Merton option model's call and put options, which are path-independent, a barrier option is path-dependent. A barrier option is similar in many ways to an ordinary option except a trigger exists. An `in` option starts its life worthless unless the underlying stock reaches a predetermined knock-in barrier. On the contrary, an `out` barrier option starts its life active and turns useless when a knock-out barrier price is breached. In addition, if a barrier option expires inactive, it may be worthless, or there may be a cash rebate paid out as a fraction of the premium. The four types of barrier options are given as follows:

- **Up-and-out**: In this barrier option, the price starts from down a barrier level. If it reaches the barrier, it is knocked out.

- **Down-and-out**: In this barrier option, the price starts from higher a barrier. If it reaches the barrier, it is knocked out.

- **Up-and-in**: In this barrier option, the price starts down a barrier and has to reach the barrier to be activated.

- **Down-and-in**: In this barrier option, the price starts higher a barrier and has to reach the barrier to be activated.

The next Python program is for an up-and-out barrier option with a European call:

```python
import scipy as sp
from scipy import log,exp,sqrt,stats
#
def bsCall(S,X,T,r,sigma):
    d1=(log(S/X)+(r+sigma*sigma/2.)*T)/(sigma*sqrt(T))
    d2 = d1-sigma*sqrt(T)
    return S*stats.norm.cdf(d1)-X*exp(-r*T)*stats.norm.cdf(d2)
#
def up_and_out_call(s0,x,T,r,sigma,n_simulation,barrier):
    n_steps=100.
    dt=T/n_steps
    total=0
    for j in sp.arange(0, n_simulation):
        sT=s0
        out=False
        for i in range(0,int(n_steps)):
            e=sp.random.normal()
            sT*=sp.exp((r-0.5*sigma*sigma)*dt+sigma*e*sp.sqrt(dt))
            if sT>barrier:
                out=True
        if out==False:
            total+=bsCall(s0,x,T,r,sigma)
    return total/n_simulation
```

The basic design is that we simulate the stock movement *n* times, such as 100 times. For each simulation, we have 100 steps. Whenever the stock price reaches the barrier, the payoff will be zero. Otherwise, the payoff will be a vanilla European call. The final value will be the summation of all call prices that are not knocked out, divided by the number of simulations, as shown in the following code:

```python
s0=40.                  # today stock price
x=40.                   # exercise price
barrier=42              # barrier level
T=0.5                   # maturity in years
r=0.05                  # risk-free rate
sigma=0.2               # volatility (annualized)
n_simulation=100        # number of simulations
sp.random.seed(12)      # fix a seed
#
result=up_and_out_call(s0,x,T,r,sigma,n_simulation,barrier)
print('up-and-out-call = ', round(result,3))
('up-and-out-call = ', 0.937)
```

Based on the preceding result, we know that the call price for this up and out-call is $0.94.

Liking two methods for VaR using simulation

In the previous chapter, *Chapter 11, Value at Risk*, we learnt that we could apply two methods to estimate a VaR for an individual stock or for a portfolio: it depends on the normality assumption and based on the ranking of historical returns. Monte Carlo Simulation could link those two methods, see the following code:

```
import numpy as np
import numpy as np
import scipy as sp
import pandas as pd
from scipy.stats import norm
#
position=1e6                   # portfolio value
std=0.2                        # volatility
mean=0.08                      # mean return
confidence=0.99                # confidence level
nSimulations=50000             # number of simulations
# Method I
z=norm.ppf(1-confidence)
VaR=position*(mean+z*std)
print("Holding=",position, "VaR=", round(VaR,2), "tomorrow")
#
# Method II: Monte Carlo simulaiton
sp.random.seed(12345)
ret2=sp.random.normal(mean,std,nSimulations)
ret3=np.sort(ret2)
m=int(nSimulations*(1-confidence))
VaR2=position*(ret3[m])
print("Holding=",position, "VaR2=", round(VaR2,2), "tomorrow")
('Holding=', 1000000.0, 'VaR=', -385270.0, 'tomorrow')
('Holding=', 1000000.0, 'VaR2=', -386113.0, 'tomorrow')
```

Monte Carlo Simulation offers a result of $386,113 compared with $385,270 based on the formula for a $1 million of portfolio value today.

Capital budgeting with Monte Carlo Simulation

As we mentioned at the beginning of this chapter, we can use Monte Carlo Simulation to capital budgeting when the number of variables has many different values. Our objective is to estimate the NPV for a given budget by discounting all of its future free cash flow:

$$NPV = FCF_0 + \frac{FCF_1}{(1+R)} + \frac{FCF_2}{(1+R)^2} + \cdots + \frac{FCF_n}{(1+R)^n} \quad \cdots (14)$$

Here, *NPV* is the Net Present Value of one proposal, *FCF0* will be the free cash flow at time zero, *FCFt* will be free cash flow at the end of year *I*, *R* is the discount rate. The formula to calculate free cash flows at the end of year *t* is given here:

$$FCF_t = NI_t + D_t - CapEx_t - \Delta NWC_t \quad \cdots (15)$$

Here, *FCTt* is Free Cash Flow at year *t*, *Dt* is depreciation of year *t*, *CaptExt* is the net capital expenditure at year *t*, *NWC* is for Net working capital, which is the current asset minus current liability, Δ means change. Let's look at a simple one. Assume that the company buys one price of long term equivalent with a total cost of 0.5 million with a life of five years:

Items	0	1	2	3	4	5
Price	0	28	28	28	28	28
Unit	0	100000	100000	100000	100000	100000
Sales	0	2800000	2800000	2800000	2800000	2800000
Cost of goods sold	0	840000	840000	840000	840000	840000
Other costs	0	100000	100000	100000	100000	100000
Selling, general and adm	15000	15000	15000	15000	15000	15000
R&D	20000					
Depreciation		1000000	1000000	1000000	1000000	1000000
EBIT	-35000	845000	845000	845000	845000	845000
Tax 35%	-12250	295750	295750	295750	295750	295750
NI	-47250	1140750	1140750	1140750	1140750	1140750
Add depreciation	-47250	2140750	2140750	2140750	2140750	2140750

Table 12.1 Cash flows every year

We have the following equivalent code:

```
import scipy as sp
nYear=5                    # number of years
costEquipment=5e6          # 5 million
n=nYear+1                  # add year zero
price=28                   # price of the product
units=100000               # estimate number of units sold
otherCost=100000           # other costs
sellingCost=1500           # selling and administration cost
R_and_D=200000             # Research and development
costRawMaterials=0.3       # percentage cost of raw materials
R=0.15                     # discount rate
tax=0.38                   # corporate tax rate
#
sales=sp.ones(n)*price*units
sales[0]=0                 # sales for 1st year is zero
cost1=costRawMaterials*sales
cost2=sp.ones(n)*otherCost
cost3=sp.ones(n)*sellingCost
cost4=sp.zeros(n)
cost4[0]=costEquipment
RD=sp.zeros(n)
RD[0]=R_and_D                      # assume R&D at time zero
D=sp.ones(n)*costEquipment/nYear   # straight line depreciation
D[0]=0                             # no depreciation at time 0
EBIT=sales-cost1-cost2-cost3-cost4-RD-D
NI=EBIT*(1-tax)
FCF=NI+D                           # add back depreciation
npvProject=sp.npv(R,FCF)           # estimate NPV
print("NPV of project=",round(npvProject,0))
('NPV of project=', 1849477.0)
```

The NPV of this project is $1,848,477. Since it is positive, we should accept that the proposal if our criterion is based on the NPV rule. Now, let's add some uncertainty. Assume that we have three uncertainties: price, unit of products expected to sell, and discount rates, see the following code:

```
import scipy as sp
import matplotlib.pyplot as plt
nYear=5                    # number of years
costEquipment=5e6          # 5 million
n=nYear+1                  # add year zero
otherCost=100000           # other costs
sellingCost=1500           # selling and administration cost
```

```
R_and_D=200000            # Research and development
costRawMaterials=0.3      # percentage cost of raw materials
tax=0.38                  # corporate tax rate
thousand=1e3              # unit of thousand
million=1e6               # unit of million
#
# three uncertainties: price, unit and discount rate
nSimulation=100           # number of simulation
lowPrice=10               # low price
highPrice=30              # high price
lowUnit=50*thousand       # low units expected to sell
highUnit=200*thousand     # high units expected to sell
lowRate=0.15              # lower discount rate
highRate=0.25             # high discount rate
#
n2=nSimulation
sp.random.seed(123)
price0=sp.random.uniform(low=lowPrice,high=highPrice,size=n2)
units0=sp.random.uniform(low=lowUnit,high=highUnit,size=n2)
R0=sp.random.uniform(lowRate,highRate,size=n2)
#
npv=[]
for i in sp.arange(nSimulation):
    units=sp.ones(n)*units0[i]
    price=price0[i]
    R=R0[i]
    sales=units*price
    sales[0]=0                  # sales for 1st year is zero
    cost1=costRawMaterials*sales
    cost2=sp.ones(n)*otherCost
    cost3=sp.ones(n)*sellingCost
    cost4=sp.zeros(n)
    cost4[0]=costEquipment
    RD=sp.zeros(n)
    RD[0]=R_and_D                     # assume R&D at time zero
    D=sp.ones(n)*costEquipment/nYear  # straight line depreciation
    D[0]=0                            # no depreciation at time 0
    EBIT=sales-cost1-cost2-cost3-cost4-RD-D
    NI=EBIT*(1-tax)
    FCF=NI+D                          # add back depreciation
    npvProject=sp.npv(R,FCF)/million  # estimate NPV
    npv.append(npvProject)
print("mean NPV of project=",round(sp.mean(npv),0))
print("min  NPV of project=",round(min(npv),0))
```

```
print("max  NPV of project=",round(max(npv),0))
plt.title("NPV of the project: 3 uncertainties")
plt.xlabel("NPV (in million)")
plt.hist(npv, 50, range=[-3, 6], facecolor='blue', align='mid')
plt.show()
```

The histogram of the NPV distribution is shown here:

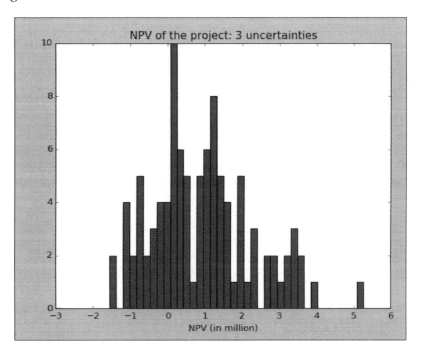

Python SimPy module

SimPy is a process-based discrete-event simulation framework based on standard Python. Its event dispatcher is based on Python's generators and can also be used for asynchronous networking or to implement multi-agent systems (with both simulated and real communication). Processes in SimPy are simple Python generator functions and are used to model active components such as customers, vehicles, or agents. SimPy also provides various types of shared resources to model limited capacity congestion points (such as servers, checkout counters, and tunnels). From version 3.1, it will also provide monitoring capabilities to aid in gathering statistics about resources and processes:

```
import simpy
def clock(env, name, tick):
    while True:
```

```
            print(name, env.now)
            yield env.timeout(tick)
    #
    env = simpy.Environment()
    env.process(clock(env, 'fast', 0.5))
    env.process(clock(env, 'slow', 1))
    env.run(until=2)
    ('fast', 0)
    ('slow', 0)
    ('fast', 0.5)
    ('slow', 1)
    ('fast', 1.0)
    ('fast', 1.5)
```

Comparison between two social policies – basic income and basic job

This example is borrowed from Stucchhio (2013). Over the development of the past several decades, the wealth of each nation is continuously commutative. This is especially true for the developed countries. One of the basic arguments supporting equity is that each citizen should have their basic standard of living. Based on this argument, many countries offer huge benefits to their citizens, such as universal healthcare, free education, and the like. One policy suggestion is basic income, under which each citizen receives a basic income annually with no strings attached. For example, if we assume that the basic hourly rate is $7.50, 40 hours per week and 50 weeks per year, then the basic income should be $15,000. Zhong (2017) reports that India is considering fighting poverty with a universal basic income plan. The obvious advantage is that the administration cost will be quite small. In addition, it is less likely that corruption would eat the lions share of government release funds for the poor. In 2017, Finland launched a pilot project, and local authorities in Canada and the Netherlands have also announced experiments. In 2016, voters in Switzerland rejected a minimum income proposal.

One alternative is a so-called basic job in which the government guarantees a low-paid job to anyone who cannot find a decent one. Each of these methods has its advantages and disadvantages. Based on a set of assumptions, such as hourly pay, number of working hours per week, number of working weeks per year, population, workforce, and the like, Stucchhio (2013) compares the cost and benefits of these two proposals. Several uncertainties exist; see the list in the following table:

Policy	Command	Description
Basic income	`unitAdmCost = norm(250,75)`	Administration cost for each person
	`binom(nNonWorkers,tiny).rvs()`	A random number from a binomial distribution
	`nonWorkerMultiplier = uniform(-0.10, 0.15).rvs()`	Multiplier for none workers
Basic job	`unitAdmCost4disabled= norm(500,150).rvs()`	Administration cost for each disabled adult
	`unitAdmCost4worker = norm(5000, 1500).rvs()`	Administration cost for each worker
	`nonWorkerMultiplier = uniform(-0.20, 0.25).rvs()`	Multiplier for none workers
	`hourlyProductivity = uniform(0.0,hourlyPay).rvs()`	Hourly productivity

Table 12.2: Costs and benefits of the two proposals

The program uses three distributions: normal, uniform, and binomial. The `uniform(a,b).rvs()` command generates a random number uniformly distributed between a and b. The `norm(mean,std).rvs()` command generates a random number generated from a normal distribution with specified mean and standard deviation. The `binom(n,k).rvs()` command generates a random number from a binomial distribution with a pair of input values of `n` and `k`:

```
import scipy as sp
import scipy.stats as stats
sp.random.seed(123)
u=stats.uniform(-1,1).rvs()
n=stats.norm(500,150).rvs()
b=stats.binom(10000,0.1).rvs()
```

```
x='random number from a '
print(x+"uniform distribution ",u)
print(x+" normal distribution ",n)
print(x+" binomial distribution ",b)
('random number from a uniform distribution ', -0.30353081440213836)
('random number from a  normal distribution ', 357.18541897080166)
('random number from a  binomial distribution', 1003)
```

Stucchhio's Python program, with a few minor modifications, is shown here:

```
from pylab import *
from scipy.stats import *
#input area
million=1e6                       # unit of million
billion=1e9                       # unit of billion
trillion=1e12                     # unit of trillion
tiny=1e-7                         # a small number
hourlyPay = 7.5                   # hourly wage
workingHoursPerWeek=40            # working hour per week
workingWeeksPerYear=50            # working weeks per year
nAdult         = 227*million      # number of adult
laborForce     = 154*million      # labor force
disabledAdults =  21*million      # disability
nSimulations   = 1024*32          # number of simulations
#
basicIncome = hourlyPay*workingHoursPerWeek*workingWeeksPerYear
# define a few function
def geniusEffect(nNonWorkers):
    nGenious = binom(nNonWorkers,tiny).rvs()
    return nGenious* billion
#
def costBasicIncome():
    salaryCost= nAdult * basicIncome
    unitAdmCost = norm(250,75)
    nonWorkerMultiplier = uniform(-0.10, 0.15).rvs()
    nonWorker0=nAdult-laborForce-disabledAdults
    nNonWorker = nonWorker0*(1+nonWorkerMultiplier)
    marginalWorkerHourlyProductivity = norm(10,1)
    admCost = nAdult * unitAdmCost.rvs()
    unitBenefitNonWorker=40*52*marginalWorkerHourlyProductivity.rvs()
    benefitNonWorkers = 1 * (nNonWorker*unitBenefitNonWorker)
    geniusBenefit=geniusEffect(nNonWorker)
```

```
        totalCost=salaryCost + admCost - benefitNonWorkers-geniusBenefit
        return totalCost
#
def costBasicJob():
        unitAdmCost4disabled= norm(500,150).rvs()
        unitAdmCost4worker = norm(5000, 1500).rvs()
        nonWorkerMultiplier = uniform(-0.20, 0.25).rvs()
        hourlyProductivity = uniform(0.0, hourlyPay).rvs()
        cost4disabled=disabledAdults * (basicIncome +
unitAdmCost4disabled)
        nBasicWorkers=((nAdult-disabledAdults-laborForce)*(1+nonWorkerMul
tiplier))

annualCost=workingHoursPerWeek*workingWeeksPerYear*hourlyProductivity
        cost4workers=nBasicWorkers * (basicIncome+unitAdmCost4worker-
annualCost)
        return cost4disabled + cost4workers
#
N = nSimulations
costBI = zeros(shape=(N,),dtype=float)
costBJ = zeros(shape=(N,),dtype=float)
for k in range(N):
        costBI[k] = costBasicIncome()
        costBJ[k] = costBasicJob()
#
def myPlot(data,myTitle,key):
        subplot(key)
        width = 4e12
        height=50*N/1024
        title(myTitle)
        #xlabel("Cost (Trillion = 1e12)")
        hist(data, bins=50)
        axis([0,width,0,height])
#
myPlot(costBI,"Basic Income",211)
myPlot(costBJ,"Basic Job",212)
show()
```

Based on the graph shown here, he concludes that the cost of basic job proposal is lower than the basic income proposal. To save space, we will not elaborate on the program. For more detailed explanation and related assumption, please read the blog posted by Stucchhio (2013):

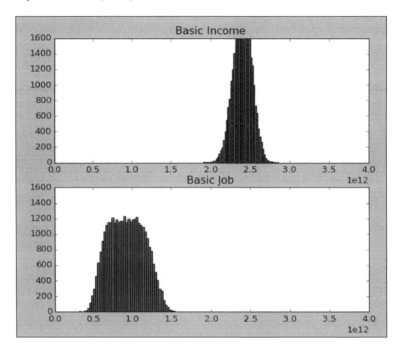

Finding an efficient frontier based on two stocks by using simulation

The following program aims at generating an efficient frontier based on two stocks with known means, standard deviations, and correlation. We have just six input values: two means, two standard deviations, the correlation (ρ), and the number of simulations. To generate the correlated *y1* and *y2* time series, we generate the uncorrelated *x1* and *x2* series first. Then, we apply the following formulae:

$$\begin{cases} y_1 = x_1 \\ y_2 = \rho x_1 + \sqrt{1 - \rho^2} * x_2 \end{cases} \quad \cdots \ (11)$$

Another important issue is how to construct an objective function to minimize. Our objective function is the standard deviation of the portfolio in addition to a penalty that is defined as the scaled absolute deviation from our target portfolio mean.

In other words, we minimize both the risk of the portfolio and the deviation of our portfolio return from our target return, as shown in the following code:

```
import numpy as np
import scipy as sp
import pandas as pd
import matplotlib.pyplot as plt
from datetime import datetime as dt
from scipy.optimize import minimize
#
# Step 1: input area
mean_0=(0.15,0.25)    # mean returns for 2 stocks
std_0= (0.10,0.20)    # standard deviations for 2 stocks
corr_=0.2        # correlation between 2 stocks
nSimulations=1000    # number of simulations
#
# Step 2: Generate two uncorrelated time series
n_stock=len(mean_0)
n=nSimulations
sp.random.seed(12345) # to get the same random numbers
x1=sp.random.normal(loc=mean_0[0],scale=std_0[0],size=n)
x2=sp.random.normal(loc=mean_0[1],scale=std_0[1],size=n)
if(any(x1)<=-1.0 or any(x2)<=-1.0):
    print ('Error: return is <=-100%')
#
# Step 3: Generate two correlated time series
index_=pd.date_range(start=dt(2001,1,1),periods=n,freq='d')
y1=pd.DataFrame(x1,index=index_)
y2=pd.DataFrame(corr_*x1+sp.sqrt(1-corr_**2)*x2,index=index_)
#
# step 4: generate a return matrix called R
R0=pd.merge(y1,y2,left_index=True,right_index=True)
R=np.array(R0)
#
# Step 5: define a few functions
def objFunction(W, R, target_ret):
    stock_mean=np.mean(R,axis=0)
    port_mean=np.dot(W,stock_mean)          # portfolio mean
    cov=np.cov(R.T)                         # var-covar matrix
    port_var=np.dot(np.dot(W,cov),W.T)      # portfolio variance
    penalty = 2000*abs(port_mean-target_ret) # penalty 4 deviation
    return np.sqrt(port_var) + penalty      # objective function
#
# Step 6: estimate optimal portfolio for a given return
out_mean,out_std,out_weight=[],[],[]
stockMean=np.mean(R,axis=0)
#
```

```
for r in np.linspace(np.min(stockMean),np.max(stockMean),num=100):
    W = sp.ones([n_stock])/n_stock              # start equal w
    b_ = [(0,1) for i in range(n_stock)]        # bounds
    c_ = ({'type':'eq', 'fun': lambda W: sum(W)-1. })# constraint
    result=minimize(objFunction,W,(R,r),method='SLSQP',constraints=c_
,bounds=b_)
    if not result.success:                      # handle error
        raise BaseException(result.message)
    out_mean.append(round(r,4))                 # decimal places
    std_=round(np.std(np.sum(R*result.x,axis=1)),6)
    out_std.append(std_)
    out_weight.append(result.x)
#
# Step 7: plot the efficient frontier
plt.title('Simulation for an Efficient Frontier from given 2 stocks')
plt.xlabel('Standard Deviation of the 2-stock Portfolio (Risk)')
plt.ylabel('Return of the 2-stock portfolio')
plt.figtext(0.2,0.80,' mean = '+str(stockMean))
plt.figtext(0.2,0.75,' std  ='+str(std_0))
plt.figtext(0.2,0.70,' correlation ='+str(corr_))
plt.plot(np.array(std_0),np.array(stockMean),'o',markersize=8)
plt.plot(out_std,out_mean,'--',linewidth=3)
plt.show()
```

The output is shown here:

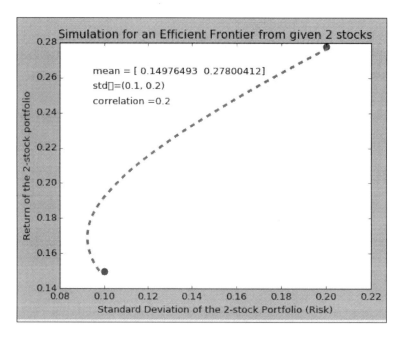

Constructing an efficient frontier with n stocks

When the number of stocks, *n*, increases, the correlation between each pair of stocks increases dramatically. For *n* stocks, we have *n*(n-1)/2* correlations. For example, if *n* is 10, we have 45 correlations. Because of this, it is not a good idea to manually input those values. Instead, we generate means, standard deviations, and correlations by drawing random numbers from several uniform distributions. To produce correlated returns, first we generate *n* uncorrelated stock return time series and then apply Cholesky decomposition as follows:

```
import numpy as np
import scipy as sp
import pandas as pd
import matplotlib.pyplot as plt
from datetime import datetime as dt
from scipy.optimize import minimize
#
# Step 1: input area
nStocks=20
sp.random.seed(1234)                      # produce the same random
numbers
n_corr=nStocks*(nStocks-1)/2              # number of correlation
corr_0=sp.random.uniform(0.05,0.25,n_corr)  # generate correlations
mean_0=sp.random.uniform(-0.1,0.25,nStocks) # means
std_0=sp.random.uniform(0.05,0.35,nStocks)  # standard deviation
nSimulations=1000                          # number of simulations
#
# Step 2: produce correlation matrix: Cholesky decomposition
corr_=sp.zeros((nStocks,nStocks))
for i in range(nStocks):
    for j in range(nStocks):
        if i==j:
            corr_[i,j]=1
        else:
            corr_[i,j]=corr_0[i+j]
U=np.linalg.cholesky(corr_)
#
# Step 3: Generate two uncorrelated time series
R0=np.zeros((nSimulations,nStocks))
for i in range(nSimulations):
    for j in range(nStocks):
```

```
            R0[i,j]=sp.random.normal(loc=mean_0[j],scale=std_0[j],size=1)
if(R0.any()<=-1.0):
    print ('Error: return is <=-100%')
#
# Step 4: generate correlated return matrix: Cholesky
R=np.dot(R0,U)
R=np.array(R)
#
# Step 5: define a few functions
def objFunction(W, R, target_ret):
    stock_mean=np.mean(R,axis=0)
    port_mean=np.dot(W,stock_mean)          # portfolio mean
    cov=np.cov(R.T)                         # var-covar matrix
    port_var=np.dot(np.dot(W,cov),W.T)      # portfolio variance
    penalty = 2000*abs(port_mean-target_ret) # penalty 4 deviation
    return np.sqrt(port_var) + penalty      # objective function
#
# Step 6: estimate optimal portfolo for a given return
out_mean,out_std,out_weight=[],[],[]
stockMean=np.mean(R,axis=0)
#
for r in np.linspace(np.min(stockMean), np.max(stockMean), num=100):
    W = sp.ones([nStocks])/nStocks          # starting:equal w
    b_ = [(0,1) for i in range(nStocks)]    # bounds
    c_ = ({'type':'eq', 'fun': lambda W: sum(W)-1. })# constraint
    result=minimize(objFunction,W,(R,r),method='SLSQP',constraints=c_,
bounds=b_)
    if not result.success:                  # handle error
        raise BaseException(result.message)
    out_mean.append(round(r,4))             # a few decimal places
    std_=round(np.std(np.sum(R*result.x,axis=1)),6)
    out_std.append(std_)
    out_weight.append(result.x)
#
# Step 7: plot the efficient frontier
plt.title('Simulation for an Efficient Frontier: '+str(nStocks)+'
stocks')
plt.xlabel('Standard Deviation of the Porfolio')
plt.ylabel('Return of the2-stock portfolio')
plt.plot(out_std,out_mean,'--',linewidth=3)
plt.show()
```

The graph is shown here:

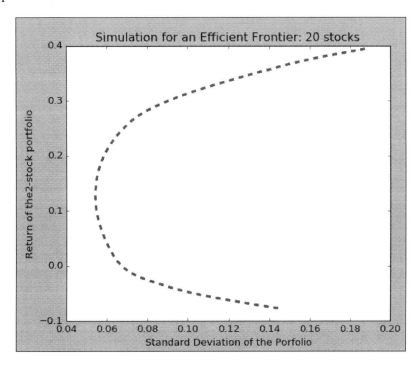

It is difficult to simulate an n-stock portfolio when n is a huge number. The reason is that it is time consuming to generate a variance-covariance matrix, see the number of covariances (correlations) here:

$$n\_pairs = \frac{n*(n-1)}{2} \qquad \ldots (17)$$

Assume that we have 500 stocks in our portfolio. Then we have to estimate 124,750 pairs of correlations. To simplify this calculation, we could apply CAPM, see the following formula:

$$R_{i,t} = \alpha_i + \beta_i R_{M,t} + e_{i,t} \qquad \ldots (18)$$

Here $R_{i,t}$ is the return for stock i at time t, a_i, and β_i are the intercept and slope for stock i, $R_{M,t}$ is the a market index return at time t, $e_i t$, is the error term at time t. Since the total risk of individual stock has two components: systematic risk and firm specific risk. Thus, the variance of stock i is associated with the market index in the following way:

$$\sigma_i^2 = \beta_i^2 \sigma_M^2 + \sigma^2(e_i) \quad \dots (19)$$

The covariance between stocks i and j is given here:

$$cov(R_i, R_i) = \beta_i \beta_i \sigma_M^2 \quad \dots (20)$$

Because of this, we can reduce our estimation from 124,750 to just 1,000. Estimate 500 βs first. Then we apply the preceding formula to estimate the covariance. Similarly, the formula to estimate the correlation between stock i and j is given here:

$$corr(R_i, R_i) = corr(R_i, R_M) * corr(R_i, R_M) \quad \dots (21)$$

Long-term return forecasting

Many researchers and practitioners argue that a long-term return forecast would be overestimated if it is based on the arithmetic mean of the past returns and underestimated based on a geometric mean. Using 80 years' historical returns to forecast the next 25-year future return, Jacquier, Kane, and Marcus (2003) suggest the following weighted scheme:

$$LT\ forecast = \frac{25}{80} R_{geometric} + \frac{80-25}{80} R_{arithmetic} \quad \dots (22)$$

The following program reflects the preceding equation:

```
import numpy as np
import pandas as pd
from matplotlib.finance import quotes_historical_yahoo_ochl as getData
#
# input area
ticker='IBM'             # input value 1
begdate=(1926,1,1)       # input value 2
enddate=(2013,12,31)     # input value 3
n_forecast=25            # input value 4
#
def geomean_ret(returns):
    product = 1
    for ret in returns:
        product *= (1+ret)
    return product ** (1.0/len(returns))-1
#
x=getData(ticker,begdate,enddate,asobject=True, adjusted=True)
logret = np.log(x.aclose[1:]/x.aclose[:-1])
date=[]
d0=x.date
for i in range(0,np.size(logret)):
    date.append(d0[i].strftime("%Y"))
#
y=pd.DataFrame(logret,date,columns=['logret'],dtype=float)
ret_annual=np.exp(y.groupby(y.index).sum())-1
ret_annual.columns=['ret_annual']
n_history=len(ret_annual)
a_mean=np.mean(np.array(ret_annual))
g_mean=geomean_ret(np.array(ret_annual))
w=n_forecast/n_history
future_ret=w*g_mean+(1-w)*a_mean
print('Arithmetric mean=',round(a_mean,3), 'Geomean=',round(g_
mean,3),'forecast=',future_ret)
```

The output is shown here:

```
('Arithmetric mean=', 0.12, 'Geomean=', 0.087, 'forecast=', array([
0.1204473]))
```

Efficiency, Quasi-Monte Carlo, and Sobol sequences

When applying the Monte Carlo simulation to solve various finance-related problems, a set of random numbers is generated. When the accuracy is very high, we have to draw a huge amount of such random numbers. For example, when pricing options, we use very small intervals or a large number of steps to increase the accuracy of our solutions. Thus, the efficiency of our Monte Carlo simulation would be a vital issue in terms of computational time and costs. This is especially true if several thousand options are to be priced. One way to increase the efficiency is to apply a better algorithm, that is, optimize our codes. Another way is to use some special types of random numbers that are more evenly distributed. This is called Quasi-Monte Carlo Simulation. A typical example is a so-called Sobol sequence. Sobol sequences belong to the so-called low-discrepancy sequences, which satisfy the properties of random numbers, but are distributed more evenly:

```
import numpy as np
import matplotlib.pyplot as plt
np.random.seed(12345)
n=200
a = np.random.uniform(size=(n*2))
plt.scatter(a[:n], a[n:])
plt.show()
```

The related graph is shown on the left panel:

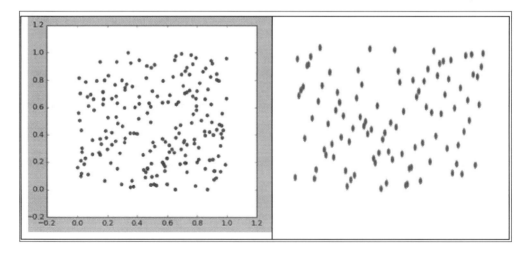

On the other hand, if we use the Sobol sequence, the distribution of those random numbers would be more even; see the preceding right panel. The related code is shown here:

```
import sobol_seq
import scipy as sp
import matplotlib.pyplot as plt
a=[]
n=100
for i in sp.arange(2*n):
    t=sobol_seq.i4_sobol(1,i)
    a.append(t)
print(a[0:10])
x=sp.random.permutation(a[:n])
y=sp.random.permutation(a[n:])
plt.scatter(x,y,edgecolors='r')
plt.show()
[[array([ 0.]), 1], [array([ 0.5]), 2], [array([ 0.75]), 3], [array([
0.25]), 4], [array([ 0.375]), 5], [array([ 0.875]), 6], [array([
0.625]), 7], [array([ 0.125]), 8], [array([ 0.1875]), 9], [array([
0.6875]), 10]]
>>>
```

For a similar example, but with more complex Python codes, see http://betatim. github.io/posts/quasi-random-numbers/.

Appendix A – data case #8 - Monte Carlo Simulation and blackjack

Blackjack is a two-player game, with a dealer and a player. Here, we assume that you are the player.

Rule #1: Cards 2 to 10 have their face value, while Jack, Quenn, and King are worth 10 points, and Ace is worth either 1 or 11 points (player's choice).

Terminology:

*   **Blackjack**: One A plus any card worth 10 points
*   **Lose**: The player's bet is taken by the dealer
*   **Win**: The player wins as much as he bets
*   **Blackjack (natural)**: The player wins 1.5 times the bet
*   **Push**: The player keeps his bet, neither winning nor losing money

- **Step 1**: The dealer draws two cards, one face up, while the player draws two cards (face up)

- **Step 2**: The player could draw the third card

- **Win or lose**: If the sum of your cards is less than 21 and is bigger than the dealer's, you win. Take a look at `http://www.pagat.com/banking/blackjack.html`

References

Please refer to the following articles:

- *Bruno, Giuseppe, Monte Carlo Simulation for Pricing European and American Basket option, Bank of Italy,* `https://www.r-project.org/conferences/useR-2010/abstracts/Bruno.pdf`

- *Easley, D., Kiefer, N.M., O'Hara, M., Paperman, J.B., 1996, Liquidity, information, and infrequently traded stocks, Journal of Finance 51, 1405–1436,* `http://www.defaultrisk.com/pa_liqty_03.htm`

- *Jacquier, Eric, Alex Kane, and Alan J. Marcus, 2003, Geometric or Arithmetic Mean: A Reconsideration,* `https://www2.bc.edu/alan-marcus/papers/FAJ_2003.pdf`

- *Stucchio, Chris, 2013, Modelling a Basic Income with Python and Monte Carlo Simulation,* `https://www.chrisstucchio.com/blog/2013/basic_income_vs_basic_job.html`

- *Zhong, Raymond, 2017, India Considers Fighting Poverty With a Universal Basic Income, Wall Street Journal,* `http://blogs.wsj.com/indiarealtime/2017/01/31/india-considers-fighting-poverty-with-a-universal-basic-income/`

Exercises

1. From Yahoo!Finance (`http://finance.yahoo.com`), download the last five years of price data for a few companies, such as IBM, WMT, and C (City Group). Test whether their daily returns follow a normal distribution.

2. Write a Python program to use the `scipy.permutation()` function to select 12 monthly returns randomly from the past five-year data without replacement. To test the program, you can use Citigroup and the time period from January 2, 2012 to December 31, 2016 from Yahoo! Finance.

3. Write a Python program to run bootstrapping with *n* given returns. For each time, we select *m* returns where *m>n*.

4. To convert random numbers from a uniform distribution to a normal distribution, we have the following formula:

$$\epsilon_{norm} = \sum_{i=1}^{12} \varepsilon_i - 6$$

Based on the formula, generate 5,000 normally distributed random numbers; estimate their mean, standard deviation, and test it.

5. Assume that the current stock price is $10.25, the mean value in the past five years is $9.35, and the standard deviation is 4.24. Write a Python program to generate 1,000 future prices.

6. Download the price data for 10 stocks over the last 10 years. Form an equal-weighted portfolio and conduct a Shapiro-Wilk test on its portfolio daily returns:

Company name	Ticker	Dell company	DELL
International Business Machine	IBM	General Electric	GE
Microsoft	MSFT	Google	GOOG
Family Dollar Stores	FDO	Apple	AAPL
Wal-Mart Stores	WMT	eBay	EBAY
McDonald's	MCD		

7. Go to Yahoo! Finance to find out today's IBM price and then download its historical-prices information to estimate its mean and standard deviation for the past five years. Generate predictions for one-year daily prices in the future.

8. For 20 tickers, download and save their daily price as 20 different CSV files. Write a Python program to randomly select five stocks and estimate their equal-weighted portfolio returns and risk.

9. Repeat the previous program, but save it as one file instead of 20 separate CSV files.

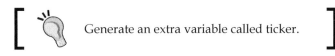

[Generate an extra variable called ticker.]

10. There are 30 students in a class. Write a program to select seven of them randomly.

11. Test the time difference between retrieving `ffMonthly.pkl`, `ffDaily.pkl`, or `ffMonthly.csv`, `ffDaily.csv` and conduct some tests.

12. Usually we observe the negative relationship between the portfolio's volatility and the number of stocks in the portfolio. Write a program to show the relationship between the variance of a portfolio and the number of stock in it.

13. What is the probability for picking up 1, 2, 3, and 4 from 10 balls marked from 1 to 10? Use two methods: a. Use the formula. b. Write a program to generate a set of five random numbers.

14. Write a program to generate 176 million sets of combinations in terms of the Mega Millions game. What is the chance to win (1, 2, 3, 4, 5) and (1)?

15. For the Powerball games, we choose five white balls from 59 white balls numbered from 1 to 59 and one red ball from 39 red balls numbered from 1 to 39. Write a program to choose those six balls randomly.

16. Retrieving seven stocks from 20 stocks, what is the probability of choosing the first seven stocks? Use simulation to prove your result.

Summary

In this chapter, we discussed several types of distribution: normal, standard normal, lognormal, and Poisson. Since the assumption that stocks follow a lognormal distribution and returns follow a normal distribution is the cornerstone for option theory, the Monte Carlo simulation is used to price European options. Under certain scenarios, Asian options might be more effective in terms of hedging. Exotic options are more complex than the vanilla options since the former have no closed-form solution, while the latter could be priced by the Black-Scholes-Merton option model. One way to price these exotic options is to use the Monte Carlo simulation. The Python programs to price an Asian option and lookback options were also discussed.

13
Credit Risk Analysis

The objective of credit risk analysis is trying to measure the probability of potential failure to pay a promised amount. A credit rating reflects the credit worthiness of a firm or a bond. A firm's rating is different from its bond's rating since the latter depends on its maturity and certain features such as whether it is callable or puttable. In *Chapter 5*, *Bond and Stock Valuation*, we have learnt the concept of **Yield to Maturity (YTM)** or simply yield, which is correlated with credit quality. The lower its credit quality; the higher its required return, that is, a higher yield. In this chapter, we will discuss many basic concepts related to credit risk, such as credit rating, credit spread, 1-year credit rating migration matrix, probability of default, loss given default, recovery rate, and KMV model. In particular, the following topics will be covered:

- Moody's, Standard and Poor's, and Fitch's credit ratings
- Credit spread, one-year, and five-year migration matrices
- Term structure of interest rate
- Simulation of future interest rate
- Altman's Z-score to predict corporate bankruptcy
- KMV model to estimate total asset and its volatility
- Default probability and distance to default
- Credit default swap

Introduction to credit risk analysis

In this chapter, we will discuss basic concepts related to credit risk, such as credit rating, credit spread, 1-year and 5-year rating migration matrices, probability of default, recovery rate, and loss given default. A credit spread, the difference between a bond's yield and a benchmark yield (risk-free rate), reflects its credit risk or default risk. For example, to estimate the present value of a coupon payment in two years for an AA rated bond, the discount rate (yield) will be a risk-free yield (treasury-note yield) plus the corresponding spread. There are many tools that we could use when analyzing a company or a bond's credit worthiness. The first tool is credit rating offered by a credit rating agent, such as Moody's or Standard and Poor's. One of the apparent advantages is that a potential user would spend less time and efforts to assess a company or a bond's credit risk. The obvious disadvantage is that the credit rating is a black box for most users. In other words, users could not replicate a credit rating. Thus, it is quite difficult to siphon the logic behind such a simple letter credit rating system, such as AA or A1. There are other ways to evaluate the worthiness of a company (bond), such as spread that is readily available. One of the most quantitative models is the so-called KMV model, which applies the options theory we have learnt in *Chapter 10, Options and Futures* to evaluate the credit risk of a firm.

Credit rating

Nowadays, there are three major credit ratings agents in the USA: Moody's, Standard, and Poor's and Fitch. Their websites are `http://www.moodys.com/`, `http://www.standardandpoors.com/en_US/web/guest/home`, and `https://www.fitchratings.com/site/home`. Although their ratings have different notations (letters), it is easy to translate one letter rating from a rating agency to another one. Based on the following link at `http://www.quadcapital.com/Rating%20Agency%20Credit%20Ratings.pdf`, a dataset called `creditRatigs3.pkl` is generated, which can be downloaded at the author's website, `http://canisius.edu/~yany/python/creditRatings3.pkl`. Assume that it is located under `C:/temp/`.

The following codes show its contents:

```
import pandas as pd
x=pd.read_pickle("c:/temp/creditRatings3.pkl")
print(x)
      Moody's S&P Fitch  NAIC  InvestmentGrade
0       Aaa  AAA  AAA     1              1
1       Aa1  AA+  AA+     1              1
2       Aa2   AA   AA     1              1
3       Aa3  AA-  AA-     1              1
4        A1   A+   A+     1              1
5        A2    A    A     1              1
```

6	A3	A-	A-	1	1
7	Baa1	BBB+	BBB+	2	1
8	Baa2	BBB	BBB	2	1
9	Baa3	BBB-	BBB-	2	1
10	Ba1	BB+	BB+	3	0
11	Ba2	BB	BB	3	0
12	Ba3	BB-	BB-	3	0
13	B1	B+	B+	3	0
14	B2	B	B	3	0
15	B3	B-	B-	3	0

The first column is for the row numbers, which have no specific meaning. The next three columns are credit levels for **Moody's**, **S&P**, and **Fitch**, respectively. **NAIC** stands for the **National Association of Insurance Commissioners**. Any ratings equal to or over BBB are classified as investment grades, see the last column (variable) that has a value of 1 or 0. Many mutual funds and pension funds are only allowed to invest bonds rated as investment grades.

When a company has an Aaa rating this year, what is its probability next year to remain as the same credit rating? According to the following table, the probability that it keeps its Aaa rating next year is 89%, Moody's (2007). On the other hand, there is 3% chance that its credit rating would be downgraded by one notch, that is, from Aaa to Aa1. For a B1 rated bond, the probability of maintaining the same credit rating is 65%. Jointly, it has 12% probability of upgrading. For a possible downgrade, it has 9% probability. The default probability of a B1 rated bond is 3%, see the last column of the following figure that gives us the one-year credit rating migration matrix:

		Aaa	Aa1	Aa2	Aa3	A1	A2	A3	Baa1	Baa2	Baa3	Ba1	Ba2	Ba3	B1	B2	B3	Caa1	Caa2	Caa3	Ca-C	WR	DEF
	Aaa	89	3	3	0		0															5	
	Aa1	3	82	5	5	0	0	0	0													5	
	Aa2	1	3	79	8	2	1	0		0	0											7	
	Aa3	0	1	3	79	7	2	1	0	0		0			0							6	
	A1	0	0	0	5	80	7	2	1	0	0	0	0	0								5	
	A2	0	0	0	1	5	79	7	3	1	0	0	0	0		0			0	0		4	0
	A3	0	0	0	0	1	8	74	7	3	1	0	0	0	0	0	0		0	0	0	4	0
Current Rating	Baa1	0	0	0	0	0	2	6	75	8	3	1	0	0	0	0	0	0	0		0	4	0
	Baa2	0	0	0	0	0	1	2	6	76	7	1	1	1	1	0	0	0	0	0	0	5	0
	Baa3	0	0		0	0	0	1	2	8	73	5	3	1	1	0	0	0	0	0	0	5	0
	Ba1		0	0	0	0	0	1	2	9	65	5	4	1	1	1	0	0	0	0	8	0
	Ba2		0	0	0	0	0	0	1	3	8	63	6	4	2	1	1	0	0	0	9	1
	Ba3		0	0	0	0	0	0	0	1	3	7	65	5	5	2	0	0	0	0	10	2
	B1	0	0		0	0	0	0	0	0	0	1	2	6	66	6	4	1	1	0	0	9	3
	B2	0		0	0	0	0	0	0	0	0	0	0	2	5	67	7	3	1	1	0	9	4
	B3		0	0		0		0	0		0	0	0	0	2	5	61	5	4	1	1	11	9
	Caa1						0			0			0	0	1	2	5	59	5	4	3	11	10
	Caa2						0			0	0	0	0	0	1	1	2	3	54	3	4	13	18
	Caa3										0		0	0	1	1	2	3	3	45	6	13	25
	Ca-C													0		0	1	1	1	35	13	20	

One-year credit rating migration matrix

Note the following abbreviations:

- WR indicates that Moody's has withdrawn their ratings
- DEF is for default probability

Similarly, the probability of an Aaa rated firm becoming an Aa2 firm is 3% next year. The values along the main diagonal line (from North-West to South-East) are the probabilities of keeping the same rating next year. The values below the main diagonal line (left and bottom triangle) are the probabilities of a downgrade while the values above the diagonal line (up and right triangle) are the probabilities of an upgrade. The last column offers the default probabilities for various ratings. For example, a Ba2 rated bond has 1% chance to default, while a Caa3 rated bond has 25%. The Python dataset called migration1year.pkl could be used, see the following codes. The dataset is available at http://canisius.edu/~yany/python/migration1year.pkl:

```
import pandas as pd
x=pd.read_pickle("c:/temp/migration1year.pkl")
print(x.head(1))
print(x.tail(1))
       Aaa    Aa1    Aa2  Aa3    A1     A2     A3   Baa1   Baa2   Baa3 ...    Ba3
B1  \
Aaa   0.89   0.03   0.03  0.0   0.0    0.0    0.0    0.0    0.0    0.0 ...    0.0
0.0
        B2     B3   Caa1   Caa2   Caa3   Ca-C     WR   DEF
Aaa    0.0    0.0    0.0    0.0    0.0    0.0   0.05   0.0
[1 rows x 22 columns]
       Aaa    Aa1    Aa2  Aa3    A1     A2     A3   Baa1   Baa2   Baa3 ...    Ba3
B1     B2\
Ca-C   0.0    0.0    0.0  0.0   0.0    0.0    0.0    0.0    0.0    0.0 ...    0.0
0.0    0.0
        B3   Caa1   Caa2   Caa3   Ca-C     WR   DEF
Ca-C   0.0   0.01   0.01   0.01   0.35   0.13   0.2
[1 rows x 22 columns]
```

The following table shows the Moody's 5-year transition (migration) matrix. Please pay attention to the column under **DEF** (for default probability):

Current Rating	Five Years Later																					
	Aaa	Aa1	Aa2	Aa3	A1	A2	A3	Baa1	Baa2	Baa3	Ba1	Ba2	Ba3	B1	B2	B3	Caa1	Caa2	Caa3	Ca-C	WR	DEF
Aaa	56	7	10	3	1	1	0	0	0	0											20	
Aa1	9	46	10	9	3	3	1	2	1	0		0									17	
Aa2	4	6	32	16	5	6	3	2	0	0	0	0									26	
Aa3	1	4	8	35	16	9	4	2	1	0		0	0								20	
A1	1	2	3	9	33	15	8	4	2	1	1	1	0	0		0		0			20	0
A2	0	1	1	3	11	34	14	8	4	2	1	1	1	0	0	0	0		0		20	0
A3	0	0	0	2	4	19	24	13	8	5	2	2	1	0	0	0	0		0		17	1
Baa1	1	1	0	1	2	6	12	29	13	7	2	2	1	1	0	0	0	0	0		19	1
Baa2	0	0	0	1	1	3	6	11	31	13	3	2	2	2	1	1	1	0	0	0	20	1
Baa3	1	0	0	0	1	2	3	6	15	26	7	4	4	2	2	1	1	0	0	0	23	3
Ba1	0	0	0	0	1	2	3	3	7	11	18	5	4	5	4	1	1	0	0	0	31	4
Ba2		0		0	0	0	1	2	3	8	9	13	7	7	5	2	1	0	0	0	36	5
Ba3	0		0	0	0	0	1	1	2	3	4	6	13	7	6	3	1	1	0	1	39	11
B1	0	0	0	0	0	0	0	0	0	0	2	2	6	13	7	5	2	1	1	1	39	17
B2	0		0				0	0	0	0	1	1	2	6	15	8	4	2	1	1	35	23
B3							0	0	0	0	0	1	1	4	4	10	3	2	1	1	38	32
Caa1									0	0	1	1	1	3	3	4	8	3	1	1	36	39
Caa2								0	0	0	0	1	1	2	1	2	2	5	1	3	41	40
Caa3													1	1	1	1	1	0	2	0	31	62
Ca-C													0	0	2	2	1	1	1	4	43	46

Moody's Average 5-year Rating Transition Matrix (1920-1992)

Source: Moody's (2007).

Note the following abbreviations:

- WR indicates that Moody's has withdrawn their ratings
- DEF is for default probability

One dataset was generated with a name called `migration5year.pkl`. The dataset could be downloaded at `http://canisius.edu/~yany/python/migration5year.pkl`. The following code will print its first and last line:

```
import pandas as pd
x=pd.read_pickle("c:/temp/migration5year.pkl")
print(x.head(1))
print(x.tail(1))
     Aaa    Aa1  Aa2  Aa3    A1    A2   A3  Baa1  Baa2  Baa3 ...   Ba3
B1   \
Aaa  0.56  0.07  0.1  0.03  0.01  0.01  0.0   0.0   0.0   0.0 ...
0.0  0.0
      B2   B3  Caa1  Caa2  Caa3  Ca-C   WR  DEF
Aaa  0.0  0.0   0.0   0.0   0.0   0.0  0.2  0.0
[1 rows x 22 columns]
      Aaa   Aa1  Aa2  Aa3    A1    A2   A3  Baa1  Baa2  Baa3  ...   Ba3
B1   \
Ca-C  0.0  0.0  0.0  0.0   0.0   0.0  0.0   0.0   0.0   0.0   ...   0.0
0.0
        B2    B3  Caa1  Caa2  Caa3  Ca-C    WR   DEF
Ca-C  0.02  0.02  0.01  0.01  0.01  0.04  0.43  0.46
```

Rating and default are negatively correlated. The higher a rating; the lower its default probability. The cumulative historical default rates (in %) are given here:

	Default rate (%)			
	Moody's		S&P	
Rating category	Muni	Corp	Muni	Corp
Aaa/AAA	0.00	0.52	0.00	0.60
Aa/AA	0.06	0.52	0.00	1.50
A/A	0.03	1.29	0.23	2.91
Baa/BBB	0.13	4.64	0.32	10.29
Ba/BB	2.65	19.12	1.74	29.93
B/B	11.86	43.34	8.48	53.72
Caa-C/CCC-C	16.58	69.18	44.81	69.19
Averages				
Investment grade	0.07	2.09	0.20	4.14
Non-investment grade	4.29	31.37	7.37	42.35
All	0.10	9.70	0.29	12.98

Table 13.3 Relationship between the credit rating and the DP (default probability)

The course of the data is from the website at `http://monevator.com/bond-default-rating-probability/`.

For example, for an `Aaa` related corporate bond by Moody's, its default probability is 0.52%. The corresponding default probability from Standard and Poor's is 0.60%. Recovery rate given default is an important concept. The status (seniority) has a great impact on the recovery rates. According to Altman and Kishore (1997), we have the following table:

	Recovery rate (% of face value)
Senior-secured debt	58%
Senior-unsecured debt	48%
Senior-subordinate	35%
Subordinated	32%
Discounted and zero coupon	21%

Table 13.4 Recovery rates based on the seniority

A secured debt is a debt on which payment is guaranteed by an asset. Senior and subordinated are referred to the priority structure. On the other hand, different industries have different recovery rates because of their unique industry characteristics, such as fixed long-term assets and the percentages of intangible assets:

Industry	Average Recovery Rate	Number of observations
Public Utilities	70.5%	56
Chemical, petroleum, rubber, and plastic products	62.7%	35
Machinery, instruments, and related products	48.7%	36
Services- business and personal	46.2%	14
Food and kindred products	45.3%	18
Wholesale and retail trade	44.0%	12
Diversified manufacturing	42.3%	20
Casino, hotel, and recreation	40.2%	21
Building materials, metals, and fabricated products	38.8%	68
Transportation and transportation equipment	38.4%	52
Communication, broadcasting, movie production	37.1%	65
Printing and publishing	NA	NA
Financial institutions	35.7%	66
Construction and real estate	35.3%	35
General merchandize stores	33.2%	89
Mining and petroleum drilling	33.0%	45
Textile and apparel products	31.7%	31
Wood, paper, and leather products	29.8%	11
Lodging, hospitals, and nursing facilities	26.5%	22
Total	41.0%	696

Table 13.5 Recovery rates based on the industry

See the article on *Recovery Rates* at: http://www.riskworx.com/resources/Recovery%20Rates.pdf.

The preceding table is sorted according to the recovery rate from the highest to the lowest. For the printing and publishing industry, there is no data according to the original source. **Loss given default (LGD)** is equal to 1 minus the *Recovery rate*:

$$LGD = 1 - Recoverary\ rate \quad ... (1)$$

Here, we explain the usage of default probability and recovery rates by using a hypothetical example to calculate the price of a bond. Assume that the face value of a one-year bond is $100 with a coupon rate of 6% and a Yield to Maturity (**YTM**) of 7%. We have the following four situations:

- **Situation #1**: No default. The price today will be its discounted future cash flow, (6+100)/(1+0.07).

- **Situation #2**: Sure default and recover nothing. For this case, its price would be zero.

- **Situation #3**: If it defaults, we receive nothing.

- **Situation #4**: If it defaults, we receive something.

The following table summarizes the preceding four situations:

#	Conditions	Default Probability Recover rate	Today's price
1	No default	P=0, Recovery Rate (NA)	$99.07
2	100% default/recover nothing	P=100%, Rrecovery=0	0
3	If default, recover nothing	O<P<100%, Rrecovery=0	$99.07 *(1-P)
4	If default, recover something	O<P<100% , Rrecovery>0	$99.07 *[1-P*(1-$R_{recovery}$)]

Table 13.6 Four situations for different default probabilities and recovery rates

The price of a bond is the summation of all present values of its expected future cash flows:

$$Price\ (bond) = PV\ (expected\ cash\ flows) \quad ... (2)$$

If P is the default probability we have the following expected future cash flow:

$$\left\{ \begin{array}{l} expected\ FV = (1-P)FV + P * FV * R_{recovery} \\ \qquad\qquad = FV - P * FV + P * FV * R_{recovery} \\ \qquad\qquad = FV - FV * P\left(1 - R_{recovery}\right) \\ \qquad\qquad = FV[1 - P * \left(1 - R_{recovery}\right)] \end{array} \right. \quad \dots\ (3)$$

Discounting all future cash flows would give us its price:

$$PV(bond\ with\ default) = PV(no\ default) * [1 - P\left(1 - R_{recovery}\right)] \quad \dots\ (4)$$

Assume that the credit rating is A based on the Moody's scale. According to Table 13.3, its default rate is 1.29%. Assume further that it is a utility firm. Thus, its recovery rate given default is 70.5% based on Table 13.5. The face value of the bond is $100 and the required return (YTM) is 5%. Based on the preceding formula, the price of a one-year bond with no default will be $95.24, that is, 100/(1+0.05). The selling price of our bond with a 1.29% chance of default will be $94.88, that is, *95.24*(1-0.0129*(1-0.705)).*

Credit spread

Credit spreads (default risk premium) reflect their default risk. For example, to estimate the present value of a coupon payment in two years for an AA rated bond, the discount rate (yield) will be a risk-free rate plus the corresponding spread. For a given credit rating, its credit spread could be found by using historical data. Here is a typical table showing the relationship between credit risk premium (spread) and the credit rating, see the following table:

We thank Prof Adamodar for making the dataset available at his website,
http://people.stern.nyu.edu/adamodar/pc/datasets/:

	A	B	C	D	E	F	G	H
1	Average for the week of 12/15/2013							
2	Rating	1 yr	2 yr	3 yr	5 yr	7 yr	10 yr	30 yr
3	Aaa/AAA	5	8	12	18	28	42	65
4	Aa1/AA+	11.2	20	27	36.6	45.2	56.8	81.8
5	Aa2/AA	16.4	32.8	42.6	54.8	62.8	71.2	97.8
6	Aa3/AA-	21.6	38.6	48.6	59.8	67.4	75.2	99.2
7	A1/A+	26.2	44	54.2	64.6	71.4	78.4	100.2
8	A2/A	32.8	46.6	54.6	67	75.6	84.4	112.4
9	A3/A-	45.6	61.8	71.6	83.6	91.6	100.2	126
10	Baa1/BBB+	57.8	80	93	109.4	120	131.8	166.8
11	Baa2/BBB	47	95.2	109.4	127.4	139.4	151.8	190.8
12	Baa3/BBB-	95.4	120.4	134.8	153.2	165.2	178.2	217.8
13	Ba1/BB+	167.6	192.6	209	228.6	243.4	258.8	297.2
14	Ba2/BB	239.6	264.8	282.8	304.2	321.2	339.4	377.2
15	Ba3/BB-	311.8	337	357.2	379.6	399.4	420.2	456.6
16	B1/B+	383.6	409.6	431.4	455.6	477.6	500.8	536.2
17	B2/B	455.8	481.6	505.2	531	555.4	581.4	615.6
18	B3/B-	527.8	553.8	579.4	606.4	633.6	661.8	695.6
19	Caa/CCC+	600	626	653	682	712	743	775
20	US Treasury Yield	0.132	0.344	0.682	1.582	2.284	2.892	3.882

Credit Spread based on credit rating

Spreads, except the last row in the preceding table, have a unit of basic-point,
which is the 100th of one percent. For example, or an A- (A minus) rated bond
with a maturity of five years, its spared is 83.6 basis points. Since the risk-free is
1.582% (for a 5-year treasury rate), the YTM for this bond will be 2.418%, that is,
0.01582+83.6/100/100. Based on the preceding table, we generated a Python dataset
called bondSpread2014.p, which is available at the author's website, http://
canisius.edu/~yany/python/creditSpread2014.pkl:

```
import pandas as pd
x=pd.read_pickle("c:/temp/creditSpread2014.pkl")
print(x.head())
print(x.tail())
   Rating     1     2     3     5     7    10    30
0  Aaa/AAA  5.0   8.0  12.0  18.0  28.0  42.0  65.0
1  Aa1/AA+ 11.2  20.0  27.0  36.6  45.2  56.8  81.8
2   Aa2/AA 16.4  32.8  42.6  54.8  62.8  71.2  97.8
3  Aa3/AA- 21.6  38.6  48.6  59.8  67.4  75.2  99.2
4   A1/A+  26.2  44.0  54.2  64.6  71.4  78.4 100.2
              Rating       1        2        3        5        7
10  \
13             B1/B+  383.600  409.600  431.400  455.600  477.600
500.800
```

14	B2/B	455.800	481.600	505.200	531.000	555.400
581.400						
15	B3/B-	527.800	553.800	579.400	606.400	633.600
661.800						
16	Caa/CCC+	600.000	626.000	653.000	682.000	712.000
743.000						
17	US Treasury Yield	0.132	0.344	0.682	1.582	2.284
2.892						

After studying the preceding table carefully, we would find two monotone trends. First, the spread is a decreasing function of credit quality. The lower a credit rating; the higher its spread. Second, for the same credit rating, its spread increases every year. For example, for an AAA rated bond, its spread in one year is 5 basis-points while it is 18 in five years.

YIELD of AAA-rated bond, Altman Z-score

From the previous sections, we have learnt that the spread between a bond's yield and a treasury bond's yield with the same maturity is the default risk premium. To retrieve the yields for AAA and AA bonds, we use the following codes. Moody's Seasoned Aaa *Corporate Bond Yield* can be downloaded at https:// fred.stlouisfed.org/series/AAA. The dataset can be downloaded at http:// canisius.edu/~yany/python/moodyAAAyield.p. Note that the .png of .p is fine for the .pickle format:

```
import pandas as pd
x=pd.read_pickle("c:/temp/moodyAAAyield.p")
print(x.head())
print(x.tail())
```

The output is shown here:

```
                AAA
DATE
1919-01-01   0.0535
1919-02-01   0.0535
1919-03-01   0.0539
1919-04-01   0.0544
1919-05-01   0.0539
                AAA
DATE
2016-05-01   0.0365
2016-06-01   0.0350
2016-07-01   0.0328
2016-08-01   0.0332
2016-09-01   0.0341
```

Note that the values of the second column, for the dataset called `moodyAAAyield.p`, are annualized. Thus, if we want to estimate a monthly yield (rate of return) in January 1919, the yield should be *0.4458333%*, that is, 0.0535/12.

Altman's z-score is widely applied in finance for credit analysis to predict the possibility of a firm going to bankruptcy. This score is a weighted average of five ratios based on a firm's balance sheet and income statement. For public firms, Altman (1968) offers the following formula:

$$Z = 3.3X_1 + 0.99X_2 + 0.6X_3 + 1.2X_4 + 1.4X_5 \quad \dots (5)$$

Here, the definitions of *X1, X2, X3, X4,* and *X5* are given in the following table:

Variable	Definition
X1	EBIT/Total assets
X2	Net sales/Total assets
X3	Market value of equity/TotalILiabilities
X4	Working capital/Total assets
X5	Retained earnings/Total assets

Table 13.8 Definitions of variables in the estimation of Z-scores

Based on the ranges of z-scores, we could classify public firms into following four categories. Eidlenan (1995) finds that the Z score correctly predicted 72% of bankruptcies two years prior to the event:

Z-score range	Description
> 3.0	Safe
2.7 to 2.99	On Alert
1.8 to 2.7	Good chances of going bankrupt within 2 years
< 1.80	Probability of financial distress is very high

Altman's Z-score belongs to the categories called credit scoring (methods). On the other hand, more advanced models, for example, the KMV model, are based on modern finance theories, such as option theory.

Using the KMV model to estimate the market value of total assets and its volatility

KMV stands for **Kealhofer**, **McQuown** and **Vasicek** who founded a company focusing on measuring default risk. KMV methodology is one of the most important methods to estimate the probability of default for a given company by using its balance sheet information and the equity market information. The objective of this section is to show how to estimate the market value of total assets (A) and its corresponding volatility (σA). The result will be used later in the chapter. The basic idea is to treat the equity of a firm as a call option and the book value of its debt as its strike price. Let's look at the simplest example. For a firm, if its debt is $70 and equity is $30, then the total assets will be $100, see the following table:

100	70
	30

Assume that the total asset jumps to $110 and the debt remains the same. Now, the value of the equity increases to $40. On the other hand, if the assets drop to $90, the equity will be valued at $20. Since the equity holders are the residual claimer, their value satisfies the following expression:

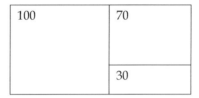

$$E = \max(assets - debt, 0) = \max(A - D, 0) \quad \dots (6)$$

Here, E is the value of equity, A is the total asset, and D is the total debt level. Recall for a European call option, we have the following payoff function:

$$\text{Payoff (call)} = \max(S_T - K, 0) \quad \dots (7)$$

Here ST is the terminal stock price at maturity date, T is the maturity date, K is the exercise price, and `max()` is the maximum function. The similarity between the preceding two equations suggests that we could treat equity as a call option with the debt level as our exercise price. With appropriate notations, we will have the following formulas for a firm's equity. The KMV model is defined here:

$$\begin{cases} E = A * N(d_1) - e^{-rT}N(d_2) \\ d_1 = \dfrac{\ln\left(\frac{A}{D}\right)+\left(r+\frac{1}{2}\sigma_A^2\right)T}{\sigma_A\sqrt{T}} \\ d_2 = d_1 - \sigma_A\sqrt{T} \end{cases} \qquad \dots (8)$$

On the other hand, the following relationship between the volatilities of the equity and the total assets holds. In the following equation, we have:

$$\Delta = \frac{dE}{dV_A} = N(d_1)$$

$$\sigma_E = \frac{A}{E}\Delta\sigma_A = \frac{N(d_1)*A*\sigma_A}{E} \qquad \dots (9)$$

Since $d1$ and d_2 are defined by the previous equations, we have two equations for two unknowns (A and σ_A); see the following formulas. Thus, we could use trial-and-error or simultaneous equation methods to solve those two unknowns. Eventually, we want to solve the following two equations for A and σ_A :

$$\begin{cases} E = A * N(d_1) - e^{-rT}N(d_2) \\ \sigma_E = \dfrac{A}{E}N(d_1)\sigma_A \end{cases} \qquad \dots (10)$$

We should pay attention to the estimated A (market value of total assets) from the preceding equation since it is different from the summation of market value of assets plus the book value of the debt.

The following Python program is for estimating total assets (A) and its volatility (sigmA) for a given *E* (equity), *D* (debt), *T* (maturity), *r* (risk-free rate), and the volatility of the equity (sigmaE). The basic logic of the program is that we input a large number of pairs of (*A*, sigmaE). Then we estimate E and sigmaE based on the preceding equation. Since both E and sigmaE are known, we could estimate the differences, *diff4E=estimatedE – knownE* and *diff4sigmaE = estimatedSigmaE – knownSigmaE*. The pair of (*A*, sigmaE) that minimizes the sum of those two absolute differences will be our solution:

```python
import scipy as sp
import pandas as pd
import scipy.stats as stats
from scipy import log,sqrt,exp
# input area
D=30.              # debt
E=70.              # equity
T=1.               # maturity
r=0.07             # risk-free
sigmaE=0.4         # volatility of equity
#
# define a function to siplify notations later
def N(x):
    return stats.norm.cdf(x)
#
def KMV_f(E,D,T,r,sigmaE):
    n=10000
    m=2000
    diffOld=1e6      # a very big number
    for i in sp.arange(1,10):
        for j in sp.arange(1,m):
            A=E+D/2+i*D/n
            sigmaA=0.05+j*(1.0-0.001)/m
            d1 = (log(A/D)+(r+sigmaA*sigmaA/2.)*T)/(sigmaA*sqrt(T))
            d2 = d1-sigmaA*sqrt(T)
            diff4A= (A*N(d1)-D*exp(-r*T)*N(d2)-E)/A   # scale by assets
            diff4sigmaE= A/E*N(d1)*sigmaA-sigmaE       # a small number
already
            diffNew=abs(diff4A)+abs(diff4sigmaE)
            if diffNew<diffOld:
                diffOld=diffNew
                output=(round(A,2),round(sigmaA,4),round(diffNew,5))
    return output
#
print("KMV=", KMV_f(D,E,T,r,sigmaE))
print("KMV=", KMV_f(D=65e3,E=110e3,T=1,r=0.01,sigmaE=0.2))
```

The output is shown here:

```
print("KMV=", KMV_f(D,E,T,r,sigmaE))
```

```
('KMV=', (65.05, 0.3287, 0.33214))
('KMV=', (142558.5, 0.1544, 0.22312))
```

Please pay attention to the result, since the summation of the book value of debt and the market value of equity 175,000 while our estimated result is 142,559. Since the equity of a firm is the call option, we could use the Black-Scholes-Merton model to double-check our result.

Term structure of interest rate

In *Chapter 5, Bond and Stock Valuation*, we have discussed the concepts of a term structure of interest rate. The term structure of interest rate is defined as the relationship between risk-free rate and time. A risk-free rate is usually defined as a default-free treasury rate. From many sources, we could get the current term structure of interest rate. For example, on 2/27/2017 from http://finance.yahoo.com/bonds, we could get the following information:

```
US Treasury Bonds Rates
Maturity     Yield Yesterday Last Week Last Month
3 Month      0.45    0.45      0.47       0.45
6 Month      0.61    0.63      0.50       0.51
2 Year       1.12    1.16      1.16       1.20
3 Year       1.37    1.41      1.45       1.48
5 Year       1.78    1.84      1.88       1.95
10 Year      2.29    2.36      2.40       2.49
30 Year      2.93    2.99      3.00       3.08
```

The plotted term structure of an interest rate could be more eye catching; see the following codes:

```
import matplotlib.pyplot as plt
time=[3./12.,6./12.,2.,3.,5.,10.,30.]
rate=[0.45,0.61,1.12,1.37,1.78,2.29,2.93]
plt.title("Term Structure of Interest Rate ")
plt.xlabel("Time (in years) ")
plt.ylabel("Risk-free rate (%)")
plt.plot(time,rate)
plt.show()
```

The related graph is shown here:

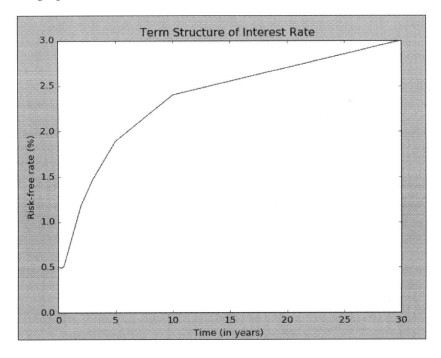

To simulate future interest movement, we could apply the so-called BIS model with the following formulas. The change in the interest rate is assumed to follow a normal distribution; see the following formula:

$$\Delta \log(R) \sim N(0, \frac{s^2}{2}) \qquad \ldots (11)$$

Here, Δ is for change, R is the interest rate, and s is the standard deviation of interest rate. Here is the equivalent equation:

$$\frac{\sqrt{2}}{s} \Delta \log(R) \sim N(0,1) \qquad \ldots (12)$$

Now, we have the following formula to tune our simulation:

$$log R_{i+1} = log R_i + \Delta \log(R_i) = \log(R_i) + z\frac{s}{\sqrt{2}} \qquad \ldots (13)$$

Here, z is the anti-cumulative normal distribution. The following codes show the `scipy.stat.norm.ppf()` function and percent point function (inverse of `cdf`) at q of the given RV:

```
import scipy.stats as stats
#
cumulativeProb=0
print(stats.norm.ppf(cumulativeProb))
#
cumulativeProb=0.5
print(stats.norm.ppf(cumulativeProb))
#
cumulativeProb=0.99
print(stats.norm.ppf(cumulativeProb))
```

The related three outputs are shown here:

```
-inf
0.0
2.32634787404
```

The related Python codes are shown here:

```
import scipy as sp
import scipy.stats as stats
# input area
R0=0.09                  # initial rate
s=0.182                  # standard deviation of the risk-free rate
nSimulation=10           # number of simulations
sp.random.seed(123)      # fix the seed
#
num=sp.random.uniform(0,1,size=nSimulation)
z=stats.norm.ppf(num)
#
output=[]
def BIS_f(R,s,n):
    R=R0
    for i in sp.arange(0,n):
        deltaR=z[i]*s/sp.sqrt(2.)
        logR=sp.log(R)
        R=sp.exp(logR+deltaR)
```

```
        output.append(round(R,5))
    return output
#
final=BIS_f(R0,s,nSimulation)
print(final)
[0.09616, 0.08942, 0.0812, 0.08256, 0.08897, 0.08678, 0.11326, 0.1205,
0.11976, 0.11561]
```

Distance to default

Distance to default (DD) is defined by the following formula; here A is the market value of the total assets and σ_A is its risk. The interpretation of this measure is clear; the higher DD, the safer the firm:

$$DD = \frac{A - Default\ Point}{A * \sigma_A} \quad \dots (14)$$

In terms of *Default Point*, there is no theory on how to choose an ideal default point. However, we could use all short-term debts plus the half of long-term debts as our default point. After we have the values of the market value of assets and its volatility, we could use the preceding equation to estimate the Distance to Default. The A and σ_A are from the output from *Equation (10)*. On the other hand, if the default point equals E, we would have the following formula:

$$DD = -\frac{\ln\left(\frac{V_A}{D}\right) + \left(r - \frac{1}{2}\sigma_A^2\right)T}{\sigma_A\sqrt{T}} \quad \dots (15)$$

According to the Black-Scholes-Merton call option model, the relationship between DD and DP *(Default Probability)* is given here:

$$DP(Default\ Probability) = N(-DD) \quad \dots (16)$$

Credit default swap

A lender could buy a so-called **credit default swap** (**CDS**) to protect them in the event of default. The buyer of the CDS makes a series of payments to the seller and, in exchange, receives a payoff if the loan defaults. Let's see a simple example. A fund just bought $100 million corporate bonds with a maturity of 15 years. If the issuing firm does not default, the pension fund would enjoy interest payment every year plus $100 million at maturity. To protect their investment, they entered a 15-year CDS contract with a financial institution. Based on the credit worthiness of the bond issuing firm, the agreed spread is 80 basis points payable annually. This means that every year, the pension fund (CDS buyer) pays the financial institution (CDS seller) $80,000 per year over the next 10 years. If a credit event happens, the CDS seller would compensate the CDS buyer depending on their loss because of credit events. If the contract specifies a physical settlement, the CDS buyer could sell their bonds at $100m to the CDS seller. If the contract specifies a cash settlement, the CDS seller would pay $Max(\$100m-X,0)$ to the CDS buyer, where X is the market value of the bonds. If the market value of the bonds is $70m, then the CDS seller would pay the CDS buyer $30m. In the preceding case, the spreads or fees is strongly correlated with the default probability of the issuing firm. The higher the default probability, the higher the CDS spread. The following table represents such a relationship:

CDS	P	CDS	P	CDS	P	CDS	P	CDS	P	CDS	P	CDS	P
0	0.0%	100	7.8%	200	13.9%	300	19.6%	500	30.2%	500	30.2%	1000	54.1%
5	0.6%	105	8.1%	205	14.2%	310	20.2%	510	30.7%	525	31.4%	1025	55.2%
10	1.1%	110	8.4%	210	14.5%	320	20.7%	520	31.2%	550	32.7%	1050	56.4%
15	1.6%	115	8.7%	215	14.8%	330	21.2%	530	31.7%	575	33.9%	1075	57.5%
20	2.0%	120	9.1%	220	15.1%	340	21.8%	540	32.2%	600	35.2%	1100	58.6%
25	2.4%	125	9.4%	225	15.4%	350	22.3%	550	32.7%	625	36.4%	1125	59.7%
30	2.8%	130	9.7%	230	15.7%	360	22.9%	560	33.2%	650	37.6%	1150	60.9%
35	3.2%	135	10.0%	235	16.0%	370	23.4%	570	33.7%	675	38.8%	1175	62.0%
40	3.6%	140	10.3%	240	16.2%	380	23.9%	580	34.2%	700	40.0%	1200	63.1%
45	4.0%	145	10.6%	245	16.5%	390	24.5%	590	34.7%	725	41.2%	1225	64.2%
50	4.3%	150	10.9%	250	16.8%	400	25.0%	600	35.2%	750	42.4%	1250	65.3%
55	4.7%	155	11.2%	255	17.1%	410	25.5%	610	35.7%	775	43.6%	1275	66.4%
60	5.0%	160	11.5%	260	17.4%	420	26.0%	620	36.1%	800	44.8%	1300	67.5%
65	5.4%	165	11.8%	265	17.7%	430	26.6%	630	36.6%	825	46.0%	1325	68.6%
70	5.7%	170	12.1%	270	17.9%	440	27.1%	640	37.1%	850	47.2%	1350	69.7%
75	6.1%	175	12.4%	275	18.2%	450	27.6%	650	37.6%	875	48.3%	1375	70.7%
80	6.4%	180	12.7%	280	18.5%	460	28.1%	660	38.1%	900	49.5%	1400	71.8%
85	6.8%	185	13.0%	285	18.8%	470	28.6%	670	38.6%	925	50.6%	1425	72.9%

CDS	P	CDS	P	CDS	P	CDS	P	CDS	P	CDS	P	CDS	P
90	7.1%	190	13.3%	290	19.1%	480	29.1%	680	39.1%	950	51.8%	1450	74.0%
95	7.4%	195	13.6%	295	19.3%	490	29.6%	690	39.6%	975	52.9%	1475	75.1%
100	7.8%	200	13.9%	300	19.6%	500	30.2%	700	40.0%	1000	54.1%	1500	76.1%

Table 13.9: Default probability and credit default swap.

The Default Probabilities Estimated five-Year Cumulative Probability of Default (P)

and five year credit default swaps (5Y CDS)

Appendix A – data case #8 - predicting bankruptcy by using Z-score

The Altman's Z score is used to predict the possibility of a firm going to bankruptcy. This score is a weighted average of five ratios based on a firm's balance sheet and income statement. For public firms, Altman (1968) offers the following formula:

$$Z = 3.3X_1 + 0.99X_2 + 0.6X_3 + 1.2X_4 + 1.4X_5 \quad \ldots (1)$$

Here, the definitions of *X1*, *X2*, *X3*, *X4*, and *X5* are given in the following table:

Variable	Definition
X1	EBIT/total assets
X2	Net sales/total assets
X3	Market value of equity/total liabilities
X4	Working capital/total assets
X5	Retained earnings/total assets

Based on the ranges of z-scores, we could classify 20 public firms into the following four categories. Eidlenan (1995) finds that the Z score correctly predicted 72% of bankruptcies two years prior to the event:

Z-score range	Description
> 3.0	Safe
2.7 to 2.99	On alert
1.8 to 2.7	Good chances of going bankrupt within two years
< 1.80	Probability of financial distress is very high

References

- *Altman, Edward I, 1968, Financial Ratios, Discriminant Analysis and the Prediction of Corporate Bankruptcy, Journal of Finance,189–209,* `http://onlinelibrary.wiley.com/doi/10.1111/j.1540-6261.1968.tb00843.x/abstract`

- *Altman, E.I., Kishore, V., 1997. Default and returns in the high yield debt market, 1991-1996,NYU Salomon Center Special Report*

- *Altman, Edward I.,2000, PREDICTING FINANCIAL DISTRESS OF COMPANIES,* `http://pages.stern.nyu.edu/~ealtman/Zscores.pdf`

- *Eidleman, Gregory J.,1995,Z-Scores – A Guide to Failure Prediction, CPA Journal Online,* `https://www.easycalculation.com/statistics/altman-z-score.php`

- *Fitch,* `https://www.fitchratings.com/site/home.`

- *KMV model,* `https://github.com/ghlingjun/kmv-model`

- *Moody's website,* `http://www.moodys.com/`

- *Moody's, 2007, Introducing Moody's Credit Transition Model,* `http://www.moodysanalytics.com/~/media/Brochures/Credit-Research-Risk-Measurement/Quantative-Insight/Credit-Transition-Model/Introductory-Article-Credit-Transition-Model.pdf`

- *Standard & Poor's,* `http://www.standardandpoors.com/en_US/web/guest/home`

Exercises

1. How many credit agencies are there in the US? Which are the major ones?

2. How many types of definition of risk are there? What are the differences between credit risk and market risk?

3. How do you estimate the total risk and market risk of a firm? What is the related mathematical formula?

4. How do you estimate the credit risk of a firm? What is the related mathematical formula?

5. Why might the credit risk of a bond be different than its company's credit rating?

6. If everything is equal, which one is for risk, long-term bonds, or short-term bonds?

7. What is the definition of credit spread? Why is it useful?

8. What are uses of the term structure of interest rate?

9. What are the definitions of *X1*, *X2*, *X3*, *X4*, and *X5* for Altman's Z-score? Explain why the higher a Z-score, the lower the probability of bankruptcy:

$$Z = 3.3X_1 + 0.99X_2 + 0.6X_3 + 1.2X_4 + 1.4X_5$$

10. Identify an issue with z score and find a way to address the issue.

11. What is the one-year migration (transition) matrix?

12. What is the relationship between the credit rating and the default probability?

13. Using the concept of the present value of a bond, is the discounted the expected future cash flows to derive equation (1).

14. What are the values on the (main) diagonal line (from NW to SE) of a credit transition matrix?

15. Walmart plans to issue a $50 million (total face value) corporate bond with a face value of $1,000 for each bond. The bonds will mature in 10 years. The coupon rate is 8% with an annual payment. How much could Walmart raise today? If Walmart manages to raise its credit rating by one notch, how much extra cash could the firm raise?

16. The following table presents the relationship between rating, default risk (spread), and time. Write a Python program to interpolate the missing spreads, such as S from year 11 to 29. The Python dataset could be downloaded from http://canisius.edu/~yany/python/creditSpread2014.p:

```
import matplotlib.pyplot as plt
import pandas as pd
x=pd.read_pickle("c:/temp/creditSpread2014.p")
print(x.head())
      Rating    1     2     3     5     7    10     30
0   Aaa/AAA   5.0   8.0  12.0  18.0  28.0  42.0   65.0
1   Aa1/AA+  11.2  20.0  27.0  36.6  45.2  56.8   81.8
2    Aa2/AA  16.4  32.8  42.6  54.8  62.8  71.2   97.8
3   Aa3/AA-  21.6  38.6  48.6  59.8  67.4  75.2   99.2
4    A1/A+   26.2  44.0  54.2  64.6  71.4  78.4  100.2
```

Summary

In this chapter, we start from the very basics about credit risk analysis such as credit rating, credit spread, 1-year rating migration matrix, **Probability of Default (PD)**, **Loss Given Default (LGD)**, term structure of interest rate, Altman's Z-score, KMV model, default probability, the distance to default, and credit default swap. In *Chapter 10, Options and Futures*, some basic vanilla options, such as Black-Scholes-Merton options and their related applications, are discussed. In addition, in *Chapter 12, Monte Carlo Simulation*, two exotic options are explained.

In the next chapter, we will discuss more exotic options, since they are quite useful for mitigating many types of financial risk.

14
Exotic Options

In *Chapter 10, Options and Futures*, we have discussed the famous Black-Scholes-Merton option model and various trading strategies involving various types of options, futures, and underlying securities. The Black-Scholes-Merton closed-form solution is for European options that could be exercised only on maturity dates. American options could be exercised before or on a maturity date. Usually, those types of options are called vanilla options. On the other hand, there exist various types of exotic options that have all sorts of features making them more complex than commonly traded vanilla options.

For example, if an option buyer could exercise their right several times before the maturity date, it is called a Bermudan option. In *Chapter 12, Monte Carlo Simulation*, two types of exotic options are discussed. Many exotic options (derivatives) may have several triggers relating to their payoffs. An exotic option may also include non-standard underlying security or instrument, developed for a specific client or for a particular market. Exotic options are generally traded **over the counter** (OTC).

In this chapter, the following topics will be covered:

- European, American, and Bermudan options
- Simple chooser options
- Shout, rainbow, and binary options
- Average price option
- Barrier options – up-and-in options and up-and-out option
- Barrier options – down-and-in and down-and-out options

European, American, and Bermuda options

In *Chapter 10, Options and Futures*, we have learnt that for a European option, the option buyer could exercise their right only on maturity dates, while for an American option buyer, they could exercise their right any time before and on maturity dates. Thus, an American option would be more valuable than its counterparty of European option. Bermudan options could be exercised once or several times on a few predetermined dates. Consequently, the price of a Bermudan option should be between a European and an American option with the same features, such as the same maturity dates and the same exercises prices, see the following two inequalities for call options:

$$ C_{European} \leq C_{Bermudan} \leq C_{Amerian} \quad \cdots\cdots\cdots (1) $$

Here is an example for a Bermudan option. Assume that a company issues a 10-year bond. After seven years, the company could call back, that is, retire, the bond at the end of each year for the next three years. This callable property is eventually an embedded Bermudan option with exercise dates in December of years 8, 9, and 10.

First, let's look at the Python program for an American call by using the binomial model:

```python
def binomialCallAmerican(s,x,T,r,sigma,n=100):
    from math import exp,sqrt
    import numpy as np
    deltaT = T /n
    u = exp(sigma * sqrt(deltaT))
    d = 1.0 / u
    a = exp(r * deltaT)
    p = (a - d) / (u - d)
    v = [[0.0 for j in np.arange(i + 1)] for i in np.arange(n + 1)]
    for j in np.arange(n+1):
        v[n][j] = max(s * u**j * d**(n - j) - x, 0.0)
    for i in np.arange(n-1, -1, -1):
        for j in np.arange(i + 1):
            v1=exp(-r*deltaT)*(p*v[i+1][j+1]+(1.0-p)*v[i+1][j])
            v2=max(v[i][j]-x,0)              # early exercise
            v[i][j]=max(v1,v2)
    return v[0][0]
#
s=40.          # stock price today
```

```
x=40.            # exercise price
T=6./12          # maturity date ii years
tao=1/12         # when to choose
r=0.05           # risk-free rate
sigma=0.2        # volatility
n=1000           # number of steps
#
price=binomialCallAmerican(s,x,T,r,sigma,n)
print("American call =", price)
('American call =', 2.7549263174936502)
```

The price of this American call is $2.75. The key for modifying the previous program to satisfy only a few exercise prices is the following two lines:

```
v2=max(v[i][j]-x,0)              # early exercise
v[i][j]=max(v1,v2)
```

Here is the Python program for a Bermudan call option. The key different is the variable called T2, which contains the dates when the Bermudan option could be exercised:

```
def callBermudan(s,x,T,r,sigma,T2,n=100):
    from math import exp,sqrt
    import numpy as np
    n2=len(T2)
    deltaT = T /n
    u = exp(sigma * sqrt(deltaT))
    d = 1.0 / u
    a = exp(r * deltaT)
    p = (a - d) / (u - d)
    v =[[0.0 for j in np.arange(i + 1)] for i in np.arange(n + 1)]
    for j in np.arange(n+1):
        v[n][j] = max(s * u**j * d**(n - j) - x, 0.0)
    for i in np.arange(n-1, -1, -1):
        for j in np.arange(i + 1):
            v1=exp(-r*deltaT)*(p*v[i+1][j+1]+(1.0-p)*v[i+1][j])
            for k in np.arange(n2):
                if abs(j*deltaT-T2[k])<0.01:
                    v2=max(v[i][j]-x,0)  # potential early exercise
                else:
                    v2=0
            v[i][j]=max(v1,v2)
    return v[0][0]
#
s=40.                    # stock price today
```

```
x=40.                    # exercise price
T=6./12                  # maturity date ii years
r=0.05                   # risk-free rate
sigma=0.2                # volatility
n=1000                   # number of steps
T2=(3./12.,4./12.)       # dates for possible early exercise
#
price=callBermudan(s,x,T,r,sigma,T2,n)
print("Bermudan call =", price)
('Bermudan call =', 2.7549263174936502)
```

Chooser options

For a chooser option, it allows the option buyer to choose, at a predetermined point of time before the option matures whether it is a European call or a European put. For a simple chooser option, the underlying call and put options have the same maturities and exercise prices. Let's look at two extreme cases. The option buyer has to make a decision today, that is, when they make such a purchase. The price of this chooser option should be the maximum of call and put options since the option buyer does not have more information. The second extreme case is the investor could make a decision on the maturity date. Since the call and put have the same exercise prices, if the call is in the money, the put should be out of money. The opposite is true. Thus, the price of a chooser option should be the summation of the call and the put. This is equivalent to buy a call and a put with the same exercise prices and maturity dates. In *Chapter 10, Options and Futures* we know such a trading strategy is called Straddle. With such a trading strategy, we bet that the underlying security would move away from our current position. However, we are not sure about the direction.

First, let's look at the pricing formula for a simple chooser option, both call and put have the same maturity dates and exercise prices. Assume that there is no dividend before maturity. A simple chooser option has the following pricing formula:

$$P_{chooser} = call(T) + put(\tau) \quad \ldots (2)$$

Here, *Pchooer* is the price or premium for a chooser option, *call (T)* is a European call with a maturity T. *put(τ)* will be defined soon. For the first *call (T)* option, we have the following pricing formula:

$$\begin{cases} call(T) = SN(d_1) - Ke^{-RT}N(d_2) \\ \quad d_1 = \dfrac{\ln\left(\frac{S}{K}\right) + \left(r + \frac{1}{2}\sigma^2\right)T}{\sigma\sqrt{T}} \qquad \ldots (3) \\ \quad d_2 = d_1 - \sigma\sqrt{T} \end{cases}$$

Here, *call (T)* is the call premium, S is today's price, K is the exercise price, T is the maturity in years, σ is the volatility, and $N()$ is the cumulative standard normal distribution. Actually, this is exactly the same as the Black-Scholes-Merton call option model. *put (τ)* has the following formula:

$$\begin{cases} put(\tau) = Ke^{-RT}N(-d_2^\tau) - SN(-d_1^\tau) \\ \quad d_1^\tau = \dfrac{\ln\left(\frac{S}{K}\right) + rT + \frac{1}{2}\sigma^2\tau}{\sigma\sqrt{\tau}} \qquad \ldots (4) \\ \quad d_2^\tau = d_1 - \sigma\sqrt{\tau} \end{cases}$$

Again, *put(τ)* is the put premium and τ is when the chooser option buyer could make a decision. To make *d1* and *d2* distinguishable from those two values in the previous equation, d_1^τ and d_2^τ are used instead of *d1* and *d2*. Note that the preceding equation is different from the Black-Scholes-Merton put option model since we have both T and τ instead of just T. Now, let's look at one extreme case: the option buyer could make their decision at maturity date, that is, τ=T. From the preceding equation, obviously the price of the chooser option will be the summation of those two options:

$$P_{chooser} = call(T) + put(\tau = T) \qquad \ldots (5)$$

The following Python program is for the choose options. To save space, we could combine both a call with a put, see the following Python codes. In order to do so, we have two time variable input called T and tao:

```
from scipy import log,exp,sqrt,stats
def callAndPut(S,X,T,r,sigma,tao,type='C'):
    d1= (log(S/X) +r*T+0.5*sigma*sigma*tao)/(sigma*sqrt(tao))
    d2 = d1-sigma*sqrt(tao)
    if type.upper()=='C':
        c=S*stats.norm.cdf(d1)-X*exp(-r*T)*stats.norm.cdf(d2)
        return c
    else:
```

```
          p=X*exp(-r*T)*stats.norm.cdf(-d2)-S*stats.norm.cdf(-d1)
          return p
    #
    def chooserOption(S,X,T,r,sigma,tao):
        call_T=callAndPut(S,X,T,r,sigma,T)
        put_tao=callAndPut(S,X,T,r,sigma,tao,type='P')
        return call_T- put_tao
    #
    s=40.         # stock price today
    x=40.         # exercise price
    T=6./12       # maturity date ii years
    tao=1./12.    # when to choose
    r=0.05        # risk-free rate
    sigma=0.2     # volatility
    #
    price=chooserOption(s,x,T,r,sigma,tao)
    print("price of a chooser option=",price)
    ('price of a chooser option=', 2.2555170735574421)
```

The price of this chooser option is $2.26.

Shout options

A shout option is a standard European option except that the option buyer can *shout* to the option seller before maturity date to set the minimum payoff as S_T-X, where S_T is the stock price at time τ when the buyer shouts and X is the exercise price. The level of the strike could be set at a specific relation to the spot price, such as 3% or 5% above (or below). The Python codes are given here:

```
def shoutCall(s,x,T,r,sigma,shout,n=100):
    from math import exp,sqrt
    import numpy as np
    deltaT = T /n
    u = exp(sigma * sqrt(deltaT))
    d = 1.0 / u
    a = exp(r * deltaT)
    p = (a - d) / (u - d)
    v =[[0.0 for j in np.arange(i + 1)] for i in np.arange(n + 1)]
    for j in np.arange(n+1):
        v[n][j] = max(s * u**j * d**(n - j) - x, 0.0)
    for i in np.arange(n-1, -1, -1):
        for j in np.arange(i + 1):
            v1=exp(-r*deltaT)*(p*v[i+1][j+1]+(1.0-p)*v[i+1][j])
            v2=max(v[i][j]-shout,0)    # shout
```

```
                v[i][j]=max(v1,v2)
        return v[0][0]
#
s=40.              # stock price today
x=40.              # exercise price
T=6./12            # maturity date ii years
tao=1/12           # when to choose
r=0.05             # risk-free rate
sigma=0.2          # volatility
n=1000             # number of steps
shout=(1+0.03)*s   # shout out level
#
price=shoutCall(s,x,T,r,sigma,shout,n)
print("Shout call =", price)
```

Binary options

A binary option, or asset-or-nothing option, is a type of options in which the payoff is structured to be either a fixed amount of compensation if the option expires in the money, or nothing at all if the option expires out of the money. Because of this property, we could apply Monte Carlo Simulation to find a solution. The Python codes are given here:

```
import random
import scipy as sp
#
def terminalStockPrice(S, T,r,sigma):
    tao=random.gauss(0,1.0)
    terminalPrice=S * sp.exp((r - 0.5 * sigma**2)*T+sigma*sp.
sqrt(T)*tao)
    return terminalPrice
#
def binaryCallPayoff(x, sT,payoff):
    if sT >= x:
        return payoff
    else:
        return 0.0
# input area
S = 40.0           # asset price
x = 40.0           # exercise price
T = 0.5            # maturity in years
r = 0.01           # risk-free rate
sigma = 0.2        # vol of 20%
fixedPayoff = 10.0 # payoff
```

```
nSimulations =10000 # number of simulations
#
payoffs=0.0
for i in xrange(nSimulations):
    sT = terminalStockPrice(S, T,r,sigma)
    payoffs += binaryCallPayoff(x, sT,fixedPayoff)
#
price = sp.exp(-r * T) * (payoffs / float(nSimulations))
print('Binary options call= %.8f' % price)
```

Note that since the preceding program does not fix the seed, for each run, users should get different results.

Rainbow options

Many financial problems could be summarized as or associated with the maximum or minimum of several assets. Let's look at a simple one: options on the maximum or minimum of two assets. These type of options are called rainbow options. Since two assets are involved, we have to get familiar with a so-called bivariate normal distribution. The following codes show its graph. The original codes are at the website of `http://scipython.com/blog/visualizing-the-bivariate-gaussian-distribution/`:

```
import numpy as np
from matplotlib import cm
import matplotlib.pyplot as plt
from mpl_toolkits.mplot3d import Axes3D
#
# input area
n    = 60                       # number of intervals
x    = np.linspace(-3, 3, n)    # x dimension
y    = np.linspace(-3, 4, n)    # y dimension
x,y = np.meshgrid(x, y)         # grid
#
# Mean vector and covariance matrix
mu = np.array([0., 1.])
cov= np.array([[ 1. , -0.5], [-0.5,  1.5]])
#
# combine x and y into a single 3-dimensional array
pos = np.empty(x.shape + (2,))
pos[:, :, 0] = x
pos[:, :, 1] = y
#
def multiNormal(pos, mu, cov):
```

```
    n = mu.shape[0]
    Sigma_det = np.linalg.det(cov)
    Sigma_inv = np.linalg.inv(cov)
    n2 = np.sqrt((2*np.pi)**n * Sigma_det)
    fac=np.einsum('...k,kl,...l->...', pos-mu, Sigma_inv, pos-mu)
    return np.exp(-fac/2)/n2
#
z    = multiNormal(pos, mu, cov)
fig  = plt.figure()
ax   = fig.gca(projection='3d')
ax.plot_surface(x, y, z, rstride=3, cstride=3,linewidth=1,
antialiased=True,cmap=cm.viridis)
cset = ax.contourf(x, y, z, zdir='z', offset=-0.15, cmap=cm.viridis)
ax.set_zlim(-0.15,0.2)
ax.set_zticks(np.linspace(0,0.2,5))
ax.view_init(27, -21)
plt.title("Bivariate normal distribtuion")
plt.ylabel("y values ")
plt.xlabel("x values")
plt.show()
```

The graph is shown here:

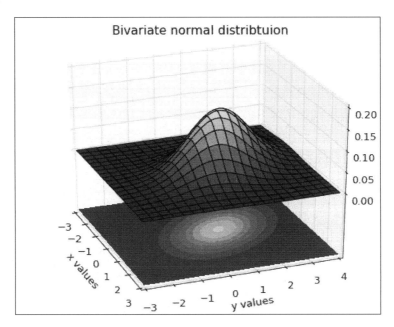

Assume that returns of those two assets follow a bivariate normal distribution with a correlation of ρ. To make our estimation a little bit easier, we assume that there is no dividend before maturity date. The payoff for a call on the minimum of two assets will be:

$$payoff\ (call\ on\ minumum\ of\ 2) = Max(min(s_T^1, s_T^2), 0) \quad \ldots (6)$$

Here, $s_T^1\ (s_T^2)$ is the terminal stock price for stock 1 (2) and T is the maturity date in years. The pricing formula for a call based on the minimum of two assets is given here:

$$Call(minium\ of\ 2\ assets) = $$
$$S_1 N_2(d_{11}, d_{12}, \rho_1) + S_2 N_2(d_{22}, d_{12}, \rho_2) - Ke^{-RT} N_2(d_1, d_2, \rho) \quad (7)$$

Here, S1 (S2) is the current stock price for stock 1 (2), N2(a,b,ρ) is the cumulative bivariate normal distribution with the upper bounds of a and b, correlation of ρ between those two assets, and K is the exercise price. The parameters of d11, d12, d21, d22, ρ1, and ρ2 are defined here:

$$d_1 = \frac{\ln\left(\frac{S_1}{K}\right) + (r - \frac{1}{2}\sigma_1^2)T}{\sigma_1 \sqrt{T}} \qquad \ldots (8)$$

$$d_2 = \frac{\ln\left(\frac{S_2}{K}\right) + (r - \frac{1}{2}\sigma_2^2)T}{\sigma_2 \sqrt{T}} \qquad \ldots (9)$$

$$d_{11} = d_1 + \sigma_1 \sqrt{T} \qquad \ldots (10)$$

$$d_{22} = d_2 + \sqrt{T} \qquad \ldots (11)$$

$$d_{12} = \frac{\ln\left(\frac{S_2}{S_1}\right) - \frac{1}{2}\sigma_a^2 T}{\sigma_a \sqrt{T}} \qquad \ldots (12)$$

$$\sigma_a = \sqrt{\sigma_1^2 - 2\rho\sigma_1\sigma_2 + \sigma_2^2} \qquad \ldots (13)$$

$$d_{21} = \frac{\ln\left(\frac{S_1}{S_2}\right) - \frac{1}{2}\sigma_a^2 T}{\sigma_a \sqrt{T}} \qquad \ldots (14)$$

$$\rho_1 = \frac{\rho\sigma_2 - \sigma_1}{\sigma_a} \qquad \ldots (15)$$

$$\rho_2 = \frac{\rho\sigma_1 - \sigma_2}{\sigma_a} \qquad \ldots (16)$$

First, we should study the bivariate cumulative normal distribution
`N2_f(d1,d2,rho)` described here:

```
def N2_f(d1,d2,rho):
    """cumulative bivariate standard normal distribution
        d1: the first value
        d2: the second value
        rho: correlation

        Example1:
            print(N2_f(0,0,1.)) => 0.5
        Example2:
            print(N2_f(0,0,0)  => 0.25
    """
    import statsmodels.sandbox.distributions.extras as extras
    muStandardNormal=0.0       # mean of a standard normal distribution
    varStandardNormal=1.0      # variance of standard normal distribution
    upper=([d1,d2])            # upper bound for two values
    v=varStandardNormal        # simplify our notations
    mu=muStandardNormal        # simplify our notations
    covM=([v,rho],[rho,v])
    return extras.mvnormcdf(upper,mu,covM)
#
```

Let's look at some special cases. From univariate standard normal distribution, we know that when input value is `0`, we expected the cumulative standard normal distribution is `0.5` since the underlying normal distribution is symmetric. When two time series are perfectly positively correlated, the cumulative standard normal distribution should be `0.5` as well, see the preceding result. On the other hand, if two time series are not correlated, their cumulative standard normal distribution when the inputs are both zero, then we expected the overlapping, that is, *0.5 *0.5=0.25*. This is true by calling the preceding `N2_f()` function. For the exotic, option, the related Python program is given here:

```
from math import exp,sqrt,log
import statsmodels.sandbox.distributions.extras as extras
#
def dOne(s,k,r,sigma,T):
    #print(s,k,r,sigma,T)
    a=log(s/k)+(r-0.5*sigma**2)*T
    b=(sigma*sqrt(T))
    return a/b
#
def sigmaA_f(sigma1,sigma2,rho):
    return sqrt(sigma1**2-2*rho*sigma1*sigma2+sigma2**2)
```

```
#
def dTwo(d1,sigma,T):
    return d1+sigma*sqrt(T)
#
def rhoTwo(sigma1,sigma2,sigmaA,rho):
    return (rho*sigma2-sigma1)/sigmaA
#
def N2_f(d1,d2,rho):
    import statsmodels.sandbox.distributions.extras as extras
    muStandardNormal=0.0     # mean of a standard normal distribution
    varStandardNormal=1.0    # variance of standard normal distribution
    upper=([d1,d2])          # upper bound for two values
    v=varStandardNormal      # simplify our notations
    mu=muStandardNormal      # simplify our notations
    covM=([v,rho],[rho,v])
    return extras.mvnormcdf(upper,mu,covM)
#
def dOneTwo(s1,s2,sigmaA,T):
    a=log(s2/s1)-0.5*sigmaA**2*T
    b=sigmaA*sqrt(T)
    return a/b
#
def rainbowCallOnMinimum(s1,s2,k,T,r,sigma1,sigma2,rho):
    d1=dOne(s1,k,r,sigma1,T)
    d2=dOne(s2,k,r,sigma2,T)
    d11=dTwo(d1,sigma1,T)
    d22=dTwo(d2,sigma2,T)
    sigmaA=sigmaA_f(sigma1,sigma2,rho)
    rho1=rhoTwo(sigma1,sigma2,sigmaA,rho)
    rho2=rhoTwo(sigma2,sigma1,sigmaA,rho)
    d12=dOneTwo(s1,s2,sigmaA,T)
    d21=dOneTwo(s2,s1,sigmaA,T)
    #
    part1=s1*N2_f(d11,d12,rho1)
    part2=s2*N2_f(d21,d22,rho2)
    part3=k*exp(-r*T)*N2_f(d1,d2,rho)
    return part1 + part2 - part3
#
s1=100.
s2=95.
k=102.0
T=8./12.
r=0.08
rho=0.75
```

```
sigma1=0.15
sigma2=0.20
price=rainbowCallOnMinimum(s1,s2,k,T,r,sigma1,sigma2,rho)
print("price of call based on the minimum of 2 assets=",price)
('price of call based on the minimum of 2 assets=', 3.747423936156629)
```

Another way to price various types of rainbow options is using Monte Carlo Simulation. As we mentioned in *Chapter 12, Monte Carlo Simulation,* we can generate two correlated random number time series. There are two step involved: generate two random time series *x1* and *x2* with a zero-correlation; and then apply the following formula:

$$\begin{cases} y_1 = x_1 \\ y_2 = \rho x_1 + \sqrt{1 - \rho^2} * x_2 \end{cases} \quad \dots (17)$$

Here, ρ is the predetermined correlation between those two time series. Now, *y1* and *y2* are correlated with a predetermined correlation. The following Python program would implement the preceding approach:

```
import scipy as sp
sp.random.seed(123)
n=1000
rho=0.3
x1=sp.random.normal(size=n)
x2=sp.random.normal(size=n)
y1=x1
y2=rho*x1+sp.sqrt(1-rho**2)*x2
print(sp.corrcoef(y1,y2))
 [[ 1.          0.28505213]
  [ 0.28505213  1.         ]]
```

Next, we apply the same technique we know in *Chapter 12, Monte Carlo Simulation* to price a rainbow option call on the minimum of two assets:

```
import scipy as sp
from scipy import zeros, sqrt, shape
#
sp.random.seed(123)    # fix our random numbers
s1=100.                # stock price 1
s2=95.                 # stock price 2
k=102.0                # exercise price
T=8./12.               # maturity in years
r=0.08                 # risk-free rate
```

```
rho=0.75                 # correlation between 2
sigma1=0.15              # volatility for stock 1
sigma2=0.20              # volatility for stock 1
nSteps=100.              # number of steps
nSimulation=1000         # number of simulations
#
# step 1: generate correlated random number
dt =T/nSteps
call = sp.zeros([nSimulation], dtype=float)
x = range(0, int(nSteps), 1)
#
# step 2: call call prices
for j in range(0, nSimulation):
    x1=sp.random.normal(size=nSimulation)
    x2=sp.random.normal(size=nSimulation)
    y1=x1
    y2=rho*x1+sp.sqrt(1-rho**2)*x2
    sT1=s1
    sT2=s2
    for i in x[:-1]:
        e1=y1[i]
        e2=y2[i]
        sT1*=sp.exp((r-0.5*sigma1**2)*dt+sigma1*e1*sqrt(dt))
        sT2*=sp.exp((r-0.5*sigma2**2)*dt+sigma2*e2*sqrt(dt))
        minOf2=min(sT1,sT2)
        call[j]=max(minOf2-k,0)
#
# Step 3: summation and discount back
call=sp.mean(call)*sp.exp(-r*T)
print('Rainbow call on minimum of 2 assets = ', round(call,3))
('Rainbow call on minimum of 2 assets = ', 4.127)
```

If we add more assets, it becomes more difficult to have a close-form solution. Here we show how to use Monte Carlo Simulation to price a rainbow call option based on the maximum terminal stock price. The basic logic is quite straight: generate three terminal stock prices, and then record the call payoff by applying the following formula:

$$Call payoff(\text{max of three}) = \max(\max(s_{T,1}, s_{T,2}, s_{T,3}) - X, 0) \quad \dots (18)$$

The final price would be the average of the discounted payoffs. The key is how to generate a correlated three set of random numbers. Here, the famous Cholesky decomposition is applied. Assume that we have a correlation matrix called C. A Cholesky decomposition matrix L that makes $L^T L = C$. Assume further that the uncorrelated return matrix is called U. Now, the correlated return matrix $R = UL$. The Python code is shown here:

```python
import numpy as np
# input area
nSimulation=5000                 # number of simulations
c=np.array([[1.0, 0.5, 0.3],     # correlation matrix
           [0.5, 1.0, 0.4],
           [0.3, 0.4, 1.0]])
np.random.seed(123)              # fix random numbers
#
# generate uncorrelated random numbers
x=np.random.normal(size=3*nSimulation)
U=np.reshape(x,(nSimulation,3))
#
# Cholesky decomposition
L=np.linalg.cholesky(c)
# generate correlated random numbers
r=np.dot(U,L)
#check the correlation matrix
print(np.corrcoef(r.T))
[[ 1.          0.51826188  0.2760649 ]
 [ 0.51826188  1.          0.35452286]
 [ 0.2760649   0.35452286  1.         ]]
```

Pricing average options

In *Chapter 12*, *Monte Carlo Simulation*, we discussed two exotic options. For convenience, we will include them in this chapter as well. Because of this, readers will find some duplicates. European and American options are path-independent options. This means that an option's payoff depends only on the terminal stock price and strike price. One related issue for path-dependent options is market manipulation at the maturity date. Another issue is that some investors or hedgers might care more about the average price instead of a terminal price.

For example, a refinery is worried about oil, its major raw material, and price movement in the next three months. They plan to hedge the potential price jumps in crude oil. The company could buy a call option. However, since the firm consumes a huge amount of crude oil every day, naturally it cares more about the average price instead of just the terminal price on which a vanilla call option depends. For such cases, average options will be more effective. Average options are a type of Asian option. For an average option, its payoff is determined by the average underlying prices over some predetermined period of time. There are two types of averages: arithmetic average and geometric average. The payoff function of an Asian call (average price) is given as follows:

$$payoff\ (call) = Max(P_{average} - X, 0) \quad \dots (19)$$

The payoff function of an Asian put (average price) is given here:

$$payoff\ (put) = Max(X - P_{average}, 0) \quad \dots (20)$$

Asian options are one of the basic forms of exotic options. Another advantage of Asian options is that their costs are cheaper compared to European and American vanilla options since the variation of an average will be much smaller than a terminal price. The following Python program is for an Asian option with an arithmetic average price:

```
import scipy as sp
s0=30.                    # today stock price
x=32.                     # exercise price
T=3.0/12.                 # maturity in years
r=0.025                   # risk-free rate
sigma=0.18                # volatility (annualized)
sp.random.seed(123)       # fix a seed here
n_simulation=1000         # number of simulations
n_steps=500.              # number of steps
#
dt=T/n_steps
call=sp.zeros([n_simulation], dtype=float)
for j in range(0, n_simulation):
    sT=s0
    total=0
    for i in range(0,int(n_steps)):
        e=sp.random.normal()
        sT*=sp.exp((r-0.5*sigma*sigma)*dt+sigma*e*sp.sqrt(dt))
```

```
        total+=sT
        price_average=total/n_steps
    call[j]=max(price_average-x,0)
#
call_price=sp.mean(call)*sp.exp(-r*T)
print('call price based on average price = ', round(call_price,3))
('call price based on average price = ', 0.12)
```

Pricing barrier options

Unlike the Black-Scholes-Merton option model's call and put options, which are path-independent, a barrier option is path-dependent. A barrier option is similar in many ways to an ordinary option, except a trigger exists. An *in* option starts its life worthless unless the underlying stock reaches a predetermined knock-in barrier. On the contrary, an *out* barrier option starts its life active and turns useless when a knock-out barrier price is breached. In addition, if a barrier option expires inactive, it may be worthless, or there may be a cash rebate paid out as a fraction of the premium. The four types of barrier options are given as follows:

- **Up-and-out**: In this barrier option, the price starts from below a barrier level. If it reaches the barrier, it is knocked out.

- **Down-and-out**: In this barrier option, the price starts from above a barrier. If it reaches the barrier, it is knocked out.

- **Up-and-in**: In this barrier option, the price starts down a barrier and has to reach the barrier to be activated.

- **Down-and-in**: In this barrier option, the price starts over a barrier and has to reach the barrier to be activated.

The following Python program is for an up-and-out barrier option with a European call:

```
import scipy as sp
from scipy import log,exp,sqrt,stats
#
def bsCall(S,X,T,r,sigma):
    d1=(log(S/X)+(r+sigma*sigma/2.)*T)/(sigma*sqrt(T))
    d2 = d1-sigma*sqrt(T)
    return S*stats.norm.cdf(d1)-X*exp(-r*T)*stats.norm.cdf(d2)
#
def up_and_out_call(s0,x,T,r,sigma,n_simulation,barrier):
    n_steps=100.
    dt=T/n_steps
    total=0
```

```
        for j in sp.arange(0, n_simulation):
            sT=s0
            out=False
            for i in range(0,int(n_steps)):
                e=sp.random.normal()
                sT*=sp.exp((r-0.5*sigma*sigma)*dt+sigma*e*sp.sqrt(dt))
                if sT>barrier:
                    out=True
            if out==False:
                total+=bsCall(s0,x,T,r,sigma)
        return total/n_simulation
    #
```

The basic design is that we simulate the stock movement n times, such as 100 times. For each simulation, we have 100 steps. Whenever the stock price reaches the barrier, the payoff will be zero. Otherwise, the payoff will be a vanilla European call. The final value will be the summation of all call prices that are not knocked out, divided by the number of simulations, as shown in the following code:

```
s0=30.              # today stock price
x=30.               # exercise price
barrier=32          # barrier level
T=6./12.            # maturity in years
r=0.05              # risk-free rate
sigma=0.2           # volatility (annualized)
n_simulation=100    # number of simulations
sp.random.seed(12)  # fix a seed
#
result=up_and_out_call(s0,x,T,r,sigma,n_simulation,barrier)
print('up-and-out-call = ', round(result,3))
('up-and-out-call = ', 0.93)
```

The Python code for the down-and-in put option is shown as follows:

```
def down_and_in_put(s0,x,T,r,sigma,n_simulation,barrier):
    n_steps=100.
    dt=T/n_steps
    total=0
    for j in range(0, n_simulation):
        sT=s0
        in_=False
        for i in range(0,int(n_steps)):
            e=sp.random.normal()
            sT*=sp.exp((r-0.5*sigma*sigma)*dt+sigma*e*sp.sqrt(dt))
```

```
        if sT<barrier:
            in_=True
        #print 'sT=',sT
        #print 'j=',j ,'out=',out if in_==True:
        total+=p4f.bs_put(s0,x,T,r,sigma)
    return total/n_simulation
#
```

Barrier in-and-out parity

If we buy an up-and-out European call and an up-and-in European call, then the following parity should hold good:

$$call_{up-and-out} + call_{up-and-in} = call \quad \dots (21)$$

The logic is very simple—if the stock price reaches the barrier, then the first call is worthless and the second call will be activated. If the stock price never touches the barrier, the first call will remain active, while the second one is never activated. Either way, one of them is active. The following Python program illustrates such scenarios:

```
def upCall(s,x,T,r,sigma,nSimulation,barrier):
    import scipy as sp
    import p4f
    n_steps=100
    dt=T/n_steps
    inTotal=0
    outTotal=0
    for j in range(0, nSimulation):
        sT=s
        inStatus=False
        outStatus=True
        for i in range(0,int(n_steps)):
            e=sp.random.normal()
            sT*=sp.exp((r-0.5*sigma*sigma)*dt+sigma*e*sp.sqrt(dt))
            if sT>barrier:
                outStatus=False
                inStatus=True
        if outStatus==True:
            outTotal+=p4f.bs_call(s,x,T,r,sigma)
        else:
            inTotal+=p4f.bs_call(s,x,T,r,sigma)
    return outTotal/nSimulation, inTotal/nSimulation
#
```

We input a set of values to test whether the summation of an up-and-out call and an up-and-in call will be the same as a vanilla call:

```
import p4f
s=40.                    # today stock price
x=40.                    # exercise price
barrier=42.0             # barrier level
T=0.5                    # maturity in years
r=0.05                   # risk-free rate
sigma=0.2                # volatility (annualized)
nSimulation=500          # number of simulations
#
upOutCall,upInCall=upCall(s,x,T,r,sigma,nSimulation,barrier)
print 'upOutCall=', round(upOutCall,2),'upInCall=',round(upInCall,2)
print 'Black-Scholes call', round(p4f.bs_call(s,x,T,r,sigma),2)
```

The related output is shown here:

```
upOutCall= 0.75 upInCall= 2.01
Black-Scholes call 2.76
```

Graph of up-and-out and up-and-in parity

It is a good idea to use the Monte Carlo simulation to present such parity. The following code is designed to achieve this. To make our simulation clearer, we deliberately choose just five simulations:

```
import p4f
import scipy as sp
import matplotlib.pyplot as plt
#
s =9.25                  # stock price at time zero
x =9.10                  # exercise price
barrier=10.5             # barrier
T =0.5                   # maturity date (in years)
n_steps=30               # number of steps
r =0.05                  # expected annual return
sigma = 0.2              # volatility (annualized)
sp.random.seed(125)      # seed()
n_simulation = 5         # number of simulations
#
dt =T/n_steps
S = sp.zeros([n_steps], dtype=float)
time_ = range(0, int(n_steps), 1)
```

```
c=p4f.bs_call(s,x,T,r,sigma)
sp.random.seed(124)
outTotal, inTotal= 0.,0.
n_out,n_in=0,0

for j in range(0, n_simulation):
    S[0]= s
    inStatus=False
    outStatus=True
    for i in time_[:-1]:
        e=sp.random.normal()
        S[i+1]=S[i]*sp.exp((r-0.5*pow(sigma,2))*dt+sigma*sp.
sqrt(dt)*e)
        if S[i+1]>barrier:
            outStatus=False
            inStatus=True
    plt.plot(time_, S)
    if outStatus==True:
        outTotal+=c;n_out+=1
    else:
        inTotal+=c;n_in+=1
        S=sp.zeros(int(n_steps))+barrier
        plt.plot(time_,S,'.-')
        upOutCall=round(outTotal/n_simulation,3)
        upInCall=round(inTotal/n_simulation,3)
        plt.figtext(0.15,0.8,'S='+str(s)+',X='+str(x))
        plt.figtext(0.15,0.76,'T='+str(T)+',r='+str(r)+',sigma=='+str
(sigma))
        plt.figtext(0.15,0.6,'barrier='+str(barrier))
        plt.figtext(0.40,0.86, 'call price  ='+str(round(c,3)))
        plt.figtext(0.40,0.83,'up_and_out_call ='+str(upOutCall)+'
(='+str(n_out)+'/'+str(n_simulation)+'*'+str(round(c,3))+')')
        plt.figtext(0.40,0.80,'up_and_in_call ='+str(upInCall)+'
(='+str(n_in)+'/'+ str(n_simulation)+'*'+str(round(c,3))+')')
#
plt.title('Up-and-out and up-and-in parity (# of simulations = %d ' %
n_simulation +')')
plt.xlabel('Total number of steps ='+str(int(n_steps)))
plt.ylabel('stock price')
plt.show()
```

The corresponding graph is shown as follows. Note that in the preceding program, since the seed is used, different users should get the same graphs if the same seed is applied:

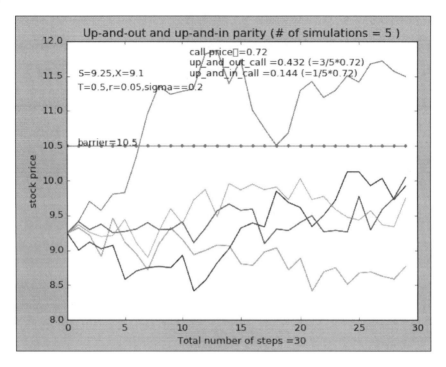

Pricing lookback options with floating strikes

The lookback options depend on the paths (history) travelled by the underlying security. Thus, they are also called path-dependent exotic options. One of them is named floating strikes. The payoff function of a call when the exercise price is the minimum price achieved during the life of the option is given as follows:

$$Payoff = Max(S_T - S_{min}, 0) = S_T - S_{min} \quad \ldots (22)$$

The Python code for this lookback option is shown as follows:

```
plt.show()
def lookback_min_price_as_strike(s,T,r,sigma,n_simulation):
    n_steps=100
    dt=T/n_steps
    total=0
    for j in range(n_simulation):
        min_price=100000.  # a very big number
        sT=s
        for i in range(int(n_steps)):
            e=sp.random.normal()
            sT*=sp.exp((r-0.5*sigma*sigma)*dt+sigma*e*sp.sqrt(dt))
            if sT<min_price:
                min_price=sT
                #print 'j=',j,'i=',i,'total=',total
                total+=p4f.bs_call(s,min_price,T,r,sigma)
    return total/n_simulation
```

Remember that the previous function needs two modules. Thus, we have to import those modules before we call the function, as shown in the following code:

```
import scipy as sp
import p4f
s=40.                # today stock price
T=0.5                # maturity in years
r=0.05               # risk-free rate
sigma=0.2            # volatility (annualized)
n_simulation=1000    # number of simulations
result=lookback_min_price_as_strike(s,T,r,sigma,n_simulation)
print('lookback min price as strike = ', round(result,3))
```

The result for one run is shown as follows:

```
('lookback min price as strike = ', 53.31)t(
```

Appendix A – data case 7 – hedging crude oil

Assume that a refinery is using crude oil every day. Thus, they have to face the risk of price uncertainty of their main raw materials: crude oil. There is a tradeoff between protecting their bottom line and running production smoothly; the company studies all possible outcomes, such as hedge the oil price or not hedge at all. Assume that the total annual crude oil consumption is 20 million gallons. Again, the company has to operate every day. Compare the following several strategies and point out their advantages and disadvantages:

- No hedging
- Use futures
- Use options
- Use exotic option

Several strategies exist, such as American options; see its specification in the following table. Some of the crude oil options contract specifications are shown in the following table:

Contract unit	A Light Sweet Crude Oil Put (Call) Option traded on the Exchange represents an option to assume a short (long) position in the underlying Light Sweet Crude Oil Futures traded on the Exchange.
Minimum price fluctuation	$0.01 per barrel.
Price quotation	U.S. dollars and cents per barrel.
Product code	CME Globex: LO, CME ClearPort: LO, Clearing: LO.
Listed contracts	Monthly contracts listed for the current year and the next five calendar years, and June and December contracts for three additional years. Monthly contracts for the balance of a new calendar year will be added following the termination of trading in the December contract of the current year.
Termination of trading	Trading terminates three business days before the termination of trading in the underlying futures contract.
Exercise style	American.
Settlement method	Deliverable.
Underlying	Light Sweet Crude Oil Futures.

Table 1: Some specification for crude oil options contract

If we use futures to hedge, we have the following formula:

$$N = \beta \frac{V_A}{V_F} \qquad \dots (1)$$

N is the number of futures contract, VA is the value of our portfolio (amount we want to hedge), β is the slope of a regression based on our material and the underlying instruments (note if our material is the same as the underlying hedging instrument, then beta is 1), and VF is the value of one futures contract:

- Source: `http://www.cmegroup.com/trading/energy/crude-oil/light-sweet-crude_contractSpecs_options.html?gclid=CLjWq92Yx9ICFU1MDQodP5EDLg&gclsrc=aw.ds`

- Source of data: *Crude Oil Prices: West Texas Intermediate (WTI) - Cushing, Oklahoma (DCOILWTICO)*, `https://fred.stlouisfed.org/series/DCOILWTICO/downloaddata`

- One related dataset is called `crudeOilPriceDaily.pkl`. The first and last several observations are shown here. The dataset is downloadable at `http://canisius.edu/~yany/python/crudeOilPriceDaily.pkl`:

```
import scipy as sp
import pandas as pd
x=pd.read_pickle("c:/temp/cruideOilPriceDaily.pkl")
print(x.head())
print(x.tail())
            PRICE
1986-01-02  25.56
1986-01-03  26.00
1986-01-06  26.53
1986-01-07  25.85
1986-01-08  25.87
            PRICE
2017-02-28  54.00
2017-03-01  53.82
2017-03-02  52.63
2017-03-03  53.33
2017-03-06  53.19
```

References

- *Clewlow, Les and Chris Strickland,1997, Exotic Options, the state of the art, Thomaston Business Press*

- *Kurtverstegen, Simulation: simulating uncorrelated and correlated random variables,* https://kurtverstegen.wordpress.com/2013/12/07/simulation/

- *Zhang, Peter, 1998, Exotic Options, World Scientific, the 2nd edition*

Exercises

1. What is the definition of exotic options?

2. Why is it claimed that a callable bond is equivalent to a normal bond plus a Bermudan option (the issuing company is the buyer of this Bermudan option while the bond buyer is the seller)?

3. Write a Python program to price an Asian average price put based on the arithmetic mean.

4. Write a Python program to price an Asian average price put based on the geometric mean.

5. Write a Python program to price an up-and-in call (barrier option).

6. Write a Python program to price a down-and-out put (barrier option).

7. Write a Python program to show the down-and-out and down-and-in parity.

8. Write a Python program to use `permutation()` from SciPy to select 12 monthly returns randomly from the past five-year data without placement. To test your program, you can use Citigroup and the time period January 1, 2009 to December 31, 2014 from Yahoo Finance.

9. Write a Python program to run bootstrapping with n given returns. For each time, we select m returns where m>n.

10. In this chapter, we have learned that a simple chooser option has the following price formula:

$$P_{chooser} = call(T) + put(\tau) \quad \ldots (1)$$

Here, T is the maturity date (in years) and τ is the time when the option makes its decision whether it prefers a call or a put. Is it possible to have the following formula?

$$P_{chooser} = call(\tau) + put(T) \quad \dots (2)$$

11. When the stock pays a continuously compounded dividend, dividend yield δ, we have the following pricing formula for Chooser options:

$$P_{chooser} = call(T) + put(\tau) \quad \dots (3)$$

Where *Pchooser* is the price or premium for a chooser option, *call (T)* is a European call with a maturity T. *put(τ)* will be defined soon. For the first *call (T)* option, we have the following pricing formula:

$$\begin{cases} call(T) = SN(d_1) - Ke^{-RT}N(d_2) \\ d_1 = \dfrac{\ln\left(\frac{S}{K}\right)+\left(r-\delta+\frac{1}{2}\sigma^2\right)T}{\sigma\sqrt{T}} \quad \dots (4) \\ d_2 = d_1 - \sigma\sqrt{T} \end{cases}$$

Where *call(T)* is the call price or premium, S is today's price, K is the exercise price, T is the maturity in years, σ is the volatility, and N() is the cumulative standard normal distribution. Actually, this is exactly the Black-Scholes-Merton call option model. Put (τ) has the following formula:

$$\begin{cases} put(\tau) = Ke^{-RT}N(-d_2^\tau) - SN(-d_1^\tau) \\ d_1^\tau = \dfrac{\ln\left(\frac{S}{K}\right)+(r-\delta)T+\frac{1}{2}\sigma^2\tau}{\sigma\sqrt{\tau}} \quad \dots (5) \\ d_2^\tau = d_1 - \sigma\sqrt{\tau} \end{cases}$$

Write a related Python program.

12. If two stocks prices are $40 and $55 today, the standard deviations of returns for those two stocks are 0.1 and 0.2, respectively. Their correlation is 0.45. What is the price of the rainbow call options based on the maximum of the terminal stock price of those two stocks? The exercise price is $60 and maturity is six months and the risk-free rate is 4.5%.

13. Explain the differences and similarities between the univariate cumulative standard normal distribution and the bivariate cumulative standard normal distribution. For both univariate cumulative standard normal distribution, `N_f()` and the bivariate cumulative standard normal distribution, `N2_f()`, we have the following codes:

```
def N_f(x):
    from scipy import stats
    return stats.norm.cdf(x)
#
def N2_f(x,y,rho):
    import statsmodels.sandbox.distributions.extras as extras
    muStandardNormal-0.0      # mean of a standard normal
distribution
    varStandardNormal=1.0     # variance of standard normal
distribution
    upper=([x,y])             # upper bound for two values
    v=varStandardNormal       # simplify our notations
    mu=muStandardNormal       # simplify our notations
    covM=([v,rho],[rho,v])
return extras.mvnormcdf(upper,mu,covM)
```

14. Write a Python program to price a call option on the maximum of two terminal prices of two assets that are correlated:

$$Call(maximum\ of\ 2) = part1 + part2 - part2 \qquad \dots (6)$$

$$\begin{cases} part1 = S_1 N_2(d_{11}, -d_{12}, -\rho_1) \\ part2 = S_2 N_2(d_{22}, -d_{21}, -\rho_2) \\ part2 = Ke^{-RT}[1 - N_2(-d_1, -d_2, \rho)] \end{cases} \qquad \dots (7)$$

 The definitions of *S1, S2, d1, d2, d11, d12, d21, d22*, and the `N2()` function are defined in the chapter.

15. Based on Monte Carlo simulation, write a Python program to price a put option on the minimum of two terminal prices of two assets that are correlated.

16. In this chapter, two programs related to American and Bermudan options, with the set of inputs of *s=40, x=40, T=6./12, r=0.05, sigma=0.2, n=1000, T2=(3./12.,4./1)*; a few dates for potential early exercise offer the same results. Why?

17. Write a Python program to price Bermudan put options.

18. Write a Python program to price a Rainbow call option based on the minimum terminal prices of five assets.

Summary

The options we've discussed in *Chapter 10, Options and Futures* are usually called vanilla options that have a close-form solution, that is, the Black-Scholes-Merton option model. In addition to those vanilla options, many exotic options exist. In this chapter, we have discussed several types of exotic options, such as Bermudan options, simple chooser options, shout and binary options, average price options, Up-and-in options, up-and-out options, and down-and-in and down-and-out options. For a European call, the option buyer could exercise their right at the maturity date, while for an American option buyer, they could exercise their right any time before or on the maturity date. A Bermudan option could be exercised a few times before maturity.

In the next chapter, we will discuss various volatility measures, such as our conventional standard deviation, **Lower Partial Standard Deviation (LPSD)**. Using the standard deviation of returns as a risk measure is based on a critical assumption that stock returns follow a normal distribution. Because of this, we introduce several normality tests. In addition, we graphically show volatility clustering—high volatility is usually followed by a high-volatility period, while low volatility is usually followed by a low-volatility period. To deal with this phenomenon, the **Autoregressive Conditional Heteroskedasticity (ARCH)** process was developed by Angel (1982), and the **Generalized AutoRegressive Conditional Heteroskedasticity (GARCH)** processes, which are extensions of ARCH, were developed by Bollerslev (1986). Their graphical presentations and related Python programs will also be covered in the next chapter.

15

Volatility, Implied Volatility, ARCH, and GARCH

In finance, we know that risk is defined as uncertainty since we are unable to predict the future more accurately. Based on the assumption that prices follow a lognormal distribution and returns follow a normal distribution, we could define risk as standard deviation or variance of the returns of a security. We call this our conventional definition of volatility (uncertainty). Since a normal distribution is symmetric, it will treat a positive deviation from a mean in the same manner as it would a negative deviation. This is against our conventional wisdom since we treat them differently. To overcome this, Sortino (1983) suggests a lower partial standard deviation. Most of the time, it is assumed that the volatility of a time series is a constant. Obviously this is not true. Another observation is volatility clustering, which means that high volatility is usually followed by a high-volatility period, and this is true for low volatility, which is usually followed by a low-volatility period. To model this pattern, Angel (1982) develops an **Auto Regressive Conditional Heteroskedasticity** (**ARCH**) process, and Bollerslev (1986) extends it to a **Generalized Auto Regressive Conditional Heteroskedasticity** (**GARCH**) process. In this chapter, the following topics will be covered:

- Conventional volatility measure—standard deviation—based on a normality assumption
- Tests of normality and fat tails
- Lower partial standard deviation and Sortino ratio
- Test of equivalency of volatility over two periods
- Test of heteroskedasticity, Breusch and Pagan

- Volatility smile and skewness
- The ARCH model
- Simulation of an ARCH (1) process
- The GARCH model
- Simulation of a GARCH process
- Simulation of a GARCH (p,q) process using modified `garchSim()`
- GJR_GARCH process by Glosten, Jagannathan, and Runkle

Conventional volatility measure – standard deviation

In most finance textbooks, we use the standard deviation of returns as a risk measure. This is based on a critical assumption that log returns follow a normal distribution. Both standard deviation and variance could be used to measure uncertainty; the former is usually called volatility itself. For example, if we say that the volatility of IBM is 20 percent, it means that its annualized standard deviation is 20 percent. Using IBM as an example, the following program is used to estimate its annualized volatility:

```
import numpy as np
from matplotlib.finance import quotes_historical_yahoo_ochl as getData
#
ticker='IBM'
begdate=(2009,1,1)
enddate=(2013,12,31)
p =getData(ticker, begdate, enddate,asobject=True, adjusted=True)
ret = p.aclose[1:]/p.aclose[:-1]-1
std_annual=np.std(ret)*np.sqrt(252)
print('volatility (std)=',round(std_annual,4))
('volatility (std)=', 0.2093)
```

Tests of normality

The Shapiro-Wilk test is a normality test. The following Python program verifies whether IBM's returns are following a normal distribution. The last five-year daily data from Yahoo! Finance is used for the test. The null hypothesis is that IBM's daily returns are drawn from a normal distribution:

```
import numpy as np
from scipy import stats
```

```
from matplotlib.finance import quotes_historical_yahoo_ochl as getData
#
ticker='IBM'
begdate=(2009,1,1)
enddate=(2013,12,31)
p =getData(ticker, begdate, enddate,asobject=True, adjusted=True)
ret = p.aclose[1:]/p.aclose[:-1]-1
#
print('ticker=',ticker,'W-test, and P-value')
print(stats.shapiro(ret))
  ('ticker=', 'IBM', 'W-test, and P-value')
  (0.9295020699501038, 7.266549629954468e-24)
```

The first value of the result is the test statistic, and the second one is its corresponding P-value. Since this P-value is so close to zero, we reject the null hypothesis. In other words, we conclude that IBM's daily returns do not follow a normal distribution.

For the normality test, we could also apply the Anderson-Darling test, which is a modification of the Kolmogorov-Smirnov test, to verify whether the observations follow a particular distribution. The `stats.anderson()` function has tests for normal, exponential, logistic, and Gumbel (Extreme Value Type I) distributions. The default test is for a normal distribution. After calling the function and printing the testing results, we see the following result:

```
print(stats.anderson(ret))
AndersonResult(statistic=inf, critical_values=array([ 0.574,  0.654,
0.785,  0.915,  1.089]), significance_level=array([ 15. ,   10. ,    5.
,    2.5,   1. ]))
```

Here, we have three sets of values: the Anderson-Darling test statistic, a set of critical values, and a set of corresponding confidence levels, such as 15 percent, 10 percent, 5 percent, 2.5 percent, and 1 percent, as shown in the previous output. If we choose a 1 percent confidence level—the last value of the third set—the critical value is 1.089, the last value of the second set. Since our testing statistic is 14.73, which is much higher than the critical value of 1.089, we reject the null hypothesis. Thus, our Anderson-Darling test leads to the same conclusion as our Shapiro-Wilk test.

Estimating fat tails

One of the important properties of a normal distribution is that we could use mean and standard deviation, the first two moments, to fully define the whole distribution. For n returns of a security, its first four moments are defined in equation (1). The mean or average is defined as follows:

$$\bar{R} = \mu = \frac{\sum_{i=1}^{n} R_i}{n} \qquad \dots (1)$$

Its (sample) variance is defined by the following equation. The standard deviation, that is, σ, is the squared root of the variance:

$$\sigma^2 = \frac{\sum_{i=1}^{n}(R_i - \bar{R})^2}{n-1} \qquad \dots (2)$$

The skewness defined by the following formula indicates whether the distribution is skewed to the left or to the right. For a symmetric distribution, its skewness is zero:

$$skew = \frac{\sum_{i=1}^{n}(R_i - \bar{R})^3}{(n-1)\sigma^3} \qquad \dots (3)$$

The kurtosis reflects the impact of extreme values because of its power of four. There are two types of definitions with and without minus three; refer to the following two equations. The reason behind the deduction of three in equation (4B), is that for a normal distribution, its kurtosis based on equation (4A) is three:

$$kurtosis = \frac{\sum_{i=1}^{n}(R_i - \bar{R})^4}{(n-1)\sigma^4} \qquad \dots (4A)$$

$$kurtosis = \frac{\sum_{i=1}^{n}(R_i - \bar{R})^4}{(n-1)\sigma^4} - 3 \qquad \dots (4B)$$

Some books distinguish these two equations by calling equation (4B) excess kurtosis. However, many functions based on equation (4B) are still named kurtosis. Since we know that a standard normal distribution has a zero mean, unit standard deviation, zero skewness, and zero kurtosis (based on equation 4B). The following output confirms these facts:

```
import numpy as np
from scipy import stats, random
#
random.seed(12345)
ret=random.normal(0,1,50000)
print('mean =',np.mean(ret))
print('std =',np.std(ret))
print('skewness=',stats.skew(ret))
print('kurtosis=',stats.kurtosis(ret))
('mean =', -0.0018105809899753157)
('std =', 1.002778144574481)
('skewness=', -0.014974456637295455)
('kurtosis=', -0.03657086582842339)
```

The mean, skewness, and kurtosis are all close to zero, while the standard deviation is close to one. Next, we estimate the four moments for S&P500 based on its daily returns as follows:

```
import numpy as np
from scipy import stats
from matplotlib.finance import quotes_historical_yahoo_ochl as getData
#
ticker='^GSPC'
begdate=(1926,1,1)
enddate=(2013,12,31)
p = getData(ticker, begdate, enddate,asobject=True, adjusted=True)
ret = p.aclose[1:]/p.aclose[:-1]-1
print( 'S&P500      n     =',len(ret))
print( 'S&P500      mean    =',round(np.mean(ret),8))
print( 'S&P500      std     =',round(np.std(ret),8))
print( 'S&P500      skewness=',round(stats.skew(ret),8))
print( 'S&P500      kurtosis=',round(stats.kurtosis(ret),8))
```

The output for the five values mentioned in the previous code, including the number of observations, is given as follows:

```
('S&P500\tn\t=', 16102)
('S&P500\tmean\t=', 0.00033996)
('S&P500\tstd\t=', 0.00971895)
('S&P500\tskewness=', -0.65037674)
('S&P500\tkurtosis=', 21.24850493)
```

This result is very close to the result in the paper titled *Study of Fat-tail Risk by Cook Pine Capital*, the PDF version of the paper could be downloaded at `http://www.cookpinecapital.com/assets/pdfs/Study_of_Fat-tail_Risk.pdf`. Alternatively, it is available at `http://www3.canisius.edu/~yany/doc/Study_of_Fat-tail_Risk.pdf`. Using the same argument, we conclude that the S&P500 daily returns are skewed to the left, that is, a negative skewness, and have fat tails (kurtosis is 38.22 instead of zero).

Lower partial standard deviation and Sortino ratio

We discussed this concept already. However, for completeness, in this chapter we mention it again. One issue with using standard deviation of returns as a risk measure is that the positive deviation is also viewed as bad. The second issue is that the deviation is from the average instead of a fixed benchmark, such as a risk-free rate. To overcome these shortcomings, Sortino (1983) suggests the lower partial standard deviation, which is defined as the average of squared deviation from the risk-free rate conditional on negative excess returns, as shown in the following formula:

$$LPSD = \frac{\sum_{i=1}^{m}(R_i - R_f)^2}{m-1}, \quad where\ R_i < R_f \quad \ldots\ (5)$$

Because we need the risk-free rate in this equation, we could generate a Fama-French dataset that includes the risk-free rate as one of their time series. First, download their daily factors from `http://mba.tuck.dartmouth.edu/pages/faculty/ken.french/data_library.html`. Then, unzip it and delete the non-data part at the end of the text file. Assume the final text file is saved under `C:/temp/`:

```
import datetime
import numpy as np
import pandas as pd
file=open("c:/temp/ffDaily.txt","r")
data=file.readlines()
```

```
f=[]
index=[]
#
for i in range(5,np.size(data)):
    t=data[i].split()
    t0_n=int(t[0])
    y=int(t0_n/10000)
    m=int(t0_n/100)-y*100
    d=int(t0_n)-y*10000-m*100
    index.append(datetime.datetime(y,m,d))
    for j in range(1,5):
        k=float(t[j])
        f.append(k/100)
#
n=len(f)
f1=np.reshape(f,[n/4,4])
ff=pd.DataFrame(f1,index=index,columns=['Mkt_Rf','SMB','HML','Rf'])
ff.to_pickle("c:/temp/ffDaily.pkl")
```

The name of the final dataset is ffDaily.pkl. It is a good idea to generate this dataset yourself. However, the dataset could be downloaded from http://canisius.edu/~yany/python/ffDaily.pkl. Using the last five years' data (January 1, 2009 to December 31, 2013), we could estimate IBM's LPSD as follows:

```
import numpy as np
import pandas as pd
from scipy import stats
from matplotlib.finance import quotes_historical_yahoo_ochl as getData
#
ticker='IBM'
begdate=(2009,1,1)
enddate=(2013,12,31)
p =getData(ticker, begdate, enddate,asobject=True, adjusted=True)
ret = p.aclose[1:]/p.aclose[:-1]-1
date_=p.date
x=pd.DataFrame(data=ret,index=date_[1:],columns=['ret'])
#
ff=pd.read_pickle('c:/temp/ffDaily.pkl')
final=pd.merge(x,ff,left_index=True,right_index=True)
#
k=final.ret-final.RF
k2=k[k<0]
LPSD=np.std(k2)*np.sqrt(252)
print("LPSD=",LPSD)
print(' LPSD (annualized) for ', ticker, 'is ',round(LPSD,3))
```

The following output shows that IBM's LPSD is 14.8 percent–quite different from the 20.9 percent shown in the previous section:

```
('LPSD=', 0.14556051947047091)
(' LPSD (annualized) for ', 'IBM', 'is ', 0.146)
```

Test of equivalency of volatility over two periods

We know that the stock market fell dramatically in October, 1987. We could choose a stock to test the volatility before and after October, 1987. For instance, we could use Ford Motor Corp, with a ticker of F, to illustrate how to test the equality of variance before and after the market crash in 1987. In the following Python program, we define a function called `ret_f()` to retrieve daily price data from Yahoo! Finance and estimate its daily returns:

```
import numpy as np
import scipy as sp
import pandas as pd
from matplotlib.finance import quotes_historical_yahoo_ochl as getData
#
# input area
ticker='F'              # stock
begdate1=(1982,9,1)     # starting date for period 1
enddate1=(1987,9,1)     # ending date for period   1
begdate2=(1987,12,1)    # starting date for period 2
enddate2=(1992,12,1)    # ending  date for period 2
#
# define a function
def ret_f(ticker,begdate,enddate):
    p =getData(ticker, begdate, enddate,asobject=True, adjusted=True)
    ret = p.aclose[1:]/p.aclose[:-1]-1
    date_=p.date
    return pd.DataFrame(data=ret,index=date_[1:],columns=['ret'])
#
# call the above function twice
ret1=ret_f(ticker,begdate1,enddate1)
ret2=ret_f(ticker,begdate2,enddate2)
#
# output
print('Std period #1    vs. std period #2')
print(round(sp.std(ret1.ret),6),round(sp.std(ret2.ret),6))
print('T value ,    p-value ')
print(sp.stats.bartlett(ret1.ret,ret2.ret))
```

The very high T value and close to zero p-value in the following screenshot suggest the rejection of the hypothesis that during these two periods, the stock has the same volatility. The corresponding output is given as follows:

```
Std period #1    vs. std period #2
(0.01981, 0.017915)
T value ,         p-value
BartlettResult(statistic=12.747107745102099,
pvalue=0.0003565601014515915)
```

Test of heteroskedasticity, Breusch, and Pagan

Breusch and Pagan (1979) designed a test to confirm or reject the null assumption that the residuals from a regression are homogeneous, that is, with a constant volatility. The following formula represents their logic. First, we run a linear regression of y against x:

$$y_t = \alpha + \beta x_t + \epsilon_t \quad \dots (6)$$

Here, y is the dependent variable, x is the independent variable, a is the intercept, β is the coefficient, and ϵ_t is an error term. After we get the error term (residual), we run the second regression:

$$\epsilon_t^2 = \gamma_0 + \gamma_1 x_t + v_t \quad \dots (7)$$

Assume that the fitted values from running the previous regression is tf, then the Breusch-Pangan (1979) measure is given as follows, and it follows a $\chi 2$ distribution with a k degree of freedom:

$$BP = \frac{1}{2}\sum_{i=1}^n f v_i^2 \quad \dots (8)$$

The following example is borrowed from an R package called `lm.test` (test linear regression), and its authors are Hothorn et al. (2014). We generate a time series of *x*, *y1* and *y2*. The independent variable is *x*, and the dependent variables are *y1* and *y2*. By our design, *y1* is homogeneous, that is, with a constant variance (standard deviation), and *y2* is non-homogeneous (heterogeneous), that is, the variance (standard deviation) is not constant. For a variable *x*, we have the following 100 values:

$$x = [-1,1, -1,1, \dots, -1,1] \quad \dots (9)$$

Then, we generate two error terms with 100 random values each. For the *error1*, its 100 values are drawn from the standard normal distribution, that is, with zero mean and unit standard deviation. For *error2*, its 100 values are drawn from a normal distribution with a zero mean and 2 as the standard deviation. The *y1* and *y2* time-series are defined as follows:

$$y_1 = x + error1 \qquad \dots (10)$$
$$y_2 = x + e_{1,i}[i = 1,3, \dots 99] + e_{2,i}[i = 2,4,6, \dots 100] \qquad \dots (11)$$

For the odd scripts of *y2*, the error terms are derived from *error1*, while for the even scripts, the error terms are derived from *error2*. To find more information about the PDF file related to `lm.test`, or an R package, we have the following six steps:

1. Go to `http://www.r-project.org`.
2. Click on **CRAN** under **Download**, **Packages**.
3. Choose a close-by server.
4. Click on Packages on the left-hand side of the screen.
5. Choose a list and search `lm.test`.
6. Click the link and download the PDF file related to `lm.test`.

The following is the related Python code:

```python
import numpy as np
import scipy as sp
import statsmodels.api as sm
#
def breusch_pagan_test(y,x):
    results=sm.OLS(y,x).fit()
    resid=results.resid
    n=len(resid)
```

```
        sigma2 = sum(resid**2)/n
        f = resid**2/sigma2 - 1
        results2=sm.OLS(f,x).fit()
        fv=results2.fittedvalues
        bp=0.5 * sum(fv**2)
        df=results2.df_model
        p_value=1-sp.stats.chi.cdf(bp,df)
        return round(bp,6), df, round(p_value,7)
#
sp.random.seed(12345)
n=100
x=[]
error1=sp.random.normal(0,1,n)
error2=sp.random.normal(0,2,n)
for i in range(n):
    if i%2==1:
        x.append(1)
    else:
        x.append(-1)
#
y1=x+np.array(x)+error1
y2=sp.zeros(n)
#
for i in range(n):
    if i%2==1:
        y2[i]=x[i]+error1[i]
    else:
        y2[i]=x[i]+error2[i]

print ('y1 vs. x (we expect to accept the null hypothesis)')
bp=breusch_pagan_test(y1,x)
#
print('BP value,     df,     p-value')
print 'bp =', bp
bp=breusch_pagan_test(y2,x)
print ('y2 vs. x    (we expect to rject the null hypothesis)')
print('BP value,     df,     p-value')
print('bp =', bp)
```

From the result of running regression by using `y1` against `x`, we know that its residual value would be homogeneous, that is, the variance or standard deviation is a constant. Thus, we expect to accept the null hypothesis. The opposite is true for `y2` against `x`, since, based on our design, the error terms for `y2` are heterogeneous. Thus, we expect to reject the null hypothesis. The corresponding output is shown as follows:

```
y1 vs. x (we expect to accept the null hypothesis)
BP value,        df,      p-value
bp = (0.596446, 1.0, 0.5508776)
y2 vs. x          (we expect to rject the null hypothesis)
BP value,        df,      p-value
('bp =', (17.611054, 1.0, 0.0))
```

Volatility smile and skewness

Obviously, each stock should possess just one volatility. However, when estimating implied volatility, different strike prices might offer us different implied volatilities. More specifically, the implied volatility based on out-of-the-money options, at-the-money options, and in-the-money options might be quite different. Volatility smile is the shape going down then up with the exercise prices, while the volatility skewness is downward or upward sloping. The key is that investors' sentiments and the supply and demand relationship have a fundamental impact on the volatility skewness. Thus, such a smile or skewness provides information on whether investors such as fund managers prefer to write calls or puts. First, we go to the Yahoo! Finance website to download call and put options data:

1. Go to `http://finance.yahoo.com`.
2. Enter a ticker, such as IBM.
3. Click **Options** in the center.
4. Copy and paste the data for call and options.
5. Separate them into two files.

If readers use the data for a maturity of March 17, 2017, they can download it from the author's website at `http://canisius.edu/~yany/data/calls17march.txt`, `http://canisius.edu/~yany/data/puts17march.txt`.

The Python program for calls is shown in the following code:

```
import numpy as np
import pandas as pd
import matplotlib.pyplot as plt
infile="c:/temp/calls17march.txt"
data=pd.read_table(infile,delimiter='\t',skiprows=1)
```

```
x=data['Strike']
y0=list(data['Implied Volatility'])
n=len(y0)
y=[]
for i in np.arange(n):
    a=float(y0[i].replace("%",""))/100.
    y.append(a)
    print(a)
#
plt.title("Volatility smile")
plt.figtext(0.55,0.80,"IBM calls")
plt.figtext(0.55,0.75,"maturity: 3/17/2017")
plt.ylabel("Volatility")
plt.xlabel("Strike Price")
plt.plot(x,y,'o')
plt.show()
```

In the preceding program, the input file is for call options. The graph of the volatility smile is shown here. The other screenshot is based on the relationship between implied volatility and exercise (strike) prices. The program is exactly the same as the preceding program, except the input file. At the end of the chapter, one data case is related to the preceding program. The next image is the volatility smile based on the call data:

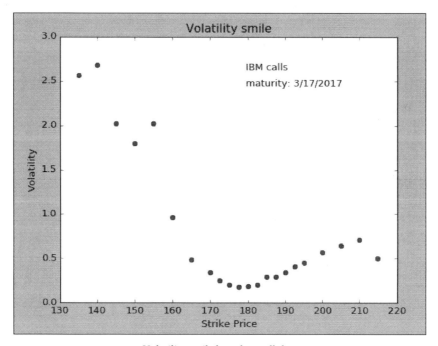

Volatility smile based on call data

Similarly, the next volatility smile image is based on put data:

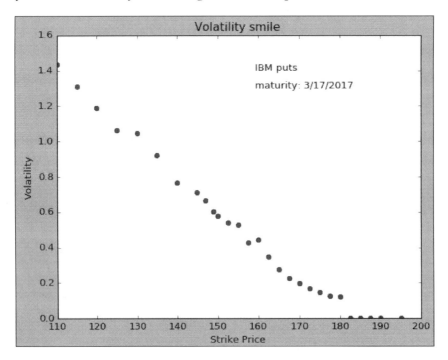

Graphical presentation of volatility clustering

One of the observations is labeled as volatility clustering, which means that high volatility is usually followed by a high-volatility period, while low volatility is usually followed by a low-volatility period. The following program shows this phenomenon by using S&P500 daily returns from 1988 to 2006. Note that, in the following code, in order to show 1988 on the *x* axis, we add a few months before 1988:

```
import numpy as np
import matplotlib.pyplot as plt
from matplotlib.finance import quotes_historical_yahoo_ochl as getData
#
ticker='^GSPC'
begdate=(1987,11,1)
enddate=(2006,12,31)
#
p = getData(ticker, begdate, enddate,asobject=True, adjusted=True)
x=p.date[1:]
```

```
ret = p.aclose[1:]/p.aclose[:-1]-1
#
plt.title('Illustration of volatility clustering (S&P500)')
plt.ylabel('Daily returns')
plt.xlabel('Date')
plt.plot(x,ret)
plt.show()
```

This program is inspired by the graph drawn by *M.P. Visser*; refer to `https://pure.uva.nl/ws/files/922823/67947_09.pdf`. The graph corresponding to the previous code is shown as follows:

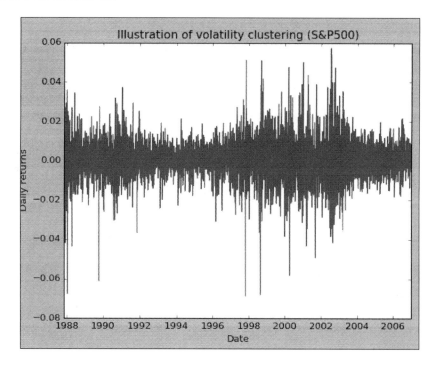

The ARCH model

Based on previous arguments, we know that the volatility or variance of stock returns is not constant. According to the ARCH model, we could use the error terms from the previous estimation to help us predict the next volatility or variance. This model was developed by Robert F. Engle, the winner of the 2003 Nobel Prize in Economics. The formula for an ARCH (q) model is presented as follows:

$$\sigma_t^2 = \alpha_0 + \sum_{i=1}^q \alpha_i \varepsilon_{t-i}^2 \quad \cdots (12)$$

Here, σ_t^2 is the variance at time t, is the ith coefficient, ε_{t-i}^2 is the squared error term for the period of *t-i*, and q is the order of error terms. When q is 1, we have the simplest ARCH (1) process as follows:

$$\sigma_t^2 = \alpha_0 + \alpha_1 \epsilon_{t-1}^2 \quad \ldots (13)$$

Simulating an ARCH (1) process

It is a good idea that we simulate an ARCH (1) process and have a better understanding of the volatility clustering, which means that high volatility is usually followed by a high-volatility period while low volatility is usually followed by a low-volatility period. The following code reflects this phenomenon:

```
import scipy as sp
import matplotlib.pyplot as plt
#
sp.random.seed(12345)
n=1000          # n is the number of observations
n1=100          # we need to drop the first several observations
n2=n+n1         # sum of two numbers
#
a=(0.1,0.3)     # ARCH (1) coefficients alpha0 and alpha1, see Equation
(3)
errors=sp.random.normal(0,1,n2)
t=sp.zeros(n2)
t[0]=sp.random.normal(0,sp.sqrt(a[0]/(1-a[1])),1)
for i in range(1,n2-1):
    t[i]=errors[i]*sp.sqrt(a[0]+a[1]*t[i-1]**2)
    y=t[n1-1:-1] # drop the first n1 observations
#
plt.title('ARCH (1) process')
x=range(n)
plt.plot(x,y)
plt.show()
```

From the following graph, we see that indeed a higher volatility period is usually followed with high volatility while this is also true for a low-volatility clustering:

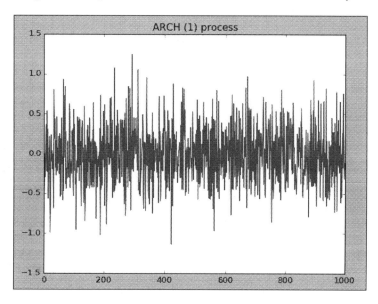

The GARCH model

Generalized AutoRegressive Conditional Heteroskedasticity (GARCH) is an important extension of ARCH, by Bollerslev (1986). The GARCH (p,q) process is defined as follows:

$$\sigma_t^2 = \alpha_0 + \sum_{i=1}^{q} \alpha_i \epsilon_{t-i}^2 + \sum_{i=1}^{p} \beta_i \sigma_{t-i}^2 \quad \dots (14)$$

Here, σ_t^2 is the variance at time t, q is the order for the error terms, p is the order for the variance, α_0 is a constant, α_i is the coefficient for the error term at t-i, β_i is the coefficient for the variance at time t-i. Obviously, the simplest GARCH process is when both p and q are set to 1, that is, GARCH (1,1), which has following formula:

$$\sigma_t^2 = \alpha_0 + \alpha_1 \epsilon_{t-1}^2 + \beta \sigma_{t-1}^2 \quad \dots (15)$$

Simulating a GARCH process

Based on the previous program related to ARCH (1), we could simulate a GARCH (1,1) process as follows:

```
import scipy as sp
import matplotlib.pyplot as plt
#
sp.random.seed(12345)
n=1000              # n is the number of observations
n1=100              # we need to drop the first several observations
n2=n+n1             # sum of two numbers
#
a=(0.1,0.3)      # ARCH coefficient
alpha=(0.1,0.3)     # GARCH (1,1) coefficients alpha0 and alpha1, see
Equation (3)
beta=0.2
errors=sp.random.normal(0,1,n2)
t=sp.zeros(n2)
t[0]=sp.random.normal(0,sp.sqrt(a[0]/(1-a[1])),1)
#
for i in range(1,n2-1):
    t[i]=errors[i]*sp.sqrt(alpha[0]+alpha[1]*errors[i-
1]**2+beta*t[i-1]**2)
#
y=t[n1-1:-1]     # drop the first n1 observations
plt.title('GARCH (1,1) process')
x=range(n)
plt.plot(x,y)
plt.show()
```

Honestly speaking, the following graph is quite similar to the previous one under the ARCH (1) process. The graph corresponding to the previous code is shown as follows:

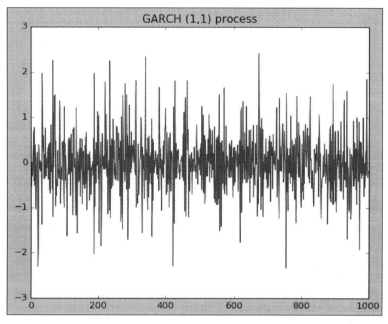

Fig15_04_garch.png

Simulating a GARCH (p,q) process using modified garchSim()

The following code is based on the R function called `garchSim()`, which is included in the R package called `fGarch`. The authors for `fGarch` are Diethelm Wuertz and Yohan Chalabi. To find the related manual, we perform the following steps:

1. Go to `http://www.r-project.org`.
2. Click on **CRAN** under **Download**, **Packages**.
3. Choose a close-by server.
4. Click on Packages on the left-hand side of the screen.
5. Choose a list and search for `fGarch`.
6. Click on the link and download the PDF file related to `fGarch`.

The Python program based on the R program is given as follows:

```python
import scipy as sp
import numpy as np
import matplotlib.pyplot as plt
#
sp.random.seed(12345)
m=2
n=100                    # n is the number of observations
nDrop=100                # we need to drop the first several observations
delta=2
omega=1e-6
alpha=(0.05,0.05)
#
beta=0.8
mu,ma,ar=0.0,0.0,0.0
gamma=(0.0,0.0)
order_ar=sp.size(ar)
order_ma=sp.size(ma)
order_beta=sp.size(beta)
#
order_alpha =sp.size(alpha)
z0=sp.random.standard_normal(n+nDrop)
deltainv=1/delta
spec_1=np.array([2])
spec_2=np.array([2])
spec_3=np.array([2])
z = np.hstack((spec_1,z0))
t=np.zeros(n+nDrop)
h = np.hstack((spec_2,t))
y = np.hstack((spec_3,t))
eps0 = h**deltainv  * z
for i in range(m+1,n +nDrop+m-1):
    t1=sum(alpha[::-1]*abs(eps0[i-2:i]))       # reverse
    alpha =alpha[::-1]
    t2=eps0[i-order_alpha-1:i-1]
    t3=t2*t2
    t4=np.dot(gamma,t3.T)
    t5=sum(beta* h[i-order_beta:i-1])
    h[i]=omega+t1-t4+ t5
    eps0[i] = h[i]**deltainv * z[i]
    t10=ar * y[i-order_ar:i-1]
    t11=ma * eps0[i -order_ma:i-1]
    y[i]=mu+sum(t10)+sum(t11)+eps0[i]
```

```
    garch=y[nDrop+1:]
    sigma=h[nDrop+1:]**0.5
    eps=eps0[nDrop+1:]
    x=range(1,len(garch)+1)
#
plt.plot(x,garch,'r')
plt.plot(x,sigma,'b')
plt.title('GARCH(2,1) process')
plt.figtext(0.2,0.8,'omega='+str(omega)+', alpha='+str(alpha)+',beta=
'+str(beta))
plt.figtext(0.2,0.75,'gamma='+str(gamma))
plt.figtext(0.2,0.7,'mu='+str(mu)+', ar='+str(ar)+',ma='+str(ma))
plt.show()
```

In the preceding program, omega is the constant in equation (10), while alpha is associated with error terms and beta is associated with variance. There are two items in alpha[a,b]: a is for t-1, while b is for t-2. However, for eps0[t-2:i], they stand for *t-2* and *t-1*. The alpha and eps0 terms are not consistent with each other. Thus, we have to reverse the order of a and b. This is the reason why we use alpha[::-1]. Since several values are zero, such as mu, ar, and ma, the time series of GARCH is identical with eps. Thus, we show just two time series in the following graph. The high volatility is for GARCH, while the other one is for standard deviation:

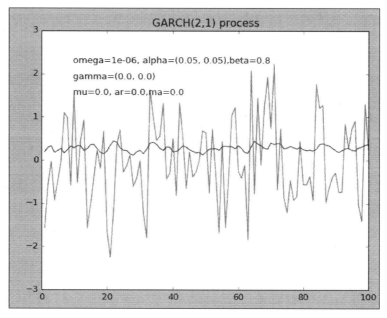

Fig15_05_two.png

GJR_GARCH by Glosten, Jagannanthan, and Runkle

Glosten, Jagannathan, and Runkle (1993) modeled asymmetry in the GARCH process. GJR_GARCH (1,1,1) has the following format:

$$\sigma_t^2 = \omega + \alpha \epsilon_{t-1}^2 + \beta \sigma_{t-1}^2 + \gamma \epsilon_{t-1}^2 I_{t-1} \quad \dots (16)$$

Here, the condition *It-1=0*, if $\epsilon_{t-1}^2 \geq 0$ and *It-1=1* if $\epsilon_{t-1}^2 < 0$ holds true. The following code is based on the codes written by Kevin Sheppard:

```python
import numpy as np
from numpy.linalg import inv
import matplotlib.pyplot as plt
from matplotlib.mlab import csv2rec
from scipy.optimize import fmin_slsqp
from numpy import size, log, pi, sum, diff, array, zeros, diag, dot,
mat, asarray, sqrt
#
def gjr_garch_likelihood(parameters, data, sigma2, out=None):
    mu = parameters[0]
    omega = parameters[1]
    alpha = parameters[2]
    gamma = parameters[3]
    beta = parameters[4]
    T = size(data,0)
    eps = data-mu
    for t in xrange(1,T):
        sigma2[t]=(omega+alpha*eps[t-1]**2+gamma*eps[t-1]**2*(eps[t-
1]<0)+beta*sigma2[t-1])
        logliks = 0.5*(log(2*pi) + log(sigma2) + eps**2/sigma2)
    loglik = sum(logliks)
    if out is None:
        return loglik
    else:
        return loglik, logliks, copy(sigma2)
#
def gjr_constraint(parameters,data, sigma2, out=None):
    alpha = parameters[2]
    gamma = parameters[3]
    beta = parameters[4]
    return array([1-alpha-gamma/2-beta]) # Constraint
alpha+gamma/2+beta<=1
#
```

```
def hessian_2sided(fun, theta, args):
    f = fun(theta, *args)
    h = 1e-5*np.abs(theta)
    thetah = theta + h
    h = thetah-theta
    K = size(theta,0)
    h = np.diag(h)
    fp = zeros(K)
    fm = zeros(K)
    for i in xrange(K):
        fp[i] = fun(theta+h[i], *args)
        fm[i] = fun(theta-h[i], *args)
        fpp = zeros((K,K))
        fmm = zeros((K,K))
    for i in xrange(K):
        for j in xrange(i,K):
            fpp[i,j] = fun(theta + h[i] + h[j], *args)
            fpp[j,i] = fpp[i,j]
            fmm[i,j] = fun(theta-h[i]-h[j], *args)
            fmm[j,i] = fmm[i,j]
            hh = (diag(h))
            hh = hh.reshape((K,1))
            hh = dot(hh,hh.T)
            H = zeros((K,K))
    for i in xrange(K):
        for j in xrange(i,K):
            H[i,j] = (fpp[i,j]-fp[i]-fp[j] + f+ f-fm[i]-fm[j] +
fmm[i,j])/hh[i,j]/2
            H[j,i] = H[i,j]
    return H
```

We can write a function called GJR_GARCH() by including all initial values, constraints, and bounds as follows:

```
def GJR_GARCH(ret):
    import numpy as np
    import scipy.optimize as op
    startV=np.array([ret.mean(),ret.var()*0.01,0.03,0.09,0.90])
    finfo=np.finfo(np.float64)
    t=(0.0,1.0)
    bounds=[(-10*ret.mean(),10*ret.mean()),(finfo.eps,2*ret.
var()),t,t,t]
    T=np.size(ret,0)
    sigma2=np.repeat(ret.var(),T)
    inV=(ret,sigma2)
    return op.fmin_slsqp(gjr_garch_likelihood,startV,f_ieqcons=gjr_con
straint,bounds=bounds,args=inV)
    #
```

In order to replicate our result, we could use the `random.seed()` function to fix our returns obtained from generating a set of random numbers from a uniform distribution:

```
sp.random.seed(12345)
returns=sp.random.uniform(-0.2,0.3,100)
tt=GJR_GARCH(returns)
```

The interpretations of these five outputs are given in the following table:

#	Meaning
1	Message describing the exit mode from the optimizer
2	The final value of the objective function
3	The number of iterations
4	Function evaluations
5	Gradient evaluations

Table 15.1 Definitions of five outputs

The descriptions of various exit modes are listed in the following table:

Exit code	Description
-1	Gradient evaluation required (g and a)
0	Optimization terminated successfully
1	Function evaluation required (f and c)
2	More equality constraints than independent variables
3	More than 3*n iterations in LSQ sub problem
4	Inequality constraints incompatible
5	Singular matrix E in LSQ subproblem
6	Singular matrix C in LSQ subproblem
7	Rank-deficient equality constraint subproblem HFTI
8	Positive directional derivative for line search
9	Iteration limit exceeded

Table 15.2 Exit modes

To show our final parameter values, we print our results with the help of the following code:

```
print(tt)
Optimization terminated successfully.    (Exit mode 0)
          Current function value: -54.0664733128
          Iterations: 12
          Function evaluations: 94
          Gradient evaluations: 12
[  7.73958251e-02   6.65706323e-03   0.00000000e+00   2.09662783e-12
   6.62024107e-01]
```

References

One of the important properties of a normal distribution is that we could use mean and standard deviation.

Engle, Robert, 2002, DYNAMIC CONDITIONAL CORRELATION – A SIMPLE CLASS OF MULTIVARIATE GARCH MODELS, Forthcoming Journal of Business and Economic Statistics, `http://pages.stern.nyu.edu/~rengle/dccfinal.pdf`.

Appendix A – data case 8 - portfolio hedging using VIX calls

The **CBOE Volatility Index (VIX)** is based on the **S&P500 Index (SPX)**, the core index for U.S. equities, and estimates expected volatility by averaging the weighted prices of SPX puts and calls over a wide range of strike prices.

By supplying a script for replicating volatility exposure with a portfolio of SPX options, this new methodology transformed VIX from an abstract concept into a practical standard for trading and hedging volatility.

In 2014, CBOE enhanced the VIX Index to include series of SPX Weekly options. The inclusion of SPX Weeklies allows the VIX Index to be calculated with S&P500 Index option series that most precisely match the 30-day target timeframe for expected volatility that the VIX Index is intended to represent. Using SPX options with more than 23 days and less than 37 days to expiration ensures that the VIX Index will always reflect an interpolation of two points along the S&P 500 volatility term structure.

References

http://www.theoptionsguide.com/portfolio-hedging-using-vix-calls.aspx.

http://www.cboe.com/micro/vix/historical.aspx.

https://www.tickdata.com/tick-data-adds-vix-futures-data/.

Appendix B – data case 8 - volatility smile and its implications

There are several objectives of this data case:

- Understand the concept of the implied volatility
- Understand that the implied volatilities are different with different exercise (strike) prices
- Learnt how to process data and produce related graphs
- What is the implication of a volatility smile?

Source of data: Yahoo! Finance:

1. Go to http://finance.yahoo.com.
2. Enter a ticker, such as IBM.
3. Click **Options** in the center.
4. Copy and paste the data for call and options.
5. Separate them into two files.

For the following companies:

Company name	Ticker	Dell company	DELL
International Business Machine	IBM	General Electric	GE
Microsoft	MSFT	Google	GOOG
Family Dollar Stores	FDO	Apple	AAPL
Wal-Mart Stores	WMT	eBay	EBAY
McDonald's	MCD		

Note that for each stock, there are several maturity dates; see the following screenshot:

A sample Python program is shown here and the input file can be downloaded from the author's website at http://canisius.edu/~yany/data/calls17march.txt:

```python
import numpy as np
import pandas as pd
import matplotlib.pyplot as plt
infile="c:/temp/calls17march.txt"
data=pd.read_table(infile,delimiter='\t',skiprows=1)
x=data['Strike']
y0=list(data['Implied Volatility'])
n=len(y0)
y=[]
for i in np.arange(n):
    a=float(y0[i].replace("%",""))/100.
    y.append(a)
    print(a)
#
plt.title("Volatility smile")
plt.figtext(0.55,0.80,"IBM calls")
plt.figtext(0.55,0.75,"maturity: 3/17/2017")
plt.ylabel("Volatility")
plt.xlabel("Strike Price")
plt.plot(x,y,'o')
plt.show()
```

Exercises

1. What is the definition of volatility?

2. How can you measure risk (volatility)?

3. What are the issues related to the widely used definition of risk (standard deviation)?

4. How can you test whether stock returns follow a normal distribution? For the following given set of stocks, test whether they follow a normal distribution:

Company name	Ticker	Dell company	DELL
International Business Machine	IBM	General Electric	GE
Microsoft	MSFT	Google	GOOG
Family Dollar Stores	FDO	Apple	AAPL
Wal-Mart Stores	WMT	eBay	EBAY
McDonald's	MCD		

5. What is the lower partial standard deviation? What are its applications?

6. Choose five stocks, such as DELL, IBM, Microsoft, Citi Group, and Walmart, and compare their standard deviation with LPSD based on the last three-years' daily data.

7. Is a stock's volatility constant over the years? You could choose **International Business Machine (IBM)** and **Walmart (WMT)** to test your hypothesis.

8. What is an ARCH (1) process?

9. What is a GARCH (1,1) process?

10. Apply the GARCH (1,1) process to IBM and WMT.

11. Write a Python program to show the volatility smile combine both calls and puts.

12. Write a Python program to put volatility smiles by using different maturity dates. In other words, put several smiles together.

13. Use the Breusch-Pagan (1979) test to confirm or reject the hypothesis that daily returns for IBM is homogeneous.

14. How can you test whether a stock's volatility is constant?

15. What does *fat tail* mean? Why should we care about fat tail?

16. Could you write a Python program to download the option data?

17. How do you download all maturity dates?

Summary

In this chapter, we focused on several issues, especially on volatility measures and ARCH/GARCH. For the volatility measures, first we discussed the widely used standard deviation, which is based on the normality assumption. To show that such an assumption might not hold, we introduced several normality tests, such as the Shapiro-Wilk test and the Anderson-Darling test. To show a fat tail of many stocks' real distribution benchmarked on a normal distribution, we vividly used various graphs to illustrate it. To show that the volatility might not be constant, we presented the test to compare the variance over two periods. Then, we showed a Python program to conduct the Breusch-Pangan (1979) test for heteroskedasticity. ARCH and GARCH are used widely to describe the evolution of volatility over time. For these models, we simulate their simple form such as ARCH (1) and GARCH (1,1) processes. In addition to their graphical presentations, the Python codes of Kevin Sheppard are included to solve the GJR_GARCH (1,1,1) process.

Index

49018466R00326

Made in the USA
Middletown, DE
03 October 2017